THE CONTINUITY OF
POETIC LANGUAGE

THE CONTINUITY OF POETIC LANGUAGE

The Primary Language of Poetry, 1540's — 1940's

BY

JOSEPHINE MILES

OCTAGON BOOKS

A DIVISION OF FARRAR, STRAUS AND GIROUX

New York   1972

Originally published by University of California Press
1948, as The Primary Language of Poetry in the 1640's
1950, as The Primary Language of Poetry in the 1740's and 1840's
1951, as The Primary Language of Poetry in the 1940's

New preface copyright © 1965 by Josephine Miles

Reprinted 1965

by special arrangement with University of California Press

Second Octagon printing 1972

OCTAGON BOOKS

A DIVISION OF FARRAR, STRAUS & GIROUX, INC.

19 Union Square West

New York, N. Y. 10003

LIBRARY OF CONGRESS CATALOG CARD NUMBER: 65-25896

ISBN 0-374-95644-8

Printed in U.S.A. by

NOBLE OFFSET PRINTERS, INC.

New York, N.Y. 10003

ACKNOWLEDGMENT

THE John Simon Guggenheim Memorial Foundation and the Research Committee of the University of California aided in the writing of this book, and Professors B. H. Lehman, James R. Caldwell, George P. Elliott, Earl Lyon, Charles Muscatine, David Reed, Mark Schorer, in the rewriting. I thank all these, Mrs. James Lynch, the Editorial Committee, and the Editor, Mr. Harold A. Small.

J. M.

PREFACE TO THE
OCTAGON EDITION

The studies of the primary language of English poetry from the 1540's to 1940's, begun in 1945, had as their purpose to discover the degree of continuity in the range of the poetry. Six years later, when the series here reprinted was completed, the degree of continuity appeared to be much greater than I had expected. In later studies therefore, *Eras and Modes* 1957, *Renaissance and Modern Language* 1960, and *Eras and Modes* second edition 1964, I tried to explore more systematically the full variety in the temporal span of five centuries, and in the spatial extension to America, discovering the levels between the extremes.

For the reader of the recent work, it may be difficult to return to these less generalizing studies, not only because many later questions remain unexplored in them, but more particularly because the tables of proportions are less ample and extensive. On the other hand, the focus here on specific centers of poetic action can provide a useful density.

I would remind the reader therefore to be cautious in various ways. Though the second edition of *Eras and Modes* has made all possible corrections of errors, some still appear, along with new ones, omitting a number of Langland's major words, for example. For corrections I am most grateful to readers who check by using, and the *Continuity* volume has been thus aided. But, in addition, the *Continuity* volume is based on publications in the forties, and thus lacks birthdates. It also lacks the word-counts which are more reliable than line counts. It makes more detailed distinctions of numbers of occurrence, between 10 and 30 than I later do. A few different authors and different works are present in these early studies. *Concordance* omissions, as of the count of *say,* are early taken more seriously, and proper names are included. Most of the differences between this volume and the later *Eras,* therefore, arise either from typographical error or from differences in degree of distinctions and discriminations. Words which, on further study, appear to be major are, for example: for Langland, *foul, kind, wise, cat, rat, mercy, people, ask, like, maintain;* for Chaucer, *young, lady, wine;* for Ballads, *child, leave;* for Douglas, *eloquence;* for Barclay, *lady, people;* for Sternhold, *just;* for Lindsay, *arms, steed, play;* for Heywood, *ill, merry, old, young, friend, speak;* for Baldwin, *mind;* for Sackville, *chief, murder, tyrant, bear;* for Turberville, *yield;* for Gascoigne, *filthy, trusty, steel;* for Breton, *art, ass, scholar, give;* for Jonson, *friend, fly, grow, meet;* for Wither, *pride, believe, take;* for Herrick, *dead;* for Quarles, *common, flock;* for Carew, *cold, flame;* for Shirley, *flame;* for Waller, *care, grow;* for Suckling, *dear, little, mind, move;* for Crashaw, *soft;* for Vaughan, *wing;* for Young, *seem;* for Thomson, *fierce, mighty, swell;* for Armstrong, *breathe;* for Johnson, *general, wealth;* for Shenstone, *fool;* for Collins, *silent;* for Thomas Warton, *mark, shine, strike;* for Landor, *daughter;* for Hemans, *own, art;* for Hood, *gloomy, lofty, daunted, haunted;* for Browning, *last, own, blood;* for Tennyson, *dreary;* for Tupper, *own, precious;* for Stevens, *own;* for Pound, *set;* for Millay, *own;* for Cummings, *mountain.*

As for the gist of what is proposed here, I think it holds good for further work. The poetry of the forties—the work published in this decade by writers born from thirty to sixty years before it—represents a lively two-thirds of the century's poets, leaving to the others, the poets born in mid-century and thus publishing toward the end of it, the mode of moderation, of balance between extremes, of consolidation of forces, which has so often been called classical, and which we see here to have become cumulatively the mode of the twentieth century. It is said that the process of natural selection moves toward a balance between the frequencies of different genes, and it is possible that we see in the progressions of an art some of the similar processes of selection among identifying characteristics. The metaphor of the pendulum's centering swings may also be relevant—to preserve the eighteenth century's mechanical figure along with the twentieth's natural one. In the poetry of the mid-centuries some of the strongest varieties of power in language, its widest swings, become visible.

Berkeley
1965

JOSEPHINE MILES

CONTENTS

PART I

The Primary Language of Poetry in the 1540's and 1640's

I. THE POETRY OF THE 1540's
AND THE 1640's

To DESCRIBE the common materials of language through
which poets work is to describe at once the limitations
and the potentialities of their medium. The language
which the makers speak is not amorphous and not by any means
susceptible of free improvisation. Its sounds and sentence structures, and the references and associations of its words, are well
set for poets as for everyone else by social situation in time and
place; and the poets' language is even further set by literary conventions. Among the arts, in fact, literature may be distinguished
by this very intense conditioning of its medium. The tones of the
musician, the stones of the sculptor, are full of their own character at the outset, but that character has not been so strongly
socialized, so loaded with meaningful and valuable forms and
associations, as has the language which the man of letters accepts
to work with. Sentences and words cannot be neutral, nor can,
for the poet specifically, the sounds and measures of sentences
and words. Whether one is interested, then, in the personal
achievement of the individual, the persistence of convention,
the social matrix, or the sheer quality of the work of art as it
embodies and transforms all these, it is necessary to distinguish
between them, not to attribute to conventional demand the free
choices of the artist, nor to the artist the full powers of the medium itself.

The methods for such discrimination are not easy, because individual and medium too readily pull apart. The study of the
common language of the poet's time and country tends to persuade us now of potentialities he never saw; the study of the
poet's own work, on the other hand, tends to persuade us of his
own singular inventive capacities. The aspects of interaction
come clearer, I propose, in a sort of study which makes a com-

promise between individual and society by its focus on the contemporary agreements in the practice of individual poets. In such agreements, not consciously compacted, the poets indicate what they together accept from their language as valuable for their poetry; they show shared choices and stresses in meanings, statement forms, and sound patterns; they present in all its variation the common poetic material of their time. From such agreement one may attempt to define some of the mass, the density, of poetry as a human production in which form celebrates value and makes it most weighty.

The descriptions I am attempting here are limited in two main ways: to brief periods in English poetry, and to some of the main emphases of the poetry. The study can do no more than make representative suggestions, observing the poems of a decade in each century, and taking them at their own face value—for which reason I should like to call the work "a superficial history," in the sense that surfaces, themselves describable, may make a further indication of depths. At any rate, the selections of decades and stresses are not random samplings, but are provisionally representative and are worked out fully, each within its own frame. The data of description are verifiable at least for the areas of their concern, and their implications may possibly be wider.

The decade of the 1640's seems to me a good one for study because so much happened in it, such various poetry was published. Donne's and Jonson's works appeared posthumously, Milton's first volume, and Dryden's first poem. All this production has especially interested us lately, whether for its "baroque," "metaphysical," "witty," or "paradoxical" qualities, and there is much confusion about the relationship of these qualities. Further, the parallel decades in other centuries are lively: in the 1540's, the first concerted emergence from anonymity; in the 1740's the power of Pope, the inventiveness of Collins; in the 1840's, the sense of a "new" poetry; in the 1940's, our own immediate questions.

The standard of verifiability for the description of the decade's poetry makes necessary that the emphases discerned be the poets' and not the discerners'. Elsewhere[1] I have argued the importance of quantitative emphasis in poetry, the sheer repetition of terms, and sentence and sound forms, as indicative of the poet's interest, and recently Professor Yule, in his statistical study of literary vocabulary, has offered support for this belief, saying, "the savour of an author's text must ... be determined in the main not by the exceptional words but by the common words, the common everyday working words which the author uses over and over again."[2] Not only the words, but their contexts in sound and structure, make the primary pattern, and it is with this, at its simplest level of common recurrence, that description may perhaps profitably be concerned. The variety of melodies in a decade does not turn out to be infinite, nor does the variety of making statements, nor does the variety of choosing terms. A poet tends to use a dozen nouns and a dozen verbs and a half-dozen adjectives so much more frequently than any others that these two dozen or so words amount to a fifth of all his uses of nouns, adjectives, verbs, and thus to a tenth of his total uses, since connectives, articles, pronouns, and so on, make up the other half of language.[3] To identify these two dozen primary terms by plain count, then, is to identify the major substance, quality, and predication of the verse. To discover further, beyond the major terms and the sorts of sentence and rhyme schemes which employ them, the proportioning of substantival and predicative forms, is to see single stresses in relation to the whole balance of the language. To many readers such analysis of quantity and connection will

---

[1] In the Introductions to the three studies in *The Vocabulary of Poetry* (Univ. of California Press, 1942–1946).

[2] G. Udny Yule, *The Statistical Study of Literary Vocabulary* (Cambridge Univ. Press, 1945), pp. 222–225 and p. 2. What Mr. Yule indicates for major nouns (pp. 10–12 and p. 50), I have extended to adjectives and verbs, because the proportions he has established statistically seem to parallel those established by my counts of frequency.

[3] See preceding footnote.

seem alien to the modes of poetic creation. But is it not possible that proportions once poetically felt, and then numerically discovered, may be poetically reperceived?

If my hypothesis is just, that every poem is poetically typical and social as well as individual—a part of its kind and its time as well as its poet,—the major vocabulary of the 1640's, as representative, should share in the major vocabulary of all English poetry, yet should share also some terms characteristic of the 1640's particularly, and should reveal within it individual stresses, some linked in type and time and some singular. The proportioning of these shares should be a strong defining factor, as should their contexts in structure and melody. Thus the sections of descriptive procedure: First, the major poetic vocabulary of the 1640's and some attempt to distinguish it from the language of the preceding century. Second, its proportions and contexts for individual poets published in the decade. Third, some of its relations to the decade's prose vocabulary and order. Fourth, in the light and shadow of some standard critical views, some descriptive generalizations.

The words appearing most often in the volumes of poetry in the bookstalls of the 1640's were these: 4 adjectives, *fair, good, great, sweet;* 10 nouns, *day, earth, eye, god, heart, heaven, love, man, soul, time;* 11 verbs, *bring, come, find, give, go, know, make, see, take, tell, think.* They took logical shape in complex declarative or exclamatory sentences about relationship, and they took melodic form to the beat of the iambic and the couplet. The poetry sounds like this "Divine Mistris" of Carew, in which are a half-dozen of these words at work:

> In Nature's peeces still I see
> Some errour that might mended bee;
> Something my wish could still remove,
> Alter, or adde; but my faire Love
> Was fram'd by hands farre more divine;
> For she hath every beauteous line:

> Yet I had beene farre happier,
> Had Nature, that made me, made her;
> Then likenes might (that love creates)
> Have made her love what now she hates:
> Yet I confesse I cannot spare
> From her just shape the smallest haire;
> Nor need I beg from all the store
> Of heaven for her one beautie more:
> Shee hath too much divinity for mee:
> You Gods! teach her some more humanitie.

These couplets make a play of reason, an argument for preference, a choice between divinitie and humanitie, by a hyperbole of too perfect beauty, and a plea to perfection for more human kindness. Starting with a beautiful piece of nature, putting it in a human relationship of love and desire, finding its flaw in feeling, in natural relation, the poem makes its "explanation" by extension into a supernatural realm, and thus by an exaggeration beyond the physical, literally metaphysical, requests correction direct from the gods through their own powers over the human rather than the divine. It is a complicated situation, being in love: the realms of the natural, the human, the divine—all are involved in it.

The same involvement shows itself in the major nouns of the decade as a whole. *Day, earth, time* are nature's; *eye, heart, love, man,* human, with divine overtones; and *god, heaven, soul,* divine with human connections. The adjectives suggest the split between the sensory affection of *fair* and *sweet* and the more moral standard of *good* and *great;* and the verbs are equally useful in either sphere of activity, human or divine, *giving, knowing, making, seeing, taking, telling* being especially suited to heavenly intercessions, and *coming, going, thinking* more mortal. In Carew's poem, the human *fair love* which is the center as object, creator, and activity is *seen* by the poet who has been *made* by nature, and who turns to *heaven* and the *gods* in his overpowering sense of divinity—a sense not qualitatively lofty or sublime, but abstractly reasoned or conceived by the logical extensions of metaphorical trope. So the terms are blended by interchange from realm to realm, the very function of trope, and the love by being part of all realms, by being fair, beautiful, perfect, divine, yet subject to nature and humanity, maintains the center of the argument and the petition, the structure of "In Nature ... but my Love ... Yet I had beene ... Yet I confesse ... You Gods! teach her ... ," which sounds so logically formed within the bounds of human reference, yet which, by its interchange of reference, is spread to the bounds of metaphysics. The couplets which carry the argument are five-accented, end-stopped, with some easy variations in foot and caesura and carry-over; they provide most strongly the sound effect of measure, with little else of assonantal or consonantal interplay; the intricacy, therefore, is left to concept, and the trope does the major job of creation in the piece, the creation of a love both natural and divine.

As Carew's poem, like many of his time, exalts the human and is therefore, at least in his not wholly humanistic world, playful, so other poems, like Vaughan's, exalt the divine, in human humility, and are called sacred. The shift is one of tone and emphasis, not of content, not of vocabulary, in its major forms. The heart, the love, the god, the natural, here in the aspect of dust and stone, even so singular a poet as Vaughan many times repeats:

> Blest be the God of harmony and love!
> The God above!
> And Holy Dove!
> Whose interceding spirituall grone
> Make restless mones
> For dust, and stones;
> For dust in every part,
> But a hard, stonie heart.

This is a more Christian and less classical god than Carew's, and a more individually echoed, less classical meter. But couplets make still the major sound pattern, enclosing still the exclamation of invocation, and emphasizing the steps of connection between God and dust and the stony but naturally and divinely loving heart of man. Carew stresses the naturalness, Vaughan the divinity, of the loving heart, and in so doing the two make different poems from common concerns. In 1,000 lines, Vaughan's primary *comes* and *sees* and *days* build up his sense of bright vision freshly gained, *fair* as Cowley's and Crashaw's are fair, seen with Carew's and Sandys' *eyes, heart* and *soul,* upon Dryden's and Lovelace's *earth* and in Waller's *heaven,* in Quarles' and Wither's own good *time,* with the *making* and the *giving* of them all.

So Donne, collected and admired in the 1640's, makes a characteristic combination: the play on a common verb *give,* through the sacred and profane powers of love, as in "Loves Exchange"; in coupleted address:

> Love, any devill else but you,
> Would for a given Soule give something too.
> At Court your fellowes every day,
> Give th'art of Riming, Huntsmanship, or Play,
> For them which were their owne before;
> Onely I have nothing which gave more,
> But am, alas, by being lowly, lower.

And Milton in his "Comus" songs weaves the life and sight of love with more visual harmony:

> Sweet Echo, sweetest Nymph that liv'st unseen
>   Within thy airy shell
>   By slow Neander's margent green,
> And in the violet embroider'd vale
>   Where the love-lorn Nightingale
> Nightly to thee her sad Song mourneth well.

The difference between slow Neander's margent and the play of the court is part of the difference in local reference between poets of the 1640's. The likeness of the personified power of love, working in more than one realm of human belief, rhymed closely and addressed by the poet, is part of the likeness by which these poets met. For them, heart and soul, earth and heaven, man and God, fair and good, made, by philosophical interconnection and by poetic device, a universe of planes, an interconnected life and love.

Such a poetic universe may strike the reader as common to all times, with its literal and figurative complexity of human and spiritual reference; but actually, poets of other times have selected other, or partly other, views. The study of major adjectives has shown the decline of words for standard and the rise of words of quality, and has suggested that a modern vocabulary would remove the superior plane of God, heaven, and soul, and substitute an intensified stratum of earthly atmosphere and physical feeling, in the form of concentrated symbol. At any rate, a contrast to the poetic vocabulary of a century earlier, to the words of Heywood, Skelton, Sternhold, Baldwin, Wyatt, Surrey, round and about the 1540's, will serve to show with some degree of detail that the major vocabulary of poetry does not last even a hundred years entire, but loses and takes on those words which are characteristic of the change in its mode and thought.

The 1540's stressed no *fair* and *sweet,* not even that much quality, but *good* and *great* alone. Nor did they favor the sight of *eye,* the physical *earth* on the one hand, nor the speculations of *heaven* and *soul* on the other. By the shunning of extremes they were directly less metaphysical. Rather, they were more humanistic, employing human *life,* the persons of *king* and *lord,* and the catchall of *thing.* So their world was almost completely one world in its main forces. So Baldwin's speakers are less lovers than rulers, citizens less of the universe than of England: the *day* is the day of a reign, the *king* has a specific kingdom.

> Yet at the last in Henryes dayes the sixt,
> I was restored to my fathers landes,

Made duke of Yorke, wherthrough my minde I fixt,
To get the crowne and kingdome in my handes.
For ayde wherin I knit assured bandes
With Nevels stocke, whose doughter was my make
Who for no wo would ever me forsake.

(*Yorke,* ll. 64–70)

Even Sackville, writing in the same *Mirror for Magistrates* much more like Milton's Neander's margent than like this practical plot, comes after the wealth of his descriptive and allusive induction to his practical point, the analogy, not the union, of heaven and earth.

Then looking vpward to the heauens leames
with nightes starres thicke powdred euery where,
which erst so glistened with the golden streames
That chearefull Phebus spred down from his sphere,
Beholding darke oppressing day so neare:
The sodayne sight reduced to my minde,
The sundry chaunges that in earth we fynde.

(*Induction,* ll. 57–63)

And thus he comes to his vast procession of earthly passions. This passage is significant not so much for vocabulary as for the non-metaphysical character of its connections, as the supernatural is used for a sort of colored background to the natural. Such writing suggests the Spenserian or Miltonic mode in its use of elaboration, yet shares with the rest of the writing in the *Mirror for Magistrates* the downright humane vocabulary of the 1540's.

In like manner, Surrey elaborates upon Wyatt, and Lindsay on Skelton, yet all four, with Baldwin and Sackville, make a nucleus of agreement. The verse of *Colin Cloute* goes like this:

Bysshopes, if they may,
Small howsoldes woll kepe,
But slumbre forth and slepe,
And assay to crepe
Within the noble walles
Of the kynges halles,
To fat theyr bodyes full,

> (Theyr soules lene and dull;)
> And have full lytell care
> How evyll theyr shepe fare.
>
> (ll. 122–131)

And Lindsay's *Squyer Meldrum* (ll. 133–142), in the midst of much social criticism like Skelton's and much history and lineage like Baldwin's:

> Than said the Squyer courteslie,
> Gude freindis I pray yow hartfullie,
> Gif ye be worthie men of weir,
> Restoir to hir againe hir geir,
> Or be greit God that all hes wrocht,
> That spuilye sall be full deir bocht.
> Quod thay to him, We thee defy:
> And drew thair swordis haistely,
> And straik at him with sa greit ire,
> That from his harnes flew the fire;

In these sorts of mortal narrative and social comment much of the poetry of the 1540's proceeded, in short, hard-hitting couplets, with much repetition of terms and of sounds, less free and varied, less complex than the poems of a century later.

Indeed, there seems no vast difference between this verse and that of its more illustrious predecessors, of Langland and Lydgate, or even Chaucer, for example. Many of the stiff rigors of formal repetition are present in all, and most of the major terms are shared. There is continuity in *good* and *great*, in *God, heart, love*, and *man*, in *lord, life, king, thing* characteristic of the 1540's, and in most of the verbs. There is even more stress, in fact, by the early poets on such human terms as *worthy, false, poor, woe, work, word, tale, tell, conscience, people, truth, joy*. And, on the other hand, there is an early shunning of terms most important later to the 1640's characteristically: the *day, earth, eye, heaven, soul* of physical and metaphysical connection.

Therefore, in the 1540's, that Tudor decade in which anonymity began so visibly to fade that almost a dozen well-known poets were published then by name, including the old masters in new editions, poetry made a sort of consolidation for itself. Loyal to the main verbs and adjectives of Chaucer, Langland, Lydgate, and some of the main nouns, interrupted slightly by Skelton's vagaries and Sternhold's hymnal specializations, it gathered, in Lindsay, Heywood, Baldwin and Sackville, Wyatt, Surrey, Gascoigne, and Googe, an assurance of emphasis, despite the great varieties of these poets' topics and intentions, which amounted to three-fourths agreement and which set a stamp of poetic value by poetic usage on 2 adjectives of standard, 10 nouns of human life, and 10 verbs of simple activity. Some of these, notably *day, thing, time, think,* the terms of speculation, led away from Tudor society toward the Stuart-Cromwell world, with its added scope of *heaven* and *earth* in *eye* and *soul,* and so to a new scope in sound and structure, playfully juggled or solemnly encompassed or thoughtfully seasoned as the new various tone might be.

It will be noted that, from century to century, adjectives, nouns, verbs do not equally carry the burden of representative change. *Come* and *go, make* and *see* and *know,* and in less degree *give* and *take,* seem to be basic and stable actions for most of these poets, as one supposes they may be for most poets. *Think,* by its early scarcity, seems more limited. The adjectives are few and tentative, but with that great strength for *great* and *good* which is to continue through so much English poetry. It is the nouns, as they represent sheer content, that vary most from poet to poet and from period to period. The *king, lord, life* of Sternhold, Surrey, Baldwin, Gascoigne, Barclay, and the ballads, are part of the prime plain content of their time, and are lost, by 1640, for Vaughan, Crashaw, Cowley, Donne, Sandys, into the more disparate realms of *earth* and *eye, heaven* and *soul.* The noun names of actors, objects, scenes all strongly change, though actions and qualities are steadfast.

Not only the vocabulary itself, but its proportioning, reveals change within stability and idiosyncrasy within the common cause of poetry. In the 1640's, the poets seem consistently to use about one verb to a line, varying no more than from Milton's 8 to Donne's 12 verbs in 10 lines, with some noteworthy early exceptions. In construction as in content the verb seems least variable. The noun, on the other hand, normally varies from one to two in a line, from Donne's 11 in 10 lines to Waller's 19, and thus may equal or double the verb. The adjective may range at extremes from one-half to one and one-half per line, from Jonson's 6 to Milton's 12 and Fletcher's 14 in 10 lines, and thus displays the widest variety in support of its nouns. A plenitude of nouns seems usually to make for a plenitude of adjectives, so that the two may be considered together as a substantival force, as very strong for example in Waller, Milton, and More, where substantival vocabulary is three times as great as predicative, in contrast to the decade's standard twice as great. Proportioning may well be a defining aspect of style.[4] There is a describable difference between the poet who crowds his lines, themselves relatively inflexible in their usual four- or five-foot length, with the separately meaningful nouns and adjectives of substantiation, and the predicating poet who intercomplicates with connectives. There is a vivid technical difference between the highly predicated, meagerly modified poetry of the 1540's and at least part of the highly modified poetry of the 1640's. The difference may suggest, too, the nature of a difference in two styles which persist through the century, the difference between a Skelton, Wyatt, Jonson, Donne sort of predicative style and a Sackville, Spenser, Quarles, Waller, Milton sort of qualitative style. Both sorts are

---

[4] Little systematic study has been made, more in German than in English, and more with emphasis on prose than with interest in poetry. David Boder's suggestion for an "Adjective-Verb Quotient" (*Psychological Record,* III: 309–344) is interesting, although its bases of classification are difficult. Vernon Lee's distinguishing, in *The Handling of Words,* p. 74, of two prose styles, the active (a two-to-one proportion of substantival elements) and the qualitative (three-to-one), is surprisingly close to what the poetry presents here.

to be seen in the great Elizabethan years between: Breton, Gascoigne, Googe, Turberville, Daniel continue the Wyatt line toward Jonson and Donne and the majority of the 1640's, but more poets in the decade after Spenser are more fully substantial, in the Miltonic direction. We may therefore see proportioning in parallel as well as in nucleus, and, as most directly important, in the simple impact of the individual poem.

A stanza from Sternhold's translation of the Twenty-third Psalm has a direct effect very different from that of Denham's translation, which was a hundred years later and obviously part of another poetic mode. Sternhold's:

> My shepeheard is the living Lord
> Nothing therefore I need;
> In pastures faire with waters calme
> He set me forth to feede.
> He did convert and glad my soule
> And brought my mind in frame;
> To walk in paths of righteousnesse,
> For his most holy name.

And Denham's:

> My Shepherd is the living Lord;
> To me my Food and Ease
> The rich luxuriant fields afford;
> The Streams my Thirst appease.
> My Soul restor'd he'l gently lead
> Into the Paths of Peace;
> To walk in Shades among the Dead,
> My Hopes, not Fears, increase.

Denham's editor thinks Denham's stanza obviously better.[5] At least it is different, with that difference in proportion which puts much stress on noun and adjective over verb. For Sternhold the ratio is 2 to 1; for Denham, 3 to 1. "Food and Ease" take the place of "I need," and the soul seldom receives in the second such active ministration as in the first; in consequence, the sound

---

[5] T. H. Banks, ed., Denham's *Poetical Works* (Yale Univ. Press, 1928), p. 45. Sandys' version is like Denham's in proportion.

pattern itself is shifted, for though rhyme and rhythm are the same, the serial rather than clausal structure opens the line ends and lengthens the periods in Denham's.

Whole eras, whole poets, like their stanzas, appear to have a whole sense of the proportioning of materials and of their choice. Sternhold's living lord was a more active lord than many of the Carolines knew. A decade of poetry has a homogeneity definable in terms of its language, describable in the relation of primary vocabulary to sound and sentence structure, and in the proportioning of the vocabulary itself. Of twenty poets publishing in a decade, a majority agree in using a certain two dozen words more than any others and on epitheting and predicating in certain limited though seldom identical proportions. Almost every poet participates in a majority of agreements. It is possible to say, then, that sheer contemporaneity gives to poetry a special character of content, context, and proportion, in the order, structure, and reference of sentences and the measure of lines. The words in simplest reference name directly what we have already known in general about the general interest of the time, as the long-accepted humanism of the Tudors, for example, is named by their favorite *lord* and *life,* and the scope of the metaphysical is spread by *heaven* and *earth.*

Further, the extremes of usage in a decade, if they group themselves, as they do about Wyatt, about Donne or Milton, suggest kinds or types of poetry, the life of poetry apart from the life of its time, the traditions and conventions of poetizing, which may extend scarcely altered through decade after decade. One is not sure whether type or time is the stronger force; in the closest continuity between 1540's and 1640's, that between Wyatt and Donne or Cowley, the two sorts of bond seem fairly even, perhaps because Wyatt as individualistic, or as bearer of a new convention, moved forward out of his own period. At any rate, here is also the third power which the language speaks for, the individual consistency of the single poet. The temporal or craft agreement of poets is never static, because always in the two-thirds likeness there is the one-third difference, always in the voice of time and kind there is the note, sweet or sour, loud or soft, of the one poet with his own singular values. And sometimes the values do not stay singular. It is to these individuals, as they spoke and agreed or disagreed in the 1640's that I would now turn, to learn the degrees of difference in their *earths* and *heavens*. By way of looking from the whole to the part, I spread out both in outline as a sort of sum, not to appall the unmathematical, but to condense in figures approximately accurate the poetic justices of quantitative stress.

Table 1 for the 1540's shows the restraint of poetry in that decade, which was one of the earliest of active publication. To make out a roster of twenty poets, one must include the late publication, or republication, of great predecessors like Chaucer, Langland, Lydgate, Douglas, as well as the work of successors like Turberville, Breton, Gascoigne, Spenser, and Shakespeare. The figures are not much altered, they are merely extended, by such inclusion. The newly strong and responsible poets of mid-century, from Skelton to Googe, set up the norm of proportion which was itself restrained and which embraced Chaucer, Lydgate, and Baldwin, as well as Wyatt and Surrey.

Note the relatively short lines of this verse, its narrative structure, the scantiness of its adjectives, the persistently low proportion, 2 to 1, of adjective-and-noun to verb. Note how characteristic are the traditional ballads of the preceding century, with their dominance of verb over epithet. Note how faithful are the Chaucerians, and not less Wyatt and Surrey, to the Chaucerian proportions. Skelton and Sternhold are most exaggeratedly economical. Heywood and Sackville, on the other hand, work toward the richer substantival vocabulary of the later Shakespeare and Spenser, the newer masters.

1540's: TABLE 1

THE POEMS IN CHRONOLOGICAL ORDER: THEIR SOUND AND
STRUCTURE AND PROPORTION

First 1,000 lines (with exceptions noted):	Form	In average ten lines		
		Adj.	Noun	Verb
Chaucer, Geoffrey. 1st 860 ll. , *Prologue*, 140 ll. *Knight's Tale. Works*, ed. F. N. Robinson (Cambridge, 1933). (Thynne ed., 1532.)	5' couplet Narr.	7	15	11
Langland, William. *Piers Plowman*, thr. III. Publ. 1550. Ed. W. W. Skeat (Oxford, 10th ed., 1932).	4' allit. Narr.	6	21	18
Lydgate, John. 1st 500 ll. each, *Temple of Glas, Fall of Princes*. Publ. 1554. Ed. resp. J. Schick (London, 1891) and Henry Bergen (Carnegie Inst. Wash., 1923).	5' cpl., st. Narr.	6	16	9
English Popular Ballads, ed. Walter Morris Hart (New York, 1916). 1st 18 ballads.	4—' stanza Narr.	6	13	11
Douglas, Gavin. 1st 500 ll. each, *Palice of Honour* and *Eneados* (London, 1553). *Poetical Works*, Vols. I, II (Edinburgh, 1874).	5' st. Narr.	8	18	9
Skelton, John. *Colin Cloute*. Publ. 1545. *Poems*, ed. Richard Hughes (Heinemann, 1924).	2' cpl. Narr.	4	10	7
Barclay, Alexander. *Eclogue V*, from *The Eclogues*, 1521 (London, Oxford Univ. Press, for E.E.T.S., 1928).	5' epl. Arg.	8	22	12
Sternhold, Thomas. *One and Fiftie Psalmes of David* (1st 25). (Huntington Library Facsimile.) Publ. 1547 ff.	4–3' st. Song	4	11	8
Lindsay, Sir David. *Squyer Meldrum*. Publ. 1548. *Poetical Works*, ed. David Laing (Edinburgh, 1879).	4' cpl. Narr.	6	13	9
Wyatt, Sir Thomas. *Songs, Rondeaus, Odes*. *Poetical Works* (Boston, 1854.)	5' st. Addr.	7	12	11

1540's: TABLE 1—(*Continued*)

First 1,000 lines (with exceptions noted):	Form	In average ten lines		
		Adj.	Noun	Verb
Surrey, Henry Howard, Earl of. Sonnets, etc. Ed., with Wyatt, by Tottel, 1557. *Poems*, ed. Morgan Padelford (rev. ed., Univ. of Washington Press, 1928).	5′ st. Addr.	7	18	13
Heywood, John. *Proverbs*, 1546, and *Epigrams*, 1st 500 ll. each, ed. resp. Julian Sharman (London, Bell, 1874) and Spenser Society, 1867.	5′ cpl. Stat.	9	17	15
Baldwin, William. *Cambridge, York, Clarence* (and 1st 400 ll. of vol.) in *Mirror for Magistrates* 1549–1559, ed. Lily B. Campbell (Cambridge Univ. Press, 1938).	5′ st. Narr.	7	20	12
Sackville, Thomas. *Induction* and *Buckingham*, in *Mirror for Magistrates*, 1563.	5′ st. Narr.	9	18	10
Googe, Barnabe. *Eglogs, Epitaphes, and Sonettes*, 1563, ed. Edward Arber (London, 1871).	4′ st. Descr., narr.	5	12	9
Turberville, George. *Epitaphes, Epigrams, Songs and Sonets*, 1567, ed. J. Payne Collier, in *Illustrations of Early English Poetry*, Vol. I (London, 1866–1870).	4–′ st. Narr. addr.	5	13	10
Breton, Nicholas. *School* and *Fort of Fancie*, in *Works*, ed. Grosart, 1879.	3′ st. Descr.	5	11	8
Gascoigne, George. *The Steele Glas*, 1576, in *Works*, Vol. II, ed. Cunliffe (London, 1912).	5′ blank Descr.	9	18	12
Spenser, Edmund. *Faerie Queene, Amoretti*, 1st 500 ll. each. 1582, 1594 ff. *Works*, Oxford ed., 1910.	5′ st. Narr. addr.	12	16	11
Shakespeare, William. *Sonnets*, to 1609. *Works*, Cambridge ed., 1906. 1050 ll.	5′ st. Addr.	10	17	10

1540's: TABLE 2

PROPORTIONS IN ORDER OF ADJECTIVAL EMPHASIS

Poet	Average in ten lines		
	Adj.	Noun	Verb
Skelton..	4	10	7
Sternhold.....................................	4	11	8
Breton..	5	11	8
Googe...	5	12	9
Ballads.......................................	6	13	11
Turberville...................................	5	13	10
Langland......................................	6	21	18
Lindsay.......................................	6	13	9
Lydgate.......................................	6	16	9
Wyatt...	7	12	11
Chaucer.......................................	7	15	11
Surrey..	7	18	13
Baldwin.......................................	7	20	12
Douglas.......................................	8	18	9
Gascoigne.....................................	9	18	12
Barclay.......................................	8	22	12
Heywood.......................................	9	17	15
Sackville.....................................	9	18	10
Shakespeare...................................	10	17	10
Spenser*......................................	12	16	11

*That Spenser and Shakespeare fairly represent their contemporaries may be seen in the following proportions: Marlowe (*Hero and Leander* and 5 *Elegies*, ed. Martin, 1931), 9–16–13; Sidney (*Écloges*, 1593, and *Astrophel*), 10–21–13; Daniel (*Delia*, 700 ll., and *Rosamund*) 8–17–13; Drayton (*Idea* and *Pastorals*), 9–18–12: Sylvester (*Divine Weeks*, ed. Grosart, 1880), 11–19–9; P. Fletcher (*Purple Island*, ed. Grosart, 1869), 14-18-10.

1540's: TABLE 3A—(*Continued*)

Word	Sk.	St.	Br.	Go.	Ba.	Tu.	La.	Li.	Ly.	Wy.	Ch.	Su.	Bl.	Do.	Ga.	Bc.	He.	Sa.	Sh.	Sp.
night												15						10	20	10
pain				15		10				30		10				15				
woe					10		10		10	10		20						10		
word			10								15			10						10
world		10	10												15				15	10
begin							10				10						10	10		
bring				10	10												10			
die		15					10				10	10	10					10	10	
hear		15													10					10
keep			10	10	25			10		10	10									
lie				10	10										15	15			10	10
live									15								15			
look								10		10	10	20							20	10
love							10			15		10	10		10			10	10	
seek															10		20	10	20	
show	10				15									15	10					
speak											20				10					

1540's: TABLE 3B

INDIVIDUAL USES

Word	Sk.	St.	Br.	Go.	Ba.	Tu.	La.	Li.	Ly.	Wy.	Ch.	Su.	3l.	Do.	Ga.	Bc.	He.	Sa.	Sh.	Sp.
black																				10
blind										10										10
bonny					25															
bright																			10	
common										10					20					
dead								10												
English			15				20													
false													20							
fine																				
foul															10					10
friendly						10			15											
fresh														10						
full																				10
gentle														10						10
golden					10															10
green					10							10								
happy					10														10	
handsome					10															
holy	10													10						
little		10	10																	
lusty		10																		
merry																	10			
new									10											10

1540's: TABLE 3B—(Continued)

Word	Sk.	St.	Br.	Go.	Ba.	Tu.	La.	Li.	Ly.	Wy.	Ch.	Su.	Bl.	Do.	Ga.	Bc.	He.	Sa.	Sh.	Sp.
noble	10							10												
pleasant				15								10			10					
proud					15		10													10
red																	10			
rich			10													10				
rural					10							10								
sad							10													10
secret																				
silver															10					
strange											10									
wicked		10									10						15			
wise												10	30		10			10		
woful									15								10			
worthy										10				10			10			
young					25			10												
bed					10															
bishop	10																	10		
blood															10					
book												20								
breast																				
brother																				
cause					10		10													
check							10													
Christ																55				
church	10																			
city																				
conscience							20													
cupid																				

1540's: TABLE 3B:—*(Continued)*

Word	Sk.	St.	Br.	Go.	Ba.	Tu.	La.	Li.	Ly.	Wy.	Ch.	Su.	El.	Do.	Ga.	Bc.	He.	Sa.	Sh.	Sp.
deed								10							15					
delight			10									10			10					
desire										10		10								
tace																				
faith			35			10				15										
tame				10																
fancy				10																
father					10								10					15		
tear																				
field																				
fire						10		10		10										
flame			10									10								
flower		15										15								
foe	10																			
friar			10																	
friend							10										10			
glass															40					
grief				10							10									
ground																10				
head			10																	
Helena						10														
hell											10									
home					10											10				
honour				10																
hope						10														
horse								25												
joy									15		10									
kind			10																	
knight											10				15					

1540's: TABLE 3B—*(Continued)*

Word	Sk.	St.	Br.	Go.	Ba.	Tu.	La.	Li.	Ly.	Wy.	Ch.	Su.	Bl.	Do.	Ga.	Bc.	He.	Sa.	Sh.	Sp.
labour																15				
land								10					15							
law							15						15							
lust									10						10					
manner																				
mede					40		65													
mercy		10					10													
mother				10															10	
name																				
nature												10		10		10				
people	10											15				15				
place										10				10		10				
pleasure		10				10														
plowman																				
poet																				
power														10						
priest													15		25			10		
prince						10									20					
Pyndara																				
right			15										10							
school								25												
Scots				10												15				
shepherd																				
ship								10		15										
sigh			20																	
sir					10															
sister																				
soldier															15					

1540's: TABLE 3B—(*Continued*)

Word	Sk.	St.	Br.	Go.	Ba.	Tu.	La.	Li.	Ly.	Wy.	Ch.	Su.	Bl.	Do.	Ga.	Bc.	He.	Sa.	Sh.	Sp.
son					10								10							
soul		15					10													
spear								20												
squire								60										10		
state					10			10												
steed									10											
story																				
sun																			10	
tale										10	15	10						10		
tear																				
thought							15					20				15			20	
tongue											10									10
town			15								10									
toy																				
tree																				
truth														10						
Virgil							30							30						
war														10						
water			20					20			10									
way																				
wedding																	20			
widow																	15			
wife																	25			
winter																				
wit							10					10		10		10				
work							10							20						
year												10					10			
youth			10												10				10	

1540's: TABLE 3B—(Concluded)

Word	Sk.	St.	Br.	Go.	Ba.	Tu.	La.	Li.	Ly.	Wy.	Ch.	Su.	Bl.	Do.	Ga.	Bc.	He.	Sa.	Sh.	Sp.
begin											10						10	10		
behold															10	10				
dwell																		10		
fall						10														
fight								15												
follow														10						
get											10			10	10					
keep		15																		
kill			10																	
learn				10											15	15				
let				10																
live																				
lose												10								
pass					10			15												
play								10												
please										10									;	
pray																				
put							25	15							25		30			
quoth								20			25									
ride											25									
rise								15												
run																				
seem																				
serve					10	10						10			10					
sing								10							15					
slay															15					
stand																				
teach		10					10					10								
win			15								10									
work																				

1640's: TABLE 1

THE POEMS IN CHRONOLOGICAL ORDER: THEIR SOUND AND
STRUCTURE AND PROPORTION

Date	Poet and work (first 1,000 lines)	Form	In average ten lines		
			Adj.	Noun	Verb
1640	Carew, Thomas. *Poems*. Preface by W. C. Hazlitt. Roxburghe Library, 1870.	4'–5' cpl. Addr.	8	15	11
	Donne, John. Songs and Sonets. *Works* (London, 1640).	4'–5' st. Addr.	7	13	12
	Harvey, Christopher. *The Synagogue.CompletePoems*,ed.Grosart, Fuller Worthies' Library, 1874.	5'–3' st. Addr.	6	12	10
	Jonson, Ben. *Under-woods. The Poems*, ed. B. H. Newdigate (Oxford, Blackwell, 1936).	5'–4' st. Addr.	6	14	12
1641	Sandys, George. *Song of Solomon, Jeremiah. Poetical Works*, ed. R. Hooper (London, 1872), Vol. II.	5'–4' cpl. Addr.	8	17	9
1642	More, Henry. *Psychozoia Platonica. Complete Poems*, ed. Grosart. Chertsey Worthies' Library, 1878.	5', Sp. st. Narr., addr.	12	18	10
	Denham, John. *Cooper's Hill* (1668 text), etc. *Poetical Works*, ed. T. H. Banks (Yale Univ. Press, 1928).	5' cpl. Descr.	7	15	9
1644	Quarles, Francis. *Shepheards Oracles. Complete Works*, ed. Grosart, Chertsey Worthies' Library, 1881	5' cpl. Descr., dial.	10	17	13
1645	Milton, John. "Christ's Nativity," "L'Allegro," "Il Penseroso," "Lycidas," "Comus." *Minor Poems*, ed. M. Y. Hughes (New York, Doubleday-Doran, 1939).	4'–5' ll. Narr., addr.	12	16	8
	Waller, Edmund. Poems. *Poetical Works*, ed. Chas. C. Clarke (Edinburgh, 1862).	5' cpl.	11	19	10

1640's: TABLE 1—(*Continued*)

Date	Poet and work (first 1,000 lines)	Form	In average ten lines		
			Adj.	Noun	Verb
	Wither, George. *Vox Pacifica.* *Misc. Works*, Pub'ns. Spenser Society, No. 13, 2d coll., 1872	5' st. Narr., addr.	7	14	11
1646	Crashaw, Richard. *Steps to the Temple. Poems*, ed. A. R. Waller (Cambridge Univ. Press, 1904).	4'–5' st. Descr., addr.	10	18	11
	Shirley, James. *Poems*, ed. Ray L. Armstrong (New York, King's Crown Press, Columbia Univ., 1941).	4' cpl., st. Narr., addr.	7	14	11
	Suckling, John. *Fragmenta Aurea. The Works*, ed. A. Hamilton Thompson (London, 1910).	4' cpl., st. avg. Narr., addr.	6	13	12
	Vaughan, Henry. *Silex Scintillans*, 1650, and *Poems. Works*, ed. Grosart. Fuller Worthies' Library, 1871.	2'–5', avg. 4' st Addr.	7	13	9
1647	Cleveland, John. "Poems," ed. Berdan, 1903.	4'–5' st. Addr.	7	17	10
	Cowley, Abraham. *The Mistress. Works* (8th ed., London, 1693).	4'–5' st.	7	13	11
1648	Herrick, Robert. *The Hesperides. Complete Poems*, ed. Grosart, 3 vols. (London, 1876).	4'–5' st. Addr., narr.	7	13	11
1649	Lovelace, Richard. *Lucasta. The Poems*, ed. C. H. Wilkinson (Oxford, Clarendon Press, 1925).	4'–5' cpl., st. Addr.	8	13	10
1649	Dryden, John. Upon the Death of Lord Hastings," in *Lacrymae Musarum*, 1649; and later elegies, in *Poetical Works*, ed. W. D. Christie (New York, Macmillan, 1921).	5' cpl. Addr.	10	16	10

1640's: TABLE 2

PROPORTIONS IN ORDER OF ADJECTIVAL EMPHASIS

Poet	Adjs.	Nouns	Verbs
Harvey..................................	6	12	10
Suckling...............................	6	13	12
Wither.................................	7	14	11
Jonson.................................	6	14	12
Donne..................................	7	13	12
Vaughan................................	7	13	9
Cowley.................................	7	13	11
Shirley.................................	7	14	11
Herrick.................................	7	13	11
Denham................................	7	15	9
Cleveland..............................	7	17	10
Lovelace...............................	8	13	10
Carew..................................	8	15	11
Sandys.................................	8	17	9
Dryden.................................	10	16	10
Quarles................................	10	17	13
Crashaw...............................	10	18	11
Waller.................................	11	19	10
Milton.................................	12	16	8
More...................................	12	18	10

1640's: TABLE 3

MAJORITY VOCABULARY: IN 1,000 LINES 10 USES BY 10 POETS OR MORE

Word	Ha.	Su.	Wi.	Jo.	Do.	Va.	Co.	Sh.	He.	De.	Cl.	Lo.	Ca.	Sa.	Dr.	Qu.	Cr.	Wa.	Mi.	Mo.	Total no. of users
fair		10				10	20	15				15	20	15		15	35	30	10	10	12
good	30	20	10		20			10	10	10	10	10		10	20	25	10	15	10	30	16
great	10	15	15	10			15			20	10		15	10	20	10	20	20	10	25	14
sweet						30		15	15				10	15	15	10	15	10		10	10
day	10	10	15	10	15	10	10	10	10			15	10	15	15	20	15	20	10	10	15
earth		15	10			10	15				10	10	25	20	10	15	10				10
eye	30			15	20	10	15	30	10	10	20	20	25	30	10	25	50	20	15	10	19
God	30	15	25	15	25		15	25	10	10	15	10	15	30	10	20	15	10	10	15	15
heart	10	15	15	10		15	15	10	10	15	25	15	30	15	40	10	45	15		10	16
heaven	10	50	20	30	110	10	60	35	40	20		15	65	10	15	10	15	30	15	15	11
love	30	30		45	20	15	30	15	20	15	20	15	10	20	15	10	15	15	10	25	16
man	10	15	15		15	10	10	15		15	15	10	10		35	10	10	15	10	15	18
soul	10	20	15	10	30	15	15	20	10	20	10		10	15	20	20	20	15	10	15	13
time		15	15	15	10	10	20	10	20	20	10	10		10	25		10	20		10	10
bring	10	10		25	15	15	20		20	15	10	15	20	15	20	25	10	15	10	10	12
come	10	20	15	45	30	15	30	35	30	30	20	20	20	15	15	45	45	30	10	25	15
find		15	15	25	20	25	25	30	20		15	25	15	15	10	15	55	15	10	25	18
give	10	15	10	20	10	10	15				15			10		15				15	19
go		10		15	10		20	10	10	10	10	10	10	10	25	10	10	10	10	10	11
know	10	20		15	15	15	20	10	10	20	20	15	20	15	20	25	10	15	10	25	18
make	25	25	15	25	30	15	30	35	15	30	15	20	20	15	15	45	45	30	10	25	20
see	25	15	25	45	20	25	25	30		20	15	25	15	10	10	15	55	15	10	25	20
take	15	10	10	20	10	10	15	10	10				10	10	10	15		10		10	12
tell		20	10	15	10				10	10	15			10		20	10			10	11
think	10		10	15	20	10	15		10	10	10					20	10	10			12
Total of major words used	16	20	18	19	17	19	22	19	17	15	14	18	16	19	19	23	22	18	15	17	

1640's: TABLE 3A

MINORITY VOCABULARY: 10 USES BY 4 POETS OR MORE

Word	Ha.	Su.	Wi.	Jo.	Do.	Va.	Co.	Sh.	He.	De.	Cl.	Lo.	Ca.	Sa.	Dr.	Qu.	Cr.	Wa.	Mi.	Mo.
bright	:	:	:	:	:	:	:	:	:	:	:	15	:	:	:	:	15	10	:	10
dark	:	:	:	:	:	10	:	:	:	10	:	:	:	:	:	:	10	:	10	:
full	:	:	:	:	:	10	10	:	:	:	:	:	:	:	:	10	10	:	:	10
happy	:	:	:	:	:	:	:	:	:	:	:	10	:	10	10	:	:	:	:	10
high	:	10	:	:	15	:	:	:	:	:	:	:	:	:	:	15	10	10	15	10
new	:	:	:	10	:	:	:	10	:	20	10	10	:	:	10	:	15	10	15	:
old	:	:	10	:	10	:	:	:	10	:	:	:	:	:	:	15	10	10	10	10
poor	10	:	:	10	:	:	:	:	10	:	:	10	:	:	:	:	15	:	:	:
rich	10	:	:	:	:	:	:	:	10	:	:	10	:	:	10	10	10	:	:	:
true	:	:	10	:	20	10	:	10	10	:	:	10	10	:	:	10	10	:	:	:
blood	:	:	:	:	:	10	:	10	:	:	:	:	10	:	:	10	:	:	:	:
death	:	:	:	10	10	10	:	:	:	:	:	10	:	10	15	:	20	:	:	:
face	10	10	:	10	10	:	10	10	:	:	:	:	15	:	10	:	:	:	:	10
fire	10	10	:	10	:	:	:	10	:	:	:	10	10	10	:	:	10	10	:	:
grace	15	10	:	10	:	:	:	:	:	:	:	:	:	:	10	15	:	:	:	:
hand	:	:	:	10	:	10	:	:	:	10	:	:	10	:	:	:	:	:	:	:
king	10	:	10	:	:	:	10	10	:	:	:	:	:	:	:	10	:	:	:	:
life	:	:	:	10	10	10	10	:	:	10	10	10	:	10	10	:	:	:	:	15
name	:	:	:	10	:	:	10	10	:	:	:	:	10	:	:	:	:	:	:	:
nature	:	:	:	10	:	10	:	:	:	:	:	:	:	:	:	:	:	:	10	10
night	:	:	:	:	:	:	:	:	10	:	:	:	:	10	:	:	10	:	10	10
part	10	:	:	:	:	10	:	:	10	:	:	:	:	:	15	10	:	10	:	:
power	:	:	10	:	:	:	:	:	:	:	:	:	:	10	:	:	10	15	:	:
sin	:	:	15	:	:	10	:	:	:	:	:	:	:	10	:	:	:	:	:	:
son	:	:	:	10	:	:	:	:	:	10	:	:	:	:	:	:	:	:	:	10

1640's: TABLE 3A—(Continued)

Word	Ha.	Su.	Wi.	Jo.	Do.	Va.	Co.	Sh.	He.	De.	Cl.	Lo.	Ca.	Sa.	Dr.	Qu.	Cr.	Wa.	Mi.	Mo.
sun		10			10	10							10						10	
tear					15	10						15	15				20			
thing	10	15	25		15	10	20			10	10				10	10				15
world			10	10	15		15			15		10			15		15	10		
year					10	10	10						10							
appear		10	10				10							10	10					
call	10	10		10	10		10		10				10							
die		10			10	10			10						10					
fall							10	10	10	10		15	10	15						
fly				10					10											
grow			15	10	10		15	10	10			10		10	10	10		10	20	
hear		10		10					15				10		10	10		15	10	
keep		10		10			10	10	10				10			20			10	
lie					15				20			10	10		15	10	10		10	
live		10	10					10	10			10		10			10			
look				10		10	10						10	10	10					10
love		25		25	25		25	10	10			20			10					
shine					10	10	10		15		10		10		10	10	10			
show												10			10				10	
sing			10				10					10		10	10			15		
seem									10	10								10		
speak										10	10					10	15		10	10
stand			10							10						10	10	10		10
teach																10				10
weep						10						10					15			

1640's: TABLE 3B

INDIVIDUAL USES

Word	Ha.	Su.	Wi.	Jo.	Do.	Va.	Co.	Sh.	He.	De.	Cl.	Lo.	Ca.	Sa.	Dr.	Qu.	Cr.	Wa.	Mi.	Mo.
bad					10															
black												10					10	10		
bold					10															
false																				
foul																				10
gentle	10															10				
holy																		10	10	10
just																				
kind		10																		
mortal										10					10					
noble										10								10		
pious				10																
proud													10				10	10		
pure																				
quick						10		10												
sad									10								10		10	
small											10									
strange																				
white		10					10		10						10					
wise																				
young															10					
age																				
air																			10	
art																				
beauty							10						20	10						
bed							10		10											

1640's: TABLE 3B—(Continued)

Word	Ha.	Su.	Wi.	Jo.	Do.	Va.	Co.	Sh.	He.	De.	Cl.	Lo.	Ca.	Sa.	Dr.	Qu.	Cr.	Wa.	Mi.	Mo.
body							15													
breast												10		10						
cloud						20								15					10	
daughter																20		10		
ear																				
fate					10		10													
fear																				
flower			10						10											
foe			10											30						
folly																				
hope																				
hour		10				10														
joy																				
lamb												15		10		15			10	
light																				
lips						20	10		10		10	10	10							
lord	15													15						
place		15																		
poet									10	10										
rose																				
seas																				
sense																		15		10
sheep																30				
shepherd																75				
star						10													10	
swain																25				

1640's: TABLE 3B—*(Concluded)*

Word	Mo.	Mi.	Wa.	Cr.	Qu.	Dr.	Sa.	Ca.	Lo.	Cl.	De.	He.	Sh.	Co.	Va.	Do.	Jo.	Wi.	Su.	Ha.
thought									10						10					
tongue										10										
virgin							15													
virtue						10												10		
voice																				
water					10														10	
way																				
woman														10					10	
wit							10													
woe	10						15													
wrath																				
word	10				15														10	
awake																				
begin	15																			
fear					10															
feed					20															
hasten																			10	
hight	15																			
hold												10							10	
kiss														10						
move														10						
prove								10	10											
rise																				
sit		10																		
sleep															10					
swear										10										

Between the extremes, the period has character; it has a poetry. Skelton was published in compilation, as was Chaucer in Thynne's edition, Langland in the B text, 1550, and Lydgate in Chaucer editions and his own of 1554. Heywood brought forth the first installment of his Proverbs, Sternhold of his Psalms. Wyatt and Surrey, both of whom died in the decade, were famous in it, and were to form the basis of that milestone miscellany, Tottel's, in 1557. Googe and Breton kept to convention. The greatest innovation, within the period's reassertion, was to be seen in the new and full style of Sackville, as he elaborated upon Baldwin and the *Mirror for Magistrates* style in general. Just so, the 1550's and 1560's elaborated upon the 1540's, translating more from Vergil and Ovid than from the psalms which were the focus of such characteristic poets as Baldwin, Wyatt, Sternhold. The Biblical style, the spare, hortatory, historical, restricted the poetical proportions of the decade, and was supported, interestingly enough, by the mastership of Chaucer and the courtly gifts of Wyatt. The measured couplet of report or address, with stanzaic modifications into sonnet or rhyme royal, maintains through all these variations about 7 adjectives, about 15 nouns, about 11 verbs, in every ten lines, a moderation like that of only the strictest in the next century.

Table 2, by arrangement in increasing adjectival (and roughly substantival) order, emphasizes the kinds of style in the decade. The early lyricists differ partly because of their shortness of line, but even with doubled line their verbs would exceed their adjectives in exceptional degree. In this lyrical technique the traditional ballads are central. In the period as a whole, the different and major figures of Chaucer and Wyatt, each a borrower in his own day, borrow evidently toward the central result. Their 7-15-11 pattern is close to the conservative, though not the central, proportion of the 1640's as well; they set up, then, a sort of mode which is also an average in their day. Spenser is another

matter, and a new matter. He presents the extreme of substantival emphasis, the 3 to 1 proportion, the heavy modification,
toward which we see earlier poets like Heywood and Sackville
working. The power of Sackville's blank verse in this new form
is noteworthy; yet it is not merely the blank verse, which others
used less fully; it is also Sackville's whole habit of expression.
Nor is the difference to be solved by chronology; although there
is not in this list an early poet with the fullness of Sackville and
Spenser, in the main the two modes, substantival and predicative,
elaborate and sparing, seem to run parallel in time.

Table 3 shows that 2 particular adjectives, 10 nouns, and 10
verbs are used frequently, ten times or more, by a majority of the
poets in the period. One notes that verbs are shared unusually
much, adjectives unusually little, in relation to proportions of
usage as indicated in preceding tables. *Good, man, make,* and *see*
are the great common terms. Beyond these, agreements occur
most often in the middle group, for Surrey, Gascoigne, Sackville,
and for Spenser, perhaps partly because they use most words.
There is no clear school of usage. Skelton, Googe, Douglas are
most eccentric. From Lindsay on, especially, the emphasis is on
subjects secular and humane. The most particular of these, the
lord and king, will vanish in the lists of the 1640's, these and other
terms giving way to a more metaphysical emphasis.

The subordinate list of minor uses makes two close relationships evident. The first is that of Lydgate, Chaucer, Wyatt, and
Surrey, in their main line of poetic tradition. They mark a central
emphasis on many adjectives and nouns of feeling and on the
verb *love* itself. The second relationship is the close one between
Sackville, Spenser, even Heywood, and Shakespeare, who, as
they use the full poetic line, seem also to agree on what content
to measure with it. All the minor terms are strongly words of
affection and interrelation, of active life and attitude. In the individual lists, on the other hand, more variations are visible: the

adjectival color of the ballads, the outer world of church, city, field, and family, the active verbs of Langland, Lindsay, Gascoigne.

The turn to the lists of the 1640's is a turn to a more complex realm of heaven and earth, and some even clearer poetical divisions.

The tables for the 1640's show, in the full detail of a decade, the wide range of agreed experiment, the deep sort of individualism, the clear division into kinds. It was a full-bodied poetic decade which began with the posthumous poems of Carew, Donne, and Jonson, moved to Milton, Waller, Crashaw, and ended with the maturity of Herrick, the youth of Dryden. Its titles are religious, philosophical, pastoral, political, amorous, elegiac. Its forms are more often now stanzaic than coupleted, though the couplet maintains its strength within the stanza. Its vocative address is most common, in the tradition of Wyatt and Surrey, and the older narrative structure is subordinate. Its average proportioning is much like that of the preceding century's, with a slightly increased stress on the adjectival. Carew's 8–15–11 closely represents it. Its range has widened considerably: from the usual 6 or 7 adjectives in 10 lines of Jonson and Donne to the 12 in 10 of Milton and More: in this decade are a half dozen poets who employ one epithet or more per line, making with their many nouns and few verbs a substantival ratio sometimes three times the predicative, and therefore collaborating in a style of effect strongly different from the average in the period and from most but Sackville's in the 1540's. Verbs and nouns have consolidated rather than widened; from Milton's 8 to Quarles' 13 verbs and from Donne's 11 to Waller's 19 nouns is not so wide a gap as that of the 1540's, for both noun and verb have lessened somewhat in extremes, as adjective has expanded. In other words, in the 1640's there is less variety in the proportioning of parts of speech and, indeed, a good deal of close agreement; but at the same time, through the agency of adjectival usage, two stylistic extremes are clarified, the larger, the Donnic, in continuity from the 1540's, the smaller, the Miltonic, in continuity it may be surmised from the intervening decades of Spenser. Table 2, by its arrangement on the adjectival basis, makes clear the two sorts of proportions which amount to styles, with Donne's few nouns, Milton's few verbs, not idiosyncratic but individualistically typical.

Table 3 presents the higher ratio of adjectives in specific form, two more major ones, *fair* and *sweet*, of a sense quality to accompany increase of *day, heart, love,* and addition of *earth, eye, heaven, soul,* most closely and consistently massed at the Miltonic or adjectival side of the page. Verbs, both old and new, are stronger at the Donnic side, as proportioning also would have led one to expect. In major unanimities, *eye* has been added to *man* while both *find* and *give* have supplemented *make* and *see.* The decade is a more receptive, a more admiring, a more closely interworking one, as the many pairs of opposites suggest. Extra-strong uses like Vaughan's *day,* Shirley's and Crashaw's *eye,* Harvey's and Sandys' *God,* Carew's *heart,* the many Miltonic *heavens,* Donne's great *love* outverbalizing all the rest in his characteristic repetition, Jonson's *man,* Dryden's *soul,* and the many *makes,* represent again, as one reads down the list, the consolidations in the 1640's both in agreement and in emphatic repetition. Across the page, on the other hand, the blanks in the interest of Denham, Cleveland, Milton in most of the standard nouns reveal an individualism still strong as Skelton's, a 50 per cent disagreement. And, further, the two sides of the page present two sides of the poetry, one predicative, the other substantive, even in the mass of major words.

Supplementary to table 3 are lists showing minor agreements and individual stresses in vocabulary. They substantiate the adjectival emphasis of the Milton group (only *new* and *true* are pre-

dominantly Donnic); show a special subject matter for Donne
and Jonson in words like *face, grace, hand, name, thing, tear,
world,* the older human meanings; and make special pointers,
as toward Crashaw's many adjectives, Herrick's many verbs,
Quarles' loyalty to the literal terms of his pastoral topic. Much of
this will turn up later, in the text of section II. At least, the generalization which all the tables and their supplements serve is
the generalization of poetic continuity, pervasive in the technical
medium, in the words and contexts of the poems, and varied in
specific and constant degree by individual and kind in their time.

The procedures of study upon which the tables are based must
now be described in greater detail for those who may be interested in the technique employed.

The poets included are those listed by Ghosh's *Annals of English Literature* as published in the decade, and are poets then
living or less than a decade dead. Any other basis would require
complexities of distinction not pertinent to this study; the basis
of composition in the decade, for example, would demand a
volume of research with special problems of its own. The exclusion of poets recently dead would remove too arbitrarily the force
of work still actively sold and read and considered, as Yeats' has
been in the 1940's. If, as for Dryden, no large amount of work
was published within the decade, I have extended the study into
later work, noting that no important change in technique occurs.
Because more than twenty poets have seemed unwieldly to tabu-
late, I have merely checked the five others least available to the
general reader, to show their place in the scheme, with Marvell
as an interesting parallel to Dryden.

Nathaniel Whiting, *Albino and Bellama,*   5′ st. narr.   8   19   10
     1641. *Caroline Poets,* III, ed. Saintsbury
     (Oxford, 1921).

Francis Kinnaston, *Leoline and Sydanis,*   5′ st. narr.   9   17   10
     1642. *Caroline Poets,* II, ed. Saintsbury
     (Oxford, 1906).

Richard Corbet, *Poems,* 1647. *Works of* *English Poets,* ed. Chalmers, 1810.	5′–4′ st. addr.	7	16	11
John Hall, *Poems.* 1647. *Caroline Poets,* II, ed. Saintsbury (Oxford, 1906).	5′ cpl. addr.	7	15	11
Joseph Beaumont, *Psyche,* 1648.	5′ st. narr.	9	17	11
Andrew Marvell, *State Poems,* 1670.	5′ cpl. narr.	10	18	10

It will be noted that these poets maintain the same average as the rest, with Corbet and Hall most Donnic, Marvell, even in his State Poems, Miltonic, and the long poems in the middle. In addition, the first five ballads, 530 lines, in Hyder Rollins' *Cavalier and Puritan: Ballads ... 1640–1660,* employ the Donnic average of 6–13–18 in 10. Others who wrote in the period but are not listed by Ghosh as publishing volumes are Benlowes, Chamberlayne, Godolphin, King, Philips, Randolph, Stanley.

The 1,000-line amount I take as representative, at least provisionally. Usually it is the first 1,000 lines of the work named; sometimes it is divided, if two works of the poet in the period seem very different: in most such poets, except Denham, the proportions do not greatly differ. In my study of some other poets, Wordsworth, Gray, Collins, Hopkins, Yeats, for example, I have learned that a poet is apt to employ one style in main proportion throughout his work, and I am working with some assumption of this generalization. But there may be many, if not a majority, of exceptions, and I therefore mean to make no statement about any more than the lines under consideration. Any remark that Herrick works in a certain fashion refers, in this study, only to the Herrick of the first 1,000 lines of *Hesperides.*

In these 1,000 lines every adjective, noun, and verb has been listed and counted. Adjectives include descriptive ones like *good,* participial modifiers like *coming,* or *fallen,* limiting modifiers like *some, ten, few.*[6] Nouns include substantive forms except verb

---

[6] It is interesting to note that while the proportion of descriptive adjectives is fairly steady, emphasis on limiting or participial seems to vary with other aspects of style. The predicating poet seems to be the limiting, the epithetical the participial, poet. As a whole,

forms or pronouns. Verbs include auxiliaries, infinitives, gerunds, each counted separately except the *has* and *is* and *do* auxiliaries. These most common terms, and a number of others, like *one* and *say,* so frequent that they are traditionally omitted from concordance tabulation (see Preface to the Wordsworth concordance, ed. Lane Cooper), are not included in the word-reference tables since they may be assumed to be common and since no check is provided by concordances; but they are accounted for in totals of verb or adjective occurrence.

The 1,000 lines, at least in the 1540's and 1640's, are apt to be five-accented lines; that is, one may assume a normal line length of which to speak, and this assumption is welcome since the line, despite its flexibilities, is by poetry's very structure much more integral a unit than any other. It is necessary, when the average of lines is much less than five-accented, as in the poetry of Sternhold or Vaughan for example, to compute the ratio of difference if one wants exact numerical parallelism. But since the use of shorter lines is itself of stylistic significance, I have not made this computation in the tables. The reader will, I trust, be willing to make the just allowances for variation, to surmise that a longer line for Vaughan or Suckling might consistently make for another adjective, one or two more nouns and verbs in ten lines, but no deeply different style.

The main measures and stanza structures I have combined with main sentence structure in the statement of "form," and the standard sorts of simple sentences I take to be declarative or narrative, in the third person; vocative address, interrogative or imperative, in or including the second person; exclamatory or lyrical, in the first and sometimes the third person. It will be seen that the characteristic form of the 1640's was that of coupleted

---

the participial construction is much less strong than in modern poetry (see my *Major Adjectives*), only Cleveland, Sandys, and Milton using the 30 per cent or more now common, while Wither, Donne, Shirley used for limitation an equal proportion, now rare.

address, the sound pattern strongly dependent upon variation of measure and the rhyme marking it, the statement-pattern commonly argumentative, beginning with the address to love, friend, or lord, developing one or both sides of the thought, and ending with conclusion often a petition. This form was only beginning in the 1540's, set by Wyatt and Surrey against a background of recommendatory narratives; and in the 1640's it was not the only form, countered as it was by a different sort of narrative, smoother and more sweeping in measure and more allied to exclamation, as the ode intended to be, and as the epithetical range of Waller and Milton demanded.

In content as in proportion, in table 3: 1640's as in tables 1 and 2, the limitation of "in the main" or "primarily" is to be held. The central concern is with the measures and structures and words most used by each poet and then also perhaps most used by most poets, at least within the bounds of the decade. Table 3 shows the majority terms, the words used ten times or more (and "ten" means, in this word enumeration, between eight and twelve, allowing a range of five as close enough for significance) by at least half the poets. Tables 3A and 3B add a view of some minority agreements and some individualisms in the 1640's. Individual word counting presents problems of combination, and I have followed the practice of combining singulars and plurals (man–men), comparatives and superlatives (good–better–best), verb forms (make–made). I have also included the gods with God. A check upon the major terms has been provided by the concordance lists of poets writing in the period, by Donne, Herrick, Herbert, Milton in the 1640's, for example; almost every word most used in the concordances was most used also by a majority of poets in the decade. Certainly a count twice checked must still have missed some major terms by oversight or error; this study would not pretend to purities of detailed accuracy past the simplest counting which will always need its corrections. But most of the major terms are here, in their proportions and proportionate contexts, and their principle is here, the principle of quantitative emphasis as clue to qualitative whole, as this study has proposed it.

If to the reader the tables look wearyingly and obtusely numerical, full of a mechanics which can never comprehend a poetry, I would ask him not only to read further in this text, which aims at some comprehension, but more seriously to read again in the poetry of the 1640's. Part of what he finds there is his own method and spirit; part is what the critics have found of wit, high seriousness, the metaphysical, the baroque; part, I submit, may well be what the poets themselves put there, knowingly or not, of their own individual, social, and poetical values, in the agreements of their own time. These values still speak to us in the *good* and *great, heart* and *soul, heaven* and *earth,* by which they spoke most strongly and constantly in the 1640's.

Moreover, these values, as they are part of a poetry, may speak in part for all poetry. One may surmise about poetic language that its nouns in proportion and emphasis are most numerous and various, representing individuality most clearly; that its verbs represent stability and unity of usage, its adjectives type and style. One may surmise about poets that they deeply share their language, in its sound and its sense and its sentencing; that they stress nevertheless their individual choices; that they maintain types, of which both major and minor poets support the extremes. One may surmise, indeed, that likeness, difference, and kind of language are important to the definition of a poetry, since language is its medium.[7]

---

[7] It is often said, as by Edith Rickert in *New Methods for the Study of English Literature* (Univ. of Chicago Press, 1927), that words rather than language are the medium of literature, a reduction which seems to me parallel with that which makes H_2O the medium of the Seven Seas. Even in its most irrational, magical forms literature makes as much use of syntax as of sound and reference. Language is not the sum of words, for their relationship is part of its character. Studies of the language of poetry have usually not taken it direct, but rather have focused on special derived forms of it, aureate terms and tropes in the sixteenth century, numbers and imagery in the eighteenth, symbols in the nineteenth, sound and imagery (by which is often meant figure) in the twentieth.

II. TWENTY POETS OF THE 1640's

No two poets of the 1640's wrote alike. Out of most of the same main words, main motifs, and meters, each man made up his special brand. Of some of these many brands one may profitably be reminded, to hear again the intonations, with and against the main tune, of Cowley or Quarles, Lovelace or Sandys. A beginning in the middle, with Cowley and his colleagues, Shirley and Carew and Herrick, sets the main tune going—the middle of greatest agreement, its variety, force, and direction. Then one may turn, surer of the norm, to some petty and some mighty opposites.

Abraham Cowley was not petty or mighty. He was the poet of his day. *The Mistress, or, Several Copies of Love-Verses* begins with a seven-stanzaed situation entitled "The Request," a situation in which the speaker complains of the need for a double wooing: of Love himself, the cruel Boy, as well as of a Mistress.

> I'have often wisht to love; what shall I do?
> Me still the cruel Boy does spare;
> And I a double taske must bear,
> First to woo him, and then a Mistress too.
> Come at last and strike for shame;
> If thou art anything besides a name;
> I'll think Thee else no God to be;
> But Poets rather Gods, who first created Thee.

The speaker is self-conscious as poet as well as lover: he makes the situation not only double, but quadruple: he informs the audience of the ambiguity of his search, and then informs the object of his search of its own ambiguity, putting the whole in the lap of fancy, at the outset.

The stanza form provides the same double play in accent and rhyme, in the first four lines rhyming five-accent lines with five-accent and fours with fours, then shifting to alternates in couplet rhyme, with a final extra accent at the end, suggesting in effect, as does the thought, the undependability of obvious expectations. The syntax is rhetorical, full of punctuational gesture aware of audience, mixing statement, question, statement, imperative, threat, in quick succession. The structure of the whole poem follows the same succession, from a two-stanza statement of the speaker's eagerness at all costs to love, to one stanza's command to strike the burning arrows in, to two stanzas' figurative questioning of man's place among the beasts and fishes as game for Love, for Venus or Diana, and a final stanza of challenge:

> Come; or I'll teach the World to scorn that Bow:
> I'll teach them thousand wholsom Arts
> Both to resist and cure thy Darts,
> More than thy skilful Ovid e'r did know.
> Musick of Sighs thou shalt not hear,
> Nor drink one wretched Lovers tasteful Tear:
> Nay, unless soon thou woundest me,
> My Verses shall not only wound, but murther Thee.

So the six stanzas are an elaboration of the first, and the last stanza directly of the first's last line: the structural neatness is complete, and devoted to the neatness of the thought which maintains through thick and thin, through rhyme and accent, myth and figure, question and imperative, that art is master over nature, and so the artist over his love.

The words in this poem are the words of the 1640's: *love,* cruel, *come,* thing, name, *God,* beauties, grow, seem, desires, fly, happy, *eyes,* noble, sin, fire, *heart,* move, flame, mighty, light, *men, make,* hear, sing, year, anger, sea, world, sighs, art, tear, all frequent, the major ones here italicized. They are worldly words and heavenly, moral words and emotional, earthly words and bodily, concrete and abstract, natural and human. They make here the blend which they tend to make throughout the 1640's, putting all materials in the explicit power of the poet, so that love may flit from wing to breast within the line; and God, sin, murder weigh the whole, yet not very heavily; and the things of nature, birds, woods, lions, and mute fishes, be interspersed with passionate deities slightly Roman.

The second piece, "The Thraldom," more briefly compares death to love's harder slavery, in the galley, the tomb, the quarry, the mine, of earth and of body. Four and five stresses vary the couplets, the intricacies of slavery modify the abruptness of the narrative of death. The next, "The Given Love," tightens all its couplets to four-stress to treat of the economy of the problem: the price put upon beauty and its pricelessness, the demands of beauty for the wealth of the Indies, the counteroffer of poetic immortality. Here King, Puritan, Adam, Spaniard, and Pope are the external references which give the repeated paradoxical play of love, avarice, heaven, and nature its local point and position. In "The Spring," it is the season which localizes, since love can be a season as well as a slavery and a wealth, and the springtime of the mistress' presence encloses the stanzas of physical and mythical spring as, within the stanza, the five-accent couplets enclose the four-accent quatrain. Again, in "Written in Juice of Lemon," love is given body as a writing on paper, to be brought out by warmth, or to be burnt in sacrifice; in "Inconstancy," couplets defend love's changes; in "Not Fair," couplets attack its falsehood, seeing it "As Puritans do the Pope, and Papists Luther do"; in the stanzas of "Platonick Love," "The Change," and "Clad all in White," heart and body and soul of love are contrasted and made one. These first ten poems of *The Mistress* are representative of the whole. The constant basic reference is to the human relationship of love. The abstract is made concrete in arbitrary metaphor which supports the power of the artist to use the pertinences of nature and myth, the features of Egyptian tombs, or Orpheus' song, or trees in shade, or Moor or Succubus, or Autumn Fruits, or maze, or court, or robe, or flag, to make a bodily construction for the intricacies of spirit. This "as it were" or "let's pretend for the sake of clarity" construction keeps always the artistry as part of the subject matter, implying not that this is a love poem, but rather that this is a poem by and about a poet in love; the self-consciousness makes for the constant double aspect of the reference: being a poet, I love through metaphor, and loving through metaphor I love thus. The syntaxes suggest most fully pleasure in argument and awareness of audience. The metaphoric structure has its own sort of dialectic which demands display. "It would be inconstant to keep on loving you: the seasons change: in nature, change is constancy." Either the figure of love as a color or season of nature calls up the paradox from nature's other qualities, or the paradox itself seeks an analogy in nature. Man's mind is, at any rate, the mediating force between abstract and concrete, and it is the process of that mediation which the poem portrays. Question and answer, argument and resulting imperative, theory and expected action upon exhortation, catch the process before it is complete and make its direct application to lady and to audience, rhetorically if not dramatically. The ends of the universe are marshaled to the situation and varied to fit. And rhyme and accent, too, vary to fit, blending or conflicting as the argument proceeds, in an effect of rather intricate weaving of emphasis and sound. Actually, most of the intricacies of sound in vowel and consonantal, or even phrasal, pattern are missing; not this sort of "color" or "melody" absorbed Cowley, but rather the punctuational, the sound patterns of a deft, variable, but measured reason. Donne's deeper emotional roughness, and Herrick's lighter lyrical point on the one hand, and Dryden and Pope's more tensely controlled measure on the other, have a sort of middle level in Cowley's poised, woven, and balanced five-and-four-stress speeches to his love.

The rest of the titles in *The Mistress*—"The Vain-Love," "The Soul," "The Passions," "Wisdome," "The Despair," "The Thief," "The Bargain," "The Prophet," "The Welcome," "The Parting," for example,—suggest the continued feelings and activities of the poems. The objects which make the body of reference are absent from the titles: they are not subjects, but accessories. At the last is "Love given over":

> It is enough; enough of time, and pain
> Hast thou consum'd in vain;
> Leave, wretched Cowley, leave
> Thyself with shadows to deceive;
> Think that already lost which thou must never gain.

(Refuse to be burnt, like helpless Ships, again. Or is one wound, by Love or Death, too much?)

> Alas, what comfort is't that I am grown
> Secure of be'ing again o'rethrown?
> Since such an Enemy needs not fear
> Lest any else should quarter there,
> Who has not only Sack't, but quite burnt down the Town.

In turning from his mistress, Cowley does not abandon address and argument; he addresses and argues with himself, asks himself the question, caps his own answer, is consumed and immortalized in his own conflagration. *The Mistress,* then, is his construction of the world, in all its verses, set in the scheme of its love and involved in everything the world can offer, if the poet has the wit to handle the involvement.

James Shirley is another who has the wit. He comes as close to Cowley as any poet in the decade comes, and as close to the decade's central procedures. He shares with Cowley and Herrick the approximate norm of 7 adjectives, 14 nouns, 11 verbs in ten lines. He shares with Cowley most main terms except *earth, god,* and *think,* all three a bit too serious for him, and with Herrick most but *great, heaven, soul,* and *time.* A measure of the cosmical, part of the metaphysical, is what many poets of mid-range fail to emphasize. Cleveland and Lovelace, Carew and Sandys, their colleagues, all shun the standards of *good* and *great,* the height of *heaven,* the abstraction of *time,* the activities of *coming* and *going, telling,* and *thinking.* They stress the *fair* and *sweet, love* and *eye, giving* and *making.* Shirley's minor terms, too, like Cowley's, stress the earthly and feeling. His *sad, warm, merry, joyful, beauty, blood, flame, name, face, tears, voice and bird, call and sing,* like Cowley's *wise, wretched, rich, art, beauty, body, nature, woman, name, fear, grow, take, seem, prove, move, fly, call, appear, shine,* participate in the poetry of worldly sense. So he writes, "To his unkind M[istris].":

> Sure thy heart was flesh at first,
> For what sin hath it been curst
> Into that stubborn thing of late,
> Above the reach of wonder? what,
> In some winter was it lost,
> And its blood drunk up by frost,
> Grew stiffe, and so a rocke became?
> Yet this would soften at a flame.
> Or didst thou bathe thy pretty limbs
> In some cold and fatal streams,
> Which turn what they embrace to stone,
> And by degrees thy heart grew one?
> I know not, but too true I find
> A Quarry of prodigious kind:
> Yet since I lov'd it, I will try
> From the warm Limbeck of my eye,
> In such a method to distil
> Tears on thy marble nature, till
> Their frequent drops by loves new Art,
> Write my Epitaph on thy heart;
>   That men may know for whom I die,
>   And say beneath that stone I lie.

The four-accent couplet, and the reasoning structure working from question to suitable answering solution, within an elaborately continued metaphorical context, are, though they seem lighter here, characteristic of Cowley's method. The relationship is personal, the mistress is addressed and reasoned with, and the nature of frost and stone is invoked to clarify the problem.

Throughout Shirley's *Poems*, of 1646, the titles to the Mistress are a little more lively, a little more active, than Cowley's. "To his Mistress confined," "Loves Hue and Cry," "Upon his Mistris Dancing," "Upon his Mistris sad," "Presenting his Mistris with a Bird," "Taking leave when his Mistris was to ride," suggest less interest in the concept of situation and more in the graces or conventions. Shirley likes grace very much: "A jest, in answer of your merriment"; "Beauty was darknes till she came"; "One gentle language, or a smile"; "Love a thousand sweets distilling"; "Her voice that heavenly musick bears"; "Joyes multiplyed, to your eternity"; "To kisse your white hand, and receive from thence, / Both an authority, and innocence." Employing these pleasant phrases the more, and enjoying especially the pleasant sounds of voice and bird, Shirley the less involved himself in complex arguments. He accepted the paradox as good poetic center, but did not worry it, letting it come along naturally in the last stanza:

> So farewel my Odelia, be thou just,
> For when I die I'le love thee in my dust;
> And when I fail thee most, secure thy trust.

So also, by token of less scope in learned and mythological reference, Shirley intensified the reference of simple sights and public celebrations, with nonchalant epitaphs and pretty speeches like his typical "Presenting his Mistris with a Bird":

> Walking to taste the welcom Spring,
> The Birds with cheerful notes did sing
> On their green Perches, 'mong the rest,
> One whose sweet warble pleas'd me best,
> I tempted to the snare, and caught,
> To you I send it to be taught;
> 'Tis young, and apt to learn, and neer
> A voice so full of art, and cleer
> As yours, it cannot choose but rise
> Quickly a Bird of Paradise.

The ease with which London's formerly leading playwright turns his verse marks his great difference from Cowley; but in many matters of substance and structure they are colleagues as well as contemporaries.

Others of their contemporaries, too, worked in close, if only tacit and unconscious, or if only in technical and conventional, agreement. The major vocabulary, sound, and logic were shared. Herrick, the closest sharer, set forth his *Hesperides* in the normal four- and five-accent couplets, with quatrain variations: addressing his muse and his love, with double consciousness of his own artistry, full of nods, becks, smiles at his audience, reducing his comment often, with characteristic simplicity, to a couplet and a phrase. Cleveland, though longer-winded, took up in couplets the same attitudes of witty address, speaking to his mistress as Herrick to his Perilla, Anthea, Julia. His too are the adjectives of good and sweet, the nouns of love and sight, the verbs of giving and taking. Fewer of his words are typical, more are special, like the pair of adjectives *strange* and *common* and the great bodily stress of his nouns *lips, kiss, head, ear, tongue;* like Sandys, he worked to use and then exaggerate the norm.

Lovelace, for all his ups and downs, struck the standard fairly true.

> Though Seas and Land betwixt us both,
>   Our Faith and Troth,
>   Like separated soules,
>   All time and space controules:
> Above the highest sphere wee meet
> Unseene, unknowne, and greet as Angels greet.

Here in the first "Song" of his *Lucasta* of 1649 the mixed couplets confront the love addressed with a physical scene to make a paradox, an articulated logic mixed with grace and heavenly reference. In "To Chloe" are the mixed pastoral and political references, in "Gratiana dauncing and singing" the familiar actions and analogies; in "An Elegie" the longer serious accents "mixe your joyes with cries" in the contrast which lingers even when paradox does not unfold.

> Here, here, oh here Euridice,
>   Here was she slaine;
> Her soule 'still'd through a veine:
>   The Gods knew lesse
> That time Divinitie,
>   Then ev'n, ev'n these
>   Of brutishnesse.
>
> Oh could you view the Melodie
>   Of ev'ry grace,
> And Musick of her face,
>   You'd drop a teare,
> Seeing more Harmonie
>   In her bright eye,
>   Then now you heare.

In this song of Orpheus, the lighter quicker pace and fancy still nevertheless maintain those pertinences and paradoxes of nature which sovereign love makes possible: divine divinity less than brute brutishness, and the sound of sight more harmonious than the sound of sound. The thought, less heavily constructed than Cowley's, is the same thought, in the same deftly irregular rhyming pace. And the adjectives *fair, good,* and *sweet* prevail, and all the nouns, and all the verbs but *come* and *go* and *think;* and of Lovelace's own special terms the qualities and graces predominate, in *bright, black, rich, joy, tear, breast, light,* and the lover's verbs to *fly* and *hasten.* There is a speed and savor in these terms which other lists fail to present, because these have all the effect of enjoyment, and this indeed is almost a defining quality of the poetry of Lovelace.

The busy and learned and traveling George Sandys, making his study in Virginia an English study, his Mediterranean pen an English pen, made Ovid and the Bible English also; in 1636, for example, he turned Psalms into the regular measure and vocabulary of Lovelace, Cowley, Carew. Despite the special problems of flora, fauna, and feeling, which the Song of Solomon brought to him, and which the Lamentations of Jeremiah insisted upon, the *virgins* and *children* and *daughters* of the *Lord,* the *cruel wrath* and *woes,* the *falling* and *rising,* Sandys translates much of his material into the special content of his decade: into the major epithets of *fair, great,* and *sweet,* into all the major nouns but *time,* into most of the major verbs. To the King, in 1641, Sandys writes:

Sir, I presume to invite you to these Sacred Nuptials: the Epithalamium sung by a crowned muse. Never was there pair of so divine a beauty, nor united in such harmonious affections:

and to the Queen,

> Chaste nymph, you who extracted are
> From that swift thunderbolt of war;
> Whose innocence and meekness prove
> An eagle may beget a dove;
> In this clear mirror you may find
> The image of your own fair mind;
> With each attractive excellence,
> Which feasts the more refinèd sense:
> The crownèd muse from heav'n inspir'd
> With such rich beauties hath attir'd
> The Sacred Spouse; for what below
> The sun could more perfection show?

and then, in the voice of the Sponsa,

> Join thy life-breathing lips to mine;
> Thy love excells the joys of wine.
> Thy odours, O how redolent!
> Attract me with their pleasing scent:
> These, sweetly flowing from Thy Name,
> Our virgins with desire inflame.
> O draw me, my Belov'd, and we
> With wingèd feet will follow Thee.

All this wording, the sacred, the divine, the beautiful, the war, prove, dove, image, and fair mind, the sense, heaven, rich beauties, and sun, the lips, love, flowing, name, flame, desire, is the accustomed wording of the poets, whether the lady be Herrick's lass, somebody's Saccharissa, or the Bride of the Lord. The tetrameter couplets, too, are familiar, and the structure of address and persuasion. A difference arises, however, in the liberality of the Song of Solomon. It allows the usual poet's monologue to be a dialogue. And it has a richness which intermittently outdoes itself in cedar roofs and galleries of cypress, in citrus and aromatic powders, more than the usual mistresses received. Nevertheless, these added spices do not alter the character of the seventeenth-century love poem. They reduce argument and paradox, they increase sensory description, but they serve still to bind the thoughts of heaven and earth.

So also the paraphrase of the Lamentations of Jeremiah serves to bind thoughts of heaven, earth, and the social state.

> How like a widow, ah! how desolate
> This city sits, thrown from the pride of state!
> How is this potent queen, who laws to all
> The neighboring nations gave, become a thrall!
> Who nightly tears from her salt fountains sheds,
> Which fall upon her cheeks in liquid beads.
> Of all her lovers none regard her woes,
> And her perfidious friends increase her foes.

Vassals are sovereigns, children cry for bread, wives are ravish'd, the foxes dwell among the ruins, Jeremiah cries to the Lord. There is much reference by indirection to the poet's own times, to any times of trouble, and the longer pentameter line carries the fuller exclamations of dismay. Yet still the sacred and profane terms repeat and ally themselves; and the mode of address, good for the lady, is good also for the Lord. How prayer and petition, religious, political, personal, kept form in the minds of the seventeenth century!

Thomas Carew figures well at the center of this norm. He was, along with Sandys, another of his poetic type, a courtier to Charles I. He was a friend of Jonson, of Cotton, of Kenelm

Digby. He died, and his works were published, just as the decade began. Men praised him for his wit, his fancy, his elegance, his grace. Some said that his sonnets were more in demand than any other poet's of his time. Suckling reported his labors in his *Sessions of the Poets,* 1646, and let him speak in a dialogue of *Fragmenta Aurea.* By reputation a poet of his times, by style he was so too, employing the average 8 adjectives, 15 nouns, and 9 verbs in ten lines, stressing *fair, good, sweet,* and his own *pure;* the major nouns with his own *face* and *beauty,* with *love* in an extra-abundance of 70 times; most of the major verbs with *to love* again as a verb and *to fly,* which he shared with his fellow lyrists of love. His irregularly rhymed and measured lyrics in all their elaboration of scheme were devoted to "His Mistress, Retiring in Affection," his Divine, his Perplexed, his Beautiful, his Cruel, his Demanding, his Inconstant Mistress, Sitting by a River side, Looking in a Glass; and to his friends, and to his king. They treated reasonably and passionately of the logics of love and such well-plotted relationship. Their moderate terms were bodily terms, of cheek and tear, blood, lips, and hands, perhaps cool, or fresh, or bright; their figures an amplification of crystal streams and youthful fires, pearly treasure, angry Jove, ivory hills, warm and cold seasons of the heart, Egyptian serpents, panting wings, holy Hymen, silken wreaths, mystique knots, hard fates, stout foes, and tender maids; their actions of waking, singing, smiling, daring, grieving, teaching, imploring, kindling, repining, blessing: a very lively poetic world, indeed, all mixed of classical, religious, political, personal loves, aerated by their combination.

Carew's poems make a kind of composite for the decade. More elaborate and adjectival than Cowley's, they are still full of Cowley's arguments.[1] The first of the poems, "The Spring," begins elaborately.

---

[1] See, for Carew's anti-Ovidian loyalty to Donne, his "Elegie upon the Death of Dr. Donne."

> Now that the winter's gone, the earth hath lost
> Her snow-white robes; and now no more the frost
> Candies the grasse, or casts an ycie creame
> Upon the silver lake or chrystall streame:

This narrative pictorial mode looks toward extremes we have not seen to be characteristic; it looks toward the Miltonic school. The second poem, "Perswasions to Love," on the other hand, employs just the tetrameter arguments of paradox and address which Cowley and his colleagues employ.

> Thinke not, 'cause men flatt'ring say,
> Y'are fresh as Aprill, sweet as May,
> Bright as is the morning starre,
> That you are so; or, though you are,
> Be not therefore proud, and deeme
> All men unworthy your esteeme:
> For, being so, you loose the pleasure
> Of being faire, since that rich treasure
> Of rare beauty and sweet feature
> Was bestow'd on you by nature
> To be enjoy'd;

Or, as a complete and brief example in mixed stanza, "His Perplexed Love":

> If she must still denye,
>   Weepe not, but dye:
> For my Faire will not give
> Love enough to let me live,
> Nor dart from her faire eye
> Scorne enough to make me dye.
>   Then let me weepe alone, till her kind breath
>   Or blow my teares away, or speake my death.

All through these is the familiar vocabulary of fair, bright, rich, sweet, man, star, pleasure, treasure, beauty, nature, eye, tear, breath, death. In major terms, Carew agrees with Lovelace, for example, except that, like Herrick, Denham, and Cleveland, he understresses *heaven*. His own special epithets are cold, cruel, pure, pale, his subjects the bodily beauties of face, lips, hands, tears, his activities the paradoxically and figuratively combined loving and dying. His center then is much the decade's center: the artful, regularly patterned joining of spiritual and bodily opposites in figurative language through rhetorical plaint, argument, and persuasion, drawing together heart and soul, sight and knowledge, Lady and Lord.

These seven poets of middle range and main agreement were not friends, formed no school, were neither of one age nor of one location in the 1640's, yet were of one poetic mind. Carew died as the decade began. Shirley avoided exile while Cowley flourished in it; Lovelace was back and forth between countries, in jail and out; Cleveland was in; Sandys had traveled and retired; Herrick had retired, at least from London life, in his own busy fashion. All were touched by the great Parliamentary war, but lightly, by imprisonment or exile or retirement, but not by military force or even lack of publication. *The Mistress, The Song of Solomon, Lucasta, The Hesperides* grew out of the deliberations of the decade, which were for the poets literary deliberations and which shared the arguments of religious and secular love, poet direct to beloved in tetrameter or pentameter accent, in the logic of metaphoric body and soul.

The frequencies of their adjective, noun, verb uses differ little. The range is from Cowley's 7 A–13 N–11 V to Sandys' 8 A–17 N–9 V: essentially a kind of poetry in which verb-frequency is about half of adjective-and-noun combined. The range of reference is not much wider. Most of the decade's main terms are shared, those of location, time, thought being most omitted, and those of the personal vigor of life, name, face, beauty most stressed. Cleveland is most idiosyncratic, not because he writes another kind of poetry, but because he writes this kind with such bodily particularization. This kind is in the main more particular in argument than in major reference, bringing all its abstractions to bear upon the point of human relationship.

The type's extreme is extreme in just such abstraction. Its extreme outdoes it in the use of predicates and connectives, in the use of *time* and *earth*, in the use of subordinated structures. In Harvey, in Suckling, in Jonson, Wither, Donne, and Vaughan the sparest and strictest major language is to be found: like that of the whole decade, but with least variety, least addition, least substantiation in noun and adjective. Some of this is poetry with more verbs than nouns, a ratio of 6 A–11 N–12 V, the like of which would seem to be exceptional in English literature and to provide a pole for all other decades as well as the 1640's.

But the other extreme, most distant from Donne and Jonson, seems to share much less in the materials of the middle range. It stresses more adjectives, in a ratio of 12 A–18 N–10 V, and more specific adjectives of sense like *sweet* and *fair* and *bright*. It stresses more scenic and cosmic nouns, and more static verbs. One of the poets of middle range wrote in this style as well, and provides, in one volume of work, the very mixture, in separate fashions, which the decade itself provides. This poet is John Denham, and it is significant that his own contemporaries recognized in his *Cooper's Hill* a special contribution.

> My eye, which swift as thought contracts the space
> That lies between, and first salutes the place
> Crown'd with that sacred pile, so vast, so high,
> That whether 'tis a part of Earth, or sky,
> Uncertain seems, and may be thought a proud
> Aspiring mountain, or descending cloud.

These lines provide, despite the familiar terms of *eye, place, sacred, high, earth, proud, thought,* a poetry rather different from his other characteristic sort, like "Friendship and Single Life," for example:

> Love! in what poyson is thy Dart
> Dipp'd, when it makes a bleeding heart?
> None know, but they who feel the smart.

> It is not thou, but we are blind,
> And our corporeal eyes (we find)
> Dazzle the opticks of our Mind.

The eyes in these verses participate in a technical figure for a feeling, while the eye of *Cooper's Hill* surveys a magnificent scene. In this difference is plain the decade's major contrast and Denham's double talent. Most of the poets wrote one way or the other, but not both, for this span of years. Harvey and Vaughan were consistently relational, Crashaw and More consistently scenic, at their respective extremes. But Denham, perhaps not a large enough figure to be insistent, not even so thorough as his colleague Waller in the composition of the new "reformed" verse, is one poet to strike a middle range because his two types of practice strike an average, his "clarity" meets his "conceit," his first of the great English local views does not outsweep his more compact abstract conceptions, yet the *proud, noble, bold* of the one serve to glorify the other's *old, name, world*.

Cooper's Hill looks toward one section of the decade's poems, then, the scenic, the grand, the adjectival and substantival and participial, the extended rather than the argued, the poems of Quarles and Dryden, of Waller and Milton, of Crashaw and More. "Friendship," on the other hand, looks to the poetry of relation, the predicated, subordinated, and reasoned, closer to the middle range of the decade but maintaining its own extreme: sparely in Wither and Suckling, strongly in Jonson and Donne. From the double view of Denham in his average place, we may turn to the closer view of major extremes.

An example of the plain and predicative procedure of the Donnic extreme is Wither's *Vox Pacifica* of 1645.

> I Who (before my Harp was tun'd or strung)
> Began to play a descant on the Times,
> And was among the first of those that sung
> The scorn and shame of VICE, in English Rymes.

> I, that have, now, just halfe the Age of Man,
> Been slashing at those Hydra's heads of sin,
> Which are, yet, more then when I first began;
> And more deformed growne, then they have bin;
> I, that have spoke of Truth, till few believe it;
> Of taking heed, till Follie hath her doome;
> Of Good-advice, till no man will receive it;
> And, of Deserved-Plagues, till they are come: . . .

This verse allows no smoothness for eye or ear. It scolds the negatives of sin and vice, and praises the positives of good. It uses almost as many verbs as nouns, and almost no adjectives at all. Nor does the moral topic necessarily establish this mode, for Milton's equally Puritan poems and More's Platonical poems are at the opposite extreme of style. The pentameter lines here, alternately rhyming and almost alternately subordinating, put their stress of reference upon action, concept, and relation, and in so doing employ the vocabulary of goodness, man and sin, and truth in the major terms; these along with *seem*ing and *appear*ing, *voice, king, God, folly,* and *foe,* and a scattering of infrequent adjectives like *private* and *public,* make up Wither's major and secondary emphases. The vocabulary seems indeed a Puritan one; at least it seems a vocabulary of state and social responsibility; and the poetry is more ostensibly didactic than we have seen since the 1540's. *Hope* and *fear, darkness* and *pride,* the richer shades and feelings of the average of his time, are scattered through Wither's work, but not, in the 1640's, the bodily beauties of the Cavaliers, and largely this one great omission accounts for his removal from the norm of vocabulary. Yet Suckling the Cavalier is almost as sparing.

In major vocabulary, Suckling agrees with Wither all down the line, showing his further alliance with the school of Donne by secondary emphasis on such terms as *new, face, fire, sun, thing, call, die,* and by his own personal *kind, wise, hope, wit,* his *way, place,* and *awake.* Suckling's *Fragmenta Aurea* is a poetry, published in 1646 posthumously, which seems staunchly to strip and dull the cavalier tradition. Though like Carew's, it is nevertheless not so rich and fanciful; though like Cowley's, it is not so fully argued; though like Jonson's, it is not so artful. In the 1630's, before his loyalist flight to and death in Paris, he was "a prominent figure among men of fashion at Court and a distinguished amateur of letters."[2] His editor relates him to Donne rather than Jonson, and praises his happy simplicity over his ingenuity,[3] yet the prominence, the amateur freshness, the simplicity seem to do little that is new to the old materials. What Mr. Henry Lawes set to music was what he had set before.

> I prithee spare me, gentle boy;
> Press me no more for that slight toy,
> That foolish trifle of an heart:
> I swear it will not do its part,
> Though thou dost thine, employ'st thy power and art....

"Awake, great sir, the sun shines here"; "There never yet was honest man"; "In each man's heart that doth begin / To love"; "Dost see how unregarded now"; "It is so rare and new a thing to see"; "What mighty princes poets are"; "Thou hast redeem'd us, Will"; "Wonder not, if I stay not here"; "Fie upon hearts that burn with mutual fire"; "I tell thee, Dick"; "My dearest rival." About half of the twenty poems are thus addressed; the rest begin with some declarative or exclamatory statement; and all develop a friendly sort of relationship in simple and standard metaphorical terms, in standard stanza or couplet in four- or five-accented lines. Suckling's own major words *place* and *way* are, indeed, characteristic of him, in their neutral functioning.

Of the religious poetry of the 1640's, Christopher Harvey's is one extreme. Composed by "a very venerable and lovable man and a genuine singer,"[4] arranged in a variety of common seven-

---

[2] *The Works of John Suckling,* ed. A. Hamilton Thompson (London, 1910), p. x.
[3] *Ibid.,* p. xi.
[4] Grosart, Introd. to *Works.*

teenth-century stanza patterns, constructed upon a familiar An-
glican series of moral imperatives and descriptive norms, and
since its first publication anonymously in 1640 linked closely with
George Herbert's more famous *Temple,* Harvey's *The Synagogue; or The Shadow of the Temple* speaks a poetic language
not central but peripheral to its decade.

> Lord, my first-fruits should have been sent to Thee;
> For Thou, the tree
> That bare them, only lentest unto me.

This, the beginning of his "Dedication," sounds standard
enough; but it is not; it is, for the 1640's, spare in the extreme.
Fewest of the major poetic terms of the decade, fewest nouns
and adjectives of any sort, least of inventive and substantiated
subject matters are to be found in *The Synagogue.*

At the opposite limit of elaboration for the decade is another
religious poem, published two years later by another divine,
*Psychozoia, or The first part of The Song of the Soul, Containing
a Christiano-Platonicall display of Life,* by Henry More, later
Master of Arts and Fellow of Christ's College, Cambridge. Here
in numbered Spenserian stanzas and cantos, in invocation, address to the reader, mythological background, narrative and
scenic structure are to be found the fullest contents and modifications of the time.

> Nor Ladies loves, nor Knights brave martiall deeds,
> Ywrapt in rolls of hid Antiquitie;
> But th'inward Fountain, and the unseen Seeds,
> From whence are these and what so under eye
> Doth fall, or is record in memorie,
> *Psyche,* I'll sing. *Psyche!* from thee they sprong.
> O life of Time, and all Alterity!
> The life of lives instill his nectar strong,
> My soul t'inebriate, while I sing *Psyches* song.

Characteristically, in the first stanza, as throughout the long
poem, qualities prevail over actions, sensations over relations.

These alternatives, of More and of Harvey, do not seem to belong to the 1640's alone. The reader of More's stanza, "Nor Ladies loves, nor Knights brave martiall deeds,..." will cry at once (in spite of the *nor*), *Spenser!* and, of "Lord, my first-fruits...," *Herbert!* These are two traditions familiar to us in all their opposition, and not limited to minor poets or to minor spaces of time. Nevertheless, it is noteworthy that they do serve in minor as well as major fashion, and in objective as well as subjective fashion, to characterize the differences both between two poetically laboring divines and between the limits of poetical invention in so crucial a decade as the 1640's. They define as well as support their colleagues.

On a scale representing the decade's range of poetic reference, with Harvey at one end and More at the other, Jonson and Donne rest beside Harvey; Waller and Milton beside More. The minor men mark the limits, the major men are beside them just within the limits. The matter of difference, then, is more than a matter of minor followers of two great traditions, the Elizabethan and the Jacobean, the Spenserian and the Metaphysical, the Neo-Platonic and the Neo-Aristotelian, the Cavalier and the Puritan; and it is less than the matter of these traditions themselves with all their ramifications. Centrally it is a matter of how poets write poetry, and how in any one time, while sharing the interests and manners of that time, poets make choices as wide apart as possible, within the range of choice afforded them by the idiom of the time. So *Under-wood* opposes "Lycidas," the posthumous work, the youthful; so Wither's poems oppose Waller's in 1645; so Vaughan as one kind of metaphysician opposes Crashaw as another in 1646; so the mature Herrick's *Hesperides* of 1648 opposes the immature Dryden's "Hastings" of 1649. So the focus of a unity of time brings clear the variety of type; and so in converse the individual reaches are seen to be bound and confirmed in the common grasp.

Perhaps the poet best to represent the solidest ramifications of the extreme position is Ben Jonson, to whom many younger poets were pleased to call themselves "son," as they modified his position toward the central agreement of their own.[5] Most modern critics think of Jonson, I suppose, as a strong and mild but somewhat dull example of what was most standard in his age. Rather, he was a radical poet, allied with Donne against a large field. He was a poet of the power of predicates and infrequent epithets. He was a poet of both Lord and Lady.

> Heare mee, O God!
> A broken heart,
> Is my best part:
> Use still thy rod,
> That I may prove
> Therein, thy Love....

and,

> Let it not your wonder move,
> Lesse your laughter; that I love.
> Though I now write fiftie yeares,
> I have had, and have my Peeres;
> Poets, though devine are men:
> Some have lov'd as old agen.
> And it is not always face,
> Clothes, or Fortune gives the grace;
> Or the feature, or the youth:
> But the Language, and the Truth,
> With the Ardor, and the Passion,
> Gives the Lover weight, and fashion.

Thus he begins a hymn to God the Father, thus he begins "A Celebration of Charis" in *Ten Lyrick Peeces*. Love is again the bond between, and art is again the immortalizing force. Every word in the two passages is essentially familiar to the reader of the poetry of the 1640's. Adjectives are scarce, and there is a verb

---

[5] Saintsbury would agree, calling Jonson "the greatest single tutor and teacher of the verse of the mid-seventeenth century"—that era which revealed the "almost incomprehensible blowing of the wind of the spirit in a particular direction for a certain space of time." *Minor Poets of the Caroline Period*, I, vii.

to almost every line. The structure is rhymed, coupleted, addressed. These are indeed poems of the 1640's, but with resraint.

For Jonson, three of the time's four major adjectives, six of the ten nouns, ten of the eleven verbs, were major. He stressed *good, great, sweet,* but not *fair; day, eye, god, heart, love, man,* but not the abstractions of *heaven, soul,* and *time;* his verbs were active and strong, *know, make, see, tell* used more often apiece than most other poets used them. Among secondary terms, he ignored the sensory in favor of epithets like *poor* and *true,* nouns like *face, life, name, nature, son, world,* verbs like *call, grow, look, love.* He ignored the *bright, dark, rich, soft* of a Crashaw, the *king* of a Wither, the *sun* and *tear* of a Donne or Carew, the *seem* and *shine* of a Cowley. His common, active language was neither one of appearances nor one of speculations, but rather one of event in thought or deed, and so slighted the aesthetics of substance and quality.

Most of the poems in *Under-wood* are stanzaic, the rest tetrameter couplet, or pentameter. The stanzas have not so much the intricate qualities of songs as the neat qualities of couplets. Here is one of the most metrically complex of the brief poems:

On A Lovers Dust
Made Sand for an Houre Glasse

Doe but consider this small dust,
    Here running in the Glasse,
        By Atomes mov'd;
Could you beleeve, that this,
    The body was
        Of one that lov'd?
And in his Mrs. flame, playing like a flye,
    Turn'd to cinders by her eye?
Yes; and in death, as life unblest,
    To have't exprest,
Even ashes of lovers find no rest.

The variations of accent play around the four-accent base of the first and last lines, which in themselves provide the idea of the poem, and which carry the echo of the major rhyme. The various rhymes set up in the first three lines are extended through the rest, with the exception of the couplet of former life, the *fly–eye* couplet; and the last line finishes with a sort of delayed couplet neatness. Not so elaborate in rhyme and accent interweaving as Cowley for example, Jonson exhibits a sense of patness, and perhaps more ear for inner pattern in the cross reference of consonants in this poem.

Note, too, how it is characteristic of his use of language. Adjectives, except verbal ones, are at a minimum. Dust, glass, atoms, body, flame, fly, cinders, ashes, lovers, the nouns extend the central figure. The central thought, on the other hand, in either first and last line, or the first question, is carried by verbs in the now familiar structure of address: "Do but consider . . . / Could you beleeve, that this, / The body was /Of one that lov'd?"

Of the two dozen or so first poems of *Under-wood,* two-thirds begin with some form of address: Let . . . , See, . . . , Guess, . . . , Come, let us . . . , Oh, doe not . . . , Consider, . . . , Take pity . . . , If, Sackville, . . . , Wake, friend, . . . , and so on,—and many then proceed through persuasion or illustration to a conclusion or question which keeps involved the subject of address. Only a few contain a simple narrative or listing progression, as "A Nymph's Passion" begins, "I love, and he loves me againe, / Yet dare I not tell who"; and then lists the qualities of her lover throughout five stanzas of telling yet not telling. Full of "eyes so round and bright," Summer sky, and love's Torches, such lines still contain some complexity of argument, and as so complex are more actually characteristic than the more famous "O so white! O so soft! O so sweet is she!" of the fourth Charis lyric.

I should suggest as representative of the true idiosyncrasy of Jonson's style the first lines of "An Epistle to Master John Selden."

I know to whom I write: Here, I am sure,
Though I am short, I cannot be obscure:
Lesse shall I for the Art or dressing care,
Truth, and the Graces best, when naked are.
Your Booke, my Selden, I have read, and much
Was trusted, that you thought my judgement such
To aske it: though in most of workes it be
A pennance, where a man may not be free,
Rather than Office, where it doth or may
Chance that the Friends affection proves allay
Unto the Censure. Yours all need doth flie
Of this so vitious Humanitie.

The sixteen verbs in these twelves lines are a great excess for poetry, but they are the very excess which Jonson, like Wither, Vaughan, and Donne felt to be poetic. The couplets are average enough, the address and argument familiar, the vocabulary of art, truth, grace, office, and friendship, strong and common; the special sound which Jonson gives to the language lies in brevity and persistency of statement. Sentences are to be weighed as sentences.

Fond of paradox like his time, Jonson presents to us, then, his own stylistic paradox. He is at once radical and conventional. He invents no new major or even secondary vocabulary, he shares the verse forms and thought forms of the decade following his death; yet he uses to an extreme that trait of his time which put up to poetry the activity of predication, which made the poem a process in which reader and writer both proposed, demonstrated, argued, disproved, questioned, responded, and so participated. Such a process and emphasis colored sound and syntax, as well as reference, filling the poem with the tone and structure of talk. As adjective and noun present substance, so predicate presents relationship and response. It was this sense of relationship which Jonson drew upon, if not always with skill, yet always with sympathy, to make a significance for his poetic sons, who moderately, and each in his own way, went to do likewise.

John Donne, whom Jonson admired and referred to with refrain-like consistency in his talks with Drummond, shared the poetic speech, yet spoke likewise in his own way. Elsewhere[6] I have tried to describe his way with adjectives and adjective structures, his scanty and conceptual use of them. Now it is possible to see that much of his method he shared with his late contemporaries, and that it was associated also with scant use of nouns and strong use of verbs. Donne, in fact, used fewer nouns than any other of the twenty poets, and more verbs than any but Jonson. He, too, pushed to an extreme the style which he shared. Most of the major terms he agreed on with Wither, Jonson, Vaughan, and then used one of these, *love,* more than a hundred times in a thousand lines, more than twice the amount of anybody else's most enthusiastic repetition. In his own special adjectives, the thousand lines of *bad, new, old, true,* reflect the emphasis of his whole concordance. In his secondary nouns, to the Jonsonian *face, name, world,* he adds characteristically more concrete emphases, on *death, tear, sun, thing,* and his temporal interest in *year.* In secondary verbs, his noun insistences are repeated in to *die* and to *love.* The traits which seemed so strong in adjective usage, then—the strong repetitive use of a few terms, the vivid appearance of some emphasis upon objects in the outer world, the preoccupation with negatives, and with time,—seem to be repeated through all the textures of his reference, and to singularize him in the midst of his wide stylistic agreements upon man, love, goodness, death, and thought, in stanza and couplet arguments with his love, and with, in his intensive fashion, himself.

"Love's Usury" sets forth many of its author's qualities in these matters.

> For every houre that thou wilt spare mee now,
>   I will allow,
> Usurious God of Love, twenty to thee,
>   When with my browne, my gray haires equall bee;

---

[6] *Major Adjectives in English Poetry.*

> Till then, Love, let my body raigne, and let
> Mee travell, sojourne, snatch, plot, have, forget,
> Resume my last yeares relict: think that yet
> We'had never met.

The couplet rhyme in stanzaic form is familiar, and the structure of address and request. The God of Love is familiar, even under the special epithet put upon him. The browne and gray are characteristically used by Donne as epithets not of sense but of concept. The hour and year are part of his preoccupation, the body too, and the relict one of his noted technical references. The rest are verbs in great variety and some familiarity in *let, think, met,* their excess of fourteen in eight lines suggesting Donne's active emphasis. The stanza is a 1640 stanza, earlier written though it was, in vocabulary, sound, and structure of argument; it is especially Donne's in its self-assertion. The next two stanzas develop an excessive paradox with authority. The average petition takes on a kind of bargaining power with Donne's desperate and direct attack.

> Spare mee till then, I'll beare it, though she bee
> One that loves mee.

This is the poetry, the music, the rhyme, the thought, the argument, of pure verbs.

Or recall "A Feaver," for an example of Donne's neatness:

> Oh doe not die, for I shall hate
> All women so, when thou art gone,
> That thee I shall not celebrate,
> When I remember, thou wast one....
>
> These burning fits but meteors bee,
> Whose matter in thee is soone spent.
> Thy beauty, and all parts, which are thee,
> Are unchangeable firmament.
>
> Yet t'was of my minde, seising thee,
> Though it in thee cannot persever.
> For I had rather owner bee
> Of thee one houre, than all else ever.

In these verses the address is to the love rather than the god, the phrasing compacter, the rhyming closer, the argument still involved in analogies, but the stress is the same, assertive and predicative. Adjectives, except for the numerals, and *unchangeable,* are minor; nouns provide a selection for illustrative reference; it is the verbs which make the sense, as the whole of the first stanza suggests.

Like Jonson, like his sons, Donne varies the patterns of his many poems, but maintains as close norm the four- or five-beat line rhymed in couplets. He maintains, too, the norm of conversation, in plea, query, imperative, beginning: "I wonder, by my troth, what thou, and I"; "Goe, and catche"; "Now thou hast lov'd me"; "Busie old foole"; "For Godsake hold your tongue"; "Sweetest love"; " 'Tis true, 'tis day"; "Ill tell thee now"; "Let me powre forth"; "Marke but this flea"; and so on; and ending in a kind of agreement or resolution in "none can die"; "I may thinke so too"; "thy spheare"; "A patterne of your love"; "ne'r parted bee"; "to marke when, and where the darke eclipses bee"; "and hastes the others death"—these concluding phrases being the last part, often, of a coupleted, a fully completed, ending. Recognizably Donne's as many of these phrases are to us, in content and structural suggestion they could begin or end most poems of the decade, except when some felicity or audacity even in so brief compass marks the extra power of mind and skill of craft. And of that skill of craft Donne, like Cowley and his colleagues, was aware. He shared the self-consciousness which analogized lover and poet, body and book, and which therefore expressed in every double turn of phrase a seriousness of relative vision.

His "metaphysical" disciples Vaughan and Crashaw chose differing forms of the metaphysical, providing another contrast between the relational and the substantial. Vaughan liked a short line, with few adjectives, nouns, verbs; of major adjectives he stressed only *fair,* and he preferred his own special emphasis on *day* to the more common *love* and *heart.* His was a heavenly view and vocabulary, and the metaphysical relation of himself to this view was given vigor by his own set of choices: the nouns of *cloud, light, year, hour, star, sun, night,* modified by the epithets of *dark, full, quick, young,* supported by *shine* and *fall,* as his *tear, death, sin,* by *weep.* The stress in these terms is more upon nature and more upon feeling than usual in the 1640's, with a special look to the height and light of the heavens, the dark of man, and it is this stress which has often been noted in Vaughan, allying him with Wordsworth, or, as one may suggest, with Hopkins. In some of his heavenly sense Donne particularly shared, in *sun,* for example, and the time of *year* and *hour,* and the expression of *thought,* in *tear* and *weeping.* But Donne's interest in human forms and standards, in *good, eye, heart, love,* in *bad, false, true, name, world,* was just specifically not Vaughan's; in it lay their great difference, in Vaughan's rejection of much earthly metaphysical substance and in his ignoring of human standard, especially the negative.

Crashaw, a poet of fuller measure in accent and vocabulary, was more apt to include than ignore, though he too lacked interest in Donne's concepts of abstract value. He employed with major stress most of the major words of the decade, especially the visual and structural *fair, eye, heaven, make,* and *see,* along with Donne's and Vaughan's *death, tear,* and *world,* the metaphysical negatives, a vast store of precious adjectives like *bright, dark, full, high, new, old, poor, rich, true,* most of the terms stressed by anyone else in the decade, along with his own *black* and *proud.* Where Vaughan differs in nouns, in the direct subjects and means of his attention, Crashaw differs in adjectives, in the world of sense which he elaborates. As Crashaw sensed, Donne judged, and Vaughan felt, and all, as they recognized their mortality, wept.

So the village doctor of Scethrog and Lower Newton, protesting the vanities of "sweet love" and "mistress fair," addressed with art and wit, but directed his art and wit heavenward.

> My God! Thou that did'st dye for me,
> These Thy death's fruits I offer Thee
> Death that to me was life and light,
> But dark and deep pangs to Thy sight.
> Some drops of Thy all-quickning blood
> Fell on my heart; those made it bud,
> And put forth thus, though Lord, before
> The ground was curst and void of store.

Word by word this vocabulary is characteristically Vaughan's and his time's, the quick bud and fruit most closely his, and all set in the decade's pattern of octosyllabic-couplet address and paradox. The pangs of the lover are here religious, his love is toward God; but again, as ever, death and the heart are counterpoised. The Dedication ends,

> I nothing have to give to Thee,
> But this Thy own gift, given to me.
> Refuse it not; for now Thy token
> Can tell Thee where a heart is broken.

It is the ending of a Cavalier poem. But the text is Revelations I, 5: "Unto Him that loved us, and washed us from our sins in His own blood"; and *Thee* is capitalized.

Vaughan wrote in his Preface, regretting his own earlier frivolous work, that "the complaint against vitious verse, even by peaceful and obedient spirits, is of some antiquity in this Kingdom.... The true remedy lies wholly in their bosoms, who are the gifted persons, by a wise exchange of vain and vitious subjects, for divine themes and celestial praise." The exchange of secular for divine did not necessitate, however, an exchange of meters, syntaxes, or vocabularies. All the time, the divine had helped to figure forth the secular; now, the exchange could be made to mutual benefit.

> 'Tis now cleare day: I see a rose
> Bud in the bright East, and disclose
> The pilgrim-sunne; all night have I
> Spent in a roving extasie
> To find my Saviour;

Or,

> O joyes! Infinite sweetnes! with what flowres
> And shoots of glory, my soul breakes and buds!
> All the long houres
> Of night and rest,
> Through the still shrouds
> Of sleep, and clouds,
> This dew fell on my breast;

Vaughan was conscious of the life and grace in his language, and swore to sober its direction, as in "Mount of Olives":

> Sweete, sacred hill! on whose fair brow
> My Saviour sate, shall I allow
> Language to love
> And idolize some shade, or grove,
> Neglecting thee? such ill-plac'd wit,
> Conceit, or call it what you please,
> Is the braine's fit,
> And meere disease.

So Cooper's Hill, with all of Denham's descriptiveness, Vaughan seriously rejected in its own day, for a mountain more *sacred* but still *sweet*.

The lines of this metaphysic were somewhat shorter, interweaving many two-accent units among the usual tetrameter and pentameter couplets, and some quatrains. Twenty of some thirty poems begin with the structure of address and are based upon it; the rest are narrative in procedure, as, for example, "Farewell, you everlasting hills!" on the one hand, and " 'Tis dead night round about: Horrour doth creepe," on the other. The short, closely rhymed, exclamatory is in some contrast to slower paced narrative and descriptive, and doubles it in amount, whereas for

most of the sons of Ben the two types were blended in the form
of the varied and elaborated tetrameter.

Crashaw extends the poetic line into a fairly steady pentameter,
coupleted or alternated, even in his mixed lyrical forms lengthening the line away from its intermittent two-accent articulations.

> Tell me, bright boy, tell me my golden Lad,
> Whither away so frolick? why so glad?
> What all thy wealth in consaile? all thy state?
> Are huskes so deare? troth 'tis a mighty rate.

This the epigram, "The Prodigal." Or, the beginning of "On a
treatise of Charity":

> Rise then, immortall maid! Religion rise!
> Put on thyself in thine owne lookes; t'our eyes
> Be what thy beauties, not our blots have made thee,
> Such as (ere our darke sinnes to dust betrayed thee)
> Heav'n set thee down new drest; when thy bright birth
> Shot thee like lightning to the astonisht earth.

Or, the beginning of the 500-line "Sospetto d'Herode":

> Muse, now the servant of soft Loves no more,
> Hate is thy Theame, and Herod, whose unblest
> Hand (o what dares not jealous Greatnesse?) tore
> A thousand sweet Babes from their Mothers Brest:
> The Bloomes of Martyrdome.

This, the main line for Crashaw, may be contrasted with his less
frequent briefer Vaughan or Herrick line,

> How life and death in thee
> Agree!

or the regular tetrameter couplet, as in the poem "On Mr. George
Herbert's booke":

> Know you faire on what you looke;
> Divinest love lyes in this booke:
> Expecting fier from your eyes,
> To kindle this his sacrifice.

This last is recognizably closest, in both measure and vocabulary, to the repeated 1640 standard, in which fair, eye, love, and divine mingle in close tetrameter progress of reasoning address. When Crashaw alters this standard, he does so, as we have seen in both vocabulary and measure, by extension, by certain filling out of extremes, not changing but increasing. The primary structure of address is still evident, but it is filled out by many exclamations, questions, imperatives. The line is lengthened and increased with adjectives, nouns, verbs, abundant all three. And the eye's fair sight and tear are the fully repeated theme.

By his amplificatory stresses, then, Crashaw writes apart from his fellow poets of the metaphysical divine, and closer to the cosmical divine of More, Quarles, Milton. Like Vaughan, he has protested the frivolity of contemporary verse; like Vaughan he is said to have taken Herbert for his model. But unlike Vaughan and Herbert, and unlike Herbert's fellow Donne, he has wished to make poetry soar on wings very broad and well feathered. Said "the authors friend" in the preface to *Steps to the Temple:*

Divine Poetry, I dare hold it, in position against Suarez on the subject, to be the Language of the Angels; it is the quintessence of Phantasie and discourse center'd in Heaven; 'tis the very Out-goings of the soule; ... Oh! when the generall arraignment of Poets shall be, to give an accompt of their higher soules, with what a triumphant brow shall our divine Poet sit above, and looke downe upon poore Homer, Virgil, Horace, Claudian? &c. who had amongst them the ill lucke to talke out a great part of their gallant Genius, upon Bees, Dung, froggs, and Gnats, &c. and not as himself here, upon Scriptures, divine Graces, Martyrs and Angels.

The contrast thus made by the defense is that between the classical or profane subject and diction and that which he calls the "primitive" or original heavenly divine. It is a contrast between sacred poems and "madrigalls" ("Love-Sonnets, and Epithalamiums"). Behind this highly ethical justification lies the clear quality of Crashaw's taste for the elaborate rather than the homely, the cosmical rather than the social, the angel rather than the gnat. All in the 1640's loved the divine; the simpler question is whether they wrote of it in gnat or in angel. The gnat required the figures and predicates of relationship; the angel asked for the epithets of admiration.

Another in 1645 to publish his choice on the side of the angels was Francis Quarles. His publisher apologized for the secular aspect of the shepherds in the *Shepheards Oracles,* but assured the seriousness of the eclogues in their mixture of heavenly with earthly.

> Heaven-blest Britannus; thou, whose Oaten Reed
> Sings thy True-Love, whilst thy proud flocks do feed
> Secure about thee, on this fruitful Brow
> Above all Shepheards, o how blest art Thou!

So speaks Gallo to Britannus in beginning the first Eglogue, and he speaks in type for the whole series. Pan talks with Gentilla, Nullfidius with Pseudo-Catholicus, Anarchus with Canonicus, Iudex with Romastix, and all their representation of problems pertinent to their names is veiled in the terms of Arcadian festival. In each of the eleven eglogues the point comes clear, despite the abundance of pastoral care, that what England needs in 1646 is cessation of hostilities on all counts, and return to a peaceful status quo.

The major terms which Quarles employs to convey this message through many lines of epitheted iambic pentamer couplet are just as standard as any poet's in his time, even Cowley's. *Fair, good, great, sweet,* all the major adjectives are stressed, and all the major nouns, with emphasis on *day, eye, heart,* and *time;* and all the verbs but *bring,* with emphasis on *give, know, make,* and *tell,* and *think.* Of his fellow "divine" poets, Quarles is closer to Crashaw than to Vaughan, and to More than to Harvey, in these choices; he joins with his qualifying rather than his predicating colleagues, but comes nearer than others to compromise in common usage. His secondary epithets, for example, are Donne's commonplaces *new, poor,* and *true,* his nouns more forceful, in *blood, hand,* and *power,* yet his verbs quiet, in *keep, look, speak, stand, teach.* More than any other poet, too, he uses with his own singular emphasis those terms which are directly important to his subject and his allegory: *gentle, shepheard, flock, sheep, lamb, swain, feed,* and words of speaking and hearing. Quarles is a wordy poet, in thought and practice, and his words are all the obvious ones in the frame of his subject and his time. Not typical in the fullness and repetitiveness of his structures, he is, nevertheless, most typical as most inclusive of the materials of his decade.

It was the poetry of this decade, remember, which was later said to have needed reform, and which Waller, one of its own members, was said to have helped reform. Waller and Dryden purified the century's poetry, it was said. What did they do to it? By practice they allied it, in structure and reference, to the extremes at which Milton's poetry rested, and More's, and Quarles', and Crashaw's: "divine poetry," then; but theirs was not divine. Evidently the reform was not one of subject or attitude, for other divines, and Wither the Puritan, wrote at the other end of the scale. Nor was the matter one of reference, for Waller and Dryden did not especially agree either with one another or with their colleagues. Waller stressed all the major adjectives, Dryden only *good* and *great;* Waller slighted such main nouns as *day, earth, soul, time,* while Dryden slighted only *man;* Waller slighted the metaphysical *thinking,* Dryden did not. Among secondary terms Waller stressed *bright, high, new, fire, power, grow, seem, sing,* and Dryden, *happy, new, rich, death, life, part, die, live, keep, shine, sing.* The difference seems to lie in Waller's greater pomp, and this impression is borne out by the more singular stresses: Waller's *noble, bold, care, seas, fate,* all in large terms;

and Dryden's *young, mortal, sacred, virtue, grace,* more modified
and conceptual. Though the poems of Dryden here under observation are of limited kind, taking their cue from the elegiac
"Hastings," nevertheless the generalization holds for his other
poems also, that their central vocabulary is a moderate and conceptual one, fairly strong on adjectives, emotional rather than
sensory. Waller, in his Occasional Poems, as in his Epigrams and
Epistles, presents more ceremony of vocabulary. Is ceremony his
reform?

An early poem on King Charles, "Of the Danger His Majesty
(Being Prince) Escaped in the Road at St Andero," begins:

> Now had his Highness bid farewell to Spain,
> And reach'd the sphere of his own power—the main;
> With British bounty in his ship he feasts
> Th'Hesperian princes, his amazèd guests,
> To find that wat'ry wilderness exceed
> The entertainment of their great Madrid.
> Healths to both kings, attended with the roar
> Of cannons, echo'd from th'affrighted shore,
> With loud resemblance of his thunder, prove
> Bacchus the seed of cloud-compelling Jove;

If the occasion seems to provide the ceremony, consider one of
the love poems for which Waller was noted, "Of the Lady who
Can Sleep When She Pleases":

> No wonder sleep from careful lovers flies,
> To bathe himself in Saccharissa's eyes.
> As fair Astraea once from earth to heaven,
> By strife and loud impiety was driven;
> So with our plaints offended, and our tears,
> Wise Somnus to that paradise repairs;

Both passages are different from the by now familiar beginnings
of plaint and complex persuasion. They do not accost, or address
from bended knee, or take the hand and press the syllogism.
Rather, they build behind an incident a background panorama

of scenery. It is significant that while half of Waller's poems are
titled "To . . . " and begin, like the poem "To the Mutable Fair,"
in the familiar octosyllabics, familiarly:

> Here, Caelia! for thy sake I part
> With all that grew so near my heart,

their logic is not complex or figured, but swung through heaven
and through "ancient tales" to draw down parallels, making a
journey more in physical space than in mental time. And, moreover, the other half of Waller's poems is another kind, the occasional kind, beginning in new fashion with narrative analogy:

> As when a sort of wolves infest the night
> With their wild howlings at fair Cynthia's light,
> The noise may chase sweet slumber from our eyes,
> But never reach the mistress of the skies;
> So with the news of Sacharissa's wrongs,

or,

> As in old chaos (heaven with earth confused)
> And stars with rocks together crush'd and bruised),

So Saccharissa . . .

The followers who praised Waller, including Dryden himself,
and Pope, and Samuel Johnson, praised him for his "sweetness,"
his "softness," his "loftiness," his combination of "feminine"
grace and "masculine" force. These terms applied to sound as
well as sense, to the use of the French closed and rounded couplet,
to the turns upon key words by repetition, to the fullness of lines
and vowels within the lines. There are fewer breaks, fewer conflicts of consonants, fewer plays upon silence, implication, conversation in these accretive verses; they make their pattern from
what is in them, and therefore control by structural rhymed
sections, by harmonies rather than dissonances, by onomatopoeias, by references which give direct sensory effects, by cumulative subjects and epithets. Denham wrote this way, too, in
Cooper's Hill, though not so consistently as Waller in his other

work and with some tendencies toward roughness of sound with power of subject which won him more often the labels "masculine" and "strong" than Waller's "soft." "Denham's strength and Waller's sweetness join," said Pope in the *Essay on Criticism*. And Dryden in his dedication of the *Aeneid* made the four "Thames" lines from *Cooper's Hill* a poetic touchstone:

> Oh could I flow like thee, and make thy stream
> My great example as it is my theme!
> Though deep, yet clear; though gentle yet not dull;
> Strong without rage; without o'erflowing, full.

These are the very value terms of the type, and they suggest the sort of representative natural magnificence to which poetry then aspired. It is the new, and yet the old, poetry of *things,* of Spenser's mellifluous and handsome glories and of cosmic scope and continuity, which by their very name and state in suitable numbers are aesthetic and so poetic.[7]

In this ceremonial manner, something thoroughgoing and persistent has been added to the poetry of the 1640's. Waller's occasional poems, with their scenic backgrounds, are not characteristic of the number of poets we have been observing; not of Cowley, Carew, Donne, not even of the masque-writing Jonson or the Biblical Sandys. Rather, suggestions of Waller's descriptive pomp may be remembered from poets of the epithetical pole, from More's Spenserians, Crashaw's lengthening decorative line, the pastoral backgrounds to Quarles' dialogues. The poets of epithet and substantive are the poets also of an altered or altering structure, a structure descriptive rather than discursive.

Dryden was the most temperate of these reformers, steering his poetic course down center and only gradually shifting from

---

[7] The rhetorical argument for words vs. things, as old as Quintilian vs. Cicero, was illustrated in the sixteenth century by Wyatt vs. Spenser, the "manly" vs. the "luxurious," and here Waller in odd accord with Sprat makes the antiverbal, antimetaphysical reassertion. See T. H. Banks' Introduction to his edition of Denham; the *Poems to the Memory of Waller;* A. C. Howell's *"Res et Verba;* Words and Things"; F. P. Wilson's *Elizabethan and Jacobean;* and C. S. Lewis' "Donne and Love Poetry" in *Seventeenth-Century Studies.*

Donne's "wit" to Waller's "poetry."[8] His first poem "Upon the Death of Lord Hastings," published together with thirty-two other elegies on the young lord's death, in *Lachrymae Musarum* in 1649—and by this date justifying Dryden's inclusion here, though most of his poems are later—[9] begins in medium fashion with an addressed question rather abstractly assumed, a ceremonious but not a descriptive manner:

> Must noble Hastings immaturely die,
> The honour of his ancient family?
> Beauty and learning thus together meet
> To bring a winding for a wedding sheet?
> Must Virtue prove Death's harbinger? must she,
> With him expiring, feel mortality?

The sharpness of the sad inquiring paradox is its "wit"; the smoothness of even-paced, poised, and balanced line is its "poetry," for Dryden.

Though the sharp and abstract terms of wit maintain the nature of Dryden's writing, they are increasingly modified toward the smooth and descriptive. Epistle or "To . . ." poems are relatively infrequent, and occasion poems have taken their place. Set beside the active personal address of "To the memory of Mr. Oldham,"

> Farewell, too little and too lately known,
> Whom I began to think and call my own,

the more static frame of "On the Monument of the Marquis of Winchester," which is filled to its limits with far-reaching epithets:

> He who in impious times undaunted stood
> And midst rebellions durst be just and good, . . .
> Such souls are rare, but mighty patterns given
> To earth were meant for ornaments to Heaven.

---

[8] "Doctor Donne, the greatest wit, though not the best poet, of our nation." Dedication to "Eleonora," 1692.

[9] Andrew Marvell, also appearing early in the same volume, uses much the same reference and structure pattern as Dryden's.

Or the first of "Eleonora":

> As when some great and gracious monarch dies,
> Soft whispers first and mournful murmurs rise
> Among the sad attendants; then the sound
> Soon gathers voice and spreads the news around, . . .
> So slowly, by degrees, unwilling Fame
> Did matchless Eleonora's fate proclaim,
> Till public as the loss the news became.

In the latter regular and substantial procedures of numbers
rather than in the former colloquialism is to be seen the major
framework of Dryden's verse. Wit and master of the abstract
though he seems in comparison with Pope, the frame even of his
satires is descriptive and ceremonial in Waller's and Milton's
manner. So "Absalom and Achitophel":

> In pious times, ere priestcraft did begin,
> Before polygamy was made a sin,
> When man on many multiplied his kind,
> Ere one to one was cursedly confined,

and "MacFlecknoe":

> All human things are subject to decay
> And, when Fate summons, monarchs must obey,

and "Religio Laici":

> Dim as the borrowed beams of moon and stars
> To lonely, weary, wandering travellers
> Is Reason to the soul: . . .

and "The Hind and the Panther":

> A milk-white Hind, immortal and unchanged,
> Fed on the lawns and in the forest ranged;
> Without unspotted, innocent within,
> She feared no danger, for she knew no sin.

These stately beginnings employ the standard vocabulary and
substance of the 1640's, of goodness and soul, earth and heaven,
greatness and fate, fear and mortality, piety and sin, monarch
and man, for Dryden was faithful to the major terms, and not

highly inventive of his own. But the vocabulary here is given a
fuller measure than by most poets of the 1640's: every line
marked to its full extent, more substantives, and more epithets
for them, a range of generalization and liberality of remark
which is limited less by logic of situation or extent of the at-
tender's listening and reasoning powers than by the poise and
balance of the even lines themselves. Here is almost the classical
"golden" line of Ovid, as Dryden describes it in his *Essay on
Translation:* "two substantives and two adjectives, with a verb
betwixt them to keep the peace." It is a line which omits, in the
spirit of the Dedication to the *Aeneis,* articles, pronouns, "and
other barbarities on which our speech is built by the faults of our
forefathers." It is a full and framing line. Short poems are fewer;
the ends, being farther from the beginnings, are less poetically
conditioned by them in close patterns, and provide often a kind of
descriptive frame, rather than an end in any directed sense. The
famous ode to Mrs. Anne Killigrew, for example, begins with
semiscene:

> Thou youngest virgin-daughter of the skies,
> Made in the last promotion of the blest;
> Whose palms, new plucked from Paradise,
> In spreading branches more sublimely rise,
> Rich with immortal green above the rest:

and ends with semiscene, after a wide tracing through the realms
of poetry, pastoral, and politics:

> There thou, sweet saint, before the quire shall go,
> As harbinger of Heaven, the way to show,
> The way which thou so well hast learned below.

Not exposition of the central point of death, but amplification
of the central quality of goodness, has been achieved. In this
manner of narrative sweep and setting, under precise and in-
genious variety of metrical control with the regular line, the
poetry of qualification expands.

Milton is, as may be surmised, such poetry's major master. He sweeps and expands every part of it: loosens its rhyme, draws out its sentence structure, extends its periods, elaborates its argument, piles up its scenes, increases its epithets, originates its main terms' emphases, and moves farthest from its central agreements as from the agreements of all the poetry in its time. What Crashaw does in exaggerating and intensifying the metaphysical norm, and what More does in earnestly and thoroughly following a borrowed mode as far from the norm as possible, Milton combines, making, with the fervor of the one and the persistence of the other, a massive shift in the decade's tone and content.

His poems published in 1645 have many metrical styles. The "Nativity" plays in complex lyrical fashion upon the short couplet base, as do so many cavalier love poems. "L'Allegro" and "Il Penseroso" are in standard octosyllabics. But "Lycidas" frees the rhyme and accent pattern, upon a blank verse base, and "Comus" works in blank verse, with interludes. This volume at the middle of the decade mixed much that was familiar with much that was surprising in sound; so too in sense.

Milton used fewer, less than two-thirds, of the major terms than almost any other poet. He was short on the standard epithets of *good, fair, great, sweet;* he stressed almost none of the nouns but *god, heaven, eye;* he used with any enthusiasm only *come,* and *go,* and *see.* Among secondary terms, he shared with Waller a preference for *high;* with Vaughan, Herrick, Lovelace, Sandys, Crashaw, More, a preference for *night;* with Donne, Vaughan, and Carew for *sun;* with many for *hear* and *live,* with Cowley, Shirley, Dryden for *sing.* All these terms share a tone, I think; not one of cerebration, but one of sensory range and vitality. So too his own special repetitions caught not verbs, not actions, but felt nouns like *air* and *light,* and minor epithets like *bright, dark, gentle, solemn, foul, mighty, mortal, loud, sad, soft, fresh, green,* making a steady sensory adjectival texture.

Milton used more adjectives and fewer verbs in these poems of 1645 than any poet of the decade. And he made this shift in poetic emphasis without any great change in poetic line, using about the same proportion of four- and five-accent lengths that Jonson did with reverse emphasis. Milton said no more in the line, but something different. Not "I know to whom I write," but

> Hence loathed Melancholy
>   Of Cerberus and blackest midnight born,
> In Stygian Cave forlorn
>   'Mongst horrid shapes, and shrieks, and sights unholy, . . .

The structure follows from this approach. As address here takes the formal and "passionate" shape of invocation, and as paradox here takes the more sensuous shape of simple contrast, so:

> But come thou Goddess fair and free,
> In Heav'n yclep'd Euphrosyne, . . .

> And if I give thee honour due,
> Mirth, admit me of thy crew
> To live with her, and live with thee, . . .

> To hear the Lark . . .

> Straight mine eye hath caught new pleasures
> Whilst the Lantskip round it measures,
> Russet Lawns and Fallows Gray, . . .

> Hard by, a Cottage chimney smokes, . . .

> Tow'red cities please us then, . . .

> These delights if thou canst give,
> Mirth, with thee I mean to live.

The progression is serial, not syllogistic; descriptive, not reasoning; and within each separate stage, a list of items, of color, variety, allusion, provides the illustrative substance.

In many separate poetical aspects, then, and in their interrelation, Milton constructed what was in his time an extreme of style. One may venture to call "Miltonic," at least Miltonic for the 1640's, a verse in which the content and structure require more adjectives than verbs, and in which participial adjectives dominate numerical, and descriptive all others, and in which few conceptual terms are shared, the nouns and verbs like the epithets being scenic and sensory; in which the linear pattern has an extreme length, flow, and fullness, the sharpness of rhyme exchanged for the sonority of internal correspondences, the amount of content as distinguished from connectives greater per line; in which the structure of thought is demonstrative and cumulative, a structure of description.

"Lycidas" may serve as an example of the way these traits function, and may suggest the major contrast to the elegiac technique of Donne or Jonson. Its open sound and motion, and ceremonial stress, and regular qualitative series are all familiar as a kind.

> Yet once more, O ye Laurels, and once more
> Ye Myrtles brown, with Ivy never sere,
> I come to pluck your Berries harsh and crude,
> And with forc'd fingers rude,
> Shatter your leaves before the mellowing year.
> Bitter constraint, and sad occasion dear,
> Compels me to disturb your season due:
> For Lycidas is dead, dead ere his prime,
> Young Lycidas, and hath not left his peer:
> Who would not sing for Lycidas?

The strongest content of these lines consists in the brown, sere, harsh, crude, rude, mellowing, bitter, sad, dear, due, young, dead, dead, rather than in I come, shatter, compel, hath not left, would not sing, which are less frequent and less full of the significance of atmosphere. The sound, like the sense, repeats its theme, in the length of once more ... once more, the fall from *b*s *to d*s in dead, and dead, the linear and cross-linear alliteration. The structure of sentence begins by address, as we may expect, but it is the ceremonial address of invocation. From then on, there is little complexity of subordination; the statements work in an accumulating parallel fashion. The steps of the whole poem move thus: Lycidas must not go unwept. Begin, then, to sing as I would be sung. We saw together the rural sights. Now Lycidas will see them no more. Where were ye Nymphs, and where your aid, when he died? What avail the earnest shepherd's labours? Neptune, Camus, report upon Lycidas, and St. Peter regrets the sacrifice of good shepherds for bad. Return, Sicilian Muse, and bid the Vales cast their beauties here for Lycidas, wherever far away his bones are hurled. Weep no more, Shepherds, for Lycidas has mounted high and will be the Genius of the shore. So sang the swain, and rose: Tomorrow to fresh Woods, and Pastures new. Each of these stages, simple and uncomplicated in its logic, is made elaborate by its scenes and allusions. Each is given scope by pastoral, classical, political, or Biblical reference, and is given substance by the epitheted setting: first the bitter shrubs, then the dewy fields, the face of Orpheus down the swift Hebrus, Amaryllis in the shade, the level brine, the scrannel Pipes of wretched straw, the Bells and Flowrets of a thousand hues, the stormy Hebrides, the Saints above, the Oaks and rills, all listed in their features and associations.

The richness of "Lycidas" resides in these features and associations, the scope and density of their coverage, rather than in the working out of thought in syntax. Once more—Begin—the change—Alas—But now—Next—Last—Return—Weep no more —Thus sang—is the syntax of demonstrative performance, pulling the stops in the tones of music, now loud, now soft, now near, now far. Within its simplest frames comes the full variety of qualitative reference.

Much of this reference is central to the decade: sad occasion, denial vain, gentle Muse, fair peace, flock and fountain, fresh dews of night, bright, Heav'n's descent, glad sound, sacred head, foul contagion, dread voice, flowers, eyes, tears, world, great vision, nuptial song, blest Kingdoms, joy and love, death, weeping, singing, glory. Some is especially Milton's: forc'd fingers rude, wat'ry bier, high Lawns and mood, sultry horn, westering wheel, gadding Vine, shaggy top, hideous roar, gust of rugged wings, Inwrought with figures dim, lean and flashy songs, the Pansy freakt with jet, whelming tide, fable of Belleros, In solemn troops, and sweet Societies—all these which by accentuation of sound pattern, of sensory quality, of participial suspension, of height, power, decoration, and ceremony, did not abandon the standard content but increased and dowered it.

In an equally conventional elegy by Donne at the decade's opposite extreme of style there is, on the other hand, a condensation and interworking of the standard content. Sorrow, strange chance, to weep, life, work, praise, tears, eyes, sweet briar, paradise, holy sacrifice, soul, heaven, foe, virtue, hope, death, children, pictures, marble Tomb, stone, all are again central usage, most of them shared with Milton, but they are much barer of descriptive adjectives, and abstracter in their emphasis, and are supported by such other terms characteristic of Donne as house, heir, cold tongues, fit, store, wither, familie, rigg'd, discoverie, Venturers, friends, practice, subtile Schoolmen, senseless, turn'd, which give the context that familiar, colloquial, technical, and active turn for which he has become famous. This "Elegie on the L(ord). C(hamberlain).," ceremonious like Milton's, proceeds as follows:

> Sorrow, who to this house scarce knew the way:
> Is, Oh, heire of it, our All is his prey.
> This strange chance claims strange wonder, and to us
> Nothing can be so strange as to weepe thus:
> 'Tis well his lifes loud speaking workes deserve,
> And give praise too, our cold tongues could not serve:
> 'Tis well, hee kept teares from our eyes before,
> That to fit this deepe ill, we might have store.
> Oh, if a sweet briar, climbe up by'a tree,
> If to a paradise that transplanted bee,

> Or fell'd, and burnt for holy sacrifice,
> Yet, that must wither, which by it did rise,
> As we for him dead: though no familie
> Ere rigg'd a soule for heavens discoverie
> With whom more Venturers more boldy dare
> Venture their states, with him in joy to share.

After a passage on the gaining of life in death, it concludes,

> His children are his pictures, Oh they bee
> Pictures of him dead, senselesse, cold as he.
> Here needs no marble Tombe, since hee is gone,
> He, and about him, his, are turn'd to stone.

The beginning exclamation of sorrow has no visual appurtenances. Sorrow as heir to the house demands a thought about legal custom, not a glance at ivy. Three meanings of the epithet *strange* are suggested: its oddity, its alienation, its unfamiliarity. The negative self-consciousness of the cold tongues differs from Milton's invoking of the Muses. The character of the Lord is set forth not by epithet but by the store of tears which his life had never caused to be shed. Then notably the sweet briar decks no Vale, mourns no death, but figures forth the relationship of dependence which is the theme of the poem. And the final stone, rejecting the convention of a fine marble memorial, doggedly insists upon the negative aspect of death for those left behind. What little decoration the poem at first seems to possess, its briar and its marble tomb, are denied and discarded by the poem's thought, just as, conversely, in "Lycidas," what there is of thought of sorrow and dismay is resolved by the beds of flowers, the choirs of angels, the twitching of the mantle blue.

The structure of the poem, although more serial than some of Donne's in its separate sections of metaphor, nevertheless involves itself in those subordinations of *if, yet, that, though, whom, when, since,* which make for complexity in the reasoning process, and for the forty verbs, as compared to the twenty adjectives, in twenty-six lines. The adjectives, strange, loud, cold, deep, sweet, holy, dead, worst, subtile, senselesse, marble, do not carry the theme, but play about it, sometimes affirmed, sometimes denied; the verbs, knew, claims, weep, deserve, climb, wither, share, lose, love, gain, grew, die, needs, is gone, are turn'd, carry in variety more of the main line of theme. While predicates are accessories for Milton, qualities are accessories, even accidents, for Donne. From this philosophical and technical difference, many of the other differences of sound pattern, of vocabulary kind, of argument follow, and the Donnic elegy becomes a problem in personal relationship while the Miltonic is a ceremonial survey.

If these seem two individualistic extremes of the 1640's, some lesser examples may serve to extend the contrast. Dryden's one poem of the 1640's, for example, "Upon the Death of the Lord Hastings," an even more youthful elegy than Milton's, and for another schoolfellow, tempers the abstract arguments of Donne and Jonson by a fuller, more epitheted and portentous, Miltonic line.

> Must noble Hastings immaturely die,
> The honour of his ancient family?
> Beauty and learning thus together meet
> To bring a winding for a wedding sheet?
> Must Virtue prove Death's harbinger? must she,
> With him expiring, feel mortality?
> Is death, sin's wages, grace's now? shall art
> Make us more learned, only to depart?

There follows an elaborated figure of Hastings' soul as a complete orb, compacted of all virtues and scannable so by the astronomers; then the painfully elaborate picture of the pox; then the inclusion in Hastings' character of all seasons, and all classical figures; then a railing at the old and sick who yet live; and finally an exhortation to the "virgin widow" to wed Hastings' soul, platonically to mother his ideas.

> Let that make thee a mother; bring thou forth
> The ideas of his virtue, knowledge, worth;

> Transcribe the original in new copies; give
> Hastings of the better part: so shall he live
> In his nobler half; and the great grandsire be
> Of an heroic divine progeny:
> And issue which to eternity shall last,
> Yet but the irradiations which he cast.
> Erect no mausoleums; for his best
> Monument is his spouse's marble breast.

The reader feels, and with a sense of eternity rather than of time, that this is a bad poem. Instead of unity in variety, there is monotony in excess. It is a young poem, and unskillful. But its attempted combinations are of interest in a youthful poet who in 1649 may be expected to follow the main standard of the decade. Dryden does not. True, he accepts the elegy tradition, chooses the longer of the common couplet forms, employs the familiar form of address and question rather than a more ceremonious survey to begin with, exercises standard wit in such colloquial yet complex questions as "Is death, sin's wages, grace's now?" and works within the major vocabulary, shunning only a few, impartially, the concept words of time and thought, the descriptive *sweet* and *fair*.

But upon this standard base he elaborates, as his admired Waller did, a smoother sort of structure. He likes the scope of *good, great, heaven, soul,* and the epithets *rich* and *noble*. He likes a full and smooth-sounding line, not a rough, colloquially broken one, with some attention to sonority, as in the first "Must noble Hastings immaturely die," with some attention to balance as in "If merit be disease, if virtue death," with some attention to elevating epithet as in "Now thy beloved, heaven-ravished spouse is gone." The structure of thought when it is additive and descriptive, as in the passage on the seasons and the old men, is serene and formal in Dryden's maturer manner; when it attempts metaphysical argument, it dashes itself into the absurdities of "wit" against which the century was to rebel, and of which the "spouse's marble breast" is so unhappy an example, its semi-descriptive figure as "monument" made foolish by the mixture of abstract and concrete, in contrast to Donne's purer and more thematically abstract memorials of stone. The tendencies toward descriptive value in Dryden made him use more epithets and fewer verbs than the decade's average, and made, even in this early poem, for the cosmical sort of range, the celestial over domestic framing, which Waller, Milton, Pope were to extend.

The apparent consistency of the extremes of poetic practice, as between Donne and Milton, Jonson and Waller, Vaughan and Crashaw, and in stiffest fashion Harvey and More, suggests that there may be discerned two groups, or schools, if by school one does not mean conscious and theoretical agreement, in the 1640's. The uses of structure, sound, vocabulary, in their interrelations, seem to separate into two, with Dryden, Quarles, Crashaw, Waller, More, Milton, in one group, and Harvey, Suckling, Wither, Jonson, Donne, Vaughan, Cowley, Shirley, Herrick, Denham, Cleveland, Lovelace, Carew, Sandys, in the other—an outnumbering of more than two to one. This split is established primarily upon the character of poetic statement, the pattern of sound and sentence. It is apparent not merely at extremes of practice, but also at the center, where the moderate configurations of Dryden are nevertheless, by a break from the moderateness of Lovelace and Carew, allied with the Miltonic rather than the Donnic. And these two labels I employ not because Milton and Donne seem most characteristic in their groups, but simply because they appear in them and their qualities are most conveniently known to us. The grouping is not a conventional one, but Dr. Johnson in his Cowley essay comes close to it.

The poets allied with Donne and Jonson use the sparer line, fewer substantives and epithets, more predicates and connectives. What epithets they do use are less descriptive and participial, more conceptual and numerical (25 to 30 per cent as compared with the Miltonic 10 to 15 per cent). Their average of 7 adjectives, 14 nouns, 11 verbs in every ten lines, represented exactly by Shirley and Herrick and near enough by Cowley, is in contrast to the 10–17–10 average of Dryden and his group. Both groups use, to convey their statements, mainly four- and five-accented couplets and varied stanza forms, with total average line length between four and five feet. Vaughan's numerous short lines are exceptional, on the one hand, as are More's Spenserian stanzas and Milton's sometimes freer forms, on the other. Length of measure does not necessarily correlate with fullness of substance, though in some cases it may. At least it may be said that the Miltonic abundance seemed to favor pentameters, whether in couplets or in blank verse.

In the midst of great general agreement with respect to vocabulary, some clear distinctions are to be met, not in the major but in the secondary terms. Donne's *bad* and *false,* Herrick's *dead* and *last,* Herrick and Lovelace's *white,* the many nouns of this group, *fire, heart, man, sin, time, world, beauty, face, grace, flame, name, hand, king,* and its verbs, *die, find, know, tell, love, think, call, fly, appear,* are less common in the Miltonic, which especially employs, instead, *high, bright, sad, foul, gentle, noble, power,* and *stand,* and *sing.* It is noteworthy that the Miltonic makes little special stamp among verbs, and the Donnic little among epithets; abundance and inventiveness seem to flourish together. In nature of reference, the Miltonic special uses are strongly descriptive, static in *stand,* and with a certain magnitude in *high, noble,* and *power.* The Donnic uses are, on the other hand, very alert and active, more critically negative, and more involved in a subject matter of physical beauty abstractly set in world and time. Face and grace, tear and year, bliss and kiss, flame and name, are their popular rhymes, while the Miltonic preferred high and sky, loud and proud, power and flower, strong and song, of larger and less personal scope.

Finally, in structure some further and repeated distinctions seem pertinent: that the Miltonic poets tended to construct longer and more serial and more declarative survey poetry, while the Donnic worked in shorter, more reflexive and self-involved analytical and lyrical units. The normal Donnic thousand lines contains thirty or forty lyrics, many set to music; in pattern of address, "To . . . ," the earthly lady, and the heavenly or earthly lord, working out a problem of relationship, however lightly, in devious personal, abstract, and metaphorical terms, and using only to minor degree, in a third or fourth of the poems, the framework of narrative description or occasional celebration. Many of the Miltonic poems, on the other hand, were of this latter kind, longer and fuller because committed to more range or ceremony. Quarles' *Shepheards Oracles* are dialogues of extensive political and social reference in pastoral survey. More undertakes a tremendous Platonic history of the soul, which he later expands. Milton and Dryden lengthen their lyrics past song form. When Denham, indeed, undertakes the first notable descriptive survey, in his *Cooper's Hill,* he shifts his style toward his associate Waller's, and contrives, in spite of his average spareness, to strike just the proportions of the Miltonic norm, with its allusive spread, and impersonal cosmic reach.

There seems, then, a close connection between practices in reference, in sound pattern, and in structure, so that one may speak of these together as the functioning form of poetry. It is not unnatural to assume that what is said will condition sound and syntax, and vice versa, into a definable shape; and two such major shapes, out of twenty more individual ones, seem to be observable in the 1640's: the substance and color of extensity, the action and relation of intensity.

It may be suggested that one of these modes was moving into the other: that there was a relation of development between them.[10] But social, political, biographical correlations do not seem to indicate such development. As we have seen, the lines were not drawn on the basis of Puritanism (Wither was farthest from Milton), nor on the basis of religiousness (More was farthest from Harvey), nor on the basis of political or love theme (Quarles was far from Denham, Waller from Suckling), but rather on the basis of a whole poetic mode. It would remain, then, to consider age and association as possible influence. Nine of the twenty poets were born before the turn of the century, so that they were elders, in their fifties or forties, by 1640; Donne, Jonson, Carew indeed had died in the preceding decade, leaving Sandys in his sixties, Wither in his fifties, and Herrick, Quarles, Shirley, and Harvey in their forties, to establish convention. But these were mixed. Harvey and Wither were more extreme than Jonson in his Jonsonism; Shirley was a good and typical "son of Ben"; Sandys nearly and Quarles extremely were Miltonic before Milton. One would guess, then, that both ways of writing were traditions of writing which came into the decade with its elder poets. The middle generation, in its twenties and thirties, also varied and continued, with Waller, Milton, Suckling in their thirties at the decade's beginning, and Crashaw, Cleveland, More, Denham, Lovelace, Cowley in their twenties, representing both styles. Even the youngest two split in their choices, Vaughan eighteen when the decade began, and Dryden nineteen when it ended.

Nor do the single volumes which here have been taken to represent these poets in the decade present any pattern of order in their publication. Volumes in Donne's style were published in 1640, '41, '45, '46, '47, '48, '49, beginning with Harvey, Jonson, Donne, and Carew, ending with Herrick and Lovelace. Volumes

---

[10] The development from beginning to end of the century from conceit to clarity has often been stated: as by F. W. Bateson; Leah Jonas, p. xi; Mario Praz, pp. 12, 18; R. L. Sharp. See also, for philosophy of periods, A. O. Lovejoy, L. L. Schücking, Max Förster, and, for continuity as expressed by color, Alice E. Pratt.

in Milton's style were published in 1642, '44, '45, '46, '49, beginning with More and Quarles, ending with Dryden's small first venture. Within the decade's area, no course of development seems apparent. If one is to speculate, certain guesses outside the decade seem plausible: if we accept Donne and Milton as lively extremes of their respective groups, it looks as if Milton's force might grow and influence after Donne's had subsided. Offhand, too, the Elizabethan and Jacobean poetry preceding this era looks more succinct and Donnic than the eighteenth-century panorama which follows. On the other hand, crosscutting this picture of a trend from Donne to Milton, is the Elizabethan elaboration of Spenser and his kind to precede, and the simplification of Prior and Gay to follow, representing a possible trend from the Miltonic to the Donnic, the decorative to the rational. Obviously, the matter of style is too complicated to allow for surmise on the basis of major characteristics alone; it is the interworking of these characteristics, the relation between major sound and major sense and syntax, which may allow for statements about styles, or about groups and trends in styles. The limitations of such analysis, therefore, at least for this study, preclude a vision of the decade in its relationship to its past and future, even the past and future of its twenty poets.

Most of the twenty, I conclude from a random sampling, wrote consistently, either fully or sparely, throughout their careers. Very different works of Sandys, translated from different sources, are, for example, stylistically alike. The poet whose work shows the clearest split in the 1640's is Denham, whose *Cooper's Hill* differs widely from his later work. Certainly Milton's *Paradise Lost,* and probably Cowley's *Davideis,* alter from their authors' more lyrical beginnings. Therefore every poet's name must stand in this analysis for just those poems which are here analyzed, though the validity of extension is, for most of them, probable.

The poets themselves claimed alliances. Jonson as the personal leader in court and out had his disciples Shirley and Carew to succeed him in his masque-writing during the 1630's. Herrick, Suckling, and through Suckling the younger Lovelace, were his "sons"; and, says his editor, "During his last years at least, Jonson was generally held by his contemporaries to be the first poet of the age." Says his editor also, of his friendship with Donne, which showed so strongly in the conversations with Drummond, "Both in different terms challenged the supreme poet of the previous generation, Spenser. Both stood for a masculine spirit in poetry, weighty, pregnant, concentrated, against a poetry of facile method and melting phrase." "Pure and neat Language, I love, yet plaine and customary," wrote Ben Jonson. And concerning this language Donne was the speaker in Jonson's lost *Ars Poetica.*[11]

Indirectly, Donne had other friends; through their love of George Herbert's poetry, Harvey and Vaughan followed him. And Wither, Cowley, Denham, Sandys, out of separate pastoral paths, turned toward the Donne fashion. Cowley and Denham, with Waller and, briefly, Crashaw, spent the crucial years of the 1640's in Parisian exile, at the court of Queen Henrietta Maria, and debated there the ways and means of poetry, apparently leaning toward the religious and heroic which Cowley's unfinished *Davideis* and Davenant's unfinished *Gondibert* were to represent. All seemed to feel remembrance of an early fondness for Spenser, and it was upon the strong basis of this fondness that Quarles and More and Dryden early wrote. Those who seemed to move in relative isolation from court centers, Cleveland in his judgeship and prison at Yarmouth, Sandys in his eastern and western travels and scholarly study, Crashaw in his last years at Rome, Wither on his Puritan campaigns, Vaughan and More in meditation, Milton in the quiet Horton years, seemed also to move more idiosyncratically through their decade's standard

---

[11] Herford and Simpson, *Ben Jonson*, Vol. II, pp. 409, 411, 448, 450.

style, but with no one alliance; rather with their own variations upon either of the main alliances. The positions they stated in their introductions were not loyalties to one or another style, but rather defenses of one content or another: the critical argument of 1640 was notably that between secular and religious attitudes and materials, as far as the poets were concerned. Yet agreement in attitude did not make, as we have seen in Vaughan and Crashaw, in Wither and Milton, agreement in poetic construction. Religion, politics, friendship, social position, daily life, schooling and reading, all help to group the poets of the decade, but none can signify what kind of poet any one will be.

The life of the poet is the life of his poetic medium; it comes to him from the past, speaks to him and through him in the present, survives for him into the future. It is never his life alone; even in the rarest materials of measure, word, and syntax, and more complexly in the whole sentences and sentiments of his time and type of poetry, it is shared. The highest degree of individuality makes choices and uses of major material less than halfway original, commonly agreeing, if not with a contemporaneous majority, at least with a minority kind, or with an earlier or later majority. So Cowley and Shirley were of the majority in their time, and shared with yet differed from Quarles, who agreed with a somewhat fuller emphasis; so Harvey and Wither looked back to earlier uses as Baldwin and Sackville had looked forward. So Donne with his many verbs, negatives, abstractions, repetitions, and Milton with his many epithets, qualities, heights and depths, and Vaughan with his condensed clouds and Crashaw with his expanded tears, and Harvey and More with their deliberate imitations of the extremes of types, and Jonson and Dryden with their radical neutralities, all stressing as they did their particular variations upon theme, yet assumed the presence and the power of the theme as the language of their time and of their poetic heritage enunciated it.

To define this central and primary theme of the language of the 1640's in all its character would take more knowledge than I now have of other decades and other centuries. How much all poetic language shares, how divides into type, how moves with changing times, I do not know and hope to learn. But at least, though the distinguishing characteristics may not always be recognized, the contained qualities may be discerned. Certain very specific qualities mark the theme the poets of the 1640's spoke: qualities rising, as we have seen, from the opposition and interplay of the realms of the human and divine. The major vocabulary speaks for just these realms, as in the 1540's it had not; the four-accented couplet measure, its variety in length, stress, rhyme, and their relations, rather than in inner harmonizings, indicates the tight external control of the poetic craftsman over these double worlds; the vocative petition and supplication and argument of structure temper this control with the suggestion of mortal humility under the poetic arrogance, the tenuous position of earthly lover and spiritual sinner and traditional subject of the muse.

The storytelling, third-person narrative, primarily human though often allegorical, of the sixteenth century has turned to prayer, first- and second-personal, playful or solemn but in forms intensely rational, binding, such is the classical power of art and the force of metaphysical belief, the worlds of earth and heaven not naturally bound. Activities of construction and discovery are primary for almost all poets; the nouns of man, his love and his vision, his epithet of goodness, belong to most. The world of secondary stresses is a world of physical parts, of temporal measures, of human values and standards conditioned by the divine. Few external objects are major, and these of the heavenly landscape, air, cloud, sun, fire, or of the pastoral, lamb, sheep, water, flower, rose, in the special contexts of individual choice or tradition. Few sheer feelings are major—love, tears, joy, woe, and the adjectival happy, proud, sad. Neither strongly objective nor strongly subjective, the secondary vocabulary is rather one of concept: of old, high, true, of death, nature, power, sin, of fate, foe, folly, wit, and word; and in this character it matches the primary terms of earth and heaven, God and man, heart and soul.

This is the poetry often called witty, conceited or conceptual, figurative, Cavalier, Puritan, Platonic, Petrarchan, heroic, lyric, baroque, metaphysical. Its major language shows how easily it is all of these. The structure is one of reason, the terms abstract, the minor earthly detail figuring forth the spiritual, the Cavalier making a heaven of earth, the Puritan an earth of heaven, the various secular and religious versions of Platonism preserving the idea in the object, the expanse of imagination magnificent and domesticated, the individual cry strong and controlled, the reaches and juxtapositions daring and elaborate, the physical always and powerfully subordinated to and informed by the metaphysical, God in heart, soul in eye, time in day.

A language of a poetry with so many interrelated attributes is more than a language of poetic technique; it is the language of thought and expression, of belief and communication; else it were not so unanimous and useful. To look at the prose of the 1640's is to see again the language, or at least the vocabulary and some of the structure, of the poetry, the forces of poetic number and measure being a special matter. For prose I have made no count, and I refer to and quote from items of the decade with only the roughest sense of representation. But I think the passages may serve a general sort of purpose, to renew acquaintance with the common vocabulary in a different form, to note some theoretical backgrounds of the vocabulary, and to suggest by context and structure its several modes. The important suggestion to be made is that the language of the decade's poetry is not unlike the language of the decade's prose.

III. MATERIALS AND ATTITUDES
IN PROSE

THE PROSE of the era supports the poetry in its substance,
even in much of its structure. Local problems and politics were subordinated to universal issues. In the midst
of the revolutionary Long Parliament in 1640, Robert Greville,
Baron Brooke's *Nature of Truth* was published, and Donne's
and Jonson's prose, Walton's life of Donne, Heywood's *Exemplary Lives,* and finally Selden's *Power of Peers and Parliament.*
It was an active year. In 1641, the Episcopacy Controversy, in
which Milton participated, shared place with Habington's *Observations upon Historie,* and John Johnson's *Academy of Love.*
The next years grew more political, elevated by Taylor, Fuller,
Milton, tempered by James Howell's *Instructions for Forraine
Travell,* Peacham's *Art of Living in London,* the continuity of
Evelyn's diary, Hammond's *Practical Catechism,* Digby's treatise
Of Bodies, Howell's letters, the rich speculations of Sir Thomas
Browne, and Stearne's *Confirmation and Discovery of Witchcraft,* until the decade ended with Milton and Donne again, the
Fifty Sermons, the *Tenure of Kings and Magistrates.* Always,
in these titles and books, the spiritual and political, the profane
and divine, the lofty and trivial, the warmhearted and cold, the
plain and esoteric, keep meeting, as they do in the poems, in *The
Synagogue, Vox Pacifica, Under-wood, The Mistress, Hesperides,
Cooper's Hill, Psychozoia Platonica, Song of Solomon, Shepheards Oracles, Lucasta, Steps to the Temple, Saccharissa,* "L'Allegro," "On the Morning of Christ's Nativity." And as in the
poems so in the prose, the categories are not so far apart as they
sound, for religious belief informs the speculation, metaphysics
the love, love the politics, myth the geography, morals the biography, and man, with his enquiring and enjoying eye, the whole.
Henry Peacham, the decade's schoolmaster, includes a little

of everything in his prose of practical guidance, and provides a fair sampling of what thoughts one could be raised up on, if one preferred not to search them out through the linear intricacies of verse. *The Art of Living in London* and *The Worth of a Penny* are handy and ironical guides, full of the sense of class, pity, fate, and significant detail of which Vaughan or Lovelace was more musically aware. *"The Worth of a Penny, or a Caution to Keep Money, With the causes of the scarcity and misery of the want thereof, in these hard and mercilesse Times: As also how to save it, in our Diet, Apparel, Recreations, &c. And also what honest Courses men in want may take to live. By Henry Peacham, Mr. of Arts, sometime of Trinity College,* Cambridge, 1641." The simple worth of a single penny includes, among other things, charity, several commodities such as nuts, vinegar, grapes, oatmeal, onions, liquorice, and a weekly newsbook, time, thrift, coffee, a nosegay, a prophecy. The mixture of such a parcel of words is the mixture of the poetry, the small trivial given the more humanity by the large abstract, and *man, life, time,* at the center.

What Peacham thinks of poetry itself is set forth in a work some years earlier, *"The Compleat Gentleman,* Fashioning him absolute in the most necessary and commendable Qualities concerning Minde or Body, that may be required in a Noble Gentleman." Some qualities and knowledges of the Cavalier are: "Nobilitie in Generall, the dignitie and necessitie of Learning, stile in speaking, writing, and reading History, the knowledge of Cosmography, Geometry, Poetry, Musicke, Statues and Medalls, Armory, Exercise of Body, reputation and carriage, Travaile, Warre, Fishing." Much grace, at the expense of much responsibility, has been added since Bacon's not so much earlier day.

To sweeten your severer studies, by this time vouchsafe Poetry your respect; which howsoever censured and seeming falne from the highest Stage of Honour, to the lowest staire of disgrace, let not your judgement be infected with that pestilent ayre of the common breath, to be an infidell; in whose beleefe, and doer of their contrary Actions, is to be religious in the right, and to merit if it were possible by good works.

The Poet, as that Laurell Maia dreamed of, is made by miracle from his mothers wombe, and like the Diamond onely polished and pointed of himselfe, disdaining the file and midwifery of forraine helpe.

Hence Tully was long ere he could be delivered of a few verses, and those poore ones too: and Ovid, so backeward in prose, that he could almost speake nothing but verse. And experience daily affoordeth us many excellent yong and growing wits, as well from the Plow as Pallace, endued naturally with this Divine and heavenly gift, yet not knowing (if you should aske the question) whether a Metaphore be flesh or fish.

Three pertinent points in this introduction are the condemnation of much secular verse in Peacham's time, the note of special character and inspiration for the poet, the synonymity of wits and poets. A fourth matter of importance is the style of the prose which, like the poetry we have seen, especially Donne's kind, blends moral abstraction with homely particularity. But the poetry Peacham praises is not Donnic. It seems to rise from the tradition of Vergil and Ovid, rather, and to move to the graces of Sidney, Daniel, Spenser. His eight pages of survey first treat of poetry as human and divine knowledge "sweetned with the pleasance of Numbers," and from then on stress more the sweetness than the knowledge. The standards by which he measures the height of the great master Vergil are "lively descriptions and lively similitudes," and Scaliger's requirements Prudence, Efficacie, Varietie, Sweetnesse. Prudence is learned skill; Efficacie is the vivid presenting of scenes "as if we saw them with our eyes"; Varietie covers persons, times, places, manners, and similitudes—"Never the same wounds, but given with divers weapons," a policy foreign to Donne; and Sweetnesse, finally, is deliciousness, opposite to harshness, what "Plutarch tearmeth

Flowery, as having in it a beautie and sweete grace to delight, as a Flower." Peacham quotes the Aeneid, Book IX, and translates,

> Purpureus veluti cum flos succisus aratro,
> Languescit moriens, lassove papauera collo
> Demisere caput, pluvia cum forte gravantur.

> Looke how the purple Flower, which the Plow
> Has shorne in sunder, languishing doth die;
> Or Poppies downe their weary necks doe bow,
> And hang the head, with raine when laden lie, . . .

None of these signal qualities, except perhaps the first, Prudence, seems to belong to the Donne tradition. Nor does the "sweetnesse and smooth current of his stile," applied to Ovid; nor the "elegant, pure, and sinewy," to Horace; nor the "easie, cleare, and true Elegiacke," to Propertius; but perhaps only the negative bitter and tart, "broken, froward, unpleasing and harsh," applied to Juvenal and Persius. With such old-fashioned taste guiding his choice, Peacham can make at best a compromise for Chaucer: "under a bitter and rough rinde, there lyeth a delicate kernell of conceit and sweet invention": a nut to crack; and for the wits of Queen Elizabeth's golden age he must make distinctions, omitting Donne and Jonson entirely, and climaxing with "our Phoenix, the noble Sir Philip Sidney, M. Edward Dyer, M. Edmund Spenser, Master Samuel Daniel, . . . Thus much of Poetry." It would seem that Peacham wrote prose with the vigor, roughness, and detail of a plain wit, but in poetry expected a smooth and flowery one. His whole book, past the Poetry chapter into Fishing, ended more roughly, as it began.

The Perch biteth at the red Worme about the middest of the water. Thus have I briefly set downe the art of Angling, and will conclude with all seasons which are naught to Angle in, as the violent heate of the day, high Winds, great Raine, Snow and Haile, Thunder, Lightning, or any wind that bloweth from the East, Land flouds, and thicke waters, the falling of the leaves into the water, and such like impediments which are enemies to Anglers.

Thus the colloquial density of some prose in the 1640's. The *Familiar Letters* of James Howell, though often repetitive in their gossip and travel notes and protestations of affection, are often equally lively and specific, in the currency of the time.

Surely, God Almighty is angry with England, and it is more sure, that God is never angry without cause. Now, to know this cause, the best way is, for everyone to lay his hand on his breast, and examine himself thoroughly to summon his thoughts and winnow them, and so call to remembrance how far he hath offended Heaven, and then it will be found that God is not angry with England, but with Englishmen. When that doleful charge was pronounced against Israel, "Perditio tua ex te, Israel," it was meant of the concrete (not the abstract), "Oh Israelites, your ruin comes from yourselves." When I make this scrutiny within myself, and enter into the closest cabinet of my soul, I find (God help me!) that I have contributed as much to the drawing down of these judgments on England as any other. When I ransack the three cells of my brain, I find that my imagination hath been vain and extravagant. My memory hath kept the bad, and let go the good, like a wide sieve that retains the bran and parts with the flour. My understanding hath been full of error and obliquities; my will hath been a rebel to reason; my reason a rebel to faith, which, I thank God, I have the grace to quell presently with this caution,
          "Succumbat Ratio Fidei, et captiva quiescat."
    When I descend to my heart, the centre of all my affections, I find it hath swelled often with tympanies of vanity and tumours of wrath; when I take my whole self in a lump, I find that I am naught else but a cargazon of malignant humours, a rabble of unruly passions, amongst which my poor soul is daily crucified, as betwixt so many thieves. Therefore, as I pray in general, that God would please not to punish this island for the sins of the people, so more particularly I pray, that she suffer not for me in particular; who, if one would go by way of induction, would make one of the chiefest instances of the argument.[1]

In this passage of self-searching, written in 1644, appears much of the material content of the decade's poetry: the religious awareness, the Biblical reference, the homely figures of cabinet and sieve, the emotional stress and swelling, the sense of argu-

---

[1] II, 83–84.

ment and petition. What is most lacking, the vocabulary of face and grace, is present in other letters.

Howell was a son of Ben, a traveler, royal clerk, and historiographer seemingly a typical man of the town and time, and while he saw fit to write all blithely and shortly in prose, he too, like Peacham, had a sense of the floweriness of poetry. In his Instructions for Forreine Travell[2] he especially recommended the elaborate poetry of Du Bartas; he praised the "rich and elaborate" Latin poems of Benlowes; he praised madness in Jonson: "The madness I mean is that divine fury, that heating and heightening spirit which Ovid speaks of";[3] and he wrote such elaborations as involved over and over sweets, flowers, and perfumes, and "Methought I felt my heart melting within my breast, and my thoughts transported to a true elysium all the while, there were such flexanimous strong ravishing strains throughout it."[4] At the same time, he is capable of a drier wit. "Never did cavalier woo fair lady as he [King Charles] woos the Parliament to a peace; it is much the head should so stoop to the members.... If the cedar be so weather-beaten, we poor shrubs must not murmur to bear part of the storm.... There is not such a windy wavering thing in the world as the common people."[5]

Howell and Peacham agree, then, on a mixed view and practice of style. Both seem to accept the tradition of a flowery poetry, yet to write more often a peppery prose. The parallel is made exactly by Howell, in fact, when he first introduces his "familiar letters" and compares them with rhetoric.

It was a quaint difference the ancients did put betwixt a letter and an oration, that the one should be attired like a woman, the other like a man. The latter of the two is allowed large side robes, as long periods, parentheses, similes, examples, and the other parts of rhetorical flourishes: but a letter or epistle should be short-coated, and closely couched;

---

[2] Ed. Edward Arber, 1869, p. 25.
[3] *Familiar Letters, or Epistolæ Ho-Elianæ* (3 vols., London, Dent, 1903), II, 241; I, 307.
[4] *Ibid.,* I, 303.
[5] *Ibid.,* II, 261; I, 156.

a hungerlin becomes a letter more handsomely than a gown. Indeed we should write as we speak, and that's a true familiar letter which expresseth one's mind, as if he were discoursing with the party to whom he writes in succint and short terms.[6]

The rhetorical tradition which Howell accepts and employs he nevertheless sees as separate from the main line of his familiar discourse; and one may be tempted to borrow his terms to extend the distinction: between poetry long and poetry short. The school of Jonson was indeed often called masculine, in opposition to the Spenserian feminine, and this may be the contrast which the 1640's reveals, the familiar versus the rhetorical, the short-coat versus the gown. It becomes then a contrast which Milton turns upside down, when in his essay on Education he opposes to logic not the succinct and familiar but the simple, sensuous, and passionate.

As Howell and Peacham, writing on manners, practiced and theorized upon the familiar especially, so Hammond in his *Practical Catechism* practiced in moral conventions of response the familiar vocabulary, and suggested, on the other hand, in his motto "Theologia est Scientia Affectiva, non Speculativa," a distinction which his style itself did not follow. His "Catechist" replies to his "Scholar" in the simplest standard 1640 terms:

C. A covenant is a mutual compact, (as we now consider it) betwixt God and man, consisting of mercies on God's part made over to man, and of conditions on man's part required by God.
S. It will be necessary for me to demand, first, what you mean by the first Covenant.
C. I mean that which is supposed to be made with Adam, as soon as he was created, before his first sin, and with all mankind in him.
S. What then was the mercy on God's part made over to him in that Covenant?
C. It consisted of two parts, one sort of things supposed before the Covenant, and absolutely given to him by God in his Creation: another promised, and not given but upon condition.
S. What is that which is absolutely given?

---

[6] *Ibid.*, I, 1.

C. 1. A Law written in his heart, teaching him the whole duty of man. 2. A positive law, of not eating the fruit of one tree in the garden, all others but that one being freely allowed him by God. 3. A perfect strength and ability bestowed on him to perform all that was required of him, and by that a possibility to have lived for ever without ever sinning.

S. What is that which was promised on condition?

C. 1. Continuance of that Light and that strength, the one to direct, the other to assist him in a persevering performance of that perfect obedience. 2 A crown of such performance, assumption to eternal felicity.

S. What was the condition upon which the former of these was promised?

C. Walking in that light, making use of that strength; and therefore upon defailance in those two, (on commission of the first sin) that light was dimmed, and that strength (like Sampson's when his locks were lost) extremely weakned.

S. What was the condition upon which the Eternal felicity was promised?

C. Exact, unsinning, perfect obedience, proportioned to the measure of that strength; and consequently upon the commission of the first sin, this crown was forfeited, Adam cast out of Paradise, and condemned to death, and so deprived both of Eternity and felicity: and from that hour to this there hath been no man living (Christ only excepted, who was God as well as man) justifiable by that first Covenant, all having sinned, and so coming short of the Glory of God promised in that Covenant.[7]

Aside from terms of the topic, like *Covenant, promise, condition,* the words are the major or secondary words of the poetry, Cavalier and Puritan alike: *God, man, mercy, part, thing, make, give, law, heart, fruit, tree, strength, sin, live, die, light, eternal, crown, death, hour, glory.* And the prose is simply argumentative, in the rational way of much of the love poetry, using divisions, causes, figures, illustrations succinctly. This is the matrix of the decade's language, its sense of relationship between two worlds, in place, time, and feeling, and moral responsibility. The commonest lesson books caried the terms and tone.

---

[7] Henry Hammond, *A Practical Catechism* (11th ed., London, 1677), pp. 3–4.

The loftier lesson books of the great divines are less direct and more decorated. So the Rt. Rev. Joseph Hall, Bishop of Exeter and afterward of Norwich, begins his *Christian Moderation* of 1646 with an elaboration:

I cannot but second and commend that great clerk of Paris, who, as our witty countryman Bromiard reports, when king Louis of France required him to write down the best word that ever he had learnt, called for a fair skin of parchment, and in the midst of it wrote this one word, *measure;* and sent it sealed up to the king. . . .

Neither could aught be spoken, of more use or excellency: for what goodness can there be in the world without moderation; whether in the use of God's creatures or in our own disposition and carriage? Without this, justice is no other than cruel rigour; mercy, unjust remissness; pleasure, brutish sensuality; love, frenzy; anger, fury; sorrow, desperate mopishness; joy, distempered wildness; knowledge, saucy curiosity; piety, superstition; care, wracking distraction; courage, mad rashness: shortly, there can be nothing under heaven without it but mere vice and confusion. Like as in nature, if the elements should forget the temper of their due mixture, and encroach upon each other by excess, what could follow but universal ruin? or what is it that shall put an end to this great frame of the world but the predominancy of that last devouring fire?[8]

This is argument concerned as much with quality as with connection; and with the quality, in particular, of magnitude; it reaches out by series, epithets, repetitions, and suspensions, and large reference, to attain the fullest sweep. As Sir Kenelm Digby in his treatise *Of Bodies* concludes with a metaphor of a hilltop "from whence looking down over the whole region of bodies, we may delight ourselves, with seeing what a height the weary steps we ascended have brought us to," so Bishop Hall, like many another orator or essayist of his generation essayed the cosmic reach, the lofty view, the cumulative epitheted survey, in prose as in poetry.

Christian Moderation emphasizes the passions, leaning not toward homely application, but toward inclusiveness and feeling.

---

[8] *Works,* Vol. VI, pp. 387–388.

Divided into Practice and Judgment, the book first considers pleasures, lust, conjugal society, wealth and honor, the passions sorrow, fear, and anger, then persons, truths, opinions, manners, ending with reference to the sacred walls of Jerusalem. The piling up of evidences and allusions and emotional atmospheres is characteristic of its mode; it is more moving, less dry and minute, than the commoner pamphlets.

Consider, then, the sweep of Jeremy Taylor: how his voice revealed the Universe. Consider the mere cadences of his simple prayer, for example, in contrast to the closer argument of a Bacon, or the familiar ease of a letter writer, however devout.

Almighty God, our glory and our hope, our Lord and master, the Father of mercy and God of all comfort, we present to Thee the sacrifice of a thankful spirit, in humble and joyful acknowledgment of those infinite favours by which Thou hast supported our state, enriched our spirit, comforted our sorrows, relieved our necessities, blessed and defended our persons, instructed our ignorances, and promoted our eternal interests.[9]

This prose moves, again, by the power of addition: just enough at a time. Or, more complicatedly, but still by paralleling and adding, "A discourse of the Nature and Offices of Friendship" concludes:

for as an eye that dwells long upon a star must be refreshed with lesser beauties and strengthened with greens and looking-glasses, lest the sight become amazed with too great a splendour; so must the love of friends sometimes be refreshed with material and low caresses; lest by striving to be too divine it become less humane: it must be allowed its share of both: it is humane in giving pardon and fair construction, and openness and ingenuity, and keeping secrets; it hath something that is divine, because it is beneficent; but much, because it is eternal.[10]

The more famous *Holy Living* is compounded with the same rich roll, with a fullness of speech which in verse would require an unrhymed pentameter at the least, and a skillful caesura to hold the uneven balances in control. Taylor lamented "a thou-

---

[9] *The Whole Works,* ed. Heber and Eden, Vol. I, p. 67.
[10] *Ibid.,* p. 98.

sand times" "that the beaux esprits of England doe not think divine things to be worthy subjects for their poesy and spare hours."[11] And his prose was in a sense the kind of poetry which Milton was to write, had already written, full of *altitudos,* like Crashaw's, Quarles', even Denham's. For though he was a practical man, full of good rules for the daily actions of the clergy, Lord Bishop, after all, of Donn, Connor, and Dromore, and loyal to His Majesty through the hard years of the 1640's and 1650's, he was not a familiar man, and preferred, as Crashaw did, in the passage quoted in § II, to the techniques of the gnat, the techniques of the angel.

Thomas Fuller was less angelic. His London sermons in the 1640's were extremely popular, but perhaps less enchanting than Taylor's. *Growth in Grace,* 1640, begins drily, and with homely emphasis.

Philosophers make a double growth. One *per aggregationem materiae,* by gaining of more matter: thus rivers grow by the accession of tributary brooks: heaps of corn wax greater by the addition of more grain: and thus stones grow as some would have it, though this more properly be termed as augmentation, or increase, than a growth. The other *per intro receptionem nutrimenti,* by receiving of nourishment within, as plants, beasts, and men grow. Of the latter growth, we understand the Apostle in the text, and will prosecute the metaphor of the growth of vegetables, as that which the Holy Spirit seems most to favour, and intend in these expressions.[12]

And *A Christening Sermon:*

In this chapter, Naaman the Syrian comes hurrying with his horses and rattling with his chariot to the door of the prophet Elisha, to be cured of his leprosy. Now, he said in his heart (I could not have told his thoughts, except first he had told them to me), he will surely come out to me, and stand and call on the name of the Lord his God, and strike his hand over the place, and recover the Leper.[13]

---

[11] Letters to Evelyn, *Works,* I, liv.

[12] *Pulpit Sparks. Being XIX Sermons of . . . Thomas Fuller,* ed. Morris Fuller (London, 1886), p. 2.

[13] *Ibid.,* p. 58.

And, A Sermon Preached in the Collegiate Church of St. Peter in Westminster, on the 27th of March, being the day of His Majesty's Inauguration (1643), upon the text from Samuel, "Yea, let him take all, foreasmuch as my Lord the King is come again in peace unto his own house."

> It is as natural for malicious men to backbite, as for Dogs to bite, or Serpents to sting, see this in Ziba, who raised a false report on his master Mephibosheth and accused him to David (when he departed from Jerusalem) of no less than high Treason, as if in David's absence he affected the Kingdom for himself.[14]

Here is learning more crabbed and colloquial than flowing in its eloquence; its highest periods are dogged with direct conversational tone. Always the metaphysical minutiae are called to Fuller's aid, gnatlike as they may be, and he seems the more complicated for being so particular. His topics make the standard admonishments, by more than the standard repetitive and brief declarative sentences.

The differences between Hall's and Taylor's grand style and Fuller's plain one indicate that, in prose as in poetry, subject matter does not seem necessarily to dictate style, even within one era. Divines as well as letter writers sometimes elected to be witty and familiar. Yet a doctor, Sir Thomas Browne, seemed to see, at least for himself, a distinction in practice for subject. His choice for religion sides with Taylor: "In Philosophy when truth seemes double-faced, there is no man more paradoxicall than myself; but in Divinity I love to keepe the road ... As for those wingy mysteries in Divinity, and ayery subtilties in Religion, which have unhindg'd the braines of better heads, they never stretched the *Pia Mater* of mine; I love to lose my selfe in a mystery to pursue my reason to an *oh altitudo.*"[15] So the soaring style was Browne's for *Religio Medici,* in dealing with the mysteries of

---

[14] *Ibid.*, p. 115.
[15] Browne's *Religio Medici*, with Digby's *Observations* (Oxford, Clarendon Press, 1909), §§ VI, IX.

Trinity, Eternity, and First Causes, and the poetry he quoted mostly Miltonic. Neither he, nor Digby in commenting upon him,[16] made much use of the personal, homely, mixed, but rather expanded the flow of thought by series, epithets, colons, and *ands* to an effect of range and power.

XXXV. Now for the immaterial world, methinks we need not wander so far as the first movable; for even in this material fabric the spirits walk as freely exempt from the affection of time, place, and motion, as beyond the extremest circumference: do but extract from the corpulency of bodies, or resolve things beyond their first matter, and you discover the habitation of angels, which if I call the ubiquitary and omnipresent essence of God, I hope I shall not offend divinity: for before the creation of the world, God was really all things.

One will notice in this prose, as has been noted many times before, Browne's special characteristic of inventive nouns and epithets. He adapts the single words rather than the subjects or structures.

Again, in the beginning of *Pseudodoxia Epidemica,* Browne suggests two ways of thought, with expression perhaps consequent, himself choosing for this work on the exposition of common errors about minerals, animals, men, emblematical, geographical, historical, and Biblical, the middle steady style fairly enough, but intimating the grandeurs of the Universal style at every step. To the Reader:

in this Encylopedie and round of Knowledg, like the great and exemplary wheels of Heaven, we must observe two Circles: that while we are daily carried about, and whirled on by the swing and rapt of the one, we may maintain a natural and proper course, in the slow and sober wheel of the other.

Mostly Browne is reasonable, patient, exploratory, setting forth and examining detail upon detail: "How beer and wine come to be spoiled by lightning"; "That Coral is soft under water, but hardneth in the ayr"; "Of the musicall notes of Swans before their death"; "A Digression of the wisdom of God in the site

---

[16] *Ibid.*

and motion of the Sun"; "A digression of Blackness"; "Of the death of Aristotle"—all this miscellany which yet fits into the standard realms. Sometimes the very piling up of his knowledge and his vivid sense of it will carry him into "the swing and rapt," but he never loses touch with the slower wheel and the particular. So the famous passages in *Urn-Burial* lift and fall back: as on the first page:

The treasures of time lie high, in urns, coins, and monuments, scarce below the roots of some vegetables. Time hath endless rarities, and shows of all varieties; which reveals old things in heaven, makes new discoveries in earth, and even earth itself a discovery. That great antiquity, America, lay buried for a thousand years; and a large part of the earth is still in the urn unto us.

I should surmise that Browne might be held to be a great mixer and animator of style, no more grand like Taylor than rough like Fuller, employing his own vocabulary with the central sort of idiosyncracy which in poetry Cleveland used. At any rate, he blended with peroration a brief and abrupt address, with tonal an explanatory structure, with his special Latinic monuments the major terms of time and earth.

The boundaries of the era's prose as set by Donne and Dryden chronologically suggest in some measure also the stylistic boundaries. Neither poet is so plain in prose as one might expect, for both make prose an occasion to soar; but Donne still is bound by the familiar, the short-coat method, as Dryden is not. Compare Donne's sermonizing,

Man is but earth; Tis true; but earth is the center. That man who dwels upon himself, who is alwaies conversant in himself, rests in his true center. Man is a celestial creature too, a heavenly creature; and that man that dwels upon himselfe, that hath his conversation in himselfe, hath his conversation in heaven. If you weigh anything in a scale, the greater it is, the lower it sinkes; as you grow greater and greater in the eyes of the world, sinke lower and lower in your owne. If thou ask thyself *Quis ego,* what am I? and beest able to answer thyselfe, why now I am a man of title, of honour, of place, of power, of possessions, a man fit for a Chronicle, a man considerable in the Heralds Office, goe to the Heralds Office, the spheare and element of Honour, and thou shalt finde those men as busie there, about the consideration of Funerals, as about the consideration of Creations; thou shalt finde that office to be as well the Grave, as the Cradle of Honour; ...[17]

and Dryden's beginning of "An Essay of Dramatic Poesy," which, though of later date, is characteristic of Dryden's style:

It was that memorable day, in the first summer of the late war, when our navy engaged the Dutch; a day wherein the two most mighty and best appointed fleets which any age had ever seen, disputed the command of the greater half of the globe, the commerce of nations, and the riches of the universe. While these vast floating bodies, on either side, moved against each other in parallel lines, and our countrymen, under the happy conduct of his Royal Highness, went breaking, by little and little, into the line of the enemies; the noise of the cannon from both navies reached our ears about the City, so that all men being alarmed with it, and in a dreadful suspense of the event which we knew was then deciding, every one went following the sound as his fancy led him; and leaving the town almost empty, some took towards the park, some cross the river, others down it; all seeking the noise in the depth of silence.[18]

This setting of Dryden's moves along an extended line in time and space: the scene, the summer's day, the two parallel lines of the navies on one hand, the City on the other, with its radial lines of river and park, up and down. The structure is preparatory in the first *It was . . .*, balanced in the *while,* and *so that,* and even in the *some . . . some* phrases. The tone is emotional and atmospheric, carried by *memorable, our, most mighty and best appointed, greater half, riches of the universe, happy conduct, alarmed, dreadful suspense,* "the noise in the depth of silence." Adjectives and nouns convey the tone, while the verbs of engaging, disputing, breaking, seeking, take the narrative.

---

[17] *Complete Poetry and Selected Prose,* ed. John Hayward (New York, Random House, 1930), pp. 590–591.
[18] *Essays of John Dryden,* ed. W. P. Ker (Oxford, Clarendon Press, 1900), p. 28.

Donne's passage, on the other hand, sets no scene, and concerns no particular time or space, though it uses a place, the Herald's Office, for illustration. Donne's structure is centripetal, circling and repeating around his point of individual centrality. A man conversant with himself rests in his true center, both human and divine: this is the concept which the repetitions state, and which the example of official honor negatively illustrates. Any spatial sense there is is abstract: vertical from heaven to earth, from high to low in the scale; horizontal from cradle to grave. The connectives, too, are abstractly relational: *but, who, if, if;* and the nouns carry no atmospheric but much conceptual continuity in man, earth, true center, heavenly creature, scale, eyes, world, title, honour, Chronicle, Heralds Office, spheare and element, Funerals, Creations, Cradle, and Grave. Epithets are scant, and verbs of *dwells, is, weighs, ask, find,* are the thread of the plot of thought, in man's learning of himself.

There is thus a great contrast between Donne's paragraph of interior conceptual relationship, reflexively organized, and Dryden's of exterior atmospheric scene, extensively organized. Whether this contrast is characteristic of the prose within the 1640's, and in what proportion, is a matter for conjecture. I have not in the prose that set of basic usages to measure by, which it has been this study's purpose to contrive; and certainly in this contrast between Donne and Dryden I have made an extreme, not a representative, choice. Both passages were written outside the 1640's, though their authors are represented within it, and neither may be said to be wholly characteristic. Nevertheless, they seem to me good striking models of the contrast which all the prose we have looked at shows in some degree and of which the writers seem well aware, the difference between prose of discourse and prose of description, between predicative and epithetical, between conceptual and atmospheric, between centripetal and centrifugal, intensive and extensive, "short" and "long," "masculine" and "feminine," "familiar" and "rhetorical," "harsh" and "sweet," "plain" and "flowery," "gnat" and "angel," "short-coat" and "gown." The lines between these various polar terms are certainly not all parallel; they cross-cut each other to a degree; but all come near the same point of distinction, at least within the decade. For within the 1640's, it can at least be suggested from a large amount of sampling, some prose writers tended to write with the combined devices of logical connectives in syntax, rough conversational patterns in sound, juxtapositions of the abstract and the petty familiar in sense: the metaphysicians, whether religious or secular, on the side of Crashaw's ill-favored gnat. And other prose writers tended to combine cumulative spatial and temporal structures with prolonged harmonies of sound and extended cosmical epitheted sense: the metaphysicians, whether religious or secular, on the side of the angels. Fuller, Howell, Peacham, Walton, Donne, wrote much of the first kind; and Taylor, Hall, Browne, Milton, Dryden, much of the second. Dryden, as readers will rise to protest, was putting the loftier prose to a new rational and simple use; it is nevertheless noteworthy that in prose as in poetry it was the Miltonic and not the Donnic which he seemed to adapt to these new ends.

What can be speculated about the decade's prose is most pertinent as it suggests three points in the decade's poetry. First, that the distinction of type which we have been observing is a larger matter than poetic tradition and goes as deep at least as the literary tradition of the time. Second, and of more general import, that poetry and prose in any one time seem to draw from the same resources of language in sound, syntax, sense, sharing perhaps least in sound and most in sense, as the force of poetic form works most specially in sound and as the force of poetic expression draws rather on a common fund of denotative and connotative reference. Such statement is counter to the critical belief of such contemporary theorists as I. A. Richards, Max Eastman,

Philip Wheelwright, Kenneth Burke, that poetic language, even as poetic vocabulary, is a special matter and separate from prose. Many modern critics and semanticists hold that poetic language is a distinct *kind* of language, representing a distinct kind of human attitude, with certain words more suitable or characteristic than others. I should suggest that not the words nor their auras of tone and reference are the characteristically poetic as apart from prosaic, but rather the measures which order and emphasize them. At least in the 1640's, a decade more various but possibly as much integrated as most, the primary vocabulary of poetry is important also in prose, the two forms seeming to draw not only upon their disparate conventions but also upon their common store of the terms of value. In addition, as third point, the poets and prose writers themselves were aware of their common store, theorized about its qualities, noted its functions and its powers.

The friend of Jeremy Taylor who preached his funeral sermon recognized this character of shared affection and value in the language of his day, and spoke of it as the language not of men only, but of the Holy Ghost through men. Through the words of value, naming the things of value, spoke the Holy Ghost to men, and men to poetry.

> Glorious things are spoken in scripture concerning the future reward of the righteous; and all the words that are wont to signify what is of greatest price or value, or can represent the most enravishing objects of our desires, are made use of by the holy Ghost to recommend unto us this transcendent state of blessedness. Such are these "rivers of pleasures," a "fountain of living water," a "treasure that can never be wasted, nor never taken from us," and "inheritance of light," an "incorruptible crown," a "kingdom," the "kingdom of God."[19]

These value terms of his represent the fields of thought and metaphor which the major word lists also represent: the *earthly* and *heavenly* kingdoms, in political metaphor, with such terms

---

[19] Taylor, *Works,* Vol. I.

as lord, lady, royal, power, rule, mighty, noble, as subsidiary; then, the crown, jewel, gem, wealth, golden, bright, magnificent, *treasure* group, with its countertone of poverty, dust, and corruption; also the *light* group, with its words of day and sky, purity, and heaven, contrasted with cloud, sin, and darkness; and finally the terms of *water,* floods, tears, fountains, rivers, blood by one analogy, purification by another, refreshment by another, sorrow by another, and sacrifice and atonement. There were other realms also, not touched upon in this list: the realm of sweetness and beauty, for example, and the realm of time; but mainly the double aspects of the major word list, its heaven and earth, God and man, heart and soul, and its visionary eye, find place in the double aspects of these more particular terms of value, the fountain, the light, the treasure, the kingdom.

Equally, poetic terms, removed from their contexts of rhyme and measure, as in concordance lists for example, may be seen to carry these same values, in the same realms of reference. Milton's *heaven* is kingdom, light, and treasure in the path to heaven, strength of heaven, the will and arm of heaven, mild heaven, Son of heaven's eternal King, heaven's high council-table, heaven's deep organ, heaven's queen, heaven's youngest teemed star, heaven's richest store, heaven's heraldry, sheeny heaven, heaven's door. Here even briefly the motion moves between site, person, power, standard, scene. Or Milton's *heart:* ambitious, stubborn. storehouse, minstrelsy, seat of bliss. Or *day:* prosperous, miserable, riddling, feastful, laborious. Or *earth:* mother, dim spot, mould, base, brute, green, frozen, aged, the stage of air and earth. Or *eye:* day's garish eye, the eye of day, my great task-master's eye, awful, love-darting, pure, quaint enamelled, His special eye. Or *great:* event, Oceanus, mistress, vision, sun, bards, Emathian conqueror. Or *make:* defence, memorable, game, fierce sign of battle, reckoning, marble, his eternal bride. Henry Vaughan writes, Fair and yong light! Fair prince of life, Fair, shining

mountains of my pilgrimage, Fair, solitary path! Fair Vessell of
our daily light, And Milton: fair silver-buskined nymphs, fair
wood, fair peace, fair guerdon, thou goddess fair and free, fair
sight, edifice, morning, and Jerusalem. The realm, the vision, the
treasure, could exist for both heaven and earth. The temporal
kingdom of Tudor poetry had now in Caroline poetry, as in
prose, a vaster as a double range.

The difference recognizable in even the few contexts, between
the interior lyrical quality of Vaughan and the exterior decorative quality of Milton is mediated by Herrick's uses, which are
not so architectural as Milton's, but still full of sensory enjoyment, as in *fair* day, maid, signs, Dawne, Injewel'd May, Constellations, Daffadils, Pearles, Wind, Hellen, Transfiguration,
Fates, Auspice, Predestination, fring'd canopies, rare stately neck.
The contrast lies strongly in the last four items, and Herrick uses
much of both kinds, the Donnic abstraction of Auspice and predestination, the Miltonic concrete pomp of stately neck and
fring'd canopies. Herrick's *Heavens* are more functional than
structural, a place to go to, but not pictured except for the sun's
lamp. His *hearts* feel and bleed, his *eyes* sparkle and weep, his
days are more a mark of time than of scene, his *earths* are scant,
neither very conceptual nor very architectural, but flowery and
cold. Herrick helps center the decade's usage, then, employing
a little of Milton's epitheted descriptiveness, a little of Donne's
abstracter juxtaposition, in the contexts of his major terms, but
on the whole relying upon the simpler relationships of concept
and feeling.

Among epithets, *fair* and *sweet* were, for the 1640's, terms of
pleasant value, more of concept than of literal sense: a sweet eternity of love, a sweet disorder in the dress, sweet sound, and soul.
Great and *good* were terms largely of moral value, with some
emphasis by the Miltonic group on sheer physical scope. All four
terms were much used by the Miltonic group, and were most

slighted, on the other hand, by the Donnic, with *sweet* especially scant for all but Herrick and Carew. The secondary *bright* and *high* are descriptive and notably Miltonic, while *new, old, poor, rich, true,* all more conceptual are more evenly distributed through the two groups, with lacks in Herrick and Carew to balance, perhaps, their extra-use of the *sweet* terms.

The contexts of the vocabulary of action differ mainly for such verbs as *see* and *make* as they may mean physical or conceptual action. Love can *make* the lover's state, the poet can *make* a poem, or man his marble tomb. Herrick can *see* the beauties of a maid, or, surprisingly, much more often an abstraction,—these Transgressions, a wilde civility, the wiles, ways, walks of wit. *To think, to die, to love, to fly, to seem,* on the surface a mixed lot of verbs, are in context close to the Donnic uses as they stress relationship, appearance, time, in meditative context; while *stand, hear, speak, sing* suggest in context a ceremonial procedure in the verse characteristic of the Miltonic.

Nouns, varying most by subject, are most varied in connection. The time words, *day, year,* and *time,* by suggesting event and mutability and change, seem to fall short of the Miltonic major list, as do also the human words *man, life, death, earth, soul, blood, face, hand, name, sin,* with their usual problems of daily action, intercourse, and identity. Rather, the Miltonic poet developed the contexts of sight and scope, in *eye, God, heaven, fire, night, power, world,* giving to these common subjects the valued associations of sublimity, in scale exterior to man.

The poetic contexts are like the prose contexts of the main vocabulary. Differing like the prose, in aspects of sublimity and in some of the terms thus involved, they establish in metrical pattern the departments of thought and analogy which the prose too concerns: heavenly and earthly love, in treasures, fountains, rays, and kingdoms; heavenly and earthly kingdoms, in wealth and war; heavenly and earthly souls, in sin and tears, in time and vision, light and love. Some work by elevation, by a line of ascension from world to heaven and soul to God. Others work by confrontation, not leaving the earth, but rearguing upon it the presences of sin, death, and time in the midst of love and life. Both poetry and prose, and continuously their common vocabulary, are useful to either method, and to the combined agreed method of the decade in conveying the life of the loving, envisioning, and aspiring soul.

IV. CRITICAL ATTITUDES AND DESCRIPTIVE CONCLUSIONS

SOME MODERN views of the 1640's, or of the era of which they were part, provide a series of tangents to the center as this study sees the center in terms of quantitative and qualitative emphases, and, whether tangential or central in a more general view, bear upon the nature of the poetry and its effects. For a generation, seventeenth-century poetry has greatly concerned scholars and critics, providing twice as many studies as the nineteenth century has, and occasioning even a suggestion that the concern may well be outworn.[1] One of the most recent interests has involved the nature of the baroque in art. A definition has been set up, fixed in a certain period and place, and applied to the inclusion or exclusion of certain examples. The 1630's and 1640's in England marked the height of its baroque in literature which is defined by Morris Croll as motion, contortion, obscurity, spiral, anti-Ciceronian and antilogical, as opposed to status, suavity, copiousness, ease, Ciceronian symmetry:[2] "Expressiveness rather than formal beauty was the pretension of the new movement, as it is of every movement that calls itself modern."[3] Croll makes Donne the poetic leader of this movement, away from Spenser; and indeed one recognizes his strong predicating force as part of the activity which Croll describes as baroque. Yet there is difficulty in the combination with "antilogical," with the flashing, unconnected motion of the thought; for Donne's structures are so evidently rational, his connectives poetically important. The end of Mr. Croll's essay shows that he has a special kind of logical and rational in mind, the Cartesian, with its subordination of im-

---

[1] Theodore Spencer and Mark Van Doren, *Studies in Metaphysical Poetry: Two Essays and a Bibliography* (Columbia Univ. Press, 1939), pp. 3, 17.

[2] Morris W. Croll, "The Baroque Style in Prose," *Studies in English Philology: A Miscellany in Honor of Frederick Klaeber,* ed. Kemp Malone (Univ. of Minnesota Press, 1929), pp. 427-456.

[3] *Ibid.,* p. 428. And note the excellent summary of the problem by René Wellek in the *Journal of Aesthetics and Art Criticism* for December, 1946.

agination to the intellectual categories. It seems to me unwise, however, to ignore the special sort of Donnic logic which sets that argued poetry and prose apart from the quite different soaring flash of Taylor or of Crashaw.

Again, but with slightly different distinction, Wylie Sypher's "The Metaphysicals and the Baroque"[4] sets *impulsiveness* as the key, and thus joins Milton, Crashaw, and Donne, stressing a mixture of the incongruous, exuberant, ornamental, the ritualistic, rhetorical, metaphysical, and grand style, which he contrasts to Jonsonian congruity and to modern expressionism. In the single decade of the 1640's this melange of qualities is certainly to be seen. Contrasts with other eras, we are not yet capable of weighing; the contrast to Jonson looks much too strong, but upon a more particular basis of the use of figurative language it may possibly be justified. The danger in Sypher's description is that it functions widely upon many levels of analysis. Common qualities may be discerned and grouped and named, even by an analogy name like "baroque"; but it would seem finally to be not merely the presence of qualities, but their relationship, which would serve to define a style.

Arthur Mizener has recently noted a likeness between such modern poets as Barker, Shapiro, and Thomas, and Cleveland and other Carolines, calling the likeness "decorative baroque" and pointing out the interest in verbalized detail rather than subject itself, with elastic syntax, stretching for the decoration of appositions and epithets, making "a poem in which a very simple structure of meaning supports a vast and intricate elaboration of highly colored details."[5] This use of "baroque" covers the Miltonic but I think not the Donnic school, for it stresses all the qualities of expansion, none of rational complication.

The dangers of confusion in the use of "baroque" to describe

---

[4] *Partisan Review* (Winter, 1944).
[5] "Verse and Poetry," *Kenyon Review* (Winter, 1944), pp. 125–126. See also Austin Warren's definition in *Richard Crashaw: A Study in Baroque Sensibility*, p. 65.

abstractly a sort of style are apparent even among these three variations of use. Each critic selects a number of qualities to demonstrate the term, but they vary from man to man and suggest, consequently, the inclusion of different representative works. Some definitions would center in Milton, others in Donne, still others would blend the two; some would suggest alliances with the present, all with other arts. But alliance in the use of qualities is not so pertinent to definition as alliance in the relating of these qualities. If the rough, technical, obscure, rational, individual combine in formalized metrical and syntactical pattern of lyrical address to make the baroque, then perhaps Donne is it, but none in our own time. If the smooth, elevated, expansive, cosmic, descriptive, general, and ceremonious combine in a little more sensory heaven-and-earthly vocabulary and a lengthened, internally articulated line to make the baroque, then perhaps Crashaw and Milton are it, and perhaps Hart Crane and Dylan Thomas in our time. If a full and restless combination of all these qualities (not possibly of all these relationships) makes the baroque, then certainly the 1640's are it, but not through any one poet or set of poems, and not in any very thorough agreement with the present. The relating of mood and content to medium raises immediately, too, the problem of significant relation to arts of other media, and brings the question of baroqueness to a level where it appears to be all question and no answer. What seems to me most pertinent here to note, until more clarification of history and terminology has been made, is that in the 1940's a kind of poetry is being written, syntactically loose, epithetically and sensuously elaborate, tonally harmonized, generally and even cosmically extended, which sounds like a modern parallel for Quarles and Crashaw, Waller and Milton.

The critical concern of a decade ago was different. It centered upon the meaning of the term "metaphysical," and the unification of sensibility which Eliot proposed as of chief importance.

The 1920's and 1930's felt that ours was a dissociated age, full of confusions, discrepancies, specializations unresolved. Through the leadership of Eliot and Grierson they discovered the resolutions of the seventeenth century, and in many searching studies documented the biographical, philosophical, social, technical procedures of such unification. The essays in the well-known *Garland* and *Tradition*[6] the items listed in the 1939 *Bibliography* by Spencer and Van Doren,[7] concentrate upon an explanation of how, how, how the metaphysicals managed such unity of spirit and of art. A good part of the problem was textual and factual; manuscripts needed discovering, dating and identifying, and editing; dates and episodes and associations needed ordering; there was always an impetus of a direct liking for the poetry. The poetry was about as far from current Imagism and Symbolism as one could appear to get, and yet it presented exactly that live sort of sensation which modern symbolism was working for. Research into medieval doctrine, the stars, patristic lore, Neo-Platonism, Petrarchism, the writings of Bacon and Ramus, the poetry of Du Bartas, the rhetoric books, the masque, Puritan doctrine and pamphleteering, Stuart social and home life, renderings of Horace, Ovid, Vergil, the newsbooks and ballads, voyages and witch burnings, all widened and complicated the world of the metaphysical poets, taking it apart in order to see how they had managed to put it together. Then, too, there was the question who was a metaphysical poet: not Milton or Jonson usually, but always Donne; usually Cowley, Crashaw, Herbert, Marvell, Traherne, and Vaughan; less frequently Carew, Cleveland, Herbert of Cherbury, Henry King, and Katherine Philips. Exclusions are thus made of the Cavalier poets or some of the sons of Ben, Herrick, Suckling, Lovelace, of Waller and Denham the reformers, though their fellow Marvell is included; and of such

---

[6] George Williamson, *The Donne Tradition,* 1930; Theodore Spencer, *A Garland for John Donne,* 1931.

[7] *Op. cit.*

serious popular poets as Quarles, Sandys, Wither, Harvey, More, within one central decade.

The line defining the metaphysical is not, then, based on any one matter of subject, secular or religious; or attitude, serious or humorous; or form, succinct or extended; or structure of thought, complexly reasoned or simply sung or elaborately accrued. Rather, the term "metaphysical" seems to cover a certain nucleus in the midst of all these factors combined, a nucleus of figurative language which binds the disparates from heaven and earth. Here is the "wit," the "conceit," of which we hear so much, the "far-fetched" metaphor, the "radical" metaphor[8] which put down its roots deeply and obscurely. It is expressive of that philosophical understanding of the universe as a whole which the metaphysical poets are said to have possessed. It is witty, knowledgeable, conceited, full of perceptive connections; it is able to consider sense and soul in one sentence, even one metaphor; to blend feeling and thinking in a way which the twentieth century envies. Metaphysical poetry is a complex excluding much seventeenth-century poetry like Lovelace's as being too easily lyrical and profane, and much seventeenth-century philosophical and religious verse as being too easily meditative and divine. The divinity and profanity must in the metaphysical come together, clash, and resolve. It is by this standard of conflict and dramatic resolution that many modern poets judge all English poetry, or all poetry, and by which they find the metaphysical to be so good.[9]

Such evaluation helps to interpret and explain our modern reading of the seventeenth-century contexts more objectively here established, by clarifying some connections and ignoring others. About sound and syntax little is said, but about reference

---

[8] Henry W. Wells' term for the peculiarly Donnic figure, in his *Poetic Imagery* (1924).

[9] See Cleanth Brooks' *Modern Poetry and the Tradition,* for example; also Friedrich's *Englishe Barocklyrik.* Grierson earlier held a wider philosophical view which is exemplified by the introduction and selections in Genevieve Taggard's anthology, *Circumference.*

and especially figured reference much is revealed. The conception of unified sensibility makes significant the appearances upon the major word lists, their notably consistent mixture of heavenly and earthly reference. It applies, in fact, to all the poets of the decade and may as well include Herrick and Quarles and Jonson as Cowley and Crashaw, since all share the power, expressed in their fullest vocabulary, to bind together soul and body, divinity and profanity, in the bonds of figure. Some, even of the metaphysical poets, protested the union, finding any combination with the profane itself profane. Cowley worried about the problem, and kept turning to his unfinished *Davideis* for consolation, but kept feeling the strong responsibility of the poet to love; Vaughan and Crashaw protested the gnat in favor of the angel; Herrick divided his responsibilities. But all actually, as the major words show, made persistent reference to both worldly and heavenly levels, if not as literal subjects, then as figurative enforcements, in which the whole syntax, indeed, was turned to the task of reasoning validities in one realm in terms of their validity in the other. It was the very power of the metaphysician, as the term "unified sensibility" suggests, that his figures could work both ways: body could speak for soul and soul for body, as familiarly as possible. "Think thy shell broke, think thy soul hatched but now." (Donne's "Progress of the Soul"). "As men in hell are from diseases free" (Cowley's "The Usurpation"). "In the clear heaven of thy brow" (Cowley, in imitation of Horace). "The sacred tree midst the fair orchard grew" (Cowley's "Knowledge"). So *fair* and *sweet face* and *hand* and *eye* are spoken by, or speak for, *good* and *great God, heaven, time;* and *lord* and *lady* are ambiguous in their divinity. The major words are of two realms in reference, and further, each word bespeaks a double realm.

This sort of philosophical and practical unification, as part of the decade's assumption, whether Calvinist or Platonical, Puritan or Cavalier, shows itself in all the poets' language and device, and perhaps helps to explain the unanimity of usage which seems, though without as yet much basis of comparison to other decades, to be so particularly strong. The whole decade may in this sense be called metaphysical, in prose as well as poetry, and every poet of it be included in the term, as every one of them seems to have been included at one time or another. Or, by a specification, by a definition of degree, those poets who most employed the play between realms, who most juxtaposed by far-fetching and fused by passionate belief and skill the glorious divine and familiar domestic, may alone be called metaphysical—in which case it becomes a sort of value term, with Donne, not Jonson on the one hand or Milton on the other, as norm for us.

Eliot's and other moderns' stress upon the sensory element in the definition can, in any case, be misleading, if one thinks of sensory in modern terms, or of Eliot's own practice. The metaphysical poets, busy between gnats and angels, worked relatively little in ostensible speech upon the medial line of their own sensations and feelings; and the objects which they chose for figuring forth abstractions were by this very purpose only secondarily to be sensed. The external facts do not for Donne "terminate in sensory experience,"[10] but rather terminate in abstract relationship, his nouns technical or pronomial, his adjectives evaluative, his verbs actively functioning, even his characteristic *sun* not so *warm* or *bright* as *busy*. Possibly vocabulary was less sensory for Donne's age than for any later age in English poetry;[11] at least it was less sensory for Donne's and Jonson's schools than for Milton's, and the distinction is one of the clearest to be seen in the whole decade. The vocabulary of sense, then, the use of sensable objects and qualities as poetic material, defines negatively rather than positively the metaphysical school if it is to be centered in

---

[10] Part of Eliot's explanation of the objective correlative, in "Hamlet," *Selected Essays, 1917–1932* (Harcourt Brace, 1932), pp. 124–125.

[11] As my study of *Major Adjectives in English Poetry* seems to indicate.

Donne, Cowley, Vaughan, Carew, Cleveland, and that kind, and represents positively the counter or parallel school of Milton, Crashaw, Waller, with its emphasis upon image and description. This is not to say that sensation and quality were not vivid in the metaphysical poets, but to say rather that they were vivid in their individuality, particularity, and subordination more than in their consistent poetic focus. The literal expressive materials of Milton were, one may explicitly say, twice as sensuous as the materials of Donne. Their respective effects upon a modern reader may not suggest this fact, because the modern reader is much more sensitive to implication than to explication, and can build upon Donne's metaphors more imagery than he meant their contexts to hold. But their respective choices of poetic substance distinctly deviate in terms of a sensuous versus a conceptual medium, a descriptive versus a dramatic result.

What does seem to me, on the other hand, positively to define the Donnic metaphysical practice is its stress upon negative material and upon the mutability of time. As we have seen, the poets most commonly called metaphysical are apt to employ a vocabulary of *false, bad, poor, time, hour, day, year, old, new, sin, thought.* This is by no means a pictorial list, but rather one of a troubled pondering and abstract speculation, setting any event it may deal with rather in the course of time and change than in visual scene. It makes another kind of unification, too, and perhaps a more complex one than that of human and divine, that of good and evil. It reports the vices of the physical world in order to redeem them, the pleasures of the physical world in order to alter them. The poetry of this kind is able to employ much negative because it has set out to make something of this negative, to premise it, argue it, and involve it in divinity. The poetry of the counter kind, stressing substance rather than relationship, hesitates to present evil quality as the substance of its poetry and stresses rather its obligation to present images of the elevating and the sublime, to translate negatives, if necessary, into the scenic *awful,* the emotive *sad,* the atmospheric *dark,* in subordination. The Donnic poet is most committed to the expressiveness of temporal problems, not of spatial views, and therefore may most closely be recognized, if one wishes to isolate him particularly within his decade, by his concepts of the negative. In this sense the term metaphysical becomes, I think, most closely narrowed and specified for its time. But in its fuller sense, covering most or all of the poets of the 1640's and suggesting their common juxtaposition and rationally figured unification of the realms of heaven and earth, the term is perhaps most generally usefully employed.

In earlier years, in the nineteenth century representatively, discussion of the Carolinian poets centered not so much in the nature of the "metaphysical"—which meant to most romantics not contrast but spiritual height—as in the nature of "wit," that curious kind of mind and technique which saw fit to deal in concept and contrive contrast. Most nineteenth-century critics, like Arnold, saw in wit frivolity, because it rationally played with differences rather than emotionally constructing likenesses as "high seriousness" should. For these critics, the decorum rather than the drama of relationship still prevailed.

So from even so late a work as Courthope's *History of English Poetry* we may draw mostly the light of curiosity upon our speculations, the notion, at which Eliot's first essay centrally rebelled,[12] of "quaintness." Perhaps it was, indeed, the feeling of need to refute this notion in its extreme that led modern critics to the equally extreme notion of the metaphysical as mainline in the English poetic tradition.[13] At any rate, *wit* troubled Courthope and his kind as too cerebral and therefore superficial rather than "organic." While the nineteenth-century philosopher wanted fusions made, he wanted them to seem to unfold and grow, not

[12] T. S. Eliot, "The Metaphysical Poets" (1921) and in *Selected Essays.*
[13] Cleanth Brooks, *Modern Poetry and the Tradition.*

to be speculated upon and verbally forced by the creative power of the poet. The poet would do better to report actual fusions and especially his own feelings of unity, than to create unity out of figures of speech. Courthope lays the fresh interest in Donne at the end of the century to "the revival of medieval sentiment, which has coloured English taste during the last three generations," and proceeds:

Poetical creation implies that organic conception of Nature, and that insight into universal human emotions, which make the classical poets of the world—Homer and Dante, and Chaucer and Milton; and to this universality of thought, as I have endeavoured to show, Donne has no claim. Nor can he be reckoned among the poets who, by their sense of harmony and proportion, have helped to carry forward the refinement of our language from one social stage to another.[14]

What was there in the major language, metrics, structure of Donne's poetry as we have seen it which would lead to such conclusion? For Eliot, Donne's poetry is universal; for Courthope, Milton's. Again the split is made in the interpretation of one decade.

The main sections of Courthope's history of seventeenth-century poetry cover first the successors of Spenser (Daniel, Drayton, Browne, Davies, Hall, Marston); then the schools of "wit": the Theological School (Southwell, Davies of Hereford, and the Fletchers), Quarles, Herbert, Crashaw, Vaughan), the Metaphysical School (Donne), the Court School (Campion, Wotton, Jonson, Drummond, John Beaumont, Carew, Suckling), the "New Wit" (Habington, Waller, Denham), the Cavaliers, Roundheads, and last of the Wits (Cowley and Butler); then Milton, the Restoration poets, Dryden and the satirists. Courthope identifies the early wit with the difficulties and roughness of Johnson's phrase *discordia concors;* the late wit of Waller, Denham, Cowley, and perhaps Dryden, with smooth and correct rationality. He likes the smoother better, but he finds all wit

---

[14] W. J. Courthope, *A History of English Poetry*, Vol. II, p. 168.

poetry local, individualistic, social, idiosyncratic, un-universal, limitedly and medievally representative, relatively slight but without the "tough reasonableness beneath the slight lyric grace" which Eliot found there,[15] or without a pleasure in that tough reasonableness. Milton seems to him in the greater tradition, on the side of the angels rather than the gnats, and he traces the Miltonic line from Spenser through the Fletchers. Here is a serious intent, a large scope, a correspondent spread of imagery which seems to Courthope "organic" in its consistency, "universal" in its attitude and material.

In thoroughly derogating "rhetorical" wit at the expense of the "more simple, sensuous and passionate," Courthope throughout the seventeenth-century volume of his History helps clarify the distinction between the kinds, as the distinction more objectively seen helps clarify Courthope's typically nineteenth-century position. He defines clearly a Spenserian tradition and a Wit tradition, both within and outside these then grouping poets by subject and attitude: metaphysical, religious, courtly, political. He prefers among these, like Arnold, the poets who write from the soul rather than the brain; since these are Spenserian and religious rather than metaphysical and political, sublime and descriptive rather than familiar and argumentative, we see that what soul meant for Courthope was a blend of sense and emotion in general nature and humanity, while what wit meant was a forcing of concept and objects in particular individual relationships. The smooth, harmonious, lofty is universal; the rough dramatic lowly is particular; and because the nineteenth century was more sympathetic with the first it saw more passion in the first.

Courthope's opposition fits the objective distinction between substantive and predicative kinds in the 1640's, and supports our sense of major modes. But he does not, on the one hand, indicate the great unanimity to be seen in the period, nor, on the other,

---

[15] "Marvell," *Selected Essays*, p. 252.

the sort of alliances we have noted. His smaller groupings are
so strongly by external connections of politics and religions that
he looks little at the basis of form and usage. He sees little of the
connection between Cavalier and metaphysical, between Milton,
Dryden, and "later wits" like Waller, and little of the opposition
of such men as Vaughan and Crashaw, More and Harvey, within
the religious field. Maintaining the traditional division between
metaphysical, classical-courtly, and religious, he does not perceive how closely in poetic form and substance the poems of
many of each of these, of Donne, Jonson, Wither, of Cowley,
Herrick, Harvey, joined. Attitude being more pertinent to him
than technique, he would not see Jonson close to Donne or Dryden to Milton, because he would see poetry as an embodying
rather than as a transforming force, and so take materials at face
value. Only at the extremes of technique, in Donne and Milton,
would its powers be plain, and its alliances for good and evil be
drawn up. The 1640's show a more serious and skillful world of
poetry than readers were long able to allow: unified, yet with a
double tradition which Courthope's kind with its blinding sense
of black and white has best made plain.

Although Samuel Johnson a century before established in his
essay on Cowley much of the material of "metaphysical" and
"wit" upon which Courthope built, he did not see the poles of
particularity and universality as the nineteenth century saw them.
He designated the poles in Cowley and Milton, "of dissimilar
genius, of opposite principles,"[16] and, as Pope did, related Cowley
to Donne: "He as well as Davenant borrowed his metaphysical
style from Donne";[17] but Johnson did not favor the one extreme
over the other; he liked the middle course, as in Dryden, as well
as any.[18] He took from Dryden the appellation "metaphysical"
("Donne affects the metaphysics not only in his satires but in his

[16] Samuel Johnson. *Lives of the Most Eminent English Poets* (2 vols., New York, 1857), Vol. I, p. 46.
[17] *Ibid.*, p. 51.
[18] *Ibid.*, p. xxiv.

amorous verses where Nature only should reign," *Dedication of Juvenal,* 1693), and stressed in the term not only Dryden's sense of forced and inappropriate learnedness, but also his own sense of the roughness of the metrical numbers. Johnson wrote from a strong opinion of the nature of reality: representative images, generalities, emotions, were realest. The metaphysical poets emphasized none of these. They "neither painted the forms of matter, nor represented the operations of intellect."[19] "Their courtship was void of fondness, and their lamentation of sorrow. Their wish was only to say what they hoped had never been said before."[20] Thus, they were not even good wits, either in Pope's verbal sense or in Johnson's "more noble" conception of wit as that which is at once natural and new, for the metaphysicals though new were not natural.

Nor was the sublime more within their reach than the pathetic; for they never attempted that comprehension and expanse of thought which at once fills the whole mind, and of which the first effect is sudden astonishment, and the second rational admiration. Sublimity is produced by aggregation, and littleness by dispersion. Great thoughts are always general, and consist in positions not limited by exceptions, and in descriptions not descending to minuteness.[21]

Certainly everything the metaphysical poets tried, even the mildest of Cavalier metaphysical fashion, ran counter to this standard. There was too much range and conflict even between the major terms, and the secondary terms of *sun, face, flame* descended too far to minuteness. Yet these were the most common; the idiosyncratic varieties of usage went infinitely farther into techniques, daily affairs, alchemies, for their resources. These Johnson hated, the "recesses of learning," "disgusting hyperboles," "violent fictions," mixed high and low, the very juxtapositions which to Eliot proved a unified sensibility. Furthermore, metaphysical "numbers" were not representative, did little to fit or

[19] *Ibid.,* p. 51.
[20] *Ibid.,* p. 53.
[21] *Ibid.,* p. 53.

"represent," by a kind of onomatopoeia, the flow of thought, and the arguing syntax misled into particularity. "The fault of Cowley, and perhaps of all the writers of the metaphysical race, is that of pursuing his thoughts to the last ramifications, by which he loses the grandeur of generality."[22]

See how well Johnson illustrates the very difference between the poetry of description and the poetry of relationship which we have thought to be fundamental. It is a good critic who makes his points so clear that they fit discrimination, even if taste is in reverse, a century and a half later. Taking Dryden's and Milton's side against Cowley he writes:

One of the great sources of poetical delight is description, or the power of presenting pictures to the mind. Cowley gives references instead of images, and shows not what may be supposed to have been seen, but what thoughts the sight might have suggested. When Virgil describes the stone which Turnus lifted against Aeneas, he fixes the attention on its bulk and weight:

>   Saxum circumspicit ingens,
>   Saxum antiquum, ingens, campoquod forte jacebat
>   Limes agro positus, litem ut discerneret arvis.   .

Cowley says of the stone with which Cain slew his brother:

>   I saw him fling the stone as if he meant
>   At once his murther and his monument.[23]

Bulk and weight versus conceptual relationship is the very counterpoise which comes so alive in the 1640's, which the critics of baroque confuse, which the dogmatists of wit, like the dogmatists of organicity, deplore. Johnson is not any of these, but a champion of general uniformity, praising Cowley as well as blaming him, liking him at his light Anacreontics, for "Real mirth must always be natural, and nature is uniform, . . ."[24] ranking him, just as our formal study suggests, between Donne and Jonson on the one hand, Waller and Milton on the other.[25] Neither extreme suits Johnson. He finds much metaphysical

[22] *Ibid.,* p. 75.
[23] *Ibid.,* p. 80.
[24] *Ibid.,* pp. 70–71.
[25] *Ibid.,* p. 54.

harshness of rhyme and epithet still in Milton and deplores many of his vast imaginings, but likes in *Comus* "his power of description and his vigour of sentiment employed in the praise and defense of virtue.... A work more truly poetical is rarely found; allusions, images, and descriptive epithets, embellish almost every period with lavish decoration."[26] This is the good side of Milton, and it is the side toward Waller and Crashaw and the eighteenth century, toward, indeed, *Paradise Lost;* "his great excellence is amplitude."

But this extreme, like Donne's, represented for Johnson, at least on the formal level of language and substance, "a half a century of forced thoughts, and rugged metre," which Dryden brought his refined diction to reform. We have noticed, even in Dryden's major words, their moderateness of abstraction, their middle path between the familiar and the remote. This is what Johnson has to praise.

Words too familiar, or too remote, defeat the purpose of a poet. From those sounds which we hear on small or on coarse occasions, we do not easily receive strong impressions, or delightful images; and words to which we are nearly strangers, whenever they occur, draw that attention on themselves which they should transmit to things.[27]

Here is one end of the age-old nominalist-realist seesaw put down hard and flat, as Sprat and others of Dryden's colleagues and the eighteenth-century poets had been trying to put it: that it was not the language or the makers of the poetry that made the poetry, but what they referred to. This is the poetry not of words, but of things.

In Dryden, the roses have been plucked from the bramble. The concise has been separated from the diffuse, the lofty from the humble. The smooth numbers and elegant and easy diction of Denham and Waller have been defended against their century and given their place in the sun. It took time for Dryden to learn

---

[26] *Ibid.*, p. 171, 179.   [27] *Ibid.*, p. 365.

to give up the conceit and the particular, and to base his senti-ments upon a more uniform nature, and in the verses on Claren-don he first arrived, says Johnson, "at those penetrating remarks on human nature, for which he seems to have been peculiarly formed."

> Let envy then those crimes within you see,
> From which the happy never must be free;
> Envy that does with misery reside,
> The joy and the revenge of ruin'd pride.[28]

Here is the *via media* in the smooth and general human which poetry had long worked to achieve. "It is a general rule in poetry, that all appropriated terms of art should be sunk in general ex-pressions, because poetry is to speak a universal language."[29] Liking the particularities of argument and wit, Dryden skirted the abyss of them and stayed mainly in the field of a natural meditation. His universal language, then, rhymed and reasoned as it is, rhymes more fittingly than Milton's, reasons more gen-erally than Donne's, and thus achieves a universality not that of Courthope's Miltonic sublime, not that of Eliot's unified sensi-bility, but that of Johnson's uniform nature.

As the twentieth century likes a unity of thought and sensation, and the nineteenth a unity of emotion, and the eighteenth a unity of exterior nature, the seventeenth century itself took a critical position in regard to unity, when in 1650, just at the end of the decade and reflecting critically back upon it, Davenant and Hobbes took the occasion of *Gondibert* to expound the function of the Heroic Poem. Theirs was a unity of genre, of psychological aim and effect corresponding to compartments of aim and effect in nature. It looked back to the classificatory methods which the Elizabethans accepted as technical guides, and forward to Dr. Johnson's norms in nature. The shift is to be seen even between Davenant and Hobbes, for Davenant lays the basis for his Heroic

---

[28] *Ibid.*, p. 373.   [29] *Ibid.*, p. 376.

usages by a brief survey of the great heroic poems of tradition, ending with Spenser, while Hobbes in reply strengthens the basis by reference to natural and social analogies, paralleling the Heroic to Celestial and Court subjects, as the Pastoral to Terrestrial and Country. The interest of both writers is so much more in Heroic than in Pastoral that the general problem of unity within genres, with its standard of "appropriateness," becomes overshadowed by the details of appropriateness within the one genre, which seems so much the "highest" and "noblest" (note Waller's and Milton's poetic value epithets) that it tends to spread as wide as the Nature which is to be Johnson's basis. Thus Davenant looks back with a sort of scorn on "lower" forms of epigram and lyric in his time, writes against the inclusion of low or evil materials or the preoccupation with death and negatives, explaining that "the distempers of Love and Ambition are the only Characters I design'd to expose as objects of terrour."[30] He accepts "wit" not as a sense of "bitter moralls," or of wonders or conceits, but as the power of universal survey,[31] and deems the force of leadership in poetry always constructive, positive, uplifting, rather than dramatic or disturbing.

For Nature performs all things by correspondent aids and harmony. And 'tis injurious not to think Poets the most useful Moralists, for as Poesy is adorn'd and sublim'd by Musick, which makes it more pleasant and acceptable, so Morality is sweetned and made more amiable by Poesy.[32]

It looks here as if, even in the decade when it still most flourished, the gnat were losing critically to the angel. Davenant has not even had time to reform his prose style to fit; he writes in the rough, reasoned, and minutely illustrative prose characteristic of metaphysical wit, but his argument moves toward the smoother elevations of Dryden and of Johnson.

---

[30] Preface to *Gondibert. Critical Essays of the Seventeenth Century*, ed. J. E. Spingarn, Vol. II, p. 16.

[31] *Ibid.*, pp. 20–22.   [32] *Ibid.*, p. 49.

Hobbes supports his friend's tendencies toward elegance, and in smoother prose. He too condemns vulgar material and "Illustration of any thing from such Metaphors or Comparisons as cannot come into mens thoughts but by mean conversation and experience of humble or evil Arts, which the Person of an Epique Poem cannot be thought acquainted with."[33] He thinks poetry needs no wonders either, no flying horses or iron men, but rather the painting and resemblance of Truth, truth, that is, in nature and men's manners, and no dark truths or riddles in language, but as many words as needed and many distinct images to set forth the facts.

> As the description of Great Men and Great Actions is the constant of a Poet, so the descriptions of worthy circumstances are necessary accessions to a Poem, and being well performed are the Jewels and most precious ornaments of Poesy.[34]

Hobbes later lists among the virtues of a Heroic Poem elevation, description, and amplitude of subject.[35]

The very qualities which appear to be objectively discernible in a third of the poets of the 1640's are those which Hobbes and Davenant praise in 1650: the smoothed, corresponding, and expanding meter, the descriptive structure, the words of sense impression and of praise. The rest of the poetry, even their friend Cowley's *Mistress,* with its accents of conversation, structures of debate, homely, technical, and far-fetched references, is not so favored. Therefore, the term "wit," which they still favor, they redefine, shifting it from the area of Donne to their own and, like Dryden, who substitutes "metaphysical" for Donne, identifying it with scope and suitability. The steps of change in terms are mixed between changes in facts and changes in values, and both "wit" and "metaphysical" as they grew more and more loaded with value, the first in the eighteenth, the second in the

---

[33] *The Answer of Mr. Hobbes. Ibid.,* p. 64.
[34] *Ibid.,* p. 62.
[35] *The Virtues of an Heroic Poem* (1675). *Ibid.*

twentieth century, covered altering sets of qualities within the poetry they applied to.

The fact remains, and is pertinent to our study, that each approach of criticism has been both discerning and partial, seeing the details of poetry in 1640's but by specifically stated standards ignoring some of them. All help interpret the characteristics of the era, but none helps interpret all of them. Each is thorough in its own terms. Davenant meticulously eliminates the qualities of predicative poetry in the 1640's, and sponsors what we have called epithetical, at least for his favored heroic form. Johnson, from the vantage point of a longer view and a fuller thought, analytically describes both types of poetizing in their Miltonic and Donnic extremes, and chooses to value the moderated form of the epithetical in Dryden, who himself was sympathetic in both directions. Courthope, having distinguished in full historical detail between Spenserian poetry and Wit poetry, both as local and limited in "schools," draws out and favors the separate magnitude of Milton. Eliot and his colleagues, in reaction against a hundred and fifty years of accumulating critical build-up of Dryden, Milton, and the epithetical kind, remind us that most of the good functioning poetry of mid-seventeenth century was actually an opposite "metaphysical" kind, the better for being so, and the better for us to inherit.

On whichever side the valuation has fallen, an idea of two main types in the formal sense has been maintained. But variations in valuation have made for variations in classification, especially in the middle range, where formal distinctions are most easily mixed with social or biographical or other distinctions. So, while in the early seventeenth century Spenser, Jonson, and Donne were seen as three different kinds, the first representing "melodie, clarté, abondance," the second "reasonableness, simplicity, directness," the third "harshness, subtlety, intensity,"[36]

---

[36] Robert Lathrop Sharp, *From Donne to Dryden* (Univ. of North Carolina Press, 1940), p. 3.

by the eighteenth century the last two kinds were merged as "low," and even the reasonable directness of Jonson was too familiar and obscure by a standard which had elaborated harmony and abundance. Now, in a century which has elaborated subtlety and intensity, the simplicity of Jonson is blended the other way, with the Elizabethan clarity of Spenser. So terms of classification change ground to fit critical attitude, and Jonson and Dryden are sometimes seen close as "metaphysical" or "reasonable," sometimes apart as "Elizabethan" versus "Augustan," while Milton is sometimes metaphysical, sometimes Spenserian, sometimes "baroque," Crashaw and Marvell waver, and Cowley is everywhere seen on both sides.[37]

Hence the value, at least to literary history, if not to criticism, of provisionally strict temporal and formal limitations, which function somewhat apart from contemporary values. Of course, the interest in formal analysis, the desire to "state material parts in formal collocation,"[38] is itself a limitation of our own time, but its bias does lead in the direction of relatively objective as well as subjective knowledges, and of arts as well as sciences. It leads, that is, to some bases of general agreement, and to some bases for the poetry of the 1640's more specific than the sense of a metaphysical, or a metaphysical and Miltonic, type. Much of the study of formal collocations, the relations in poetry between the sound, reference, and syntax components of its medium, bears out, as one should hope and suppose, the intuitions of poetry's readers and critics in all times, and indeed illuminates, amid the

---

[37] Note, for example, the reasoned or assumed classifications of Austin Warren's *Richard Crashaw*, pp. 65, 74; Ruth Wallerstein's *Richard Crashaw*, p. 136; Pope's *Anecdotes; Observations, and Characters of Books and Men*, by Joseph Spence, ed. S. W. Singer (2d ed., London, 1858), pp. 6, 16 ff., 102, 109, etc.; Rosamund Tuve's "Imagery and Logic: Ramus and Metaphysical Poetics," *Journal of the History of Ideas*, Vol. III, No. 4 (October, 1942); Theodore Spencer's "Antaeus, or Poetic Language and the Actual World," *ELH: A Journal of English Literary History*, Vol. X, No. 3 (September, 1943); F. W. Bateson's *English Poetry and the English Language;* Leah Jonas' *The Divine Science*, p. xi; John W. Good's *Studies in the Milton Tradition;* and earlier references.

[38] Elder Olson, "Recent Literary Criticism," *Modern Philology*, Vol. XL, No. 3 (February, 1943); and see "Two Essays in Practical Criticism," *University Review*, Vol. VIII, No. 3 (Spring, 1942).

variety of terms and attitudes, the bond of understanding between readers in all times. But further, such study, by its analytical limitations, shows much diversity and accord and much general pattern which the self-selecting critic is not apt to notice, or to care about.

In relation to critical discussion of the seventeenth century's poetry, for example, I think this study of the media in the mere 1640's makes newly evident certain very specific and certain very general matters for critical consideration. First of all, and most centrally to traditional discussion, it specifies the technical nature on a general level of the two types of poetic work within the decade, and suggests a parallel distinction in prose. It notes that on the general level of selected media in major use one type emphasizes the vocabulary of concept and relation, the other of sense and scene; one the accent of voice in conversation or song, the other the smoothed and extended syllables of recitatif or descriptive oratory; one the structure of reasoning argument, the other of display. Basic to these is the proportioning of substantives and predicates in the language: the difference between a large and a small number of substantial terms, which makes, since predication remains relatively constant, for a proportionate difference in the power of the predicate, and thence for the difference between clausal and phrasal sentence pattern, between punctuated and flowing sound. Arranged upon this basis, the poetries of the 1640's indicate not only a natural extension from one pole to the other which is the result of any linear arrangement, but also a grouping at each pole, twice as strong at the predicative, and without much middle compromise, an alignment which suggests the presence of two kinds of poetic sentence-making and two resultant poetries.

The fact that no matter external to poetic form seems to parallel this grouping, neither age, fame, religion, political allegiance, friendship, nor education (except perhaps, if it could be thoroughly discovered, childhood reading), and that, on the other hand, usages of meters, stanzas, structures, and major vocabularies do run somewhat parallel, suggests that materials from the poetry itself are the best clues to its consistencies, and that, specifically, much as Donne and Jonson, or Milton and Dryden, are unlike, they share a basic poetic formula, as Donne and Crashaw, Cowley and Waller, Jonson and Dryden, differ in theirs. The sense of language underlies the sense of poetry, and underlies our feeling of its varieties.

Again, the fact that the extremes of type are shared by strongly inventive and strongly imitative poets suggests that major individuality of contribution scarcely depends one way or the other upon the uses of tradition. Crashaw, Milton, Waller, made very different individualities out of the notes of Spenser. Donne and Jonson stood side by side against Spenser, yet minutely disagreed. The men at the center of the respective types, on the other hand, men like Cowley and Quarles, shared not only with their groups but with each other, because they were most content with currency as it appeared and had least special, whether of individuality or tradition, to add. Average in one sort of usage tended to be average in another, so that vocabulary, metrics, structure, attitude, title, tone, all in a poet like Carew could be typical yet his. The same habit of language could serve radical and conformist alike, so strong was its forming power. So strong were two major patterns of habit in the 1640's.

Secondly, and apart from type, formal study helps define the special characteristics of individual poets. Vaughan, for example, uses consistently the shortest of lines, stressing the brevity and intensity of his lyrical cry, yet seldom abandoning the structural formula of reasoning. His words are most singular for his time, and most often repeated, as Donne's are, so that favorites like *light* and *cloud* are used twenty or more times apiece, and *sun* and *star, thought, year* and *hour,* in frequency intensify the

metaphysical cosmos of concept, as *dark* and *weep* stress its negatives. At the same time that Vaughan shares in his decade's
usages, he lifts and aerates many of them with his personal and
succinct poetizing of a lyrically symbolical light and shadow.
To Crashaw, Ruth Wallerstein attributes just this preoccupation
with dark and light, saying that "the image of man as dust, as
the dark son of dust and sorrow," is common to Crashaw, and
that no image is more frequently repeated than those of contrasting day and night, darkness and light."[39] Though it is a question
what many modern writers on poetry mean by "image," since
many, like Milton Rugoff on Donne and Caroline Spurgeon on
Shakespeare, and perhaps Miss Wallerstein here, treat it as "figure," rather than as sense reference, I think it is fair to suggest,
by either meaning, even if I have not tabulated "figures," that
not light and dark but rather *weeping* is most central and
abundant for Crashaw. *Seeing, making, speaking, lying, weeping* are major verbs for him, *heaven, death, eye,* and *tear* the
major nouns, and *fair, great, good, sweet, bright, new,* the major
adjectives. At least, one must recognize by either count that
Crashaw's poetic spirit, like that of his era but literally doubly
so, is in his eye. It would be surprising, then, if *sweet* and *delicious*
were his favorite adjectives, as Austin Warren says they are.[40]
Sweet is "favorite" for only Herrick, Cleveland, and Milton
among the poets of the decade; for Crashaw *great* and *fair* were
much more pleasant.

Another sort of individuality is to be seen in Cleveland. He
did not, in Vaughan's and Crashaw's fashion, differ by intensifying the standard interests of his time, but rather worked in
them obliquely, so that "Clevelandizing" came to mean the
twisting of meanings.[41] He among all the poets used fewest, only

---

[39] Ruth Wallerstein. *Richard Crashaw: A Study in Style and Poetic Development;*
Univ. of Wisconsin Studies in Language and Literature, No. 37 (Madison, 1935), p. 50.

[40] Austin Warren, *Richard Crashaw: A Study in Baroque Sensibility,* p. 172.

[41] *Poems of John Cleveland,* ed. J. M. Berdan (Yale Univ. Press, 1911), p. 54.

half, of the shared major terms, quite ignoring fairness and greatness, the human heart, the heavenly God, the earthly day and
time, even the commonest actions, and concentrating upon a
multiplicity of bodily terms more played upon than stressed. As
Royalist Judge Advocate in Newark in 1645, he did not participate in the poetic exiles of Royalists, and maintained his own
circle of admirers, by 1668 having been published ten times as
often as the popular Waller.[42] Thomas Fuller called him "A General Artist, Pure Latinist, Exquisite Orator, and (which was his
Master-Piece) Eminent Poet. His epithets were pregnant with
Metaphors, carrying in them a difficult plainness, difficult at the
hearing, plain at the considering thereof. His lofty Fancy may
seem to stride from the top of one Mountain to the top of another, so making itself a constant Level and Champion of continued Elevations."[43] In such a characterization we see nothing
to set Cleveland apart from his colleagues of the "Masculine
Stile," yet apart he was, not in his practice which is here described, but in the variety and obliquity of his materials, as a
formal study perceives them. The masculine style was Donne's
and Jonson's, which they defended against the Spenserians, the
masculine wit against the feminine eye;[44] and though Cleveland
has been connected with Marinism, the rich repetition and excess
of Marino did not affect him as it did Crashaw; he was and re-
mained a predicative poet because the elaboration of concept
meant more to him than the elaboration of sense. Nevertheless,
in the multiplicities of his vocabulary and his lack of heavenly
stress he was apart from both schools.

Other characteristics we have seen, the freed rhyme and line
pattern of Milton, the Spenserian stanza and style of More, the
strongly pastoral vocabulary of Quarles' special piece in combination with the strongly standard vocabulary of his average

[42] *Ibid.*, p. 55.
[43] *Ibid.*, p. 49.
[44] Sharp, *op. cit.*, pp. 4–5, 11, 57.

usage, the mild and level abstractness of Dryden in such terms
as *mortal, age, grace, virtue,* which Theodore Spencer calls
Dryden's best kind, less commonly represented by such terms
as *candidate* and *deviate;*[45] the "masculine" rigors of Sandys and
Wither in their denunciatory passages; the stylistic split in Denham between *Cooper's Hill* and his other poems, and his "nobility" shared with Waller; the verve of Shirley and Lovelace in
their mixture of quality and feeling; the flowers and kisses and
pointed brevities of Herrick; the self-conscious artistry of Cowley; the negatives of Donne: all these characteristics and others
are definable as individualistic, and perceivable as representatively idiosyncratic, when they are seen in the context of their
era's practice.

Thirdly, and at the pole opposite idiosyncrasy, study of the
formal relations of major poetic materials discovers the degree
of unanimity in the poetry of the time. It shows, as little other
study tends to, how closely contemporary poets work together,
whether consciously or no; how closely contemporaries feel and
analogize and sound and argue in common; how limited are a
poet's choices by the choices of his times and how directly he
himself participates in those choices and helps establish them.
Fifty words, a couple of metrical forms, a pattern of address,
provide the common large defining center of the poetry of the
1640's, maintaining the majority of uses in almost every poet, and
pervading in at least minor degree the poetry of every one. Milton
turned from couplets more than most, and Cleveland from
heavenly terms, and Vaughan from long lines and phrases, and
all sometimes from invocation, yet address and invocation, octo-
syllabic and decasyllabic couplets, and the terms of heaven and
earth were just what even they shared with their contemporaries,
many of whom employed mainly these basic norms. It is surprising, I think, to readers of an era in which the idea of "expres-

---

[45] Theodore Spencer, *op. cit.*

siveness" has had some power, and in which the closest criticism has been most concerned with individual rather than shared characteristics, to observe how much of self-expression is common expression, how much of poetic sound and sense is drawn in for nourishment like the air we breathe. It is surprising to find over and over in the intricate stanzaic structures and arguments of the 1640's the simple basic couplet rhyme without any internal sound patterning, and the recurrent vocative, and the unanimous verbs. It is surprising to think that of twenty poets' twenty or thirty words used most apiece, twenty-five are shared by ten or more poets, fifty by five or more, and only another seventy-five, or half of all, used individualistically, and then within the common limited realm of usage. If every poet used a different major list, there would be five or six hundred major terms to deal with. If every poet used the same list, there would be twenty or thirty. The actual total of about a hundred and fifty major terms for the 1640's is nearer to agreement than to disagreement by about 70 per cent.

Consider the degree of diversity and agreement in the lives of these poets. All but the three who died in the 1630's shared in the 1640's the Revolution and all it stood for in social, political, and religious loyalties. The keynote of the age is said to be revolt against authority, by science, by sects, by the middle classes.[46] The Bishops were too earthly in behavior, the Crown too divine; the Parliament took to power and then to war. Puritan prescriptions being so grim, most of the sympathies were with Charles, in his sorties, and at his beheading in 1649. Royalists, which most of the poets were, were loyal to king, to church, and to the land. Sandys, Herrick, Harvey, Quarles, in their forties, lived quietly, or died, amid the conflict. Shirley fought for the king, after an era of dramatic success; Wither, scorned as a rabble-rouser, hymn maker, and reformed love poet, seized Farnham Castle

---

[46] Godfrey Davies, *The Early Stuarts* (Oxford, Clarendon Press, 1937), Introd.

from Denham for Parliament in 1642, and was an active participant in the war. Little community in this older generation, either of friendship or belief, justified the description by Spencer: "The poets of the seventeenth century lived, as we have lived, in a difficult and transitional age; they were aware, as we have been aware, of conflicts that more ordinary periods ignore, but they had a community of reference, a generally accepted sense of values which we lack, and their conflicts were within definite limits as ours are not."[47]

The younger generation had more of this reference in common, for though Suckling early died a suicide in exile and Cleveland held position outside London, many of the rest, driven by the Puritans from Cambridge, were friends at the Queen's exiled court in Paris. Waller and Cowley and Denham, at least, were there in the 1640's, Crashaw came briefly as an old Cambridge friend, Lovelace was there abroad on the king's business. Those who stayed at home, and not in jail, had various reasons: Vaughan his youth, More his meditation, Milton his learned political campaign. The battles, with a total of 20,000 or so ahorse and afoot on either side, and mostly in small forays and sieges, charged back and forth across the country, with a scope which now seems petty, but with a brutality now recognizable. Those at home and abroad, in retirement, on horseback, in prison, or disguise, shared indeed a situation which affected all, but no evident notion of its solution. All were apart by birth or choice from the "merchant class" for whom the fighting was done, and the topical preoccupations of most were far from the centers of activity, in heavenly dialogues, in ladies who did not exist, in pastures greener than England possessed. Perhaps Herrick and Donne spoke most directly from the world they inhabited, yet each shared strongly the materials of all. I see little in the lives of poets in the 1640's which would make directly for unity of

---

[47] Spencer and Van Doren, *op. cit.*, p. 16.

method and material; the best friends and associates differed as widely as any; the unity came through existing unities of language and of poetry.

Homogeneity of poetic medium spread wide enough to enclose the types and individualisms of the 1640's, yet never so deeply as to obscure them. Poets who seem as unlike as any in our history yet shared closely a substance and syntax of speech. This socially expressive force of poetic language and, as we have seen by some analogies, of prose language also, must underlie and interpret daily activities, social structures, philosophical and religious beliefs, literary models, and critical theories, since through major usage it provides a common pattern for all of them. Whether this pattern was more unified in the 1640's than now, as the school of Eliot has suggested, is a question to be answered by comparative analysis. The study of Major Adjectives has indicated, at least in slightly representative fashion, that we too have our linguistic and poetic homogeneity, material and qualitative. Perhaps, also, all poetry through all times provides a continuity and limitation of expression stronger than we realize. At any rate the major language and thence the major poetic language of the 1640's speaks, through its literally and figuratively double heavenly, earthly, temporal, conceptual, and scenic reference, and through its rational, descriptive, and petitional structures, for a world conscious of a double life, half mutable in time and death, half divine in love and the nobility of aspiration, half physical in the presences of bodies and familiar objects, wholly directed to authority, inner or outer, or both. No man within such a context would formulate it fully. Milton would pamphletize the right of kings; Descartes would emphasize the psychological powers of sight; Van Dyck and Overbury would consider the ins and outs of portraiture; the exiled dramatists would be won over to scenes and machines; Neoplatonists, astrologers, witchburners at their various stages of complexity, would note the occult forces in common objects, while Harvey and Hobbes would analyze the less commonly known circulation of blood and sense. But no one man could see or report the multiplicity whole. Closest could come the poets, who would accept the great spread of language which contained and ordered all this thought, who would deal with it as worthy matter to be set to the voice's formal measures, and who would, by their closely agreed devices of enrichment and order, arrive at pieces new and different but expressive, representative, communicative of the whole.

The poet as artist is, by the common nature of his medium, poet as citizen. His free choice of poetic form, material, value, is by more than half an agreed choice, his individual poetry a typical and social poetry. In poetry's vocabulary, even in its whole language of sound and structure, its life and time make sense together. To reach some conclusions about the poetry of the 1640's may be to surmise, therefore, some conclusions about poetry as a whole. A majority concurrence in primary vocabulary, sound pattern, statement, with one intenser minority concurrence apparently allied to past and to future, and with thoroughgoing individual idiosyncrasy or innovation, suggests that time provides a bond for poets and type a continuity, and both a basis for invention. Poetry like society quickly varies, slowly classifies and alters, vastly shares and conserves. Within its prime vocabulary, nouns, subjects, contents are the variables, adjectives the typical modifying forces, verbs of human activity the constants. In reference and in relation, in context and proportion, within the formalizing of poetic measure, these terms combine in individual accents, persistent styles, consensus. They are the means of thought and the medium of poetry. What values they bear as thought, poetry as art accepts and celebrates.

BIBLIOGRAPHY

(Most items of critical theory, if listed in my earlier Bibliographies, are omitted here unless they are of special pertinence. Editions of the poetry are listed in 1540's and 1640's: table 1, pp. 16 and 28.)

PRIMARY

A Concordance to the Poems of John Donne, ed. H. C. Combs and Z. K. Sullens (Chicago, Packard, 1940).

A Concordance to the Poems of Robert Herrick, ed. Malcolm L. MacLeod (New York, Oxford Univ. Press, 1936).

A Concordance to the Poetical Works of John Milton, ed. John Bradshaw (London, Macmillan, 1894).

Browne, Thomas. *Religio Medici,* with Digby's *Observations* (Oxford, Clarendon Press, 1909).

Digby, Kenelm. *Of Bodies, and of Man's Soul* (London, 1669).

Fuller, Thomas. *Pulpit Sparks. Being XIX Sermons of . . . Thomas Fuller,* ed. Morris Fuller (London, 1886).

Hall, Joseph. *Works* (10 vols., Oxford Univ. Press, 1863), Vol. VI.

Hammond, Henry. *A Practical Catechism* (11th ed., London, 1677).

Herbert of Cherbury, Lord Edward. *The Life and Raigne of King Henry the Eighth* (London, 1649).

Howell, James. *Familiar Letters, or Epistolæ Ho-Elianæ* (3 vols., London, Dent, 1903).

———. *Instructions for Forraine Travell,* ed .Edward Arber (London, 1869).

Peacham, Henry. *The Worth of a Penny* (reprint, London, 1667).

———. *Peacham's Compleat Gentleman,* 1634, ed. G. S. Gordon (Oxford, Clarendon Press, 1906).

Reynoldes, Edward. *A Treatise of the Passions and Faculties of the Soule of Man* (London, 1640).

Taylor, Jeremy. *The Whole Works,* ed. Reginald Heber and Charles Page Eden (10 vols., London, 1849–1854).

Waller, Edmond. *Poems to the Memory of . . . ,* by Several Hands (London, 1688).

Walton, Izaak. *Lives of John Donne . . . &c.* (2 vols., London, Dent, 1898).

CRITICAL

Aiken, Pauline. *The Influence of the Latin Elegists on English Lyric Poetry, 1600–1650.* Univ. of Maine Studies, Ser. 2, No. 22 (Orono, 1932).

Bateson, F. W. *English Poetry and the English Language: An Experiment in Literary History* (Oxford, Clarendon Press, 1934).

Bennett, Joan. *Four Metaphysical Poets: Donne, Herbert, Vaughn, Crashaw* (Cambridge Univ. Press, 1934).

Berdan, John M. *Early Tudor Poetry, 1485-1549* (New York, Macmillan, 1920).

Boder, David P. "The Adjective-Verb Quotient," *Psychological Record,* III (1940): 309-344.

Bradley, Jesse F., and Joseph Q. Adams. *The Jonson Allusion-Book* (Yale Univ. Press, 1922).

Bush, Douglas. *English Literature in the Earlier Seventheenth Century: 1600-1660* (Oxford, Clarendon Press, 1945).

Cawley, Robert Ralston. *Milton's Literary Craftsmanship: A Study of "A Brief History of Moscovia"* (Princeton Univ. Press, 1941).

Coffin, Charles Monroe. *John Donne and the New Philosophy* (Columbia Univ. Press, 1937).

Cory, Herbert E. *Spenser, the School of the Fletchers, and Milton.* Univ. Calif. Publ. Mod. Philol., Vol. II, No. 5 (1912).

Courthope, W. J. *A History of English Poetry* (6 vols., New York and London, Macmillan, 1895-1910), Vols. I and II.

Croll, Morris W. "The Baroque Style in Prose," *Studies in English Philology: A Miscellany in Honor of Frederick Klaeber,* ed. Kemp Malone (Univ. of Minnesota Press, 1929).

Davenant, William. Preface to *Gondibert,* 1650.

Davies, Godfrey. *The Early Stuarts, 1603-1660* (Oxford, Clarendon Press, 1937).

Dryden, John. *Essays,* ed. W. P. Ker (2 vols., Oxford, Clarendon Press, 1900).

Eliot, T. S. *Selected Essays, 1917-1932* (New York, Harcourt, Brace, 1932).

Emperor, John Bernard. *The Catullian Influence in English Lyric Poetry, circa 1600-1650.* University of Minnesota Studies, Vol. III, No. 3 (1928).

Evans, Joan. *Pattern: A Study of Ornament in Western Europe from 1180 to 1900* (Oxford, Clarendon Press, 1931).

Förster, Max. "The Psychological Basis of Literary Periods," in *Studies for William A. Read,* ed. Nathaniel M. Caffee and Thomas A. Kirby (Louisiana State Univ. Press, 1940).

Friedrich, Werner P. *Spiritualismus und Sensualismus in der englischen Barocklyrik.* Wiener Beiträge zur Englischen Philologie, LVII. Band (Vienna, 1932).

Godfrey, Elizabeth. [Jessie Bedford.] *Home Life under the Stuarts, 1603-1649* (London, Stanley Paul & Co., 1925).

Good, John Walter. *Studies in the Milton Tradition.* Univ. of Illinois Studies in Language and Literature, Vol. I, Nos. 3 and 4 (Urbana, 1915).

Grierson, H. J. C. *Cross Currents in English Literature of the XVIIth Century* (London, Chatto & Windus, 1929).

———. Introduction to *The Poetical Works of John Donne,* 1912.

Harrison, John Smith. *Platonism in English Poetry of the Sixteenth and Seventeenth Centuries* (Columbia Univ. Press, 1903).

Hartmann, Cyril Hughes. *The Cavalier Spirit and Its Influence on ... Lovelace* (London, Routledge, 1925).

Hatzfield, Helmut A. "The Language of the Poet," *Studies in Philology,* XLIII (1946): 93–120.

Herford, C. H., and Percy and Evelyn Simpson. *Ben Jonson* (8 vols., Oxford, Clarendon Press, 1925–1947).

Hobbes, Thomas. Answer to Davenant's Preface to *Gondibert,* 1650.

Holmes, Elizabeth. *Aspects of Elizabethan Imagery* (Oxford, Blackwell, 1929).

———. *Henry Vaughan and the Hermetic Philosophy* (Oxford, Blackwell, 1932).

———. "Some Notes on Milton's Use of Words," *Essays and Studies by Members of the English Association,* Vol. X (1924), ed. E. K. Chambers.

Howell, A. C. "*Res et Verba:* Words and Things," *ELH: A Journal of English Literary History,* XIII (1946): 173–192.

James, Eleanor. "The Emblem as an Image-Pattern in Some Metaphysical Poets," *Summaries of Doctoral Dissertations,* Univ. of Wisconsin, Vol. VII (1942).

———. "The Imagery of Francis Quarles' 'Emblems,'" *Studies in English, 1943* (Univ. of Texas Press, 1943).

Johnson, Samuel. *Lives of the Most Eminent English Poets, with Critical Observations on Their Works* (2 vols., New York, 1857).

Johnston, George Burke. *Ben Jonson: Poet* (Columbia Univ. Press, 1945).

Jonas, Leah. *The Divine Science: The Aesthetic of Some Representative Seventeenth-Century English Poets* (Columbia Univ. Press, 1940).

Knights, L. C. *Explorations: Essays in Criticism, Mainly on the Literature of the Seventeenth Century* (London, Chatto & Windus, 1946).

Lee, Vernon. [Violet Paget.] *The Handling of Words* (London, John Lane, 1923).

Legouis, Pierre. *Donne the Craftsman* (Paris, Didier, 1928).

Lehmann, Ruth Preston. "Characteristic Imagery in the Poetry of Henry Vaughan," *Summaries of Doctoral Dissertations,* Univ. of Wisconsin, Vol. VII (1942).

Leishman, J. B. *The Metaphysical Poets: Donne, Herbert, Vaughan, Traherne* (Oxford, Clarendon Press, 1934).

Lewis, C. S. *A Preface to Paradise Lost* (Oxford Univ. Press, 1942).

Loiseau, Jean. *Abraham Cowley's Reputation in England* (Paris, Didier, 1931).

Lovejoy, Arthur O. *The Great Chain of Being* (Harvard Univ. Press, 1936).

McEuen, Kathryn Anderson. *Classical Influence upon the Tribe of Ben* (Cedar Rapids, Iowa, Torch Press, 1939).

Melton, Wightman F. *The Rhetoric of John Donne's Verse* (Ph.D. diss., Johns Hopkins; Baltimore, 1906).

Mizener, Arthur. "Some Notes on the Nature of English Poetry," *Sewanee Review*, LI (1943): 27–51.

———. "Verse and Poetry," *Kenyon Review*, VI (1944): 123–126.

Moloney, Michael Francis. *John Donne: His Flight from Mediaevalism*. Illinois Studies in Language and Literature, Vol. XXIX, Nos. 2 and 3 (Urbana, 1944).

Nethercot, Arthur H. *Abraham Cowley, the Muse's Hannibal* (London, Oxford Univ. Press, 1931).

Neumann, Joshua H. "Milton's Prose Vocabulary," *Publications of the Modern Language Association*, LX (1945): 102–121.

Olson, Elder, and Norman Maclean. "Two Essays in Practical Criticism." University of Kansas City *University Review*, VIII (1942): 199–219.

Powicke, Frederick J. *The Cambridge Platonists* (London and Toronto, Dent, 1926).

Pratt, Alice Edwards. *The Use of Color in the Verse of the English Romantic Poets* (Univ. of Chicago Press, 1898).

Praz, Mario. *Studies in Seventeenth-Century Imagery* (London, Warburg Institute, 1939).

Read, Herbert. "The Nature of Metaphysical Poetry," *Criterion*, Vol. I, No. 3 (1923).

Rollins, Hyder E., ed. *Cavalier and Puritan: Ballads and Broadsides . . . 1640–1660* (New York Univ. Press, 1923).

Ross, Malcolm Mackenzie. *Milton's Royalism: A Study of the Conflict of Symbol and Idea in the Poems* (Cornell Univ. Press, 1943).

Rugoff, Milton Allan. *Donne's Imagery: A Study of Creative Sources* (New York, Corporate Press, 1939).

Saintsbury, George. Introductions to *Minor Poets of the Caroline Period* (3 vols., Oxford, Clarendon Press, 1905–1921).

Schücking, L. L. *The Sociology of Literary Taste*, trans. E. W. Dickes (Oxford Univ. Press, 1944).

Seventeenth Century Studies, Presented to Sir Herbert Grierson (Oxford, Clarendon Press, 1934).

Sharp, Robert Lathrop. *From Donne to Dryden: The Revolt against Metaphysical Poetry* (Univ. of North Carolina Press, 1940).

Spencer, Theodore. "Antaeus, or Poetic Language and the Actual World," *ELH: A Journal of English Literary History,* X (1943): 173–192.

———. *A Garland for John Donne* (Harvard Univ. Press, 1931).

Spencer, Theodore, and Mark Van Doren. *Studies in Metaphysical Poetry: Two Essays and a Bibliography* (Columbia Univ. Press, 1939).

Spingarn, Joel, ed. *Critical Essays of the Seventeenth Century* (Oxford, Clarendon Press, 1908–1909).

Stallman, Robert Wooster. "Dryden in Modern Poetry and Criticism," *Summaries of Doctoral Dissertations,* Univ. of Wisconsin, Vol. VII (1942).

Stebbing, William. *Some Verdicts of History Reviewed* (London, 1887).

Stein, Arnold. "Donne's Obscurity and the Elizabethan Tradition," *ELH: A Journal of English Literary History,* XIII (1946): 98–118.

Stewart, George R. "Color and Science in Poetry," *Science Monthly,* XXX (1930): 71–80.

Stoll, Elmer Edgar. *From Shakespeare to Joyce* (New York, Doubleday, Doran, 1944).

Sweeting, Elizabeth J. *Early Tudor Criticism, Linguistic and Literary* (Oxford, Blackwell, 1940).

Sypher, Wylie. "The Metaphysicals and the Baroque," *Partisan Review,* 11 (1944): 3–18.

Taggard, Genevieve, ed. *Circumference: Varieties of Metaphysical Verse, 1456–1928* (New York, Covici, Friede, 1929).

Taylor, George Coffin. *Milton's Use of Du Bartas* (Harvard Univ. Press, 1934).

Thorpe, Clarence DeWitt. *The Aesthetic Theory of Thomas Hobbes* (Univ. of Michigan Press, 1940).

Tuve, Rosamund. *Elizabethan and Metaphysical Imagery* (Univ. of Chicago Press, 1947).

Van Doren, Mark. *The Poetry of John Dryden* (New York, Harcourt, Brace, 1920).

Wallerstein, Ruth C. *Richard Crashaw: A Study in Style and Poetic Development.* Univ. of Wisconsin Studies in Language and Literature, No. 37 (Madison, 1935).

Warren, Austin. *Richard Crashaw: A Study in Baroque Sensibility* (Louisiana State Univ. Press, 1939).

Wellek, René. "The Concept of Baroque in Literary Scholarship," *Journal of Aesthetics and Art Criticism,* V (1946): 77–109.

White, Helen C. *The Metaphysical Poets: A Study in Religious Experience* (New York, Macmillan, 1936).

Whiting, George Wesley. *Milton's Literary Milieu* (Univ. of North Carolina Press, 1939).

Wiggins, Elizabeth Lewis. "Logic in the Poetry of John Donne," *Studies in Philology,* XLII (1945): 41–61.

Willey, Basil. *The Seventeenth-Century Background* (London, Chatto & Windus, 1934).

Williamson, George. *The Donne Tradition* (Harvard Univ. Press, 1930).

Wilson, F. P. *Elizabethan and Jacobean* (Oxford, Clarendon Press, 1945).

Wright, Louis B. *Middle-Class Culture in Elizabethan England* (Univ. of North Carolina Press, 1935).

Yule, G. Udny. *The Statistical Study of Literary Vocabulary* (Cambridge Univ. Press, 1945).

PART II

The Primary Language of Poetry in the 1740's and 1840's

I. POETRY OF THE 1740's

THE PURPOSE of this study is to describe in a very simple way the language most used in the poetry of two decades, the 1740's and the 1840's. The study is based on certain hypotheses: that the materials much used and much shared by poets have significance for the description of the poetry of which they are a part; and that time is a force in the establishing of the materials. For each decade each first chapter sets forth the primary language, the selection and proportioning of the parts of speech in their main contexts of sound and sentence structure; each second chapter suggests some of their parallels in prose and some of their status in critical theory. Tentative conclusions concern the great amount of agreement in usage within a decade, its power to unify as well as to distinguish.

The language of poetry appears to be a special selection from and formalizing of the language of prose. Prose statement, in syntax, sound, and reference, finds certain accentuation in poetry: its sounds more closely patterned, its structures and references chosen and repeated. The care involved involves also choice toward special forms which represent the sense of worth. And because the poet is a social being he chooses to stress not only singular forms of values but shared ones, the sorts of statement-forms stressed by his fellow writers, the sorts of line-forms stressed by his fellow poets. This is the common language of poetry in its simplest sense, not yet linguistically analyzed into basic units of meaning, not yet formally constructed into figure, connotative patterns, and thematic types, but in common use as it is available to the poet, the structures, words, sounds of remarks. With this agreed-on material I am concerned. What the poet does with it, what attitude he takes toward it, what point he carries it to, the style in which he treats it, all are further problems; it is my idea that they can be better considered after we know more about the basic medium itself, the primary, that is, the most frequently used, terms, forms, and proportions of poetic language.

What will be the relation between tables listing numerical frequencies of main parts of speech and their proportionings in main line and sentence forms, and any whole poem or body of poems? What is the relation between "primary language" and poetry? It is the relation, I think, of main ingredients to the whole works made from them. Each special use may be singular, but to a degree all combinations are affected and bound by the shared choices of material. So I think it may be of some use eventually to critics and historians to know the shared choices in certain eras, and so I list provisionally representative works of twenty poets in a decade to show the amount of agreement in choice of forms and proportioning of terms and the nature of the terms themselves, in their contexts. The passages quoted in illustration give a direct sense of the way the language works and establish whatever generalizations are made about common tone and practice. The focus of both tables and quotations is upon the similarities which unite poetic practices, rather than upon the equally interesting differences which distinguish them.

The argument is often made that the most frequent patterns of statement are after all so familiar, there is no use to point them out. To learn in round numbers how strongly adjectival is eighteenth-century poetry is to learn nothing one could not as roundly, and more easily, have guessed from reading. But on the other hand, the argument is made that frequency is not especially pertinent in literary study, that what one learns from it has no echoes in intuition or genuine feeling. So, if one finds two poets very much alike in the language they use, one may say either, "I knew their styles were alike anyway, so the mere likeness of language doesn't matter," or, "I knew their styles as a whole were different, so the mere likeness of language doesn't matter." But one cannot consistently speak both these ways. Language usage, as one part of style, is one clue to the whole of likeness or difference, and, as a part closely observable, may be a check upon what we think we know.

Consider the poetry of the 1740's. We know it well, its reasonableness, its sublimity, its formal couplet, its graveyard gloom, its sharpness of antithesis, its splendor of scene and personification. We think of Pope old and Johnson young, Thomson's *Seasons* and the *Gentleman's Magazine.* Yet we may well be reminded that seldom else have we had so many long poems, wide views, high emotions, vast conceptions. The primary vocabulary is a vocabulary of nature, and power, and air, day, heaven, in all their scope. The emotions are more positive than graveyard associations would lead us to expect, in *love* and *joy,* and adjectives like *fair, great, soft,* and *sweet.* The human figure is expansively present in *eye, hand, head, heart, soul,* and in perceptive verbs. And for all our sense of strict rhyme and balance we note that sound pattern has become more interior, moving toward such harmonies as onomatopoeia will effect. The harmonizing of sound and sense in invocative as well as descriptive statement seems to reveal as well as to contrive the harmony of man and nature, and similitude is central to attitude.

This is not the poetic world familiar to a reader of verse a century earlier. Then another sort of agreement had prevailed: on negative and rough metaphor, on pause and argument, on death and time and thought in active shape. Now the laborious way has been smoothed, as wit in wisdom has come to recognize more correspondence, less discrepancy, between the passions of man and the qualities of nature. Man is not shadow and dust under the kingdom of God,—not that harshness of metaphor. Man is a part of nature, his joy like sunshine,—that pleasure of simile.

Two songs from the respective centuries illustrate the contrast. Both mourn the fleetingness of time, an enduring theme.

Shirley's from the "Contention of Ajax and Ulysses" argues and instructs in the metaphysical and irregular couplet (it is dated 1646 in Frederick Boas's collection of Songs from the Playbooks):

> The glories of our blood and state
>   Are shadows, not substantial things:
> There is no armour against Fate
>   Death lays his icy hand on Kings:
>   Sceptre and crown
>   Must tumble down,
> And in the dust be equal made
> With the poor crooked scythe and spade....
>
> The garlands wither on your brow,
>   Then boast no more your mighty deeds:
> Upon Death's purple altar now
>   See where the victor-victim bleeds:
>   Your heads must come
>   To the cold tomb;
> Only the actions of the just
> Smell sweet and blossom in the dust.

This is the seventeenth-century mode. The song from *The Fathers, or The Good-Natured Man,* in 1743, a century later, sings otherwise to the same theme, for Fielding:

> While the sweet blushing Spring glowing fresh in her prime
>   All nature with smiles doth adorn,
> Snatch at each golden joy, check the ravage of time,
>   And pluck every bud from the thorn.
> In the May-time of life, while gladsome and gay,
>   Each moment, each pleasure improve,
> For life, we shall find, is at best but a day,
>   And the sunshine that gilds it is love.
>
> The rose now so blooming, of nature the grace,
>   In a moment is shrunk and decayed,
> And the glow which now tinges a beautiful face
>   Must soon, alas! wither and fade.
> In the May-time of life then, while gladsome and gay,
>   Each moment, each pleasure improve,
> For life, we shall find, is at best but a day;
>   And the sunshine that gilds it is love.

This song is based upon the analogy of age to season, of emotion to sunlight, and all the rest of it contributes to such likenesses. Spring blushes, like a person. A rose is like a face. The May season is joyous, as well as smiling, as well as golden. The result is directly to be sensed, as both scene and portrait; the body and scene share the same qualities of color and pleasure. The older poem, on the other hand, is not sensably, but rather conceptually, centralized. Shadows, armour, icy hand, dust, garlands, altar, make not one picture or effect, but a number, in their play upon idea. The central metaphor of glories as shadows is developed not by the similitudes of shadowiness, not by an increased sense of the atmosphere of shadow, but rather by other metaphors, of scepter and scythe, of action and blossom, so that we get a flash of battle, a flash of agriculture, a flash of sacrifice and of fragrance, to give to us the power of the mind in its construction of the thought.

The poetic construction differs too, therefore. The 16 tetrameter and dimeter lines of the seventeenth century make about a dozen statements, which are related logically, working from metaphorical definition to metaphorical recommendation, to metaphorical conclusion. The *must* refrain is structural. The nouns and verbs carry the meaning; the adjectives *substantial, icy, equal, poor, crooked, mighty, purple, cold,* do so only partially, in abstraction. In the 16 pentameter lines of the eighteenth-century piece, on the other hand, the twice-as-many adjectives do more than twice as much work of significance, as they develop a consistent atmosphere for the moral statement. *Sweet, blushing, fresh, glowing, golden, gladsome, gay,* and *shrunk* and *decayed* vs. *blooming* and *beautiful,* fill out the lines with a positive joy in sense; and *all, each, every, each, each,* provide the sort of structural balance which the verbs provided in the earlier poem. Feelings and sensations are not opposed, but correlated. The statement structure is one not of argument, but of repetition, as the simple recommendation with its fitting atmosphere is varied down the lines and in refrain.

The eighteenth-century song is more substantial, more literally rich in substance, in length and regularity of line, in epithet and noun, in repetition and variation upon one main statement, in the unfolding of a central similitude, in the positive warmth of its sense impression. That our life is a day and our love its sunshine is a more pleasant and poetic notion than that the glories of our blood and state are shadows; more pleasant and poetic, that is, in certain terms: in terms of physical sensation, humane feeling, continuity of spiritual reality with natural, and so, technically, in terms of a harmonious, substantial, atmospheric, and similitudinous verse.

A reader may fairly question the description of a by-the-way song as representative; certainly it cannot present the depths and varieties of poetry in the 1740's. But a song can catch, in material and arrangement, some of the basic pattern of poetry in its time, and this is my concern. It seems to me important to recognize not only the vast differences but the shared likenesses between poems, not only their individuality but their commonalty, in the matrix of language both traditional and contemporary. Such recognition requires a discerning of main emphases in the language, and the verification of main emphases must be quantitative, if the reader is not to run the risk of emphatic projections of his own. Therefore in this study of the 1740's, as in the study of the 1640's earlier and of the 1840's to follow, I have tried to establish a simple system of observation, by representative selection and the counting of frequencies within that selection. The method is not statistical; it is merely provisionally descriptive. Working upon an assumption of relative homogeneity in individual and contemporary styles, it seeks to discover the main lines in the style of language, which is poetry's medium—the main words used, the guiding sound patterns and sentence structures. Then it examines the way these work together in the poetry. The recurring pattern of relationship should come clear.

The tables which follow serve to summarize the data of texts, and of forms, proportions, and vocabulary to be found in them. The details of technique are summarized in footnote form,[1] because they have already been discussed more fully in the *1640's,* chapter i. What all the figures should show is not the mere matter of quantitative usage of twenty poets in a decade, but more seriously the interrelationships of usage which make for

---

[1] The main traits of language I take to be sound, vocabulary, and syntax. When used as medium for poetry, all these will be formalized in some degree, sound in rhythm (meter or cadence, etc.), and in rhyme (end rhyme, assonance, consonance, alliteration, etc.); vocabulary, in repetitions emphasized or unemphasized, and in special selectivity; syntax, in its control of the poem's logical structure. The relation between these formalizations helps define the total style. Given unifying time and place, or social context, one can learn some of the nature of the poetry by finding main emphases agreed on from poet to poet: sound patterns, words, structures most frequently and consistently employed and combined. Yule has shown in his *Statistical Study of Literary Vocabulary* that two or three dozen adjectives, nouns, and verbs tend to be used so often by an author that they make up a large and significant portion of his total vocabulary. (The half of language made up of connectives is no less important but requires a different sort of consideration.) Therefore the main words, together with sound and sentence structures, should suggest a good portion of the verse. The finer shadings, the pauses and silences, the uses of synonym and trope, are not counted here and are suited to more delicate study. The word "roughly" should be assumed to precede every statement of quantity in art. But roughly quantitative emphasis can show, and better than impressionistic reading at times, the likenesses and differences between poets and between periods and between kinds.

A decade is an arbitrary and convenient span of time, and I have gone on from the first-chosen decade of the 1640's to the forties in other centuries to see what sort of general continuity is describable. In Ghosh's *Annals of English Literature,* the listed poems of a decade seem to be written by about twenty poets, published and living in that time or not more than a decade dead, and I have taken just twenty as a basis for comparison. This method of selection does not allow for precise discrimination between two successive decades, since the published poems may have been written over a period of years, or later work added to make 1,000 lines. The published poetry of a decade tends indeed to represent the work of one or two generations, thirty or forty years.

The 1,000 lines of work taken as representative, provisionally, allows for a count of every adjective, noun, verb, and structural pattern, as a larger amount would not. As I have written before, experience seems to warrant the assumption of a certain homogeneity in the work of a single writer. But the facts are only for the poetry of the 1,000 lines. These lines are usually either the first or the last in the volume considered, or are divided between two works if a great difference seems apparent.

Adjectives, epithets, include descriptive terms like *good, green;* participials like *coming, made;* limiting modifiers of number like *one, many, no, all.* Nouns include substantive forms except verb forms or pronouns; I include nouns used as modifiers, as in *summer*

definable style, and which can by their presence in the poetry, even in so slight a piece as the sunshine-is-love song, justify its representative qualities. Through the 1,000-line selections of the twenty poets published in the decade, selections possibly but not necessarily representative of further work by the poets, run certain repeated forms of sound and sentence structure, in five-accented couplet, in invocation and description, in proportioning of adjectives, nouns, verbs, in chosen terms, and in the inter-association of all these. Table 1 presents the predominant forms and proportionings of the specific texts, arranged in an order of agreement based on proportioning, which is in many ways substantiated by table 2, the lists of adjectives, nouns, verbs most used in the texts of a majority, a minority, or an individual.

---

days (except for materials, like *iron* cross), because form is a more steady guide than function in a work which is considering forms. Verbs include auxiliaries, infinitives, gerunds, each counted separately except the *is, has, do* auxiliaries. In addition to these common verb forms, there are a few words, notably limiting adjectives like *one,* and the verb *say,* too common to be listed fully in concordances. These do not appear, therefore, in the lists of major words, but they are counted in total occurrences.

The statement of proportion by line unit, 10 Adjectives–20 Nouns–10 Verbs in 10 lines, for example, depends on a fairly stable line of four or five accents. For a writer of dimeter, adjustments must be made for comparison's sake, and his proportions doubled; his 5–10–5 in 10 would be comparable to a regular 10–20–10 in 10. But there are not many extremes, and there is almost as much variation between poets of one line length as of many. Line length is just one of many considerable factors, and the reader will find the adjustments to be made minor on the whole.

"Form" is the label in table 1 for the predominant structures of sound and syntax. Rhythm is noted roughly by number of stresses, rhyme as setting up couplet or stanza. In other eras cadence or alliteration might be dominating. The sorts of sentences which control the whole depend partly on person, first, second, third, and partly on form, exclamation, question, statement. Third-person statement, narrative or descriptive, tends to be characteristic of the 1740's, with infusions of lyrical invocation in ode and elegy, as second-person address and argument is characteristic of the 1640's.

Together, form and proportion work in the major vocabulary. Twenty or thirty words are shared by a half or more of the poets; fifty or so by a minority group of at least four, the rest of the major terms by only one or two poets. The term is considered major when it is used at least ten times in a thousand lines, and its frequency is listed by fives, so as not to make the point too fine. The notation "10," then, stands for 8 to 12, and so on. Singulars and plurals, comparatives and superlatives, the various tenses, have been counted together. Of course it is common, especially in the individual lists, to find words which have occurred 10 times for some highly insignificant and unrepresentative reason, the mere chance of refrain in a long poem included, for example. But most of the recurrences are so scattered yet so persistent that they suggest a deeper sort of interest.

1740's: TABLE 1

THE POEMS IN ORDER OF ADJECTIVAL EMPHASIS*

Texts: First 1,000 lines (with exceptions noted)	Form	Proportion in average 10 lines		
		Adj.	Noun	Verb
Cooke, Thomas. *Original Poems* (London, 1742) and *Battel*, 200 lines	5' couplets Lyrical and satirical	9	21	11
Gray, Thomas. Poems, 1747 ff. *Poems of Gray and Collins*, ed. Poole (Oxford Univ. Press, 1937)	5' stanzas Lyr.	10	17	8
Akenside, Mark. *Odes*, 1745. *Works*, 1808	5' blank verse, etc. Meditative	10	17	8
Young, Edward. *The Complaint, or Night Thoughts*, 1742. (New York, 1868 ed.)	5' blank verse Medit.	10	20	10
Johnson, Samuel. *Drury Lane Prol.*, *London*, *Vanity*, 12 misc., 1738 ff. *Works*, ed. Osgood (New York, 1909)	5' cpl. Descriptive	9	21	10
Blair, Robert. *The Grave*, 1743, 800 lines. *Works of English Poets*, ed. Chalmers, XV (London, 1810)	5' b. v. Medit.	11	17	9
Blacklock, Thomas. *Poems on Several Occasions*, 1746. (Edinburgh, 1793)	4' cpl., etc. Exclamatory	11	18	9
Montagu, Lady Mary. *Town Eclogues*, 1747, etc. *Letters and Works*, 3d ed., Vol. II (London, 1861)	5' cpl. Narrative	11	18	12
Walpole, Horace. *Fugitive Verses*, 1746. Ed. W. S. Lewis (Oxford Univ. Press, 1931)	4' cpl., st. Invoc., narr.	11	19	9
Pope, Alexander. *Dunciad* (B version), 1743. *Poems*, Vol. V, ed. James Sutherland	5' cpl. Narr.	11	22	10

* For explanatory note see foot of page 171.

1740's: TABLE 1—*Continued*

Texts: First 1,000 lines (with exceptions noted)	Form	Proportion in average 10 lines		
		Adj.	Noun	Verb
Collins, Wm. *Persian Eclogues, Hanmer, Dirge, Odes, Thomson,* 1742 ff., in *Poems of Gray and Collins,* ed. Poole (London, 1937)	5′ st. Narr., lyr.	12	17	9
Mason, William. *Musaeus,* 1747, etc. *Poems* (London, 1764)	5′ st. Lyr.	12	18	10
Lyttelton, George. "Progress" ff. thru "Monody," 1130 ll. 1747. *Works* (Dodsley, 1774)	5′ cpl., st. Voc.	10	17	9
Shenstone, Wm. *Judgment of Hercules, Schoolmistress, Progress of Taste* (175 lines), 1741 ff. *Works in Verse and Prose* (2 vols., London, 1764)	5′ st. Narr.	12	19	11
Warton, Joseph. *The Enthusiast, Odes,* 1746. *Works of English Poets,* ed. Chalmers, XVIII (London, 1810)	5′ b. v., cpl. Descr., invoc.	13	19	8
Dyer, John. *Ruins of Rome* (550 lines), *Fleece* (500 lines), 1740, 1757. *Poems* (London, 1859)	5′ cpl. Descr.	13	20	8
Armstrong, John. *Art of Preserving Health,* 1745 (London, 1804)	5′ cpl. Descr.	15	18	9
Thomson, James. "Winter," rev. in *The Seasons,* 1748, *Complete Poetical Works,* ed. Robertson (Oxford Univ. Press, 1908)	5′ b. v. Descr.	15	18	7
Warton, Thomas. *Odes* and *Isis,* 1747. Chalmers, XVIII (London, 1810)	5′ cpl., st. Invoc., narr.	15	19	8
Somerville, Wm. *Hobbinol, or Rural Games* (London, 1740)	5′ b. v. Narr., satir.	17	19	8
Average..............................	....	12	19	9

Here one can see in coldest array the ingredients of the sunshine-is-love song: its regularity of accent and line length, its full proportion of nouns and adjectives, the richness of its reference to sense and feeling. Of twenty poets, only the most reserved, like Gray, Young, Johnson, or the most prodigal, like Thomson and Thomas Warton, or Cooke and Somerville in mockery of extremes, fail to write the middle mode of richly controlled and harmonized similitude employed by such varied poets as Blair, Blacklock, Montagu, Walpole, Pope, Collins, Lyttelton, Mason, Shenstone, Dyer, Armstrong. Different as Pope and Collins may be, one consolidating the past, the other inventing the future, they are also, with a great significance for poetry, alike in the moderation, for their time, of substantiality, and in their secondary qualities of sense. Different as Young and Thomson may be, at extremes of proportioning, they yet share in the adjectival emphasis of that proportioning, as it subordinates the predicative force of the metaphysical school in the

---

Note to Table 1

Adjectival emphasis tends to mean substantival emphasis also; nouns tend to increase with adjectives, as verbs decrease. Statements using a high proportion of adjectives and nouns I call "substantival"; a high proportion of verbs, "predicative."

The texts used were those most available for working, not always the most authoritative.

The first 100 lines of Virgil's *Aeneid* and *Georgics,* Ovid's *Metamorphoses,* and Horace's *Odes* show, with minor variations, proportions that are close to Young's and Johnson's—about 10 adjectives, 20 nouns, and 10 verbs, in 10 lines. Since such balance, with a substantive dominance of 3 to 1, is characteristic also of Dryden, it is possible that further study of this pattern would lead to a more exact understanding of neoclassical in relation to classical verse. Philip Francis, whose translations of Horace into English were published in the 1740's, used a like proportion through 1,000 lines, namely, 10-18-11.

Of the scattered books of poems published in America about the 1740's, I have seen only the *Poems on Several Occasions,* by a Gentleman of Virginia (Facsimile Text Society, New York, 1930). Its strong dominance of adjectives over verbs was close to the English average in the decade, and closer to Pope or Dyer than Young or Johnson. Perhaps the Gentleman recognized his adjectival and scenic materials as going beyond a classical balance, toward romanticism, as the decade was moving, because he called his colleague Pope "romantic": "Taught by *Pope's* romantic Song, / Sequester'd Scenes and Muse's Seats." The Oxford Dictionary shows the early association of the term with emotionally associative scene—scene which would make for a heavy proportion of nouns and adjectives.

seventeenth century. Different as any one is from another, yet in one decade they all join to agree on twenty or thirty primary poetic terms and to set up a distinguishing vocabulary of value in the sense of *soft* and *air,* the sociability of *friend* and *youth,* the anatomy of *hand,* the emotion of *joy,* the general force of *nature* and of *power.* The tables give clues to these connections, and to many more which may interest the speculative reader.

Table 1, in adjectival order, shows the regular publication of all sorts of volumes during the decade, without indicating any sort of evident progression. Narrative pentameter couplets are prominent; so are odes and blank verse. Proportions persistently vary chronologically, but in table 1 they show in arrangement by adjectival, and in the main substantival, order, a strong central grouping at the average and median of 11 and 12, with few extremes at 9, 15, 16. As in the 1640's also, poets of greatest reputation appear both centrally and extremely, Gray as restrained, Thomson as lavish, Blair, Pope, Collins, Shenstone as variously moderate and typical. Note how nouns are relatively stable throughout, how verbs tend to decline with the increase of adjectives, so that in the last six epithetical poets the dominance of substantive over predicate has risen to 4 to 1.

Note too that the average for the decade, 12–19–9, as compared with 8–15–10 in the 1640's, shows a firm increase in both adjectives and nouns, with a slight decrease of verbs. Predication, subordination, action are simply of less relative importance for these poets, for James Thomson especially.

Table 2 adds more of the same sort of evidence, showing that while the words agreed on by at least half the poets of the decade are in number about the same as those in the preceding century, there are half a dozen more major nouns and fewer verbs than before. Note the new ones: *soft* instead of *good,* as more to be sensed; *air* instead of *earth,* as softer too; *friend* and *youth* as pleasant and sociable; *hand* and *joy* as bodily, personal, feeling;

nature and *power* instead of *time,* more present, visible, forceful; *hear* and *rise* for *make, take, tell, think,* and others, the responsive sensory for the active intellectual. The almost unanimous *see, fair, day* of the decade carry on from the past but shift the emphasis from the past *make, great, man* to nature and appreciation.

Reading down the columns of table 2, we see the full participation of Cooke, and of the middle men, Montagu, Mason, Lyttelton in their time's vocabulary, the expectable idiosyncrasy of Thomas Warton, the odd idiosyncrasy of Pope. Again, in tables 2A and 2B Mason's and Montagu's local enthusiasms are primary, along with Young's clear reaction in vocabulary, and Thomas Warton's special new world. The minor and individual terms are notably terms of sense and affection, *gay, happy, tender, beauty, breast, flower, maid, muse, night, scene, sky, song, virtue, behold, call,* as characteristic minor terms, for example; and even the few individual verbs carry the tone, scant and scattered as they are, in *bid, bless, cry, draw, fall, feel, flow, meet, move, please, pursue, sing, sit, yield, view,* and so on, in the fine passivities of sympathy. Or else the secondary and individual terms are old terms, sixteenth-century poetic language as they are for Young. And thus we get a sense of three parties in this vocabulary: the conservatives, who preserve the old abstractions and stress verbs still; the experimenters, who create a new set of landscape and color terms in noun and adjective; and most of the rest, who deal epithetically and atmospherically in the vocabulary of sensibility.

But these are large generalizations to draw from small sets of numbers on a page. It will be better to look at poems themselves, first Mason's poems, as central in vocabulary and proportion, for example, to see how runs in context this rune for the 1740's of sweet friend and love and nature, of proud beauty and muse and song.

1740's: TABLE 2

MAJORITY VOCABULARY: WORDS USED 10 TIMES IN 1,000 LINES, BY 10 POETS OR MORE

Word	Ck.	Gr.	Ak.	Yg.	Jn.	Bl.	Bk.	Mo.	Wa.	Pp.	Cl.	Ma.	Ly.	Sn.	J.W.	Dy.	Ar.	Th.	T.W.	Sm.	Total no. of users
fair	15	··	10	10	··	··	10	10	10	··	10	15	15	20	15	10	··	10	10	10	15
great	15	15	··	10	10	15	··	15	15	15	··	··	··	··	10	··	··	10	··	10	10
soft	··	··	··	10	··	··	··	10	··	··	10	10	10	15	10	10	10	··	··	10	10
sweet	10	10	··	10	··	··	10	··	··	··	15	10	20	10	10	10	··	··	··	··	10
air	··	15	10	··	10	··	20	10	10	··	10	··	··	10	10	10	30	10	··	10	13
day	25	10	10	25	15	15	15	10	10	15	15	10	10	10	··	10	10	15	15	10	19
eye	25	25	15	10	15	10	30	20	15	15	20	10	15	25	15	10	··	10	10	30	19
friend	15	10	10	15	15	··	··	10	··	··	··	··	10	20	10	··	··	10	··	10	12
God	10	15	10	10	··	··	25	10	10	··	··	15	15	··	10	··	10	··	··	··	11
hand	10	10	15	··	··	15	··	10	15	20	20	10	25	10	10	10	··	10	10	25	10
heart	25	10	15	20	15	10	15	20	··	15	15	··	··	··	10	··	10	15	··	20	14
heaven	··	··	··	15	10	··	35	15	··	··	10	··	20	··	10	··	15	10	··	··	12
joy	15	10	10	20	··	··	15	15	10	10	··	10	10	10	10	··	··	··	··	15	12
life	10	10	10	40	25	10	10	35	··	··	30	10	35	15	··	10	30	25	··	··	13
love	50	··	10	··	15	30	15	20	10	··	10	15	··	··	10	··	··	··	··	15	15
man	15	10	15	65	10	··	20	··	··	··	10	15	··	10	··	··	15	20	··	15	13
nature	10	··	··	25	20	··	10	10	10	··	15	10	20	··	··	10	25	15	10	15	13
power	15	··	15	··	25	10	··	··	··	··	10	10	10	10	10	··	20	20	10	··	14
soul	15	10	25	15	··	··	35	10	10	··	20	10	10	··	··	10	10	··	··	10	11
youth	10	··	10	··	10	··	··	··	10	··	··	10	··	··	··	··	10	10	10	10	12
come	10	10	··	··	10	10	··	20	10	··	··	10	10	··	··	10	10	··	··	··	12
give	25	10	10	15	15	10	··	15	··	15	20	10	10	10	10	··	10	10	··	··	13
hear	10	15	··	10	··	10	··	25	10	··	··	··	··	··	15	10	··	··	··	10	11
know	15	10	10	··	10	10	10	··	15	··	10	10	··	10	··	··	10	10	··	··	15
rise	15	20	10	10	15	··	20	··	25	··	20	20	20	25	10	20	10	15	10	··	15
see	30	··	··	··	··	10	10	··	··	30	··	··	··	··	··	··	··	··	25	10	19
Total of major words used	23	19	19	18	18	13	18	22	18	8	20	21	20	17	19	13	17	19	9	16	··

1740's: TABLE 2A

MINORITY VOCABULARY: WORDS USED 10 TIMES BY 4 POETS OR MORE

Word	Ck.	Gr.	Ak.	Yg.	Jn.	Bl.	Bk.	Mo.	Wa.	Pp.	Cl.	Ma.	Ly.	Sn.	J.W.	Dy.	Ar.	Th.	T.W.	Sm.
divine	10		10								10								10	
gay					10			10						10		10		10		
happy								10		10	10		15			10		10		
new					10		10	10	10	10		10					10		10	
proud									10		10					10			10	10
tender								10	10			10	10				10			10
vain					10			10	10										10	
art	10		10		15			10	10			10		10			10			10
beauty								25	15					10						
breast	15	10	10	20	10		10			10		10	10	10	10					
fate		10	10				10								10	10				15
flower			15	10							10	20		15		10				
head	10	10								20					10					
hour	10								10		15								10	20
king	20	10			10				10					10				10		
land	20				10									10		10			10	10
maid	15		10					15	10		35	20	10					10		
mind		10	10						10		10	10							10	
muse			10																15	
name	10								15				10							

1740's: TABLE 2A—*Continued*

Word	Ck.	Gr.	Ak.	Yg.	Jn.	Bl.	Bk.	Mo.	Wa.	Pp.	Cl.	Ma.	Ly.	Sn.	J.W.	Dy.	Ar.	Th.	T.W.	Sm.
night		10		10		10								10	10			20		
scene			10	10	10						15	10		15	10			10		
sky			10		10		30									10	10	15		
song	10		10	10							10	15					10			
thought		10		35	10	10					10		10	10				10		
time	40			50	10							10								
virtue				10	10						10			10	10					
world				20									10		10		15	15		
bear	10		10		10			10								10	10			10
behold			10						10	10										
call	10			10	10	10			10	10	10	10							10	
die	10			10	10							10	10							
find	10		10	10	10		10	10			20									
fly	15	15		15			20						10	15						10
love	10	10			10	10		15			15			10	10					
make	15			20				15		15	10		10						10	
stand	15									15									10	15
take	10			10		10	10			10			10					10		
tell						10		10	10	10										
think	10			10				10												

1740's: TABLE 2B
INDIVIDUAL USES

Word	Ck.	Gr.	Ak.	Yg.	Jn.	Bl.	Bk.	Mo.	Wa.	Pp.	Cl.	Ma.	Ly.	Sn.	J.W.	Dy.	Ar.	Th.	T.W.	Sm.
ancient	.	.	.	.	.	.	.	.	.	.	.	.	.	.	.	.	.	.	15	.
bold	10	.	.	.	.	.	.	.	.	.	.	.	.	.	.	.	.	.	10	10
brave	.	.	.	.	.	.	.	10	.	.	.	10	.	.	.	.	.	.	.	.
bright	.	.	.	.	.	.	.	10	.	.	.	.	.	.	.	.	.	.	10	.
cruel	.	.	.	.	.	.	.	.	.	.	.	.	.	.	.	.	.	.	.	.
conscious	.	.	.	.	.	.	.	.	.	.	.	.	.	.	10	.	.	.	10	.
dark	.	.	.	10	.	.	.	.	.	.	.	.	.	.	.	.	.	.	.	.
dear	10	.	.	.	.	.	.	.	.	.	.	.	15	.	.	15	.	.	.	.
deep	.	.	.	.	.	.	10	.	.	.	.	.	.	.	.	.	.	10	.	.
endless	.	.	.	.	.	.	10	.	.	.	.	.	.	.	.	.	.	.	.	.
eternal	.	.	.	.	.	.	15	.	.	.	.	.	.	.	.	.	.	.	.	.
false	.	.	.	.	.	.	.	10	.	.	.	.	.	.	.	.	.	.	.	.
free	.	.	.	.	.	.	10	.	.	.	.	.	.	.	.	.	.	.	.	.
full	.	.	.	.	.	.	.	.	.	.	.	10	.	.	.	.	.	.	.	.
generous	.	.	.	.	.	.	.	.	.	.	10	.	.	.	10	.	10	.	.	.
gentle	.	.	.	10	.	.	.	.	.	.	10	.	10	.	.	.	.	.	10	.
golden	10	.	.	.	.	.	.	.	.	.	.	10	.	.	.	.	.	.	.	.
good	.	.	.	.	.	.	.	.	.	.	.	.	.	.	.	.	.	.	10	.
gothic	.	.	.	.	.	.	.	.	.	.	10	.	.	.	10	.	10	.	.	.
green	.	.	.	.	.	.	.	.	.	.	.	.	.	.	.	.	.	.	10	.
high	.	.	.	.	.	.	.	.	.	.	.	.	.	.	.	.	.	.	.	.
holy	.	10	.	.	.	.	10	.	.	.	.	.	.	.	.	.	.	.	10	.
human	.	.	.	10	.	.	.	.	.	.	.	.	.	.	.	.	10	.	.	.
immortal	.	.	.	10	.	.	.	.	.	.	.	.	.	.	.	.	.	.	.	.

1740's: TABLE 2B—Continued

Word	Ck.	Gr.	Ak.	Yg.	Jn.	Bl.	Bk.	Mo.	Wa.	Pp.	Cl.	Ma.	Ly.	Sn.	J.W.	Dy.	Ar.	Th.	T.W.	Sm.
little		10												10		10				
lonely			10																	
long						10								10				10		
lovely	10																		10	
mild	10																			
noble										15								10	10	
old																			10	10
pensive				10																
poor																			10	10
proud												10						10	10	10
pure																			10	
rich									10		10				10				10	10
royal																		10		
rude																				
sacred												10					10			
sad		10									15									
solemn	10	10																		
strong				10																
true				10														10		
various	10						10									15		10		
virtuous																				
wide							10				10							10		
wild	10	10									25				10			10		
wise				10														10		
young									10											

1740's: TABLE 2ʙ—*Continued*

Word	Ck.	Gr.	Ak.	Yg.	Jn.	Bl.	Bk.	Mo.	Wa.	Pp.	Cl.	Ma.	Ly.	Sn.	J.W.	Dy.	Ar.	Th.	T.W.	Sm.
age					15				10											
Albion	10																		10	
arm																	15			20
blood			10									10								
care																				
charm																		10		
cloud																		10		
country																				
crowd																				20
dame														15						
Damon														10						
death				30		20												10		
dust																				
ear																				
earth			10	20						10						10				
eternity				10																
face									10	10									10	
the fair	15																			
fame	10																			
fancy									10			10								
father	10																			
field	10														10					
flame																				
flood					10											10		10		
foe																				10

1740's: TABLE 2B—*Continued*

Word	Sm.	T.W.	Th.	Ar.	Dy.	J.W.	Sn.	Ly.	Ma.	Cl.	Pp.	Wa.	Mo.	Bk.	Bl.	Jn.	Yg.	Ak.	Gr.	Ck.
food				10																
fool							10				10									
freedom		10																		10
glory		10										10				10				
goddess															10					
gold															10					
grave																				10
hero					10															
hill			10																	15
honour																				
hope	10																10			
Isis																				
lay									20											
liberty			10								10	10						10		
light																	10	10		
Lorenzo																		10		
lyre																				
mead						10						10								
monarch																				
mountain			15			10												10		10
nymph	10							10												
pain								15												
poet									10		10									
praise									10											
priest												10								

1740's: TABLE 2B—Continued

Word	Ck.	Gr.	Ak.	Yg.	Jn.	Bl.	Bk.	Mo.	Wa.	Pp.	Cl.	Ma.	Ly.	Sn.	J.W.	Dy.	Ar.	Th.	T.W.	Sm.
pride					10							10								
prince	10								15											
queen																10				10
rage																				
ruins												15								
shade												10								
sheep										20	15					20				
shepherd										20						15				
snow											10							20		
son	15																		10	
state	10																			
storm																		15		
strain		10	10						20			15						10		
sun		10	10						10											
sweets														10						
thing																				
toil						10								10						
tongue			10								10	10								
truth	10																		15	
virgin		10			10															
voice	10																			
war		10																		10
way																		10		
wind									15		15									
wit										15										
winter												10						10		

1740's: TABLE 2B—*Concluded*

Word	Ck.	Gr.	Ak.	Yg.	Jn.	Bl.	Bk.	Mo.	Wa.	Pp.	Cl.	Ma.	Ly.	Sn.	J.W.	Dy.	Ar.	Th.	T.W.	Sm.
woe					10															
world				20	10															
year																		10		
bid							10					15								
bless	10																			
cry				10					10											
draw											15									
fall												10						10		20
feel	10						15													
flow		10				10														
go																				15
hang											10	10			10					
lead		10									10									
leave					10											10				
lie					10							10		10						
live																				
meet																				
move			10														10			
please					10															
pursue								10												
sing									10		10								10	
sit																				
teach												10			10					
view													10							10
yield																	10			

II

William Mason's "Musaeus: A Monody to the Memory of Mr. Pope, In Imitation of Milton's *Lycidas*" represents the elegiac kind, as *Lycidas* had done a century before, and so doing represents much of its own decade.

> Sorrowing I catch the reed, and call the muse;
> If yet a muse on Britain's plain abide,
> Since rapt Musaeus tun'd his parting strain:
> With him they liv'd, with him perchance they dy'd....
> Yet ah! ye are not dead, Celestial Maids;
> Immortal as ye are, ye may not die:
> Nor is it meet ye fly these pensive glades,
> E'er round his laureat herse ye heave the sigh.
> Stay then awhile, O stay, ye fleeting fair;
> Revisit yet, nor hallow'd Hippocrene,
> Nor Thespiae's grove; till with harmonious teen
> Ye sooth his shade, and slowly-dittied air.

After speeches by Chaucer, Spenser, Milton, reference to Donne and Horace, imitation of Virgil, and quotation from Pope himself, the poet concludes.

> But now dun clouds the welkin 'gan to streak;
> And now down-dropt the larks, and ceas'd their strain:
> They ceas'd, and with them ceas'd the shepherd swain.

Here are three hundred lines of descriptive invocation and allusion. Muse moves from Greek glade to Thames shore, Chaucer invokes old Time, Spenser raises the simile of a village of birds, Milton calls Pope "last and best / of all the train! Poet, in whom conjoin'd / All that to ear, or heart, or head, could yield / Rapture; harmonious, manly, clear, sublime." The seraphic heights of heaven are predicted. Pope's verse is compared to a peaceful cave, and he speaks his more vigorous standards. Fate cuts the thread, and the nymphs weep.

All this world of poetic reference is interwound. Mason's major vocabulary of *fair, soft, sweet, bright, vain,* of *muse, shade,*

song, man, nature, hand, head, heart, of *bid, come, call, flow,*
and others, suggests the character of the interwinding. It is pur-
posefully smooth and harmonious, even when humbly "Doric."
The spirits of old poets, the forms of new, move in a sort of Ely-
sian field under a Christian heaven, with some local English
appurtenances. Virgilian classicism, a guide in Dante's world, is
a resolver still in this, making handsome combinations. The main
words of human body and form, stronger now than in earlier
centuries, work still with soul and nature, muse and fate, in partial abstraction, with feelings of love and pride, with qualities
of sweetness, softness, youth, in day and scene. This blend of
body, concept, emotion, and setting is made ceremoniously, as
if the ceremony would justify the blend, by an invocative and
exclamatory serial structure held within a temporal scene.

The Odes are much the same. "To Memory" introduces the
woodbine, the cygnet, and the vine, its instances of local reality,
with a larger sweep.

> Mother of Wisdom! thou, whose sway
> The throng'd ideal hosts obey;
> Who bidst their ranks, now vanish, now appear,
> Flame in the van, or darken in the rear;
> Accept this votive verse. Thy reign
> Nor place can fix, nor power restrain.
> All, all is thine. For thee the ear, and eye
> Rove thro' the realms of Grace, and Harmony:
> The Senses thee spontaneous serve,
> That wake, and thrill thro' ev'ry nerve.
> Else vainly soft, lov'd Philomel! would flow
> The soothing sadness of thy warbled woe:...

The throng'd ideal hosts, the votive verse, the power and reign,
the ear and eye, the nightingale and its soothing sadness, all are
the natural parts, by which sensation, feeling, nature, and idea
served together in verse to make its serious whole.

Mason's proportioning was medial and average for his time.
His 12 adjectives, 18 nouns, 10 verbs in 10 lines was close to that

of Lyttelton, Shenstone, Collins, to Blacklock, Montagu, and Walpole, in general stress on more adjectives than verbs, half again as many nouns as adjectives, and a combined substantival dominance of 3 to 1. His lines were pentametric, using couplet and quatrain rhyme with variation; they were not extra long but rather extra-weighted with reference. "Else vainly soft, lov'd Philomel! would flow / The soothing sadness of thy warbled woe" is the sort of combination wherein the verb singly serves paired items and multiple unfolding epithets. Onomatopoeia too serves substance as well as motion, as song and feeling are liquid, and alliteration braces noun with adjective. The effect of sound in separating and then linking its parts of speech is to mold the verse as if it were material.

The main words bear out this stress. Mason uses more of the major words of his time than almost any other poet, and the ones he does not use are abstract *life* and *joy*. He agrees with that same group to whom he is closest in verbal proportioning in an emphasis on beauty, bodily form, and Collins' *scene* and *song,* the terms which his minority agree on sharing. Close to the center of poetic practice in the decade this emphasis in reference, in sound pattern, in structural proportion, achieves special sorts of beautiful material, in shape sensable, in unit phrasal, set up, bound, and linked by harmonious qualitative connections, including the vital connection of human feeling.

So Lyttelton's *Monody,* equally representative in construction, begins:

> At length escap'd from every human eye,
> From every duty, every care,
> That in my mournful thoughts might claim a share,
> Or force my tears their flowing stream to dry;
> Beneath the gloom of this embowering shade,
> This lone retreat, for tender sorrow made,
> I now may give my burden'd heart relief,
>   And pour forth all my stores of grief;

Of grief surpassing every other woe,
Far as the purest bliss, the happiest love
    Can on th' ennobled mind bestow,
    Exceeds the vulgar joys that move
Our gross desires, inelegant and low.

Ye tufted groves, ye gently-falling rills,
    Ye high o'ershadowing hills,
Ye lawns gay-smiling with eternal green,
    Oft have you my Lucy seen!
But never shall you now behold her more:
    Nor will she now with fond delight
And taste refin'd your rural charms explore.
Clos'd are those beauteous eyes in endless night,
Those beauteous eyes where beaming us'd to shine
Reason's pure light, and Virtue's spark divine.

Beside these scenes, passions, and abstractions we have Dryads, shepherds, Philomel again, Nature and Nature's God, Fate, Muses, and Aeonian maids, Castalia's plain and other Greek and Roman places, Petrarch's Laura, and Death himself. In these sequester'd dales and flower-embroider'd vales Lucy practiced the conjugal and the maternal virtues. Where, in what foreign spot, were the Muses, that they let her die? Now let them keep her fame, her beauty, grace, expressive eyes, soul, manners, innocence, tenderness, kindly-melting heart, gentle tears, elevated mind, bright wit, sweet benevolence, and bashful modesty. Let Petrarch teach me to sing a woe greater than his. The orange blossom was blighted by the Apennine wind, the fabric of felicity broken. The soul must arise from these low abodes of sin and pain, to the heavenly radiance of eternal light, the throne, the regions of serene delight.

It is possible to see how in this procedure, which is a lament like Mason's though more variously formed in ode fashion, with rhyme range in pairs and alternates, and lines from three to six feet, the same sort of Masonic mood and landscape has been constructed. It is a freer poem, a more personal poem, yet its major reference is *Musaeus*'s, the fair, soft, sweet qualities of day, eye, hand, heart, joy, love, power, soul, and youth, with the regular actions of coming and giving, hearing and seeing. Nor do Lyttelton's special choices of epithets, *happy, tender, dear,* and *gentle,* lead away except by excess from the path through feeling nature. There is much "sensibility," much statement of emotional response, in both poets, and the same sorts of human and natural traits provide the material responded to.

So too Shenstone, though in *The School-Mistress* he is writing not a monody, and an imitation not of Milton but of Spenser, orders the familiar descriptive and emotional materials.

> Ah me! full sorely is my heart forlorn,
> To think how modest worth neglected lies;
> While partial fame doth with her blasts adorn
> Such deeds alone, as pride and pomp disguise;
> Deeds of ill sort, and mischievous emprize!
> Lend me thy clarion, goddess! let me try
> To sound the praise of merit, ere it dies;
> Such as I oft have chaunced to espy,
> Lost in the dreary shades of dull obscurity.
>
> In ev'ry village mark'd with little spire,
> Embowr'd in trees, and hardly known to fame,
> There dwells, in lowly shed, and mean attire,
> A matron old, whom we school-mistress name;
> Who boasts unruly brats with birch to tame;
> They grieven sore, in piteous durance pent,
> Aw'd by the pow'r of this relentless dame;
> And oft-times, on vagaries idly bent,
> For unkempt hair, or task unconn'd, are sorely shent.

In two ways this descriptive development is not written straight. The mock tone, the puffing up of the lowly, the "clarion" for "brats," is one alteration; the other, the pseudo-Spenserian vocabulary of "grieven," of "shent," of "piteous durance," along with the pseudo-Spenserian grace and formality of the stanza. Nevertheless, the fun which Shenstone is having here does not sway him from the pastoral norm. *Fair, soft,* and *sweet* are still his major qualities, *day, eye, friend, love, nature, youth,* his substantial subjects, and *seeing* his central action. He had a special light sense for the *gay,* the *little,* the *lovely,* for the *beauty* and the *flowers* of a *scene;* he could *find* and *fly;* he was a light and pretty poet, even when a mock one, and liked his verse-making colleagues.

The School-Mistress moved (with Spenser's appropriate particulars, "his language, his simplicity, his manner of description, and a peculiar tenderness of sentiment," as Shenstone said in his introductory note) through details of the situation, the mistress' garb, chickens, herbs, psalms, furniture, power, the crisis of punishment, the speculations of greatness, the play of noon, the survey of seasons and of cakes. The juxtapositions because they are mock, startle, but they are inwound and presented with familiar poetic terms of "No vision empty, vain, his native bliss destroy," and "Where comely peace of mind, and decent order dwell," and "marj'ram sweet, in shepherd's posie found," and "Eyes her bright form in Severn's ambient wave." Mock or straight, Shenstone knew what his decade's poetry should sound like.

His elegies and his essay on them show his straight understanding of the technique and theme. His moral *Judgment of Hercules,* smooth in couplets, reference, structure of choice and survey, exemplifies again the main line of poetic action, exhibiting a moral through a natural and physical beauty. Local in introduction:

> Will *Lyttelton* the rural landskip range,
> Leave noisy fame, and not regret the change?
> Pleas'd will he tread the garden's early scenes,
> And learn a moral from the rising greens?

general in application:

> Happiest of these is he whose matchless mind,
> By learning strengthen'd, and by taste refin'd,
> In Virtue's cause essay'd its earliest pow'rs;
> Chose virtue's paths, and strew'd her paths with flow'rs.

classical in central illustration:

> 'Twas youth's perplexing stage his doubts inspir'd,
> When great *Alcides* to a grove retir'd.
> Thro' the lone windings of a devious glade,
> Resign'd to thought, with ling'ring steps he stray'd; ...

balanced in choice between the two beautiful figures, invocative
and argumentative in its speeches, happy in the wisdom of its
final decision for the real light of the sun over the false light of
the moon: the *Judgment* sets up the perfect array of sense impressions and moral abstractions in an atmosphere of immediate
though mythical order.

The most notable colleague of these three poets, sharing most
enthusiastically in their major and minor uses, and inventive
along the very lines they followed, was William Collins. His
special *maid, shepherd, song, scene, way* emphasized the constancy of his characters in setting—pastoral, alliterated, and harmonious. His adjectives of feeling, *happy, tender, gentle, sad,
solemn,* gave to his new qualities *green, wild,* and *wide,* and to
his attributions *royal* and *divine,* the sense of most delicately
shaded response. His slighting of common poetic abstractions
like *joy, life, God,* and *love* in favor of *hand* and *eye, hearing* and
seeing, set him with Mason, Lyttelton, and Shenstone apart from
many others. Yet his full agreement on two-thirds of the major
terms, like *sweet, day, heart, power, youth,* and the verbs, gave
him a central place in the decade's practice, as did his average
proportioning of 12 adjectives to 17 nouns to 9 verbs. The verses
of the young Oxford student were exactly, indeed almost humor-
ously, as they seem to me, up to par. There was no backward
look to an earlier generation for the youthful scholar; the backward look in the text of the *Eclogues* was part of their recent
fashion. Collins suggested that they were written probably in
the beginning of Shah Sultan Hosseyn's Reign, the Successor of
Sefi or Solyman the Second, and that Collins himself "received

them at the Hands of a Merchant." Translation and antique discovery were both good businesses for the poetry of this merchant era.

> Ye Persian Maids, attend your Poet's Lays,
> And hear how Shepherds pass their golden Days:
> Not all are blest, whom Fortune's Hand sustains
> With Wealth in Courts, nor all that haunt the Plains:
> Well may your Hearts believe the Truths I tell,
> 'Tis Virtue makes the Bliss, where'er we dwell.
>
> Thus Selim sung; by sacred Truth inspir'd;
> No Praise the Youth, but her's alone desir'd:
> Wise in himself, his meaning Songs convey'd
> Informing Morals to the Shepherd Maid,
> Or taught the Swains that surest Bliss to find,
> What Groves nor Streams bestow, a virtuous Mind.

Here immediately is the central vocabulary and structure. The
Maids are addressed and they *hear*. *Shepherds* pass golden *days*.
Hand sustains, *hearts* are *told*, *Virtue* makes bliss, the *Youth*
sung, and *taught* to *find* a virtuous *Mind*. In a golden daytime
country, youthful figures listen to songs of beauty and virtue;
analogies of Doe and Falcon bear out the later song, and a train
of Faith, Pity, Meekness, Love concludes it.

The Second Eclogue is more rough and negative: days are
luckless, hours sad, sorrow wild, heart breaking, only the poor
happy. The Third Eclogue is softened by its evening setting:
"Fair happy Maid! to other Scenes remove, / To richer Scenes
of golden Pow'r and Love!" And the Fourth, at awful Midnight,
hears "Shrieks and Sorrows load the sad'ning Wind," "No more
the Dale with snowy Blossoms crown'd."

> Th' affrighted Shepherds thro' the Dews of Night,
> Wide o'er the Moon-light Hills, renew'd their Flight.

Each of the poems sets its time and scene in narrative fashion,
addresses its occupants, invokes abstracter figures, ranges a world
of geographic reference, lists vices, or flowers, or foreign places,

within the very regular confines of its couplets. Strong caesuras make phrasal divisions which then may be alliteratively linked and epithetically balanced. Each molded part, each substantive phrase of person, place, or thing, by suiting of sound or sense moves on into the whole, as above for example the four items in two lines are joined by the long *i* which runs through them and by onomatopoeia suggests the long and open quality of their reference.

This is fairly simple descriptive stuff for the young Collins. Setting blends emotion, character, and concept easily enough. His next poem was more difficultly abstract: *Verses, Humbly Address'd to Sir Thomas Hanmer on his Edition of Shakespear's Works*. By a Gentleman of Oxford. London, 1743. Yet it makes again the simple solution, by imaginatively scenicizing the abstraction.

> Sir,
> While, own'd by You, with Smiles the Muse surveys
> Th' expected Triumph of her sweetest Lays:
> While, stretch'd at Ease, she boasts your Guardian Aid,
> Secure, and happy in her sylvan Shade:
> Excuse her Fears, who scarce a Verse bestows,
> In just Remembrance of the Debt she owes;
> With conscious Awe she hears the Critic's Fame,
> And blushing hides her Wreath at Shakespear's Name.

Though the occasion here is a book, a text, an edition, the narrative motion persists: settling the muse with her emotions in the grove, calling up a survey of poets from Greece to Rome to Florence to London to France, and coming finally to the muse's great English future in art, the manly and moral passions of a Shakespearean nature.

One sees the pervasion of a poetic mode. The extraordinary abundance of the poetic terms of bodily form, scene, and feeling is a necessary part of the "poem" which builds itself in regular fashion upon the basis of passionate and personified survey.

There is a good deal of verbal and metrical variety in the texts we have briefly observed; no phrasal or thematic lack of invention, but a solid sense of the structural order in which phrases should move and themes be expressed. Certain subjects and formulations mark off the realm of poetry: poetry itself, with its personification in the muse; history, with its muse; the human type, abstracted into nymph and shepherd forms; the natural world, framed in landscape with certain types of natural forms; the human sensibility, in sensation and feeling. So the later poems, of 1746/7, the *Odes on Several Descriptive and Allegoric Subjects,* which make even in their title that fast combination of descriptive and normative modes characteristic of the time, are addressed to feeling concepts of Pity, Fear, Simplicity, Mercy, Liberty, Peace, and the Poetical Character, and give all of these immediate body in the text by physical and natural location: the familiar vocabulary of Friend of Man, balmy Hands, destin'd Scene, Pella's Bard, old Ilissus, gentlest Otway's infant Head, the Buskin'd Muse, Monsters, ghastly Train, Hybla's Dews, Cypress Wreath, Attic Robe, Hall or Bow'r, Waller's Myrtle Shades, Pilgrim grey, smiling Bride, Spartan fife, Albion's Fame. The major counters of proper names and characteristic qualities can be combined and recombined, as each is an expected part of the normal poetic whole. England calls up France and Rome, Rome calls pastoral scenes, scenes shepherds, shepherds love, love the human eye and head, eye color and shape and train, train ceremony, ceremony the muses, the muses Greece and Rome, and so on over the great surface of the globe. The predicative motion of the procedure is, moreover, also ceremonious and enlarging. The "O Thou, ... Receive" of *Ode to Pity* becomes "let the Nations view," and "wander wide," "has heard," "shed," "sung," "Come," "shall raise," "prevail," and finally "There let me oft ... melt away, / Allow'd with Thee to dwell." Verbs of sight control the *Ode to Fear: is shown, seest, appear, behold, trace, meet*

my blasted View, along with *hearing, wandering,* and *dwelling.*
Simplicity stresses feeling and the *Poetical Character* construction, yet through these also the large verbs of *Pity* run. The
poetry predicates position or change of position, seeing, hearing,
and recognition, with responses of feeling suitable to situation.

Collins, actively engaged in this mode, varied it in two ways:
one, by intensification of sense detail; the other, by subtlety of
melody. The "Ode to Evening," which modern readers seem to
admire most, is most varied in these ways. The phrasal units are
not much altered, the structure again carries the line from invocation to the requested teaching "To breathe some soften'd
strain" and "let me rove some wild and heathy scene," and finally
to a survey of seasonal change and a prediction of Eve's gentlest
Influence. But along the way are some smaller discriminations
for which modern lovers of small discriminations praise Collins:
the weak-ey'd Bat, the leathern Wing, the paly circlet, the dim-
discover'd Spires, the gradual dusky Veil. There is a continuity
of atmosphere in these, a unity of quality, which makes them all
seem new as they intensify each other not through concept but
through the simplest qualitative reference. More than usual, too,
the sounds of these phrases ease their sense, not by an enforced
onomatopoeia but by a delicate sort of shading, as for example
the sound of *gradual* moves into *dusky,* and as in the line "Prepare thy shadowy Car" with its shadowy extra syllable, the *car*
is a shadowy assonance for *prepare.* Most individualistic too is
Collins' omission of rhyme in this poem, in keeping with its
gentleness of sound. The alternating five and three accented
couplets are written but not rhymed as couplets, so that the measure does double work and becomes particularly memorable. All
sorts of other sound devices make gentle links of sound at the
line ends: the assonance of *Strain* and *Vale,* the consonance of
Strain and *Return, Song* and *Springs, Sport, wont,* and *Light,*
the alliteration of *Wing* and *winds,* the rhyme of *Vale* and *hail,*

Eve and *Leaves,* and many more in variation back into the lines. In the poetry of Collins is vivid the influence of personal skill within an accepted technique. With all the poets of his time Collins shared most of a material and structure; and with some of the poets of his time he shared almost all. And it was within this shared mode, not outside it, that he made his special contributions to poetry: his terms of pastoral scene, his "green" color and quality, his fresh and shaded melody. Taking for granted that poetry's function was the giving of form in a very literal sense to thought, feeling, history, and nature in a very literal sense, Collins worked with the ceremonious formalizing of his colleagues, and beyond it, giving evening a full and human figure and at the same time giving the things of evening a more immediately perceivable quality; making the ode form more and more delicate, its echo of sound to sense more and more inward.

III

A very different sort of poet is Gray, with whom Collins is regularly linked in our minds by the Oxford Press and a hundred brief histories. Gray's place in his time was conservative, idiosyncratic in a noncommittal and not very emphatic way. He had no clear group of poetical colleagues like Collins, but rather maintained in the decade an extreme of restraint at the same time that he went along in general with the general practice. We move back from the central current of the decade, when we look at Gray, to its steadier reserve. There are fewer nouns and adjectives in this verse than in almost any other of the period, a period in which an abundance of nouns and adjectives is characteristic. Since the verse is almost normally extended, the line more frequently 4 feet than 5, we must suppose in addition that, lacking such substantial content and lacking also a high degree of predication, it employs more of the nonsubstantial connective words for its poetry and in this choice is more like the standard poets of the preceding century. Akenside, Cooke, Young, and Johnson share this moderation of substantives with Gray, though in somewhat different material.

The major material is of less defining consequence than the minor. Gray stresses two-thirds of the terms and tends to agree with his reactionary colleagues in avoiding mostly the new terms, like *soft, air, nature, power,* and *youth,* keeping, on the other hand, many of the abstract terms which Collins avoided. More strongly in the minor list we see Gray's reticence: no special adjectives, unless one counts his slight emphasis on *human* and *solemn;* no verbs either, except the conventional *to fly* which is characteristic of the older type; nouns like *fate, time, king,* also older, and then just one or two, like *flower, head, muse, night,* which point in the direction of Collins' bodily and atmospheric interest. Gray's favorite vocabulary was as a whole abstract. It is significant of his tentative consideration, however, that if one counts beyond the 1,000 lines to Gray's complete work, as exhibited in the Concordance, for example, the new sort of word appears often enough to seem major: *soft, deep, golden* then appear along with the older *fair, great, little, old* among the epithets. Gray's very lack of emphasis in length of line and statement makes for a scant count and an apparent subdual of the experimental qualities which Collins stressed; and even the full concordance count shows Collins to be by far the greater innovator (or participator in innovation) by his narrowing to, his intensification of, the new.

Gray's beginning of "Ode on the Spring" is pleasantly familiar in its figurative time setting. The poem had first been called "Noontide" and it establishes its atmosphere much as Collins' "Evening" does.

> Lo! where the rosy-bosom'd Hours,
> Fair Venus' train appear,
> Disclose the long-expecting flowers,
> And wake the purple year!

> The Attic warbler pours her throat,
> Responsive to the cuckow's note,
> The untaught harmony of spring:
> While whisp'ring pleasure as they fly,
> Cool Zephyrs thro' the clear blue sky
> Their gather'd fragrance fling.

But Gray's great difference, his summary abstraction, his more common evaluative terminology, ends the second stanza.

> With me the Muse shall sit, and think
> (At ease reclin'd in rustic state)
> How vain the ardour of the Crowd,
> How low, how little are the Proud,
> How indigent the Great!

So also the other poems which begin with invoked spires, daughter of Jove, Aeolian lyre, ruthless king, conclude by abstraction with "folly to be wise"; with "Teach me to love and to forgive, / Exact my own defects to scan, / What others are, to feel, and know myself a Man"; "Beyond the limits of a vulgar fate, / Beneath the Good how far—but far above the Great"; "To triumph and to die, are mine." These thoughts are more than scenic and ceremonious and passionate, they are recommendatory; they are concerned with standards.

Like Collins' "Evening," Gray's most admired poem has not been his most characteristic in form and technique; but unlike Collins, Gray played in it even more than usual upon the poetic conventions of his type and decade.[2] The narrative quatrains stabilize and regularize the beat of the pentameter. The plowman, beetle, owl, elms, yew, establish the time and place as usual. The survey is achieved for the dead by listing what they do *not* see.

> For them no more the blazing hearth shall burn,
> Or busy housewife ply her evening care:
> No children run to lisp their sire's return,
> Or climb his knees the envied kiss to share.

---

[2] A fact which the intricate interpretations in Empson's *Versions of Pastoral* and Brooks' *Well-Wrought Urn* could well have stressed further.

Then that ninth and most quoted stanza generalizes the situation into concept, not by figure merely, not by personified form, but by almost straight abstraction from the scene:

> The boast of heraldry, the pomp of pow'r,
> And all that beauty, all that wealth e'er gave,
> Await alike th' inevitable hour.
> The paths of glory lead but to the grave.

This measure of abstraction we have never since forgotten, and it draws not only a truth which we may like to recognize from the humanity we are, but also a simplicity of statement from the ode's pomp and the welter of generalization and innumerable established scenic displays.

The poem proceeds to address and personify, until it comes again, by way of the standard survey of idea's range, to the gem, the flower, the Milton mute, the Cromwell guiltless, "Along the cool sequester'd vale of life." Here again it is able to draw on the forces of association in term and structure. The strongly poetic *flower* of the decade was normally no person, but a decoration and embroidery, a gem, to be *seen,* so that the personal, human quality and the *unseen* are in directest contradiction to poetic expectation. And this very negative force controls these stanzas, as it does the whole poem, in the difference between expected and received, the standard poetic life and this negative yet still poetic death. Thus the shift to *thee* and *him* and the Swain and the Epitaph toward the end of the poem: the removal from the immediacy of scene, the negative even of involvement, "Nor up the lawn, nor at the wood was he"; "A Youth to Fortune and to Fame unknown"; "No farther seek his merits to disclose." The final positive line, "The bosom of his Father and his God," withdraws completely from the local poetic world alive or dead and makes a final negation of the stuff of poetry with which Gray has been working. Its vocabulary, as partly alien to the eighteenth century's poetry, confirms it by contrast, and we see that the pastoral, historical, and cosmic panorama to which we have grown accustomed in the decade is the very world, of reality as well as of poetry, which the churchyard poet must name and deny as he writes of death, the absence of it all.

Young and Blair, whose melancholy denials of this same standard life were published even earlier than Gray's, won a long popularity like his for their moral and often negative abstractions. The eighteenth-century reader seemed troubled by the soft and colorful view of life which the poets were setting up and liked poems which rejected while they constructed it. Or rather, perhaps, the reader was accustomed to the strong quality of Gray's abstraction as we have seen it, and found adequate in Young and Blair, even excessive in Gray and Collins, the construction of a visible world. Certainly Young's *Night Thoughts* are more of thought than of night and mix their figures toward concept more than view.

> Tired Nature's sweet restorer, balmy Sleep!
> He, like the world, his ready visit pays
> Where Fortune smiles; the wretched he forsakes;
> Swift on his downy pinion flies from woe,
> And lights on lids unsullied with a tear.
>
> From short (as usual) and disturbed repose
> I wake: how happy they who wake no more!
> Yet that were vain, if dreams infest the grave.
> I wake, emerging from a sea of dreams
> Tumultuous....
>
> Night, sable goddess! from her ebon throne,
> In rayless majesty now stretches forth
> Her leaden sceptre o'er a slumb'ring world.
> Silence how dead! and darkness how profound!
> Nor eye nor list'ning ear an object finds;
> Creation sleeps.

Little of the poem is more visual than this for long:

> What though my soul fantastic measures trod
> O'er fairy fields, or mourn'd along the gloom
> Of pathless woods, or, down the craggy steep
> Hurl'd headlong, swam with pain the mantled pool, ...

though the poet has asked,

> O lead my mind,
> (A mind that fain would wander from its woe,)
> Lead it through various scenes of life and death,
> And from each scene the noblest truths inspire.

It is not surprising that Young's vocabulary is even more abstract than Gray's. He scants *eye, hand, youth,* and stresses *life* and *man* with unusual repetitiveness. Among minor terms again he repeats the more traditional sort, *fate, thought, time,* and *world.* Though not highly adjectival, he maintains the main adjectives and adds a few special stresses on such wide epithets as *eternal, human, immortal,* and on such out of an earlier era as *good, poor, wise.*

His fellow mourner Blair, of *The Grave,* and his fellow surveyor Blacklock both show that the common consideration of humanity, even of human sorrow and decline, is in the 1740's somewhat more lively and colorful. Young's conservatism is in fact almost singular as we compare it with those who wrote most like him. Few were content with his restrained 10–20–10 proportioning, well-balanced as it seemed. Blair and Blacklock tended to agree on more epithet, less verb, in a ratio of 11–18–9. Blair shunned the main aesthetic line of *soft, sweet, air, nature, power, youth,* but was also shy of the more abstract line of *friend, God, life.* His overtones were still, like Young's, overtones of the metaphysical, of *time* and *night, death* and *grave,* with verbs of *thinking* and *dying.* Yet more solidly the *eye, hand, heart* of *man* flourish for him, and the poem thinks in "painting" as it begins:

> Whilst some affect the Sun, and some the shade,
> Some flee the city, some the hermitage;
> Their aims as various as the roads they take
> In journeying through life; — the task be mine
> To paint the gloomy horrors of the tomb;
> Th' appointed place of rendezvous, where all
> These travellers meet.—Thy succours I implore,
> Eternal King! whose potent arm sustains
> The keys of Hell and Death....

> The wind is up: hark! how it howls! Methinks
> Till now I never heard a sound so dreary:
> Doors creak, and windows clap, and night's foul bird,
> Rook'd in the spire screams loud: the gloomy ailes,
> Black-plaster'd and hung round with shreds of 'scutcheons,
> And tatter'd coats of arms, send back the sound,
> Laden with heavier airs, from the low vaults,
> The mansions of the dead.

This sort of fancy tapestry does not add up to the main text of Blair, which is less specific, more surveyed, characteristically on the order of

> Proud lineage! now how little thou appear'st
> Below the envy of the private man.
> Honour! that meddlesome officious ill,
> Pursues thee ev'n to death; nor there stops short.

But all of it through thick and thin makes panoramic illustration of its old and grisly abstractions which show sympathy with Gray and Collins as well as Young.

The sober hymns, odes, elegies of Dr. Thomas Blacklock maintain the tone and much of the vocabulary of Blair. Many of them were imitations of classical and Biblical themes, with some appropriate Spenser added, and they were thought by Blacklock's friends and editors to be necessarily at second hand simply because he could not see. The extraordinary fact that a man could be blind yet a poet is the main point of Chalmers' introduction, and it testifies to the stress on the poetics of sight throughout the century. At any rate, the clear imitative force of the poems does ally them to the most characteristic of the decade, in gloom, pomp, and range.

> O Thou, whose goodness unconfin'd
> Extends its wish to human kind;
> By whose indulgence I aspire
> To strike the sweet Horatian lyre;
> There are who, on th' Olympic plain,
> Delight the chariot's speed to rein;

> Involv'd in glorious dust to roll;
> To turn with glowing wheel the goal;
> Who by repeated trophies rise
> And share with gods their pomp and skies....

This is an adaptation of Horace's first Ode. "A Hymn to Fortitude" proceeds somewhat more darkly:

> Night, brooding o'er her mute domain,
> In awful silence wraps her reign;
> Clouds press on clouds, and, as they rise,
> Condense to solid gloom the skies.
>   Portentous, through the foggy air,
> To wake the demon of despair,
> The raven hoarse, and boding owl,
> To Hecate curst anthems howl....

And, with the suitable extreme of emotion, an elegy "On the Death of Mr. Pope,"

> While yet I scarce awake from dumb surprise,
> And tepid streams profusely bathe my eyes;
> While soul-dissolving sighs my bosom strain,
> And all my being sinks oppress'd with pain;
> Deign you, whose souls, like mine, are form'd to know
> The nice poetic sense of bliss and woe;
> To these sad accents deign a pitying ear:
> Strong be our sorrow, as the cause severe.
>   O Pope, what tears thy obsequies attend!
> Britain a bard deplores, mankind a friend:
> For thee, their darling, weep th' Aeonian choir,
> Mute the soft voice, unstrung the tuneful lyre:...

Both Blacklock and Blair by furnishing out to such an excess of substance in their regular couplets and blank verses the natural feelings and connections of humankind, climatic or sepulchral, show us how inevitably used was the poetic material of the decade. In their sorts of range the two poets are little alike, but in the fact of their range and spread, and in the main points constantly hit upon: the great heart beating thick, the far-seen orb of day, the pride of man, the fatal causes, the uni-

versal laws of nature, the rising and beholding of fair or grue-
some sights: we see a common confidence. These materials are
so good because true, so beautiful because good, that the more
we get of them the better.

Even the satirist, or I suppose naturally the satirist since it
is his intention to shift attitude through common means, employs these means. Thomas Cooke's *Battel of the Poets,* though
extreme, along with Cooke's other poems, in proportioning,
9–21–11, with fewer nouns and more verbs than normal in the
decade, uses almost every major word the poets of the decade
proposed and proceeds in the couplets which most of them preferred. The few omissions he makes are *gentle, soft, air, heaven;*
all the minor words he shares belong to the reactionary minority, the seventeenth-century words of *beauty, fate, hour,
king, land, maid, mind, name, thought, virtue,* with their older
epithets *brave, dear, good,* and all the old major verbs as well
as the new ones.

Cooke's satirical verse, although giving us an extreme for
the period, a moral, political, and temporal sense, with strong
predicative emphasis, characteristic of the majority of poets a
century before, nevertheless does not give us a poem alien to
the 1740's, since the new emphases of sense and structure have
been adapted in it.

> The bloodless Warfare, and the dreadful Day
> To Bards tenacious of the dying Lay,
> The happy few who back with Conquest came,
> The pensive many who return'd with Shame,
> I sing. Indulge, *Calliope,* my Verse,
> While I the Horrors of the War rehearse,
> How Poets doubly in their Works were slain,
> When the big Volumes cover'd all the Plain,
> How little Witlings like Enthusiasts fought
> For the same Cause, they knew not why, they wrote.
> First, Goddess, for thou know'st, instruct my Tongue
> To tell the Source whence the Dissention sprung. . . .

> In that soft Season when the fruitful Show'rs
> Call from the Womb of Earth the infant Flow'rs,
> In the full beauty of the fragrant May,
> When Nature smiles, and ev'ry Field is gay,
> When George and Caroline begun their Reign, . . .

and so on. The mock-heroic conflict is given all the beautiful aspects of the generally poetic: a classical invocation, a sense of scope and range, a seasonal setting, a political or national setting, later a survey of poets, the electing of Philips chief over Pope with the gods' approval, and an eventual scenic peace. Though most of the poets involved are of an earlier day, the *Battel* first having been published a decade earler, the choice they make of leader is an anti-Popean choice, one pointing forward to the mode we have been observing, as successor to Dryden's. Philips is their choice, over Swift, Tickell, Dennis, Theobald, Savage, and the like. And

> *Philips* charms all Hearers with his Strain,
> A skilful, pure, and unaffected, Swain;
> His Numbers flow with Harmony and Ease,
> And like the Country in her Beauty please.

So does this satire move, though antagonistic never rough. That a battle becomes a pageant is a tribute to the compelling values of the era, though the change may not be a helpful one for satire.

What was the mode of Pope that the conservative Cooke objected to? Why was it not easy and harmonious enough? At this time in the century it was the *Dunciad* of course that loomed largest, revised as it was into the 1740's; and it was the *Dunciad* style that many meant when they spoke of Pope. Yet the proportioning and much of the vocabulary of this style placed Pope as a normal conservative, like Cooke himself but more pleasantly substantial. It begins:

> The Mighty Mother, and her Son, who brings
> The Smithfield Muses to the ear of Kings,

> I sing. Say you, her instruments the Great!
> Call'd to this work by Dulness, Jove, and Fate:
> You by whose care, in vain decry'd and curst,
> Still Dunce the second reigns like Dunce the first;
> Say, how the Goddess bade Britannia sleep,
> And pour'd her Spirit o'er the land and deep.

Here is the familiar invocation and beginning of survey; yet a local particularity and sharpness of juxtaposition alters it somewhat. The oddity of particularity increases, until, about line 120, there is lively and special phrasing such as

> Round him much Embryo, much Abortion lay,
> Much future Ode, and abdicated Play;
> Nonsense precipitate, like running Lead,
> That slipp'd thro' Cracks and Zig-Zags of the Head;
> All that on Folly Frenzy could beget,
> Fruits of dull Heat, and Sooterkins of Wit.

Even the ceremonious pomp of the poem's ending is more broken than roundly rolled by its specialized reference.

> Physic of Metaphysic begs defence,
> And Metaphysic calls for aid on Sense!
> See Mystery to Mathematics fly!
> In vain! they gaze, turn giddy, rave, and die.
> Religion blushing veils her sacred fires,
> And unawares Morality expires.
> For public Flame, nor private, dares to shine;
> Nor human Spark is left, nor Glimpse divine!
> Light dies before thy uncreating word;
> Thy hand, great Anarch! lets the curtain fall,
> And universal Darkness buries All.

Throughout this writing, the lack of fidelity to image is surprising to the faithful reader of Pope's colleagues. For Pope, particularity of language entails not objects and qualities so much as notions, relations, slang bits, odd instances, startling and thoughtful combinations. In the absence of progressing picture, perhaps, is the absence of smoothness and enthusiasm which troubled the poets of the 1740's. There is an absence of enthusiasm for major vocabulary in Pope, too. He likes *great, day, eye, God, heaven,* well enough, but no more of the sweet adjectives and no more of the joyful, soulful, and sensory nouns. He stresses the verb *to see* and its kind, but not so much what is seen. *New* and *old* are minor adjectives he insists on, and *fate* and *head*. He neither invented new varieties nor piled up old ones; he stressed merely a third of the main words but put no others in place of them. And the reason for this restraint was, as we have seen in even a few lines, that he put his care and enthusiasm in a greater variety of instance, a more common as well as a more usual particularity.

So Pope, for all his normal proportioning and structuring of verse, was, as Cooke said, less than Cooke characteristic of the decade of his death because he played more curiously and precisely. Others whom we associate with him and whom we think of as "classical" did more tempering to the mode of general image. Akenside's *Pleasures of Imagination* begins thus "smoothly."

> With what attractive charms this goodly frame
> Of nature touches the consenting hearts
> Of mortal men; and what the pleasing stores
> Which beauteous imitation there derives,
> To deck the poet's or the painter's toil;
> My verse unfolds.

And even better the *Hymn to the Naiads:*

> O'er yonder eastern hill the twilight pale
> Walks forth from darkness; and the God of day,
> With bright Astraea seated by his side,
> Waits yet to leave the ocean. Tarry, *Nymphs* ...

These Nymphs and "attractive charms" are not vivid images, but they suggest at least the possibility of vision. This was the suggestibility of the 1740's, the hint of sight, the figure veiled, the shadowy anatomy of an abstraction; and Akenside employed it steadily. "Beauteous imitation" is said to "deck," as if it were a visible garland; the twilight "walks forth" and the God of day "sits" by implication and "waits," like a person on a cosmic stage.

Akenside, like Cooke, Blacklock, and Walpole, accepts *fair* as a major adjective, but not *soft;* he employs most of the other major terms except the personal *friend, heart, youth;* his minor emphases are on the aesthetic, *divine, art, breast* and *head, muse, scene, sky, song;* he is clearly a compromiser.

Mrs. Montagu was another enthusiastic collaborator in the mode, both aesthetic and humane. The proportioning of 11–18–12 shows a good many substantives along with an undue dominance of verbs, and the verbs were of many kinds: the major *see* and *know* most of all, the others except *hear,* the older *love* and *make,* the newer *shine.* Her eclogues actively cover their ground. Their ground is mixed, too, strongly abstract in *life, love, man, mind* and in *great* to modify them, but aesthetic also, like Akenside, in *air, day, beauty, art,* in most of the major physiological terms, and in the varied and mixed epithets of *fair* and *soft, bright, cruel, false, gay, happy, tender, vain,* some like *false* echoing the seventeenth century, some like *gay* characteristic of eighteenth-century innovation. The poems are early, written in 1715 though not published complete under Mrs. Montagu's initials until 1747, by Walpole. Their likeness at once to Blacklock's and to Walpole's, to Pope's and to Johnson's, suggests the persistence through the first half century of the conservation of abstraction in the midst of growing sensory detail, with a mediation between the two materials by the vocabulary of sensibility.

> Roxana, from the court retiring late,
> Sigh'd her soft sorrows at St. James's gate.
> Such heavy thoughts lay brooding in her breast,
> Not her own chairmen with more weight oppress'd;
> They groan the cruel load they're doom'd to bear;
> She in these gentle sounds express'd her care.

> "Was it for this that I these roses wear?
> For this new-set the jewels for my hair?
> Ah! Princess! with what zeal have I pursued!
> Almost forgot the duty of a prude.
> Thinking I never could attend too soon,
> I've missed my prayers, to get me dress'd by noon.
> For thee, ah! what for thee did I resign?
> My pleasures, passions, all that e'er was mine...."

This beginning of the "Monday" eclogue takes in its regular couplets a middle course between Pope's local particularity and the general eclogue's generality, of which latter the "Wednesday" opening is a closer example:

> "No, fair Dancinda, no; you strive in vain
>   To calm my care, and mitigate my pain;
>   If all my sighs, my cares, can fail to move,
>   Ah! soothe me not with fruitless vows of love."
> Thus Strephon spoke. Dancinda thus replied;
> "What must I do to gratify your pride?
> Too well you know (ungrateful as thou art)
> How much you triumph in this tender heart:
> What proof of love remains for me to grant?
> Yet still you teaze me with some new complaint.
> Oh! would to heaven!—but the fond wish is vain—
> Too many favours had not made it plain!
> But such a passion breaks through all disguise,
> Love reddens on my cheek, and wishes in my eyes...."

Here the address and dialogues, the serial description, the emotional diction, and a little later the personification of Love as god and tyrant, show the normal eclogue form so characteristic of the decade and perhaps the early century, with its statement and restatement of sensibility and the support of recurrent physiological, political, classical figures.

When Lady Mary, with Lord Hervey, wrote some verses against her old friend Pope, she called his writing "crabbed" and thorny, hard and obscure, rough descriptive terms in her day as in any. And we can see, by a comparison with her own poems, what she may have meant by the terms: the varied sound and acute particularity of much of Pope, which stands out as idiosyncratic against the smooth and moderate flow of these moderately descriptive verses.

Walpole's *Beauties* echoed her in proportioning and substance. A few standard adjectives, not as tender; the main verbs, particularly of sight; and a great number of repeated nouns, not only the main group but also an array of lofty, official, and royal ones, make up the poem. *Art, beauty, face, fame, goddess, king, land, liberty, monarch, muse, name, priest, queen, son,* and *state* indicate the pomp of Walpole's ceremony. They indicate also how a poet may unfold the potentialities of a standard vocabulary in a special direction without much altering the standard structure.

> Desponding artist, talk no more
> Of Beauties of the days of yore,
> Of Goddesses renown'd in Greece,
> And Zeuxis' composition-piece, ...
> In Britain's isle observe the Fair,
> And curious chuse your models there; ...

The nationalism of Walpole's survey of beauty does not affect its thoroughness or its range of reference. The official monarchial terms add splendor to the local celebration, as *Emily* is *Queen*.

Some grandness needed always to be drawn into the picture, to give it significance beyond the common. Otherwise it turned funny. Walpole's glorifications were more official and physical than cosmic or pastoral or passionate in the manner of many of his colleagues, even the most soberly reserved, yet in his set variations he was still a good standard classicist; he analogized and balanced terms at a lofty level. Good moderation needed to be grand, because the norms of man and nature were grand, in even trivial verse.

We come finally to the mid-century's most classic poet, young in this decade and fond producer of early poems, and we find

that he is most proper, as one might expect. He is moderate in
adjectives, strong in verbs, in a 10–21–11 ratio. He maintains the
five-accented and the four-accented couplet. He prefers abstract
terms, *great, new, fate, friend, life, love, nature, power,* most
strongly among the major ones, and his own *age, foe, king,
land, pride, virtue, woe, wealth;* and at the same time he employs the newer *gay, air, day, youth, scene, gold,* and *art,* and
most of the main verbs. He is not so conservative as Young and
Gray, not so individual as Pope; he never goes so far toward new
forms as even the typical Lyttelton; he is close to Blacklock, Mrs.
Montagu, and Walpole in the moderation of their poetics, in a
sense of *life, nature, power.* His *London* begins:

> Tho' grief and fondness in my breast rebel,
> When injur'd *Thales* bids the town farewel,
> Yet still my calmer thoughts his choice commend,
> I praise the hermit, but regret the friend,
> Who now resolves, from vice and *London* far,
> To breathe in distant fields a purer air,
> And, fix'd on Cambria's solitary shore,
> Give to St. David one true Briton more.

And his *Vanity of Human Wishes* is even more familiar in its
generality:

> Let observation with extensive view,
> Survey mankind, from China to Peru;
> Remark each anxious toil, each eager strife,
> And watch the busy scenes of crowded life;
> Then say how hope and fear, desire and hate,
> O'erspread with snares the clouded maze of fate,
> Where wav'ring man, betray'd by vent'rous pride,
> To tread the dreary paths without a guide;
> As treach'rous phantoms in the mist delude,
> Shuns fancied ills, or chases airy good.
> How rarely reason guides the stubborn choice,
> Rules the bold hand, or prompts the suppliant voice,
> How nations sink, by darling schemes oppress'd,
> When vengeance listens to the fool's request.

> Fate wings with ev'ry wish th' afflictive dart,
> Each gift of nature, and each grace of art,
> With fatal heat impetuous courage glows,
> With fatal sweetness elocution flows,
> Impeachment stops the speaker's pow'rful breath,
> And restless fire precipitates on death.

This is a survey not only of mankind but of the conservative poetry of the 1740's. The first line of the *Human Wishes* stresses sight and its scope. The next few concern general mankind, in range and activity, with the power of vitality in *anxious, eager, busy,* and *crowded,* and the focus on *scene.* The next set passions in the scene, the *maze* and *paths* of fate; and then move to illusion, in *mist* and *airy.* Then through *rules* the verses take a step toward nations as extensions of people, past the by-figure of fate's afflictive dart, to the demagoguery of passion. Life, nature, power are all in force here, denotatively as well as connotatively. The imperative *look* dominates the series of phrases and clauses, of subjects and actions. A number of half lines balance, and a number of pairs, as the coördinate *and* extends by apposition. The stress is, familiarly, then, on the phrasal unit, the series and progress of thoughts and sights subsumed under the key exclamation, "How rarely reason guides the stubborn choice," but developing a general substance far more than the exclamation would demand. In the twenty lines are about twenty verbs, piece by piece: Let ... survey, Remark, And watch, Then say ... how o'erspread ... to tread ... delude, ... Shuns. How guides, Rules, or prompts, How sink, when listens, Wings, glows, flows, stops, precipitates. There is an essence of eighteenth-century survey action in this sort of predicative structure, starting slowly with the span, ending in an acceleration of more qualitative suggestion and vividness. Again, more than half the nouns are modified by adjectives, and an easy play goes on between the single and the phrasal units, as in "Fate wings with ev'ry wish th' afflictive dart, / Each gift of nature, and each grace of art." This is the sort of close variety to which we have grown accustomed. Even the reference speaks in major terms or synonymous variation in *view, mankind, scene, life, fate, man, pride, good, reason, hand, voice, wish, nature, art, sweetness, powerful, fire, death.* The wide worlds of geography, politics, passion, and fate themselves possess a sort of synonymous variety.

We see in these lines of poetry the poetry of the decade.

IV

Yet the decade's poetry had more ways than one of enlivening itself; and Johnson's neutral norm, though it provides a fine and sober instance of structure and content, does not indicate the heights and extremes. As we have seen, the most conservative Gray-Young-Pope-Johnson group, which balanced modification and predication as it balanced couplets, phrases, and abstractions, was not as close to the center of the decade's procedures as was the Collins-Lyttelton group, which closely agreed on special stress of epithets and the vocabulary of feeling scene. But even this central stress was mild in contrast to the further extreme of James Thomson and the Wartons, of Dyer, Armstrong, and Somerville. This group agreed less within itself concerning materials and patterns of usage; it agreed most on a sort of various excess, not particularly inventive, but selective and emphatic. It tended to ignore certain major terms like *God, joy, love, youth, give, know,* usually those which had had the longest inheritance of poetic usage. It slighted certain characteristic minor terms like *divine, beauty, breast, fate, name, hour, time, virtue,* and all the minor verbs, suggesting its lack of interest in abstraction and in predication. It was most lively, on the other hand, in the use of the major *fair, soft, air, day, nature,* and *rise* and *see,* which suggest a mild visibility, and in the minor *gay* and *sky* which extend it. One, Thomas Warton, seems to add to this line by invention, in his free use of many epithets, his *an-*

cient, bold, bright, conscious, golden, Gothic, holy, mild, pensive, proud, rude, sacred, his *fame, freedom, glory, truth, state,* which commit to history his sense of view. Another, James Thomson, adds with more agreement those natural images for which Wordsworth commended him: modified by *gay, happy, deep, pure, wild,* the *land, night, scene, sky, world,* and more singularly *cloud, country, flood, mountain, snow, storm, sun, wind.* We are led to expect a motion away from man as central substance, toward a spread of quality and view.

Joseph and Thomas Warton indicate the quality and development. Joseph Warton's *The Enthusiast, or the Lover of Nature,* written in 1740, begins:

> Ye green-rob'd Dryads, oft at dusky eve
> By wondering shepherds seen, to forests brown,
> To unfrequented meads, and pathless wilds,
> Lead me from gardens deck'd with art's vain pomps.
> Can gilt alcoves, can marble-mimic gods,
> Parterres embroider'd, obelisks, and urns,
> Of high relief; can the long, spreading lake,
> Or vista lessening to the sight; can Stow,
> With all her Attic fanes, such raptures raise,
> As the thrush-haunted copse, where lightly leaps
> The fearful fawn the rustling leaves along,
> And the brisk squirrel sports from bough to bough,
> While from an hollow oak, whose naked roots
> O'erhang a pensive rill, the busy bees
> Hum drowsy lullabies?

The bards of old, says the Enthusiast, often met in such a spot to learn the Muse's moral strains, as Aegeria whispered sacred laws to Numa. Versailles may have its fountains, let me choose a foamy stream like Anio. Can Titian or Raphael vie with tulip or rose? Happy the man who lived in Earth's infancy. What is artful Addison to wild Shakespeare? I invoke Contemplation to lift my soul above this little Earth, to hear the spheres, to meet the procession of Virtues to the Isles of Innocence.

The reader will probably find this poem not unfamiliar; more, in fact, of the same. But the same is more indeed. Amid invocation, survey, pastoral and classical scene, the richly descriptive epithets are thicker than we have found before. Three-fourths of the nouns here are modified, to Johnson's one-half, and the epithets are colored as well as sensitive. The verbs, on the other hand, are far fewer than the familiar one per line. This is verse excessively substantial, less active than almost any we have noticed in English poetry before 1740. What was, in the seventeenth century, a regular 2 to 1 ratio between substantives and verbs, and usually in the 1740's a 3 to 1 ratio, becomes here 4 to 1 for Warton as for his group. This means a richer, denser, more static poetry. And while Joseph Warton is content with a proportioning of 13–19–8, his brother raises the adjectival to 15–19–8, sounding even more elaborate:

> Mother of musings, Contemplation sage,
> Whose grotto stands upon the topmost rock
> Of Teneriff; 'mid the tempestuous night,
> On which, in calmest meditation held,
> Thou hear'st with howling winds the beating rain
> And drifting hail descend; or if the skies
> Unclouded shine, and thro' the blue serene
> Pale Cynthia rolls her silver-axled car,
> Whence gazing stedfast on the spangled vault
> Raptur'd thou sitt'st, ...

This the beginning of the *Pleasures of Melancholy,* written at 17; or, when he was 21, *The Triumph of Isis,* in handsome couplets,

> On closing flowers when genial gales diffuse
> The fragrant tribute of refreshing dews;
> When chants the milk-maid at her balmy pail,
> And weary reapers whistle o'er the vale;
> Charm'd by the murmurs of the quiv'ring shade,
> O'er Isis' willow-fringed banks I stray'd:
> And calmly musing through the twilight way,
> In pensive mood I fram'd the Doric lay.

To whom the muse came from the dimply flood, saying to sing no more of love but rather of Freedom, and giving along with the *sacred glory* and *truth* of a *free state* the persistently discriminating and modifying vocabulary of *ancient, bright, golden, Gothic, mild, pensive,* and *rude,* broadening the tolerances of eighteenth-century acceptance further into the old, rough, and dazzling than they had before gone.

Both the Wartons are *conscious,* a favorite word, of the mode which they are extending or altering. The Doric, the pastoral, Mason's popular elegiac, these Thomas Warton explicitly surrenders to the more wide historical and political, but implicitly employs to give Liberty its local habitations. These are more visible habitations than it is used to, colored and stylized. The concepts of freedom and the feelings of melancholy which have been thematic all through the century are here most figured, clothed, and located, so that pageantry reaches an extreme of enthusiasm, and the poetry of thought, in becoming for Thomas Warton most conscious, ceremonious, historical and pictorial, substantival and adjectival, has become more objectified though emotional, perhaps more objectively emotional, than any before in an era of poetic thought.

There is one poem of the decade, of the year 1740 itself to be exact, more extremely adjectival and visual even than the experimenter Warton's, and that is *Hobbinol,* the burlesquer Somerville's. Here is the startling proportion of 16 adjectives to 8 verbs, the adjectives double the verbs and almost equal to the nouns. Why? Well, as Somerville wrote to Hogarth in his Dedication, "You have some Advantage of your poetical Brethren, that you paint to the Eye"; and, as he wrote in his Preface, "If, therefore the Heroic is the proper Measure, where the low Character is to be rais'd, Milton's Style must be very proper in the Subject here treated of; because it raises the low Character more than is possible to be done under the Restraint of Rhyme;

and the Ridicule chiefly consists in raising that low Character."
Milton's style is visual and epithetical as well as unrhymed, and
as Somerville makes it suit the subject of rural games, and the
purpose of ridicule, it raises its satire "against the Luxury, the
Pride, the Wantonness, and quarrelsome Temper of the mid-
dling sort of People," thus:

> What old *Menalcas* at his Feast reveal'd
> I sing, strange Feats of antient Prowess, Deeds
> Of high Renown, while all his list'ning Guests
> With eager Joy receiv'd the pleasing Tale.
>
> O Thou! who late on *Vaga's* flow'ry Banks
> Slumb'ring secure, with *Stirom* well bedew'd,
> Fallacious Cask, in sacred Dreams wert taught
> By antient Seers, and *Merlin* Prophet old,
> To raise ignoble Themes with Strains sublime,
> Be thou my Guide! while I thy Tract pursue
> With Wing unequal, thro' the wide Expanse
> Advent'rous range, and emulate thy Flights.

Here only a handful of the many nouns are unepitheted, while
the verbs are scant, and even scanter in the passages of sport
where one would suppose action necessary. The action, rather,
is epithetical:

> Rage, and Revenge, and ever-during Hate,
> Blacken'd his stormy Front; rash, furious, blind,
> And lavish of his Blood, of random Strokes
> He laid on Load; ...   (Canto II)

This style we are to recognize as high, forceful, visual, and
heroic; and in its many *eyes, hands, hearts, heads, breasts,* all
rich, bold, and *proud,* with few actions except the Miltonic
stand, we may recognize, after a fashion, its own burlesque.

Two poets of the decade who make their epithetical abundance perfectly serious, using it, as it seems, to mold the mundane
into the beautiful, without either the burlesque of Somerville on
the one hand or the fervor of Thomas Warton on the other, are

Armstrong and Dyer, the practical poets of health and architecture in landscape form. Both maintain the substantial 4 to 1 proportion in regular narrative, expository and invocative blank verse. Both stress the major descriptive terms of *soft, air, day, life, nature, come, rise,* and *see;* and the minor *various* and *sky;* but both are led to specialize also in their own fields, Armstrong in the *human, generous, tender* words of *man, power, world, blood, live, bear,* and *yield;* Dyer in the more outward *deep* and *lofty* and *little* aspects of *fleece, flock, flood,* and *flower, hill, sheep.* In characteristic differences, then, they represent two main material divisions of the period, the human world and the natural, split here in individual emphasis, but linked always in major effect.

> Daughter of Paeon, queen of every joy,
> Hygeia; whose indulgent smile sustains
> The various race luxuriant nature pours,
> And on th' immortal essences bestows
> Immortal youth; auspicious, O descend!
> Thou cheerful guardian of the rolling year,
> Whether thou wanton'st on the western gale,
> Or shak'st the rigid pinions of the north,
> Diffusest life and vigour thro' the tracts
> Of air, thro' earth, and ocean's deep domain.

This is the beginning of *The Art of Preserving Health,* and Armstrong is able, by a survey of proper airs and climates, to describe many beautiful natural scenes along with his human miseries of "the languid frame, / Vapid and sunk from yesterday's debauch." The blood itself is scenic:

> The blood, the fountain whence the spirits flow,
> The generous stream that waters every part,
> And motion, vigour, and warm life conveys
> To every particle that moves or lives; ...
> Besides, the flexible and tender tubes
> Melt in the mildest most nectareous tide
> That ripening nature rolls; as in the stream
> Its crumbling banks; ...

Health is throughout a sort of gentle adaptation to nature, its climates and forms, to "One Power of Physic, Melody, and Song."

Dyer works, on the other hand, from the outside inward, to much the same effect of interinfluence. The famous, and earlier, *Grongar Hill* begins outside:

> Silent Nymph! with curious eye,
> Who, the purple ev'ning, lie
> On the mountain's lonely van,
> Beyond the noise of busy man,
> Painting fair the form of things,
> While the yellow linnet sings,
> Or the tuneful nightingale
> Charms the forest with her tale;
> Come, with all thy various hues,
> Come, and aid thy sister Muse; ...

But the long description turns at the end to a soothing human application much like Armstrong's:

> Be full, ye Courts! be great who will;
> Search for Peace with all your skill:
> Open wide the lofty door,
> Seek her on the marble floor:
> In vain ye search, she is not there;
> In vain ye search the domes of Care!
> Grass and flowers Quiet treads,
> On the meads and mountain-heads,
> Along with pleasure close-ally'd,
> Ever by each other's side,
> And often, by the murm'ring rill,
> Hears the thrush, while all is still,
> Within the groves of Grongar Hill.

And on the way, Armstrong's likening of blood to stream is reversed, in

> And see the rivers how they run
> Thro' woods and meads, in shade and sun! ...
> A various journey to the deep,
> Like human life to endless sleep: ...

The 1740 *Ruins of Rome* brings up the further mediating force of art and antiquity.

> Enough of Grongar, and the shady dales
> Of winding Towy, Merlin's fabled haunt,
> I sung inglorious. Now the love of arts,
> And what in metal, or in stone remains
> Of proud Antiquity, thro' various realms
> And various languages and ages fam'd,
> Bears me remote o'er Gallia's woody bounds, ...

And the later *Fleece* adds the serious moral technicality of the pastoral.

> The care of sheep, the labours of the loom,
> And arts of trade, I sing. Ye rural Nymphs!
> Ye Swains, and princely Merchants! aid the verse.
> And ye, high-trusted Guardians of our Isle
> Whom public voice approves, or lot of birth,
> To the great charge assigns! ye Good of all
> Degrees, all sects! be present to my song.

That famous *Winter,* which outlasted all Thomson's revisions from 1726 to 1746, startled its readers by its natural and sensory elaboration yet fits very easily into the poetic field of the 1740's as we see that field as a whole. It says, as most of the poems say, literally *See!* It invokes, lifts the soul, traces place and time, in blank verse like the Wartons', with the modified unit of phrase, and the balanced pattern of sound within the line.

> See, Winter comes to rule the varied year,
> Sullen and sad, with all his rising train—
> Vapours, and clouds, and storms. Be these my theme;
> These, that exalt the soul to solemn thought
> And heavenly musing. Welcome, kindred glooms!
> Congenial horrors, hail! With frequent foot,
> Pleased have I, in my cheerful morn of life,
> When nursed by careless solitude I lived
> And sung of Nature with unceasing joy,
> Pleased have I wandered through your rough domain;
> Trod the pure virgin-snows, myself as pure;
> Heard the winds roar, and the big torrent burst;
> Or seen the deep-fermenting tempest brewed
> In the grim evening-sky.

Two-thirds of the nouns are modified, mostly by emotion, so
that they load the scene with feeling, as the use of *I* does also,
in a fashion which seems newly personal. But the poem grows
impersonal as it further engages the Muse. It is far more often
the scenic than the personal that the critics have praised in Thomson. His Oxford editor calls his presentation of the snowstorm
(ll. 223-235) his highest achievement in natural description (p.
x), "a splendid specimen of Thomson's peculiar art in the reali-
zation of a scene."

> The keener tempests come; and, fuming dun
> From all the livid east or piercing north,
> Thick clouds ascend, in whose capacious womb
> A vapoury deluge lies, to snow congealed.
> Heavy they roll their fleecy world along,
> And the sky saddens with the gathered storm.
> Through the hushed air the whitening shower descends,
> At first thin-wavering; till at last the flakes
> Fall broad and wide and fast, dimming the day
> With a continual flow. The cherished fields
> Put on their winter-robe of purest white.
> 'Tis brightness all; save where the new snow melts
> Along the mazy current.

Part of this, the lines of the falling flakes, has indeed a directness
of observation new to us and the decade, but much is standard
figure: the anatomy of *womb,* attribution in *saddens,* and ceremonial personification in *winter-robe.* In the next lines the summary figure is "Earth's universal face." It cannot be said,
therefore, that Thomson does any extended describing in our
literal sense of the term; he is fully a part of his era, figuring and
abstracting his description for the sake of its human significance;
and he writes, moreover, many of the most standard abstract
passages; like lines 322 ff.:

> Ah! little think the gay licentious proud,
> Whom pleasure, power, and affluence surround—
> They, who their thoughtless hours in giddy mirth,
> And wanton, often cruel, riot waste—

> Ah! little think they, while they dance along,
> How many feel, this very moment, death
> And all the sad variety of pain; ...

This, outside the flow of the whole blank verse, sounds so much like Pope that there seems a couplet echo. Even the Spenserian stanzas of the *Castle of Indolence* generalize grimly as Spenser never would:

> O mortal man, who livest here by toil,
> Do not complain of this, thy hard estate; ...

But the stanzas do go on to:

> Was nought around but images of rest:
> Sleep-soothing groves, and quiet lawns between;
> And flowery beds that slumbrous influence kest,
> From poppies breathed; and beds of pleasant green,
> Where never yet was creeping creature seen.

And one must note that in this vein of correspondent image so valuable to his time Thomson effected more than the "restoration of nature to the domain of poetry from which it had been banished by Pope and his school" (p. vi); he brought into poetry an amount of plain nature, of sun and mountain, land and wind, which had simply never been there before. As his titles of seasons name a direct preoccupation with their facts and qualities, we accept the temporal surveys along with the spatial ones of "Hills" and "Forests," and gain new dimensions in the observation of scene which grow finally more precise as they grow wider and deeper.

In brief survey of the eighteenth-century order we may see that Thomson for all his natural objects and Young for all his abstractions shared very closely in a poetic tradition whose extremes, even when satirized by a Cooke or a Somerville, were never very far apart. The 1740 poem, whether brief lyrical ode or extended moral essay, assumed scope of the natural, historical, and mythological world, gave immediacy by human figure and physical setting, harmonized by linear regularity and syllabic

shading, and constructed by full syntactical sequence the ceremony of its inclusiveness.

Within the sweep of agreement were some definite distinctions. Those poets who, like Thomson, Armstrong, Dyer, and
the Wartons, delighted in an abundance of everything to be
seen and felt, a wealth of temporal and spacial variety, rich and
soft words, physical nouns, a substantival dominance of 4 to 1,
as many as 3 epithets in 2 lines, were balanced to a degree by
Gray, Blair, Young, Johnson, who liked more abstract terms and
more predication of them. For these, verbs were apt to equal
nouns and were more various, especially in the actions of knowing and thinking; and thoughts about life and death, time and
fate, God and virtue, were more often the central poetic material.

In Johnson's *Vanity of Human Wishes* the lines (291–296) are
characteristic:

> But few there are whom hours like these await,
> Who set unclouded in the gulphs of Fate.
> From Lydia's monarch should the search descend,
> By Solon caution'd to regard his end,
> In life's last scene what prodigies surprise,
> Fears of the brave, and follies of the wise?

And these may be contrasted to Thomson's characteristic beginning of *Summer:*

> From brightening fields of ether fair-disclosed,
> Child of the sun, refulgent Summer comes
> In pride of youth, and felt through nature's depth:
> He comes, attended by the sultry hours
> And ever-fanning breezes on his way;
> While from his ardent look the turning Spring
> Averts her blushful face, and earth and skies
> All-smiling to his hot dominion leaves.

In structure and texture the passages do not differ greatly, except
that Thomson's is the more specifically to be sensed. Both poets
may be highly abstract yet concrete, highly moral yet scenic, but
they are distinguished by their choice of emphasis.

The poetic sentence for the whole decade, for all the twenty poets, would say, *Rise, fair day, before the eyes and soul of man,* and thus would combine generally and gently the abstract and the visual in its moral imperative. This was its major vocabulary, the fair day, in its natural and airy setting; the eye, soul, hand, heart of man in youth and power; above, heaven and God. It was a world viewed, felt, and considered, and its great poetizing power was to bring more and more of what it considered and felt into view. At the level of minor terms this creation is even more apparent; the minor epithets themselves suggest that though for conservative poets the conservative terms of *dear, good, noble, solemn, virtuous, eternal, poor, strong, true, wise, young, old, various* were adequate, what the more lavish poets had to add was not more terminology of idea and value but more of sense: of *bright, green, high, dark, golden, deep, lofty, little, rude, wild.* Thus it was the *fair day,* not man, that was *rising,* in the decade's poetry; for the strangest, the least familiar, the newest terms were the terms not of man and soul and heaven but of day and air and light and height, the youthful power of present nature, the joy of atmosphere.

II. GROUNDS OF PROSE IN THE 1740's

THE PROSE of the decade was concerned with the same
"poetical" subjects: the passions of man, the varieties of
natural landscape, the eternal power of heaven. The
main difference in the prose was that the conditioning force of
the second, or natural, subject was not so strong; morals and
eternal verities were less often scenicized. Even so, much of the
prose of drama heightened its effects by atmosphere and insisted
on the seriousness of its intent, as for example Garrick's·farcical
Miss in Her Teens bespoke in its prologue "nature's laws," "more
gen'rous views," real life and passions; and Mallet's *Alfred,* very
different in weight and kind, was different not only by the standard variation between farce and tragedy but by the new sublimity of its atmospheric reference. "All the world's a stage" became
significant in a new sense: not in the conflict and confrontation
of character so much as in the scenic properties, the formal focus
and expansive backdrop, the draperies and fitting tonal reso-
nances, the large scale of production, the renewed use of Shakespeare to these large, passionately reforested, ends. Histories of
the English stage, like Betterton's and Chetwood's, commentaries
like Hanmer's, Upton's, Johnson's, collections like Dodsley's, all
contributed to the sense of long view, of temporal survey, and
of local immediate participation in the truths of history, the
visions and verities of the ancient and great.

The novel in its new solidity was an even stronger localizer
of moral problems and spiritual forces in specific times of day,
in specific houses, towns, and shires. The reader under the light
could live in the panorama. This is not to say that *Pamela,
Shamela, Joseph Andrews, David Simple, Clarissa Harlowe,
Roderick Random, Tom Jones,* the novels of the 1740's, were
full of "poetic" descriptive passages; rather, they seem to us bare
of local fact and atmosphere. Pamela lives in a world of sensi-

bility rather than of sensation, and her vocabulary is intensely one of human virtue and vice rather than of the spiritual or natural orders; but even *Pamela* brings to its reader what the devout moral essay never could, a sense of placement within the boundaries of a situation. Mr. B's house, though we know little of its aspect, is in one place, Pamela's parents' house in another, and the letters must go between. There is an upstairs and a down-stairs, Lady Davers comes and goes, Pamela is kidnapped: still the mail gets through. How much more satisfactory to the visual, even to the spatial, imagination this consistency of development within a frame than on the one hand the vaporous non-world of romance or on the other the moral advices of highly hypo-thetical characters, typical and familiar though they may be. Richardson's *Familiar Letters on Important Occasions* have all the paraphernalia of situation, but none of its setting. In their "To a Father, against putting a youth of but moderate Parts to a Profession that requires more extensive Abilities," "From an Uncle to a Nephew, on his keeping bad Company, bad Hours, etc., in his Apprenticeship," there are far more recommendatory and illustrative Biblical quotations than there are items of sight and sound. In *Pamela* there is at least a constant riding out, some strolling about the grounds, some clothing and furniture, the substantial evidences of the "walk of life."

It was the walk of life that Richardson aimed to convey, the idea of type of comportment in everyday which, by its very meta-phor, suggested a literal setting. He was, as he said in various prefaces and letters (*The Novels,* London, 1824, Vol. VI, to Aaron Hill, etc.), opposed to the improbable and the marvelous, to rant and bombast, to language "coldly abstract and metaphysi-cally absurd" (though he had Lady Davers admire Cowley very sincerely); and he wanted to promote the cause of religion and virtue by writing in an easy and natural manner, in an "ordinary tone of feeling." The great talking point for the book, by author, editor, reader alike, was its natural emotion. "For it abounds with lively images and pictures; with incidents natural, surprising, and perfectly adapted to the story: with circumstances interesting to persons in common life as well as to those in exalted stations." "Blest be thy powerful pen, whoe'er thou art, / Thou skill'd, great moulder of the master'd heart!"; "My dear Father and Mother, I have great trouble, and some comfort, to acquaint you with. The trouble is, that my good lady died of the illness I mentioned to you, and left us all much grieved for the loss of her; for she was a dear good lady, and kind to all us her servants"; "...above my degree...God...my good lady's heart...the squire a little wildish ... take by the hand ... die a thousand deaths ... looked like an angel ... Lie still, my throbbing heart, divided as thou art, between thy hopes and thy fears!" Letter I from Pamela, like the prefatory texts which praise it, is written in the vocabulary of emotion, with some sense of nature and deity but much more of the path which reached from low to high, tremulous with feeling all the way.

As the decade progressed, this highly simplified novelistic view complicated itself in attitude, vocabulary, and substance. Fielding made much more happen concretely, and mixed the tones of the heart; and Smollett renewed the scope of romance in combination now with vivid instance. But the basic saga of feeling in the stages of its adventure did not alter, and the landscape through which it passed, the roads, fields, towns, valleys, hills grew more and more dark or bright, common and sympathetic, as one novel followed another. The Gothic, which would shift emphasis to scenery itself as well as to the grotesques of scenery, would shift title from personal to local name in the *Castle of Otranto,* but especially the domestic novel and sentimental comedy took into their normal tones the passages of field and stream, and the *Vicar of Wakefield* came to inhabit a very characteristic as well as delightful spot.

The straightest essays of the decade, the prose arguments of the age of prose and reason, are also full of a pictorial and an emotional rather than a metaphysical vigor. Cibber's auto-biographical *Apology,* Middleton's, Campbell's, North's, Birch's, Bower's, Johnson's *Lives,* of poets, popes, orators, admirals, and gentlemen, carry their subjects from first to last with an epic sweep and civility. Middleton prefaces his Life of Cicero, 1741, with the remark that "there is no part of History, which seems capable of yielding either more instruction or entertainment, than that which offers to us the select lives of great and virtuous men, who have made an eminent figure on the public stage of the world." He points out the danger of panegyric, the need for observance of chronological order, councils first, then acts and events; he hopes to create, first, admiration of Cicero, then imitation of him, believing, as his dedication says, that "human nature has ever been the same in all ages and nations, and owes the difference of its improvements, to a difference onely of culture, and of the rewards proposed to its industry...." This is the steady note struck by historians and biographers. It makes the historical figure a model actor and universal man.

The travelers of the period were hard put to it to find universal man, and they dealt with their curiosities rather askance, making not the wonders but the technical procedures of their journeys the significant center. The ending of Pococke's Holy Land tour is standard enough.

The next day we came in sight of the tower of Arabia, and the day after saw Alexandria; as we approached it we had a very agreeable prospect of the famous column, of the walls of the old city, of the country covered with palm trees, which grow to a great height, rising up above the buildings of the city. And on the twenty-ninth we arrived in the port of Alexandria, after a very pleasant and agreeable voyage of twenty-three days.

The chronological method blends easily with the scenic. Pascoe Thomas, mathematician, reported Anson's voyage round the globe with equal accuracy of spirit,

The End of all publick Writings is, or should be, either Instruction or Diversion; and as my Talent does not lye the latter Way, I have, in the following Sheets, made it my only Aim to Instruct; ... [Preface]

September 1740. Being quite ready about the Beginning of September the same Year, we put to Sea three different Times, but were as often put back to the Road of St. Helen's by contrary Winds and stormy Weather.

(December, off Brazil) The Men throughout the whole Squadron began now to drop off apace with Fevers and Fluxes, occasion'd chiefly, I believe, by the violent Heat of the Climate, and the bad Air; the Country being so very woody that the Air must needs be stagnated, and render'd very unhealthful.

(March, Tierra del Fuego) ... consisting of high craggy Hills, towering above each other, mostly covered with Snow, with deep horrid Valleys, some few scattering Trees, no Plains, nor one chearful Green thro' all the dismal Scene; so that the whole may not improperly be termed the *Land of Desolation.*

The authors who journeyed not historically or geographically but only through regions of the mind were apt to arrive at the same sort of scenic properties. In *The Improvement of the Mind,* Isaac Watts's "Direction for the Attainment of useful Knowledge" began:

No man is obliged to learn and know every thing; this can neither be sought nor required, for it is utterly impossible; yet all persons are under some obligation to improve their own understanding; otherwise it will be a barren desert, or a forest overgrown with weeds and brambles. Universal ignorance or infinite errors will overspread the mind, which is utterly neglected, and lies without any cultivation.

James Hervey, a much-beloved minister, in 1746 published "Reflections on a Flower-Garden," to make a different sort of scene, shadowed with personification, serve the same sort of ends.

It was early in a summer morning, when the air was cool, the earth moist, the whole face of creation fresh and gay. The noisy world was scarce awake. Business had not quite shook off his sound sleep; and riot had but just reclined his giddy head. All was serene; all was still; every thing tended to inspire tranquillity of mind, and invite to serious thought.

Robert Dodsley's *Economy of Human Life,* of 1750, presented
also the duties and virtues of man through the scene of the world.
His outline was abstract: man's Consideration, Modesty, Application, Emulation, Prudence and so on as Duties; man's Hope
and Fear, Joy and Grief, as Passions; Providence and Religion
leading to the wider second part, Man in General. Within this
frame were more figured passages, as in "Joy and Grief,"

> Look now on the other side, and behold, in that vale overshadowed
> with trees, and hid from the sight of men, the habitation of Sorrow.
> ... [In the bower of Tranquillity] dwelleth Peace, with her dwelleth
> Safety and Contentment. She is cheerful, but not gay; she is serious,
> but not grave; she vieweth the joys and the sorrows of life with an
> equal and steady eye.

So the abstractions after a long literary tradition came home to
man in moral prose through the human, larger than life-size
figure, with its steady eye.

The literary critics were consciously aware of this tradition,
in both prose and verse, which bodied forth its abstractions to
the reception of sense. *Taste* was their aesthetic term, and they
opposed it to *wit,* as image to that sort of conceit which worked
by turns and twists rather than by direct presentation. So Shenstone (*Works,* London, 1764, Vol. II, pp. 312, 203) wrote firmly,
"The object of taste is corporeal beauty," and, "The difference
between a witty writer and a writer of taste is chiefly this. The
former is negligent what ideas he introduces, so he joins them
surprisingly.—The latter is principally careful what images he
introduces, and studies simplicity rather than surprize in his
manner of introduction." The important realm of human morals
was thus made available to the realm of taste by a corporeal framing, an anatomical, architectural, or pictorial design, which could
serve not only the most actively artistic forms of literature but
also the most purely didactic, so that we see shades of boundaries
and personifications looming wherever we look and finding a
specific justification in literary theory.

The Memories of the Extraordinary Life, Works and Discoveries of Martinus Scriblerus, the mock and mythic figure of the Pope-Arbuthnot circle, began in just the mode:

What thou seest in me is a body exhausted by the labours of the mind. I have found in Dame Nature not indeed an unkind, but a very coy Mistress: watchful nights, anxious days, slender meals, and endless labours, must be the lot of all who pursue her through her labyrinths and meanders. My first vital air I drew in this island (a soil fruitful for philosophers), but my complexion is become adust, and my body arid, by visiting lands (as the poet has it) *alio sub sole calentes.*

The subject, the state of a student, is partly set forth by its translation into personified and geographized terms. Arbuthnot suggests how formulized the method is by 1714 in a letter to Swift (*Works,* Oxford, 1892, p. 71):

I was going to make an epigram upon the imagination of your burning your own history with a burning glass. I wish Pope or Parnell would put it into rhyme. The thought is this: "Apollo speaks, 'That since he had inspired you to reveal those things which were hid, even from his own light, such as the feeble springs of some great events; ...'" And then you must conclude with some simile: thus, &c. There are two or three that will fit it.

The mere conception, even if it is a playful one, is not enough; it must be "imagined" first into Apollo's realm and finally into a large "thus" simile to fit.

Swift himself, in so special a work as *The Art of Punning,* subtitled "The Flower of Languages," supports the abstract with the anatomical in his definitions.

Moral Definition-Punning is a Virtue that most effectually promotes the End of Good Fellowship, which is Laughing. . . . Physical Definition-Punning is an Art of harmonious Jinggling upon Words, which passing in at the Ears, and falling upon the Diaphragma, excites a titillary Motion in those Parts, and this being convey'd by the Animal Spirits into the Muscles of the Face, raises the Cockles of the Heart.

Mocking as this attitude and Arbuthnot's were, the assumptions they made were standard, so that the styles they assumed were intensified by the mockery. Warburton's edition of Shakespeare, professing to work by Nature rather than by Rules, found natural the same sort of elaboration. It saw in the atmospheric story of a damsel in a cave "the very spirit of Romance-adventure" (note to *Love's Labour's Lost,* Act I, sc. 1), and described Shakespeare, in the scenic image of Pope's preface, as "an ancient Majestick piece of Gothick Architecture, compar'd with a neat Modern building: The latter is more elegant and glaring, but the former is more strong and more solemn."

Thomas Edwards' "Introductory Sonnet" in his mock *Canons of Criticism* condemned excessive flight by its own excessive flight:

> Tongue-doughty Pedant; whose ambitious mind
>   Prompts thee beyond thy native pitch to soar;
>   And, Imp'd with borrow'd plumes of Index-lore,
> Range through the Vast of Science unconfin'd!
>
> Not for Thy wing was such a flight design'd:
>   Know thy own strength, and wise attempt no more;
>   But lowly skim round Error's winding shore,
> In quest of Paradox from Sense refin'd.
>
> Much hast thou written—more than will be read;
>   Then cease from *Shakespear* thy unhallow'd rage;
> Nor by a fond o'erweening pride mis-led,
> Hope fame by injuring the sacred Dead:
>   Know, who would comment well his godlike page,
> Critic, must have a Heart as well as Head.

And the introduction to that greatest of mockeries, "The Dunciad," stressed the very mode in which it worked:

This Poem, as it celebrateth the most grave and antient of things, Chaos, Night and Dulness, so is it of the most grave and antient kind.
... The Fable being thus according to best example one and entire, as contain'd in the proposition; the machinery is a continued chain of Allegories, setting forth the whole power, ministry, and empire of Dulness, extended thro' her subordinate instruments, in all her various operations.

This was the task of the prose of the time, mock or not, dull or not, fictive, argumentative, didactic or not, to set forth the "whole power, ministry, and empire" of its subject. Therefore its effect of range was usually great; the force of feeling was joined with the force of material; a pattern of typical arrangement and rule was accepted; and the metaphor of *empire,* for its scope, political and majestic pomp, was most suitable. If a voyage or tour were to be reported, one followed its visual and technical continuity, with perhaps a touch of interpretive allegory at times. If, on the other hand, the soul's characteristics in all men were to be set forth, one employed a few appurtenances of an imagined journey or pictorial view. The most concrete subjects of observation were spread and generalized, given universal force if only by metaphor. The most abstract ideas of human virtue and relationship were focused and pictorialized by anatomical and scenic image. Most vividly the new novel form took up the task of verbal embodiment by putting the whole story before one's eyes, minimizing aural temporal qualities and stressing the direct participation of the reader, scene by scene. It was all an art of presentation, in the 1740's, presentation to the understanding, the eye, the taste; and, following the psychology of sense, it was for a purpose, to keep alive and vivid in the human consciousness the universal qualities of human nature and of natural order which were felt to be the greatest truths. Art, even prose, was the direct aesthetizing, the embodying, of truth and goodness; so that we see in almost every prose document some attempt at aesthetic translation, some simile of body or scene which will provide an analogy of scientific or moral order.

All trees have a character analogous to that of men. Oaks are in all respects the perfect image of the manly character: In former times I should have said, and in present times I think I am authorized to say, the British one. As a brave man is not suddenly either elated by prosperity, or depressed by adversity, so the oak displays not its verdure on the sun's first approach; nor drops it, on his first departure. Add to this its majestic appearance, the rough grandeur of its bark, and the wide protection of its branches.

A large, branching, aged oak, is perhaps the most venerable of all inanimate objects.

This passage from Shenstone on "Gardening" does not suggest a landscape allegory; it rather, granted the primacy of human character, shows how signs and likenesses of human character may be seen everywhere, the more vividly for their separate shapes. Shenstone's prose, like Wordsworth's later, stresses the natural norm, the classic natural and perspicuous simplicity as opposed to his own modern affectation, witticism, and conceit ("On Writing and Books," viii), the normality of natural objects as opposed to the artifice which brings "night, gothicism, confusion and absolute chaos" ("Gardening"). Everywhere the absence of natural order, the conceit and chaos, troubled the prose writers, so that they vigorously set up abstract norms and concrete instances for voyages, sciences, love affairs, letter writing, politics, punning, and then made a mode of the very excess they disliked, the burlesque, to heighten the absurdity of what they disapproved.

I do not quote the prose writers of the decade with any systematic order, nor do I suggest that their techniques of statement, their stores of vocabulary, make any exact parallel to the procedures of the poetry. Merely the prose seems to me interesting as it reflects the sort of state of mind which enforces abstractions by images, and norms by instances, and man by nature, and reason by sense, and thus contrives a regular texture in poetry and in prose. We may see directly from the constant prose statements of human virtue in natural setting how *man, friend, youth, soul* came to be major terms, how *eye, hand, heart* substantialized them, how *air, day, nature* focused them, how *God* and *heaven* and their own *life, joy, love, power,* gave them feeling. We may see why the major actions were of most general motion and response, in *rising, coming, giving, knowing, hearing, seeing,* and how the qualities were qualities of scope and sensory appreciation in *great, fair, soft, sweet.*

II

A more systematic inquiry into the prose structures and arguments of the decade would concern itself not only with the typical terminology and interest but also with the large philosophical pattern. What was the theoretical concept, what the aesthetic "taste," that made metaphysical poetry bad and neoclassical poetry good? What was the relation between the neoclassicism of Dryden and 1700 and this fuller more scenicized form of the 1740's?—or should we call this preromantic? These are larger problems than can be treated in this technical study; they are difficult, and have been discussed with an extreme range and skill in such books as Monk's *Sublime,* Becker's *Heavenly City,* Lovejoy's *Great Chain of Being.* They have not been closely applied to poetry in any noteworthy way I know of; the critical approach to the eighteenth century has not been so distinguished as the scholarly, nor so lively and immediate as the critical approach to the seventeenth.

For a simple critical interpretation of the eighteenth century I think Samuel Johnson still our best guide. The later critics, from Wordsworth and Arnold and Courthope to Brooks and Eliot, move too much in an atmosphere of toleration. Johnson was sympathetic to most of his major and minor predecessors, and undertook in the *Lives* to say why. He developed, through one description of practice after another, a set of describable principles, and they do, I think, help us see in terms close to the eighteenth century what the eighteenth century thought poetry had been and should be. From his prose, and his prose alone, so far as I know, one could reconstruct the poetry of the 1740's.

First of all, Johnson is negative about what has been. In his introductory and favorite Life of Cowley (*Lives,* 2 vols., New York, 1857, I, xix) he summarizes what was wrong with metaphysical poetry, with a descriptive if not an evaluative justice. Primarily, "The fault of Cowley, and perhaps of all the writers of the metaphysical race, is that of pursuing his thoughts to the last ramifications, by which he loses the grandeur of generality." The odd, the excessive, the actively fictive, the fanciful, the farfetched, the last ramifications are bad for poetry, as they are minute and particular, not grand and general. The values of the universe reside in its large basic central structures, both natural and human; the human, by this value, are natural too, as all are part of a natural and divine order. General human nature, then, the likenesses between men, is important; and general general nature, the likenesses between men and the external world, between objects and feelings, is important too. Poetry, like thought, becomes a matter of generalizing, instancing by normal forms, and similitudinizing. Says Johnson again, "Great thoughts are always general, and consist in positions not limited by exceptions, and in descriptions not descending to minuteness." And, in more poetic image, he says that the metaphysical particulars cannot represent true scenes of life any more than "he who dissects a sunbeam with a prism can exhibit the wide effulgence of a summer noon." Always the metaphysical poets are criticized for being too analytic, eccentric, willful; they sought too much difference and surprise, what they thought rather than what they saw. "In forming descriptions, they looked out, not for images, but for conceits." "To the disproportion and incongruity of Cowley's sentiments must be added the uncertainty and looseness of his measures." "In all the examples it is apparent that whatever is improper or vicious is produced by a voluntary deviation from nature in pursuit of something new and strange."

These principles, these rebellions against the metaphysical, had been set up as early as 1650 in that classic of neoclassicism, the preface to *Gondibert*. There Hobbes and Davenant brought the news straight from France—as Longinus, rediscovered, also would; as Milton did from his books at Horton, and Locke from his scientific meditation,—that great passions and great qualities are alike universal, and great nature is alike their source. This magnitudinous cosmical unity was a "restoration" to English theory of a view it had never fully had; assimilation was by no means instantaneous. But the classical genre theory, main types defined by main shared qualities and effects, was easily shifted to its neoclassical form, the subordination of all other genres to the highest and best, as Hobbes and Davenant, and later Dryden and Dennis, did it when they put their major defining emphasis upon the heroic poem. In such a type, the noblest characters, actions, scenes could come together and, by the theory of correspondence, raise the noblest passions to the noblest effects. How much more rewarding a univeral heroism and good manners than the mixed negatives and complexities of metaphysical relationship, which, while it more humbly preserved two realms, of human and divine, yet too arrogantly allowed the human, participating in the divine, to play with and distort the natural. Neoclassical art would be more modest, more receptive, more truthful, as it would take "invention" to mean not creation but discovery and synthesis of the truth, as it would take human and natural truth to be the same. It would go on being classical in talking about the best of the kind, but would be especially neoclassical in stressing the best kind, and its pervasiveness.

Locke continued Hobbes's idea of Imagination as similitudinous, removing it further from Hobbes's admission of "surprise." The Royal Society asked for quantitative fitness even in language—"so many things almost in an equal number of words" (Sprat, *Hist. Roy. Soc.*, II, 22); by 1690 Sir William Temple was able in his essay on poetry to blend most analysis and discrimination of type into the more general aspects of attitude and feeling. All this progress toward the poetry of feelings, images, and connections, had the philosophical support not only of the moderns, the scientists, but of the ancients, like the revived Longinus. Milton and Dryden read and recommended him, and Dryden on Milton is a direct appropriate reflection of him. "You must consider those sublimities fine and genuine which are pleasing at all times to all men," said Longinus. And what are these sublimities? Not inflated truths on the one hand, nor the frigid overrefinements of rhetoric on the other, but aspects of natural grandeur, great souls, amplifications, harmonies of sound and sense, and images—"you think you actually see of which you are speaking and make your hearers behold it." Different as were Longinus and Locke in their views of art and truth, both felt that art and truth came direct through eye and ear; they were philosophers of sense and of correspondent sense; a great object made for a great thought. And at just this point, Johnson showed, the school of Donne and Cowley failed the truth.

Milton was a better, though an ambiguous, seventeenth-century poet, Johnson thought, just because he did have great ideas and great images. See *Comus:* "A work more truly poetical is rarely found; allusions, images, and descriptive epithets embellish almost every period with lavish decoration." *Paradise Lost* was great, too, because it assembled great powers, truths, and precepts. Its virtue was *amplitude.* On the other hand, the peculiarity of some of the diction, its foreign quality, the absence of rhyme pattern, the originality in harshness, obscurity of the early verse particularly, make Milton a poet not to be imitated though admired. He was full, general, noble, and rich, by neo-classical standards, but many of his words, lines, periods were not classical, following early the earlier English line of Spenser. It would have been hard for Johnson to deal with Spenser, and he did not do so. That was a Life he never wrote. For while he recognized Spenser's mastery of poetry, especially in sound, he was not an admirer of either allegory or odd antiquity, and Spenser meant both to him. Neither the early fashionableness of heroic poetry nor the later fashionableness of mellifluous antiquity gave a mid-road classicist an excuse for understanding Spenser.

Two poetic schools in the seventeenth century presented dangers, then, to the eighteenth: the metaphysical overconceit, the mixed blessings of the native epical. But from a modest middle ground of Waller and of Dryden grew a third group, more general, more smooth, more pictorial, more universal, to be imitated as well as admired. Though not yet "grand" enough, too soft, sweet, and occasional, Waller had polished the English language for common use and saved it from antiquity. He had reformed the metaphysical: "He seldom indeed fetches an amorous sentiment from the depths of science; his thoughts are for the most part easily understood, and his images such as the superficies of nature readily supplies"; Dryden further "refined the language, improved the sentiments, and turned the numbers of English poetry." He found English brick and left it marble. He fostered strength, variety, ratiocination. He was probably Johnson's favorite poet. And we have seen in Dryden's style the regularization of a common vocabulary, the regularization of stress and caesura, the poiseful survey of cosmic and human situation.

By the norm of Johnson's own work, the firmly and regularly moving iambic pentameter, the modest and impressive couplet rhyme, the accepted and positive vocabulary of *gay, generous,* and *great—friend, nature, power, pride, scene, voice, virtue*— the serious negatives of *foe* and *woe* and *vain*—good poetry is emotionally evaluative and personally general and deliberately steady. The controlled power of a Dryden is a more central force than the tricky farfetching, the alien soaring, of a Cowley or a Milton. The metaphysical mode is so verbal and figurative as to be unclear to literal sense and feeling; its abrupt lowness cannot encourage the pleasures and truths of great similarities. The epical mode is best as elevated, worst as harsh and extravagant. The middle, the golden, the neoclassical mode of Dryden abstracts from and neutralizes the metaphoric, tempers the sublime, and binds English and Roman, natural and human truths together in the measure of statement and sound.

In his own eighteenth century Johnson saw these kinds continuing, and criticized accordingly. Pope made a good successor to Dryden. Thomson and others showed some of Milton's vices and virtues, including his originality. Gray and Collins were often odd enough to be condemned as harsh and obscure.

This is what mid-eighteenth century blame sounds like, as applied to Gray's bardic odes: "These odes are marked by glittering accumulations of ungraceful ornaments: they strike, rather than please; the images are magnified by affectation; the language is laboured into harshness. The mind of the writer seems to work with unnatural violence. . . . His art and his struggle are too visible, and there is too little appearance of ease and nature." (*Lives,* ed. Hill, III, 44.) The *Elegy,* on the other hand, may be accepted for its universality: "The *Church-yard* abounds with images which find a mirrour in every mind, and with sentiments to which every bosom returns an echo." But Collins had no such saving grace. He, even more than Gray, stressed the fictive, the fanciful, past the bounds of nature; he used obsolete words and uncommon orders; "the grandeur of wildness and the novelty of extravagance were always desired by him, but were not always attained"; "and perhaps, while he was intent upon description, he did not sufficiently cultivate sentiment." Edward Young bore some of the same judgment of oddity.

James Thomson is more to be favored, for his originality, like though different from Milton's, his poetic eye, smooth numbers, luxuriant diction. "The poet leads us through the appearances of things as they are successively varied by the vicissitudes of the year, and imparts to us so much of his own enthusiasm that our thoughts expand with his imagery and kindle with his sentiments" (III, 299). Here is the double richness of the natural: the scenes, the feelings, in full correspondence. Nature provides the appearances of things, man responds with fitting feelings, the poet guides and glorifies the whole. The difference between Thomson and Collins is in a way a difference of literalness, and this meant much to Johnson. The literal progression of the Seasons kept nature before us in clearest form and smoothest numbers. Fictions, phantoms, allegories, like seventeenth-century wit, troubled him as too much created, not enough discovered in the natural world.

He makes this very distinction in discussing Pope and defending the fictive sylphs and gnomes of the *Rape of the Lock,* because they are an active and useful machinery, whereas allegorical persons as normally used "may produce effects, but cannot conduct actions; when the phantom is put in motion, it dissolves; thus Discord may raise a mutiny, but Discord cannot conduct a march or besiege a town" (III, 233). Johnson's clarification is a good one for his time; the production of effects far overweighed the conducting of actions in the usual poetry, and allegorizing may have been a cause; but it makes a further descriptive point for him, that as a whole the supernatural should not be welcomed any more than the metaphysical or the religious by poetry. His essay on Watts specifically excludes the divine; his comment on Pope's *Essay on Man,* even the new metaphysical.

Most of what he praises in Pope is the natural. "Of his intellectual character the constituent and fundamental principle was Good Sense, a prompt and intuitive perception of consonance and propriety" (III, 216), plus a genius which "collects, combines, amplifies, and animates." "The *Eloisa* is one of the most happy productions of human wit.... The heart naturally loves truth.... So new and so affecting is their story that it supersedes invention, and imagination ranges at full liberty without straggling into scenes of fable." (III, 235.) This imagination of Pope's, it must be remembered, is that quality of genius which impresses the forms of nature and feeling on the mind; it need not create new trains of events like Invention, nor be carefully selective like Judgment, nor provide elegant expression like the Colours of Language, all of which are the other components of genius (p. 247); Imagination is the most receptive, the most wisely passive of the four, and records a sort of deeply emotional nature which Wordsworth later will reassert.

The natural, too, must be ennobling. Johnson finds the *Essay on Criticism* so, especially the comparison of the student to the traveler in the Alps; one of the best similes in the language: "A simile, to be perfect, must both illustrate and ennoble, the subject; must shew it to the understanding in a clearer view, and display it to the fancy with greater dignity: but either of these qualities may be sufficient to recommend it" (III, 229). The very vocabulary must be dignified, except in the correctives of satire, and there Pope sometimes lets himself fall too low; and the combinations of noun and epithet Johnson especially remarks, admitting now and then in Pope "an epithet rather commodious than important," but agreeing with Watts that "there is scarcely a happy combination of words or a phrase poetically elegant in the English language which Pope has not inserted into his version of Homer."

Essentially there is the contrast with Dryden: "If the flights of Dryden therefore are higher, Pope continues longer on the wing. If of Dryden's fire the blaze is brighter, of Pope's the heat is more regular and constant. Dryden often surpasses expectation, and Pope never falls below it. Dryden is read with frequent astonishment, and Pope with perpetual delight." (III, 223.) The adverbs and adjectives of degree in this comparison make Pope a model of steady and lasting practice.

The nouns which set up the poetic standard in this prose, *flight, fire, height,* and *delight,* summarize too the theory by which neoclassic practice functioned. The *delight* is the central effect, long emphasized by all critics, but in the eighteenth century elaborated in its psychological ramifications. The *flight, fire,* and *height* are its natural parallels, its corresponding stimuli from the outer world. The senses of loftiness, of soaring, of warmth and flame, are senses which lift and irradiate the body and thus the soul; they are good and beautiful senses as they correspond with natural goods, moving toward the heights of heaven, and they please, since pleasure makes a natural co-operation with universal goodness. Whether these natural-human-divine connections be the rather fixed ones of Hobbes, the more casual and habitual ones of Locke and Hartley and Addison, the more artistic one of Longinus, they provide a firm basis for the central critical thought and poetic vocabulary of the eighteenth century, by which man as one of the great works of God speaks as he feels in universal value-terms of height and force, of power and order.

If Johnson is a good classical critic, his contemporaries, or at least his distinguished immediate predecessors, should find a center of agreement with him, and indeed it seems clear that they have been doing so ever since 1650. Dryden, though he wrote no full descriptions of English poets in the Johnsonian fashion, though he devoted much debate to the difficulties of the language, and of heroic and satiric structures, nevertheless, in passing sentences of appraisal wrote with standards not un-Johnsonian. In the "Essay on Translation," 1685, he wrote of

Virgil: "He is everywhere above conceits of epigrammatic wit, and gross hyperboles: he maintains majesty in the midst of plainness; he shines, but glares not; and is stately without ambition." Of Horace's odes: "There is nothing so delicately turned in all the Roman language. There appears in every part of his diction, or (to speak English) in all his expression, a kind of noble and bold purity." Of Milton: "Cannot I admire the height of his invention, and the strength of his expression, without defending his antiquated words, and the perpetual harshness of their sound?"

Worse than antiquity and harshness was lack of a proper seriousness in the greatest verse. Turns of words are to be shunned in strong passion, "because passions are serious, and will admit no playing," says the Preface to the *Fables*. How natural, then, that John Dennis could write in 1692, as Johnson would years later, "In short, no sort of imagery ever can be the Language of Grief" (*Works*, ed. Hooker, I, 2), when imagery is taken in the sense of elaborated figure. "There is nothing in Nature that is great and beautiful, without Rule and Order; and the more Rule and Order, and Harmony, we find in the Objects that strike our Senses, the more worthy and Noble we esteem them" (I, 202). "There is certainly no Subject so great as the Power of God, and both Homer and Virgil have handled it to Admiration" (I, 267). "I esteemed Dryden," said Dennis, "for the solidity of his Thought, for the Spring, the Warmth, and the beautiful Turn of it; for the Power and Variety, and Fulness of his Harmony; for the Purity, the Perspicuity, the Energy of his Expression" (I, 400).

We recognize a vocabulary of praise, a feeling of value, which extends through the century, and which has carried its cues from Dryden on to Johnson. Nature, order, harmony, nobility are the framing terms, and fire, energy, power, the enforcements. The plenitude and vigor of natural order are important. So such reigning concepts as Lovejoy's "great chain of being" are articulated in the details of poetic selection. For such terms as *nature* and *power* are the very ones which distinguish eighteenth-century major vocabulary from seventeenth, and their characteristic of abstract force is the very characteristic of Dryden's developing verse, while their sensory glorification in *high, bright, heaven, world, stand,* is characteristic of Waller's and Milton's. Milton and Dryden were opposed though allied in the building up of the cosmic classical frame.

Dryden debated with himself and his public the problem of outreaching nobility, finding, as his contemporaries did, support in classical sources for the rich, dignified, majestic, and heroic. He noted the strength of Homer, sweetness of Ovid, melody and nobility of Virgil, even the serious passions and images of Spenser, Milton, Waller—"our lineal descents and clans," as he praised them in the Preface to the *Fables,*—in preference to the rough and undignified poetizing of older wits like Donne and Cowley, with their conceits, epigrams, hyperbole, their lack of measure.

Dennis, agreeing with him on the beauty of the classics, the primacy of visual and emotional powers, added a new magnitude to the heroic, the religious. He condemned the mixed "Rhyming Heroick Fustian" of the 1660's, in his essay on *Arthur* (1696), in favor of the great natural works of God as they are visible to the human eye, moving, through their magnificent natural order, the moral order of man. So the cosmology of Milton, the works and days of Sylvester, came into their own in Dennis' "Reformation of Modern Poetry" in 1701. And the preparation of their justification had long been readied by Longinus, as he set up the art of the sublime against the art of rhetoric—qualities rather than species, parts rather than wholes, genius rather than skill, sensation rather than argument, transport rather than logic,—all accepted by a universal taste, the magnitude of soul the shadow of the magnitude of nature, as a "great style is the shadow of a great soul." Here from its long tradition comes to life, to enforce a neoclassical unity of truth in man, a neo-Platonic unity of truth in nature, so enthusiastically, with such enthusiastic reception, that the term *truth* itself gives way to the term *nature* in neoclassical consciousness.[1]

By 1713, Parnell's "Essay on the Different Styles of Poetry" was satirizing four ways in which injustice was poetically done to the natural in the opening decade of the century. The ways will be recognized as belatedly metaphysical. The first was verbal—puns and acrostics. The second Parnell called frigid—dry and sententious. The third was low—petty, pastorally metaphorical. The fourth was extravagant—full of comets, gods, machines, and glare. Finally, above all these realms of false poetry,

> Stands the great palace of the Bright and Fine,
> Where fair ideas in full glory shine; ...
>
> And just Proportion all, and great Design,
> And lively Colours, and an Air divine....
>
> Whence images, in charming numbers set,
> A sort of likeness in the soul beget, ...

It is this likeness, suiting idea, design, image, soul at once, that made eighteenth-century poetry have sense for eighteenth-century philosophy, creating a world reasonable yet visible, ideal yet sensational, universal yet measured, at once sublime and beautiful.

Pope, too, satirized the verbal, frigid, extravagant, low. His moderate classical spirit, touched by the Miltonic sublime, would not tolerate much more of extremes than a noble sort of passion

---

[1] Basil Willey, *The Eighteenth Century Background*, p. v. Willey notes also that "Cogito ergo sum" became "Je sens donc je suis." See also Olson's introduction to Longinus.

would allow. In poetic usage he was moderate, as we have seen, at least in relation to his era as he left it; in relation to Dryden, he seems full to overflowing with the Miltonic, the epithetical, the harmonically various, the sensory. His *Eloisa* is as good a rich eighteenth-century poem as one can find. His satire of the exaggerations of sublimity and metaphysicality in *Peri Bathous, the Art of Sinking in Poetry* is satire, then, which comes from the verge of understanding and use as well as from distaste.

Wherefore considering with no small grief, how many promising geniuses of this age are wandering (as I may say) in the dark without a guide, I have undertaken this arduous but necessary task, to lead them as it were by the hand, and step by step, the gentle down-hill way to the bathos; the bottom, the end, the central point, the *non plus ultra,* of true modern poesy! (Chap. i)

The sublime of nature is the sky, the sun, moon, stars, etc. The profund of nature is gold, pearls, precious stones, and the treasures of the deep, which are inestimable as unknown. But all that lies between these, as corn, flower, fruits, animals, and things for the meer use of man, are of mean price, and so common as not to be greatly esteemed by the curious. It being certain that any thing, of which we know the true use, cannot be invaluable: which affords a solution, why common sense hath either been totally despised, or held in small repute by the greatest modern critics and authors. (Chap. iv)

Nothing seemed more plain to our great authors than that the world had long been weary of natural things....

He ought therefore to render himself master of this happy and anti-natural way of thinking to such a degree, as to be able, on the appearance of any object, to furnish his imagination with ideas infinitely below it. And his eyes should be like unto the wrong end of a perspective glass, by which all the objects of nature are lessened.

For example: when a true genius looks upon the sky, he immediately catches the idea of a piece of blue lustring, or a child's mantle. (Chap. v)

Many painters, who could never hit a nose or an eye, have with felicity copied a small-pox, or been admirable at a toad or a red-herring. (Chap. vi)

It may be expected, that, like other critics, I should next speak of the passions: but as the main end and principal effect of the Bathos is to produce tranquillity of mind, (and sure it is a better design to promote

sleep than madness) we have little to say on this subject. (Chap. ix)
... we shall content ourselves to range the principal [figures], which
most powerfully contribute to the Bathos, under three classes.

    I. The Variegating, Confounding, or Reversing Tropes and
      Figures.
    II. The Magnifying; and
    III. The Diminishing. (Chap. x)

A genuine writer of the Profund will take care never to magnify any
object without clouding it at the same time: his thought will appear in
a true mist, and very unlike what is in nature. It must always be remembered that darkness is an essential quality of the Profund, or, if
there chance be a glimmering, it must be as Milton expresses it,

       No light, but rather darkness visible.   (Chap. xi)

The virtues of great men, like those of plants, are inherent in them,
whether they are exerted or not; and the more strongly inherent, the
less they are exerted; as a man is the more rich, the less he spends. ...

    As to what are commonly called the colours of *honourable* and *dis-
honourable,* they are various in different countries: in this they are
blue, green, and red. [Orders of Garter, Bath, and Thistle.] (Chap. xiv)

As these comments are characteristic of "The Art of Sinking,"
so they are indirectly of the "Arts of Poetry" of the era. They
reflect by exaggeration the exaggerations already in the verse and
the judgment. They ask, by implication, for the natural, the
human, the visual, the passionate, the analogical, the clear, the
representative. They satirize not only the false extremes of all
these but even more their lack, in artificialities of natural reference too far from the human, in minor, ugly, unpleasant detail,
in a dullness of temper for which Pope uses Wordsworth's later
word "tranquillity," in elaborate metaphors and the whole
Renaissance system of classifying metaphors—the Vulgar, the In-
fantine, the Inane, taking their place in an older terminology,—
in the obscure and even the literal dark, and in symbolic expression of the "inherent."

It is surprising that even this satire maintains a sort of classic
balance: it mocks what is to come as well as what has been. Most
of the faults which Pope finds, in the especial objects of his attack,

come from an older seventeenth-century tradition of metaphoric expression. But some are to be most characteristically nineteenth-century—the stars, the deep, the toad, the child's mantle, the tranquillity, the mist and cloud, the symbolic colors. Pope is the better definable, then, and the better defines his kind, as it lies between two seemingly absurd extremes: the normal, between the witty and the wild.

Pope's sensitivity to the metaphor of height and depth, his desire both to soar and to keep a middle way, and his treatment of the problem in satire are all characteristic of the time. The satirist is not just the rationalist, but the passionate man excessively aware of extremes and troubled by them. Without the metaphysical solution of microcosm in macrocosm, the neoclassical man had to try to blend, or moderate, or check extremes, whether of geography or of passion. Then the uncheckable extremes, the resistant vices, poverties, extravagances, or mere things, he had to call absurd. In an age when the heroic, the general, the sublime were all possible and even normal, the satiric with its balancing vices and particularities and lownesses made life tolerable. In an age which canceled the double view of metaphysics, the double view became humorous, a mock, and that was satire. *Absalom* and the *Dunciad* preserved the ugly detail of life for poetry and provided a major transition between *microcosm* and *empire*.

The empire early was Roman, for Dryden and for Pope; it was still Roman for Johnson: Virgilian in height and nobility, Horatian in moderation, Juvenalian in the low depths where absurdities and crudities abounded. The empire was classical, then, in more ways than one: classical in its sense that the work of the best models corresponded to and heightened the work of nature, classical in its sense of kinds and levels, classical with its special emphasis on the best kind, the noble level, the cosmic and physiographic altitudinous level as it corresponded to and heightened human feelings, classical as it recognized these correspondences by reason and mocked their discrepancies by satire. Pope and Johnson, and in part Mrs. Montagu, Gray, Akenside, Young, represent this empire.

But further, its various levels were being smoothed away, so that even the mildest recognitions of satire seemed too rough to be first-rate, and Joseph Warton's ranking of poets in mid-century brought both height and depth inward to the feelings where both should be taken seriously, even as extreme, without mockery. A Greek classicism, less imperial, allowed for such a move, as the "genius" and "fire" of Homer, for whom even Pope was major speaker, burned from within and blurred the outlines of their own epic heroism. Pindaric odes and Theocritean lays made further allowance for soaring and spreading without boundary, and provided the Miltonic with respectable ancient models. Therefore the main part of poetry in the 1740's was smoother than Roman classicism would make for, than satire would permit, and the *Bathous* of Pope was an extreme which was already becoming less extreme, already less humorous and more blended in the new metaphysical sort, in Gray and Collins.

Nevertheless, the renewed acceptance of depths and obscurities did not make, as *Peri Bathous* had suggested, for a new metaphysical poetry of wit. Wit did not return to duality and incongruity. It kept and extended its genteel Lockean form (*Hum. Und.*, II, xi, 2), "lying most in the assemblage of ideas, and putting those together with quickness and variety, wherein can be found any resemblance or congruity, thereby to make up pleasant pictures, and agreeable visions of the fancy." Wit, as for Pope, became agreeingly normal rather than surprisingly sharp. In fact, pleasant uniformity was so important in mid-century[2] that if a

---

[2] See the good article by Alex Aronson, "Eighteenth-Century Semantics of Wit," *Etc.*, V, 182–190. See also interesting work in F. L. Huntley, "Dryden's Discovery of Boileau," *MP*, XLV, 112–117; Scott Elledge, "English Criticisms of Generality and Particularity,"

man insisted on calling it the opposite of witty, then Dullness was to be praised, as in the *Gentleman's Magazine* in 1737: "It is no small Recommendation of Dullness that it is a Thing of a uniform, fix'd Nature; not subject to Uncertainty and Change; not whimsical and fantastical; not ebbing and flowing; not rising and setting; not turning with every wind and tossed and blown about like a feather." Gradually *wisdom,* as propriety (*Gent. Mag.,* 1738, VIII, 478), and *genius,* as the higher power of imagination, came to do some of the serious work of the much worked and now prim *wit,* so that by 1753 in the *Gentleman's Magazine* (XXIII, 330), for example, *genius* has that old faculty of searching for likeness at great height. It is *"a tall faculty of the intellect* (if I may be pardoned the expression) which looks around on every side, finds out all that has any native relation to the object we contemplate, perceives relations which are not obvious to others, and from their connections can infer certain truths and distant conclusions." This genius or wit of poetry stands at an eminence, looks around, and makes or rather finds native connections. Though perhaps newly exploratory, it is still a receptive and a primarily visual faculty.

One would expect, then, that the old handbooks of poetry would have gone out of date, that instead of the long lists of rhetorical figures, the definitions of types, the aphorisms of poetic action, there would be new handbooks of images. And so there were. The dicta of Bacon or Ben Jonson, even the "copiousness" of the commonplace books, the systems of Wilson or Puttenham, could not do for an eighteenth-century genius any more than for Spenser or Milton what a sense of classical and divine imagery could do. The scattered cries in the seventeenth century of poets like Crashaw and orators like Taylor, for the high, serious, and

---

PMLA, LXII, 147–183; Alfred Aldridge, "Akenside and the Hierarchy of Beauty," *MLQ,* March, 1947; A. R. Humphreys, "The Friend of Mankind, 1700–1760," *RES* (July, 1948), pp. 203–219; and Spence, *Anecdotes,* p. 6.

angelic, were more in the right direction. That distinction between two modes which we saw to be so clear in the 1640's, between what Sir Thomas Browne called the familiar philosophical and the divine sublime, grew heavy-sided toward the sublime. The philosophical as human, logical, rhetorical, relational, gave way to the divine as sensed, felt, universal, surveyable, sympathetic. Early in the 1670's by Poole, and again in 1703 by Bysshe,[8] and again in 1718 by Gildon, along with numerous others, appeared the new handbooks of verse which would teach the new manners to the next whole century.

Bysshe is representative as he provides his readers, who as they are geniuses cannot really be taught, but who as they are mortal can be helped now and then, with three major aids to the memory: Epithets and Synonyms, Sentiments, and Rhymes. These are just the special features of the poetry as we have seen it. The epithet reigns, and it reigns not only as selectively descriptive and generally qualitative, but also as "numerous" in syllabic number proper for a space in the line. Gildon, some years later, maintains this same emphasis. Once he had defended Cowley and Waller as not farfetched and glittering but rather natural, tender, and elevating; now he abandons Cowley for Spenser and formulizes the natural into rules—rules in general and for special types, supported by quotation from Locke, Milton, Dennis, and by a vast array of "Descriptions, Similes, Allusions." Gildon says he is stronger on image and design than Bysshe, but certainly both are strong on both; their whole poetic assumption involves the fitting color and sound of contexts rather than the earlier sort of listing as on a "bead-roll," as Bysshe remarks, where the items isolated "appear bald, insipid, uncouth, and offensive both to the Eye and Ear." The contexts are the very sensory contexts of the 1740's; "for," says Bysshe, "what are Epithets, but Adjectives that

[8] See the excellent recent work on Bysshe by A. Dwight Culler, "Edward Bysshe and the Poets' Handbooks," *PMLA*, LXIII (September, 1948), 858–886.

denote and express the Qualities of the Substantives to which they are joind, as *Purple, Rosy, Smiling, Dewy,* Morning: *Dim, Gloomy, Silent,* Night. What Synonymas, but words of a like Signification as *Fear, Dread, Terrour, Consternation, Affright, Dismay,* &. Are they not then naturally to be sought for in the Descriptions of Persons and Things? And can we not better judge by a piece of Painting, how beautifully Colours may be dispos'd; than by seeing the same several Colours scatter'd without Design on a Table?" Bysshe does not wish to be, then, as arbitrary as he sounds when he begins, ". . . for the sake of a Syllable or two, more or less, to give a verse its true Measure, (a man may) be at a stand for Epithets and Synonymas." But he wishes verse of eight or ten syllables, avoiding alliteration, and concordance of vowels, and final adjectives; and he revises such lines as Cowley's "None think Rewards render'd Worthy their Worth" to "None think Rewards are equal to their Worth," wherein the feet are more neatly iambic and the verbal play of wit or turn on *worthy–worth* is eliminated.

What Bysshe tried to jog his geniuses to remember was, in the main, the importance of the full smooth line, the full smooth sentiment. Metrically he aided them by examples of well-measured lines and by a rhyming dictionary. Thoughtfully he aided them by his prized "contexts," his fine thoughts listed under their main abstractions and representing, as the years went by in new editions, less and less of Cowley, more and more of Spenser, always much of Milton. Most specifically he aided them by his discussion of an emphasis on those fillers the epithet and the synonym, which served so easily to cushion substantially the gaps in either meter or sentence and thus to fulfill the poem. Bysshe was for Truth. He wanted poetry to speak Truth. He knew that the True was the Natural, and he knew that the bad, the ugly, the obscene, the satirical were not True. Therefore, the more goodness, beauty, scene, straight description and feeling in the poem the better, and his handbook made its notations to that end. What he called Rules he considered to be descriptive, rather than prescriptive; he simply reminded people how to get the best effects by showing them what Spenser had done with the same subjects. In a world of general truth a gentle reminder may well be as strong as law. Mornings are, by general truth, Purple, Rosy, Smiling, Dewy, while Nights are Dim, Gloomy, Silent; and the poet had best just not forget these facts, these beauties.

A number of good recent works have shown us the strong literary influences on such thinking.[4] Especially Earl Wasserman's *Elizabethan Poetry in the 18th Century* has organized the details of usage, showing what qualities of earlier verse flourished or were altered. Eighteenth-century editions of such poets as Quarles, Fairfax, Drayton, all, it will be noted, poets of the full line before its fullest day, made hundreds of unnoted revisions which moved in the direction a Bysshe would have approved. Meter and syntax were regularized, diction and grammar were modernized, vulgarities and affectations were modified, and the repeated adjective *dear* was given synonyms, so as to function less as verbal turn, more as perception. In discussing Spenser's power, Wasserman makes clear, as Cory does also, its sweetness and visibility. Hughes's edition in 1715 called embellishments of description the most striking part of poetry. Aaron Hill praised Spenser because he presents "the very substance of the Things he thought of." The very borrowing from Spenser was first his picture-making epithets. He became, then, along with Milton, the master of the 1740's, because of his rich substance, his visual force, his full line. Despite the difficulties of his allegory and his stanza for poets who wanted to be clear and direct couplet makers, he prevailed finally over the short-coat school of Jonson, by his very

---

[4] Herbert E. Cory, *The Critics of Edmund Spenser;* Raymond D. Havens, *The Influence of Milton on English Poetry;* Ants Oras, *Milton's Editors and Commentators from Hume to Todd, 1695–1801,* and such good works on individuals as Tillotson's *Pope* and McKillop's *Background of Thomson's "Seasons."*

presentation of *things* and noble thoughts, so that Warton was able to explain what he felt to be the poetic decline in the metaphysical period after Spenser by the fact that "poets began now to be more attentive to words, than things and objects; and a manner of expressing a thought prettily, was more regarded than that of conceiving one nobly."[5] The truth of things is nobler than the truth of art.

Most impressive evidence for this evaluation is the fact that in the 1740's, with continuing force strongest again in the 1780's and 1790's, Spenser served as a favorite model for the verse in the "very erudite and deadly commemorative volumes" at the universities.[6] His was recognized as the way to write poetry. When Cory suggests (p. 108) that "the earliest exponents of what they vaguely termed Gothic or romantic were often not strong men with a new faith, but decadents weary of the old," he emphasizes the minor rebellions of the Wartons, Hurd, and Beattie; but also I think he might emphasize the continuity of their faith, mild though it was, as it reasserted a vivid and definable older value, a sense of the fictive, bright and new.

Moreover, the common scholarly descriptions of eighteenth-century thought and practice fit together to help enforce and explain this reassertion of the Spenserian-Miltonic kind as it participated in the philosophy of the era. Myra Reynolds' early statement of stages between Waller and Wordsworth in the poetic view of nature itself accepts the eighteenth-century notion of the "view of nature"; and its three aspects: nature as storehouse of similitudes, nature as detailed external beauty, nature as cosmic sense of unity, reveal not only the sequence of thought but also its center in descriptive similitude: the visible harmony of *things*. Hussey, Durling, Deane, Aubin, and others make clear the interconnections, the further harmonies, between Virgilian

---

[5] Quoted by Wasserman, p. 219.

[6] Wasserman, p. 149. Note Havens, p. 27, for Miltonic university exercises also, and many *Gentleman's Magazine* papers in 1730's and 1740's.

description and Claudian landscape painting, the precise observation, the generalized form, which Reynolds was to lecture on and Wordsworth was in part to accept. Wordsworth accepted Dyer's imagination as best since Milton, and, as Hussey has shown (p. 19), "Thomson and Dyer enlarged poetic landscape by describing what the painters had borrowed from earlier poets," as Claude did from Virgil. Throughout the era, from Du Fresnoy's *De Arte Graphica* to Spence's *Polymetis,* the books on picturing, the assumptions of visual art as general truth, prevailed.

They prevailed because they did not appear alone. They worked in accord with the "New Science," as Carson Duncan has suggested; they pictured forth the realities of material which lay at the other end of microscope and telescope; they provided stimuli for the circulation of sensations and feelings with the blood. It is surprising to think that the writings of Hobbes would have led away from, rather than toward, the study of the manners of men which he specifically recommended; but, for one reason, men studied by science seemed to be more subjects of satire than heroes of noble poems, and, for another, as the great central question of science, the Royal Society's science, was *cause,* men were led out from themselves, into the natural world as it acted upon them. They were concerned by the relation between the sight of a storm and their own fear, the sight of a pleasant field and their own pleasure. They felt that knowledge lay, as John Locke said, in *connections;* that reason found out and followed connections, that imagination discerned and pictured connections, in the special sense of noble and universal similarities, so that a sober revelation could in that sense bring the same result as the new wit, the assembling of ideas by correspondences between man and nature. "Extended views a narrow mind extend," as Kenneth MacLean in his book on Locke justly quotes from *Night Thoughts* (IX, 138). This is the sort of direct effect, the one-to-one correspondence, which makes similarity so important to the era, and error so hard to handle. Error is extravagance, wide-wandering farfetchedness; it is off the beam. It is fitting, on the other hand, to reach far, if not to fetch far, because reaching, looking to countryside, mountain, night sky, classical Rome, Olympus, Timbuctoo, still kept the reacher in a central position at home; kept the poet at the mean, and let the exhorted Muse do the necessary errands.

MacLean sets the highest popularity of Locke from 1725 to 1765, when the Miltonic reach was at its height, and when, as Samuel Monk says, the Longinus cult was also at its height, about 1740. In 1749, Pope was dead, and Johnson not yet established. "In poetry, at least," writes Eleanor Sickels in her *Gloomy Egoist,* "the 1750's were a moment of pause. The neoclassic tradition was moribund, the true romantic tradition was unborn, or, at most, still in unconscious infancy, and the precarious balance of disparate emotional and intellectual elements ... was apparently capable for the moment of producing nothing more." (P. 6.) But the era of Locke and Longinus does not seem to me to call for such negative description. It was an era, rather, of a rich, full poetizing, whether that should be called classic or romantic, substantial with sense impression and with the feelings derived therefrom.

For by feelings the scenes of nature got back to man, and by feelings they were expanded and interpreted. Locke, Shaftesbury, Wesley, Hartley, the novels, all provided what John Draper in his *Funeral Elegy and the Rise of English Romanticism* calls "a diction and metaphor of emotions" (p. 306). Dennis and Addison subordinated the classical genres to emotions; Addison's and Akenside's *Pleasures of Imagination* built systems of aesthetics upon emotional reactions to qualities in space, so that the "beautiful" and the "sublime" themselves became terms definable both by feelings like "calm" and qualities like "vast"; and this whole double structure rested easily on Locke's major principle (*Hum.*

Und., II, i, 2) : "Our observation, employed either about external sensible objects, or about the internal operations of our minds, perceived and reflected on by ourselves, is that which supplies our understanding with all the materials of thinking. These two are the fountains of knowledge, from whence all the ideas we have, or can naturally have, do spring."

From such thought springs also the *ode,* the meditative and rhapsodic celebration of a noble universe. The ode is the form of the 1740's, in measured coupleted meditation or in the "romantic" stanza 8*a* 8*a* 6*b* 8*c* 8*c* 6*b.* The presence of the stanza itself is a tribute more to Spenser's regular stanzas than to the irregular ones of seventeenth-century odes; the abstract forces of nature marshal themselves here in patterns rounded and sustained. Both Yost on the poetry of the *Gentleman's Magazine* and Havens on the Dodsley *Miscellanies* stress the odelike invocations and personifications of the 1740's, the ceremony rather than moral sharpness, the emotional celebration, the full poetic tone in popular publication. And W. L. Renwick in his notes on some lesser poets of the century (*Essays to David Nichol Smith*) remarks in the Dodsley collection of 1748 especially the lively presence, by imitation and assimilation, of Horace, Virgil, Spenser, Milton, in poet after poet who "assumed the value of a pictorial sense." From the pictorial ode-poem comes not only the *friend, maid, youth,* the *hand* and *head* of portrayed figure, but the *soft air, nature, scene* of surroundings, and the *gay, happy, beauty, joy, power, virtue,* of response.[7] There is no *time* here, or *death* or *pain,* or even *good,* but rather, in the special major terms of the poetry, the idea of the philosophy, the collaboration of man with nature in a magnificent order of sights and feelings.

The change between seventeenth- and eighteenth-century theory and practice was phrased as neatly as one could ask by Addi-

---

[7] There are many pleasant articles on these poetic phenomena in the eighteenth century; for example, H. O. White's on Purney's "Gloom" and B. H. Bronson's on Personification.

son in his essay on "True and False Wit." He said that "a bosom white as snow" was a true simile; "a bosom cold as snow," false. Here is the distinction between two great poetries finely simplified if oversimplified. Seventeenth-century metaphysical or "false" wit made a conceptual rather than a sensual comparison. The bosom was not literally cold to touch; it represented coldness of feeling, of attitude. Further, the concept was a relational one; the simile suggested not a sense, not even merely an abstract quality of coldness, but a relationship between two persons, a coldness toward. Therefore the figure was a complex one, situational, personal in its abstraction, immediate though conceptual, and in that sense arbitrary, created, farfetched, not simply received from observation. This was the wit which forced similarity from difference; the bosom could not "really," by a sense of the literal experienced coldness of snow, be cold as snow. On the other hand, the bosom white as snow could be literally, pleasantly, and appreciatively observed. The observation was not only more true to the facts of bodies and of snows; it was more positive and delightful, and thus more good and poetic. *White,* calling upon sight, was also more vivid than *cold,* calling upon touch; there was more psychological power in it. So in all ways the bosom white as snow was an exact example of the truth of nature and its correspondence to truth and beauty as they could be set forth in art. The central importance of bodily beauty could be enhanced, for the sake of pleasure and understanding, by natural, external beauty, which in certain important qualities naturally corresponded. In that one world the sciences worked together. Anatomy, meteorology, and the psychology of receptive sight were, in the art of the bosom white as snow, in complete coöperation, and the reader like the poet felt the better for it.

III. POETRY OF THE 1840's

By the 1840's it was the spirit within the breast that guided, with all its mysteries, silences, hints, and hesitations, the course of poetic construction. Its powers of discernment being delicate, it dealt with an increasingly minute world, and found spirit everywhere, in flower as well as field, in child as well as man. It encouraged scrupulous observation and detailed narration because significance was omnipresent. As more and more natural objects received more and more human feeling, and sponsored more, the object came to imply the feeling, the thoughts too deep for tears. In the earlier century, readers had rejected the literal connections which Wordsworth made as too minute and personal; now they could accept even Coleridge's "strong underimport."

Therefore, the fullness of poetic statement lessened. "Ballads" and "Songs" came back into titles. In form, lines shortened and varied, adding odd short syllables, hesitating over dactyls and anapests, leaving a breath where a word might have been. Statements left off in mid-air, did not always draw conclusions, or by their downright literal intensity indicated that even more was being said. The major vocabulary gave up *nature* and *power* for *light, night,* and *spirit.* Adjectives declined. Adjectival poets like Lowell, Tupper, Hemans, Wordsworth wrote the more accustomed poetry of the day, but not the most exciting; their epitheting seemed reactionary. Emerson, Clough, and the Brownings were new, and their likeness to Landor indicates a new sort of reserve. For the twentieth century such reserve may not be enough; there may still be too much cosmos in the poetry, and too much obvious feeling. But at least the feeling was being drawn inward, the cosmos shaded and implied. The pervasion of light, and passive verbs, distinguish the vocabulary of the majority, and familial affections the minority. In form and pro-

portion and terminology, as the tables following show,[1] the most
curious of individual poets come to much agreement about poetry
as they feel it, an art of infinite suggestion from the realm of
earthly atmosphere and inward affection.

We may see how the tables summarize these characteristics.
The representative works in table 1 show us the great poetic
activity at the beginning of the decade, the variety in proportioning all through the decade, the slight falling of epitheting
and narrative structures toward the end. Most especially, we
note in very few works the epitheting or adjectival emphasis
of the preceding century, and we note in major sound and sentence patterns a shortening of line, a shift to stanzaic organization, and a narrative, "objective," statement, combined with
lyrical exclamation.

The grouping of works based on proportion, in table 1, shows
the adjectival and substantival moderation of the majority, and
even the dominance of verbs over adjectives in many. Landor,
Emerson, the Brownings, and even Macaulay, with his narrative
objectivity, are strong for predicative action. Clough, Arnold,
Poe, Hawker, Bryant, and Longfellow write an easily balanced
style, with a moderation of classical poise. Hood and Tennyson
not only use more adjectives but stress them especially in proportion, their nouns and verbs are so exceptionally scant. In
Campbell, Wordsworth, Lowell, and their associates we see
a stronger substantiality, an emphasis closer to that of their
eighteenth-century predecessors; in Tupper, finally a singularity
of heavy stresses on all forms, especially nouns, which is oc-
casioned not merely by his long line but by his great weight
of material.

Compared with the corresponding table 1 for the 1740's, this
table shows that in the main the poetry of the 1840's functions
at a different level of usage. Gray, Young, Johnson, Pope, the

---

[1] See note 1 to chap. i for technical detail.

1840's: TABLE 1

THE POEMS IN ORDER OF ADJECTIVAL EMPHASIS*

Texts: First 1,000 lines (with exceptions noted)	Form	Proportion in average 10 lines		
		Adj.	Noun	Verb
Landor, Walter Savage. *Hellenics*, 1847. First 9 (London, 1847, compl.)	5' b. v. Narr., dram.	8	16	12
Emerson, Ralph Waldo. *Poems*, 1847. "Sphinx" to "Woodnotes I" (Boston, 1899)	4' stanzas Medit.	7	15	8
Macaulay, Thomas B. *Lays of Ancient Rome*, London, 1842. (Rev., 1848)	4'–3' st. Narr.	7	15	7
Browning, Robert. "Pippa," 500 lines. "Dramatic Lyrics" to "Laboratory," 500 lines. 1841 ff. *Works* (Boston, 1887)	5' st. Exclamatory	8	16	12
(Browning), Elizabeth Barrett. "Romaunt of the Page," Sonnets, "Rosary," III, 8, 1844. *Poetical Works* (New York, Macmillan, 1903)	4' st. Lyr., narr.	8	16	10
Clough, Arthur. *Ambarvalia*, 1849 (London, Chapman & Hall, 1849)	4' st. Lyr.	9	13	9
Arnold, Matthew. *The Strayed Reveller*, 1849. (Oxford ed., 1922)	5' st. Addr., lyr.	9	15	9
Poe, Edgar Allan. "Raven" through "Israfel," 1845. *Poems* (New York, Crowell, 1892)	5' st. Excl., lyr.	9	17	8
Hawker, Robert. *Reeds Shaken with the Wind*, 1843. Thirty-two poems of the 1840's in *Poetical Works*. (London, 1899)	5' st. Narr., lyr.	9	18	9
Bryant, William Cullen. "Later Poems" to 1842. *Poems* (Philadelphia, 1851)	5' st., b. v. Descr.	9	17	9
Longfellow, Henry. *Ballads and Other Poems*, 1842 (4th ed.)	4' st. Narr.	9	19	10

* Adjectival emphasis tends to mean substantival emphasis also; nouns tend to increase with adjectives, as verbs decrease. Statements using a high proportion of adjectives and nouns I call "substantival"; a high proportion of verbs, "predicative."

The texts used were those most available for working, not always the most authoritative.

1840's: TABLE 1—*Continued*

Texts: First 1,000 lines (with exceptions noted)	Form	Proportion in average 10 lines		
		Adj.	Noun	Verb
Hood, Thomas. "Song of the Shirt," "Tree," "House," "Sighs," 1843. *Poems* (London, 1846)	4' st. Narr., excl.	10	14	6
Tennyson, Alfred. *Poems Published in 1842* (Oxford, Clarendon Press, 1914), Vol. I, first 21 poems	4' st. Narr., address	10	14	6
Campbell, Thos. *Theodoric* and *Pilgrim*, collected 1842. *Poetical Works*, ed. Robertson, (Oxford ed., 1907)	5' cpl. Narr.	10	21	12
Keble, John. *Lyra Innocentium:* "Holy Baptism," 6; "Cradle Songs,"13,1846. (London, Methuen, 1903)	4' st. Lyr.	11	16	8
Wordsworth, William. *Poems of Early and Late Years*, 1842. *Complete Poetical Works* (London, Macmillan, 1930), "Poems 1840–45" through "The Westmoreland Girl"	5' st. Excl.	11	19	9
Horne, Richard H. *Orion*, 1843. (London, Scholartis Press, 1928)	5' b. v. Narr.	12	13	9
Lowell, James Russell. "Prometheus," 1st 100 ll. "Brittany," "Launfal," 1843. *Poetical Works* (Cambridge ed., 1897)	5' st. Narr.	12	19	11
Hemans, Felicia. *Collected Works*, 1839. From "Restoration of Works of Art . . ." 518 ll. to "Edith" (Boston, 1864) 106 l.	4' st. Narr., lyr.	13	20	9
Tupper, Martin. *Proverbial Philosophy*, 1842. (Philadelphia, 1845 ed., from 5th London)	6' lines Medit.	13	30	15
Average..............................	....	10	17	9

Shelley's 1820 poems, published in 1840, show just about this proportion: 9–19–8. One thousand lines of Wordsworth's *Lyrical Ballads* and all of Coleridge's show about 10–16–10, with fewer adjectives for Coleridge. Keats's *Odes* and *Hyperion* use more. The 1840's do not seem to have broken away from the great poets of earlier decades. The romantic poets as a whole have moderated eighteenth-century substantiality.

most moderate of their time, using a proportion of about 10 adjectives, 20 nouns, 10 verbs, the "classical" balance, parallel only the most extreme in amplitude, like Campbell, Wordsworth, Lowell. The most ample in the 1740's, like the Wartons, Thomson, Dyer, Armstrong, with 14 adjectives and 19 or 20 nouns to only 7 or 8 verbs, are far out of the normal range for the next century, except for Mrs. Hemans. In other words, the majority in the 1740's is over 10–20–10; the majority in the 1840's, under 10–20–10. The extrasubstantiality of late classicism and preromanticism becomes the undersubstantiality of the 1840's. The high average of 12–19–9 becomes the sign of postclassical qualitative description; the later subdued 10–17–9, of postromantic suggestion. The relationship of poets to the norm is therefore also shifted, the extreme of innovation in Thomson seeming reactionary in Lowell and Hemans, the conservatism of Young and Johnson seeming a radical change in the Brownings and Emerson.

Note also the amount of variation. In the 1740's, except for extremes, adjectives ranged from 10 to 15 in ten lines, the nouns from 17 to 22, the verbs from 7 to 12, a range of 5 in each. In the 1840's, adjectives from 7 to 13, nouns from 13 to 20, verbs from 6 to 12, the range is about 6 in each, and lower for all but verbs. In other words, more forms and combinations were being tried in the 1840's, but they were being tried at a level of substantial statement consistently below that in the preceding century. There is no doubt, then, of the temporal force in style.

Remembering the predicative proportions of the sixteenth and seventeenth centuries, 7–15–11 and 8–15–10 respectively, we may see in the nineteenth century a sort of return, though no more than halfway, to the earlier stages of poetic construction. But the return through a differing, narrative, structure, and a differing, atmospheric, vocabulary, alters the style. Table 2 sets forth the new central vocabulary.

Reading across the page, in the order established in table 1 and in an approximate count by fives, we see in table 2 that the main adjectives are used (10 times or more apiece) by a bare majority of the poets. The words most agreed upon are traditional: *eye, heart, love, man, come,* and *see.* In these the 1840's preserved the classic human norm as Wordsworth wished. Reading down the page, we see that the most participating poets are Elizabeth Barrett (who seems to have agreed closely with Robert Browning even before she met him); Longfellow, who is representative in vocabulary as well as proportion; and Lowell and Tupper, perhaps out of enthusiastic excess. Those who share fewest terms, Macaulay and Hood, do so perhaps because of the specializing quality of their story material. It is surprising that poets busy telling stories, as most of these are, and calling lyrically upon individual qualities in nature, should come to so much agreement about so many terms, almost forty in majority and fifty more in minority, or ten more in each category than in the century before.

The majority terms emphasize light in *bright, light, night,* and *sun;* interior consideration in *heart, soul, spirit, thought, word,* and some of the verbs; time in *old, day, night, time;* and a sort of responsiveness in the verbs *come, fall, lie, hear, look, love, rise, take.* The minority terms specify qualities of light even further, and of size, and of affection. The minority nouns preserve much of the eighteenth century, as they are used by the substantival poets especially, and they add also a new realm: *child, death, dream, father, flower, mind, mother, prayer, sea, sky, star,* of further specified natural detail, inward thought, and childlike relationship, submissive in a sense like the verbs *bring, feel, find, seem.* The individual terms extend these kinds, specifying proper names, sorts of flowers and trees. Innovation in terminology seems strongest for the middle range of poets, for the Brownings, Arnold, Tennyson, Poe, Longfellow; theirs

1840's: TABLE 2

MAJOR VOCABULARY: WORDS USED 10 TIMES IN 1,000 LINES BY 10 POETS OR MORE

Word	Ld.	Em.	Mc.	R.B.	E.B.	Cl.	Ar.	Po.	Hk.	Br.	Lg.	Hd.	Tn.	Cb.	Ke.	Ww.	Ho.	Lo.	He.	Tp.	Total no. of users
bright	:	:	:	:	:	10	:	:	10	10	10	:	:	10	20	15	10	10	25	:	10
good	:	10	15	15	10	15	:	:	:	:	10	:	20	:	10	10	:	10	:	15	11
old	10	15	:	:	:	10	10	:	30	10	15	15	:	15	10	10	:	10	:	:	12
sweet	10	10	:	:	15	10	10	10	:	10	:	:	10	10	10	:	:	10	:	10	12
day	20	10	20	25	10	30	25	10	30	15	25	:	10	25	20	:	:	10	20	:	16
earth	:	15	:	:	10	:	10	:	20	20	25	:	10	:	20	10	10	:	15	15	12
eye	20	20	10	10	20	10	40	20	10	15	25	10	20	15	30	20	15	25	15	15	20
God	35	20	:	25	35	20	10	10	35	10	30	:	:	:	:	30	30	10	:	30	15
hand	15	:	10	15	20	:	10	:	15	15	25	15	:	15	30	10	35	55	10	15	15
heart	10	10	:	10	20	35	:	15	20	10	20	:	15	15	25	15	10	15	25	25	18
heaven	:	:	:	10	15	:	20	20	10	15	40	:	:	15	15	20	:	20	15	10	12
life	:	:	:	10	10	10	:	:	10	15	20	:	15	20	15	15	15	10	20	25	15
light	:	:	:	:	:	10	10	15	10	10	15	10	20	10	20	10	10	25	15	:	11
love	15	15	:	25	20	20	50	10	35	15	20	10	15	15	10	15	15	15	20	10	19
man	25	20	25	10	10	20	10	30	10	15	25	:	:	20	:	:	10	10	:	100	18
night	10	:	10	15	15	:	10	30	20	:	15	:	20	:	15	:	10	25	:	:	12
soul	:	:	:	:	10	20	:	:	:	:	:	:	:	20	10	:	:	10	30	15	11
spirit	:	:	:	:	10	10	:	:	10	10	10	15	:	10	10	15	:	10	25	35	10
sun	:	15	:	15	10	:	:	:	:	10	15	:	10	:	:	10	:	25	:	10	11

1840's: TABLE 2—*Continued*

Word	Ld.	Em.	Mc.	R.B.	E.B.	Cl.	Ar.	Po.	Hk.	Br.	Lg.	Hd.	Tn.	Cb.	Ke.	Ww.	Ho.	Lo.	He.	Tp.	Total no. of users
thought	:	10	:	:	10	15	:	10	10	10	:	:	:	:	10	15	15	10	25	10	12
time	:	10	:	10	:	10	10	15	10	:	:	10	15	10	:	10	10	:	10	10	13
word	15	:	:	10	10	10	:	10	10	:	:	:	:	15	15	10	:	:	:	15	10
world	:	15	:	10	10	:	10	10	:	10	10	:	:	:	10	15	:	10	20	20	12
come	20	10	25	20	15	20	20	15	25	10	20	10	25	20	10	15	10	20	:	15	19
fall	10	10	10	10	10	:	:	10	20	10	15	10	10	:	10	:	:	15	10	:	14
give	10	:	10	20	10	20	10	:	10	:	:	:	:	15	10	10	10	15	10	10	13
go	20	15	10	15	10	15	20	15	10	:	10	:	10	15	:	10	:	15	:	10	15
hear	25	10	10	:	20	20	10	10	15	:	20	:	:	15	:	10	:	15	:	:	15
know	15	10	10	10	10	25	20	15	10	10	15	:	10	10	15	:	10	10	10	30	15
lie	10	10	:	10	20	:	10	:	:	10	15	10	:	:	10	10	:	20	:	10	14
look	15	:	10	10	10	10	:	:	10	25	15	:	:	10	:	15	:	10	:	15	12
love	25	:	10	15	20	:	:	:	:	10	15	:	:	:	15	10	:	10	:	10	10
make	:	10	:	10	10	10	20	:	10	10	15	10	10	10	10	:	10	:	10	10	14
rise	15	10	15	:	15	15	:	:	:	15	:	:	:	20	10	15	10	10	:	10	10
see	25	15	25	20	:	25	35	20	15	15	10	10	:	20	20	10	20	25	10	15	18
take	10	:	:	15	10	10	:	:	:	10	20	:	10	:	10	15	15	:	10	10	10
think	10	:	:	10	10	10	:	:	10	:	10	:	:	10	10	:	10	10	:	:	11
Total of major words used	24	23	15	27	31	27	22	21	29	28	30	12	19	26	28	26	23	32	20	30	:

1840's: TABLE 2A

MINORITY VOCABULARY: WORDS USED 10 TIMES BY 4 POETS OR MORE

Word	Ld.	Em.	Mc.	R.B.	E.B.	Cl.	Ar.	Po.	Hk.	Br.	Lg.	Hd.	Tn.	Cb.	Ke.	Ww.	Ho.	Lo.	He.	Tp.
dark			10				10			15	10	10						10	15	10
dear								10	10			10			10	10				
deep											10		10		10		20	15	15	10
dim					10										10			10	10	
fair						15		10	10	20				10				10	15	
gold		10	10	15	10		15	10	10		10		25				10	10		
great			25		10	10		10					10			10	10			
happy					10	10			10	10					10				15	10
high		10	10	10			10					15			20					
holy					10	10								10		10	15	15	15	
human						10					10					10	15	10		
little			10											10	10	10				
long	10		10				10	10	10	10	10			10				10	15	10
mighty			15				10		10		10		10		15	10			10	
poor			10	10	10	10			10				10						15	
proud	10					10		10		10				10	20		10			
soft																				10
strong		10	10					10		10					10		15	10		
true									10	10	10			10				10	10	
white		10	10						10	20	25			10				10		
wild											15			10	20		15		10	10
wise	10				10							10	10							
air								10	10	20							15	10		
beauty	10							10	15	10	10							10		10
breast									20	15	25				20	15				
child										10	15	10	10			20			10	
death					10				10			10			20					
dream					15			10							10		10	15		10

1840's: TABLE 2A—*Continued*

Word	Ld.	Em.	Mc.	R.B.	E.B.	Cl.	Ar.	Po.	Hk.	Br.	Lg.	Hd.	Tn.	Cb.	Ke.	Ww.	Ho.	Lo.	He.	Tp.
father	25				20					10	25			10	10	15				
flower				10		10		10		15	10		15	10	10		10			10
friend						15	10	10								10		15		10
hope				15			35	10					10		10	10			10	
hour										10					15	10			10	
joy															20					10
king	10				10		15		10		10						15		10	10
Lord							10		15		15				15					10
maid	10			10	15			10							15	10				
mind		20			10					10			10	20		10	10		10	
mother				10		15	10			15	10				15	10		10		35
nature		10			10		10	15	10			10		15		20	10	10	25	
power	10	10				10		10	15	10				10	10	10				
prayer		10		10		10	10		10		10	10			10					20
sea	10			10		10	10	15			15		10			10		15		
sky							10		10											
song		10		10		10												10		
star						10	10									10		10		
thing	15	10														10				
youth								10												25
bring	10	10		10			10										15			
feel				10	10	10	10						10	10			10	10		
find	10	10				10		10		10		10							10	10
live				10		10		10								10			15	10
seem		10									10									10
sing	10			10	15				10		10					10		15		
speak	15		10		25			10	10		15									10
stand					10											10				
tell														15					10	10

1840's: TABLE 2ᴮ

INDIVIDUAL VOCABULARY: WORDS USED 10 TIMES OR MORE BY INDIVIDUAL POETS

Word	Ld.	Em.	Mc.	R.B.	E.B.	Cl.	Ar.	Po.	Hk.	Br.	Lg.	Hd.	Tn.	Cb.	Ke.	Ww.	Ho.	Lo.	He.	Tp.
aweary													15							
awful									10						10					
beautiful				15							10									
black																				
blessed									10											
brave			15		10															
brown																				
calm									10							10				
clear											10		10							
dead													10				10			
divine																				
earthly						10										10				
eternal			10												10					
false																				
free										10										
full									10	10									10	
gentle									10											
glad									10	10										
green										10										
grey																				
hollow												10								
loud			10																	
new																	10			

1840's: TABLE 2B—*Continued*

Word	Ld.	Em.	Mc.	R.B.	E.B.	Cl.	Ar.	Po.	Hk.	Br.	Lg.	Hd.	Tn.	Cb.	Ke.	Ww.	Ho.	Lo.	He.	Tp.
plain												10								
pure																			15	
rich								10	10			10							10	
sad																				
secret																10		10		10
silent													10						10	10
silver																				
solemn																				
wide					10				10			10								
young																		10		
angel					10			15							10					
arm	15														15					
art																			10	
Artemus																				
atonement											10						15			
babe								65							25					
bell								10	10											
bird																				
birth																				
bough																				
bride					10							10								
bridge			15																	
character																				10
Christ											10									

1840's: TABLE 2B—*Continued*

Word	Ld.	Em.	Mc.	R.B.	E.B.	Cl.	Ar.	Po.	Hk.	Br.	Lg.	Hd.	Tn.	Cb.	Ke.	Ww.	Ho.	Lo.	He.	Tp.
door								20												
dust										10										
duty						10														
ear												10								10
Edenhall											15	20								
elm																				
evil																10				25
faith											10				10	10				
fool																				10
giant															10					
good																				25
grace													15				15			
Haroun	15																			
head								10	20								10		10	
home		10	10																	
Horatius																				
house				10											10					10
humility																				
Jesus																				
Julian																				
knight					15	10								15						
lady					20															
land									15											
law							15													
Launcal																		15		

1840's: TABLE 2B—*Continued*

Word	Ld.	Em.	Mc.	R.B.	E.B.	Cl.	Ar.	Po.	Hk.	Br.	Lg.	Hd.	Tn.	Cb.	Ke.	Ww.	Ho.	Lo.	He.	Tp.
Lenore								10												
Annabel Lee								10												
length																		15		
Margaret							10										10			
memory																				10
might				15				10											10	
moon																				
morning													10							
music		10				10		10							10					
name								10							10					10
nothing																				
nymphs																	15			
Onora					10															
Oriana													45				35			
Orion																				
page					25			10												
prime								10					10							
raven																				
right	10																			15
Raicas									10											
river			20																	
Roman																				
rose								10							10					
rosary		10			10															
saviour																				

1840's: TABLE 2B—*Continued*

Word	Ld.	Em.	Mc.	R.B.	E.B.	Cl.	Ar.	Po.	Hk.	Br.	Lg.	Hd.	Tn.	Cb.	Ke.	Ww.	Ho.	Lo.	He.	Tp.
scene									15										20	
sense												10					10			
shadow																	10			15
sin															15					
smile														10						
son																	10			
stag																				
stream										15										
teacher											10									
token												20			10					
tree																10				20
truth						15														
Udolph.									15											10
virtue									25					15						
wall																				35
water																				
wisdom					15															
woman																	15			
woods								10												
year	10																			
Zeus																				
bear									10								10			
become																				
behold									10											10

1840's: TABLE 2B—*Concluded*

Word	Ld.	Em.	Mc.	R.B.	E.B.	Cl.	Ar.	Po.	Hk.	Br.	Lg.	Hd.	Tn.	Cb.	Ke.	Ww.	Ho.	Lo.	He.	Tp.
breathe									15										10	
daunt												10								
die								10	10	15										10
dwell								10	10											
fear																				
forbear				10	10															
gallop																				
grow										10		20						20		
hang												10								
haunt																				
hearken									10				10				10			
hold																				10
kiss																				
laugh				10																
learn																				
leave	15																			
listen						10														
pray					10															
ride				30	10													10		
sit																				
stitch												10								
teach									10								10			10
weep																				
work												30								
yield																			15	15

is the minority of atmospheric specification which most distinguishes their era from preceding ones. Individual emphases suit the rest: Keble's *babe*, Poe's *bell* and *door*, Tupper's *good* and *evil*, Lowell's older *scene*, Hemans' *water*, Browning's *ride*, Hood's *work*. Both seventeenth-century and eighteenth-century terms are frequent throughout. The choices are personal, yet they work with a strong amount of agreement and a concerted modification of tradition.

The tables as basis of generalization lead further into the work of individual poets. We may turn to passages which represent individual working out of the language in form first for the typical poets, then for the extremes. The next succeeding chapter will show at random the presence of some of the same materials in prose. The concluding chapter will consider critical theory of the change in poetic emphasis between the eighteenth and nineteenth centuries.

II

At the center of poetic practice in the 1840's were the American poems of Longfellow, Bryant, Poe, as well as the English poems of Arnold and Tennyson. Their moderate proportioning of adjectives and verbs, their full employment of a shared vocabulary, were characteristic of the period. Not only to us does Longfellow's verse seem familiar; it must have seemed familiar as first it was read, with its strong recollections of eighteenth-century scene, its nineteenth-century refinements of sensation and of melody. One must brace oneself to hear as if anew, in its authenticity, the nineteenth-century tone.

> Under a spreading chestnut tree
>   The village smithy stands;
> The smith, a mighty man is he,
>   With large and sinewy hands;
> And the muscles of his brawny arms
>   Are strong as iron bands.

His hair is crisp, and black, and long,
   His face is like the tan;
His brow is wet with honest sweat,
   He earns whate'er he can,
And looks the whole world in the face,
   For he owes not any man.

Week in, week out, from morn till night,
   You can hear his bellows blow;
You can hear him swing his heavy sledge,
   With measured beat and slow,
Like a sexton ringing the village bell,
   When the evening sun is low.

And children coming home from school
   Look in at the open door;
They love to see the flaming forge,
   And hear the bellows roar,
And catch the burning sparks that fly
   Like chaff from a threshing floor.

He goes on Sunday to the church,
   And sits among his boys;
He hears the parson pray and preach,
   He hears his daughter's voice,
Singing in the village choir,
   And it makes his heart rejoice.

  .   .   .   .

Thanks, thanks to thee, my worthy friend,
   For the lesson thou hast taught!
Thus at the flaming forge of life
   Our fortunes must be wrought;
Thus on its sounding anvil shaped
   Each burning deed and thought!

Here, in either identical or similar terms, are both the primary and the secondary stresses of the decade: *mighty man, hands, strong, long, looks, world, morn, night, hear, sun, children, come, love, see, sing, make, heart, friend, life, thought.* We see the basic terms of other centuries colored by association with two new kinds, the *children* and the *sunny morning* kind, highlighting the human qualities of joy and strength. The poem's minor vocabulary carries out this emphasis, setting the time of day and week, the visible scene, the family and church relationships, the final positive interpretation in the anvil metaphor. Moreover, the singing and speaking qualities, of which the poem itself speaks, are strong in it; it is not a poem of picture but of narrative declamation: You can hear . . . You can hear . . . Thanks, thanks to thee. The ballad measure enforces the vocal quality, along with the ease and simplicity of the words and rhymes, the traditional *stands–hands, can–man, slow–low, door–floor, voice–rejoice, taught–thought,* which makes the lines seem possibly extemporaneous. The studied naïveté of sound suits that of sense, without undertone or implication. The man is honest, the day is open and sunny, and there are children present.

In the word list of the nineteenth century there are also, more than Longfellow's poem would indicate, the terms of *wild, dark, death, thought,* and, among actions, *falling* and *lying.* There are stormy weather, danger, and submission to power; but to these in the total poetic effect the blacksmith's anvil supplies the answer: the trouble is all to the good. The "Skeleton in Armour," which begins with the wild, dim, and dead,

> "Speak! speak! thou fearful guest!
> Who, with thy hollow breast
> Still in rude armour drest,
>   Comest to daunt me!
> Wrapt not in Eastern balms,
> But with thy fleshless palms
> Stretched, as if asking alms,
>   Why dost thou haunt me?"

ends with light and elevation:

> "Thus, seamed with many scars
> Bursting these prison bars,
> Up to its native stars
>   My soul ascended!
> There from the flowing bowl
> Deep drinks the warrior's soul,
> *Skoal!* to the Northland! *skoal!*"
>   —Thus the tale ended.

In "The Wreck of the Hesperus" it is the holiness of the final invocation which lifts the soul.

> It was the schooner Hesperus,
>   That sailed the wintry sea;
> And the skipper had taken his little daughter,
>   To bear him company.
>
> Blue were her eyes as the fairy-flax,
>   Her cheeks like the dawn of day,
> And her bosom white as the hawthorn buds,
>   That ope in the month of May.

But:

> Such was the wreck of the Hesperus,
>   In the midnight and the snow!
> Christ save us all from a death like this,
>   On the reef of Norman's Woe!

Nor does an alteration of rhythm, as in Longfellow's adaptation of "The Children of the Lord's Supper," alter the simplicity of tone.

> Pentecost, day of rejoicing, had come. The church of the village
> Stood gleaming white in the morning's sheen. On the spire of the
>   belfry,
> Tipped with a vane of metal, the friendly flames of the Spring-sun
> Glanced like the tongues of fire, beheld by Apostles aforetime.
> Clear was the heaven and blue, and May, with her cap crowned with
>   roses,
> Stood in her holiday dress in the fields, and the wind and the brooklet
> Murmured gladness and peace, God's-peace!

This is more lyrical prose than the eighteenth century's exposition just because it sets forth less of scene and arrangement, despite its literalness, as it utters more of feeling through metaphor. The fairy-flax of Hesperus, the cap of roses which May wears, the friendly flames and glad brooklet, are not framed for presentation; rather they are invented for expression. The simplicity of procedure, the effect that this is just how things were on the stormy sea or in the quiet village, is achieved partly by the direct narrative method; yet it is complicated by much metaphorical attribution. The naïveté artfully contrived by this mixture of direction and indirection makes in itself a sort of subject; the poet's lyrical attitude of pleasure toward or in it establishes the central tone.

Longfellow's *Ballads and Other Poems* of 1842 are in these ways very different from the central verses of a century earlier, and represent what the poetic mode has come to. It has come to lyricism by abdicating the full frame of exposition, toward the partial and echoing expression, and has come by way of the narrative, the ballad, shortening the five-foot shelf of meter, assuming a simple literalness of audience and atmosphere, making personal attributions of metaphor and symbol. It is not of course the burden of innovation that belongs on Longfellow's shoulders; the *Lyrical Ballads* themselves carry that weight; but by Longfellow's time the mode had become familiar, and it is the burden of representation that his poetry bears.

Bryant, his elder, whose poems of the 1840's were "Later Poems" and whose reputation as representative of Americans was well established in England, temporized in his adoption of the new mode, feeling still and strongly the old responsibilities of framework and survey but alien to the learned antiquities involved. The first of the "Later Poems" is as "classical" as he wrote: addressed to the Apennines, pairing the pictures of *serenest skies, aerial shelves, fair earth, glimmering deep;* surveying history as it spread below, the "Libyan host—the Scythian and the Gaul," "Jove, Bacchus, Pan, and earlier, fouler names." The sweeping view is impressive; but its conclusion has not the abstract scope to which the 1740's were earlier accustomed.

> In you the heart that sighs for freedom seeks
>   Her image; there the winds no barrier know,
> Clouds come and rest and leave your fairy peaks;
>   While even the immaterial Mind, below,
> And Thought, her wingèd offspring, chained by power,
> Pine silently for the redeeming hour.

The serious personification of chained Thought and Mind is confused by the cloud line and the fairy peaks and even by the personal, wishful tone of "the heart that sighs for freedom."

Throughout Bryant's work continues the pomp, though a personal pomp, as of "Earth,"

> A midnight black with clouds is in the sky;
> I seem to feel, upon my limbs, the weight
> Of its vast brooding shadow.

But there runs also through the later poems an easier, more literal, less boundary-bound note of, for example, "The Hunter of the Prairies,"

> Ay, this is freedom!—these pure skies
>   Were never stained with village smoke:
> The fragrant wind, that through them flies,
>   Is breathed from wastes by plow unbroke.

Or "Catterskill Falls,"

> Midst greens and shades the Catterskill leaps,
>   From cliffs where the wood-flower clings;
> All summer he moistens his verdant steeps
>   With the sweet light spray of the mountain springs;
> And he shakes the woods on the mountain side,
> When they drip with the rains of autumn-tide.

Or "The Strange Lady,"

The summer morn is bright and fresh, the birds are darting by,
As if they loved to breast the breeze that sweeps the cool clear sky;
Young Albert, in the forest's edge, has heard a rustling sound,
An arrow slightly strikes his hand and falls upon the ground.

Or "Earth's Children Cleave to Earth,"

> Earth's children cleave to Earth—her frail
>   Decaying children dread decay.
> Yon wreath of mist that leaves the vale,
>   And lessens in the morning ray:
> Look, how, by mountain rivulet,
>   It lingers as it upward creeps,
> And clings to fern and copsewood set
>   Along the green and dewy steeps.

The same contrast that is noteworthy here, between the steady pace and the full five-accented line of "Earth," and the alternate rhymes, or easy dactyls, or carried-over stresses of the rest—the contrast between a closely framed and an openly hovering poetry—is especially vivid in Bryant's two famous early poems, "Thanatopsis" and "To a Waterfowl." Note the last lines of each:

> So live, that when thy summons comes to join
> The innumerable caravan, that moves
> To that mysterious realm, where each shall take
> His chamber in the silent halls of death,
> Thou go not like the quarry-slave at night,
> Scourged to his dungeon, but, sustained and soothed
> By an unfaltering trust, approach thy grave,
> Like one who wraps the drapery of his couch
> About him, and lies down to pleasant dreams.

And, with more tenuous measure and symbolic image,

> Thou'rt gone, the abyss of heaven
> Hath swallowed up thy form; yet, on my heart
> Deeply hath sunk the lesson thou hast given,
> And shall not soon depart.
>
> He who, from zone to zone,
> Guides through the boundless sky thy certain flight,
> In the long way that I must tread alone,
> Will lead my steps aright.

The first of these pieces has the fullness of formalized scope and picture which we remember from the mid-eighteenth century. The caravan moves as pageant across the stage, the rational and emotional alternatives of slave and freeman are made personages with appropriate stage gestures. Eight steady epithets for a dozen nouns give substance to the prediction in processional fashion, though without the balanced weight that once would have been used. *Innumerable* and *mysterious,* foreign to the solidity, are nevertheless impressive enough not to destroy it. In the second passage there is no solidity to speak of. The more the waterfowl becomes spirit, the less bird, the better for the poem. The abyss of heaven is a fine example of an emotional rather than pictorial figure, its zones and its guide conceptual; the heart with a lesson sunk on it cannot be a very anatomical heart; the long way and the boundlessness have more force than their equivalents in the *Thanatopsis* lines to set the tone, because they are almost the only epithets and are thematically set against *certain,* while they sustain it. While both poems are concerned in these last lines with the nature of death, they find two very different ways of setting it forth, the first pictorial, the second conceptual; the first imaged, the second symbolized; the first explicative in both sound and sense, the second implicative. The "Waterfowl" meter is not a common one for Bryant; it may be compared to Collins' "Evening" experimentation, perhaps, in its arrangement of long and short lines and the consequent stress on silence as well as sense; it suggests at least the sort of celestial and metrical implications Bryant liked to make when he made them in their most special form. At any rate, this seriously traditional and American poet, using the modes available to him from English reading and American experience, made various choices at various times, but often the "Waterfowl," the symbol choice, by which poetry kept saying as it had for a century, Look! and then adding, "There is more here than meets the eye." There was an open sort of wonder, and there was an American sort of God.

Wonder and spirit made the poetic conditions for Poe also, the third American representative of the normal mode. Poe's Heaven was less orthodox than some, but not less influential, as it constantly tempered substance by its vaguer and sublimer spirit. So "Lenore" begins, "Ah, broken is the golden bowl!— the spirit flown forever!—" and ends,

"Avaunt! To-night my heart is light! no dirge will I upraise,
  But waft the angel on her flight with a paean of old days!

Let *no* bell toll!—lest her sweet soul, amid its hallowed mirth,
Should catch the note, as it doth float up from the damnèd Earth!
To friends above, from fiends below, the indignant ghost is riven,—
From Hell unto a high estate far up within the Heaven,—
From grief and groan to a golden throne, beside the King of Heaven."

Sound, sense, and structure combine to emphasize the non-material quality. The merged ballad line hastens the motion with its effect of internal rhyme; the feminine rhymes and refrain sustain each other toward the unevenness of echo; consonance and assonance promote the effect of interweaving rather than of substantial balance. Never do the exclamations and imperatives move, as they did in the eighteenth century, into an ordered exposition which they serve to introduce; rather, exclamation is the stuff of the piece. And even the substantial nouns are altered in this direction: *heart, day, soul, earth, friends, high estate, throne* and *king*, are wafted by *light, waft, angel, flight, mirth, note, bell, float, ghost,* and *golden* to a less concrete and social sphere than they have earlier functioned in, while they are at the same time shadowed by the atmospheric negatives of *dirge, night, toll, damned, fiends, indignant, grief,* and *groan.* All these qualities of sound and reference unsubstantialize the normal worldly terms, taking them out of landscape into soulscape, and thus subjectivizing in the most literal sense the materials of poetic construction.

Like Longfellow, Poe gave the poetic soul a good deal of torment in its flight, letting it fall as well as rise, making the night dark as well as the day bright, as if to add to the lyrical power by emotional inclusiveness. Poe is more apt than Longfellow or Bryant to play with and end with the gloomy, in his paraphernalia of tombs, but all share their decade's stress on that darkened atmosphere which the word *night* represents for them. It is important that the negative, with its positive accompaniment of *light* and *sun,* appears in atmospheric rather than in moral terms. On this level of feeling and sensation, this Gothic world, the negative seems more easily sustained by the poets. Customary trouble and evil, like customary scene, is poetized by translation out of custom into concept, out of morals into aesthetics.

> And the Raven, never flitting, still is sitting, still is sitting
> On the pallid bust of Pallas, just above my chamber door;
> And his eyes have all the seeming of a demon's that is dreaming,
> And the lamplight o'er him streaming throws his shadow on the floor;
> And my soul from out that shadow that lies floating on the floor
>   Shall be lifted—nevermore!

Even the structural *ands* and the ending *-ings* of this stanza aid its effect of suspension, its *still, seeming, floating,* and *shadow,* so that they shape into sensation the abstraction *nevermore*. One would say at first that these lines have little in common with Longfellow's except their almost humorous familiarity to us; but at a closer look the Raven shares with the Blacksmith the character of symbolic focus. Both are directly perceived objects distinctly located in reference to door and floor, domestically viewed, in an effortless and bouncing sort of rhythm, and both are shifted quickly to a function of symbolic analogy or representation. In the light of lamp as of forge the soul is discerned and exclaimed, and bird like blacksmith is blended into a larger and much more tenuous whole than it seemed at first prepared for. Where in an eighteenth-century poem the invocation and survey at the outset would establish range into which objects could be suitably fitted, in these poems of 1840 the objects establish centers, particularly centers in time of day, which may widen cosmologically and spiritually by the swift association of light and spirit.

Poe's birds, bells, and girls diffuse particularly speedily, as in "Ulalume,"

> The skies they were ashen and sober;
>   The leaves they were crisped and sere,—
>   The leaves they were withering and sere,—
> It was night in the lonesome October
>   Of my most immemorial year;

> It was hard by the dim lake of Auber,
>   In the misty mid-region of Weir,—
> It was down by the dank tarn of Auber,
>   In the ghoul-haunted woodland of Weir.

No place is more highly specified and less fully developed. So, in "To Helen," Helen is seen in line after line but less and less as bodily form:

> I saw thee once—once only—years ago:
> I must not say *how* many—but *not* many.
> It was a July midnight: and from out
> A full-orbed moon, that, like thine own soul, soaring,
> Sought a precipitate pathway up through heaven,
> There fell a silvery silken veil of light,
> With quietude, and sultriness, and slumber,
> Upon the upturned faces of a thousand
> Roses that grew in an enchanted garden,
> Where no wind dared to stir, unless on tiptoe.

One will read these lines and think, "But they are characteristically Poe's; they are eccentric, not standard." Rather, one may come to learn, they are at a significant center of the standard, and heighten, and even predict, as Baudelaire was to see. The night of the soul was a nineteenth-century night, as it deliberately blurred the edges and the expected shapes of objects toward a more ineffable vision, and often a darker one. The vision made for a common mode of poetry, different from that of the eighteenth century as it modified substantiality toward suggestion, as it worked to combine literalness with inexpressibility. This mode the English shared with the Americans; the sea did not divide. Nor did time, in the 1840's, strongly split; for elders like Campbell and Bryant and Hood, younger men like Tennyson, Hawker, Arnold, Clough, shared, as the tables indicate, a style generally characteristic in structure and vocabulary. I do not mean to say, of course, that these very different poets all wrote one sort of poem; Poe is no Longfellow, and Clough no Campbell. But the individualities do unite in some main lines of poetic practice, and these are lines, of atmospheric spirit and stanzaic susceptibility, which distinguish mid-nineteenth from mid-eighteenth century.

Minor poets as well as major catch the spirit and follow the practice. The poems of Robert Hawker's *Ecclesia* in 1840, for example, though not now famous, though written by a some-time Vicar of Morwenstow, Cornwall, and speaking for him, as the writer of his Memoir says, "in language that is entirely his own," yet speak the famous English poetic language of the era. The opening poem, "The Western Shore":

> Thou lovely land! where, kindling, throng
> Scenes that should breathe the soul of song;
> Home of high hopes that once were mine
> Of loftier verse and nobler line!
>
> 'Tis past—the quench'd volcano's tide
> Sleeps well within the mountain-side;
> Henceforth shall time's cold touch control
> The warring Hecla of my soul.
>
> Welcome! wild rock and lonely shore,
> Where round my days dark seas shall roar;
> And thy gray fane, Morwenna, stand
> The beacon of the Eternal Land!

Morwenna was Hawker's home, a real place and no Auber, but it holds him no longer than Auber to descriptive fact. Land and scene move quickly into soul and hope, literal home leads to symbolic volcano, and the gray fane, when we return to it, stands, like Longfellow's anvil, for spiritual conceptions.

Hood is a less simple representative, but a surprisingly accurate one in some ways. With the verve of a minor and not responsible individualism he stresses the key new terms of the decade and ignores the traditional ones, counteracts a normal moderation in epithets with an abnormal paucity of verbs, and with an effect of excessive devotion to the mode seems almost to satirize its major qualities one by one. Notice the literal narrative beginning of (and notice the title) "The Dream of Eugene Aram":

> 'Twas in the prime of summer time,
>   An evening calm and cool,
>   And four-and-twenty happy boys
>   Came bounding out of school:
>   There were some that ran and some that leapt,
>   Like troutlets in a pool.
>
> Away they sped with gamesome minds,
>   And souls untouched by sin;
>   To a level mead they came, and there
>   They drave the wickets in:
>   Pleasantly shone the setting sun
>   Over the town of Lynn.

The summer and evening setting, the natural background, the immediate souls aid the short and simply rhymed sentences to convey a lyricism of childlike sublimity.

"The Elm Tree" gives us that nineteenth-century preference of music to picture:

> 'Twas in a shady Avenue,
>   Where lofty Elms abound—
>   And from a Tree
>   There came to me
>   A sad and solemn sound,
>   That sometimes murmur'd overhead,
>   And sometimes underground.
>
> Amongst the leaves it seem'd to sigh,
>   Amid the boughs to moan;
>   It muttered in the stem, and then
>   The roots took up the tone;
>   As if beneath the dewy grass
>   The dead began to groan.

Even in such direct description the spirits soon appear. In the "Haunted House," indeed, they begin:

> Some dreams we have are nothing else but dreams,
> Unnatural, and full of contradictions;

Yet others of our most romantic schemes
Are something more than fictions.

It might be only on enchanted ground;
It might be merely by a thought's expansion;
But in the spirit, or the flesh, I found
An old deserted Mansion.

A residence for woman, child, and man,
A dwelling place,—and yet no habitation;
A House,—but under some prodigious ban
Of excommunication.

.   .   .   .

O'er all there hung a shadow and a fear;
A sense of mystery the spirit daunted,
And said, as plain as whisper in the ear,
The place is Haunted!

One will recognize this, in the aura of the Blacksmith and Ulalume and the Strange Lady and the Western Shore, as intensely
of the 1840's. (Poe, in *The Poetic Principle,* called it one of the
truest poems ever written.) Its iambic pentameters are insubstan-
tial, broken by the fourth lines, the feminine endings, the short
words and sentences, the dashes and exclamations, the lack of
serious subordination in either epithet or predicate. Called "A
Romance," the poem at the outset stresses the romantic insub-
stantiality of its subject, the confusion of spirit and flesh, the
domestic certainties of a familial establishment blurred by
shadow, mystery, and whisper,—the key of Haunted! heightened
by its punctuation. Later in the poem we get more of the natural
scene we expect; wild flower, wren, rabbit, wary crow, coot,
moping heron, pear and quince, marigold, spicy pink, fountain
and statue, give way to bat and screech-owl, wood-louse and
spider, and mystic moth; and all are described with the sort of
fine detail which made famous the nearsightedness of Tennyson. But all are dissolved in the secret which we never learn, the
secret of the *Bloody Hand,* more violent than Mariana's mystery
but of the same sort unrevealed. In total, the effect is one of great

sensory detail made suspect or abandoned by the mysterious force of extrasensory phenomena mysteriously yet not very explicitly involved in good or evil, at the same time that the sensory detail enforces the reality of the illusion. In this way, the characteristic literalness in the decade, seeming almost absurd, is actually used for a special poetic purpose: the grounding, the oblique confirmation, of unpicturable realities.

Hood's more well-known "Bridge of Sighs" serves further to enfold and aestheticize the implications of evil. Again it sets the evil against the stabilities of home and family, coloring and vaporizing it.

> One more Unfortunate,
> Weary of breath,
> Rashly importunate,
> Gone to her death!
>
> Take her up tenderly,
> Lift her with care;
> Fashion'd so slenderly,
> Young, and so fair!
>
> .   .   .   .   .   .
>
> Loop up her tresses
> Escaped from the comb,
> Her fair auburn tresses;
> Whilst wonderment guesses
> Where was her home?

> Who was her father?
> Who was her mother?
> Had she a sister?
> Had she a brother?
> Or was there a dearer one
> Still, and a nearer one
> Yet, than all other?
>
> .   .   .   .   .   .
>
> Where the lamps quiver
> So far in the river,
> With many a light
> From window and casement,
> From garret to basement,
> She stood, with amazement,
> Homeless by night....

Like "The Wreck of the Hesperus" this poem devotes itself to a vigorous conveying of atmosphere, rhymed to recite; it examines its additional social and moral materials less verbally than it does its body and its night. The states of body and night, it feels, tell much and suggest all.

"The Song of the Shirt" sings the symbols yet again. The mass of a society is not given a picture or a stage, is not exposited and discoursed upon in survey; rather it is given an object, a shirt, set in an easy ditty of signification.

With fingers weary and worn,
  With eyelids heavy and red,
A woman sat, in unwomanly rags,
  Plying her needle and thread—
    Stitch! stitch! stitch!
In poverty, hunger, and dirt,
  And still with a voice of dolorous pitch
She sang the "Song of the Shirt"!

  "Work! work! work!
While the cock is crowing aloof!
  And work—work—work,
Till the stars shine through the roof!
It's O! to be a slave
  Along with the barbarous Turk,
Where woman has never a soul to save,
  If this is Christian work!

    .   .   .   .

"O! Men, with Sisters dear!
  O! Men! with Mothers and Wives!
It is not linen you're wearing out,
  But human creatures' lives!
    Stitch—stitch—stitch,
  In poverty, hunger, and dirt,
Sewing at once, with a double thread,
  A Shroud as well as a Shirt.

Here is Death again in the familiar object, morals again in the familiar, the backing of both the family and the stars.

You will say that Tennyson does this better, and he does, but it is just this. He arrives at an identical proportioning, 10 adjectives to 14 nouns to 6 verbs, average except for the scantness of verbs. He shares the basis of the nouns and verbs of sight, time, fall, but is much more general in his use of *good, life,* and such terms. The subtilizing of the mode of song is done by a sense of literary convention richer than Hood's, who stressed mostly a few new key terms like *spirit;* rhyme and refrain weight the individual tone of *gold, good, come, eye, light, night,* the moral and moving within the atmospheric.

> Where Claribel low-lieth
>   The breezes pause and die,
>   Letting the rose-leaves fall:
> But the solemn oak-tree sigheth,
>   Thick-leaved, ambrosial,
>   With an ancient melody
>   Of an inward agony,
> Where Claribel low-lieth.

> At eve the beetle boometh
>   Athwart the thicket lone:
> At noon the wild bee hummeth
>   About the moss'd headstone:
> At midnight the moon cometh,
>   And looketh down alone.

From the poems of 1830, republished in the first of the major two lyrical volumes of 1842, this "Claribel, a Melody," through its musical mode, with beetle booming and bee humming, presents other qualities central to its matured decade: the vocabulary of lying, dying, falling, the temporal setting, especially night, the natural objects without much frame, the suggestion of old and ancient time and mysterious inward feeling. The suspended and feminine rhyme characteristically echoes these verbs and inward voices.

So also "Mariana":

> With blackest moss the flower-plots
>   Were thickly crusted, one and all,
> The rusted nails fell from the knots
>   That held the peach to the garden-wall.
> The broken sheds look'd sad and strange,
>   Unlifted was the clinking latch,
>   Weeded and worn the ancient thatch
> Upon the lonely moated grange.
>   She only said, "My life is dreary,
>   He cometh not," she said;
>   She said, "I am aweary, aweary;
>   I would that I were dead!"

Her tears fell at even, at night she heard the cock crow, she saw the gusty shadow sway, old faces and voices glimmered in the dreamy house, she wept, "Oh God, that I were dead!" Not so violent as the "Hesperus," not so moral as the "Bridge of Sighs," this is still like them a poem of objects of suggestion, of feminine and implicative sense, fainting and falling, with God at the horizon to be called upon.

Women are often subjects in these early poems, and if not women then atmospheric ditties as they might seriously sing them, or as sensitive children might.

> When cats run home and light is come,
>   And dew is cold upon the ground,
> And the far-off stream is dumb,
>   And the whirring sail goes round,
>   And the whirring sail goes round;
>   Alone and warming his five wits,
>   The white owl in the belfry sits.

While this observation is finely oblique it is still simple, and in the same straight structure as "Under a spreading chestnut tree / The village smithy stands."

The third sort of poem which Tennyson wrote in these years was fuller of abstract elaboration, looking toward the blank-verse processions of the *Idyls,* conditioned the most perhaps by his practice in imitation of Thomson, Pope, and Byron. "Ode to Memory" and "The Poet's Mind" are such poems, and they show how for him even abstraction lyricizes and fragmentizes itself.

> i
> Vex not thou the poet's mind
>   With thy shallow wit:
> Vex not thou the poet's mind;
>   For thou canst not fathom it.
> Clear and bright it should be ever,
> Flowing like a crystal river;
> Bright as light, and clear as wind.

ii

Dark-brow'd sophist, come not anear;
 All the place is holy ground;
 Hollow smile and frozen sneer
  Come not here.
 Holy water will I pour
 Into every spicy flower
Of the laurel-shrubs that hedge it around.
The flowers would faint at your cruel cheer.
 In your eye there is death,
 There is frost in your breath
Which would blight the plants.
  Where you stand you cannot hear
  From the groves within
  The wild-bird's din.

With its broken quality, this was not orthodox elaboration of concept. In the second volume of his 1842 *Poems,* Tennyson developed the orthodoxy more neatly, coming to write that smooth yet rather breathless and implicative blank verse for which he has been much admired. This blank verse had already taken on two major qualities of the decade which we have noted: the flat literal statement of a Bryant or Longfellow, which seems in "Dora" to go too far toward a numbness of objectivity, and the individual impressionism which alters the nature of descriptiveness from its eighteenth-century past.

As a matter of fact, even the heroic couplet had altered in this latter direction. Thomas Campbell, who was ceasing rather than beginning to write in the 1840's, had presented in his two last large poems a pleasant modification toward the new mode, with temporal setting, mixed colors, bees and weeds to intensify the pictorial perspective, and the feeling form of Earth rather than its personification.

 'Twas sunset, and the *Ranz des Vaches* was sung,
 And lights were o'er the Helvetian mountains flung
 That gave the glacier-tops their richest glow
 And tinged the lakes like molten gold below.

Warmth flushed the wonted regions of the storm,
Where, phoenix-like, you saw the eagle's form
That high in heaven's vermilion wheeled and soared; ...
'Twas transport to inhale the bright sweet air!
The mountain-bee was revelling in its glare,
And roving with his minstrelsy across
The scented wild weeds and enamelled moss.
Earth's features so harmoniously were linked,
She seemed one great glad form, with life instinct,
That felt Heaven's ardent breath, and smiled below
Its flush of love with consentaneous glow.

This seems to me an elegant example of the transition between Thomson and Tennyson. There remains in it the old sense of a formal piece, a scene in the couplets making one by one their spatial arrangements. There is added in it the strong impression of light in almost every line, the variation of perspectives, and most appreciably a new kind of physical effect. Where, earlier, thoughts had moved personified among sensations like figures on a stage, here sensations themselves are attributed to the whole concept, so that the stage setting gives way to "one great glad form," the structure becomes organism. It was the combination of just these two views with which Wordsworth was dealing in the "Westminster Bridge" sonnet with its triumph of the mighty heart over the panorama, and the triumph continued for Campbell even though he was a most conventional and popular writer of couplets and tales of pomp. The 1842 "Pilgrim of Glencoe" echoes his fidelity.

The sunset sheds a horizontal smile
O'er Highland frith and Hebridean isle;
While, gay with gambols of its finny shoals,
The glancing wave rejoices as it rolls
With streamered busses that distinctly shine
All downward pictured in the glassy brine;
Whose crews, with faces brightening in the sun,
Keep measure with their oars, and all in one
Strike up th' old Gaelic song, "Sweep, rowers, sweep!
The fisher's glorious spoils are in the deep."

> Day sinks; but twilight owes the traveller soon,
> To reach his bourne, a round unclouded moon,
> Bespeaking long undarkened hours of time; . . .

Despite the finny shoals and glassy brine, the Gaelic song in the twilight guides the story, accustoming hundreds of faithful readers to the lights and shades, the fragmentary snatches of music which were to appear in the new thin volumes on the shelves alongside Campbell's thick ones.

Arthur Hugh Clough's *Ambarvalia* was one such thin volume, shared with a brother poet in 1849, and breaking into pieces the massive poems of tradition, yet holding within the pieces the characteristic style of its own era. Most of these verses had no titles even; they were snatches of personal meditation, echoes from the realm of spirit. The book begins:

> The human spirits saw I on a day,
> Sitting and looking each a different way;
> And hardly tasking, subtly questioning,
> Another spirit went around the ring
> To each and each: and as he ceased his say,
> Each after each, I heard them singly sing,
> Some querulously high, some softly, sadly low,
> We know not,—what avails to know?
> We know not,—wherefore need we know?
> This answer gave they still unto his suing,
> We know not, let us do as we are doing.

The informality of the couplet form, the spirits themselves, their speaking and singing, the vagueness of their implications, all are characteristic of Clough and of the times. There follow some lyrics of love—"A light of more than mortal day"—and then a poem which well exemplifies the flat obviousness of statement which we have noted before.

> As, at a railway junction, men
> Who came together, taking then
> One the train up, one down, again

> Meet never! Ah, much more as they
> Who take one street's two sides, and say
> Hard parting words, but walk one way:
>
> Though moving other mates between,
> While carts and coaches intervene,
> Each to the other goes unseen, ...
>
> Ah, joy! when with the closing street,
> Forgivingly at last ye greet!

The justification for this plainness of material is, as it was Wordsworth's, its involvement in greater theme, its participation in
emotional whole. The exclamation of joy is able to dissolve mates,
carts, and coaches in an aura of unity. Another kind of enfold-
ment indicates the power of the new major term *night* for the
1840's, under that title traditionally accepted as thematic for the
mid-Victorians: "Blank Misgivings of a Creature moving about
in Worlds not realised":

> Here I am yet, another twelvemonth spent,
> One-third departed of the mortal span,
> Carrying on the child into the man,
> Nothing into reality. Sails rent,
> And rudder broken,—reason impotent,—
> Affections all unfixed; so forth I fare
> On the mid seas unheedingly, ...
>
> viii
>
> O kind protecting Darkness! as a child
> Flies back to bury in his mother's lap
> His shame and his confusion, so to thee,
> O Mother Night, come I! within the folds
> Of thy dark robe hide thou me close; for I
> So long, so heedless, with external things
> Have played the liar, that whate'er I see,
> E'en these white glimmering curtains, yon bright stars,
> Which to the rest rain comfort down, for me
> Smiling those smiles, which I may not return,
> Or frowning frowns of fierce triumphant malice,
> As angry claimants or expectants sure
> Of that I promised and may not perform
> Look me in the face! O hide me, Mother Night!

Clough in an inward fashion, like Hood in an outward, is exploring the world of the child in man, its terrors and uncertainties, its poverties and rebellions, finding relief in an aestheticizing of expression that is in symbol, making sea and sky, dark and light, the natural and sympathetic substitutes for God and man.

So, though there is much reason and religion in the poems, much *God, heart, man,* and *soul,* and a high degree of abstractness and feeling, a poise is often reached in a very simple objectification, in standard *things.* And in one sense, the poems are more inventive when not attaining to this poise, when not too standardly objectified, but when, in one of Clough's minor modes, they stress rather the fluidity of both melody and human understanding, and play over a doubt of sound and sense. So, for example, the untitled poem which is a sort of nineteenth-century ode to music, troubled, personal, wavers intentionally with an abstract and colloquial repetitiveness and suggests with what special skill the nineteenth-century stress on hearing could be exploited.

Why should I say I see the things I see not,
    Why be and be not?
Show love for that I love not, and fear for what I fear not?
And dance about to music that I hear not?
    Who standeth still i' the street
    Shall be hustled and justled about;
And he that stops i' the dance shall be spurned by the Dancers' feet,—
Shall be shoved and be twisted by all he shall meet,
    And shall raise up an outcry and rout;
      And the partner, too,—
      What's the partner to do?
While all the while 'tis but, perchance, an humming in mine ear,
    That yet anon shall hear,
    And I anon, the music in my soul,
    In a moment read the whole;
    The music in my heart,
    Joyously take my part,

And hand in hand, and heart with heart, with these retreat, advance;
   And borne on wings of wavy sound,
   Whirl with these around, around,
  Who here are living in the living dance!

· · · · · · · · · · · · ·

Yea, and as thought of some belovèd friend
By death or distance parted will descend
Severing, in crowded rooms ablaze with light,
As by a magic screen, the seër from the sight,
(Palsying the nerves that intervene
The eye and central sense between;)
   So may the ear,
   Hearing, not hear,
Though drums do roll, and pipes and cymbals ring;
So the bare conscience of the better thing
Unfelt, unseen, unimaged, all unknown,
May fix the entrancèd soul mid multitudes alone.

The variation in this kind of poem makes partial quotation particularly unjust; its negatives themselves are thematic; but even in a few lines one may hear the blending of a full eighteenth-century line's smooth scope with a seventeenth-century's pause and return and the heavily commonplace Stitch, stitch, stitch, Break, break, break, of Hood and Tennyson, in complex indication of the soul's tentative compasses and compassions.

Matthew Arnold, who is often linked with Clough in the light of their shared lyrical dismay, shares much also of technical construction. His proportioning is like Clough's and the average, moderate all round, a bare 3 to 1 substantival dominance. The nostalgic terms of *old, long, sweet, joy, time* are common to both, along with the main actions of man and soul; and the motion of poems like "The Voice" could be characteristic of both.

     As the kindling glances,
     Queen-like and clear,
     Which the bright moon lances
     From her tranquil sphere
     At the sleepless waters
     Of a lonely mere,

> On the wild whirling waves, mournfully, mournfully,
>   Shiver and die.
> As the tears of sorrow
>   Mothers have shed—
> Prayers that to-morrow
>   Shall in vain be sped
> When the flower they flow for
>   Lies frozen and dead—
> Fall on the throbbing brow, fall on the burning breast,
>   Bringing no rest.

But Arnold's volume of 1849 is much less consistently like this than Clough's. Arnold's poety all through his life sounds basically schooled in an older descriptive tradition, less intensely fragmented. The school poems of the early 1840's are strictly stanzaic and filled to the brim with images of construction. Thus the "Cromwell" sets up the cradles of Freedom, surveys the life of the man, and finally disperses the vision with all the aplomb of a stage master, though the sleepless waves, voice of fear, mystic tone, childhood of its smile, speechless impulse, deep stillness, song of liberty, all suggest the presence in Arnold's ear of the new phrasing, with a consequent paucity of substance for the stage design.

"Mycerinus" and the sonnets seem to me to be thinned by the same difficulty, a mixing of modes, a pouring of new implications into the outward forms of old explications, so that the weaknesses of both come through. The iambic pentameters are full of the sound of exposition but little of its sense; the meanings full of the reference of overtone, with little overtone to be heard; nor does the conflict between the two seem allowed to make a point of its own. Arnold recognized the difference between two cultures and expressions, but while he consciously denied the attitudes of the earlier, he did not so clearly abandon its poetic mode, as the sonnet "Written in Butler's Sermons" illustrates.

> Affections, Instincts, Principles, and Powers,
> Impulse and Reason, Freedom and Control—

So men, unravelling God's harmonious whole,
Rend in a thousand shreds this life of ours.
Vain labour! Deep and broad, where none may see,
Spring the foundations of the shadowy Throne
Where man's one Nature, queen-like, sits alone,
Centred in a majestic unity;
And rays her powers, like sister islands, seen
Linking their coral arms under the sea:
Or cluster'd peaks, with plunging gulfs between
Spann'd by aerial arches, all of gold;
Whereo'er the chariot wheels of Life are roll'd
In cloudy circles, to eternity.

The distinct abstractions of the eighteenth century and later seem to Arnold to rend God's harmonious whole, and denouncing that destruction, he builds up not in the sestet but in the octave itself the alternative picture of the enthroned and queen-like Nature in her majestic unity. The octave's structure, balanced and visualized, is thus close to an eighteenth-century one. What then will be the function of the sestet? Arnold suspends it with a mere semicolon and *and;* confuses the picture immeasurably by a metaphysical rather than physical figure of rays, islands, gulfs, and arches, and chariot wheels of Life; ends triumphantly with another sort of substitution, the imponderable release of "cloudy circles, to eternity." The sestet rays off into the modern vocabulary of suggestion, which he likes, but which he must suspend like a cloud since it does not work well in direct opposition to "Affections, Instincts, Principles, and Powers."

In like fashion, from the serious and relatively monumental poems for which Arnold, possibly by his standard of touchstones, felt most responsible, in what he called in the preface to "Merope" his "supposed addiction to the classical school in poetry," from "Merope" itself, and "Sohrab" and "Balder," ray off the more fragmentary and the more famous melodies of the "Merman" and the "Strayed Reveller" and of "Dover Beach," the cloudy circles of Arnold's easiest rest in the mode of his time. How natural he was at it! "A Modern Sappho" says,

> They are gone: all is still: Foolish heart, dost thou quiver?
> Nothing moves on the lawn but the quick lilac shade.
> Far up gleams the house, and beneath flows the river.
> Here lean, my head, on this cool balustrade.
>
> Ere he come: ere the boat, by the shining-branch'd border
> Of dark elms come round, dropping down the proud stream;
> Let me pause, let me strive, in myself find some order,
> Ere their boat-music sound, ere their broider'd flags gleam.

So a lady of Tennyson, of Clough, of Poe might speak, or, as the bells or merman of Poe or Longfellow,

> Come, dear children, come away down.
> Call no more.
> One last look at the white-wall'd town,
> And the little grey church on the windy shore.
> Then come down.
> She will not come though you call all day.
> Come away, come away.

In such lines Arnold made poetry of his own wishes and mystifications, and in so doing he was closer to his contemporaries than he knew.

If it seems an irony that the self-split Arnold was an "average" poet, practicing much as other poets practiced in his time, then it is an irony too that all these individuals of the decade, so self-searching, had so much in common. Not the Atlantic, not relative maturity or popularity, not varying verse traditions, not degree of subtlety, kept Longfellow, Bryant, Poe, Hawker, Hood, Campbell, Tennyson, Arnold, Clough from a kind of agreement in the nature of poetry. It was a poetry too substantial for the seventeenth century, with its adjective and verb per line and its doubled nouns; with its lack of extra substantives it was too thin for the eighteenth; it took a middle course. Clough used few nouns and Campbell many, Hood and Tennyson as few verbs,

6 in 10 lines, as one would think a decent poetry could get by
with; Bryant and Hawker in their oversea agreement came as
close as any to the 10–17–9 norm, but with all these variations
the poets sounded more like each other than like any poet of
the eighteenth or seventeenth century. Part of the reason for this,
too, was their vocabulary, which shared both centuries, with additions of its own. On its immediately inherited basis of *sweet day,
eye, God, heart, heaven, life, love, man, soul, come, give, hear,
know, rise, see,* it reconstructs the older *good, earth, time, world,
go, love, make, take, think,* and adds its new own *bright, old,
night, spirit, sun, thought, word, fall, lie, look.* It adds, that is,
the passivity of atmospheric implication to the activity of metaphysics and the vision of sublimity, filtering scenic structure and
spiritual interaction through the light and shadow of a receptive,
often a feminine, often a childlike, sometimes a mysterious and
troubled, always a feeling and dreaming mind.

III

A mind so capricious, at least steadily hinting caprice, must have
its expressions of extreme; and these we see in Landor, Emerson,
Macaulay, the Brownings on the one hand, in the later Wordsworth, and Keble, Hemans, Horne, Lowell, Tupper on the other.
The distance in practice and attitude between Emerson and
Lowell, that great American distance between Concord and Boston, spans the Atlantic, stretches from Landor's fit audience
though few to Tupper's vast array, and is nevertheless mediated
and mellowed by most poets of the decade.

The strict Emersonian poetics is an art which comes closer to
seventeenth-century than to eighteenth-century forebears. Yet it
would be wrong to call it "metaphysical," because it has been so
colored and altered by its procedure through time and by the
thought of the minds which contrive it. The proportioning is
tight like Donne's or Jonson's, with 7 or 8 adjectives in 10 lines

and twice as many nouns, and more verbs than epithets, though not enough, except for Landor's, to establish the verbs as half the substantives. At least, the 7–15–8 or 8–16–10 sort of proportion indicates an active predication and subordination in preference to modification and thus suggests the discursive rather than the descriptive mode.

The emphasis on terms supports this suggestion. Among epithets the Emersonian poets stress the seventeenth-century *good* and even *great* rather than their own modern *bright;* among nouns they ignore likewise the modern *light, soul, spirit* as well as many characteristically eighteenth-century terms; they are shy of the eighteenth-century verb *rise,* and stress instead most typically the new verb *speak,* with *word* its accompanying noun; actively fond of verbs as they are, they participate in all the new predicative stresses, the *loving, falling, lying, hearing* of their colleagues. Thus they are predicatively progressive and adjectivally reactionary, their substantives maintaining a middle, a most closely eighteenth-century ground. The result is a poetic texture at once more abstract and more actively, aurally, tenuously sensed than heretofore.

The result is evident on the first page of the first book of Emerson's poems, in 1847.

> The Sphinx is drowsy,
>   Her wings are furled:
> Her ear is heavy,
>   She broods on the world.
> "Who'll tell me my secret,
>   The ages have kept?—
> I awaited the seer
>   While they slumbered and slept:—
>
> "The fate of the man-child,
>   The meaning of man;
> Known fruit of the unknown;
>   Daedalian plan;

> Out of sleeping a waking,
>   Out of waking a sleep;
> Life death overtaking;
>   Deep underneath deep?"

To readers of Clough or Hood this phrasing by a colleague will be familiar. Its rhythm is regularly broken in line and in foot, yet carried by simple statement and rhyme. The statement is, in fact, as direct and simple as "Under the spreading chestnut tree / The village smithy stands," but in reference it takes the shadier complex side of *slept,* and *secret,* and *broods,* and *deep,* so that one feels at once there is more here than meets the eye, or even the heavy ear. No survey explains the scope, but rather *Sphinx* and *Daedalian* alone hint that vast geographic and historical worlds are involved. The *seer* is mysterious, the *man-child* innocent and sympathetic, the fruit ripely figurative, and *life* and *death* the commonest of familiar abstractions.

This is highly contemporary material, then, fitted to its time in motion and the variety of acceptable implication, in its stress on hearing, brooding, and the mystery of life (Ah, sweet mystery of life! is the purest nineteenth-century); and it is not metaphysical, for lack of human relationship; not neoclassical, for lack of a solid frame. It makes its own new combination of abstraction, implication, and centered symbol, bathing the thrush, the waves, the babe, the great mother, the oaf, the poet, the lover, and Jove in an infusion of joy, and bringing all in the end back to color, sensation, Monadnoc, and riddle, that jumble of physical being which neither metaphysician nor sublime satirist could muster.

> Uprose the merry Sphinx,
>   And crouched no more in stone;
> She melted into purple cloud,
>   She silvered in the moon;

> She spired into a yellow flame;
>   She flowered in blossoms red;
> She flowed into a foaming wave;
>   She stood Monadnoc's head.
>
> Through a thousand voices
>   Spoke the universal dame;
> "Who telleth one of my meanings,
>   Is master of all I am."

The quotation marks themselves are significant of the mode, as they suggest voice, speech, dialogue, not in the rational argument sense of the seventeenth century nor in the formally invocative sense of the eighteenth, but as a sort of matter of course, a direct personal tone. So "Each and All" begins, "Little thinks, in the field, yon red-cloaked clown / Of thee from the hill-top looking down"; and "The Problem," "I like a church; I like a cowl; / I love a prophet of the soul"; and "The Visit," "Askest, How long thou shalt stay? / Devastator of the day!"; and "The World-Soul," "Thanks to the morning light, / Thanks to the foaming sea"; and "Alphonso of Castile," "I, Alphonso, live and learn," and so on, to that most famous "Good-bye, proud world! I'm going home." Much of the difficulty of phrasing and connection in Emerson's poetry is attributable to his colloquial assumptions, his suggestion of explanatory gesture and tone which are not on the page; and this difficulty is but another aspect, like Longfellow's refrains and Poe's repetitions and Hood's heavy rhymes, of the highly auditory quality of the decade's verse. It does not conflict with the couplet, but it urges the couplet to conversation and to song.

> There's a melody born of melody,
> Which melts the world into a sea.
> Toil could never compass it;
> Art its height could never hit;
> It came never out of wit; ...

This from "Destiny," yet also from "Hamatreya,"

> Bulkeley, Hunt, Willard, Hosmer, Meriam, Flint,
> Possessed the land which rendered to their toil
> Hay, corn, roots, hemp, flax, apples, wool and wood.
> Each of these landlords walked amidst his farm,
> Saying, " 'Tis mine, my children's and my name's.
> How sweet the west wind sounds in my own trees! ..."

So melodized in more ways than one the old *eye, God, man,* and *nature,* to which Emerson was most loyal.

No less in Landor is the oral quality memorable. The "Imaginary Conversations" even in title suggests the spirit. The "Hellenics" of 1847, Landor said in an introductory note, were "rude frescoes," "scenes and figures which we venture once more to introduce in poetry"; and indeed their classical titles and settings and the firm regularity of their blank verse seem to indicate a poetical return to neoclassic phrasing as well. But the poetry does not so.

> Who will away to Athens with me? who
> Loves choral songs and maidens crown'd with flowers,
> Unenvious? mount the pinnace; hoist the sail.

The first Hellenic begins in this way, moves on to dialogue, petition, and exclamation, and never sets a stage securely. The end, moreover, trembles on the very brink of implication where the lyric likes to hover. Thrasymedes in a long impassioned cry before the prince admits he should not have loved the prince's daughter, and awaits punishment.

> He would have wept, but one
> Might see him, and weep worse. The prince unmoved
> Strode on, and said, "To-morrow shall the people,
> All who beheld thy trespasses, behold
> The justice of Peisistratos, the love
> He bears his daughter, and the reverence
> In which he holds the highest law of God."
> He spake; and on the morrow they were one.

The lasting and satisfying *one* of the nineteenth century! Zoe, in "Theron and Zoe," after a tortuous dialogue asking and denying words of love, after a kiss interrupting and lingering past the end of the poem, says,

> My voice is gone.
> Why did you kiss me, if you wisht to hear it?

Accepting the major terminology, as Emerson does, and adding the minor *father, mother, youth* of the decade, the *love, hear, see, speak* of their familial and dramatic actions, Landor, though the most predicative in proportioning and the most aware of his eccentricities, shares strongly the poetic manners and materials of his time.

Macaulay, though more popular, was somewhat less adaptable in vocabulary, because he narrowed his field of concentration in his Roman lays to a few major nouns and the lot of major verbs, adding his own *bridge* and *Roman* to the list, as one would expect. Nevertheless, it is pleasant to recognize in the old fifth-grade warhorse of school memory the speaking tones of the severer Landor, the regularly modified ballad rhythms of the decade, and the gentle domesticity of setting and sentiment in the midst of the historic survey.

> Lars Porsena of Clusium
>   By the Nine Gods he swore
> That the great house of Tarquin
>   Should suffer wrong no more.
> By the Nine Gods he swore it,
>   And named a trysting day,
> And bade his messengers ride forth,
> East and west and south and north,
>   To summon his array.
>
>   .   .   .   .
>
> When the goodman mends his armour,
>   And trims his helmet's plume;
> When the goodwife's shuttle merrily
>   Goes flashing through the loom;

> With weeping and with laughter
>   Still is the story told,
> How well Horatius kept the bridge
>   In the brave days of old.

"The Battle of Lake Regillus," "Virginia," "The Prophecy of Capys," in the same volume of 1842, proceed in the same manner, the ballad meter softened by the alternate feminine endings, as stanzas of village customs soften the battles, and the activity of the "old" becomes a value.

"The early history of Rome is indeed far more poetical than anything else in Latin literature," Macaulay wrote in his preface to these poems. "The loves of the Vestal and the God of War, the cradle laid among the reeds of Tiber, the fig tree, the she-wolf, the shepherd's cabin, the recognition, the fratricide, the rape of the Sabines, the death of Tarpeia, the fall of Hostus Hostilius, the struggle of Mettus Curtius through the marsh, the women rushing with torn raiment and disheveled hair between their fathers and their husbands, the nightly meetings of Numa and the Nymph by the well in the sacred grove, . . . are among the many instances which will at once suggest themselves to every reader." These are episodes not only *old* but *bright* and *good, dark* and *gold* and *high* and *wild*. In so many words, they are fine nineteenth-century episodes, loving, childlike, natural, violent, familial, emotional, atmospheric in the mysteries of marsh, night, and sacred grove. They have not what Macaulay decries some paragraphs later, "the quaint forms and gaudy coloring of such artists as Cowley and Gongora." Yet they have a simplicity of material and structure that is absent from the neoclassical as well as the metaphysical. They neatly supplement Longfellow in their narrative speed, Hood in their social conscience, Landor in their antiquity, Bryant and Hawker in their native objects, and echo the most downright in thumping enthusiasm.

In what better connection may "How They Brought the Good News from Ghent to Aix" be thought of? Or the "Cavalier Tunes," or even

> Just for a handful of silver he left us,
>   Just for a riband to stick in his coat—
> Found the one gift of which fortune bereft us,
>   Lost all the others she lets us devote; . . .

Or, more softly,

> Here's the garden she walked across,
>   Arm in my arm, such a short while since:
> Hark, now I push its wicket, the moss
>   Hinders the hinges and makes them wince!
> She must have reached this shrub ere she turned,
>   As back with that murmur the wicket swung;
> For she laid the poor snail, my chance foot spurned,
>   To feed and forget it the leaves among.

Or, full of both inner and outer dialogue,

> At the meal we sit together:
>   *Salve tibi!* I must hear
> Wise talk of the kind of weather,
>   Sort of season, time of year:
> *Not a plenteous cork-crop: scarcely*
>   Dare we hope oak-galls, I doubt:
> *What's the Latin name for "parsley"?*
>   What's the Greek name for Swine's Snout?

Or, the "Lost Mistress'" catching of situation and abstraction in a half parallel of atmosphere,

> All's over, then: does truth sound bitter
>   As one at first believes?
> Hark, 'tis the sparrows' good-night twitter
>   About your cottage eaves!

Or, finally, in a magical sort of formalizing of the nineteenth-century mode, its caught-up echoing line, its twilit scene, its colloquial interpolation, its antique re-creation, its narrative motion into the feeling and statement of love,

Where the quiet-colored end of evening smiles
    Miles on miles
On the solitary pastures where our sheep
    Half-asleep
Tinkle homeward through the twilight, stray or stop
    As they crop—
Was the site once of a city great and gay,
    (So they say)
Of our country's very capital, its prince
    Ages since
Held his court in, gathered councils, wielding far
    Peace or war.

All these Brownings and the others of *Dramatic Lyrics* and *Dramatic Romances* are the poets of the decade. They vary the pattern, from villa to city, from Spain to Florence, from sea to fireside, from Galuppi to Gismond, and the Piper to Roland, they stumble as the speaking tongue of Emerson did over the complexities and ellipses of what they wish to say; but their ethic of reach and grasp, their aesthetic of the lit lamp and the blown horn, make them directly expressive of the force of symbol in their poetic day.

Much of the variety was too complex for the immediate readers, but Pippa's song suited everyone, moving in and out of verse freely and dramatically, as Arnold could also, but with more ebullience, as of livelier beat.

Day!
Faster and more fast,
O'er night's brim, day boils at last;
Boils, pure gold, o'er the cloud-cup's brim
Where spurting and suppressed it lay;
For not a froth-flake touched the rim
Of yonder gap in the solid gray
Of the eastern cloud, an hour away;
But forth one wavelet, then another, curled,
Till the whole sunrise, not to be suppressed,
Rose, reddened, and its seething breast
Flickered in bounds, grew gold, then overflowed the world.

The dramatic songs of Elizabeth Barrett Browning are less flexible, though ecstatic: her "Drama of Exile" began her volume of
1844, its final chorus characteristic, and characteristically not far
from R. B.'s.

> Calm the stars and golden
>   In a light exceeding:
> What their rays have measured
>   Let your feet fulfil!
> There are stars beholden
>   By your eyes in Eden,
> Yet across the desert,
>   See them shining still!
>
> .   .   .   .
>
> Patiently enduring,
>   Painfully surrounded,
> Listen how we love you,
>   Hope the uttermost!
> Waiting for that curing
>   Which exalts the wounded,
> Hear us sing above you—
>   *Exiled, but not lost!*

But more especially in her own voice are the many sonnets of
the 1840's, which say as if in essay form what are the states of
feeling that seem true and important, and set forth in greatest
emotional literalness the poet's attitude. So "The Soul's Expression":

> With stammering lips and insufficient sound
> I strive and struggle to deliver right
> That music of my nature, day and night
> With dream and thought and feeling interwound,
> And inly answering all the senses round
> With octaves of a mystic depth and height
> Which step out grandly to the infinite
> From the dark edges of the sensual ground.
> This song of soul I struggle to outbear
> Through portals of the sense, sublime and whole,
> And utter all myself into the air:
> But if I did it,—as the thunder-roll
> Breaks its own cloud, my flesh would perish there,
> Before that dread apocalypse of soul.

Both the Brownings lend a sense of effort and intense difficulty to their work which, within a tight form, suggests their mastery over strong emotion, yet at the same time its force beyond their words, and this again is a phase of the suggestibility of the nineteenth century's poetry, its more than meets the understanding as well as the eye. The wife and husband, bringing the family biographically as well as referentially into poetry, wrote with remarkable likeness even before their marriage. The small difference in proportioning lay in Browning's extra verbs, with a referential difference in their kind, Browning's being more active, in *give, bring, live,* Mrs. Browning's passive, in *hear, stand, sing,* but all of the rest alike. Except for Mrs. Browning's *sweet, fair, holy, true,* they agreed on most adjectives, and with like distinction chose most nouns alike except for Mrs. Browning's more abstract *earth, soul, spirit, thought, death, dream, nature, prayer,* and her especial *father.* They worked, in other words, on a standard basis, emphasizing the *good day, God,* and *love,* along with the new *little, mother, night, sun, song,* and in addition Mrs. Browning added the frills of the spiritual, the receptive, and the chivalrous. Browning made a sturdy conservatism masculine, Mrs. Browning an intenser acceptance of new styles feminine. Both told with much intensity the tales of the adventures of spirit, the notion of otherworld in the trappings of this, and carried the antique fortunes of Landor's and Macaulay's characters further into the solidities of life and the symbolisms of dream.

IV

Another sort of conservatism obtains at the other pole of poetic practice in the decade, in the most fully amplificatory poetry of Wordsworth, Keble, Horne, Hemans, Lowell, Tupper. This seems a mixed lot of poets, not one to think of or consent to except perhaps in what seems to us a sort of mid-century mediocrity. But for its own age it was not mediocre, but rather extreme, and most popular, following the normal proportionings of the eighteenth century, not its own, and following also the terms of sense rather than of standard, the major *bright, eye, hand, heart, life, light, man, rise, see,* and the minor *dark, deep, high, joy, mind, power, seem,* which in the main continue or increase the descriptive stresses of the eighteenth century.

Mrs. Hemans was Mrs. Browning's elder by many years, her collected poems printed just as the first of Elizabeth Barrett's were beginning to appear, and her vocabulary reflects her closer eighteenth-century alliances, to more adjectives than verbs, to strong sense adjectives of the *bright–dark, strong–wild* kind, to weak verbs of the envisioning kind; to a substantial emphasis on feelings. Her titles make a résumé of early nineteenth-century procedures, the early "Restoration of the Works of Art to Italy" in its heroic couplets sounding very early indeed,

> Land of departed fame! whose classic plains
> Have proudly echo'd to immortal strains;
> Whose hallow'd soil hath given the great and brave,
> Daystars of life, a birthplace, and a grave;
> Home of the Arts! where glory's faded smile,
> Sheds ling'ring light o'er many a mould'ring pile;
>
> . . . .
>
>   Awake, ye Muses of Etrurian shades,
> Or sacred Tivoli's romantic glades;
> Wake, ye that slumber in the bowery gloom
> Where the wild ivy shadows Virgil's tomb; . . .

The later "King of Arragon's Lament for his Brother" has the newer lilt and vocality,

There were light sounds of revelling in the vanquish'd city's halls,
As by night the feast of victory was held within its walls;
And the conquerors filled the wine cup high, after years of bright blood
   shed;
But their Lord, the King of Arragon, 'midst the triumph, wail'd the
   dead.

The themes of home, song, death, ancient times, seasons, and selected natural objects like birds, seas, flowers recur in the titles, and variations of four- and five-stressed rhymed lines are commonest, as for the decade.

> Sing them upon the sunny hills,
>   When days are long and bright,
> And the blue gleam of shining rills
>   Is loveliest to the sight!
> Sing them along the misty moor,
>   Where ancient hunters roved,
> And swell them through the torrent's roar,
>   The songs our fathers loved!

This "Songs of Our Fathers" is a clear nineteenth-century song, and one of the many which readers of Mrs. Hemans accepted and loved. The heavier, more visual language she used appears more clearly in sonnet than in song and illustrates what one who began in coupleted surveys can make by way of compromise with the lyric. Consider, for example, "To the Sky," the second of "Records of the Spring of 1834":

> Far from the rustlings of the poplar bough,
> Which o'er my opening life wild music made,
> Far from the green hills with their heathery glow
> And flashing streams whereby my childhood play'd;
> In the dim city, 'midst the sounding flow
> Of restless life, to thee in love I turn,
> O thou rich sky! and from thy splendors learn
> How song-birds come and part, flowers wane and blow.
> With thee all shapes of glory find their home,
> And thou hast taught me well, majestic dome!
> By stars, by sunsets, by soft clouds which rove
> Thy blue expanse, or sleep in silvery rest,
> That Nature's God hath left no spot unbless'd
> With founts of beauty for the eye of love.

Less personal and spiritual, more richly verbally explicative than a sonnet by Mrs. Browning, yet full of the details of a nineteenth-century sensibility, this poem has the smoothness of compromise between modes.

So has the sonnet written by the elder Wordsworth on the first day of 1840, on a portrait of I. F. It deals with the visual, but etherealizes it.

> We gaze—nor grieve to think that we must die,
> But that the precious love this friend hath sown
> Within our hearts, the love whose flower hath blown
> Bright as if heaven were ever in its eye,
> Will pass so soon from human memory;
> And not by strangers to our blood alone,
> But by our best descendants be unknown,
> Unthought of—this may surely claim a sigh.
> Yet, blessèd Art, we yield not to dejection;
> Thou against Time so feelingly dost strive.
> Where'er, preserved in this most true reflection,
> An image of her soul is kept alive,
> Some lingering fragrance of the pure affection,
> Whose flower with us will vanish, must survive.

The smooth and dignified flow is aided by the archaic and reverential *thou,* by the feelings and the symbolizing flower, and by the *precious, bright, human, best, blessed, lingering, pure* epithets, which here, though more scantily than usual for Wordsworth, maintain a qualitative continuity.

The poems of Wordsworth's last decade, mostly sonnets, some pieces, on flowers, clouds, people, pictures, and events, tend all to share this eighteenth-century smoothness, not to be broken by much tone of voice. His proportioning of 11–19–9 in these years is closer to eighteenth-century proportions than are the *Lyrical Ballads* of a half century before. His vocabulary, too, is conservative, omitting the new *day* and *night, fall* and *lie,* stressing *power* and the terms of feeling, though some terms of outward nature survive from the *Ballads.* It would seem, in the history of this poet, that the more experimental practices and patterns came in his earlier years and influenced younger poets more than the aging Wordsworth himself; for his work of the 1840's is less singular, more like an older poet like Blair, than one would ex-

pect from the *Ballads* author. The sonnet gave him, as it gave
Mrs. Hemans, a chance to ease up on experiment with lyrical
colloquial techniques and to compromise between lyric and exposition, softening discourse and implication with the substance
of a flowery nature.

See how smooth in this process the epic has become. Horne's
"farthing epic," "Orion," with five editions in its year of publication 1843, makes the blank verse flow with a sequence of easy
epithets, ceremonious as the eighteenth century but more solidly
sensory. This is what has become of orthodox survey.

> Ye rocky heights of Chios, where the snow,
> Lit by the far-off and receding moon,
> Now feels the soft dawn's purpling twilight creep
> Over your ridges, while the singing dews,
> Like creatures on a mission from the spheres,
> Swarm down, and wait to be instinct with gold
> And solar fire!—

It is softened and blurred in the realm of sense, made not structural but wholly atmospheric. And the story of Orion, developed
in narrative and dialogue, nevertheless is laden with atmosphere,
so that such an ending is suitable as:

> The song ceased; and at once a chorus burst
> From all the stars in heaven, which now shone forth!
> The Moon ascends in her rapt loveliness;
> The Ocean swells to her forgivingly;
> Bright comes the dawn, and Eos hides her face,
> Glowing with tears divine, within the bosom
> Of great Poseidon, in his rocking car
> Standing erect to gaze upon his son,
> Installed midst golden fires, which ever melt
> In Eos' breath and beauty; rising still
> With nightly brilliance, merging in the dawn,
> And circling onward in eternal youth.

The classically divine personages have tended to lose both their
abstract and their physical figures within a universal glow of
nature, as moon, ocean, and dawn with their blended outlines

have absorbed the scene. The many epithets, especially participial, *all, rapt, glowing, divine, bright, great, rocking, standing, golden, rising, nightly, merging, circling, eternal,* carry the theme almost exactly, as Keatsian epithets were apt to do, suspending the few active verbs of ascension in, as the text suggests, a sort of eternal circle of spiritual height. The cosmical framework has been spread and smoothed by its adaptors.

For Keble and for Tupper the smoothing came in rather different fashion, also epithetical, but more moral. His editor has said that Keble's favorite words in *Lyra Innocentium* were *duteous* and *healing,* and these "Thoughts in Verse on Christian Children Their Ways and Their Privileges" as they soothe us with early encouragements and warnings, lessons of nature and grace, holy places and things, holy seasons and days, do read the offices of comfort through the natural world. Keble's favorite words actually are those of sight (his *bright* is twice his *good*), of feeling, and of family; he cares for few verbs, but likes most of the new adjectives of his day, the *dear, deep,* and *dim.* So the introductory "To All Friendly Readers" infuses its air with ethics:

> There are, who love upon their knees
>   To linger when their prayers are said,
> And lengthen out their Litanies,
>   In duteous care for quick and dead.
> Thou, of all Love the Source and Guide!
>   O may some hovering thought of theirs,
> Where I am kneeling, gently glide,
>   And higher waft these earth-bound prayers.
>
> There are, who gazing on the stars
>   Love-tokens read from worlds of light,
> Not as dim-seen through prison-bars,
>   But as with Angels' welcome bright.
> O had we kept entire the vow
>   And covenant of our infant eyes,
> We too might trace untrembling now
>   Glad lessons in the moonlight skies.

Though the effect here seems very different from such an epical sweep as Horne's, the difference is more in the rocking meter than in the vocabulary. The technique of suspensive participles, in *hovering, kneeling, gazing, untrembling,* still dominates, the dim and bright feelings dominate, and the otherworld of the Angels, like the otherworld of the gods, is high, moonlit, and symbolical. And on the cosy domestic side, "Cradle Song" 4:

> While snows, e'en from the mild South-west,
>   Come blinding o'er all day,
> What kindlier home, what safer nest,
>   For flower or fragrant spray,
> Than underneath some cottage roof,
>   Where fires are bright within,
> And fretting cares scowl far aloof,
>   And doors are clos'd on sin?

The *Proverbial Philosophy* of Martin Tupper too is a book of "thoughts," "A Book of Thoughts and Arguments," and it too develops the eighteenth-century abstractions of feeling: Anticipation, Memory, Ambition, Humility, Pride, Hatred, and Anger, and so on, with its modern variations in Hidden Uses, Compensation, Indirect Influences, Experience, Prayer, Mystery, Solitude, and Yesterday, Today, and Tomorrow. Its method is startling, because unlike anything we have seen in poetic history; its long six-foot line, its common feminine endings, its alliterative and metaphorical joinings, its personal tone, all are slightly related to Longfellow's freedoms but beyond them, speaking across an ocean in the decade-later voice of *Leaves of Grass.*

Thoughts, that have tarried in my mind, and peopled its inner chambers,
The sober children of reason, or desultory train of fancy;
Clear running wine of conviction, with the scum and the lees of speculation;
Corn from the sheaves of science, with stubble from mine own garner;
Searchings after Truth, that have tracked her secret lodes,

And come up again to the surface-world, with a knowledge grounded
    deeper;
Arguments of high scope, that have soared to the keystone of heaven,
And thence have swooped to their certain mark, as the falcon to its
    quarry;
The fruits I have gathered of prudence, the ripened harvest of my
    musings,
These commend I unto thee, O docile scholar of Wisdom,
These I give to thy gentle heart, thou lover of the right.

Even the special vocabulary of Whitman is Tupper's sooner:

There is use in the prisoned air, that swelleth the pods of the laburnum;
Design in the venomed thorns, that sentinel the leaves of the nettle;
A final cause for the aromatic gum, that congealeth the moss around a
    rose:
A reason for each blade of grass, that reareth its small spire.
How knoweth discontented man what a train of ills might follow,
If the lowest menial of nature knew not her secret office?

The voice of Whitman and the voice of Pope may join together.

Where art thou, storehouse of the mind, garner of facts and fancies,—
In what strange firmament are laid the beams of thine airy chambers?

These lines "Prefatory," "Of Hidden Sources," and "Of Memory," take the pattern of the hundreds more, and the hundreds
which would not appear until another century, following their
good gray poet.[2]

Yet the orthodoxy of Tupper's 1840 vocabulary is not dis-
turbed. He used most of the major terms, except the important
atmospheric group of *bright–light–day–night,* with especial stress
on the elder strengths of *God, spirit, man, know.* He used strong
minor adjectives, and nouns of *mind, power,* the *lord* and *king*
synonyms for God. While his high moral tone seems foreign to
the sensory allusiveness of Poe, the colored myth of Horne, yet

---

[2] Little has been written on the connection between Tupper and Whitman, but see:
American Notes and Queries, I (October, 1941), 101–102; F. O. Matthiessen, *The James
Family,* pp. 490–492, and Edna Romig, "More Roots for Leaves of Grass," *Elizabethan
Studies and Other Essays* (Univ. of Colorado Studies, II, 4).

more seriously all three share with their colleagues the simple sense of natural fact, as in earth, sun, flower, of physical being in hand and heart, of emotional and spiritual order, as in love and soul, thought and word. The conservatism which they shared in the decade was closely allied to its most experimental practice, as the qualities of earth were shaded, the physical being was made sensitive and passive, and the spiritual order was made at once more intellectual and more dim and childlike in the questioning lyrics of Arnold and Poe, of Tennyson, Hood, and Clough. The Proverbial Philosophy of Tupper provides the matrix for such lyricizing and questioning.

The one of the conservatives who perhaps most represents them all, and their time, with least idiosyncrasy and most enthusiastic participation is Lowell. He is highly substantial because he puts everything in. He has the solidity of an eighteenth-century Shenstone or Dyer, 12 adjectives, 19 nouns, 11 verbs in ten lines, almost the eighteenth-century norm. Like Horne, Wordsworth, Keble, and Hemans he likes plentiful reference and modification, and strengthens verbs in addition. He shares in more of the major terms than anybody but Elizabeth Barrett Browning, and especially flourishes among the minor epithets, fostering Bryant's *dark,* Horne's *deep,* Poe's *dim,* Hemans' *fair,* Keble's *holy,* Clough's *little,* Hood's *poor,* and others including the full array *bright, good, old,* and *sweet.* As may be expected, he stresses the nouns and verbs of sight, but he adds also the newer and freer *feeling* and *hearing, hope* and *dream.*

The well-remembered beginning of "The Vision of Sir Launfal" speaks for this richest variety of the verse.

> Over his keys the musing organist,
>   Beginning doubtfully and far away,
> First lets his fingers wander as they list,
>   And builds a bridge from Dreamland for his lay:
> Then, as the touch of his loved instrument
>   Gives hope and fervor, nearer draws his theme,

> First guessed by faint auroral flushes sent
>   Along the wavering vista of his dream.
> Not only around our infancy
> Doth heaven with all its splendors lie;
> Daily, with souls that cringe and plot,
> We Sinais climb and know it not.
>
> Over our manhood bend the skies;
>   Against our fallen and traitor lives
> The great winds utter prophecies;
>   With our faint hearts the mountain strives;
> Its arms outstretched, the druid wood
>   Waits with its benedicite;
> And to our age's drowsy blood
>   Still shouts the inspiring sea.

The story itself comes to symbolic point.

> As Sir Launfal mused with a downcast face,
> A light shone round about the place;
> The leper no longer crouched at his side,
> But stood before him glorified,
> Shining and tall and fair and straight
> As the pillar that stood by the Beautiful Gate,—
> Himself the Gate whereby men can
> Enter the temple of God in Man.

Here is the finest infusion of spirit into scene. Some of Lowell's poems in the 1840's are more purely scenic, like "Prometheus," which begins with a cosmic survey, "One after one the stars have risen and set"; and some more lightly lyrical, like "A Legend of Brittany's" "Fair as a summer dream was Margaret." In Launfal's vision the modes blend.

The beginning melody subordinates the whole vision to the intangibles of spirit, and thus to symbol. Yet the vision is a fuller, more sensuously splendid one than Emerson, for example, would allow. The rhythms are prolonged, yet subtly. The first trochaic substitution makes an excellently easy onomatopoeia of improvisation; the shift to tetrameter makes a direct emphasis; the series of nature's actions in the second stanza makes structural variety part of its effectiveness. The play of sound for Lowell, in other words, is full and meaningful, showing, like Clough's and Arnold's and not like that of the other very substantival poets, a recognition of new harmonies for verse to temper its substantiality.

The play of sense, though ponderous, is more varied here than Lowell often managed. It is full of immediately sensed convention. The *far away,* the *faint,* the *wavering,* the *drowsy* maintain that air of suspended suggestion which was orthodox. The music, dream, and infancy are proper poetic states. Heaven and nature participate as one in the guidance of man, in the reversed *splendor* of heaven and *benedicite* of the wood. And feelings infuse all, in *hope* and *inspiration.*

In such a poem as this, though he was sometimes more downright, Lowell was able to catch that nineteenth-century flower of sense in spirit at its fullest bloom. More than his most like contemporaries, Horne or Wordsworth or Mrs. Hemans, he could blend June with moon to achieve the quality of rich suggestion and spiritual gleam which seemed quintessentially poetic. He was most unlike the poets who interpreted this essence in another way, the poets like Landor and Emerson and the Brownings who tried less melody and more conversation, less music and more speech, less sensory feeling and more active thought. Lowell smoothed and filled in the rough extremes of Emerson and the central simplicities of Longfellow; his aestheticizing of their thought was, in the 1840's, a conservative and "literary" procedure as it rested in a mode of the past, yet a liberal one as it spread and blended.

IV. GROUNDS OF PROSE IN THE 1840's

A BOOK like R. H. Horne's *New Spirit of the Age,* written in 1843 to clarify the characteristics of new writing as Hazlitt had in decades earlier, speaks most strongly of the mysteries in nature—a crushed human heart, a touch, an echo. And these are good. We find them in the new Charles Dickens: "Nor is the squalid place so bad as it was before he entered it, for some 'touch of nature'—of unadulterated pathos—of a crushed human heart uttering a sound from out the darkness and the slough, has left its echo in the air, and half purified it from its malaria of depravity" (I, 13). This new sentiment allows a depth of feeling to the uncorrespondingly deep, to the minor, squalid, crushed, malarial. And "a touch" is all that is needed; it leaves its lingering "echo." The hint and the suggestion are taken as moving and refining.

Horne was no rebel or anticlassicist. He admired Landor especially for his clear nobility. "He is classical in the highest sense. His conceptions stand out, clearly cut and fine, in a magnitude and nobility as far as possible removed from the small and sickly vagueness common to this century of letters." Horne was not proud of the 1840's, completely. But he knew what he didn't like about the late neoclassical poets, and he knew that he did like the new "dawn" in Wordsworth, and in these feelings he was representative (I, 308–310):

For several generations, had the cadences of our poets (so called) moved to them along the ends of their fingers. Their language had assumed a conventional elegance, spreading smoothly into pleonasms or clipped nicely into elisions. The point of an antithesis had kept perpetual sentry upon the "final pause"; and while a spurious imagination made a Name stand as a personification, Observation only looked out of window ("with extensive view" indeed…"from China to Peru!") and refused very positively to take a step out of doors. A long and dreary decline of poetry it was, from the high-rolling sea of Dryden, or before Dryden, when Waller first began to "improve" (bona verba!) our versification—down to the time of Wordsworth. Milton's far-off voice, in the meantime, was a trumpet, which the singing-birds could not take a note from: his genius was a lone island in a remote sea, and singularly uninfluential on his contemporaries and immediate successors. The decline sloped on.... And England did not wait in vain for a *new* effluence of genius—it came at last like the morning—a pale light in the sky, an awakening bird, and a sunburst—we had Cowper—we had Burns—that lark of the new grey dawn; and presently the early-risers of the land could see to spell slowly out the name of William Wordsworth.

Taking this long view back, one sees that the "renascence of wonder" involves a special sort of wonder, not so much of admiration as of delicacy and sympathy and doubt;—let not all be said. Such wonder lurked always in sublimity, as in the simplicity of classical explication, but had little function as guiding force. Johnson was not a man of hints and echoes. But along with Johnson were the new critics of the last half century, who cried for mystery, novelty, the Gothic surprise, and who gradually managed a blend of crude wonder with general nature to achieve that delicate mystery of a single flower which would gracefully epitomize the new poetic mode.

Bishop Hurd's dissertation "On the Idea of Universal Poetry" represents the transitional approach very neatly, speaking in the regular terms of pleasure, images, variety, adornment, nature, power, sublimity, virtue, soul, but shifting emphasis toward the strange, away from the noble general (*Works,* II, 8–9).

For there is something in the mind of man, sublime and elevated, which prompts it to overlook all obvious and familiar appearances, and to feign to itself other and more extraordinary; such as correspond to the extent of its own powers, and fill out all the faculties and capacities of our souls....

Hence it comes to pass, that it deals in apostrophes and invocations; that it impersonates the virtues and vices; peoples all creation with new and living forms; calls up infernal spectres to terrify, or brings down celestial natures to astonish, the imagination; assembles, combines, or connects its ideas, at pleasure; in short, prefers not only the agreeable and the graceful, but as occasion calls upon her, the vast, the incredible, I had almost said, the impossible, to the obvious truth and nature of things.

This is the very attitude, well known in its seventeenth-century form, which Pope satirized in his "Art of Sinking" forty years before. The words are almost the same as Hurd's, but for the neoclassicist of common generality the tone must be satiric. Chapter v describes the poet with "true genius for the profund":

He is to consider himself as a grotesque painter, whose works would be spoiled by an imitation of nature, or uniformity of design. He is to mingle bits of the most various, or discordant kinds, landscape, history, portraits, animals, and connect them with a great deal of flourishing, by heads or tails, as it shall please his imagination, and contribute to his principal end, which is to glare by strong opposition of colours, and surprize by a contrariety of images.

Serpentes avibus geminentur, tigribus agni.—Hor.

His design ought to be like a labyrinth, out of which nobody can get clear but himself. And since the great art of poetry is to mix truth with fiction, in order to join the credible with the surprising; our author shall produce the credible, by painting Nature in her lowest simplicity; and the surprising, by contradicting common opinion.

This absurd "lowest simplicity" of Nature will come to be, within the century, not metaphysical mixed birds and serpents indeed, but Wordsworth's modest celandine, not low, but deep, in its significance of spirit.

The development was not an easy one. Longinus' was for many years the most liberal and progressive critical philosophy, and it did not provide in any very vivid way for either negative or microcosmic views. It tended rather to support the Aristotelian heroic and to supplement it in the realms of nature and inner feeling, to correlate scene, action, passion. Only gradually, through interpreters like Beattie and Burke, was the darker and lower side of life, Pope's comic profund, taken seriously, developed from suggestions of simplicity and mystery in Longinus, and brought through all the tortures of the Gothic, all the straits of Crabbe and Cowper, up to the subtle dawn which Horne in 1843 hailed and accepted for the new poetic world.

Obvious and *familiar, conventional* and *shared,* are negative critical terms for Horne, as they had been for Hurd and his later colleagues in the romantic spirit, and the strange, the fine-drawn, the delicately shaded have come to seem more truthful and poetic. The value of *commonness* is no longer its highest normal shared or *in common* quality, but rather its lowest descriptive everyday quality. The plane of thought has moved downward and inward, and value works with refinement, intensification, rather than with elevation.

Says Horne, "Refinement is an essential property of the Ideal, and whatever is touched by ideality is so far redeemed from earth" (I, p. 147). He uses the figure of "a vital flower of ideality through the heavy fermenting earth of human experience" (II, p. 29). He praises "a certain consciousness of dreamy glories in the soul" for Tennyson, and finds the poetic fire "one simple and intense element in human nature; it has its source in the divine mysteries of our existence" (II, p. 3). Wordsworth, too, as the "laurelled veteran," spoke for the personal, even the mean, from the heart: "He would take no leap at the generalization of the natural; and the brown moss upon the pale should be as sacred to him and acceptable to his song, as the pine-clothed mountain" (I, pp. 311–312).

This evaluative phrasing, natural to Horne and his time and new in its wide acceptance, was not of course new entirely. It had grown slowly stronger as classicism had widened its range in the eighteenth century. Pope's vast minor vocabulary of particularity prepares for it, and much of Addison's appreciation, and Hume's essays, and Blair, and Thomas Warton's view of Elizabethan poetry, and the young Romantics, through a hundred years and more, or even from Spenser and before, to the 1840's.

The details of the course of accrual have begun to be traced.[1] But at least we may see in the contrast between two centuries the new consolidations and consistencies.

Horne has much excited praise for Carlyle, for the newness of him, his "window to the east"; "how deep and like a new sound, do the words 'soul,' 'work,' 'duty,' strike down upon the flashing anvils of the age, till the whole age vibrates!" (pp. 257, 264). And Carlyle sounds, in his *Hero* lectures of 1840, the same note of discovery at the source of things.

We cannot look, however imperfectly, upon a great man, without gaining something by him. He is the living light-fountain, which it is good and pleasant to be near. The light which enlightens, which has enlightened the darkness of the world; and this is not as a kindled lamp only, but rather as a natural luminary shining by the gift of Heaven; a flowing light-fountain, as I say, of native original insight, of manhood and heroic nobleness;—in whose radiance all souls feel that it is well with them. (P. 2)

The fountain and the light as metaphors of source suggest a divine power, and one not ordered like the eighteenth century's, but mysteriously welling up, within even the smallest objects. Time, too, takes on the quality of vague, as indefinable, power:

That great mystery of *Time,* were there no other; the illimitable, silent, never-resting thing called Time, rolling, rushing on, swift, silent, like an all-embracing ocean-tide, on which we and all the Universe swim like exhalations, like apparitions which *are,* and then *are not:* this is forever very literally a miracle; ... Force, Force, everywhere Force; we ourselves a mysterious force in the centre of that. "There is not a leaf rotting on the highway but has Force in it: how else could it rot?" (P. 8)

And again,

To us also, through every star, through every blade of grass, is not a God made visible, if we will open our minds and eyes?

---

[1] See, for example, Blair, pp. 214, 244. And *Guardian* 12, *Spectator* 253. A recent dissertation by Paul Roberts at the University of California has shown the importance of Scott also in the increase of the poetic vocabulary of particularity.

Now this, in 1840, is a new time and universe, apparitional, exhalational; and a new leaf, made to *rot* in nevertheless noble prose, and a new visibility, not in human form, since we see God in grass blades, and not of the eyes only but of the mind. More hints. More echoes. We recognize the Germanic quality of much of this thought. Indeed Carlyle makes direct reference, to Fichte's idea, for example, that literature is a "continuous revelation" of the Godlike in the Terrestrial and Common (p. 151), and to the "infinitude" in a Poet, and to his "Inspiration" (pp. 76, 144). Always the sense of depth, source, search, is present, the veil, the sigh, the spring, the breath, and always the sense of the ultimately inexpressible hovering close to the surface.

One would expect this feeling to have some effect on the discussion of metrics, and so it does directly for both Horne and Carlyle. The problem of harmony no longer seems as important as the problem of melody, and melody fades off into overtone.[2] A major force in sound for the eighteenth century had been onomatopoeia—outward harmony, that is, in the simultaneity of sound and reference, the play of correspondences. But now the song qualities and half-suggested significances of melody come to be considered. The point is important in "The Hero as Poet" (pp. 77–78):

> For my own part, I find considerable meaning in the old vulgar distinction of Poetry being metrical, having music in it, being a Song.... A *musical* thought is one spoken by a mind that has penetrated into the inmost heart of the thing; detected the inmost mystery of it, namely the *melody* that lies hidden in it; the inward harmony of coherence which is its soul, whereby it exists, and has a right to be, here in this world.... Poetry, therefore, we call *Musical Thought*. The Poet is he who *thinks* in that manner. At bottom, it turns still on power of intel-

---

[2] There is no fully useful general book to read on the new metrics following Coleridge, but such studies of earlier metrics as George Williamson's and Ruth Wallerstein's provide a good basis for Bracher on blank verse and George Stewart on ballad measures, this last being especially helpful. The surveys of meters are usually specialized and technical. But see Karl Shapiro's bibliographical essay.

lect; it is a man's sincerity and depth of vision that makes him a Poet. See deep enough, and you see musically; the heart of Nature *being* everywhere music, if you can only reach it.

Close to music is the eloquence of silence, as in Dante's poetry. "Let us honour the great empire of *Silence,* once more! The boundless treasury which we do *not* jingle in our pockets, or count up and present before men! It is perhaps, of all things, the usefulest for each of us to do, in these loud times" (p. 93). Horne too feared the loudness of the times, and so looked back with pleasure to the skill of an early Wordsworthian undertone.

The major prose of the time supported Horne, vividly and stylistically, if not with such specifically literary application. Emerson's Nature as dramatically as Carlyle's Heroes asserted the new depths of spirit.

> The eye reads omens where it goes,
> And speaks all languages the rose; ...

begins the first 1836 essay on Nature, and shows an eye immediately not an eighteenth-century eye, a rose not an eighteenth-century flower. *Omens* are only partly to be seen; they are more to be guessed at and interpreted. The *rose* is neither to be seen, nor even to be taken as personified speaker, since it speaks, rather than represents, all it contains; it is symbol rather than image. Emerson immediately asks:

Why should not we also enjoy an original relation to the universe? Why should not we have a poetry and philosophy of insight and not of tradition, and a religion by revelation to us and not the history of theirs? Embosomed for a season in nature, whose floods of life stream around and through us and invite us by the powers they supply to action proportioned to nature, why should we grope among the dry bones of the past or put the living generation into masquerade out of its faded wardrobe? The sun shines today also. There is more wool and flax in the fields. There are new lands, new men, new thoughts. Let us demand our own works and laws and worship.

Already this very writing is characteristic of the new poetry. *Original, insight, revelation* have become words of value. The figure of the flood of life is set in favorable contrast against the figure of the wardrobe, that great old metaphor of visual beauty in adornment now turned to the superficiality of masquerade. The straight assertion of sun shining and flax in the fields, in its particularity characteristic of Emerson especially, asserts by implication the significance behind, beneath, these common appearances. Their very commonness makes them the more significant. *"Nature,* in the common sense, refers to essences unchanged by man: space, the air, the river, the leaf. *Art* is applied to the mixture of his will with the same things, as in a house, a canal, a statue, a picture." These are not the classical examples of nature, they are both more abstract and more particular; and the list of phenomena thought inexplicable, "language, sleep, madness, dreams, beasts, sex," possesses even more an interest extravagant in classical terms. The Introduction to *Nature,* then, is not to norm, or to human form, or to scene, but to a seemingly almost arbitrary diversity of wonders and participations.

The chapter titles mix their worlds equally. "Commodity" is homely and economical, shifting to the plane of "Beauty." "Language" and "Discipline" seem to work at a general social level; "Idealism" and "Spirit" give us the new terms which dissolve the social; finally, "Prospects" has a benign eighteenth-century sound. Emerson happily blends all these. Under "Nature":

To speak truly, few adult persons can see nature. Most persons do not see the sun. At least they have a very superficial seeing. The sun illuminates only the eye of the man, but shines into the eye and the heart of the child.... The greatest delight which the fields and woods minister is the suggestion of an occult relation between man and the vegetable.

Under "Beauty":

But besides this general grace diffused over nature, almost all the individual forms are agreeable to the eye, as is proved by our endless imitations of some of them, as the acorn, the grape, the pine cone, the wheat ear, the egg, the wings and forms of most birds, the lion's claw, the serpent, the butterfly, sea shells, flames, clouds, buds, leaves, and the forms of many trees, as the palm.

Under "Language":

Man is conscious of a universal soul within or behind his individual life, wherein, as in a firmament, the natures of Justice, Truth, Love, Freedom arise and shine. This universal soul he calls Reason: it is not mine, or thine, or his, but we are its; we are its property and men. And the blue sky in which the private earth is buried, the sky with its eternal calm and full of everlasting orbs, is the type of Reason. That which intellectually considered we call Reason, considered in relation to nature, we call Spirit. Spirit is the Creator. Spirit hath life in itself. And man in all ages and countries embodies it in his language as the *Father*.

Under "Discipline":

What is a farm but a mute gospel? The chaff and the wheat, weeds and plants, blight, rain, insects, sun—it is a sacred emblem from the first furrow of spring to the last stack which the snow of winter overtakes in the fields.

Under "Prospects":

He will perceive ... that a guess is often more fruitful than an indisputable affirmation, and that a dream may let us deeper into the secret of nature than a hundred concerted experiments.

The childlike, the occult, the diffused, the particular, the abstract, the fatherly, the mutely emblematic, the guessed and dreamed, these make a combination, a cosmos, clear, rugged, and new, not smooth, but various. I would not outline Emerson's argument here, because outline is not a form to suit him, and because I think the plain texture represents his world as well as the form; and this texture has a special quality in the prose of the 1840's. It is at the same time familiar and lofty, concrete and abstract, and it is able to be both because it is less interested in general qualities, more in partial suggestions. The same is demanded of poetry.

Things admit of being used as symbols because nature is a symbol, in the whole, and in every part. Every line we can draw in the sand has expression; and there is no body without its spirit or genius. ...

No wonder then, if these waters be so deep, that we hover over them with a religious regard. The beauty of the fable proves the importance of the sense; to the poet, and to all others; or, if you please, every man is so far a poet as to be susceptible of these enchantments of nature; for all men have the thoughts whereof the universe is the celebration. I find that the fascination resides in the symbol....

The world being thus put under the mind for verb and noun, the poet is he who can articulate it. For though life is great, and fascinates and absorbs; and though all men are intelligent of the symbols through which it is named; yet they cannot originally use them.... The poet, by an ulterior intellectual perception, gives them a power which makes their old use forgotten, and puts eyes and a tongue into every dumb and inanimate object.... The condition of true naming, on the poet's part, is his resigning himself to the divine *aura* which breathes through forms, and accompanying that.... The poet knows that he speaks adequately then only when he speaks somewhat wildly, or "with the flower of the mind"; not with the intellect used as an organ, but with the intellect released from all service and suffered to take its direction from its celestial life; ...

Swedenborg, of all men in the recent ages, stands eminently for the translator of nature into thought. I do not know the man in history to whom things stood so uniformly for words. Before him the metamorphosis continually plays. Everything on which his eye rests, obeys the impulses of a moral nature.... There was this perception in him which makes the poet or seer an object of awe and terror, namely that the same man or society of men may wear one aspect to themselves and their companions, and a different aspect to higher intelligences.

Characteristically, then, Emerson can find no model poet. Homer is too historical, Milton too literal; there were too many wits in Chalmers' *English Poets*. But the richest poets, Homer, Chaucer, Shakespeare, at least are not limited; they "resemble a mirror carried through the street, ready to render an image of every created thing."

So we find the prose focus on, the philosophical justification of, the symbol, as the heart of thinking and writing. The mirror ready to render an image of every created thing can be of special significance only if every thing is significant; and if every thing is, then we have no eighteenth-century hierarchy, nor even a seventeenth-century convention, but rather a meaning which must inform all objects equally. Nature is in this way a symbol "in every part." And inwardness, depth, aura, discovery, changing aspect become important concepts. Not the thing-in-itself, but the thing as symbol is the center, and idea gives it life. Therefore Emerson is able to admire an exact reversal of the eighteenth-century standard for words and things. He does not want words to stand for things, as the Royal Society did; his things are not his basis. Rather, he praises Swedenborg, "to whom things stood so uniformly for words." Objects, in other terms, are significant as they stand for ideas, as they represent a meaning beyond themselves. This is the idealism of the nineteenth century; the divinity of idea in the human spirit is primary, and objects take their life, all objects take the fullest sort of life, through this divinity.

Another contemporary of Emerson, Ruskin, makes just this sort of distinction, with this sort of preference stated strongly. He contrasts in the *Stones of Venice* (II, viii, LV) the rightness of symbol to the wrongness of that sort of personification which moves from idea or abstraction *into* the limitations of human form instead of vice versa.

This general tendency to a morbid accuracy of classification was associated, in later times, with another very important element of the Renaissance mind, the love of personification; which appears to have reached its greatest vigor in the course of the sixteenth century, and is expressed to all future ages, in a consummate manner, in the poem of Spenser. It is to be noted that personification is, in some sort, the reverse of symbolism, and is far less noble. Symbolism is the setting forth of a great truth by an imperfect and inferior sign (as, for instance, of the hope of the resurrection by the form of the phoenix); and it is almost always employed by men in their most serious moods of faith, rarely in recreation. Men who use symbolism forcibly are almost always true believers in what they symbolize. But Personification is the bestowing of a human or living form upon an abstract idea: it is, in most cases, a mere recreation of the fancy, and is apt to disturb the belief in the reality of the thing personified. . . .

§LVI. Nevertheless, in the hands of its early and earnest masters, in whom fancy could not overthrow the foundations of faith, personification is often thoroughly noble and lovely; . . .

Beside this general preference for moving out of, rather than into, objective forms, Ruskin sets his important defense of imperfection. The two work together, the imperfect and symbolic; both strain toward perfection; neither is ever satisfied. Both allow, therefore, for all the fragments, husks, even distortions of life, as materials of art, as the neoclassicist could not.

§XXII. Enough, I trust, has been said to show the reader that the rudeness or imperfection which at first rendered the term "Gothic" one of reproach is indeed, when rightly understood, one of the most noble characters of Christian architecture, and not only a noble but an *essential* one. It seems a fantastic paradox, but it is nevertheless a most important truth, that no architecture can be truly noble which is *not* imperfect.

§XXIV. This for two reasons, both based on everlasting laws. The first, that no great man ever stops working till he has reached his point of failure; . . .

§XXV. The second reason is, that imperfection is in some sort essential to all that we know of life. It is the sign of life in a mortal body, that is to say, of a state of progress and change. Nothing that lives is, or can be, rigidly perfect; part of it is decaying, part nascent. The foxglove blossom,—a third part bud, a third part past, a third part in full bloom—is a type of the life of this world. And in all things that live there are certain irregularities and deficiencies which are not only signs of life, but sources of beauty. (*Stones of Venice,* II, vi)

Here again is the nineteenth-century flower, so specific as foxglove, yet Emerson's wild "flower of the mind," standing for the imperfection, the irregularity, the spontaneity, the color, the smallness, the fleetness, of nineteenth-century beauty and spirit. Ruskin's Gothic, whose form and expression he defined as savage, changeful, natural, grotesque, rigid, and redundant, was not so delicate as this later manifestation, just as Gray's Bard was not so delicate as Shelley's, yet some of the qualities of that Gothic, of wildness, nature, changefulness, we see surviving as admirable to Ruskin and his time.

His first work on *Modern Painters,* in the 1840's, made a persistent plea for more naturalness, by which he meant more fidelity to detail and relation, and more sensitivity to changefulness. Under the old heading of Power he added such new variables as "mystery," "inadequacy," "velocity"; to Truth and Beauty he added Relation, and to General Truths the Truth of Skies.

A man accustomed to the grace and infinity of nature's foliage, with every vista a cathedral, and every bough a revelation, can scarcely but be angered when Poussin mocks him with a black round mass of impenetrable paint, diverging into feathers instead of leaves, and supported on a stick instead of a trunk. (Everyman ed., p. 69)
It is a strange thing how little in general people know about the sky....Sometimes gentle, sometimes capricious, sometimes awful, never the same for two moments together; almost human in its passions, almost spiritual in its tenderness, almost divine in its infinity, its appeal to what is immortal in us, is as distinct as its ministry of chastisement or of blessing to what is mortal is essential. (Pp. 194–196)

The eighteenth-century Gothic here, in the awe, infinity, cathedral structure, is tempered into a gentler symbolism, a variety of foliage and caprice. And what Ruskin likes, as the almost breathlessness of his prose at times shows, is not so much the majesty as the multiplicity, the depth, persistence, and intricacy of structure.

God is not in the earthquake, nor in the fire, but in the still small voice. They are but the blunt and the low faculties of our nature, which can only be addressed through lamp-black and lightning. It is in quiet and subdued passages of unobtrusive majesty, the deep, and the calm, and the perpetual,—that which must be sought ere it is seen, and loved ere it is understod,—things which the angels work out for us daily, and yet very eternally,... it is through these that the lesson of devotion is chiefly taught, and the blessing of beauty given. (P. 195)

In his somewhat more pious and painter-like way, Ruskin is saying what Carlyle and Emerson said also: the truth of the deep, the secret, the underlying—intensely structured, and to be worked for, yet intensely simple.

This truth we tend to call romantic, as it is not obvious and general, but hidden and particular, with an aura. We know its quality well from Wordsworth and Coleridge and slightly from others of their era. We recognize it in Poe's pieces of 1831 and 1845, the arguments for the lyrical cry, the swift flight, the height, the star, the praise of Ossian. We see it in the symbols of Hawthorne's notebooks—the flower growing in the mud. In rough ways the acceptance of the lowly, delicate, and speaking symbol was widespread. Bernard Smith said that "by the beginning of the third decade of the century ecstatic references to the beauties of nature, the simple life, the humble people, the truths of the spirit, and so on were commonplace" (*Forces in American Criticism,* p. 28). Yvor Winters in *Maule's Curse* (p. 105, etc.) emphasized the pleasure in mystery in the time, the linking of beauty and sadness, so that neither is too clear, the techniques of diffusion, the concentrations of obscurity. "An air of mystery, of strangeness, will then be of necessity, not an adjunct of poetic style, but the very essence of poetic style." The critical world had grown conscious of this defining essence.

Carlyle, in fact, in 1827, reported the turn, and made its center, as Poe did, not only in the Gothic but in Germany:

Criticism has assumed a new form in Germany;—the grand question is not now a question concerning the qualities of diction, the coherence of metaphors, the fitness of sentences, the general logical truth in a work of art, as it was some half-century ago among most critics; neither is it a question mainly of a psychological sort, to be answered by discovering and delineating the peculiar nature of the poet from his poetry, as is usual with the best of our own critics at present, but it is . . . a question of the essence and peculiar life of the poetry itself. . . . whence comes the empyrean fire?" ("The State of German Literature," quoted in an unpublished dissertation on De Quincey's Criticism, by John Jordan, Univ. Calif.)

Carlyle is reporting here not only a shift from classic to romantic judgment, from the work as standard objectivity to the author as more or less standard subjectivity, but also a shift in the romantic itself from author back to work, and to the peculiar, the singular secret of the work itself, the work as person.

We may see then how easy it was for Arnold, beginning to write poetry in the 1840's, to function later in prose as a classical critic for his own era. He turned the fullest force of his attention upon the work as objectified person and was able to treat it both classically "of its kind" and romantically "in itself," because he could always resort to a sort of *je ne sais quoi* when it came to final definition.

The specimens I have quoted differ widely from one another, but they have in common this: the possession of the very highest poetical quality. If we are thoroughly penetrated by their power, we shall find that we have acquired a sense enabling us, whatever poetry may be laid before us, to feel the degree in which a high poetical quality is present or wanting there. Critics give themselves great labor to draw out what in the abstract constitutes the characters of a high quality of poetry. It is much better simply to have recourse to concrete examples;—to take specimens of poetry of the high, the very highest quality, and to say: The characters of a high quality of poetry are what is expressed *there*. ("The Study of Poetry")

These are the touchstones. "In la sua voluntade è nostra pace." "If thou didst ever hold me in thy heart, / Absent thee from felicity awhile"; "And courage never to submit or yield / And what is else not to be overcome..." They have a fine measure, poise, seriousness, an emotionality abstracted from the personal, and especially an implication always of further significance; thy will ... my story ... not to be overcome ... all portend as well as state, as does even that concretest touchstone in Wordsworth, "And never lifted up a single stone."

This taste for poised implication, for the magic of the Celtic as well as the brightness of the Greek, gave Arnold his chance to be classical in a special nineteenth-century way. Perfection for him was *inward* as well as *general* and harmonious as the eighteenth century would have it; "this is *an inward spiritual activity, having for its characters increased sweetness, increased light, in-*

creased life, increased sympathy" (*Sweetness and Light*). These
mainly eighteenth-century terms are stirred up by increase and
by light to a feeling of activity rather than stability, a force not
checked, an intensity more possibly personal than general. The
classical objects of poetry are for Arnold eternal, "among all
nations and at all times." "They are actions; human actions;
possessing an inherent interest in themselves, and which are to
be communicated in an interesting manner by the art of the
poet." And which actions are most excellent? "Those, certainly,
which most powerfully appeal to the great primary human affections: to those elementary feelings which subsist permanently in
the race, and which are independent of time" (*Poetry and the
Classics*). Arnold thought in this essay that the Greeks were right
to consider the whole rather than the parts. He accepted all
through the great classical sense of the formal and enduring, the
basic and structured, the noble and whole. Yet his own touchstone theory accepted partial and implicative fragments of nobility. He denied the contemporary poetics of "the allegory of a
state of mind," as confused, partial, personal, not *the best;* he supported, against such a poet as Wordsworth, the classical importance of action over passion; yet he sympathized, in his essay
on Maurice de Guérin, with the "way" of natural magic as well
as of moral profundity, the way of the "mystic, inward, and
profound." "This faculty always has for its basis a peculiar tem-
perament, an extraordinary delicacy of organization and susceptibility to impressions; in exercising it the poet is in a great degree
passive (Wordsworth thus speaks of a *wise passiveness*); he as-
pires to be a sort of human Aeolian harp, catching and rendering
every rustle of Nature."

Arnold's very sensitivity to this sort of passiveness perhaps
strengthened both his belief in the significance of objects as they
are, on the one hand, and his tendency to hierarchize, on the
other. Granting the pluralisms of nineteenth-century *things* and

responses, yet feeling the need of a strong order of values without the plain heroic scope of the eighteenth century, he set up *kinds* not in nature but in ways of feeling nature, his Hellenic, Hebraic, Celtic being subjective, felt, not fully definable, orders, his *good, better, best* functioning through a universality in which these orders seemed implicatively to participate, with nobility, simplicity, seriousness.[3] So while Arnold remembers, in essay after essay, the excitement of the 1840's at Oxford, when Wordsworth was still much loved and Carlyle and Emerson were speaking with a new difference, he remembers also to set these men in just relation to Shakespeare and Dante, thereby finding Wordsworth wanting in power, thereby finding Emerson's verse eccentric. Steadily Arnold held up to his public the importance of the noblest standards, the most serious ideas, the greatest world figures and literatures. Yet at the same time, as the author of "The Forsaken Merman," he shared with evident pleasure the less clear, less definable sensitivities which were valuable in his age, so that he could write with fullest enthusiasm, as he did for Maurice de Guérin, a paragraph sounding like Emerson, like Carlyle, with an inwardness which makes us understand the mixture not only in his classicism but in his successor Eliot's, the need for ministry.

The grand power of poetry is its interpretative power; by which I mean, not a power of drawing out in black and white an explanation of the mystery of the universe, but the power of so dealing with things as to awaken in us a wonderfully full, new, and intimate sense of them, and of our relations with them. When this sense is awakened in us, as to objects without us, we feel ourselves to be in contact with the essential nature of those objects, to be no longer bewildered and oppressed by them, but to have their secret, and to be in harmony with

[3] In *On the Study of Celtic Literature,* four ways of handling nature: conventional (eye not on object: Latin, eighteenth century, moon as refulgent lamp), faithful (eye on object: German, morning walk), Greek (eye on object plus lightness and brightness), magical (eye on object plus charm and magic). Of the Celtic earlier in the essay Arnold said, "It has all through it a sort of intoxication of style—a *Pindarism,* to use a word formed from the name of the poet on whom, above all other poets, the power of style seems to have exercised an inspiring and intoxicating effect"—others in English being Ossian, Byron, Keats.

them; and this feeling calms and satisfies us as no other can. Poetry, indeed, interprets in another way besides this; but one of its two ways of interpreting, of exercising its highest power, is by awakening this sense in us. I will not now inquire whether this sense is illusive, whether it can be proved not to be illusive, whether it does absolutely make us possess the real nature of things; all I say is, that poetry can awaken it in us, and that to awaken it is one of the highest powers of poetry.

In such prose some of the nature of modern symbolism is reflected. Not statement, not imitation or representation, not similitude, not elevation, is asked of the poet, but interpretation: the mediation of objects and their "essential nature," of things and truths, by feelings and ideas, within an aura of mystery. The sense at once of intimacy and illusion is the sense of symbolism. The object is to be known in itself very richly, yet the object can never fully enough be known, so that objectivity in its very extremes calls up subjectivity, and vice versa. Carlyle was right even for Arnold. Criticism had moved from the terms of imitation through association to essence, and there spoke the spirit in the thing.

Not merely the critics of the age wrote of this spirit. The 1840's were lively with novels which spoke more and more literally just because they were able to assume that the literal could be deeply significant. The novelist delighted in beginning with atmospheric scenes which set the tone for, and so in a sense symbolized, the book as a whole. Dickens' heights trembled in Dickens' depths. The correspondent glories of Scott were no longer necessary. Some representative passages from the novels may wake in the reader echoes of the critical prose and in so doing may set up the sort of overtone of recognition which the 1840's would have approved.

Disraeli's *Tancred, or The New Crusade* begins:

In that part of the celebrated parish of St. George, which is bounded on one side by Piccadilly and on the other by Curzon St, is a district of a peculiar character. 'Tis a cluster of small streets of little houses, frequently intersected by mews, which here are numerous, and sometimes gradually, rather than abruptly, terminating in a ramification of those mysterious regions.

It contains many scenes of deep and inarticulable emotion like this at the end:

He had clasped her hand; his passionate glance met her eye as he looked up with adoration to a face infinitely distressed. Yet she withdrew not her hand, as she murmured with averted head, "We must not talk of these things; we must not think of them. You know all."

Not the emotion, but the suppression, the sense of hidden depths, separates this writing from the eighteenth century. "Infinite" is the term. The lowliest emotions are infinitely profound.

Bulwer-Lytton makes this distinction at the beginning of his preface to *The Caxtons,* suggesting the book's *new* quality in its lack of a suitable "Romantic" significance in plot and passion.

If it be the good fortune of this work to possess any interest for the Novel reader, that interest, perhaps, will be but little derived from the customary elements of fiction. The plot is extremely slight; the incidents are few, and, with the exception of those which involve the fate of Vivian, such as may be found in the records of ordinary life.

... And thus, in any appeal to the sympathies of the human heart, the common household affections occupy the place of those livelier or larger passions which usually (and not unjustly) arrogate the foreground in Romantic composition.

... That which may be called the interior meaning of the whole is sought to be completed by the inference that, whatever our wanderings, our happiness will always be found within a narrow compass, and amidst the objects more immediately within our reach; ...

And this is a lyrical passage from the text (New York, 1860 ed., p. 495): the prose of silence, tenderness, simple cares:

O ye days of still sunshine, reflected back from ourselves—O ye haunts, endeared evermore by a look, tone, or smile, or rapt silence; when more and more with each hour unfolded before me that nature, so tenderly coy, so cheerful though serious, so attuned by simple cares to affection, yet so filled, from soft musings and solitude, with a poetry that gave grace to duties the homeliest—setting life's trite things to music.

All the terms—still, silence, hour, attuned, soft, music—make the appropriate understatement, as it seemed, for the decade.

Elizabeth Gaskell's *Mary Barton* begins somewhat more soberly, but in the same affectionately lowly way:

> There are some fields near Manchester, well known to the inhabitants as "Green Hays Fields," through which runs a public footpath to a little village about two miles distant. In spite of these fields being flat, and low, nay, in spite of the want of wood (the great and usual recommendation of level tracts of land), there is a charm about them which strikes even the inhabitant of a mountainous district, who sees and feels the effect of contrast in these common-place but thoroughly rural fields, with the busy, bustling manufacturing town he left but half an hour ago....Here in their seasons may be seen the country business of hay-making, ploughing, etc., which are such pleasant mysteries for townspeople to watch; and here the artisan, deafened with noise of tongues and engines, may come to listen awhile to the delicious sounds of rural life: the lowing of cattle, the milkmaid's call, the clatter and cackle of poultry in the old farm-yards.

Mr. Surtees' Mr. Jorrocks too lived near such a place: Handley Cross:

> It was a pretty village, standing on a gentle eminence, about the middle of the Vale of Sheepwash, a rich grazing district, full of rural beauties, and renowned for the honest independence of its inhabitants. Neither factory nor foundry disturbed its morals or its quietude—steam and railroads were equally unknown. The clear curl of white smoke, that rose from its cottage chimneys, denoted the consumption of forest-wood, with which the outskirts of the vale abounded. It was a nice clean country. The hazel grew with an eel-like skin, and the spiky larch shot up in a cane-coloured shoot. (London, 1854 ed., p. 4)

See how particular the observation has become: within a classically happy scene though lowly, hazel and larch are singled out, and thing distinguished as eel-like and cane-coloured—not classical at all in the qualitative oddity of perception. This too was part of the new mode. A little later, Mr. Holbrook, in *Cranford's* "Visit to an Old Bachelor," was to comment on Tennyson's part in it with approval and enjoyment.

... Now, what colour are ash-buds in March? Didn't know till this young man comes and tells me. Black as ash-buds in March. And I've lived all my life in the country; more shame for me not to know. Black: they are jet-black, madam.

Along with such discernment went the deeper emblemizing, so that Hawthorne in *Mosses from an Old Manse* could repeat the note of his *Notebooks* about the pond lily in the mud, "let it be a symbol that the earthliest human soul has an infinite spiritual capacity and may contain the better world within its depths," or could write of apples "that are bitter sweet with the moral of Time's vicissitude." Or at the very least the atmosphere is portent. So Harriet Martineau's *The Hour and the Man* begins,

The nights of August are in Santo Domingo the hottest of the year. The winds then cease to befriend the panting inhabitants; and while the thermometer stands at 90°, there is no steady breeze, as during the preceding months of summer. Light puffs of wind now and then fan the brow of the negro, and relieve for an instant the oppression of the European settler; but they are gone as soon as come, and seem only to have left the heat more intolerable than before.

And Trollope tells how he drew his first novel, *The Macdermots of Ballycloran,* from the atmosphere of an old house. His preface explains his walks in the country around Drumsna.

... we turned up through a deserted gateway, along a weedy, grass-grown avenue, till we came to the modern ruins of a country house. It was one of the most melancholy spots I ever visited.... We wandered about the place, suggesting to each other causes for the misery we saw there, and while I was still among the ruined walls and decayed beams, I fabricated the plot of the *Macdermots of Ballycloran.*

The plot concerned the responsibility of a young son of a down-at-heel family for his sister's honor; and this too was a common theme growing from the atmosphere of old houses and old homes. The family thrived or declined in these settings, in Whitehead's *Richard Savage,* and Gaskell's *Mary Barton,* in the

fuller complexities of Dickens and Thackeray; and indeed
Thackeray's early *Punch* burlesques of Novels by Eminent
Hands, his *George de Barnwell* neatly brought together family
and setting, to a glowing whole.

Vol. I. In the Morning of Life the Truthful Wooed the Beautiful, and
their offspring was Love.... 'Twas Noonday in Chepe. High Tide in
the Mighty River City!—its banks well-nigh overflowing with the
myriad-waved stream of Man!

But while much of the fiction was so excessively atmospheric
and emotional, every dawn, every street scene, every small child
or elder weighted with the significance of sentiment, in a fashion
which our popular novels still sometimes follow, there was in the
decade much sober expositional prose which worked to the same
ends. We have noticed how breathless was the prose cadence of
Carlyle or Ruskin, cumulative with less balance than before, colloquial and individual as if the man were speaking his enthusiasm direct to the reader, without thought of planned structural
device. Such spontaneity, such revelation of hidden perceptions,
shared the spirit of the times and the poetry. Lecturers, ministers,
astronomers, diarists shared the spirit too.

Catherine Crowe's *Night-Side of Nature,* for example, appeared in the 1840's, treating of ghosts and portents and the
mysteries beyond the rational or usual. The book criticized the
"contemptuous skepticism" of the last age and its trust in the eye
rather than inner senses. It considered not "faculties" but man's
scriptural tripartite being, Spirit, Soul, and Body, the temporary
body emblemized in leaves, flowers, fruits; and related dream
upon dream, apparition upon apparition, sounding like this in
the Preface:

The term "Night-side of Nature" I borrow from the Germans, who
derive it from the astronomers, the latter denominating that side of a
planet which is turned from the sun, its *night-side....* during this
interval, external objects loom upon us but strangely and imperfectly.

It is a mistake, said Catherine Crowe, to think the supernatural an interruption of the natural,

which latter mistake arises from our only seeing these facts without the links that connect them with the rest of nature, just as in the faint light of a starlit night we might distinguish the tall mountains that lift their crests high into the sky, though we could not discern the low chain of hills that united them with each other.

The astronomers, from whom the night-side figure came, gave support to the new feeling of change and mystery. Herschel's *Outlines of Astronomy,* growing from his first treatise in 1833, are introduced by sympathy for the reader in his confusion between appearance and reality.

Thus, the earth on which he stands, and which has served for ages as the unshaken foundation of the firmest structures, either of art or nature, is divested by the astronomer of its attribute of fixity, and conceived by him as turning swiftly on its centre, and at the same time moving onwards through space with great rapidity.... The planets, which appear only as stars somewhat brighter than the rest, are to him spacious, elaborate, and habitable worlds; several of them much greater and far more curiously furnished than the earth he inhabits, as there are also others less so; and the stars themselves, properly so called, which to ordinary apprehension present only lucid sparks or brilliant atoms, are to him suns of various and transcendent glory—effulgent centres of life and light to myriads of unseen worlds. (*Outlines,* New York, 1872, p. 2)

The scientist, in his enthusiastic prose, is able to show clearly one reason why the poet was altering his terms. He could no longer trust in or use effectively the correspondence between nature and himself, between what he saw and how he felt, because what he saw was not necessarily true to nature after all. What nature was perhaps was more mystery to be intuited than scope to be seen, and that was why truest feelings could be inward and truest representations in smallest flowers that blow.

Even the traditions of religion have taken on more mystery. Sin, once black and picturable, or bad and abstractable, now too is atmospheric and strange. Henry Edward Manning's sermons proceeded as follows:

Perhaps there is no thought more awful than this: that sin is all around us and within us, and we know not what it is. We are beset by it on every side; it hangs upon us, hovers about us, casts itself across our path, hides itself where our next footstep is to fall, searches us through and through, listens at our heart, floats through all our thoughts, draws our will under its sway, and ourselves under its dominion; and we do not know what it is. (*Sermons,* London, 1850; I, "The Mystery of Sin")

How fallen. How sensuous, domestic, and fallen, the great sin of Bunyan or of Donne. And we do not know what it is.

With sin such a hanging, hiding, listening, floating thing, it was no wonder that immediate familiar objects took on an air of good, if only by proxy. The family circle, the local scene were infused with pleasant if vague feelings. Margaret Fuller and the *Communist Manifesto* both defended women and children as frail elements subordinated by unnatural hierarchies of class and kind. Margaret Fuller said in her book on the subject,

The especial genius of Woman I believe to be electrical in movement, intuitive in function, spiritual in tendency. She excels not so easily in classification, or recreation, as in an instinctive seizure of causes, and a simple breathing out of what she receives, that has the singleness of life, rather than the selecting and energizing of art. (*Woman in the Nineteenth Century,* Boston, 1860, p. 115)

These are all central poetic values which her woman has. And they are the values of the natural and the lowly.

The candlestick set in a low place has given light as faithfully, where it was needed, as that upon the hill. In close alleys, in dismal nooks, the Word has been read as distinctly, as when shown by angels to holy men in the dark prison. Those who till a spot of earth scarcely larger than is wanted for a grave, have deserved that the sun should shine upon its sod till violets answer. (P. 17)

Here, as elsewhere, the gain of creation consists always in the growth of individual minds, which live and aspire, as flowers bloom and birds sing, in the midst of morasses; and in the continual development of that thought, the thought of human destiny, which is given to eternity adequately to express, and which ages of failure only seemingly impede. (P. 25)

This is the mild inspired cadence of the decade, time and again. The lowly individual soul yet inherits the sunlight of eternity. The spirit breathes its fear or rapture in tones no less enduring for being hushed. The light, the birds, the flowers contain minutely the good of life. The near and familiar epitomizes the far and strange. So the young Darwin on his Beagle voyage, seeing a whole new world and how "many of these creatures, so low in the scale of nature, are most exquisite in their forms & rich colours" (p. 23), was hard put to it to convey even to his diary all the newness, except by *strangeness,* the eerie silences, or by familiar reference, to Milton, Salvator, Elgin marbles (pp. 107, 178, 192), or the Opera House: "I do not know what epithet such scenery deserves: beautiful is much too tame; every form, every colour is such a complete exaggeration of what one has ever beheld before. If it may be so compared, it is like one of the gayest scenes in the Opera House or Theatre" (p. 66).

At home in England, a modest writer of the decade like John Sterling could, appropriately enough, in his *Essays and Tales* communicate the much that everyone else said. Sterling was a follower of Coleridge and Carlyle, an admirer of Milton and the Germans, a believer in the organic unity of the object, a man of faith and wonder, a lover of home and of simplicity.

The still unadulterated purity of home among large circles of the nation presents an endless abundance of the feelings and characters, the want of which nothing else in existence can supply even to a poet. (London, 1847 ed., p. 436)

He remembered his own childhood place:

...its grass to me the symbol and archetype of all verdure and tranquillity, a spiritual, not material thing; its clouds the only authentic ones of cloud-collecting Jove. For it was from these objects that I learnt to read and love the essential forms of nature and life. (Sketch of Life)

He liked the "strong under-import" of Coleridge's *Geraldine* (p. 107), the dreamy music, luminous painting, liquid intoxication of Tennyson, rather than the seriousness and the described-rather-than-shared emotion of Wordsworth (pp. 436 f.). He saw the usual image of transitoriness and re-creation in a flower—"the gruncistus plant, covered to-day with fresh white flowers, while the earth around it is strewn with those which similarly opened yesterday. The plant however abides and lasts, although its flowers fade and perish." (II, 135.) He felt the immediate warmth and presence of poetry in domestic things: "All the ordinary intercourse of life is big and warm with poetry. The history of a few weeks' residence in a circle of human beings is a domestic epic. Few friendships but yield in their development and decay the stuff of a long tragedy. A summer day in the country is an actual idyl." (II, 135.) He had the true feeling for light and music: "a poetic Light dormant in all things, to which the Music of our Feelings gives the signal of awakening"; yet he felt too the wider mysteries, deeper and beyond the gruncistus and home: "But at best we are immensely ignorant. Around us is a fulness of life, now vocal in a tone, now visible in a gleam, but of which we never can measure the whole compass, or number and explore the endless forces." ("Carlyle," §4.)

V. CLASSIC AND ROMANTIC

CONTRASTING the gleams of nineteenth-century poetry to the general powers of eighteenth, our scholars and critics have a strong impression of the difference between the two, a difference significant to define. The definitions take various forms. A favorite of the recent "close critics" is normative, setting up eighteenth-century poetry as general, and poetry in essence as particular, and thus removing the one from the realm of the other. Cleanth Brooks in *Modern Poetry and the Tradition,* Max Eastman in *The Enjoyment of Poetry,* Ransom in his *Kenyon* editorials, and many others make such discrimination.[1] We do not see these critics looking "closely" at much eighteenth-century poetry, because the sort of detail they think it significant to observe is not significantly there. Elder Olson protests this narrowness of focus when he examines Pope, yet does not explicitly consider the narrowness of his own.[2] When they come to the nineteenth century, the close critics are not so decided; they appreciate the new particularities but resent their ineffability of implication, their drifting nuance. The solidest symbol they accept most easily, Keats and Coleridge and Hopkins over Shelley and Poe and Tennyson. For no poet of either century, nor for any group, do we have the mass of affectionate critical documents that we have for Donne, Marvell, and the metaphysical poets. Yet the terms *classic* and *romantic* are both used with some affection: *classic* by and for the Yvor Winters school, in the tradition of Hulme's "hard, clear" definition; *romantic* for new young poets of a brilliantly, easily, and abundantly sensuous verse.[3]

Definitions less normative, more descriptive, should be given us by the scholars. But we are still so close to the problem that

[1] See Bibliography, and Ransom's editorial in the *Kenyon Review,* I (Spring, 1939).
[2] See note 7 below.
[3] Don Stanford's review of Winters' *Poems,* and Arthur Mizener's review of younger poets, *Kenyon Review,* III (Winter, 1941), VI (Winter, 1944).

it is hard to achieve perspective. The scholarly tradition, in alliance with nineteenth-century idealist philosophy, has been to study poetic ideology rather than practice, and to view the eighteenth century most strongly by the ideology of the nineteenth. Examples are the many studies of "nature" in both centuries. I do not mean here to be speaking of shortcomings; the major traditional scholars in English have done what was important to them; I mean merely to suggest that the reason much scholarship helps us no more than criticism toward the task of descriptive definitions is that its purpose really was not descriptive. For younger scholars it is, and we have had recent great numbers of carefully objective works, best for the eighteenth century where observation is still more the fashion, but increasing for the nineteenth century, especially for Blake, Coleridge, and Keats.'

Because such work is relatively new, careful, and limited, it has not yet arrived at an adding-up or definitional stage. It gives fine solid clues, but not full generalizations, concerning the nature of the *isms* within which it works. What is a literary *ism?* A cultural or philosophical idea, a technical style, a loose collocation of traits, a norm or type? The question recently has seemed more anthropological than literary. In 1940, *PMLA*'s symposium on romanticism ignored the very kind of question and offered one-word summaries of romantic essence, like "fusion." And some general writers like Barzun have even enjoyed setting up great world dichotomies on the basis of two terms, making one side modern and good, the other reactionary, Hitlerian. The split between such large generalizations and the finer workings of the scholars has not been much moderated.

' Keats has had an especial amount of "craft" study, by Ridley, James Caldwell, George Ford, and others, perhaps because of his part in the modern imagist tradition. So Blake's association with symbolism has brought thorough study culminating in Schorer's work. The work of Burke and Warren on Coleridge, following the line of Richards' *Coleridge and the Imagination,* is less easily catalogued as technically descriptive. In other studies of nineteenth-century poetry, Trilling's of Arnold, Guérard's of Bridges, for example, the central interest seems tangent to the poetry itself, or the poetry tangent to the interest.

Nor can such a work as this make the moderation, concerned as it is with but one manifestation of attitude, the poetic, and with but one aspect of the poetic, the primary characteristics of its language. Within these narrow limitations it may be useful, however, to summarize the contrast between two centuries and the apparent points of transition in conscious literary theory. As the 1640's represent a "late" metaphysical style, countered at their very end by the critical debate on *Gondibert,* the 1740's and 1840's also present late versions of their respective modes, and much of the critical writing between them is involved in the alteration of one to the other. It may be profitable to note that the changes in the language of poetry represent just those changes with which the criticism is concerned; that the literary development was consciously marked.

Joseph Warton's *Essay on the Genius and Writings of Pope* in 1756 provided, like the Preface to *Gondibert* in 1650, a transitional frame of judgment. It accepted the old, but with reservations, tempering it toward the new. It still based its argument on *kind,* and the highest kind, but it tended to speak of kinds of poets, not poems—of Pope, not *Gondibert.*

In the first class, I would place, our only three sublime and pathetic poets; *Spenser, Shakespeare, Milton.* In the second class should be ranked, such as possessed the true poetic genius, in a more moderate degree, but who had noble talents for moral, ethical, and panegyrical poesy. At the head of these are *Dryden, Prior, Addison, Cowley, Waller, Garth, Fenton, Gay, Denham, Parnell.* In the third class may be placed, men of wit, or elegant taste, and lively fancy in describing familiar life, tho' not the higher scenes of poetry. Here may be numbered, *Butler, Swift, Rochester, Donne, Dorset, Oldham.* In the fourth class, the mere versifiers, however smooth and mellifluous some of them may be thought, ... (4th ed., London, 1782, Vol. I, p. xii)

In this familiar passage of the Dedication, two or three items are especially pertinent to change. Reading from the end, note first that smoothness is not considered a very strong value. Note secondly that Warton does not preserve wit's more complimentary senses, but makes it third-class, elegant, fanciful, familiar, low rather, and on the way to being trivial; *imagination* is the term for more creative syntheses, which he allies to the sublime and pathetic. Note then that Cowley has been promoted to the second class, with Dryden, Waller, Denham. His metaphysical sins have been forgiven more than Donne's because they were less satirical, because they ranged higher in the realms of the ode. Note finally, of course, the famous victory of Spenser and Milton.

What was the evidence that Pope could not have been a Spenser or a Milton in epic form and in height of inspiration? Sec. V suggests that Pope would not have succeeded in a planned epic.

But shall I be pardoned for suspecting, that *Pope* would not have succeeded in his design; that so *didactic* a genius would have been deficient in that SUBLIME and PATHETIC, which are the main nerves of the epopea; that he would have given us many elegant descriptions, and many GENERAL characters, well drawn; but would have failed to set before our eyes the REALITY of these objects, and the ACTIONS of these characters: for Homer professedly draws no characters, but gives us to collect them from the looks and behaviour of each person he introduces; that Pope's close and constant reasoning had impaired and crushed the faculty of imagination; ... Add to all this, that it was to have been written in rhyme; a circumstance, sufficient of itself alone to overwhelm and extinguish all enthusiasm, and produce endless tautologies and circumlocutions. (Pp. 290–292)

Besides the rebellion against couplet rhyme, in which Pope was planning to share (as a footnote added), but which was not yet won by the end of the century, the very important rebellion against generality is made here, and I think it is the change which characterizes Warton's view most clearly. His Imagination, his Pathos and Sublimity, all ask specifically for a specific report on specific things. To give significance to the specific, there must be implication, and this too Warton praises in the looks and behavior of Homer's characters. The interest in implicative particularity seems to me an interest by which we may define the new poetry of the mid-eighteenth century, even though Johnson and Reynolds will still defend the general, even though Wordsworth will still be feared and disliked for his idiosyncratic emphasis on little objects of nature.[5] The little objects are one of the marks of the new poetry, not correspondent objects, but full of a mysterious life. This manifesto of Warton's in Sec. II is close to Wordsworth's:

A minute and particular enumeration of circumstances judiciously selected, is what chiefly discriminates poetry from history, and renders the former, for that reason, a more close and faithful representation of nature than the latter. And if our poets would accustom themselves to contemplate fully every object, before they attempted to describe it, they would not fail of giving their readers more new and more complete images than they generally do. (P. 48)

Newness is another new standard for images in poetry, then, because the old have been too general, have in fact been opposed to newness and surprise; and Warton here, like Wordsworth later, praises Thomson for his "new" images from nature, of which there were to be no more, according to Wordsworth, till his own day. Thomson actually walked in the fields, and so did not practice "that disgusting impropriety of introducing what may be called set of hereditary images, without proper regard to the age, or climate, or occasion in which they were formerly used." This is a relativism which indeed fosters newness, but which must be shocking to poets of the universal. And these are the natural details which Thomson had, which Pope lacked:

The scenes of Thomson are frequently as wild and romantic as those of Salvator Rosa, varied with precipices and torrents, and "castled cliffs," and deep vallies, with piny mountains, and the gloomiest caverns. Innumerable are the little circumstances in his descriptions, totally unobserved by all his predecessors. What poet hath ever taken notice of the leaf, that towards the end of autumn,

> Incessant rustles from the mournful grove,
> Oft startling such as, studious, walk below,
> And slowly circles through the waving air?

---

[5] See Monk's most interesting essay, "Anne Seward and the Romantic Poets," in *Wordsworth and Coleridge*, ed. Griggs (Princeton, 1939).

Or who, in speaking of a summer evening hath ever mentioned,
     The quail that clamours for his running mate?
Or the following natural image at the same time of the year?
     Wide o'er the thistly lawn, as swells the breeze,
     A whitening shower of vegetable down
     Amusive floats.... (Pp. 43–44)

The nineteenth-century poets would abandon the "castled cliffs" as too wild and glittering, in Wordsworth's view, but they would preserve the detail of leaf, quail, and vegetable down increasingly, so that Tennyson would undergo reprimand by Lockhart in 1833 for too many bees and woodbines.[6] Still these were major new poetic forces. They created the new vocabulary of detail in the poetry of the Wartons, Dyer, Thomson, and again in Wordsworth, Keats, and Tennyson, with a gradual increase of implication, through the pre-Raphaelites, into the realm of symbol.

Warton was one of the first to do what critics have been doing ever since: to call Pope rational and didactic, and then to praise him for being emotional and descriptive. Though he started out to speak firmly of genre, then, Warton's happiest moments were in making exceptions for Pope, a practice which Elder Olson has recently insisted is wrong.[7] The sections on Pope's *Pastorals* and *Windsor Forest* and *Eloisa* are lively and full of illustration; that on the *Dunciad,* bare. Warton's favorite critic was Boileau, but from Boileau he managed to draw least of classic frame and structure, most of the forceful image he rejoiced in. (P. 199.) So he was able to rank Pope ahead of Dryden, not as a better poet of his classical kind, but indeed as lesser, more mixed, more extreme.

I think one may venture to remark, that the reputation of POPE, as a poet, among posterity, will be principally owing to his *Windsor-Forest,* his *Rape of the Lock,* and his *Eloisa to Abelard;* whilst the facts and

---

[6] Nicholson, pp. 113–115.
[7] Olson, "Rhetoric and the Appreciation of Pope," *Mod. Phil.,* XXXVII, 13–35.

characters alluded to and exposed, in his later writings, will be forgotten and unknown, and their poignancy and propriety little relished. For WIT and SATIRE are transitory and perishable, but NATURE and PASSION are eternal. (Sec. VI, p. 347)

And here is the specific quality of Warton's Nature and Passion:

No part of this poem [*Eloisa*], or indeed of any of Pope's productions is so truly poetical, and contains such strong painting, as the passage to which we are now arrived;—The description of the convent, where Pope's religion certainly aided his fancy. It is impossible to read it without being struck with a pensive pleasure, and a sacred awe, at the solemnity of the scene; so picturesque are the epithets.

> In these *lone* walls, (their days eternal bound)
> These *moss-grown* domes with *spiry* turrets crown'd,
> Where *awful* arches make the noonday night,
> And the *dim* windows shed a *solemn* light;
> Thy eyes diffus'd a reconciling ray.

The essence, then, is in the adjectives, sensuous and feeling, and the feeling is not classically positive and constructive, but mixed, negative, gloomy in the new mode of mixture by which Burke defined and defended sublimity.

The effect and influence of MELANCHOLY, who is beautifully personified, on every object that occurs, and on every part of the convent, cannot be too much applauded, or too often read, as it is founded on nature and experience. That temper of mind casts a gloom on all things.

> But o'er the twilight groves and dusky caves,
> Long-sounding iles, and intermingled graves,
> Black MELANCHOLY sits, and round her throws
> A death-like silence, and a dread repose;
> Her gloomy presence saddens all the scene,
> Shades every flower, and darkens every green,
> Deepens the murmur of the falling floods,
> And breathes a browner horror on the woods.

The figurative expressions, *throws,* and *breathes,* and *browner* horror, are, I verily believe, some of the strongest and boldest in the English language. The IMAGE of the Goddess MELANCHOLY sitting over the convent, and as it were expanding her dreadful wings over its whole circuit, and diffusing her gloom all around it, is truly sublime, and strongly conceived. (Sec. VI, pp. 329–331)

The specific, small, observed, new, diffusive were values for Warton. They were not in the main the values of the 1740's, his own early decade, but they were to grow, through the sensibilities of Pope and Thomson, through a freer Burns and the ballads, to Wordsworth and Coleridge, steadfastly the while maintaining that in their accuracy lay the true classical spirit.

I take two works as representative critical landmarks, this *Essay on Pope* and the prose on the *Lyrical Ballads,* because they emphasize the consciousness of the shift to implicative particularity which the shifting poetic language most reveals. The change from *fair* to *bright,* from *nature* and *power* to *light, sun,* and *night,* and on the minor level from *fate, virtue, scene,* to *dream, mother, flower, hour, sea, sky,* is the very change which Warton and Wordsworth urged and defended, as a century earlier Davenant and Dryden had urged the access of *nature* and *power,* of *scene* and *virtue.* And already by 1740 the *soft air* of at least a general atmospheric particularity had come to prevail. The mid-century moved naturally, therefore, in its own native course receptive to later German theory, as little by little it increased the detail and the implication of its observation and made its associations more inward and more personal. Re-creations of the gothic aided this progression; but it was not the gothic which Warton and Wordsworth essentially favored. Preserving the classical idea of universal norms of feeling, they wished simply to center those norms at a more precise level of observation, a "commoner" range of feeling. And of this range, the dark, the strange seemed to them, as especially to Coleridge, an important part.

Norms and correspondences between man and nature were accepted as classical, and their importance was not denied. But inquisitive poets and critics examined them further, in two main ways. Some wanted to turn them over to see their other face, of aberration, dissimilarity, surprise. Others wanted more positively to specify them, to carry them into particularity. Coleridge and

Wordsworth divided at just this point. Coleridge took up with enthusiasm the originality, exploration, night-side, of Young, and the gothic, and the German; Wordsworth persistently rebelled against the extremes of these, and argued for a classical down-center norm, which would, nevertheless, contain literal associations and direct images more individual than eighteenth-century classicism seemed to allow. The question was, for the partners, which was the truer unfolding of classical and universal truth, the odd inner vision or the common outward one? The strange, or the familiar; the distant, or the near? It was their version of the division between sublime and beautiful.

It took form, too, in the difference between their major vocabularies in the *Lyrical Ballads*. Coleridge's distinctive major terms were of sea and night, in *white, black, strange, moon, bird, sea, ship, wind, cloud, water*. Wordsworth's were of earth and daylight, in *green, cold, warm, wide, deep, nature, woods, sun, mountains, trees*. Yet also they worked together, in establishing the increasingly valuable vocabulary of outward color and inward light, the shared major words of *sweet, little, old, bright, white, sun, day, love, joy, spirit, prayer*, a vocabulary closer to the coming 1840's than to the past 1740's, yet preserving the explicit terms of feeling from the past. In explicit feeling the classical norms of human likeness were longest maintained, and Wordsworth was their late great defender. Coleridge like many of his predecessors in the eighteenth century wished to carry them further, and to carry them inward, to be more universal still. He found mere surface likeness secondary, fanciful, trivial, as the unlikenesses of satire and wit had earlier been found trivial. He wanted trivia themselves to be seen as serious, unified as symbolic, recognized as infinitely implicative rather than visually corresponding. He joined with Wordsworth in the new literal yet implicative lyricism of the *Ballads,* yet recognized the differences in approach.

... it was agreed, that my endeavours should be directed to persons and characters supernatural, or at least romantic; yet so as to transfer from our inward nature a human interest and a semblance of truth sufficient to procure for these shadows of imagination that willing suspension of disbelief for the moment, which constitutes poetic faith. Mr. Wordsworth, on the other hand, was to propose to himself as his object, to give the charm of novelty to things of every day, and to excite a feeling analogous to the supernatural, by awakening the mind's attention from the lethargy of custom, and directing it to the loveliness and the wonders of the world before us; an inexhaustible treasure, but for which, in consequence of the film of familiarity and selfish solicitude we have eyes, yet see not, ears that hear not, and hearts that neither feel nor understand. (Chap. xiv of the *Biographia Literaria*)

The vice against which they joined was social custom, the vice of the eighteenth century also, because it was not nobly universal. But where eighteenth-century poets attacked it by satire and antithesis, the nineteenth century would prefer to look beyond it or beneath it, for stranger and deeper truths. Coleridge would look beyond, to far horizons, night skies, unknown seas, haunted castles and haunted souls, following the strange and gothic line in its new German transcendence. Wordsworth would stay at home and look beneath standard surfaces, to find the spirit of small flowers and common souls in common trouble. He would argue, as he did even in his first "Advertisement," for the implications in the lowly and the literal of a general universal truth.

In the "Advertisement" of 1798 there are five sections. The first has to say that the materials of poetry are to be found in every subject which can interest the human mind. The second has to say that these particular poems are experimenting to ascertain how far the language of conversation in the middle and lower classes of society is adapted to the purposes of poetic pleasure, and it asks that under the term *Poetry* the reader look not for gaudiness and inane phraseology, but for natural delineation of human passions, human characters, human incidents. The third places these poems, in the then conventional contrast between high and low styles, on the side of the low, along with elder, and most human modern, writers. The fourth asks for patience in the developing of taste. The fifth notes some of the literal backgrounds of some of the poems.

Much of everything Wordsworth ever said is here. He acknowledges that it is hard for the reader to change his notion of what fits under the word *Poetry*. So indeed it is always hard. He says, though, that he is experimenting with such an apparent change, admonishing his readers that nothing of interest to the human heart is not also of interest to poetry, enforcing this belief with meticulous reference to the "well-authenticated fact which happened in Warwickshire" and the "conversation with a friend." And, in consequence of the subject, he explains the style, neat but not gaudy, of only middle height, as it expresses a common denominator of human interest, in character and event. His wish is, then, to be radically literal. No object, however small or mean, needs transformation or decoration to give it poetic value. It speaks for itself through the literally expressed feelings and thoughts which it awakens in its poet's breast. *Scene* plus *love* plus *prayer* is the literal vocabulary of this poetic report.

> And then my heart with rapture fills
> And dances with the daffodils.

Now these were the faults for which Coleridge held Wordsworth responsible in 1814: the aims Wordsworth had set for them both in 1798: inconstancy of style, sometimes rudely dropping from its natural elevation; matter-of-factness, laborious minutiae, and accidental circumstances; undue predilection for dramatic form; feeling disproportionate to such knowledge and valuation of objects described as can be expected of men in general; thoughts and images too great for the subject. This was just Wordsworth's mixture: his literalness, his conversational quality with its ups and downs, his feeling for objects and incidents which others did not yet feel for; and this was just the mixture of the "Advertisement," his platform. I should say that the virtues of this mixture were just Wordsworth's characteristic virtues, as he recognized: he was able to give to conventionally insignificant objects and words and conversational verse patterns significance by the full voice of the feeling he felt for them. So Coleridge is able to praise him in more general terms: for the fitness of his language, the weight of his thought, the strength of his lines, the truth of his descriptions, the power of his imagination. But these general poetic virtues were to hold through his duller later work; the specific idiosyncracies for which he spoke weakened the "Idiot Boy," but made the best poems best.

How then did the poems of Coleridge fit the "Advertisement" which advertised them also? Not so literal and not so familiar, they nevertheless dealt with human character and incident in style free from the gaudy and inane. The more lord, heaven, and strangeness in them displaced some of the natural and good which was advertised, but still spoke in the pure plain language of human feeling in the fashion advertised. The central vocabularies of the two poets differed, as we have seen, by more loftiness of reference in image and in concept on Coleridge's side, more pedestrian daylight humanity on Wordsworth's. It is this central difference, I believe, which is reflected in Coleridge's complaint. It is the central difference in their average and their worst poems, then; and in their best also, in the "Ancient Mariner" and "Tintern Abbey," and at the heart of all their poetries, this mystery, or this obviousness, of human feeling in scenic incident.

In the Preface of 1800 and its later minor revisions, Wordsworth went on to specify further what his principles of literal report and moral relationship involved in these poems "so materially different from those upon which general approbation is at present bestowed." First, in his first now well-known paragraph, he specified more closely than before the language as, fitted to metrical arrangement, "a selection of the real language of men in a state of vivid sensation." He warned his readers to expect that "class of ideas and expressions" which would relate incidents, in language really used by men, with a coloring of imaginative point of view, and revealing the primary laws of our nature. It is these four specifications together, not separately, which define the class of expression which Wordsworth is introducing. It is the class, then, of language literal, familiar, personal, primary. What would such language logically be? Would it not comprise the words which name the objects most seen and the feelings most felt and the thoughts most thought by most people including Wordsworth himself? Would it not exclude, then, the language of city people or manor people or poets in any of their special class interests, and stress rather the ideas and expressions they would share: Biblical, philosophical, emotional, natural: the words, in fact, of sun and sea, of joy and tears, of love and prayer which do appear most frequently in the Lyrical Ballad poems? Wordsworth the literalist of language wants all the valuable objects of nature, made valuable by human thought and feeling, named and stated in just this literal order. Bad poetry for him, then, is that which either does not stress this vocabulary or distorts it by figurative confusions of natural relationship, like pageantry, personification, farfetched metaphor, balances of likeness and difference.

So the paragraphs of the Preface go on to explain. The language which rises from repeated experience and regular feelings is a more permanent and philosophical language than that rising from caprice. True, language can be too low, but lowness is in the long run less false than arbitrariness. It is the basic important feeling of men which gives importance to action and incident. The poetic style suitable to such importance is that which avoids all device not natural to the company of flesh and blood and the steady look at the subject. There is no reason why the order of words should not often, in fact should not better, be natural

prose order. Prose and poetry share the significances of thoughtful emotional statement about man and nature, the tears not
celestial but natural. It is their selection which separates the composition from the vulgarities of ordinary life; they need no foreign splendor to do so. Poetry is the image of man and nature,
and the Poet is the most skilled imaginer. He considers man and
nature as essentially adapted to each other, the seasons and the
passions full of association and similitude, from which the reader
most naturally derives his pleasure, his sense of the quality and
multiplicity of moral relations.

The Appendix to the Preface of 1802 made an added explanation of the label "Poetic Diction" which Wordsworth used for
language "arbitrary and subject to infinite caprices, upon which
no calculation whatever can be made." Such diction, like meter,
set poetry apart from everyday, and, unlike meter which employed a just and regular formalization, did so by "thrusting out
of sight the plain humanities of nature by a motley masquerade
of tricks, quaintnesses, hieroglyphics, and enigmas." The examples offered in the Preface had been lines of Gray, like

> In vain to me the smiling mornings shine,
> And reddening Phoebus lifts his golden fire;
> The birds in vain their amorous descant join,
> Or cheerful fields resume their green attire.

An example added from Cowper was

> But the sound of the church-going bell
> These valleys and rocks never heard,
> Ne'er sighed at the sound of a knell,
> Or smiled when a sabbath appeared.

This passage Wordsworth condemned as "vicious poetic diction." What the two quotations have in common is the language
which Wordsworth protests. We see, then, that it is not single
words which trouble him, wholly. *Smiling, morning, birds,
fields, green, bell, valleys, sabbath* are all good major words for

Wordsworth. One might suggest he would object to the elaborations of *Phoebus* and *descant,* but such words he used often himself to excellent effect, as Coleridge later was to point out. No, it
was rather the conceptual relation between the words which
troubled him. "Falsehood of description" was what, in the ninth
paragraph of the Preface, he connected with "poetic diction."

The falsities of the two quoted passages are the same: they
make an abstract epithetical, rather than an active sympathetical,
association of images and feelings. The scenes are "isolated" from
direct human response, as Wordsworth felt the scenes of Ossian
were, and being so isolated, are half personified so that the feelings may be self-contained rather than humanly associated. So
"church-going bell" was the phrase Wordsworth particularly
protested: the artificializing of such a natural wording as "the
bell which the church-goers heard" to the compressed and trans-
ferred epithet which to Wordsworth seemed literally and inex-
cusably false. The bell was in the steeple; the people went to
church; that was the truth. Paralleling "church-going bell" are
the golden fire of Phoebus, the green attire of the fields, the valleys ne'er smiling when a sabbath appeared. It is not that Wordsworth disliked the attribution of emotion to nature; he made
such attribution constantly; rather, he disliked any attribution
which distorted observation, as the half-personifications of lifting
fire, green garments, valleys unsmiling for sabbath well could
do. The emotions of nature were shared, sympathetic, universal
emotions, not devices of description and decoration which removed the objects from man's response.

So Wordsworth rejected the "personification of abstract ideas"
in favor of directer statement of ideas. So he preferred the Bible's
simple direction to Dr. Johnson's elaborate balance.

Go to the ant, thou sluggard; consider her ways, and be wise: which
having no guide, overseer, or ruler, provideth her meat in the summer,
and gathereth her food in the harvest. . . .

> Turn on the prudent Ant thy heedless eyes,
> Observe her labours, Sluggard, and be wise;
> No stern command, no monitory voice,
> Prescribes her duties, or directs her choice;
> Yet, timely provident, she hastes away
> To snatch the blessings of a plenteous day;
> When fruitful Summer loads the teeming plain,
> She crops the harvest, and she stores the grain. . . .

This latter "hubbub of words," as Wordsworth calls it, works in every line to create a set piece, to frame the Ant in the images of idea, by the very *the*'s and balances and personifications to abstract the thought from the world of action to the world of concept. Wordsworth preferred, therefore, the Bible's livelier interplay between the two worlds and its omission of the "plenteous day," the "fruitful Summer," the "teeming plain" which are dedicated to purposes of isolation from the sluggard rather than to connection with him. Whenever Wordsworth quotes, from Cowper, Gray, or Johnson, a line or so he likes, it is a line of human connection and sympathy: "My lonely anguish melts no heart but mine"; "These pretty Babes with hand in hand" (much more humanly significant than hat in hand!); "O tell me I have yet a friend." Problems of diction, problems of figure, problems of order, all are subordinated, the usual critic of Wordsworth's diction to the contrary, to problems of what Wordsworth called reality: the literal sympathetic connection between man and nature, between image, feeling, and thought, and between them in just these terms.

I make the suggestion that the relation between this prose theory of 1802 and Coleridge's set forth some dozen years later is the same relationship that is to be seen in the poetries of the *Lyrical Ballads,* and in the poetries of the changing century, through the major words. The majority of agreement in practice is a majority of agreement in theory, in, as Coleridge phrased it (chap. xvii), "the natural language of impassioned feeling," *love* and *prayer* in the *wide wood*. The minority of disagreement, in theory as in practice, involves the differences between naturalistic and esemplastic, between *human* and *heaven,* between *day* and *moon.* Coleridge, in a letter of 1802, reporting "lately some little controversy" between the two on problems of poetic language, suggests early the debate which went on into the *Biographia* and Wordsworth's new preface of 1815. It turned upon the meaning of Imagination, but it rested upon a broad basis of agreement in interest and usage. Like the "Poetic Diction" Appendix, many early chapters of the *Biographia* inveighed against the turgidness, the epitheting, the swell and glitter, the mixed imagery and abstraction of metaphor, the harsh incongruity, doleful egotism, low simplicity, strained thought, of conventional, and especially youthful, poetic language, stemming from Pope's Homer. Coleridge was kinder to the diction of "The Female Vagrant" than Wordsworth himself was (chap. ii vs. *Early Letters,* p. 270), but noted as example of what both poets disliked Wordsworth's "apple sickens pale in summer's ray" and "Ev'n here content has fix'd her smiling reign." Here, and in the note in esemplastic chapter x, that Coleridge worked with memorandum book in hand, with the objects and imagery immediately before his senses, the two poets were in general agreement about sound feeling and observation. But the chapters from xiii to xix spoke across and counter to Wordsworth's meaning because they denied the validities of literalism in interpretation of imagination and "the real language of men."

Coleridge here stressing the creative power of imagination, the force of poetic spirit and pattern, denied, indeed, the arguments of the Preface by arguing away from the copying of actual rustic conversations toward the creation of higher poetic pleasures, by praising Wordsworth for his soaring, not his plodding. For him it is not the rustics' thought but the poet's thought which is important. For Wordsworth, on the other hand, stressing the receptivity of the poet, the minutest qualifications of the Preface were validly descriptive in their emphasis upon outward as well as inward combinations. Wordsworth's main object, as Coleridge acknowledged in chapter xx, was to dissolve differences and discover likenesses. For him the imagination performed this service, working beneath the surface of accident and caprice: and where, then, would imagination work better than in the part of the world most natural and unspoiled, connected with the simplest objects of nature and feelings of man?

Wordsworth wrote in a letter of 1801 (*Early Letters,* p. 260) that the domestic affections were decaying in the lower orders of society but were still strong in the north of England. He wrote in 1802 (*Early Letters,* pp. 292–294) that one learned best from men "who have never known false refinements"; and that "there cannot be a doubt that in tracts of country where images of danger, melancholy, and grandeur, or loveliness, softness, and ease prevail, they will make themselves felt powerfully in forming the character of the people." Such easy similitudes were not for Coleridge. His mariners and dark ladies were more producers than products of their atmospheres, as he was more dreamer than observer of his own. He went along a long way with Wordsworth, in humanity and piety and joy and even the memorandum book, but then his imagination was off to a more complex resolving job than Wordsworth's sought for. He rightly showed how far from sheer simplicity Wordsworth was in his elevation of sense to feeling; but he wrongly, I think, suggested that Wordsworth was far from consistency also, because what was consistency for Wordsworth was a sort of literal acceptance which Coleridge could not find adequately poetic—not *strange,* not *holy,* not *black,* not *white* enough.

> I pass, like night, from land to land;
>   I have strange power of speech;

said the mariner.

> ... Nature never did betray
> The heart that loved her; 'tis her privilege,
> Through all the years of this our life, to lead
> From joy to joy:

said the brother.

> He prayeth best who loveth best,
> All things both great and small:

said the two poets together, when in the *Lyrical Ballads* they were close to one voice and mind.

This imaginative and emotional association helped successfully to reassert some romantic connections which critics had been making earlier between strangeness and familiarity, showing how each was a development from classical norms, strangeness out from, familiarity down from, and both inward from, the generally elevated center. The poetry fits the philosophical ideal. *Friend, joy, nature* yield to *light, sun, spirit.* The pleasant outward *fair, great, soft* of eighteenth-century epithet become the mixed atmospheric, moral, and nostalgic *bright, good, old* of the nineteenth. The few and standard verbs of neoclassical poise gain the active additional receptivity of romantic *falling* and *lying* and *looking* and *loving* and *taking.* And these differences themselves reside in a continuity of agreement from century to century, of modifying *sweet,* of human *eye, hand, heart, life, love, man,* of divine *God, heaven, soul* and the common *coming, knowing, hearing, seeing* of the age.

The greatest difference the nineteenth-century vocabulary shows, then, against a background of man and God, is an externalizing of values. *Bright, light,* and *sun* take the place of *fair, friend, joy, nature,* and *power.* Atmosphere takes the place of emotional force and relationship. At the same time, we know that externality is not the main effect of the nineteenth-century lyric: the use of these terms in context and especially in sound subjectively modulates them; we see then the development of symbolizing in poetry whereby external and internal realities are taken as separate, so that the one may stand for and suggest the other.

The minor vocabulary, terms much used by about a fourth of the poets, bears out this development. In the 1840's, the minor adjectives *dark, dim, gold, white* have taken the place of the eighteenth century's emotional *gay, tender, vain,* though *proud* and *happy* remain; and many dimensional terms like *deep, great, high, little, long, mighty* have increased. The nouns have moved to the family, to *child, father, mother,* as well as the earlier *friend, lord, king;* and eighteenth-century nature of *flower, land, night, scene, sky* has been specified to *star* and *sea* as well; *time* to *hour; fate, thought,* and *virtue* to *death, dream, hope,* and *prayer;* and *beholding* to *feeling* and *seeming.*

These were not vast shifts of material, but extensions, widening of the mode, tempering it to more detail. Much of the detail itself came from pioneers in eighteenth-century poetry: the *bright* and *old* from Thomas Warton and others, the *light* from Pope, the *sun* from Gray and Thomson, the *good, world, thought,* and *night* from Young and more. Most of the detail works in the one clear direction of external particularity, to be distinguished from an older metaphysical particularity by its naturalistic and associative function.

As we may see the harmony between poetical changes and critical comment on these changes, between the 1740's and the 1840's, we may recognize that poetry was consciously and evaluatively altered, and we may recognize the precise character of the alterations. In the 1740's most poets used a closely metered and rhymed control of substantial general material in descriptive statement. Their emphasis on natural and human similitudes, on temporal and special ranges, on a three-to-one, or higher, substantival proportioning, gave them a bond, made them a group with a certain number of shared standards. "Classical" was a good term for them, as for their predecessors in the century, and in a double sense: their mode was to be seen also in the verse of Virgil, Ovid, Horace, and it was a mode which valued the generalities of class. In the 1840's a new and different agreement had been made, upon a shorter, more intricately rhymed and metered stanza, upon more use of pause, short syllable, and refrain, in melody rather than onomatopoetic harmony, upon simple literal statement in combination with symbolic implication, and upon a vocabulary of atmosphere grown out of feeling. "Romantic" was gradually taken as a term for this agreement, because it connoted strange and individual atmospheres and objects, old times and inner echoes. Romanticism was, then, both a counter to and a version of Classicism; the qualities of its major opposition were conditioned by the qualities of its temporal succession.

In 1820, Byron wrote from Ravenna, "I perceive that in Germany, as well as in Italy, there is a great struggle about what they call 'Classical' and 'Romantic,'—terms which were not subjects of classification in England, at least when I left it four or five years ago." But four or five years ago Hazlitt was borrowing A. W. Schlegel's terms for explanation: "... the most obvious distinction between the two styles, the classical and the romantic, is, that the one is conversant with objects that are grand or beautiful in themselves, or in consequence of obvious and universal associations, the other, with those that are interesting only by force of circumstance or imagination."[8]

This seems to me a good distinction because it is literally applicable to both theory and practice. It centers in "objects," just as criticism since Hobbes had been centering, just as poetry since Hobbes had been first negatively, then positively, working. It specifies the qualities of the objects, as the eighteenth century persistently did, and specifies grandness and beauty, the sorts of

---

[8] Both quotations are from a helpful general study, Frederick E. Pierce's *Currents and Eddies in the English Romantic Generation* (Yale University Press, 1918) pp. 258, 288.

qualities debated over and over in central focus by critics before Burke and after. Finally, it distinguishes between the two styles by their "conversance" with objects qualified "by obvious and universal associations," or "by force of circumstance or imagination"—the difference between a classic commonness, which Wordsworth still pleaded for, and an individual situation. Furthermore, it evades two issues debated and still to be debated in the nineteenth century: one, how much acceptance, how much creation, there was in the ambiguous word "conversance"; and two, the relation between the allied phrases "objects . . . in themselves" and "in consequence of obvious and universal associations."

The poetic changes through two centuries show just these interests. The neoclassicist associated himself with orderly and grand objects in an orderly and grand universe. He used all those methods of similitude, in scansion, rhyme, onomatopoeia, simile, scene, which would strengthen the obviousness and universality. He wished not to be fictive, but sympathetic, apprehensive in the strongest sense. He mocked aberration. But sheer accumulation of correspondence carried him farther and wider, in time and space, so that his range itself became aberrant, fearful, as Gray's *Bard* seemed to Johnson, and Sublimity to Burke. But it was also pleasant, as Pope's *Eloisa* was to Joseph Warton, and, as for Warton, came to create a new standard of oddity, individuality, atmospheric detail, "force of circumstance." Against the extremes of this gothic romanticism both Wordsworth and Coleridge rebelled, because they found it arbitrary and capricious. They wanted to reassert the classicism of universality now at the level of small things, the common man, the ballad structure, the "simple" in all forms. They themselves split in emphasis, Wordsworth toward the day side, Coleridge toward the night; Wordsworth in *The Prelude* back to the full classical line, tempered by implication; Coleridge in *Christabel* forward to the stress and rest count which would provide for nineteenth-century poetry much silence, in thought as well as sound. Wordsworth stressed the old passivity, Coleridge the new activity, of the imagination. But their romanticism, therefore, and that of the 1840's, was classic as well as gothic, just as neoclassicism was metaphysical as well, so that the compound was fine and rich, not a new strain, but an enthusiastically fostered and combined one.

So the ease of contiguous and similitudinous association perseveres, from the 1740's even to Alison and Jeffery, in such phrasing as: "When an object is presented to any of our senses, the mind conforms itself to its nature and appearance, feels an emotion, and is put in a frame suitable and analogous; of which we have a perception by consciousness or reflection."[9] While by 1815 Coleridge criticizes Wordsworth's *Excursion* for not "removing the sandy sophisms of Locke, and the mechanic dogmatists, and demonstrating that the senses were living growths and developments of the mind and spirit, in a much juster as well as higher sense, than the mind can be said to be formed out of the senses!"[10] So Kames and Blair, whose handbooks of criticism were to guide a full century or more of students, emphasized effects on eye and ear of images and objects, simplified the Elizabethan system of figures, lauded good epithets and smoothly asserted: "Nothing appears to flow more of its own accord, into poetical numbers, than rivers and mountains, meadows and hills, flocks and trees, and shepherds void of care."[11] Whereas by 1850 Holman Hunt could say, "I feel really frightened when I sit down to paint a flower."[12]

For Hunt, for Tennyson, for the 1840's and the Pre-Raphaelites as for Coleridge and Keats, the contrarieties rather than the simi-

[9] From Gerard's *Essay on Taste*, 1756—a statement which Gordon McKenzie in his *Critical Responsiveness* calls representative of the later eighteenth century.

[10] Quoted from Melvin Rader's *Presiding Ideas in Wordsworth's Poetry*, p. 162.

[11] Hugh Blair, *Lectures on Rhetoric and Belles Lettres, 1762–1783* (London, 1813), p. 214.

[12] *Victoriana*, ed. Barton and Sitwell.

larities of association had asserted themselves, and pain, fear, mystery, bloomed in the most delicate flower. In 1845, Bulwer-Lytton's satire on Tennyson as "Out-babying Wordsworth and out-glittering Keats"[13] struck just the traits by which late romanticism may be characterized, the delicate and the colorful, the tender and the bright, the form and gleam and silence of suggestion and implication. But neither the affectionate school of Wordsworth nor the richer school of Keats, called "new" in the 1840's, was dominant alone. Campbell and Hemans sold most widely, as Scott and Rogers were best remembered. Longfellow was the type. For most, in agreement, despite their varieties of reticence and long-windedness, of public and private tone, of narrative progression and lyric instant, and the one in the other, the sense of inexpressible spirit was primary. In consequence, substance and enclosing stress lessened, receptive verbs increased variety, dark and sunny hearths and hearts spoke their individual prayers. The voice of universal empire as it grew stiller and smaller became the voice of domestic domain, lighter and clearer.

It seems to me just and even necessary to try to name the differing frames within which poets work: the differing frames, indeed, within which men live. But since the bounds are not arbitrarily imposed, since they are created and altered by individuals, the task of definition is not simple. I do not think that the task of defining "romantic" and "classic" can be worked out merely in the realm of idea; I think it must be carefully engaged in the realm of practice. Poetry is one sort of practice, the more complexly describable and relatable because it uses a highly social medium, language. It is possible to observe, as we have here, that all the traits of language, its sound, its sentence structure, and its vocabulary, alter together, over a period of time like a century, to compose a new major pattern with a certain stability and continuity. It is possible to observe how specifically the alterations

---

[13] George Ford, *Keats and the Victorians* (Yale University Press, 1944), p. 23.

are commented on and encouraged by the critics of the time; how conscious is the process. Such a nucleus of theoretical and practical agreement may well enough be given a name like "romantic." But first we must know much more: the limits of the nucleus, the degree of variation in change, the function of innovation, the relation of one sort of change to another, the relation of language as medium to the ideas and the feelings of authors and audiences. This present study has found certain minimum facts: contemporary agreements in some main aspects of poetic practice; the importance of general descriptive similitude for the poetry of the 1740's, as distinguished from the dual and difficult metaphorical logic of the 1640's, as distinguished from the implicative particularity of the 1840's. These facts, for all their ramifications in this text, are not adequate to suggest definitions; but they should be adequate to provide a small part of definition when poetry is read in the light of its whole world.

BIBLIOGRAPHY

(Useful prose works of the 1740's and 1840's, and studies of poetic problems in these periods, are listed here. The bibliography of poetry appears in the tables, pp. 169 f. and 260 f.)

PRIMARY

CONCORDANCES

A Concordance to the Works of Alexander Pope, by Edwin Abbott (London, 1875).

A Concordance to the Poetical Works of William Collins, compiled by Bradford A. Booth and Claude E. Jones (Univ. of California Press, 1939).

A Concordance to the English Poems of Thomas Gray, ed. Albert S. Cook (Boston, Houghton Mifflin, 1908).

A Concordance to the Poems of Robert Browning, by Leslie N. Broughton and Benjamin F. Stelter (2 vols., New York, Stechert, 1924-1925).

A Concordance to the Poems of Ralph Waldo Emerson, by George Shelton Hubbell (New York, H. W. Wilson, 1932).

A Concordance to the Poetical Works of Edgar Allan Poe, by Bradford A. Booth and Claude E. Jones (Baltimore, Johns Hopkins Press, 1941).

A Concordance to the Poetical and Dramatic Works of Alfred Lord Tennyson, by Arthur E. Baker (London, Paul, Trench, Trübner, 1914).

EIGHTEENTH CENTURY

Addison, Joseph. *Essays,* ed. Sir James George Frazier (2 vols., New York, Macmillan, 1915).

Arbuthnot, John. *Life and Works,* ed. George A. Aitken (Oxford, Clarendon Press, 1892).

Blair, Hugh. *Lectures on Rhetoric and Belles Lettres,* 1762 et seqq. (London, 1813).

Boas, Frederick S., ed. *Songs and Lyrics from the English Playbooks* (London, Cresset Press, 1945).

Bolingbroke, Henry St. John, Lord Viscount. *Works* (3 vols., Dublin, 1793).

Burke, Edmund. . . . *the Sublime and the Beautiful* (London, 1757).

Bysshe, Edward. *The Art of English Poetry,* 9th ed. (London, 1762).

Dennis, John. *Critical Works,* ed. Edward N. Hooker (Baltimore, Johns Hopkins Press, 1939).

Dodsley, Robert. *The Economy of Human Life,* 1750 (London, 1839).

Dryden, John. *Essays,* ed. W. P. Ker (2 vols., Oxford, Clarendon Press, 1900).

Edwards, Thomas. *The Canons of Criticism,* 7th ed. (London, 1765).

Fielding, Henry, ed. *The Jacobite's Journal.*

Garrick, David. *Miss in Her Teens* (London, Tonson, 1747).

Gildon, Charles. *The Complete Art of Poetry in Six Parts* (London, 1718).

Gray, Thomas. *Essays and Criticism,* ed. Clark Northrup (Boston, Heath, 1911).

Hervey, James. *The Whole Works* (6 vols., London, 1825).

Hume, David. *Essays and Treatises in Several Subjects* (2 vols., Edinburgh, 1821), Vol. I.

Hurd, Richard. *Works* (8 vols., London, 1811), Vol. II.

Johnson, Samuel. *Lives of the English Poets,* ed. George Birkbeck Hill (3 vols., Oxford, Clarendon Press, 1905).

Kames, Henry Home, Lord. *Elements of Criticism* (New York, 1830).

Mason, John. *An Essay on the Power of Numbers and the Principles of Harmony in Poetical Compositions* (London, 1849).

Parnell, Thomas. *Poetical Works,* ed. George A. Aitken (London, 1894).

Pococke, Richard. *Travel in the East,* in *A General Collection of ... Voyages and Travels,* ed. John Pinkerton (London, 1811).

Pope, Alexander. *Peri Bathous,* in Vol. X of *Works,* ed. Courthope and Elwin (London, 1886).

Pope and Warburton, eds. *The Works of Shakespeare* (8 vols., London, 1847), Vols. I, II.

Richardson, Samuel. *Familiar Letters on Important Occasions,* 1741. (English Library series; London, Routledge, 1928.)

—— *The Novels,* with Memoir, Notes (London, 1824), Vol. VI.

Rowe, Elizabeth. *Miscellaneous Works in Prose and Verse* (2 vols., London, 1739).

Scott, John. *Critical Essays, on Some of the Poems of Several English Poets* (London, 1785).

Shenstone, William. *The Works in Prose and Verse* (London, Dodsley, 1764).

Spence, Joseph. *Anecdotes, Observations, and Characters of Books and Men,* ed. S. W. Singer, 2d. ed. (London, 1858).

[Swift, Jonathan.] *The Art of Punning; or, The Flower of Languages,* 2d ed. (Dublin, 1719).

Thomas, Pascoe. *A True and Impartial Journal of a Voyage to the South-Seas* (London, 1745).

Warton, Joseph. *An Essay on the Genius and Writings of Pope,* 4th ed. (2 vols., London, 1782).

Warton, Thomas. *History of English Poetry* (12th to 17th cent.) (4 vols., London, 1871).

Young, Edward. *Works* (3 vols., London, Dodsley, 1798).

NINETEENTH CENTURY

Arnold, Matthew. *Essays in Criticism,* I, II, and *Culture and Anarchy,* 1869.

Browning, Robert and Elizabeth Barrett, *Letters, 1845–1846* (New York, Harpers, 1898).

Carlyle, Thomas. *On Heroes, Hero Worship, and the Heroic in History* (London, Chapman and Hall, 1840).

Bulwer-Lytton, Edward. *The Caxtons* (New York, 1860).

Coleridge, Samuel Taylor. *Biographia Literaria* (Modern Reader's series; New York, Macmillan, 1926).

Crowe, Catherine. *The Night-Side of Nature* (New York, 1850).

Dallas, Eneas. *The Gay Science* (London, 1866).

Darwin, Charles. *Diary of the Voyage of H. M. S. "Beagle"* (Cambridge Univ. Press, 1933).

De Quincey, Thomas. *Literary Reminiscences* (Boston, 1853).

Disraeli, Benjamin. *Tancred* (London, 1847).

Emerson, Ralph Waldo. *Nature,* 1836.

Gaskell, Elizabeth. *Mary Barton* (Oxford World's Classics), and *Cranford* (London, 1853).

Hawthorne, Nathaniel. *Mosses from an Old Manse,* and *Notebooks.*

Hazlitt, William. *Spirit of the Age,* in Vol. XI of *Works,* ed. P. P. Howe (London, Dent, 1932).

Herschel, John F. W. *Outlines of Astronomy* (New York, 1872).

Horne, R. H. *A New Spirit of the Age,* 2d ed. (London, 1844).

Hunt, Leigh. *Poetical Works* (Oxford Univ. Press, 1923).

Jones, Ebenezer. *Studies in Sensation and Event* (London, 1844).

Keats, John. *Letters,* ed. M. Buxton Forman (2 vols., Oxford Univ. Press, 1931).

Manning, Henry Edward. *Sermons* (4 vols., London, 1846–1850), Vol. I.

Martineau, Harriet. *The Hour and the Man* (London, 1841).

Ossoli, Margaret Fuller. *Woman in the Nineteenth Century and Kindred Papers* (Boston, 1860).

Peacock, T. L. *Memoirs of Shelley,* ed. H. F. B. Brett-Smith (London, Frowde, 1909).

Poe, Edgar Allan. "The Poetic Principle," in *Works,* ed. Stedman and Woodberry (Chicago, Stone and Kimball, 1894–1895).

Ruskin, John. *Modern Painters* (Everyman's Library; New York, Dutton, 1929–1935).

—— *Stones of Venice* (3 vols., New York, 1860), Vol. II.

Sterling, John. *Essays and Tales* (2 vols., London, 1847).

Surtees, R. S. *Handley Cross* (London, 1854).

Taylor, Henry. *Works* (5 vols., London, H. S. King & Co., 1877–1878).
Tennyson, Alfred. *Memoir by His Son* (London, Macmillan, 1897).
Thackeray, W. M. *Contributions to Punch* (London, 1898).
Trollope, Anthony. *The Macdermots of Ballycloran* (London, 1847).
Wordsworth, William and Dorothy. *Early Letters,* ed. Ernest de Selincourt (Oxford, Clarendon Press, 1935).

CRITICAL AND HISTORICAL

EIGHTEENTH CENTURY

Ainsworth, Edward Gay, Jr. *Poor Collins: His Life, His Art, His Influence* (London, Oxford Univ. Press, 1937).
Aldridge, Alfred. "Akenside and the Hierarchy of Beauty," *MLQ,* VIII (1947), 65–67.
Aronson, Alex. "Eighteenth-Century Semantics of Wit," *Etc., A Review of General Semantics,* V (1948), 182–190.
Arthos, John. *The Language of Natural Description in Eighteenth-Century Poetry* (Univ. of Michigan Press, 1949).
Aubin, Robert Arnold. *Topographical Poetry in Eighteenth-Century England* (New York, Modern Language Association, 1936).
Augustan Reprints, Series I and II, on Wit, on Poetry (1946, 1947).
Bate, Walter Jackson. *From Classic to Romantic* (Harvard Univ. Press, 1946).
Baugh, A. P., ed. *A Literary History of England* (New York, Appleton, 1948).
Bell, Charles C. "A History of Fairfax Criticism," *PMLA,* LXII (1947), 644–656.
Bett, Henry. *The Hymns of Methodism in Their Literary Relations* (London, Epworth Press, 1920).
Birrell, Augustine. *John Wesley: Some Aspects of the Eighteenth Century in England* (London, Epworth Press, 1938).
Bosker, Aisso. *Literary Criticism in the Age of Johnson* (Den Haag, 1930).
Bracher, Frederick. "The Silent Foot in Pentameter Verse," *PMLA,* LXII (1947), 1100–1107.
—— "Pope's Grotto: The Maze of Fancy," *Huntington Library Quarterly,* XII (1949), 141–163.
Brandenburg, Alice. "English Education and Neo-Classical Taste in the Eighteenth Century," *MLQ,* VIII (1947), 174–193.
Bray, J. W. *History of English Critical Terms* (Boston, Heath, 1898).
Bronson, Bertrand H. "Personification Reconsidered," *ELH,* XIV (1947), 163–177.
Brooks, Cleanth. *The Well-Wrought Urn* (New York, Reynal and Hitchcock, 1949).

Butt, John. "The Inspiration of Pope's Poetry," *Essays on the Eighteenth Century, Presented to David Nichol Smith* (Oxford, Clarendon Press, 1945).

Carlson, C. Lennart. *The First Magazine: A History of the Gentleman's Magazine* (Brown Univ., 1938).

Cory, Herbert E. *The Critics of Edmund Spenser,* Univ. Calif. Publ. Mod. Philol., Vol. II, No. 2 (1911), pp. 81–182.

Culler, A. Dwight. "Edward Bysshe and the Poets' Handbooks," *PMLA,* LXIII (1948), 858–885.

Deane, C. V. *Aspects of Eighteenth-Century Nature Poetry* (Oxford, Blackwell, 1935).

Doughty, Oswald. "The English Malady of the Eighteenth Century," *RES,* II (1926), 257–269.

Draper, John W. "Eighteenth-Century Aesthetics: A Bibliography," *Anglistische Forschungen,* Heft 71 (1931), pp. 1–140, esp. pp. 70–76.

—————— *The Funeral Elegy and the Rise of English Romanticism* (New York Univ. Press, 1929).

Duncan, Carson S. *The New Science and English Literature in the Classical Period* (Menasha, Wis., Banta Publ. Co., 1913).

Durling, Dwight. *The Georgic Tradition in English Poetry* (Columbia Univ. Press, 1935).

Elledge, Scott. "Cowley's Ode 'Of Wit' and Longinus on the Sublime," *MLQ,* IX (1948), 185–198.

—————— "English Criticism of Generality and Particularity," *PMLA,* LXII (1947), 147–182.

Empson, William. *Some Versions of Pastoral* (London, Chatto and Windus, 1935).

Fitzgerald, Margaret Mary. *First Follow Nature: Primitivism in English Poetry, 1720–1750* (New York, King's Crown Press, 1947).

Guyer, Byron. "Jeffrey's Essay on Beauty," *HLQ,* XIII (1949), 71–85.

Havens, Raymond D. "Poetic Diction of English Classicism," in *Kittredge Anniversary Papers* (Boston, Ginn, 1913).

—————— *The Influence of Milton on English Poetry* (Harvard Univ. Press, 1922).

—————— "Changing Taste in the Eighteenth Century: A Study in Dryden's and Dodsley's Miscellanies," *PMLA,* XLIV (1929), 501–536.

Houpt, Charles Theodore. *Mark Akenside: A Biographical and Critical Study* (Univ. of Pennsylvania thesis, 1944).

Humphreys, A. R. "The Friend of Mankind, 1700–1760," *RES,* XXIV (1948), 203–219.

Huntley, F. L. "Dryden's Discovery of Boileau," *MP,* XLV (1947), 112–117.

Hussey, Christopher. *The Picturesque: Studies in a Point of View* (New York, Putnam, 1927).

Kallich, Martin. *Association of Ideas and Criticism in the Eighteenth Century* (Baltimore, Johns Hopkins Press, 1945).

Jones, Claude. "Poetry and the Critical Revolution, 1765–1785," *MLQ*, IX (1948), 17–36.

Leedy, Paul. "Genres Criticism and the Significance of Warton's Essay on Pope," *JEGP*, XLV (1946), 140–146.

Lovejoy, Arthur O. *The Great Chain of Being: Plenitude and Continuity in the Eighteenth Century* (Harvard Univ. Press, 1936).

McKeehan, Irene P. "Some Observations on the Vocabulary of Landscape Description among the Early Romanticists," in *Elizabethan Studies and Other Essays in Honor of George F. Reynolds,* Univ. of Colorado Studies in the Humanities, Vol. II, No. 4 (1945).

McKenzie, Gordon. *Critical Responsiveness: A Study of the Psychological Current in Later Eighteenth-Century Criticism,* Univ. Calif. Publ. English, Vol. XX (1949).

McKeon, Richard. "Literary Criticism and the Concept of Imitation in Antiquity," *MP*, XXXIV (1936–1937), 1–35.

McKillop, Alan Dugald. *The Background of Thomson's Seasons* (Univ. of Minnesota Press, 1942).

MacLean, Kenneth. *John Locke, and English Literature of the Eighteenth Century* (Yale Univ. Press, 1936).

Monk, Samuel. *The Sublime: A Study of Critical Theories in Eighteenth-Century England* (New York, Modern Language Association, 1935).

Myers, Robert M. "Neo-Classical Criticism of the Ode for Music," *PMLA*, LXII (1947), 399–421.

Olson, Elder. "Rhetoric and the Appreciation of Pope," *MP*, XXXVII (1939–1940), 13–35.

—— Introd. to *Longinus on the Sublime and Sir Joshua Reynolds' Discourses on Art* (University Classics; Chicago, Packard, 1945).

Oras, Ants. *Milton's Editors and Commentators, 1695–1801* (Oxford Univ. Press, 1931).

Partridge, Eric. *Eighteenth-Century English Romantic Poetry* (Paris, 1924).

—— "The 1762 Efflorescence in Poetics," *SP*, XXV (1928), 27–35.

Platt, Joan. "The Development of English Colloquial Idiom during the Eighteenth Century," *RES*, II (1926), 189–196.

Quayle, Thomas. *Poetic Diction: A Study of Eighteenth-Century Verse* (London, Methuen, 1924).

Randall, Helen Whitcomb. *Critical Theory of Lord Kames,* Smith College Studies in Modern Languages, Vol. XX, Nos. 1–4 (1944).

Renwick, W. L. "Notes on Some Lesser Poets of the Eighteenth Century," in *Essays on the Eighteenth Century, Presented to David Nichol Smith* (Oxford, Clarendon Press, 1945).

Schelling, Felix E. "Ben Jonson and the Classical School," *PMLA*, XIII (1898), 221–249.

Sickels, Eleanor. *The Gloomy Egoist* (Columbia Univ. Press, 1932).

Starr, H. W. "Gray's Craftsmanship," *JEGP*, XLV (1946), 415–429.

Surtz, Edward L., S.J. "Epithets in Pope's 'Messiah,'" *PQ*, XXVII (1948), 209 ff.

Sutherland, James. "Wordsworth and Pope" (Warton Lecture, British Academy, 1944).

—— ed. *Dunciad* (London, Methuen, 1943).

—— "Eighteenth-Century Prose," in *Essays on the Eighteenth Century, Presented to David Nichol Smith* (Oxford, Clarendon Press, 1945).

Swedenberg, H. T. *The Theory of the Epic in England*, Univ. Calif. Publ. English, Vol. XV (1944).

Tate, Allen. "Longinus," *Hudson Review*, I (1948), 349–362.

Tatlock, J. S. P. "Origin of the Classical Couplet in English," *Nation*, XCIX (July 30, 1914), 134.

Tillotson, Geoffrey. *On the Poetry of Pope* (Oxford, Clarendon Press, 1938).

Trowbridge, Hoyt. "Joseph Warton on the Imagination," *MP*, XXXV (1937–1938), 73–87.

Tuveson, Ernest. *Millennium and Utopia* (Univ. of California Press, 1949).

Wallerstein, Ruth. "The Development of Rhetoric and Metre in the Heroic Couplet," *PMLA*, L (1935), 166–209.

Warren, Austin. "The Mask of Pope," *Sewanee Review*, LIV (1946), 19–33.

Watkins, W. B. C. *Johnson and English Poetry before 1660* (Princeton Univ. Press, 1936).

—— *Perilous Balance: The Tragic Genius of Swift, Johnson, and Sterne* (Princeton Univ. Press, 1939).

Wasserman, Earl. *Elizabethan Poetry in the Eighteenth Century*, Illinois Studies in Language and Literature, Vol. XXXII (1947).

White, H. O. "Thomas Purney," in the English Association's *Essays and Studies*, Vol. XV (Oxford, Clarendon Press, 1929).

Willey, Basil. *The Eighteenth-Century Background* (London, Chatto and Windus, 1940).

Williams, Basil. *The Whig Supremacy, 1714–1760* (Oxford, Clarendon Press, 1939).

Williamson, George. "The Rhetorical Pattern of Neo-Classical Wit," *MP*, XXXIII (1935–1936), 55–81.
—— "Strong Lines," *English Studies*, XVIII (1936), 152–159.
Wimsatt, W. K. "One Relation of Rhyme to Reason," *MLQ*, V (1944), 323–339.
—— *Philosophic Words* (Yale Univ. Press, 1948).
—— "The Structure of Romantic Nature Imagery," in *The Age of Johnson: Essays Presented to Chauncey Brewster Tinker* (Yale Univ. Press, 1949).
Yost, Calvin. *The Poetry of the Gentleman's Magazine: A Study in Eighteenth-Century Literary Taste* (Univ. of Pennsylvania thesis, 1936).

NINETEENTH CENTURY

Barzun, Jacques. *Romanticism and the Modern Ego* (Boston, Little, Brown, 1943).
Beach, Joseph Warren. *The Concept of Nature in Nineteenth-Century English Poetry* (New York, Macmillan, 1936).
Beatty, Arthur. *William Wordsworth: His Doctrine and Art in Their Historical Relations*, Wisconsin Studies in Language and Literature, No. 24 (1927).
Belden, Henry Marvin. "Observation and Imagination in Coleridge and Poe," *Papers in Honor of ... Charles Frederick Johnson*, ed. Odell Shepard (Hartford, Trinity College, 1928), pp. 131–175.
Bowra, C. M. *The Romantic Imagination* (Harvard Univ. Press, 1949).
Branch, E. Douglas. *The Sentimental Years, 1836–1860* (New York, Appleton-Century, 1934).
Bush, Douglas. *Mythology and the Romantic Tradition in English Poetry* (Harvard Univ. Press, 1937).
Caldwell, James Ralston. *John Keats' Poetry* (Cornell Univ. Press, 1945).
Campbell, O. J., and Paul Mueschke. " 'Guilt and Sorrow' [and] 'The Borderers,' " *MP*, XXIII (1925–1926), 293–306.
Davis, Herbert, ed. *Nineteenth-Century Studies* (Cornell Univ. Press, 1940).
Dobrée, Bonamy, ed. *From Anne to Victoria: Essays by Various Hands* (London, Cassell, 1937).
Duméril, Edith. *Felicia Hemans, une femme poète au déclin du romantisme anglais* (Paris, 1929).
Evans, Bertrand. *Gothic Drama from Walpole to Shelley*, Univ. Calif. Publ. English, Vol. XVIII (1947).
Ford, George H. *Keats and the Victorians* (Yale Univ. Press, 1944).
Grierson, H. J. C. *Milton and Wordsworth: Poets and Prophets* (Cambridge Univ. Press, 1937).

Griggs, Earl Leslie, ed. *Wordsworth and Coleridge: Studies in Honor of George McLean Harper* (Princeton Univ. Press, 1939). Includes Griggs's "Early Defense of Christabel," Samuel Monk's "Anna Seward and the Romantic Poets," and C. D. Thorpe's "Coleridge on the Sublime."

Hulme, T. E. *Speculations: Essays in Humanism and the Philosophy of Art* (New York, Harcourt, Brace, 1924).

Jump, J. D. "Weekly Reviewing in the 1850's," *RES*, XXIV (1948), 42–57.

Kennedy, Wilma L. *The English Heritage of Coleridge of Bristol* (Yale Univ. Press, 1947).

Ladd, Henry. *Victorian Morality of Art* (New York, Long and Smith, 1932).

Lehman, Benjamin H. *Carlyle's Theory of the Hero* (Duke Univ. Press, 1928).

Logan, James Venable. *Wordsworthian Criticism: A Guide and Bibliography* (Ohio State Univ. Press, 1947).

Mead, George. *Movements of Thought in the Nineteenth Century* (Chicago Univ. Press, 1936).

Minnegerode, Meade. *The Fabulous Forties* (New York, Putnam, 1924).

[Modern Language Association] "Romanticism: A Symposium," *PMLA*, IV (1940), 1–60.

Nicolson, Harold. *Tennyson* (Boston, Houghton Mifflin, 1930).

Pearce, Helen. *The Criticism of Tennyson's Poetry* (Univ. of California, unpublished dissertation, 1930).

Pierce, Frederick E. *Currents and Eddies in the English Romantic Generation* (Yale Univ. Press, 1918).

Rader, Melvin M. *Presiding Ideas in Wordsworth's Poetry*, Univ. of Washington Publications in Language and Literature, Vol. VIII, No. 2 (1931).

Read, Herbert. "Surrealism and the Romantic Principle," Introd. to *Surrealism* (London, Faber and Faber, 1936).

Reynolds, Myra. *The Treatment of Nature in English Poetry between Pope and Wordsworth*, 2d ed. (Univ. of Chicago Press, 1909).

Robertson, J. G. *Studies in the Genesis of the Romantic Theory* (Cambridge Univ. Press, 1923).

Rollins, Hyder Edward. "Notes on the Vogue of Keats, 1821–1848," in *Elizabethan Studies and Other Essays in Honor of George F. Reynolds*, Univ. of Colorado Studies in the Humanities, Vol. II, No. 4 (1945).

Romig, Edna Davis. "More Roots for Leaves of Grass," *ibid*.

Schorer, Mark. *William Blake: The Politics of Vision* (New York, Holt, 1946).

Shapiro, Karl. *A Bibliography of Modern Prosody* (Baltimore, Johns Hopkins Press, 1948).

Sherwood, Margaret. *Undercurrents of Influence in the English Romantic Period* (Harvard Univ. Press, 1934).

Smith, Bernard. *Forces in American Criticism* (New York, Harcourt, Brace, 1939).

Smith, C. Willard. *Browning's Star Imagery* (Princeton Univ. Press, 1941).

Sutcliffe, Emerson Grant. *Emerson's Theories of Literary Expression,* Univ. of Illinois Studies in Language and Literature, Vol. VIII, No. 1 (1923).

Thompson, Lawrance. *The Young Longfellow* (New York, Macmillan, 1938).

Tillyard, E. M. W. *Five Poems, 1470–1870* (London, Chatto and Windus, 1948).

Trilling, Lionel. *Matthew Arnold* (New York, Norton, 1939).

Victoriana. Margaret Barton and Osbert Sitwell, eds. (London, Duckworth, 1931).

Winters, Yvor. *Maule's Curse* (Norfolk, Conn., New Directions, 1938).

PART III

The Primary Language of Poetry in the 1940's

I. POETRY OF THE 1940's

THE SIMILARITIES on which generalization may be based are difficult to discern in work so close to us as the poetry of the 1940's. Not because the similarities are fewer than in other eras, but because our expectations and consequent observations are more various, the discernment is difficult. If self-knowledge is important to artist or society, then I think some descriptive generalizations about contemporary poetry are important to make. One of the simplest to arrive at should be a description of the primary materials of the poetry. The language medium provides the sorts of materials: accent and tone in sound; reference, connection, sentence structure in meaning. In their most obvious, unanalyzed appearances, prior to interpretation, prior to linguistic or stylistic study, subject only to the simplest formalities of repetition established by their use in art, these materials should reveal some of the *what* of poetry and provide a clue to its *why* and *how*.

Therefore I have extended into the present century the study of primary terms in contexts of sound and sentence structure. "Primary" I take to mean most frequently used, in representative texts by representative poets in representative eras. By this assumption of representativeness, which is tentative and provisional, dependent upon much further study, the work is barred from the realm of statistical, scientifically established sampling. For the texts chosen, the count is complete, so that even if certain assumptions of representativeness turn out to be mistaken, the frequencies in the text themselves have been reported. Frequency of usage I take to be but one of the traits of evaluative selection and formal repetition, one part of that complex of choice and order which is the art, the poem.

The poetry of the 1940's focuses the extremes of other centuries, tempering both the argumentative predicates of the seventeenth century and the descriptive modifiers of the eighteenth to a poise and balance upon the base of its own strong nouns. Lines grow short or long, syllables multiply, rhymes break away from the exteriors of stanzas to the interiors of lines, statements grow more and more declarative, whatever they may be declaring, and words, preserving most of their nineteenth-century symbolic atmosphere, intensify in addition the force of physical objects and of intellectual interpretations. The poetry is therefore a poetry of pattern. It is devoted to the linear, tonal, and qualitative arrangement of things according to a perspective in a state of mind. Its truth and beauty are in arrangements: in it explicit good is subordinate. As line and syntax, even verb and adjective, are subdued to substance, substance itself deepens and alters in its contexts to make a serious verse of objective interpretation.

For the mixed and miscellaneous poetry which we have been reading poem by poem for the past decade, such round generalizations of likeness may not easily seem valid. Yet it is my interest to point out likenesses, because they show the normal homogeneity of our poetic practice, and they show our relationship to the centuries before us. The 1940's have not produced a poetry in an alien or idiosyncratic language; like the decades in other centuries, they have modified their linguistic heritage toward their present attitude and need, and so have established their own standard medium of representation, expression, and communication.

This first chapter attempts to determine this standard medium in its primary details of vocabulary, sound, and syntax, first for its medial range, then for extremes, in the particular variations of twenty poets. The second chapter relates to poetry some of the stylistic and theoretical preoccupations of the decade's prose. The third relates the poetry to that of other centuries, in decades already studied. All attempt to exemplify the functioning of primary poetic materials of language in their general contexts, their associations with each other in structures recurrent throughout the decade's verse. In this emphasis upon general poetic context the study differs from much modern criticism, which focuses upon specific contexts of connotation in phrase and line. My concern is with the selections and formalizations within language as a whole, the third-personal statements of "fact," the assonantal patterns, the substantival phrases which we draw from contemporary language to make a poetic language like to, yet different from, the abstractions of metaphysical poetry and the descriptive generalities of the eighteenth century.

What poets most accurately represent the 1940's? For the decade in earlier centuries the question did not so awkwardly arise, because time and its conventions of choice, as represented in such a bibliographical handbook as Ghosh's *Annals of English Literature* for example, preserved from a ten-year span of publication only a dozen or two to significant remembrance. But now we have in mind literally hundreds for the past decade, and even these are a selection on the basis of most reputable publication. Is it possible to think of twenty poets as best representing the whole? Taking "best" in a very provisional sense of most recognized and reviewed, most debated, most published and imitated, in parallel to other eras though without the advantage of time's selectivity, I think agreement is fairly simple. Yeats, Eliot, Pound, Frost would appear for the fullness of their skill and influence; Stevens, Williams, Cummings, Moore, H. D., Sitwell for the various smaller perfections of their interpretations; Jeffers and Millay for their special sorts of popularity and effect; Auden, Spender, Warren for their versions of the middle generation; Crane for his lasting power of personality and symbol; Thomas, Manifold, Shapiro, Lowell for youthful success.

To this list there are recognizable objections. First, important elders, like De la Mare, Blunden, Aiken, are omitted. Even Housman should be included with Yeats and Crane, under the working principle of inclusion of those who publish in the period and have been dead no more than a decade. But the living elders are so many in our time that choice must be forced. Second, the middle generation of those in their forties and fifties numbers so many poets on what now seems an equal footing that it is impossible to include them all. So MacNeice is omitted, and Gregory, Tate, Winters, MacLeish, Fearing, Patchen, and many others. Third, the younger generation is of course least estimable. I have been guided by a sort of consensus of reviews, except that I have chosen, instead of Barker or Reed or another young

Englishman, the Australian Manifold, for the sake of variety in background and attitude. Examples of poets still in their twenties, Wilbur and Horan, appear in footnote with other additional notations.[1] I cannot pretend to recognize in this decade its youthful Dryden or Collins or Arnold. The poetry of elders dominates in the 1940's more than in the other observed decades. The 1640's were balanced between old and young; the 1740's, youthfully progressive; the 1840's, middle-aged. Those who think, then, that my list fails to represent fairly the conservative poets of the popular field will acknowledge the nevertheless heavy dominance of early twentieth-century tradition.

Given the work of twenty poets in a decade, how may one describe it so literally, so apart from imposed interest and stress, as to present its simple character? My idea is, as in preceding studies, to look for certain emphases of the work itself. I have chosen the emphasis of frequency in vocabulary, in its relation to sound and statement structures. I have counted the frequencies of the most referential parts of speech—adjectives, nouns, and verbs,—noting their proportioning and their contexts, not of complex meaning but of most obvious pattern in sentence and line.

The tables summarize the facts about this primary poetic language.[2] Table 1 lists the texts studied: usually the first 1,000 lines of a volume

---

[1] A number of other proportions, briefly stated, may serve to indicate margins not fully represented in the text. For example, Housman's 5 adjectives–15 nouns–10 verbs, in the first 500 lines of *A Shropshire Lad* and the first 500 of *Last Poems,* all four-accented lines or less, shows the line of predication from which Millay and others may have drawn their proportioning in our day. In lines almost twice as long, Ogden Nash uses the same proportion: 11–28–20 (first 100 lines of Ogden Nash *Pocket Book,* 1944). Robert Graves, Louis MacNeice, Stephen Benét represent versions of the decade's central mode: Graves, *Poems* (London, 1946) plus last 245 lines of *Collected Poems* (1938), 1,000 lines, 4' lyr. sts., 9–15–8; MacNeice, *Springboard* (Faber, 1944), 1,060 lines, 5' sts., narr. medit., 9–19–10; and Stephen Benét's popular narrative *Western Star* (Farrar, 1943), first 500 lines, 5', 9–20–9, preserve this standard proportion. On the other hand, young and recently first-published poets put more faith in epithet: Richard Wilbur, *The Beautiful Changes* (Reynal, 1947), first 500 lines, 4' descr. sts., 10–18–8; and Robert Horan, *A Beginning* (Yale Series of Younger Poets, 1948), first 500 lines, 4' descr. sts., 10–20–8. The first few hundred lines of *Paterson I* show that Williams is faithful to this mode of adjectival emphasis, in a proportion of 12–17–9 much like his earlier one, though with figures increased by line length. None of these works presents a major vocabulary in any way foreign to that of the majority studied in the decade.

[2] For readers who wish a closer analysis of the procedure by which these facts were arrived at, I append this note, repeated from the earlier studies. It seems necessary, in view of questions about and criticisms of the study of the 1640's, to emphasize again my own sense of experiment

in all these procedures. I am sure there are many errors in the counts; they have been checked only twice, and I have learned from the 1640's tables the tendencies toward error in column listing and proofreading. (Note, for example, corrections to be made in earlier tables. 1540's, table 1: Ballads 5–12–10, Shakespeare 10–17–10. 1540's, table 3A: remove *day, begin, keep, live* to 3B. 1640's, table 1: Cowley 7–13–11; table 3: Milton *give*, not Shirley *take*. 3A: Herrick *poor* and *rich*, Milton *old*, not Lovelace *full; thing* for Quarles, not Dryden; *fall* for Herrick, not Shirley; *grow* for Waller, not Milton; *fly, grow, look* for Jonson, not *look* for Donne. To 3B add *teach* from 3A, and a number of other individual terms such as *cold* Carew, *common* Quarles, *dead* Herrick, *dear* and *little* Suckling, *soft* and *sad* Crashaw, *care* Waller, *flame* Shirley and Carew, *flock* Quarles, *friend* Jonson, *move* and *mind* Suckling, *pride* and *fear* Wither, *wing* Vaughan. 1740's, table 2B: *grave* for Blair, not Blacklock. 1840's, table 2B: *hang* for *have*.) As I gain experience in relevant methods of checking frequency, I may learn that many more such items, as well as many of my assumptions, are in error. Nevertheless, the main lines of development will, I think, remain clear. I welcome suggestions with especial pleasure, because the methods are tentative and the questions many.

The main traits of language I take to be sound, vocabulary, and syntax. When used as medium for poetry, all these will be fixed in more formal pattern, sound in rhythm (meter or cadence, etc.) and in rhyme (end rhyme, assonance, consonance, alliteration, etc.); vocabulary in repetitions emphasized or unemphasized and in special selectivity; syntax in its control of the poem's logical structure. The relation between these formalizations helps define the total style. Given unifying time and place, or social context, one can learn some of the nature of the poetry by finding main emphases agreed on from poet to poet: sound patterns, words, structures most frequently and consistently employed and combined. Yule has shown in his *Statistical Study of Literary Vocabulary* that two or three dozen adjectives, nouns, and verbs tend to be used so often by an author that they make up a large and significant portion of his total vocabulary. (The half of language made up of connectives is no less important but requires a different sort of consideration.) Therefore the main words, together with sound and sentence structures, should suggest a good portion of the verse. The finer shadings, the pauses and silences, the uses of synonym and trope, are not counted here and are suited to more delicate study. The word "Roughly" should be assumed to precede every statement of quantity in art. But roughly quantitative emphasis can indicate, and better than impressionistic reading at times, the likenesses and differences beween poets and between periods and between kinds.

A decade is an arbitrary and convenient span of time, and I have gone on from the first-chosen decade of the 1640's to the forties in other centuries to see what sort of general continuity is describable. In Ghosh's *Annals of English Literature* the listed poems of the decade seem to be written by about twenty poets, published and living in that time or not more than a decade dead, and I have taken just twenty as a basis for comparison. This method of selection does not allow for precise discrimination between two successive decades, since the published poems may have been written over a period of years, or later work added. The published poetry of a decade tends indeed to represent the work of one or two generations, a half century.

The 1,000 lines of work taken as representative, provisionally, make easily practicable a count of every adjective, noun, verb, in structural pattern, as a larger amount would not. As I have written before, experience seems to warrant the assumption of a certain homogeneity in the work of a single writer. But the facts are only for the poetry of the 1,000 lines. These lines are usually either the first or the last in the volume considered, or are divided between two works if a great difference seems apparent.

Adjectives, epithets, include descriptive terms like *good, green;* attributive and appositive participles like *coming, made;* limiting modifiers of number like *one, many, no, all.* Nouns include forms which function as substantives except verbal forms or pronouns; I include nouns used as modifiers, as in *summer day* (except for materials, like *silver sea*), because form is a more steady guide than function in a work which is considering forms. Verbs include auxiliaries, infinitives, gerunds, each counted separately except the *is, has, do* auxiliaries. In addition to these common verb forms, there are a few words, notably limiting adjectives like *one*, and the verb *say*, too

published in or nearly in the decade, even though these lines may go back to an earlier date of composition; sometimes the first 500 lines of each of two texts if the two have seemed to be appreciably different. Table 1 lists also the primary sound pattern in accent and rhyme, the sort of statement, and the proportioning of terms, in order of increasing adjectival and (in the main) substantival quantity, the main modes of construction as proportioning reveals them. Table 2 lists first the primary terms (that is, those used 10 times or more in 1,000 lines) which are agreed upon by 10 or more of the 20 poets; secondly, the terms agreed upon by a minority of 4 or more poets; finally, the terms of individual emphasis. The tables thus report the language of reference most used in 1,000 lines by 20 poets published in the 1940's and so seem to me to report a language of value in our time.

Table 1 reveals the continuing force of Collected Works through the decade, the retrospective shows of Williams, Frost, Yeats, Eliot, Millay, Warren, Auden, and others, along with their new work and the new work of newer poets. I should guess that the list would reflect the 1930's

---

common to be listed fully in concordances. These do not appear, therefore, in the lists of major words, but they are counted in total occurrences.

The statement of proportion by line unit, 10 adjectives–20 nouns–10 verbs in 10 lines, for example, depends on a fairly stable line of four or five accents. For a writer of dimeter, adjustments must be made for comparison's sake, and his proportions doubled; his 5–10–5 in 10 would be comparable to a regular 10–20–10 in 10. But there are not many extremes, and there is almost as much proportional variation between poets of one line length as between poets of many. Line length is just one of many considerable factors, and the reader will find the necessary adjustments minor on the whole.

"Form" refers to line accent and organization, and to kind of statement. Rhythm is noted roughly by number of stresses, rhyme as setting up stanza grouping. The sorts of sentences which control the whole depend partly on person, first, second, or third; and partly on form, exclamation, imperative, question, declaration. Third-person declaration, narrative or descriptive, with infusions of lyrical invocation, is characteristic of the 1740's, as second-person address and argument is characteristic of the 1640's.

Together, form and proportion work in the primary vocabulary: 20 or 30 words are shared by half or more of the poets; 50 or so by a minority group of at least four; the rest by only one or two poets. The term is considered primary when it is used at least 10 times in 1,000 lines; and "10" stands for 8 to 12; "15" for 13 to 17, and so on; the count is by fives, in order not to make the point too fine. Singulars and plurals, comparatives and superlatives, and the various tenses have been counted together.

Of course it is common, especially in the individual lists, to find words which have occurred frequently for some insignificant and unrepresentative reason. But most of the recurrences are so scattered yet persistent, not only from poem to poem, but from poet to poet, that they suggest a deeper sort of interest.

TABLE 1: 1940's

THE POEMS IN ORDER OF ADJECTIVAL EMPHASIS

Texts: first 1,000 lines (exceptions noted)	Form	Proportion in average ten lines		
		Adj.	Noun	Verb
Williams, William Carlos. "Early Martyr," 465 lines, "Adam and Eve," 585 lines, 1938. *Complete Collected Poems* (New York, New Directions, 1938)	2' lines Descriptive	5	8	4
Cummings, E. E. *1×1* (New York, Holt, 1944)	3' stanzas Lyrical	6	11	7
H. D. *The Walls Do Not Fall* (London, Oxford Univ. Press, 1944) and *Tribute to Angels*, 220 lines (Oxford Univ. Press, 1945)	3' lines Meditative	6	13	6
Millay, Edna St. Vincent. *Collected Lyrics* (New York, Harpers, 1943)	5'–4' st. Lyr.	8	13	11
Auden, W. H. *Collected Poems* (New York, Random House, 1945), first 620 lines, and "In Time of War"	5' st. Descrip.	8	16	10
Lowell, Robert. *Lord Weary's Castle* (New York, Harcourt, Brace, 1946)	5' st. Descrip.	7	21	10
Frost, Robert. "A Further Range," *Collected Poems* (New York, Halcyon House, 1939)	5'–4' cpl., st. Medit.	8	15	11
Manifold, John. *Selected Verse* (New York, John Day, 1946)	5' st. Narrat.	8	17	11
Warren, Robert Penn. *Selected Poems* (New York, Harcourt, Brace, 1944)	5' lines Narr., med.	8	18	11
Pound, Ezra. *Complete Cantos* (New York, New Directions, 1948)	5'–3' lines Descrip.	7	20	6
Yeats, William Butler. "The Tower," 1928, 1,100 lines. *Collected Poems* (New York, Macmillan, 1940)	5' st. Medit.	9	16	9
Moore, Marianne. *Nevertheless* (New York, Macmillan, 1944) and first 8 from *Selected Poems* (New York, Macmillan, 1935)	4'–3' lines Descrip.	9	17	6
Spender, Stephen. *The Still Centre* (London, Faber, 1939)	5' st. Descrip.	9	18	9

TABLE 1: 1940's—*Continued*

Texts: first 1,000 lines (exceptions noted)	Form	Proportion in average ten lines		
		Adj.	Noun	Verb
Stevens, Wallace. *Transport to Summer* (New York, Knopf, 1947) 1st. 20 poems	5' st. Medit.	9	17	10
Eliot, T. S. *Four Quartets* (New York, Harcourt, Brace, 1943) and "Prufrock," 130 lines	5' lines, st. Medit.	9	19	8
Crane, Hart. "The Bridge." *Collected Poems* (New York, Liveright, 1940)	5' lines Descrip.	10	20	8
Shapiro, Karl. *V-Letter* (New York, Reynal and Hitchcock, 1944) and *Person, Place, and Thing* (1942), first 19 poems in each	5' st. Lyr.	10	21	9
Thomas, Dylan. *Selected Writings* (New York, New Directions, 1946) 1st. 29 poems	5' st. Lyr.	10	23	8
Sitwell, Edith. *Green Song* (New York, Vanguard Press, 1946) and *Street Songs*, first 350 lines	5' st. Lyr.	10	23	9
Jeffers, Robinson. *Be Angry at the Sun*, 480 lines (New York, Random House, 1941) and last 540 lines of *Selected Poems* (New York, Random House, 1938)	6' lines Narr., descr.	16	28	16
Average..		9	18	9

almost as accurately as the 1940's, except for the few younger men published toward the end of the decade. The force of survival and acceptance is itself characteristic of the decade.

Sound and sentence structures are, as usual, various; so brief and subordinate as Williams' descriptive, cadenced lines of not more than two or three accents; so long and heavy as Jeffers' swinging six-accented descriptions; so closely rhymed and normally measured as the stanzas of Frost, Manifold, Shapiro. As a whole, however, the group is distinguished from those of other centuries by its use of unrhymed lines in preference to stanzaic forms, by the variation of line length,[3] and by meditative third-personal descriptive statement.

Proportions of adjectives, nouns, verbs, appear to be moderate. That is, except for special extremes like Williams, Jeffers, Cummings, H. D., we see a common use like Spender's or Yeats' or Eliot's, 9–19–8, or so, with verbs nearly equal adjectives, and nouns twice as many. Such proportion makes for a moderate sort of statement, not adjectivally rich or predicatively complex, but substantial in nouns, particularly for the younger poets. Chronology shows little pattern, except that the strongest use of verbs is by elders, Frost, Millay, Cummings, as well as younger Auden, Lowell; while the strongest use of adjectives and nouns is in the Pound tradition and somewhat more youthful.

The more serial order of proportions shows the grouping more clearly. There should really be three lists, of course, based on noun and verb as well as adjective quantity; but the reader will note a certain consistency, as well as oversimplicity, in the one tabulation. Nouns tend to increase as adjectives do (with an extra increase for Lowell), and verbs, with a few notable exceptions, decline. At least, two main sorts of proportioning are clear: the predicative, from Cummings through Warren, which tends to emphasize verbs and underplay adjectives and often nouns; the substantival, from Moore through Sitwell, which tends to increase both adjectives and nouns at the expense of verbs. The latter sort of proportioning comes closest to the average of the decade, 9–18–9, or 1–2–1, the central balance of Yeats and Stevens. The more predicative proportion, like the 8–15–11 of Frost, seems the subordinate mode.

The primary terms of table 2, listed in majority, minority, and individual usage, bear out this structural distinction. Of the three adjectives, seventeen nouns, and ten verbs agreed on by a majority of the poets, the nouns are dominant in both quantity and new force. To the conventional *day, heart, man, time, eye* are added *death, hand, head, mind, light, night, sun,* characteristic in their temporal and intellectual emphasis. The adjectives *little, old, white* further dis-

---

[3] This variation in line length, even as roughly measured by accent, reduces the stability of line as unit of proportion. The reader should make allowances if he seeks clear parallels: double Williams' figures, reduce Jeffers' by a sixth, for example.

criminate time, size, color. The verbs, on the other hand, are not inventive, but still exceptionally receptive, with *come* and *go* the main actions.

Further, certain terms tend to be stressed by only one group of poets. The predicative poets, from Cummings through Warren, emphasize *age, death, God, heart, life, world, thing, knowing,* and *making,* the cognitive abstractions and constructions. They shun *white, light, night,* and *lying,* the atmospheric sense and long open sound of the era. The substantival poets use most of the major terms. Williams, Moore, Pound are exceptions because of scant lines or a very specialized vocabulary.

In the terms of the minority, table 2A, Pound is, on the other hand, most active, helping to establish the vocabulary of darkness, water, and standing still. Yeats and Warren add the terms of tree and sky, renew goodness, greatness, and youth. Jeffers again, with Sitwell, employs the full and common terminology. As may be expected, the substantival poets contribute adjectives, the *dark* and *green* qualities of sense, while the predicative poets contribute verbs. The words agreed on by the largest minority, *great, sky, seem, think,* echo the meanings of majority terms. The further *new, child, dream, earth, water, wind, word* set up an echo to the substance, of youth and illusion and transience.

The final table 2B, terms used individually, again supplements that of the majority. The individual adjectives *ancient, big, beautiful, blue,* are variations upon the major terms of time, size, color. Proper names, and nouns like *body, boy, brain, nothing* make particular specifications. Many verbs, at one time major, now survive in only a poet or two. Some single terms, Thomas' *blood,* Eliot's *fire,* Warren's *river,* serve to distinguish their poets, yet suggest also the commonest sort of modern reference.

The poetic vocabulary of the 1940's concerns through all its reaches the characteristics of time, size, color. It specifies *day* and *night, new* and *young* and *old, little* and *great, white* and *black, green* and *golden.* It sets these in *life* and *death, God* and *man* and *thing, sun, sky,* and the physical world, and deals with them by *hand, head, heart, mind,* by *dream, thought, love.* When the poetry is divided, it is divided in these terms, the predicative and narrative poets choosing the more abstract temporal; the substantive, the more concrete spatial. Terms of thought from the seventeenth century, of sense and feeling from the eighteenth, of dream from the nineteenth, come together here in forms as particular as poetry has found it possible to achieve. The substantive phrasal unit, by which both sound and sentence structure are subordinated to reference, focuses meaning upon object. But because of the mind and the dream, described objects are not directly recognizable; they are altered by context.

We turn to the context of the poetry itself, not to try to define or explain any poem or part of a poem, but simply to try further to define the nature of the primary materials as we see the sorts of composition in which they function. The use of the terms, the work they are put to, will help identify them. The recurring references are a part of the recurring patterns of sound and statement, at the norm of the decade's practice, and at its extremes, in its habits of art and of thought.

I

The normal selection of material, as Stevens or Eliot represents it, differs from the extremes of Cummings on the one hand and of Sitwell on the other in its balance of predication and qualification. The statements are rich with color and substance and at the same time active and mobile. The language of state of mind has both the stability of time and shape and the vivacity of emotional consideration. The terms of *come, go, think, know,* of *old, little, white,* of *eye, mind, night,* and *time,* work in the contexts of terms which substantiate them, of measures, harmonies, and sentence structures which focus and enforce their concern with perspectives.

That the poems of Wallace Stevens should provide exemplification of the characteristic poetic interest may surprise readers who treat him affectionately as a rarity. Yet we have seen that the proportioning of his recent work is that of the decade's poetry as a whole, and that even

TABLE 2: 1940's

MAJORITY WORDS: USED 10 OR MORE TIMES IN 1,000 LINES, BY 10 POETS OR MORE

	Wi	Cu	HD	Ml	Au	Lo	Fr	Mn	Wa	Pn	Yt	Mo	Sp	St	El	Cr	Sh	Th	Si	Jf	Total users
little	:	10	:	25	10	:	10	10	20	:	:	10	10	:	:	:	10	:	:	20	10
old	10	:	15	10	10	15	10	:	35	15	30	:	:	10	15	:	10	:	30	45	14
white	10	:	:	:	:	:	10	:	10	10	:	10	10	10	:	10	10	10	:	10	10
day	10	:	:	25	15	10	20	10	:	10	20	:	20	10	:	10	15	10	20	10	15
death	:	10	10	10	10	10	:	:	:	:	:	:	10	:	:	:	25	20	20	10	10
eye	10	10	10	15	10	20	10	:	20	:	20	10	40	15	:	30	25	20	15	25	17
God	:	:	10	25	:	15	10	:	:	15	:	:	:	:	:	10	:	:	15	15	12
hand	10	:	:	20	:	10	10	15	15	:	10	:	15	10	10	10	10	20	10	20	11
head	:	10	10	10	10	10	10	10	10	:	:	10	10	10	:	:	15	10	110	10	14
heart	:	10	:	20	10	10	10	:	10	:	30	:	20	15	:	:	15	20	20	:	13
life	:	15	:	:	25	15	10	:	10	:	15	10	25	:	10	:	15	15	20	25	10
light	10	:	:	10	:	10	:	10	10	10	:	:	10	30	10	:	10	30	40	20	12
love	10	20	:	:	20	15	10	:	10	:	20	15	15	20	15	10	10	35	65	85	17
man	10	20	:	:	20	:	15	30	:	25	45	15	10	25	10	:	:	:	:	10	9
mind	10	10	:	10	:	:	10	10	:	:	20	:	10	15	15	10	10	20	30	20	14
night	:	:	10	10	:	:	15	:	:	10	10	15	15	15	:	:	:	:	:	10	10
sun	:	10	:	:	10	:	10	15	:	:	25	:	15	15	15	10	10	20	55	10	11
thing	:	10	:	30	10	10	10	15	10	10	10	:	10	20	60	20	:	:	:	10	16
time	:	10	:	:	15	10	10	15	20	:	25	15	15	15	15	:	10	35	:	25	11
world	10	15	:	15	15	15	:	:	:	:	:	:	25	20	15	:	10	15	75	20	12

come	fall	give	go	hear	know	lie	make	see	take	Total majority words used
16	10	10	18	10	14	10	16	16	11	
35	:	10	35	20	25	15	15	30	20	27
40	15	15	15	10	20	25	15	25	:	24
:	10	:	:	:	:	15	20	:	:	17
20	10	:	10	10	:	15	10	15	10	24
10	:	:	10	:	20	:	:	30	10	16
20	10	:	20	:	15	:	:	10	10	15
15	10	:	10	10	15	10	20	15	:	22
:	10	:	:	:	:	10	10	:	:	20
:	:	:	10	:	10	10	20	20	:	12
20	:	10	10	:	15	10	20	:	10	20
25	:	10	20	:	10	10	10	10	:	15
25	:	10	25	10	25	:	10	15	10	17
20	:	10	25	10	:	:	10	10	10	17
40	:	15	20	:	15	:	25	20	15	23
10	10	:	10	10	:	:	:	10	15	20
15	10	10	15	15	20	:	20	20	15	21
30	10	:	25	15	40	10	15	25	:	23
:	10	:	10	:	20	:	:	10	10	12
10	:	10	20	:	10	:	10	:	:	18
10	:	:	10	:	:	:	10	10	:	14

TABLE 2A: 1940's

MINORITY WORDS: USED 10 OR MORE TIMES BY 4 POETS OR MORE

	Wi	Cu	HD	Ml	Au	Lo	Fr	Mn	Wa	Pn	Yt	Mo	Sp	St	El	Cr	Sh	Th	Si	Jf	Total users
black	10					15			15	10							15	10			5
dark										10					10				10	15	4
dead				10	10	10									10			10	20		4
good	10			10	15		10	10	10		20	10	10	10						20	5
great		10				10			10							10	10		20	25	8
green	10	10			10						10					15		15			6
long			15						20							10	10		15		5
new				20				10	15		10		10		10	10			15	15	7
young																				10	5
air	10	10	10							15		15		15			10		30	10	6
bird	10	10		10	20						10		10					15	10		4
child		10				15					10		10				10	15		10	7
dream		10	10		20											15				10	7
earth							10		30	10				10						10	7
face	10																		30		4
heaven		10		15					15							10		10	15		4
leaf			10				15				10			15				10			3
moon		15		15	10									15	15		10				4
nothing	10									20							10	10			6
sea		10				10							15	10		10	10	35			9
sky		10					10			10	10						10	10		10	4
stone						10					15	10	10					10			4
thought			10									10									4

	tree	water	wind	word	die	find	grow	live	look	love	seem	speak	stand	think	Total minority words used
	6	7	7	7	6	6	4	4	7	4	8	4	4	8	
					10	10		15	35	10	10			20	18
							20			10	10				12
	15	15	20	10											15
					10				20			10			9
		10	10												9
		10	10	15	10									15	9
						10		10				10	15	10	11
				10			10	10		10					10
							10	10							5
	10		15							20			10	15	16
		25	15			10		10					10		9
	15	15	15	10	10							10	15		14
				15	15			10				10	10		7
	10					10			15		10			20	9
	10	20	10		10										10
				10		10	15		10	10	10				13
									15	10	10	10		15	10
				10											6
	10														8
		10			10			10							9

TABLE 2B: 1940's

INDIVIDUAL VOCABULARY

	Wi	Cu	HD	Ml	Au	Lo	Fr	Mn	Wa	Pn	Yt	Mo	Sp	St	El	Cr	Sh	Th	Si	Jf
ancient											10									
beautiful																				25
big				10		10			20					10						
blue																10			20	
bright																			15	10
cold										10		10						10		
deep													10							
dry																				
fine																				
golden																			25	15
grey										10				10						
high										10				10						
human								10												
large					10															
last																				
open			10															10		
real																				
red				10		10								10	10		10		10	
small			10																	
still												15								
sweet		10																		
true											10									
wild																				
Amen			10																	
arm																10				

	Atlantis	beginning	being	bell	Billie	blood	body	bone	boy	brain	Christ	dark	ear	elephant	end	everything	faith	fate	father	fire	flame	flower	fly	foot	freedom	friend	future	glass	grave	hill
			10		20		15	15																					10	
																				10										10
															20				20								10			
		15																												
					10									10	10															
							10																							
														10										10						
	10	10			40										10						10				10					10
										10		10														20				
																					10	10								
						10	10	10			10						15	10				10						10		
	10																10	10												
																10		10		10										
															10															
																				10										

Atlantis.......... beginning........ being........... bell............. Billie........... blood............ body............. bone............. boy.............. brain............ Christ........... dark............. ear.............. elephant......... end.............. everything....... faith............ fate............. father........... fire............. flame............ flower........... fly.............. foot............. freedom.......... friend........... future........... glass............ grave............ hill.............

TABLE 2B: 1940's—*Continued*

	Jf	Si	Th	Sh	Cr	El	St	Sp	Mo	Yt	Pn	Wa	Mn	Fr	Lo	Au	Ml	HD	Cu	Wi
home	10			10												10				
house			15								10				10					
ice												10			10					
innocence																				
king				10							10				10					
kiss			10									15								
land												10								
lip																				
lord												10			10					
luck																				
moon			10				15			10										
mother										10						10				
mouth	10		10																	
music							10													
name									10			20	10					10		
neck						15							15							
Ned Kelly																				
past																				
place												10	10							
poet																				
power	20																10			
rain																				
river												30								
rose						10							10							
rhyme		10										15								
section																				
ship											10									

	Sigismunda	sleep	snow	soldier	song	soul	spirit	spring	star	stranger	summer	Sweden	tongue	tower	trunk	truth	verse	voice	wall	war	wave	way	weather	wing	woman	wood	year	ask	begin	blow	break	breathe
																		10														
		10								15		10	10			10				10											10	
					10													10														
			10					10													10											
																15		10														
			10			10																										10
														10		10								15								
				10	10																			10	10						10	
	15											10	10			10	10		10				10	10	25							
											10																					
				10																												
		10														15										10						
		10														15								10					10		
				10										15																		
				10	10																						10	10				

TABLE 2B: 1940's—Concluded

	Jf	Si	Th	Sh	Cr	El	St	Sp	Mo	Yt	Pn	Wa	Mn	Fr	Lo	Au	Ml	HD	Cu	Wi
bring				10						15				10						
call										10		10								
cry										10					10					
drive			10																	
drop			10										10				10			
fear																10				
feel		10																		
fight									15											
fly									10				10							
get			10								10	20								
hold																				
keep					10											10				
learn											10	10		10						
leave												10								
lose											10									
move						10						10								
ride				10			10					10								
ring																				15
rise																				
run																				
seek										10		10	10							
sing												10							10	
sit										10										
stare								10				10								
stop																			10	
tell	10									10		10								
try																				
turn			10										10							
walk															10					

the individual terms of his choice are the terms of his time. We may see further how this common material works in individual pattern. In "God Is Good, It Is a Beautiful Night," the beginning poem of *Transport to Summer,* for example, the summer night is qualified by qualities of its moon and bird; interrelated and interchanged by the meditating, inadequate yet creating, head; and voiced by its parallel and rising phrasal declarations, so that the head is made not only praiser but maker.

> Look round, brown moon, brown bird, as you rise to fly,
> Look round at the head and zither
> On the ground.
>
> Look round you as you start to rise, brown moon,
> At the book and shoe, the rotted rose
> At the door.
>
> This was the place to which you came last night,
> Flew close to, flew to without rising away.
> Now, again.
>
> In your light, the head is speaking. It reads the book.
> It becomes the scholar again, seeking celestial
> Rendezvous,
>
> Picking thin music on the rustiest string,
> Squeezing the reddest fragrance from the stump
> Of summer.
>
> The venerable song falls from your fiery wings.
> The song of the great space of your age pierces
> The fresh night.[*]

Much has happened since Longfellow's time, and that much appears in this poem. The nineteenth century could easily have praised God by beauty like this, and in nighttime, and by natural symbols of moon and bird, and by music. But each object would then have preserved its normal appearance, even in symbol: the moon shining with a brighter light; the bird, not the moon, flying and singing; the head, zither, book, rose, and shoe in more accustomed places, fragrance only rarely colored, summer not probably a stump; in the rich final metaphor not

---

[*] Reprinted from *Transport to Summer,* by Wallace Stevens, by permission of Alfred A. Knopf, Inc. Copyright 1942, 1947, by Wallace Stevens.

so many varieties of material raveled. Moon might have stood for the radiance of spirit, bird for the wings and voice of spirit, book and head for the thin searching of intelligence, night for encompassing nature, all simply and directly, in the early technique of symbol. These representations have not been abandoned in "God Is Good," but they have been complicated by interassociation, they have affected and altered each other. The moon, by its unstated likeness to a bird, has taken on unlikenesses which are stated, the brown color, flight, song, and fiery wings. The head, by its unstated likeness, in triviality, humility, and wear, to the objects on the ground, takes on a neuter quality which it keeps even when it speaks again, picking and squeezing while the song is able to pierce. The song, finally, by its unstated authority in the head, its humanity implied in its metaphorical venerability, fire, and masculinity, raises and reasserts the power of the poet, keeps the celestial rendezvous.

Such statement proceeds by negative rather than positive association, and so uses symbol based upon the assumption rather than the declaration of likeness. Such a mode may remind us of the seventeenth century with its consciously artful construction of unities from disparities. But the materials in the two modes differ, because the metaphysical subjects were abstract human relationships; they had not the sensuous eighteenth-century shapes of brown bird and rusty string, the atmospheres of red fragrance and fresh night.

The structure, too, differs. It does not argue; it floats. True, it goes back to simplest address: Look round, This was the place to which you came last night;—but the brown moon does not suggest a dialogue or answer, its venerable song being rather separate and invoked. Again, then, seventeenth- and eighteenth-century structures run counter and merge, the familiar second-person relation leading out to a more impersonal and suspended cosmic state. The verse structure follows, in the suspense of its parallelism. The first long lines in each stanza rise and wait, on comma or period. The shorter second lines normally run into the final period, making the line division surprising and the more suspenseful. Almost every stanza ends with a period, the next beginning at a new point of thought, so that we seem to get a parallel series of statements rather than consequences, while the transformations of the objects themselves are creating the consequences; and in this way the author does not seem to be taking responsibility for the progession; he seems passive and reportorial in a situation where his own joy is the point. Not the sentences or the verse structures, but the nouns, undergo change. Therefore, like the content, the structure works by dissociation; the song is treated as if apart from the constructions of its maker.

Sound reinforces the separation. There is no rhyme to round out, conclude, or bring home. Rather, the end sounds are thematic, the long open vowels at first ending the long moon lines, and then, with a sense of effect, taking the place of heavy *ground, door, summer* in the final *night*. The beginnings of lines play the heavier bass of repetition of phrase. The general early tone of *brown, rotted, now* shifts in the middle of the poem to the thinner *again, thin, string,* and finally to the fuller *fiery, great space, age,* and *night;* so that the sound follows the sense, not onomatopoetically, in direct imitation, but rather in parallel to feeling. The basic measure of iambic pentameter, as in "This was the place to which you came last night," is shaded also according to feeling, as in "In your light, the head is speaking. It reads the book"—where the extra syllables make a laborious sound,—and in "The venerable song falls from your fiery wings"—where the extra syllables in related pattern are triumphant. This is not to say that the sounds would make such sense without the sense; but merely that they work to this sort of combined effect, and that such internal patterning, intricate and nonemphatic, is one special characteristic of the mode.

As one reads in this poem much of the sound and sense of modern poetry, one may analyze also a characteristic vocabulary and proportioning. The verbs and adjectives are equal, and fewer than one per line. The nouns are about twice as many. The major nouns *night* and *head* are major also for the decade, *night* continuing from the nineteenth century, *head* new. The minor *moon* and *bird* are newly characteristic of the decade. The adjectives *brown* and *reddest* represent the common emphasis on color; *great* the size, *thin* and *fresh* the

quality, *rotted, seeking, picking, squeezing,* the dominance of parti-
cipial modifier, which extends and suspends action in qualification.
Look, fly, come, fall are key verbs for the era as well as for the poem.
Singular as this brown moon is, in its rising and the peculiar fire of
its song, it uses words, orders, measures, proportions which speak for
Stevens as average as well as individual poet.

This is another way the kind of poem may sound: more colloquial,
less atmospheric because it lacks a moon:

On her side, reclining on her elbow.
This mechanism, this apparition,
Suppose we call it Projection A.

She floats in air at the level of
The eye, completely anonymous,
Born, as she was, at twenty-one,

Without lineage or language, only
The curving of her hip, as motionless gesture,
Eyes dripping blue, so much to learn.

If just above her head there hung,
Suspended in air, the slightest crown
Of Gothic prong and practick bright,

The suspension, as in solid space,
The suspending hand withdrawn, would be
An invisible gesture. Let this be called

Projection B. To get at the thing
Without gestures is to get at it as
Idea. She floats in the contention, the flux

Between the thing as idea and
The idea as thing. She is half who made her.
This is the final Projection C.

The arrangement contains the desire of
The artist. But one confides in what has no
Concealed creator. One walks easily

The unpainted shore, accepts the world
As anything but sculpture. Good-bye,
Mrs. Pappadopoulos, and thanks.[5]

As in many others of his poems, Stevens makes a statement of relationship between life and art or the natural and the created. As in "God Is Good," he ostensibly gives the credit to nature, to the night and the moon, here to the unpainted shore and Mrs. Pappadopoulos. They are what we thank. Yet again the series of parallel statements sets up its interest in the human projection upon this nature. Projection A is the physical girl in the physical painting, the "thing," objective enough, but we learn about her what she isn't, what we must search for, "anonymous," "without lineage," "so much to learn." Projection B is the painter's evident idea of the thing, the slight and bright Gothic crown suspended, not painted, and in contention with Projection A. Finally, Projection C, the arrangement, floats in the contention, is neither fully the physical girl nor fully the crowned vision, but half still the contention in the artist himself. Nature is easier. One could wish this girl were Mrs. Pappadopoulos indeed.

But all the while, as in "God Is Good," it is the poet who has been doing the work, and the poem turns out to be the poet's. The construction, that is, controls the whole idea by running counter to it; does not accept and organize nature as the eighteenth century would, but abstracts and transforms it. The painting is treated not as an object but as a series of "projections," and the projections are seen to be at odds with each other. The sentence structure is complex, in the tone of a geometrical proof, packed with an effortful reasonableness. In contrast, the last two stanzas are nonchalant, indicating the absurd ease of life when it is not art. The absurdity makes the irony, and makes us prize the effort as well as the ease.

This neatly backhanded poem uses again the valued terms of the decade in its abstraction, its floating and suspension, its analytical objectivity, and its immediate detail of hip, blue eye, Gothic, and Mrs. Pappadopoulos, in the focus of complicated thought. The objects are strongly subordinate, and therefore may be as off-center, as mixed, as limited as possible. The process of figuring out relationships—of appearance to reality again—is what matters. And it is the process, not the result—the figuring, not the answer. "To So-and-So Reclining on

Her Couch" gives us not primarily So-and-So or the Couch, nor indeed what they separately stand for, but rather what a mind thinking about reclining as art may conjure up.

It is difficult for the modern reader to let go of the physical or the symbolical moon or couch as he has seen such objects functioning in earlier centuries of poetry and thought, and to accept an effect not of harmonious sensation nor of melodious mystery, but of contextual precision. Stevens' problems of thought about beauty and reality are not easily or popularly read, because they involve reëxamination as well as reconsideration of beauty and reality, and because they allow for little common generalization, being engaged in a personal abstraction. Yet, difficult or not, the problem is not special to Stevens. It has led most of the poets of the decade to stress the abstractness of head and mind, with a stress which is characterizing.

The major vocabulary of the 1940's has *death* in it, *mind* in it, *thing, time,* and *world* in it, concepts more withdrawn than the common traditional *God, day, life, man, love,* which it also maintains. To the *hand* and *heart* it has added *head.* For traditional *fair, sweet, soft* it has substituted *old, little, white,* adjectives, too, withdrawn from directest appreciation. Its verbs are not new, and preserve the passives of the nineteenth century. The structures using this vocabulary are meditative and suspended; the sound patterns are intricate and interior. The poetry of the decade is, in its whole make-up, opposed to direct apprehension or intuition through substance. It is made out of abstract consideration and requires some devotion to reconsideration.

Eliot's *Four Quartets* presents a simpler view of the process, but a similar one. Eliot's proportioning is much like Stevens' and the average 9A–18N–9V; close to this balance, though a bit short on verbs. He agrees in stressing *old* and *mind, thing,* and *time. Time* is his great major term, and in its presence dissolve the scenes and symbols of romanticism. "Burnt Norton," the first Quartet, begins,

> Time present and time past
> Are both perhaps present in time future,
> And time future contained in time past.
> If all time is eternally present

> All time is unredeemable
> What might have been is an abstraction
> Remaining a perpetual possibility
> Only in a world of speculation.
> What might have been and what has been
> Point to one end, which is always present.[6]

This is Stevens' reasoning tone; it goes on in the Latin vocabulary of the trained philosophical head; and it's poetry how?—partly by pattern, partly by jargon, partly by implied concern, and by its vestige of atmospheric setting, its roses and birds of tradition.

> Footfalls echo in the memory
> Down the passage which we did not take
> Towards the door we never opened
> Into the rose-garden. My words echo
> Thus, in your mind.
> But to what purpose
> Disturbing the dust on a bowl of rose-leaves
> I do not know.
> Other echoes
> Inhabit the garden. Shall we follow?
> Quick, said the bird, find them, find them,
> Round the corner. Through the first gate,
> Into our first world, shall we follow
> The deception of the thrush? Into our first world.

The bird for Eliot like the bird for Stevens gives a light touch of mysterious nature to the heaviness of speculation. It suits the echoes, it gives a voice to garden and dust, and by its qualities of quickness and wingedness, thus of deception, gives present quality to time, as time vanishes yet stays in memory. "Our first world" has like facets of suggestion: whole, large, and encompassing in one sense, narrow and limited by the gate and the memory in another, one of many later worlds (and what worlds are they?) in a third sense. In the autumn heat this world, further specified, holds unheard music, sunlight and cloud, leaves full of children, all the delicate appurtenances of romantic suggestion and overtone as the nineteenth century practiced it.

---

[6] These and the other lines from *Four Quartets,* copyright 1943 by T. S. Eliot, are reprinted by permission of Harcourt, Brace and Company, Inc.

Then we get another, a less atmospheric, more metaphysical joining of unlike objects.

> Garlic and sapphires in the mud
> Clot the bedded axle-tree
> The trilling wire in the blood
> Sings below inveterate scars
> And reconciles forgotten wars.

Here the control is outward, the intentions centripetal rather than centrifugal, the nouns not implicative by themselves but meaningful in their combination.

Then again atmosphere, but of the waste land, needing the commentary words *unhealthy, torpid, gloomy.* Then the scrutinizing section on words. Then the summarizing abstraction with its romantic heart of echo:

> Love itself is unmoving,
> Only the cause and end of movement,
> Timeless, and undesiring
> Except in the aspect of time
> Caught in the form of limitation
> Between un-being and being.
> Sudden in a shaft of sunlight
> Even while the dust moves
> There rises the hidden laughter
> Of children in the foliage
> Quick now, here, now, always—
> Ridiculous the waste sad time
> Stretching before and after.

Eliot uses various modes of combination, the romantic implicative, the abstract rational, the descriptive, the metaphorical, as variations upon a theme which is involved in all of them and can be drawn from all of them. The nature of *time* and our life in it, which is Stevens' problem of perception and creation in another form, is made the subject of statement and restatement, of echo, and elaborated metaphor, renamed to a total of sixty times in the four Quartets. Recapitulation emphasizes the burden and the consciousness of the poet, so that at the end of *Little Gidding,* the end of the Quartets, the consciousness is plainest.

What we call the beginning is often the end
And to make an end is to make a beginning.
The end is where we start from. And every phrase
And sentence that is right (where every word is at home,
Taking its place to support the others,
The word neither diffident nor ostentatious,
An easy commerce of the old and the new,
The common word exact without vulgarity,
The formal word precise but not pedantic,
The complete consort dancing together)
Every phrase and every sentence is an end and a beginning,
Every poem an epitaph. And any action
Is a step to the block, to the fire, down the sea's throat
Or to an illegible stone: and that is where we start.

Exact, precise, complete, rounded to end and to beginning, this is poetry and this life in Eliot's eyes. Form is asserted upon the formless, the formulable. The haunting ends and echoes of ends come to a final end, it is said. It is said that

> . . . all shall be well and
> All manner of things shall be well
> When the tongues of flame are in-folded
> Into the crowned knot of fire
> And the fire and the rose are one.

Note how much control is asserted by the spirit of the poet. He quotes an ancient text, he metaphorizes and symbolizes, he has moved from the finite rose garden to the infinite rose, from lyric to statement. Every poem an epitaph, the spirit's strength written over the body's weakness.

The major materials in the vocabulary of the Quartets are the body's weakness and the strength of time and thought. The spirit, contrary to romantic emphasis, does not have a major place; it is implied in the terms of nature like *rose* and *wind,* but its more dominant form for Eliot is intellect in its recognition of mutability. His primary verbs, besides *come* and *go,* are *know* and *think.* The rest, *die, fall, move, see, take,* are characteristic of the decade, and subordinate. Eliot is one of the most extreme in ignoring verbs like *make.* His adjectives likewise are quiet or temporal: *dark, dead, still, old, new,* with *old* the strongest. His great noun, used sixty times, is *time,* and others follow to enforce the theme, *end, future, past;* further abstractions are *God, love, mind, man, thing, way, word, world;* and the natural objects which are most invested with these meanings are *fire, light, rose, sea, voice, water, wind.* These make the characteristic specifications of the 1940's, renewing *light* and *voice* from the 1840's and *fire* from earlier, elevating *flower* in the *rose* symbol, discovering *wind* and *water,* usually in combination. These terms make for Eliot a fleeting world and an elusive one. Though he names now and again many hard edges, this main material of his vanishes almost at a touch; he keeps a nineteenth-century romantic poetics of implication. At the same time his intellectual statement explicitly controls, organizes, varies, dismisses, and recalls these elusive echoes of nature and spirit, painstakingly builds hints into arguments, blocks out wisps of melody into "quartets," and makes a sonorous poetry of assertion from the materials of suggestion.

Such control does not seem wholly a classical one. It does not discover order in nature; rather it discovers over and over a disorderly nature, which it strives to take to task. It does not accept forms of poetic harmony and bring them to a higher potential state; rather it works on an alternation between hints of form, echoes of form, and almost literal analyses of form. It seeks the normal, in its pendular swing between extremes, but it does not assume the normal, and does not indeed ever deal with it happily. It acclaims no golden mean, but a fiery point in time, a point which vanishes but persists, between a personal heaven and a personal hell, both worldly, both subordinate to the desired and the poetic abstract. One could call this method of thought, not classicism, but a Puritan romanticism, which recognizes and poetizes the evanescence of the worldly, but which claims beyond it the force of mind and its rigor, in the dilemma of Thomas Becket. Despite the metaphysical fire and thought, this "thought in sense" is too dominant in illusion to be metaphysical; its wind and water wash away the older stabilities and its mind establishes a center in the flux of time.

In this establishment the Quartets are more literal than Eliot's poems of the 1920's, but not greatly different from them. The open implicative forms varied by the tight ironical ones, the literary, the cultural, allusiveness, the jolts of meaninglessness in the specific, the repetitive incantatory sentence structures, all have been maintained. Emphasis has shifted from the mirage of roses in the waste land to the mirage of waste land under the Rose, but the proportionings and the terms are constant, the *old* and *time,* the *coming* and *going* persistent. The changes over two decades show largely Eliot's increased thematic insistence, the added epithets and varieties of terms which work all to the same point, by synonymy and repetition, and by declaration.

In the 1920's too, Yeats was writing versions of his poetry which seem to many today the best modern poetry we have, and which, published in collection in 1940, a year after their author's death, persist through this decade in affecting the concept of poetry as the Quartets do, as the *Waste Land* still does. The poems are not fundamentally far apart. Yeats in *The Tower* and elsewhere, like Stevens and Eliot, uses a proportion characteristic of the 1940's, a balanced 9A–16N–9V, odd only in a scantness of nouns. His primary vocabulary is ample by repetition, and fully part of the century: his major *old* like Eliot's and Stevens', his added *young* and *ancient,* his quantitative *great* and *long.* Nouns, in addition to the standard *eye, heart, love, man,* agree with the others in stress on *thought, mind, time,* and then on implicative nature: *birds, moon, night, stone, sun, tree, wind,* with the romantic personnel of *woman, child, mother, dream,* and *song.* Verbs are abundant and common, all the standard ones, and the especially atmospheric *call, cry, grow, run, seem, sing.* Yeats' poetry is more active, constructive, responsive, in terms of motion, than the poetry of the others, and possesses more clearly nineteenth-century words like *wild, child, cry,* and *dream;* but, like the others' poetry, it is devoted to the strength of complex and intellectual assertion of, rather than acceptance of, these active and objective significances. The reader of Yeats' life reads there, in fact, the story of search for structures in the drift of symbol.

"Sailing to Byzantium" begins *The Tower* with establishment, against the "sensual music," of "monuments of unaging intellect," and "the artifice of eternity."

> Once out of nature I shall never take
> My bodily form from any natural thing,
> But such a form as Grecian goldsmiths make
> Of hammered gold and gold enamelling
> To keep a drowsy Emperor awake;
> Or set upon a golden bough to sing
> To lords and ladies of Byzantium
> Of what is past, or passing, or to come.[7]

Time in nature is the theme, but a bird out of nature, farther even than Stevens' bird, is the artificer of the song. Again in the title poem "The Tower," discipline is set up against physical atmosphere, the "learned school" of human control against the sleepy cry of nature, at the end:

> Now shall I make my soul,
> Compelling it to study
> In a learned school
> Till the wreck of body,
> Slow decay of blood,
> Testy delirium
> Or dull decrepitude,
> Or what worse evil come—
> The death of friends, or death
> Of every brilliant eye
> That made a catch in the breath—
> Seem but the clouds of the sky
> When the horizon fades;
> Or a bird's sleepy cry
> Among the deepening shades.

Many a nineteenth-century poem has ended with the fading horizon, the deepening shades, in ever-widening circles of poignant suggestion; Yeats in irony presents these with the *but* which diminishes and will disregard them.

One may remember that the passive and the natural and the beau-

---

[7] From "The Tower," in *Collected Poems* by W. B. Yeats, copyright 1933 by The Macmillan Company.

tiful are, in Yeats' *Vision*, not so subordinate to the rigors of intellect
as my statements would indicate. The intellectual sun, opposed to the
spiritual moon, is hard, bright, primitive, or mechanical, not produc-
tive of the best men or periods in the scheme of things. Yet the very
elaborate polarization which Yeats makes is itself significant of his
consciousness of the force of intellect in the world of nature, and significant, further, of the bent of his own mind toward the invention
of structure to contain and formalize phenomena, to oppose rather
than dissolve them.

> I climb to the tower-top and lean upon broken stone,
> A mist that is like blown snow is sweeping over all,
> Valley, river, and elms, under the light of a moon
> That seems unlike itself, that seems unchangeable,
> A glittering sword out of the east. A puff of wind
> And those white glimmering fragments of the mist sweep by.
> Frenzies bewilder, reveries perturb the mind;
> Monstrous familiar images swim to the mind's eye....
>
> I turn away and shut the door, and on the stair
> Wonder how many times I could have proved my worth
> In something that all others understand or share;
> But O! ambitious heart, had such a proof drawn forth
> A company of friends, a conscience set at ease,
> It had but made us pine the more. The abstract joy,
> The half-read wisdom of daemonic images,
> Suffice the ageing man as once the growing boy.

This last section of "Meditations in Time of Civil War" dismisses
again familiar images in favor of daemonic ones; takes from the broken stone an abstract joy. But it is the presence of both sorts of images,
not the choice of one, that is the point. Yeats chooses sometimes one
way, sometimes the other, depending on the emphasis of context, and
he has fought to be master of both.

His versification provides the same combination of familiarity and
authority. The "Civil War" stanzas with their six-accented lines and
interlocking rhymes are characteristic of many poems in *The Tower*.
Note how free and nonchalant they are within a firm form. The long
lines seem easy and quick, not heavy. The comparatively regular

iambic accents of the first lines of both stanzas, reporting a simple action directly, waver and complicate themselves when they come to natural images or human thoughts; the heavy spondee in *blown snow* reverses the whole measure; the *Wonder how many times* in the second stanza does so again to more troubled effect; the many scattered extra syllables give the effect of breath hurrying or caught in conversation and in directly reflected meditation.

The statement makes the directest sort of presentation, with an air of "all should be made plain," in spite of, indeed because of, the daemonic images. Yeats, as he says many times in his prose, wishes not to mystify but to reveal, even if the revealed order is one he must himself create. So he reports his thoughts, his motions, as if with great candor and literalness, and the sentence structure is as purely declarative as one can imagine.

His early verse, like Eliot's, embodied most of the qualities of this later verse, the same primary vocabulary, proportioning, statement, speaking melody, according partly with the traits of the times. The sense of direct report of meditation increased in both poets, as both increasingly concentrated upon exposition of certain relationships which had grown to seem most important to them. So both gave up some of the more elusive appurtenances of early romanticism: Eliot the white and yellow colors, the streets, the hair, the *feel,* of the Prufrock poems, and Yeats the same sort, the pale and young, the floating hair, the misty terms and floating measures of the *Wind,* and the *Woods.* Contrary to common belief, Yeats' adjectives increased in his later work, to somewhat the same effect as Eliot's, but none of the new adjectives were used often enough to be major like the early standard *pale* and *young;* rather they were the commentary terms of immediate context, like the *broken, unchangeable, monstrous, familiar, abstract* of the stanzas above. Qualities grew more singular, less standard, for Yeats as he ceased accepting the daemonic images of others and fought for his own, and his own grew closer to the familiar images which he fought, and fought for.

At the same time, then, that both Yeats and Eliot were working toward the severer abstraction characteristic of Stevens and the 1940's, they brought along differing degrees of romantic context, Yeats tending to abandon, Eliot to preserve some most-accepted symbols like rose and fire and sea; Eliot abandoning and Yeats keeping, on the other hand, the streets and people, the women, children, friends, and the dramatic verbs of feeling. Meantime, they shared and preserved the poetic line of *old, God, man, mind, thing, time, coming,* and *going,* and *knowing,* giving it special emphasis on age and intellect: world, man, friend, song, and story *old,* and knowing their end in their beginning.

Another poet of such knowledge was Pound, their mutual friend. Yeats has told how Pound tried to wean him from abstraction, and indeed the Imagism of the 1920's still reflects in poetry today Pound's enthusiastic influence. But even in the solid color and shape of this imaged vocabulary and cadence, much of it romantic and much a further development into natural concreteness, is a trace of the learning, the temporal sense, the love of antiquity, in *old, year, end, thing, time, know,* which shows Pound's abstract alliances. The rest of his major terms outdo his friends' in color and texture; they are as solid a poetic list as one could find: the standard passive verbs and the adjectives all hues, *black, dark, dry, golden, gray, white,* and the nouns, besides *air, day, God, man, voice,* and *light,* strong *land* words, *house* and *stone* and *wood* and *wall,* and even more strong *sea* words, *water, ship, wind,* and *wave.* It is the vocabulary of the *Lyrical Ballads,* sifted and concentrated. It is that lasting natural world through which the fragments caught by a mythologizer can make their journey.

> And then went down to the ship,
> Set keel to breakers, forth on the godly sea, and
> We set up mast and sail on that swart ship,
> Bore sheep aboard her, and our bodies also
> Heavy with weeping, and winds from sternward
> Bore us out onward with bellying canvas,
> Circe's this craft, the trim-coifed goddess....

or,

> Hang it all, Robert Browning,
> There can be but the one "Sordello."

But Sordello, and my Sordello?
Lo Sordels si fo di Mantovana.
So-shu churned in the sea.
Seal sports in the spray-whited circles of cliff-wash,
Sleek head, daughter of Lir,
    eyes of Picasso
Under black fur-hood, lithe daughter of Ocean;
And the wave runs in the beach-groove: . . .

or,   These fragments you have shelved (shored).
"Slut!" "Bitch!" Truth and Calliope
Slanging each other sous les lauriers:
That Alessandro was negroid. And Malatesta
Sigismund:
         Frater tamquam
   Et compater carissime: tergo
         ...hanni de
         ..dicis
         ...entia
Equivalent to:
         Giohanni of the Medici,
         Florence.
Letter received, and in the matter of our Messire Gianozio,
One from him also, sent on in form and with all due dispatch,
Having added your wishes and memoranda.

These, the beginnings of the first, second, and eighth Cantos, indicate the sorts of fragments Pound finds worth shoring: fragments of human knowledge and creation in a sea of natural being. The lines begin and end with *ands,* having no rhymes but feminine-ending echoes to make their patterns. Their length suits to the material concerned and the style of the supposed speaker. All the arts and all the languages and nations fit side by side. Anybody speaks; Pound commands poets and patriots, and reads everybody's letters. Thus the author becomes an encyclopedist, but not dry; his land and sea, wind and wave, keep all in solution. Canto II ends:

Olive grey in the near,
    far, smoke grey of the rock-slide,
Salmon-pink wings of the fish-hawk
    cast grey shadows in water,
The tower like a one-eyed great goose
    cranes up out of the olive-grove,

And we have heard the fauns chiding Proteus
    in the smell of hay under the olive-trees,
And the frogs singing against the fauns
    in the half-light.
And...[8]

By this suspension and hyphenated qualification, Pound seems a far more submitting poet than Yeats or Eliot or Stevens. He makes nothing come of his collections and intermittent passions except their primary atmosphere. This is the "let be" tone of the Imagists, of MacLeish in *Conquistador,* and of many other moderns, and it is far more neutral than the romantics' implications because those were more carefully established by a common sense of nature. But at the same time that Pound seems to do none of the explicit or implied resolving of so early a confrère as Coleridge or so recent a one as Eliot, the freeness and variety of selection and cadence and tone themselves indicate an authority of choice. The authority is content to rest in the very intended miscellaneity of things.

Our leading elder poets present to us the median average of poetry in our decade, a poetry of moderate balance in qualification and predication, a poetry with a strong sense of natural quality involved in time and thought, a poetry of fragmented statement including much inward harmony. Pound is a part of this group, in friendship and influence, in cadence and substance. But in one way he differs strongly, in his minimum of verbs, and he shares this characteristic with Moore and Spender. These three put more emphasis than their colleagues do on a thick surface of substance. Structure and statement are more subordinate, action is rarer and less distinguished, than in most poetry of this or any other period, except for Hood's and Tennyson's in the 1840's. Before this, we have found that a small number of verbs depends proportionately on a large number of adjectives and nouns; from the middle range of Pound, Moore, Spender, as from Tennyson, we should expect more predication than we get.[9] But the difference is the imagism of our era, which supports a school of objects.

---

[8] All lines quoted are from *Complete Cantos,* by Ezra Pound, New Directions, 1948.

[9] William Carlos Williams is of the same type in proportioning, though his unusually short lines make for lower figures.

In the last 11 lines quoted from Pound, *cast* and *cranes* are the only verbs, themselves close to images, in the midst of 18 nouns and 10 adjectives. Even in the first lines quoted, the unusually active ones of going aboard ship, nouns and adjectives outnumber predicates by four to one, an average usually characteristic of only the heavily substantival eighteenth century. We see, then, in the midst of the modern type, and possibly even stronger in the Imagism of a few years back, a special excess of distinguishing features, an excess of nominal emphasis, of structural fragmentation. The poetry is less in the sentences than in the materials and their inert but interacting arrangement. Marianne Moore chooses, like Pound, the careful adjectives and hyphenated nouns which will discriminate the exactitude of the thing, around which her comment plays. Take the first brief poem in *Nevertheless,* "The Wood-Weasel":

> emerges, daintily, the skunk—
> don't laugh—in sylvan black and white chipmunk
> regalia. The inky thing
> adaptively whited with glistening
> goat-fur, is wood-warden. In his
> ermined well-cuttlefish-inked wool, he is
> determination's totem. Out-
> lawed? His sweet face and powerful feet go about
> in chieftain's coat of Chilcat cloth.
> He is his own protection from the moth,
>
> noble little warrior. That
> otter-skin on it, the living pole-cat,
> smothers anything that stings. Well,—
> this same weasel's playful and his weasel
> associates are too. Only
> woop-weasels shall associate with me.[10]

The lightly humorous conversational tone is like Pound's and the others'. The detail is serious. *Sylvan, inky, whited, glistening, ermined, outlawed* and the rest set up an interplay of odd terms at the center of which is precision. *Little* is characteristic of Miss Moore's constant

---

[10] All lines by Marianne Moore are from *Nevertheless,* copyright 1944 by The Macmillan Company.

care about size. *Well-cuttlefish-inked* wool defines to absurdity the modern structure of modification, forming adverb, verb, and noun into epithet, where once a relative clause would have functioned. The lack of clauses brings all items to one level of time, place, and grammar, serving to stuff and preserve. In contrast to the 18 preserving adjectives in these 16 lines, there are 11 verbs only, *emerges, go, smothers, stings,* the parenthetical *laugh,* and the rest *is,* enforcing again the definition of a context of being. The sentence structures carefully, oddly, describe and define, and at last assert. "Only / wood-weasels shall associate with me." ["all shall be well and / All manner of thing shall be well"].

The sound devotes itself to precision also. Nothing must get in the way of the skunk, so rhyme does not, nor alliteration, nor any obtrusive pattern. The line ends don't really end; they just deliberate before going on; their rhymes therefore make couplets which are extremely shy. The words now and then, like *adaptively, wood-warden, Chilcat cloth,* catch up the tongue and remind that the going of thought is difficult. Effort, care, good humor, a pleasure in abstracting from a clarified object, all are reflected in the sturdy progress of the sounds.

"The Mind Is an Enchanting Thing" plays the same game at an abstracter level, trying·to set forth just that mystery which enchants modern poets, but without any mystery, rather with clear *things,* like katydid-wing, dove-neck; the mind

> is an enchanted thing
>   like the glaze on a
> katydid-wing
>   subdivided by sun
>   till the nettings are legion.
> Like Gieseking playing Scarlatti;
>
> like the apteryx-awl
>   as a beak, or the
> kiwi's rain-shawl
>   of haired feathers, the mind
>   feeling its way as though blind,
> walks along with its eyes on the ground.

> It has memory's ear
>   that can hear without
> having to hear.
>   Like the gyroscope's fall,
>   truly unequivocal
> because trued by regnant certainty, . . .

The mind is netted, varied, yet unequivocal; it is "conscientious inconsistency"; it is "not a Herod's oath that cannot change." More rigorously than Pound, Miss Moore draws her objects to a generalization, but still as vigorously she scours learning, experience, dialogue, and the countryside for that miscellany of material which, at the fine point of its enforced connection, will draw a bead on a piece of truth.

Therefore her major words are odd objects, her adjectives measure them, her verbs construct, perceive, and exist, in *small, little, fine, white,* in *bird, wing, ear, body, trunk, elephant, neck, Sweden,* as well as the normal *eye, heart, life, man, thought,* and in *fight, fly, go, lie, live, look, know, make, see.* It is probable that for Moore as for Pound the idiosyncratic nouns would vary from poem to poem, as each is struck upon to maintain a certain note, but it is probable too that Moore's words would be persistently anatomical, in animal anatomy, while Pound's were concerned with the seven seas. Color and size serve as primary qualities; motion and rest, the predication.

So too for Spender in his *Still Centre. Great* and *little, deep, young,* and *white* modify his world of major terms and his especial *death, dream, children, light,* and *sky,* his thinking *head* and *mind.* His verbs, *lie,* or *seem,* or *look,* are scant. More diffuse in reference than the others, Spender is still weighty. The book begins:

> Our single purpose was to walk through snow
> With faces swung to their prodigious North
> Like compass iron. As clerks in whited banks
> With bird-claw pens column virgin paper,
> To snow we added foot-prints.
> Extensive whiteness drowned
> All sense of space. We tramped through
> Static, glaring days, Time's suspended blank.

That was in Spring and Autumn. Summer struck
Water over rocks, and half the world
Became a ship with a deep keel, the booming floes
And icebergs with their little birds:
Twittering Snow Bunting, Greenland Wheatear,
Red-throated Divers; imagine butterflies
Sulphurous cloudy yellow; glory of bees
That suck from saxifrage; crowberry,
Bilberry, cranberry, *Pyrola uniflora....*

                      Was
Ice our anger transformed? The raw, the motionless
Skies, were these the Spirit's hunger?

Spender tends to begin with the stuff, various, searched out, listed, and then to draw his questions of mind and spirit from it. Even in narrative it is the stuff that does the work. In "Easter Monday,"

The corroded charred
Stems of iron town trees shoot pure jets
Of burning leaf. But the dust already
Quells their nervous flame: blowing from
The whitening spokes ...

                But look, rough hands
From trams, 'buses, bicycles, and of tramps,
Like one hand red with labour, grasp
The furred and future bloom
Of their falling, falling world.[11]

   The falling, falling world falls because it is heavy with substance. The "corroded charred stems of iron town trees" cannot be said lightly nor taken lightly. The forces of both noun and verb have been translated into epithet for this statement, which is yet not statement at all but just a loading of substance. The iron town trees do act; they "shoot pure jets of burning leaf," and the verb is vigorous, but it is single in the three lines in which there are at least four adjectives and a half dozen nouns. *Iron* and *town* are half noun, half adjective, and it is hard to know how to classify them, since they have not adapted form to function in any way, but remain almost as if implying hyphens. They are intensely characteristic of modern verse, in its desire to

---

[11] All lines from Stephen Spender's *The Still Centre*, 1939, Faber and Faber Ltd.

qualify by the interaction of objects, with none of the weight of the objects lost. The high proportion of verbs turned to adjectives is a parallel characteristic; the action is frozen or suspended into quality. "Was / Ice our anger transformed?" The pacing lines, unreturning, and heavy with extra accents, support the sort of question.

II

But if we see in the midst of the moderate balances of median poets in the decade a nominal emphasis which tips the scale toward substance, we may see also a group of poets who agree upon a more predicative extreme. They write ballad narrative, or lyric which partakes of narrative, or lyric which participates in argument and so in clausal structure. These poets, Warren, Auden, Manifold, Lowell, Millay, Frost, both young and old, are verbally active in the way that the Brownings, Landor, Macaulay, Emerson were, or, earlier, Wyatt, Donne, Cowley, and the Cavaliers. They use seven or eight adjectives in ten lines, nouns about twice as many, and more verbs than adjectives, ten or eleven, at least one per line. They do not thereby, however, write a metaphysical or a transcendental verse. Their words are different. They agree with their own contemporaries on the vocabulary of things. Such a poet as Warren is, except for his predicative emphasis, much like Stevens in accepting the weight of interrelated symbols, toward the control of a world however strange.

Warren's words are the reëchoing wind and water words of the time; in "Billie Potts," they wrap up a story of modern poetry as well as of ambush. And further, unlike Stevens, Warren often writes a medium sort of poem that sounds like a merely slight exaggeration of half the writing going round in the country. This participation is probably a matter of personal leadership, and a matter, too, I think, of the least inventive side of Warren's own work. At any rate, it is represented at the beginning of such a poem as "Terror":

> Not picnics or pageants or the improbable
> Powers of air whose tongues exclaim dominion
> And gull the great man to follow his terrible

Star, suffice; not the window-box, or the bird on
The ledge, which means so much to the invalid,
Nor the joy you leaned after, as by the tracks the grass
In the emptiness after the lighted Pullmans fled,
Suffices; nor faces, which, like distraction, pass
Under the street-lamps, teasing to faith or pleasure,
Suffice you, born to no adequate definition of terror.[12]

The mouth-filling pomp here is not wholly serious, but it is by no means wholly ironical either. The bird which means so much to the invalid is a phony, as it has turned out, and as you can tell by the second-hand ring of the speech. But the ambiguously specific *the*'s,[13] permitted in the statement, go on and on seriously through Warren's writing;—the great man, the lighted Pullmans, the privy breath, the absurd contraption, the applauded name, the slow god, the conscience-stricken stare, proceed with others like them in this one poem to an effect of absolute truth revealed in the particular which measures and molds the whole tone toward pomp. The sound collaborates, in having regular scansion abetted by extra syllables which fill rather than lighten. Alliteration, assonance, repetition are emphatic, and meanings like *dominion, terrible, emptiness, fled, distraction* are emphatic too, tossed as they are among *picnics, window-boxes, Pullmans.* The strong speech and accent, which in their trivial company the reader may have taken to be ironical, turn out merely meager; the portent of the whole is much greater than the heaviest statements can state.

Warren, like Stevens, plays with the expectations from standard symbols, mixing them with unstandard accompaniments, never quite redeeming them or throwing them away; unlike Stevens, he does not often transform them. His *tongues, star, bird, grass, light* are all the poetic sort of our time, like the *stone, leaf, door* of Wolfe, and however much by *the* he generalizes them, or by *picnic* and *terror* jars and denies them, the residue of poetic remains. In his best poems the residue is used to a purpose, the atmospheric lingo a part of the point.

---

[12] This and other lines from Robert Penn Warren, *Selected Poems, 1923–1943,* copyright 1944 by Harcourt, Brace and Company, and used with their permission.

[13] G. Rostrevor Hamilton, *The Tell-tale Article: A Critical Approach to Modern Poetry* (London, 1949). This good book acknowledges, as I should like to, a debt to Owen Barfield.

Narrative technique, a stronger predicative sense, structurally establishes Warren's difference from Stevens and establishes, I think, his
own best way of getting his poetic materials off the ground. Contrast
to "Not picnics or pageants or the improbable" the beginning of the
first of the *Selected Poems,* "The Ballad of Billie Potts."

> Big Billie Potts was big and stout
> In the land between the rivers.
> His shoulders were wide and his gut stuck out
> Like a croker of nubbins and his holler and shout
> Made the bob-cat shiver and the black-jack leaves shake
> In the section between the rivers.
> He would slap you on your back and laugh.

Here the leaves and rivers are a bit more subordinated to man and
action, and, best of all, the extra effect of the last line quits rich terms
and Elizabethanisms in a fine abrupt fashion. The narrative continues
this way, and the humor belongs fairly enough to the narrator.

> So Little Billie took his leave
> And left his Mammy there to grieve
> And left his Pappy in Old Kaintuck
> And headed West to try his luck
> And left the land between the rivers,
> For it was Roll, Missouri,
> It was Roll, roll, Missouri.
> And he was gone nigh ten long year
> And never sent word to give his Pappy cheer
> Nor wet pen in ink for his Mammy dear.
> For Little Billie never was much of a hand with a pen-staff.

There follows this piece of narrative, and every piece in the poem, a
parenthesis; and this parenthesis returns to more "poetry" again, to a
lyrical mood and loaded natural symbols. Little Billie has been away,
but he'll be back; so we get the terms of search, identity, return, in
name, face, water, image.

> (There is always another country and always another place
> There is always another name and another face.
> And the name and the face are you, and you
> The name and the face, and the stream you gaze into

Will show the adoring face, show the lips that lift to you
As you lean with the implacable thirst of self,
As you lean to the image which is yourself,
To set the lip to lip, fix eye on bulging eye,
To drink not of the stream but of your deep identity,
But water is water and it flows,
Under the image on the water the water coils and goes
And its own beginning and its end only the water knows.

The interlocking repetitions make the lyric seem like a magical chant, and the mysterious, assumed definitions increase the effect. They give all through the narrative a portentous interpretation of name and face and self which makes the narrative action itself a symbol. But, not condensed into lyric alone, the story in turn gives to the symbol what is to me at least a welcome enlivening motion,—more than the comparable charm-making of *Four Quartets* contrives or wishes to.

After the story of Little Billie's return is over, the poetry comes down hard on main words to finish off—the poem's words, and the decade's:

And you, wanderer, back,
After the striving and the wind's word,
To kneel
Here in the evening empty of wind or bird,
To kneel in the sacramental silence of evening
At the feet of the old man
Who is evil and ignorant and old,
To kneel
With the little black mark under your heart,
Which is your name,
Which is shaped for luck,
Which is your luck.)

Wind, word, evening, bird, empty, old, man, heart, little, name, black—these, shared by many or a few, are the sliding, falling, nostalgic, exterior words of the decade, which require the thought of man, the action of the poet, to give them meaningful shape. The Waste Land must be made sense of. The old men must be acknowledged. The cadence must be checked.

With Warren the rest of the predicative poets agree in stressing age and size for epithets. *Great, little, old* are common, sometimes *good, young, new,* and colors of *black* and *white. Sun* and *sky* and *to lie,* as these suggest a possible passive enjoyment, are least common, along with *dark, green, air, moon.* This poetry makes most comment as in *good,* and subdues atmosphere. *Earth, tree, water, wind,* and *word* are more its kind, and the nouns *thing* and *nothing,* and the verbs *think* and *die.* There's a new cold *snow* in Lowell and Frost, but *making* and *seeing,* as well as *coming* and *going,* keep the poems from freezing over. Least of all in the decade the predicating poets are lighted and dreamy; most, active, and moral, and controlled.

Here, for example, is the second of Manifold's first two poems "For Comrade Katharine":

> Give me what of death you hold
> In your loins and lips and hands;
> Act and word are contraband
> At a frontier so controlled.
>
> So in earth and darkness rolled
> Sleeps the harvest of wild lands
> And again in summer stands
> Vigorously manifold.
>
> Hands from writing, lips from speech
> Turn to festival with yours,
> Mingle, play, and sleep, and then
>
> Like the sailor to the beach
> Fresh with our united force
> Rally to the task again.

Accents are tight, rhymes direct, verbs continuous, focus human and personal. A more abstract poem, "Demolition," takes the same effect:

> This was provided for: before they built
> They reckoned on demolishment: the plan
> Plotted in detail where the wiring ran
> Under the surface like a sense of guilt.
>
> The bridge stands still, and offers by the hilt
> What will undo it, closing what began
> When dynamite was planted in the span
> Of concrete our retreat returns to silt.

> So the event—something as unforeseen
> As the *amazing disappearance,* say,
> *Of Edna Brown of Highgate, age sixteen,*
>
> *Boy-friendless, bright, and helpful*—miles away
> Hangs on a tossup; but has always been
> Bedded like this, structural in the clay.[14]

Like the actions of Little Billie, apart from their atmospheric inserts, or like one of Marianne Moore's animals moving in its extreme particularity, or like Mrs. Pappadopoulos, the bridge and Edna Brown hang on the tossup, some old structural intention giving them whatever sense they have. Manifold's vocabulary puts especial stress on intention, adding to the decade's *head* and *mind* others: *brain, freedom, name, word,* and the *poet's rhyme, song, verse. Fight* and *fear, run* and *turn* increase the motion. Often he makes succinctly, as in "Quins," the sort of metaphor the whole decade implies,

> (Amphibian-like to skim the waves of passion
> Or zoom full-throttle up the sky of thought);

wherein sense, sex, natural scene, and intellect are bound in linear relation.

An Australian soldier in his thirties, Manifold shares much with a New England philosopher in his seventies. Both like brevity regular, colloquial, and sharp, as well as solid. Frost's *good, little, old, white* modify most of the same major terms, and more nature, *flower, sky, tree, leaves, snow;* and his verbs add *look, seem, ask, leave* to the standard. He is not so explicitly conscious as Manifold, but is equally quick to analyze and define.

An early poem in *A Further Range* is "The White-tailed Hornet," subtitled "The Revision of Theories." It begins:

> The white-tailed hornet lives in a balloon
> That floats against the ceiling of the woodshed.
> The exit he comes out at like a bullet
> Is like the pupil of a pointed gun.
> And having power to change his aim in flight,

---

[14] Both poems from John Manifold's *Selected Verse,* reprinted by permission of The John Day Co., Inc. Copyright 1946 by The John Day Co., Inc.

He comes out more unerring than a bullet.
Verse could be written on the certainty
With which he penetrates my best defense
Of whirling hands and arms above the head
To stab me in the sneeze-nerve of a nostril.
Such is the instinct of it I allow.
Yet how about the insect certainty
That in the neighborhood of home and children
Is such an execrable judge of motives
As not to recognize in me the exception
I like to think I am in everything—
One who would never hang above a bookcase
His Japanese crepe-paper globe for trophy?
He stung me first and stung me afterward.
He rolled me off the field head over heels,
And would not listen to my explanations. . . .[15]

The briefer lyrical poems move less deliberately but make the same combination of deliberated fact as "Leaves Compared with Flowers" does, for example, or the most famous "Desert Places,"

Snow falling and night falling fast oh fast
In a field I looked into going past, . . .

Whether the poem is tightly rounded like this one, or straighter forward like "The White-tailed Hornet," Frost makes one of its major characteristics the progression of the meditative sentence structure. Such outspoken thought represents the predicative poets; they care about clause as well as phrase, and accentuate, in a decade when most of the poetry takes the tone of speech, the fullest working out of sentences against meters in that speech. They work, in this sense, in the units of language larger than note, word, phrase, and so employ metered lines and worked-out periods.

As rhyme and period are used the more, in the emphasis on ends, and the playing of one end against the other, with a strong force of conclusion when they meet, the inner harmonies of vowel and consonant tone are used the less. It is true that *falling* and *lonely* set up onomatopoetic patterns of open vowels, but they do so fairly simply;

---

[15] From *Complete Poems of Robert Frost, 1949,* by Robert Frost. Copyright 1949 by Henry Holt and Company, Inc.

the direct report of "In a field I looked into going past," or "I have it in me so much nearer home," would be spoiled by effects of vowel pattern; they want to sound mixed and awkward. "The white-tailed hornet lives in a balloon / That floats against the ceiling of the wood-shed" is, as Frost treats it, a remark which requires a *So what* answer, not a beauty of interior arrangements.

Much in the writing of Frost, Manifold, Warren seems like metaphysical poetry. The structure is like, with its emphasis on linear control and meditative repetition; the proportioning is like, with more verbs than adjectives in narrative, reasoning, and clausal organization; the tone is like, purposely roughened by particles of speech as talk is. But mainly the relation of author to material has altered. The metaphysical poet dealt largely in a vocabulary of concept. Even the specific beauties of addressed ladies or the details of a civil life were subordinated as metaphor to the main statements of larger spiritual relation. Now the poet, in the 1940's, is much more oppressed by the concrete material of life and cannot so subordinate it. His theme is often mastery in the largest sense, but it is a theme achieved by worry, trouble, and arrangement. Things are not mastered for him by God as they were in the seventeenth century; the job of ordering is now more literally man's own, and God a part of the order.

Therefore, though in some poets we get a workmanship more metaphysical than any since the seventeenth century, the nineteenth century has intervened to give us the hornet, the bird, the wood, the desert places, their tones and atmospheres as well as the thoughts of the poet, for poetic substance. Bringing them even more closely in focus, Frost does not let them drift away as symbols of infinite sympathy, but considers them in relation to himself: in himself the desert places, as in Stevens the brown moon.

The first poem in Edna St. Vincent Millay's *Collected Lyrics,* her famous youthful "Renascence," concerns just this relationship. It sets up the oppression of natural things against the human sense. It narrates the crisis of "immensity made manifold," the weight, as well as the scope, of sympathies. It begins as follows.

All I could see from where I stood
Was three long mountains and a wood;
I turned and looked another way,
And saw three islands in a bay.
So with my eyes I traced the line
Of the horizon, thin and fine,
Straight around till I was come
Back to where I'd started from;
And all I saw from where I stood
Was three long mountains and a wood. . . ."[16]

These are the mountains and woods, the stones and trees, of the century's concrete emphasis. They are the material images which some poets presented for themselves, but which Millay like Frost early sought to make strong assertions about. The rains of sympathy dissolve their weight, and the poem ends:

The world stands out on either side
No wider than the heart is wide;
Above the world is stretched the sky,—
No higher than the soul is high.
The heart can push the sea and land
Farther away on either hand;
The soul can split the sky in two,
And let the face of God shine through.
But East and West will pinch the heart
That cannot keep them pushed apart;
And he whose soul is flat—the sky
Will cave in on him by and by.

This is the measure, and the explicit measure, of nature by the soul under pressure. It may be that twentieth-century poetry worked against nineteenth, as seventeenth against sixteenth, that is, as an age of self-consciousness against an age of enthusiastic affirmation. At any rate, the dominance of the personal, of death, of the *thing* concept, of rhyme and argumentation, are characteristic of both reacting periods. In their simple form of defiance, in the young Millay and Frost of the earlier decades, they roused immediate pleasure, and have kept on without great change, finding form in the first-published verse of

---

[16] These and the other lines by Millay from *Renascence and Other Poems*, published by Harper and Brothers. Copyright 1914, 1942, by Edna St. Vincent Millay.

younger poets still. One may note in Millay's work constantly the ease of the colloquial, whether it be Spain, Death, or Sorrow addressed. The "Sorrow" poem in *Renascence* goes:

> Am I kin to Sorrow,
>   That so oft
> Falls the knocker of my door—
>   Neither loud nor soft,
> But as long accustomed—
>   Under Sorrow's hand?
> Marigolds around the step
>   And rosemary stand,
> And then comes Sorrow—
>   And what does Sorrow care
> For the rosemary
>   Or the marigolds there?
> Am I kin to Sorrow?
>   Are we kin?
> That so oft upon my door—
>   *Oh, come in!*

The resilience of accent in this cavalier tune, as in later lyrics from *Huntsman, What Quarry*, makes it a type which still prevails for younger poets. The poise of question against meter and rhyme, the dashing finality of ending, the nonchalance of diction, the reined pathos or nostalgia, all differ from the level parallels of Imagism, and maintain some seventeenth-century concept, some nineteenth-century tune, to argue the death and truth of the universe.

The poetic leader of a younger school who is most attached to this tradition is W. H. Auden. He enjoys the outward controls of verse, the predicative assertions. He, too, is good at bringing everything to a sharp close for which rhyme and syntax have progressively prepared. He, too, declares *words* of *truth*. He represents neatly the type's emphasis on *great* and *little, new* and *old*, and *good,* on standard nouns and verbs for this time. His special emphasis, on the vocabulary of family, *children, mother, father, home,* he shares with Millay, Lowell, Spender, Shapiro, Thomas, Jeffers, but his special *nothing, death, truth,* and *word* he shares more closely with others of his type. *Fate* he adds to these, and has no main vocabulary of natural things. So he abstracts from the rest, with family his foundation.

The first of his *Collected Poetry,* "Musée des Beaux Arts," runs as follows:

> About suffering they were never wrong,
> The Old Masters: how well they understood
> Its human position; how it takes place
> While someone else is eating or opening a window or just
>   walking dully along;
> How, when the aged are reverently, passionately waiting
> For the miraculous birth, there always must be
> Children who did not specially want it to happen, skating
> On a pond at the edge of the wood:
> They never forgot
> That even the dreadful martyrdom must run its course
> Anyhow in a corner, some untidy spot
> Where the dogs go on with their doggy life and the
>   torturer's horse
> Scratches its innocent behind on a tree.
>
> In Breughel's *Icarus,* for instance, how everything turns away
> Quite leisurely from the disaster; the ploughman may
> Have heard the splash, the forsaken cry,
> But for him it was not an important failure; the sun shone
> As it had to on the white legs disappearing into the green
> Water; and the expensive delicate ship that must have seen
> Something amazing, a boy falling out of the sky,
> Had somewhere to get to and sailed calmly on.[17]

The isolations of men and things are conveyed chattily, but strictly, the things familiar but very special—you have seen just that picture, of course,—the rhymes unemphatic but inevitable.

Sometimes Auden's form is even more passive, in substantive manner, as "Letter to Iceland" begins:

> And the traveller hopes: "Let me be far from any
> Physician"; and the ports have names for the sea,
>   The citiless, the corroding, the sorrow;
>   And the North means to all: "Reject."

---

[17] These and other lines by Auden from *Collected Poetry of W. H. Auden,* copyright 1945 by W. H. Auden. Reprinted by permission of Random House, Inc.

> And the great plains are forever where the cold fish is hunted,
> And everywhere; the light birds flicker and flaunt;
>   Under the scolding flag the lover
>   Of islands may see at last,
>
> Faintly, his limited hope, as he nears the glitter
> Of glaciers, the sterile immature mountains intense . . .

But often again, as in *Journey to a War* XXV, "Nothing is given: we must find our law," or XXVI, "Always far from the centre of our names," or in cryptic narrative bits like "Gare du Midi," Auden turns not only the heaps of rubble, the alien scene, into verse, but also the logic of his thought about these. So in the *Age of Anxiety* argument and eclogue work sometimes together, sometimes at odds, according as the poet's sense is of weary acceptance or of easy control.

The combination of these traits gives Auden his characteristic quality. He is active in poetry, but he employs, or gives in to, a great amount of passive listing. At times he is as much a poet of substances and series as Spender, his friend. The trick is that he uses a serial structure with predicative material; he states but does not subordinate. So a most characteristic poem would appear somewhere between the first two quoted here, giving a moving portrayal of situation in a rather static serial form. "Voltaire at Ferney," for example, begins and ends:

> Almost happy now, he looked at his estate.
> An exile making watches glanced up as he passed,
> And went on working; where a hospital was rising fast
> A joiner touched his cap; an agent came to tell
> Some of the trees he'd planted were progressing well.
> The white alps glittered. It was summer. He was very great. . . .
>
> So like a sentinel, he could not sleep. The night was full of wrong,
> Earthquakes and executions. Soon he would be dead,
> And still all over Europe stood the horrible nurses
> Itching to boil their children. Only his verses
> Perhaps could stop them: He must go on working. Overhead
> The uncomplaining stars composed their lucid song.

The eighteen verbs in these twelve lines make the poem most unusually active. Yet the activities, reported in bits, listed as subjects, placed side by side in surprising juxtaposition like nouns, do not make the poem itself move anywhere. Nothing results. The verbs compose a state, and that state is modified, almost in supererogation, by the commentary epithets *happy, making, white, great, full, dead, horrible, itching, uncomplaining, lucid.* All these terms are standard in the decade, *great, white, dead* as major kinds, *horrible* and *itching* in their use as contrast to startle and confront, and the present participles as they fit the mode of suspension used most fully by the substantival poets and appropriated by Auden.

One gets from the poems the sense of fixed, even helpless states, which are describable in the most standard terms of the time, mixed with small violences of idiosyncrasy. So that, while Auden is a lively and technically subtle predicator, meditating like Frost, narrating like Manifold and Warren, his notion of life seems to lead away from them, as Warren's lyrical interludes lead, to a world less of assertion than acceptance, to a poetry less of structure than material. The mixture is notable, too, in the verse form; it combines outer linear controls with inner harmonies, drawing rhyme and measure inward to as- sonance and cadence, as action is drawn inward to being.

A younger poet who has been critically hailed in the past years, and descriptively related to Auden, makes much the same sort of combi- nation.

> There mounts in squalls a sort of rusty mire,
> Not ice, not snow, to leaguer the Hôtel
> De Ville, where braced pig-iron dragons grip
> The blizzard to their rigor mortis. A bell
> Grumbles when the reverberations strip
> The thatching from its spire,
> The search-guns click and spit and split up timber
> And nick the slate roofs on the Holstenwall
> Where torn-up tilestones crown the victor....[18]

So begins Robert Lowell's *Lord Weary's Castle.* Since there is less variety in his work from poem to poem, these lines are the more rep- resentative of them all, and they indicate how action can be turned to

---

[18] These and lines from "To Peter Taylor" are from *Lord Weary's Castle,* copyright 1944, 1946, by Robert Lowell. Reprinted by permission of Harcourt, Brace and Company, Inc.

quality. *Mounts, leaguer, grip, grumbles, strip, click, spit, split up, nick, crown,* all ten in nine lines, couldn't be more variously and vigorously active. The adjectives are meager and subordinated to verbs: *rusty, braced, slate, torn-up.* The twenty nouns are a tremendous load, mixed and specific. The whole is devoted to precision of context, not scene merely, but situation; the poem ends, "your life is in your hands," and it has devoted itself to telling you the particularities of event in that life. Event becomes quality.

Lowell's main verbs are, as here, besides standard actions the verbs of shattering: *break, cry, die, fall.* His adjectives, besides *old* and *dead* and *great,* are colored: *black, red, blue.* His nouns are multitudinous: besides most of the major ones, his own and his decade's *water, father, child, snow, ice, king, Christ, Lord,* the anatomy of *bones, blood, body, face,* the nature of *tree, stone, wind, sea, house, glass;* over these the major *time, head, light, death* preside. Nouns so outweigh adjectives for him because they take on the function of adjectives, as, in the lines above, the materials of pig iron and slate are used to modify. The proportion of 7A–21N–10V in its subordination of epithet links him with Frost and Auden and the seventeenth century, but in its excess of nouns links him with the most substantival poets like his contemporary Thomas. Any twenty nouns in any average ten lines are apt to make a strong substantival burden, and in Lowell it is their quality that is their burden.

We may see a good example of resulting structure in such a relatively short poem as "To Peter Taylor on the Feast of the Epiphany." The title suggests the address and the occasion of seventeenth-century verse; the eighteen verbs in twenty-two lines come close to fitting a metaphysical predication; the minor *thin, allegoric, sacred, fabulous, sharp, old,* and others, paint no scene and are subordinate to concept; the couplets are regular, the thought complex. But the more than fifty nouns control. See how the first sentences progress:

> Peter, the war has taught me to revere
> The rulers of this darkness, for I fear
> That only Armageddon will suffice

> To turn the hero skating on thin ice
> When Whore and Beast and Dragon rise for air
> From allegoric waters. Fear is where
> We hunger: where the Irishmen recall
> How wisdom trailed a star into a stall
> And knelt in sacred terror to confer
> Its fabulous gold and frankincense and myrrh:
> And where the lantern-noses scrimmage down
> The highway to the sea below this town
> And the sharp barker rigs his pre-war planes
> To lift old Adam's dollars for his pains; ...
>
> And still the grandsires battle through the slush
> To storm the landing biplanes with a rush—
> Until their cash and somersaulting snare
> Fear with its fingered stop-watch in mid-air.

The poem sets power and wealth against fear. The first sentence explains, addressing Peter, why the poet thinks only Armageddon will suffice against the shapes of fear. The second defines: Fear is where we hunger, ... where the Magi went in sacred terror, ... and where the airplane industry builds to government contract; ... there the bugs of Armageddon. The third sentence wears the time away to twilight and continues the battle which by its persistence and money power catches fear suspended, mid-air. The total effect of all three sentences is this mid-air poise. The long middle one describes a number of scenes of activity of fear; in all there is much bustling and going about, but all are framed and set off as examples. The shorter first and last statements parallel each other, making the balance of opposition, keeping the hero skating on thin ice, the grandsires battling, the stop-watch fingered, the fabulous gold offered in terror. Where is Peter? Unlike the lady or the lord of seventeenth-century address, he does not even seem to reply. The active, personal, "Peter, the war has taught me to revere," turns quickly to solid Whore and Beast and Dragon and "Fear with its fingered stop-watch in mid-air," and relationship of persons is less poetic than relationship of mass.

If such development from active to qualitative context is characteristic of Lowell, as I think it is, then his structures follow the turn of his vocabulary. They make substantives of verbs and qualities. They arrive at a generalized particularity. The sound pattern aids by subordination. The common rough five-accent couplet gives a sense of workmanship and effort; not much agility or delight in sound, but a sense of achievement in bringing a sort of serial order from a great many rough syllables and objects. "And the sharp barker rigs his prewar planes" is hard to say, but important to think and feel; in its ugliness it has a kind of onomatopoeia which is characteristic throughout. All efforts turn toward getting the significant particularity of situation built up before us; and the situation is not a pleasant one. The spirit is caught in it and must deal with it.

As Lowell's concern for difficult context turns ostensible nouns and verbs to defining qualities and makes him less a reasoning or active poet than one would surmise from his proportioning, so too the most extremely predicative poets in the decade are not as extreme as they look, though for a different reason. They do not alter the standard parts of speech so much as they alter line length. William Carlos Williams, E. E. Cummings, and H. D. belong at the extreme of the list, in other words, not because, like Googe and Barclay in the sixteenth century, or like Harvey, Suckling, Jonson in the seventeenth, they used so few adjectives and nouns in proportion to verbs, whatever the line length, but rather because the use of short and broken lines itself cuts down amounts. In proportioning, Williams and H. D. belong with Eliot, Pound, Spender, Stevens, the middle group of balance or slight adjectival emphasis. Cummings, maintaining predicative emphasis, fits closer to Frost.

Nevertheless, it is significant to consider the poets at an extreme, for the reasons that put them there. With Auden and Lowell they represent a breaking down, a revision, of traditional language structures. To the juggling of parts of speech they add the juggling of linear units. Where through four centuries we have seen a constant correlation between proportioning, linear quantity, and vocabulary, now in the twentieth we find experimentation in cross-cutting which disturbs such correlation though preserving much of it.

For such consideration Cummings is best known. The result in the first poem of *1 × 1* reads as follows:

> nonsun blob a
> cold to
> skylessness
> sticking fire
>
> my are your
> are birds our all
> and one gone
> away the they
>
> leaf of ghosts some
> few creep there
> here or on
> unearth[19]

In its words and thought this is a most familiar kind of modern poem, and, being so familiar, it can afford to try some variations on line-and-sentence structure. Stating that from this cold atmosphere most of the birds have gone away, only a few like leaf ghosts creep in a world they don't recognize, the poem breaks up the statement into pieces. It is like Stevens' "God Is Good," in that the identification of man and atmosphere is made through bird, but the continuity of identification is less. First, the atmosphere is given in nouns, made negative. Then, in the second stanza, the predicate *are* is interwoven with variations of the pronoun *our* to make the identification. Finally, in the third, the "leaf of ghosts" moves back to the early nouns, with ghosts a negative summary of the spirit in the atmosphere; the strong verb *creeps* is summary too, the play of adverbs widens the view, and *unearth* rounds back to *nonsun*.

A great lot of poetry of language must be assumed in order to make this poetry of semi- or interlanguage. The main nouns are the standard poetic nouns of the time, for example, in *sun, sky, fire, bird, leaf*. The theme of atmospheric context is central. The structure is, underneath, a simple statement. Over this base, and with echoes of common phrasing

---

[19] These and other lines by Cummings from *1 × 1*, published by Henry Holt and Co. Copyright 1944 by E. E. Cummings.

in mind, like Pound's and Eliot's but less literary, Cummings can work such a pattern as we see in the second stanza, where, in "are birds our all / and one gone," he gives us two ideas at once in "birds our all" and "birds one and all," the subjective and objective grammatically interlocked.

Cummings does not always write so closely. His poem XIV represents a fuller colloquial mood, still negative, active, and tender.

> pity this busy monster, manunkind,
>
> not. Progress is a comfortable disease:
> your victim (death and life safely beyond)
>
> plays with the bigness of his littleness
> —electrons deify one razorblade
> into a mountainrange; lenses extend
>
> unwish through curving wherewhen till unwish
> returns on its unself.
>   A world of made
> is not a world of born—pity poor flesh
> and trees, poor stars and stones but never this
> fine specimen of hypermagical
>
> ultraomnipotence....

Here he preserves both sentence and verse structure, fitting one to the other traditionally enough, on the whole. The breaks in fit have their share in meaning: the suspending of *not* to the second line implants the pity; the suspension after hell in the next-to-last line robs the colloquialism "hell of a good universe" of its enthusiasm; the attitude in both places is made double. Further, the beginning of sentences always within the line allows the less finality, the end of octave having to sustain the beginning of sestet.

But more of the variation is in words: the insertions of *un*'s, the exchange of parts of speech to make a noun of *wherewhen,* and of *born* and *made*. And there is the pleasure of joining magnificences like "hypermagical ultraomnipotence" with five-and-dime "hopeless case" and "let's go." Cummings' major terms go down the middle; they are light and lyrical, and do not participate in his games of alteration, but provide his solid core. *Green, little, true* are his adjectives, *love, man, world, life* his major nouns, with *nothing, everything, spring, bird, death, mind, heart, leaf, tree, dream, earth, sky, sun* his special additions, and his verbs standard, adding *blow* and *sing.* His idiosyncrasies are close to those of Yeats, and of Williams and H. D., picking up more than usual of the metaphysical *true, time, thing,* along with his natural detail. It is to be seen in the poem above how much Cummings loves his natural detail, poor flesh and trees, poor stars and stones, but seen too in the restless verbs, *pity, plays, deify, extend, returns, know, go,* that his is a world of *made* as well as *born.*

H. D. is more content with substance. Her strongest verb is *know,* her adjectives *old* and *new,* her *word* and *thought* controlling *leaf* and *star,* as her proportioning is balanced 6–13–6. Such a poem as the first in *The Walls Do Not Fall* has the qualities we have grown accustomed to, in Stevens, or Moore, or Pound, or Spender, the parallel lines and items, the fine objective detail, the sense of heavy significance, and less of structural variety than in most of the predicative poets. The poem moves through oddity to central quality.

> An incident here and there,
> and rails gone (for guns)
> from your (and my) old town square:
>
> mist and mist-grey, no colour,
> still the Luxor bee, chick and hare
> pursue unalterable purpose
>
> in green, rose-red, lapis;
> they continue to prophesy
> from the stone papyrus:
>
> there, as here, ruin opens
> the tomb, the temple; enter,
> there as here, there are no doors:
>
> the shrine lies open to the sky,
> the rain falls, here, there
> sand drifts; eternity endures: . . .
>
> the flesh? it was melted away,
> the heart burnt out, dead ember,
> tendons, muscles shattered, outer husk dismembered,

> yet the frame held:
> we passed the flame: we wonder
> what saved us? what for?[20]

Again, William Carlos Williams writes in this tense, qualitative fashion, colloquially irritable when he fails, as in "The Wood Thrush," in *Adam and Eve and the City:*

> Singing across the orchard
> before night, answered
> from the depths
> of the wood, inversely
> and in a lower key—
>
> First I tried to write
> conventionally praising you
> but found it no more
> than my own thoughts
> that I was giving. No.
>
> What can I say?
> Vistas
> of delight waking suddenly
> before a cheated world.

Or, more happy in technicality, as in the next poem, "Fine Work with Pitch and Copper":

> Now they are resting
> in the fleckless light
> separately in unison
>
> like the sacks
> of sifted stone stacked
> regularly by twos
>
> about the flat roof
> ready after lunch
> to be opened and strewn
>
> The copper in eight
> foot strips has been
> beaten lengthwise

---

[20] From *The Walls Do Not Fall*, Oxford University Press, 1944.

> down the center at right
> angles and lies ready
> to edge the coping
>
> One still chewing
> picks up a copper strip
> and runs his eye along it[21]

Here Williams is pleased. He has caught a still moment, significant in all its potentials, the copper carefully measured yet immeasurably more, and he is indeed so content with the vista of delight of the One still chewing that he can omit this time the "cheated world." Like his fellows in poetry, he is devoted to defining the quality of the instant as it is eternal, and the definition is not classificatory, but a kind of denotation, a pointing out, a setting down of the complex event, however simple, in all its fullness and particularity of meaning. His "so much depends / upon / a red wheel- / barrow" ("Spring and All," XXI) sort of remark is characteristic of his poetry and of much today: the simplest rift is loaded with ore which the mind is to deliberate upon.

Many of Williams' poems, especially in the later *Paterson,* are more meditatively or slangily abstract in vocabulary than the ones I have quoted. He wants to make any sort of action or material into a poem, and any sort is to be found, usually not so precious as H. D.'s or Moore's, but rich with sense. His epithets are colored, *black, white, green,* along with the common *old;* his verbs are standard, the special *ring* of Cummings' sort; his nouns are simply human as in *hand, eye, mind, dream, face,* or natural in *flower, sea, day, night, water, world.* In his details of simple sense he is more like Pound, as Cummings in more complex thought and structure is like Yeats, and so in vocabulary as in proportioning (5–8–4) shows more kinship with substantival than predicative poets.

The short lines, the delicate selection, the fond precision of Williams, H. D., Cummings bring to a narrow and intense focus the poetic mode of the decade, emphasizing the fleeting details of its natural world and the troubled loving care of mind to understand and stay

---

[21] From *Complete Collected Poems of William Carlos Williams,* New Directions, 1938.

and preserve. The major variation comes at the level of mind, whether its character be to assert itself directly in its predicative structure and speaking tone or whether its method be indirect, through the arrangements of substance. The purest predicative poets are in this decade relatively rare, since they have learned how to think even of event as at stasis; Cummings, Millay, Auden, Frost, Manifold, Warren, Yeats are most active. Past the balance of Stevens and Eliot, the group at the other, substantival, extreme fulfills what seems the wish to abound in material good, to order material redundancy.

III

The most substantival poets are characterized by a full, free line, a sequential and cumulative structure, a harmonious tone. They expand the units of order, they add to the powers of noun and adjective. Their proportioning, like that of the more restrained Pound and Moore, amounts to about four adjectives and nouns to one verb, as high an emphasis as that in the eighteenth century, though the present power has shifted somewhat from adjective to noun. Crane's 10–20–8 and Sitwell's 12–23–9 are typical proportions. They come closest to Waller and Pope; few other poets through the centuries have put such emphasis on nouns in combination with adjectival plenitude. They have material agreements: on color, green and white; on sea and sky and much nature; on living, loving, seeming, rather than thinking, acting, speaking. They are, in moderation, what substantival poets have been in other centuries, the most sensuous and receptive. In the luxury of their verse they are, for this time, most conventional.

> Be with me, Luis de San Angel, now—
> Witness before the tides can wrest away
> The word I bring, O you who reined my suit
> Into the Queen's great heart that doubtful day;
> For I have seen now what no perjured breath
> Of clown or sage can riddle or gainsay;—
> To you, too, Juan Perez, whose counsel fear
> And greed adjourned,—I bring you back Cathay![22]

---

[22] From *Collected Poems*, Liveright, 1940.

So Columbus begins at the beginning of Crane's *Bridge,* more active than usual at first, but showing in the smooth flow of line, and in such example as "Into the Queen's great heart that doubtful day," how easily the adjectives will fit.

> Here waves climb into dusk on gleaming mail;
> Invisible valves of the sea,—locks, tendons
> Crested and creeping, troughing corridors
> That fall back yawning to another plunge.
> Slowly the sun's red caravel drops light
> Once more behind us. . . .

The watery element, the sense of light, the suspending modifiers all work in the characteristic mode of Crane.

Though Crane died before the 1940's, his poetry did not; its republication in this decade is only one aspect of his strong influence. Youthful poems in contemporary magazines, if they do not sound like Millay or Auden, are apt to sound like Crane. His mode gives the wealth of imagism a greater freedom, a fuller ostensible emotional swing, enlists Whitman along with Keats, absorbs more enjoyment than the severities of other imagists like Williams and H. D. have allowed. The vocabulary is of image sense: in order of descending emphasis in each group, *long, green, new, white, bright; eye, time, dream, day, God, hand, light, night, man, sky, snow, star, wind, wing, arm, fire, heart, heaven, hill, sea, water; see, know, hear, come, go, keep, take.* The verbs have little distinction; the old *see* is still most important. The adjectives, on the other hand, are sensuous, spacious, and shining, as lively a lot as we find to represent the decade. The nouns are many and familiar to the twentieth century; they include the positive simple words of *man, God, eye, heart* from tradition, the *dream* and *light* words of romanticism, the particularities of the 1940's. Crane's list, like that of Jeffers, Sitwell, Thomas, and Shapiro, and of Pound, Williams, Lowell, in addition, is fairly purified of metaphysical terms of time, thought, and thing, the abstractions fostered by much predication.[23]

---

[23] The proportion of 10–20–8 for Crane's *Bridge* is based on the 1,020 lines through Sec. VI. The broken lines, as quoted above for example, are counted as separate lines in such literal acceptance of typography as that which we must make for Williams or Cummings. In an earlier work on *Major Adjectives* I did not make such allowance, so that the count *per line* there is higher.

Except for this omission, the list speaks for the decade fairly. See how the description runs; as at the end of Section I:

> White toil of heaven's cordons, mustering
> In holy rings all sails charged to the far
> Hushed gleaming fields and pendant seething wheat
> Of knowledge,—round thy brows unhooded now
> —The kindled Crown! acceded of the poles
> And biassed by full sails, meridians reel
> Thy purpose—still one shore beyond desire!
> The sea's green crying towers asway, Beyond
>
> And kingdoms
>   naked in the
>   trembling heart—
> Te Deum laudamus
>   O Thou Hand of Fire

Though structure dissolves in materials here, the predicate poured into invocation, the white and green reeling in the guise of cosmic ship and shore under the hand of fire, though all is quality and exclamation, with *far, desire, kingdom, heart* spreading the spacious passion of a cosmic poetry, as in the eighteenth century a Young or a Mason would spread it, yet there is still in these lines the twentieth-century cast of intellect. *Toil* makes the point of thought, asks it of the reader. *Seething wheat / Of knowledge* makes it again, and the *brows* and *purpose* of Elohim. He, the invoked, is *Inquisitor! incognizable Word,* and the whole vast flux which the Bridge spans, as at the end in "azure swing," lies under his mysterious hand, his time and mind. The poem makes the fullest effort to blend, by architecture, by exclamation, by heavily loaded suspension, a world of sense rich and oppressive with a world of "incognizable" meaning; and the terms of religious symbol are helpful again, as for Eliot and others.

Thomas is similarly possessed. The eighth of his poems swims him in just such a miraculous and cosmic nature, such a driving and suspending line.

> I dreamed my genesis in sweat of sleep, breaking
> Through the rotating shell, strong

As motor muscle on the drill, driving
Through vision and the girdered nerve.

From limbs that had the measure of the worm, shuffled
Off from the creasing flesh, filed
Through all the irons in the grass, metal
Of suns in the man-melting night.

Heir to the scalding veins that hold love's drop, costly
A creature in my bones I
Rounded my globe of heritage, journey
In bottom gear through night-geared man....

I dreamed my genesis in sweat of death, fallen
Twice in the feeding sea, grown
Stale of Adam's brine until, vision
Of new man strength, I seek the sun.[24]

Thomas' is a most bodily universe, for all its scope. *Blood, eye, hand, heart, bones, face, head, mouth, tongue* keep it expressive, and *water, house, tower, stone, bell* are analogues for it, in addition to other traditional and special terms. Most of the rainbow colors make the major qualities of this world. Against color the verbs play with unusual vigor of body, in *make, lie, fall, break, drive, hold, drop, turn,* and with much verbal individuality, echoed faintly in kind through the decade. And against all this life of sense, or partly in accord with it, the alliterative and assonantal harmonics of *sweat of sleep, -ing* and *-ong, girdered nerve,* and the slant interlocking rhyme, strains and parallels and enforces the rich charm.

Shapiro is more nonchalant, easier, and as eager. Read some of his beginnings in *V-Letter:*

Just like a wave, the long green hill of my desire
Rides to the shore-like level here to engulf us all
Who work and joke in the hollow grave and the shallow mire
Where we must dig or else the earth will truly fall.

Long as a comber, green as grass, taut as a tent,
And there far out like specks the browsing cattle drift,
And sweet sweet with the green of life and the downhill scent,
O sweet at the heart such heavy loveliness to lift! ...

---

[24] From *Selected Writings,* New Directions, 1946.

or,   Geography was violently dead,
                Hairline and parallel, Mercator, torn,
                Brushed by a finger from the finespun map
                As one might desecrate a spider's web;
                And now like Moses was our will again
                To part the sea and push all distance back
                To cross the dry land of your wavy roads
                In plotted days exuberantly home; ...

or,   Because the tree is joyous and as a child
                Lovely in posture, fresh as wind to smell,
                Bearing clear needles like a coat of hair,
                    And is well-combed and always mild,
                        And stands in time so well,
                And strong in the forest or beside a tomb
                Looks over time and nature everywhere—
                Lift it up lightly, bring it in the room.[25]

This poetizing makes a strong compromise between the mode of substantives and the natural action of enthusiasm. Its controls of melody are more outward; it experiments with patterns of accent; it moves toward ends of decision. The last verse form especially takes its beauty from its accentual relations, and its structural progress, the qualities of the tree suspended between the argument and the imperative, and patterned more than serially by the pause and return of line length. Nevertheless, the poems are firmly packed with materials as well: color in *green, black, white,* time in *new, old,* Shapiro's own calling up of *sweet;* besides the traditional terms, the present ones, *children* and *home, head* and *sky,* and *death,* and Shapiro's *war* and *kiss;* and most of the standard verbs except verbs of thought, with *come* and *look* most active. Shapiro works in simple sense and reaction, aware of tradition but of tradition where he now is, where poetry now is.[26]

How fully poetry does now participate in this world of sense the work of the most substantival poets shows. The very fact that two poets

---

[25] All from *V-Letter and Other Poems,* copyright 1944 by Karl Shapiro. Reprinted by permission of Harcourt, Brace and Company, Inc.

[26] See foreword to his *Essay on Rime,* 1945. "The metaphysician / Deals with ideas as words, the poet with things, ..."

as seemingly far apart in space and character as Sitwell and Jeffers can share their major vocabulary and linear direction makes emphatic the point of temporal absorption. Because of the long swinging and accumulative motion of their more than six-accented lines, both pile up a lot of repeated terms heavily relied on, and these terms as a whole are the same for both. In the decade's majority vocabulary they participate almost completely, and in the minority they share the *dark, great, long, young, air, earth, loving,* and *seeming* of the moderate poets, adding their own *cold.* Their enthusiasm is neither for warmth and bright color on the one hand nor for meditative abstraction on the other, but stresses the weighty pattern, the portent, in the world of phenomena.

Much of Jeffers is more active, more storytelling, than any other poetry in the decade, and therein lies his singularity, his special virtue which he has not shared. *Mara* begins:

> Walking up from the barn to the house
> In the moon cloud-light Ferguson saw a stranger standing
> Up the slope on the right: "What do you want?
> Hey, you: come here." The intruder paid no attention,
> And Ferguson went up to him; the fellow turned—
> A man as tall as himself, but backed against
> The moon-spot in the cloud it was impossible
> To see his face—Ferguson said again,
> "What do you want here?"...[27]

This peculiar familiar progression, flat and literal yet emotional, is very different from any other mode I know of. It may be related to such prose as Lawrence's or Hemingway's, but it has not, I think, a related practice in poetry. It distinguishes Jeffers. The ending of the poem is another matter. It is roughly a part of the average poetry of the decade in its qualifying of natural forces toward human meaning.

> This pallid comet announces more than kings' deaths
> To tail it with purer color I add
> That the mountains are alive. They crouch like great cats watching

---

[27] These and other lines by Jeffers from *Be Angry at the Sun*, 1941, and *Collected Poetry*, 1938, copyright by Robinson Jeffers. Reprinted by permission of Random House, Inc.

Our comic and mouse-hole tragedies, or lift high over them
Peaks like sacred torches, pale-flaming rock.
The old blue dragon breathes at their feet, the eternal flames
Burn in the sky. The spirit that flickers and hurts in humanity
Shines brighter from better lamps; but from all shines.
Look to it: prepare for the long winter: spring is far off.

This is like Jeffers too in its attitude, its large metaphor and portent; yet here the basic materials and their connections are common.

Better yet, though less frequently, these two kinds of writing, along with some philosophical abstraction, come together in a whole poem and make us see more integrally the patient and receptive nature of modern poetry as it takes in, lists, arranges, and thus makes meaning of, the wealth of sensation at hand. Here Jeffers is like Moore, Williams, Spender, even Pound, in his deliberate and curious substantiality. "Oh, Lovely Rock" is an example from *Such Counsels.*

We stayed the night in the pathless gorge of Ventana Creek,
    up the east fork.
The rock walls, and the mountain ridges hung forest on forest
    above our heads, maple and redwood,
Laurel, oak, madrone, up to the high and slender Santa Lucian
    firs that stare up the cataracts
Of slide-rock to the star-color precipices.

                              We lay on gravel and
    kept a little camp-fire for warmth.
              ... Light leaves overhead danced in the fire's
    breath, tree-trunks were seen: it was the rock-wall
That fascinated my eyes and mind. Nothing strange: light-gray
    diorite with two or three slanting seams in it,
Smooth-polished by the endless attrition of slides and floods; no
    fern nor lichen, pure naked rock ... as if I were
Seeing rock for the first time. As if I were seeing through the
    flame-lit surface into the real and bodily
And living rock. Nothing strange ... I cannot
Tell you how strange: the silent passion, the deep nobility and
    childlike loveliness: this fate going on
Outside our fates. ...

More than the rest, Jeffers feels the externality of substance, its inaccessibility except as symbol; more therefore of his symbols are explicit, external; and the relating of material to human is a labor from which, except in narrative resolution, in acted violence, he has no release. "Until the mind has turned its love from / itself and man, from parts to the whole" is a long time and an inhuman time to wait for truth. Yet it is the ending of the *Selected Poems,* and the end toward which Jeffers looks. Meanwhile the mind must discern the truth in the rock, and that is a sense not alien to the sense of the time.

With more emphasis on spirit, and in a more allegorical mode, Edith Sitwell treats the same substance. "Green Song" begins and ends:

> After the long and portentous eclipse of the patient sun
> The sudden spring began
> With the bird-sounds of Doom in the egg, and Fate in the bud
>   that is flushed with the world's fever—
> But those bird-songs have trivial voices and sound not like thunder,
> And the sound when the bud bursts is no more the sound of the
>   worlds that are breaking.—
>
>   . . . Are we not all of the same substance,
> Men, planets and earth, born from the heart of darkness,
> Returning to darkness, the consoling mother,
> For the short winter sleep—O my calyx of the flower of the
>   world, you the spirit
> Moving upon the waters, the light on the breast of the dove.[28]

The cadence takes a ritualistic turn of ceremony, the vocabulary is implicative of ancient uses, the priesthood of Sitwell is more templed than the priesthood of Jeffers, but both invoke the old dark junctures of man and earth.

> I, an old woman whose heart is like the Sun
> That has seen too much, looked on too many sorrows,
> Yet is not weary of shining fulfillment and harvest
> Heard the priests that howled for rain and the universal darkness,
> Saw the golden princes sacrificed to the Rain-god,
> The cloud that came, and was small as the hand of Man.
> And now in the time of the swallow, the bright one, the chatterer,
> The young women wait like the mother of corn for the lost one—
> Their golden eyelids are darkened like the great rain-clouds.

---

[28] These and other lines by Sitwell from *Green Song and Other Poems* (New York, Vanguard Press, 1946).

> But in bud and branch the nature of Fate begins
> —And Love with the Lion's claws and the Lion's hunger
> Hides in the brakes in the nihilistic Spring.—

As this capital Lion performs some of the nature of man in the way that the uncapital hawk of Jeffers more realistically does, so this rhythm, these vowels are arranged with somewhat more artifice than the narrative chants of Jeffers. Detail calls for attention. The surface is carefully worked, and beautiful: the diminution of sound in *small,* for example, or the carrying over of *time* to *bright,* or the noble jolt of the antique *brakes* against *nihilistic,* with its other world of association. Sitwell does not inhabit a specific Point Sur country; her book would not take a photograph for a cover. She draws upon realms of learning and allusion, as Jeffers does, and as the eighteenth century did, upon a physical or a Greek or Gothic cosmos to arrive at an effect of spacious whole. And, so drawing, she finds the terms which name the full cycle, the *young* and *dark* and *death,* which allow her spring and winter, love and hate, body and mind, the parallels which, while they reach out farthest, gather most inward to the poetic ceremony. The green and birds are blood, the stone is bone, the veins are branches, youth is gold, rose is life, and by allegories of song come together with ease, whereas Jeffers must force them. Yet some separations persist, as for other poets they persist:

> Said the Sun to the Moon—'When you are but a lonely white crone,
> And I, a dead King in my golden armour somewhere in a dark wood,
> Remember only this of our hopeless love
> That never till Time is done
> Will the fire of the heart and the fire of the mind be one.'

This from "Heart and Mind"; and again from "Girl and Butterfly":

> But the young girl chases the yellow butterfly
> Happiness ... what is the dust that lies on its wings?
> Is it from far away
> From the distance that lies between lover and lover, their minds
>   never meeting—
> Like the bright continents?—are Asia, Africa, and Cathay
> But golden flowers that shine in the fields of summer—
> As quickly dying?

Bright animals, continents, ships, branches, and constellations all gather to the question, as the poets ask it.

Perhaps Sitwell and Jeffers at their extreme perform much of the function and have much of the relation of H. D. and Williams at theirs. An intensely realistic, roughly serious and sensitive poet joins with one of delicate and ritualistic polish and formula to report the world as truly as possible. The directions of Williams, the indirections of H. D. are minutely focused, the lines short, words precise and emphasized, every new item examinable as a potential poem, the resultant poem *image* in a very clear and literal sense. For the other two the poem is always *image plus,* with the plus as literal as the image. The talk, swagger, story, technicality of Williams is expanded by Jeffers, taken miles out of town into timber, strung into episode, examined into philosophy. The tight and curious possessions and prayers of H. D. are liberated into entire services by Sitwell.

These expansions and liberations take the poetry into no foreign direction, but into the heart of the matter. Like Crane's, Thomas', Lowell's, like Pound's, Yeats', Eliot's in their earlier moderation, the full poems search for the cycle of dark in light and youth in age and body in earth and sea. The substantive poets see the more correspondences, the more colors and anatomies, embodying and substantiating discerned processes. And since in the 1940's the very discernment of substance is primary, a high degree of material elaboration cannot seem eccentric, but rather is a central unfolding, an enforcing, a making plain, of what it is that poetry now wishes to secure to itself.

The types of poetry-making in the decade, then, are not very far apart. The concentration on ordering of substance is important for all, and the modes adapt themselves to this emphasis. The extremes of type, Donnic and Miltonic, which we see in the 1640's, and even in the 1840's, are both tempered toward a middle point in the 1940's. Nevertheless, type does remain, and it may be clarified in summary, before a summary consideration of individual and of whole.

Our most decisive predicative writers are Frost and Millay and Cummings. They clearly subordinate quality to motion. They make the structure of statement a part of the primary interest, and they relate to it closely the structure of meter. The poems are externally pointed, the emphases at beginning and end of units of thought, rhyme often active, line length varied and rounded out, conclusions arrived at. Their vocabulary is active. Of majority terms they stress *little, life, love, man, world, thing, coming, going, making, knowing;* of minority terms their characteristic *earth, sky, leaf, tree, nothing,* with versions of *good* and *great,* of *find, look, seem, think.* They omit, on the other hand, such major passive verbs as *fall* and *lie,* and the qualities of *dark, light, air, sea, water.* In these choices they tend to prefer the seventeenth-century vocabulary of thought and thing to the nineteenth-century vocabulary of atmosphere. When they add modern particularities of natural detail, they use the tree rather than the sea sort. They have, then, a degree of homogeneity in practice and in material, and this they share with some other contemporaries who are less clear in mode than they.

The less clear are the younger, Auden, Warren, Manifold, Lowell. They vary the mode in different ways. All are strongly predicative, partly formal, and attached to the majority terms, especially the active and temporal, the minority of *good,* and *looking, loving, seeming, speaking, thinking.* They agree in the emphasis upon terms such as *child, father, name,* and more receptive verbs. Manifold varies by just his emphasis on these terms. His ballad making is self-conscious, as it constantly returns to the terms of the making, to name, rhyme, verse, word, and the thinking mind, head, brain. Warren too is self-conscious; only part of the time does the narrative move along its own track for him. The longer roll of the rest adopts a more sensory vocabulary. Auden's variation appears most strongly in the structural dissolution of his predicates; he treats actions so fragmentarily and objectively that they become objects in effect. Lowell by using nouns rather than adjectives for adjective functions gives predicative verse a much greater weight of material than it usually has borne. All these poets have leanings toward the more substantive mode.

So also do Pound, Moore, Spender, Williams, who proceed less by excess of substance than by lack of predication. Their devotion to the object makes us see it in stasis, caught and held. Their lines are often short and broken, to give full focus to the thing named. Their melodies and harmonies are slightest, or least obtrusive, since sight is more important. Like Auden's and Lowell's, their actions themselves become objects for presentation. In vocabulary, color, *face, body, wind, sea, sky, dream,* and *time* and passive verbs are important, with the result that the whole atmosphere is poised and passive. This we should call a more "romantic" vocabulary; at least it seems a direct extension and particularization of the nineteenth-century attempt to catch and qualify the instant. Along with sound and structure, it establishes a clear distinction between the world of Pound and the world of Frost.

But both these worlds are active, lively, colloquial in contrast to the third and most substantival kind, the newest world of Crane and Sitwell and Thomas, and the Eliot of the Quartets. Here substance as it becomes ritualized becomes most poised, quiet, masterful. Here the domination of *old, new, green, white,* of *day* and *night* and *light* and *time* and *love,* of *air* and *water,* of *coming, going, lying, seeming,* is fullest and purest, with least of *goodness, greatness, thought,* and *speech.* Here the lines are longest, the cadence richest and most lingering, the vowels roundest, consonants liquidest, onomatopoeias warmest, and sentences most invocative and accumulative and exclamatory.

Toward this status most of the poetry in the decade seems in some degree to be moving. True, there are moves also in the other direction, Shapiro's and Jeffers' toward action in abundance, but again, Jeffers' at least seems numbed toward eternity, and Shapiro in his titles makes an emphasis upon nouns. At any rate, the vocabulary of the substantival mode is nowhere alien in the decade, even to Frost, and the mode's structures of suspension fill and serialize parts of every work in the decade as they do vividly Auden's.

In other eras the direction has not seemed so single, through the decade, toward one type. In the 1640's and 1840's, both old and young wrote in each school. In the 1740's the youth seemed to be increasingly piling Pelion on Ossa, but to a breaking point rather than a future.

In the 1940's, the predicative poets are almost all the older poets, with echoes lingering in a few like Auden, Lowell, Shapiro. Even the simplest image poets, Pound and his followers, are older too. The youngest are the richest and most inclusive, Crane, Spender, Shapiro, Lowell, Thomas; and the younger still, in their twenties and beginning to be praised, like Richard Wilbur and Robert Horan, join here.

As elder mode draws into younger, the balance that we get, for this decade and indeed for a whole five centuries, is the moderate balance of Yeats, or of Stevens, lightening a little the classical balance of Dryden. For these, verbs and adjectives are equal, the substantives no more than three times the verbs, in a proportion like or near 9–18–9, the decade's average. For these, time, natural objects, thought, are all primary elements, immediate qualities and abstract standards both allowable, and construction not alien to reception. They temper both ends toward the middle, more than Cowley or Collins or Longfellow did. They use a speaking voice without flattening, rhyme reasonably, with rhyme both inward and outward, and search the margins of death and dark without floating away on a tide of significance. The era's quarrel with self they recognize and write to resolve.

The most idiosyncratic poets of the decade are Moore, H. D., and Pound, who participate least in the vocabulary of the majority, who employ most special terms and forms. As we have seen, the extremes in proportioning are not extreme by oddity but by excess of zeal; Williams, Cummings, Jeffers follow the main lines of practice with intensity or enthusiasm. H. D., on the other hand, devotes herself to special emphasis on verbal terms like *word* and *name,* Moore to the bodily parts of her animals, both to the exclusion of the great traditional *day* and *love* and *time* and *world,* and both with an exceptional concentration upon precise phrasal structure. Pound's position is a little different. Like the others he shuns the major vocabulary, *eye, hand, head, heart, mind, love, night, sun, world,* and more, and like Moore he shuns verbs; but his own major vocabulary has become the minority vocabulary of the decade. His *black* and *dark,* his *bird, sea, water, wind* are, especially for substantival poets, in the tone of the time. And the free broken form of his line and statement, not so tight as Moore's, suits the tone also.

The tone of the time includes easily these oddest poets and is strongly unified. It speaks in the main of *old, eye, man, time, coming, going, seeing,* a wandering, observing man in an old world; it speaks characteristically of *little* and *great, white, death, mind, head, thing, sky, water,* and *seeming,* a world of increasing natural particularity pondered by a meditating man. It speaks in increasing fragments of line, of phrase, of reference and melody, in increasing interarrangement, assonant and synesthetic and intersyntactic. It approximates a balance of quality and predicate upon a strong base of substance. The *things* of its devotion are not plain or free, not sympathetic or purely symbolical. They exist in time and mind, and are there colored, aged, measured, and are there altered.

II. BACKGROUNDS IN PROSE: PRACTICE AND THEORY

IN THE prose reports, stories, essays of the period the materials of mind, time, substance persist. I point them out here and there as possibly representative, not in form or frequency, but in simple parallel to poetic concern. Bertrand Russell, at the end of his *History of Western Philosophy,* says that the questions of our day are questions about number, space, time, mind, matter; and these are the characteristic materials of prose as of poetry. What is fact and how is it interpreted by mind?

I

The novel is devoted to extremely accurate reporting and, at the same time, to interpretation either intently implied or painstakingly ruminated. The much-read stories of the 1940's, the titles of which I have drawn from the selective lists of the American Library Association, represent types both subtle and simple. Faulkner's *Intruder in the Dust,* Koestler's *Darkness at Noon,* Bowen's *The Heat of the Day,* Greene's *The Heart of the Matter,* Hemingway's *For Whom the Bell Tolls,* Llewellyn's *How Green Was My Valley,* Marquand's *H. M. Pulham, Esq.,* Hersey's *A Bell for Adano* and Brown's *A Walk in the Sun,* Lewis' *Kingsblood Royal,* Porter's *The Leaning Tower,* Guthrie's *The Big Sky,* Lockridge's *Raintree County,* Betty Smith's *A Tree Grows in Brooklyn* and Lillian Smith's *Strange Fruit,* Mailer's *The Naked and the Dead,* Steinbeck's *Cannery Row,* Stewart's *Storm* and *Fire,* Waugh's *Brideshead Revisited,* Welty's *Delta Wedding,* Warren's *All the King's Men*—these and others suggest certain main types of storytelling. There is the big book of men's struggle for action and for value; there is the small book of intent psychological warfare; there is the middle-range book of ordered or disordered social texture.

Most of these share a major trait, their sense of precision in reported detail. I say "sense," because the effect seems conscious, an effort at defining, a desire to note not just accurate data but accuracy itself. Hemingway works at this numbly, Welty lyrically, Lewis ponderously, the Smiths domestically, all with care. A second trait they share is the strong effect of perspective upon the detail, to distort, highlight, and indirectly to interpret it. Many look through the eyes of children, either in memory or in the direct confusion of the child. Many use a dogged downright plodding "I was there." A few make the reporter a meditating analyst of his own or another's situation; and a few make the events pass through many minds, turned and twisted into some clarity only as they proceed. The soldier fights, the captain organizes, the politician campaigns, the child wonders, the Negro moves through southern heat, the Jew through eastern cold, the prisoner strains at bonds; all these small counters of mass pressures tell painfully what they see, and none thinks he sees a whole. Only the telling makes the whole. In this telling, the wearing away of time, the progress of minute to minute and season to season, and youth to age, has as active a force as event itself. The plots are not nineteenth-century plots full of emotional action and reaction, but are attenuated, tuned to what next may come. They move, but they wait.

Crisp factual beginnings are characteristic: here is the situation: what can be done about it.

The nickname of the train was the Yellow Dog. Its real name was the Yazoo-Delta. It was a mixed train. Laura McRaven, who was nine years old, was on her first journey alone. (*Delta Wedding*)

He lay on the brown pine-needled floor of the forest, his chin on his folded arms, and high overhead the wind blew in the tops of the pine trees. The mountainside sloped gently where he lay; but below it was steep and he could see the dark of the oiled road winding through the pass. There was a stream alongside the road and far down the pass he saw a mill beside the stream and the falling water of the dam, white in the summer sunlight.
"Is that the mill?" he asked.
"Yes."
"I do not remember it." (*For Whom the Bell Tolls*)

Invasion had come into the town of Adano.
An American corporal ran tautly along the dirty Via Faverni and at the corner he threw himself down. . . .
In the Via Calabria, in another part of town, a party of three crept forward like cats. (*A Bell for Adano*)

Or the shading of detail may be intensified; as in many of the novels of the South:

> The sugar tree's round shadow was moving past the store. At five o'clock when the first leaves were withering on the burning macadam the store-keeper raised his eyes to the fields across the road. The heat rose somewhere between the road and those distant woods. Always at this hour he looked, expecting to see it rise out of that far cornfield and always when he looked it was there. Only a light shimmer now above the green, but the shimmer would deepen as the field brimmed over. In a few minutes the first waves would beat against the porch. He got up and, walking to the end of the porch, lifted the lid of the red metal ice-chest.
> "How about you, Ed?" he asked. (Gordon, *The Women on the Porch*)

On the other hand, we may sometimes get a word of interpretation, almost startling in its abstractness, to start off.

> The Cullens were Irish; but it was in France that I met them and was able to form an impression of their love and their trouble. (*The Pilgrim Hawk*)

Usually the love and trouble grow almost without name from the gusty streets, foxholes, swamps, and come only at the end to something more of an interpretation, a worrying of meaning, or suggestion of resolution.

> "I saw where it fell," said Laura, bragging and in reassurance. She turned again to them, both arms held out to the radiant night. ·(*Delta Wedding*)

> *Let them come. One thing well done can make—*
> Robert Jordan lay behind the tree, holding onto himself very delicately to keep his hands steady.... He could feel his heart beating against the pine needle floor of the forest. (*For Whom the Bell Tolls*)

> What had the silly little thing reminded him of before? There was an answer if he could think what it was, but this was not the time. But just the same, there was something terribly urgent at work, in him or around him, he could not tell which.... He stood there feeling his drunkenness as a pain and a weight on him, unable to think clearly but feeling what he had never known before, an infernal desolation of the spirit, the chill and the knowledge of death in him. (*The Leaning Tower,* title story)

Stated or not, such terrors are thematic, and they shape the whole; they are a central concern if not the body and substance; they are seldom written out, as a James or a Wordsworth would write them, because their major force is a conditioning perspective. Not always is the restraint as pointed as in the quoted passages. Often stuff and perspective whirl and wash away in a great blur as in *Raintree County* or the novels of Pennell; often, as in the more rhapsodic poetry also, stuff piles up with feeling and sensation to an extraordinary degree. See how Steinbeck recognizes the problem in feeling, and how readily he adopts the technique. He introduces *Cannery Row:*

> Cannery Row in California is a poem, a stink, a grating noise, a quality of light, a tone, a habit, a nostalgia, a dream. Cannery Row is the gathered and scattered tin and iron and rust and splintered wood, chipped pavements and weedy lots and junk heaps, sardine canneries of corrugated iron, honky tonks, restaurants and whorehouses, and little crowded groceries, and laboratories and flophouses.
>
> ... How can the poem and the stink and the grating noise—the quality of light the tone the habit and the dream—be set down alive? When you collect marine animals there are certain flat worms so delicate that they are almost impossible to capture whole, for they break and tatter under the touch. You must let them ooze and crawl of their own will onto a knife blade and then lift them gently into your bottle of sea water. And perhaps that might be the way to write this book—to open the page and to let the stories crawl in by themselves.

Then see how the first chapter begins with the same abundance:

> Lee Chong's grocery, while not a model of neatness, was a miracle of supply. It was small and crowded but within its single room a man could find everything he needed or wanted to live and to be happy—clothes, food, both fresh and canned, liquor, tobacco, fishing equipment, machinery, boats, cordage, caps, pork chops. You could buy at Lee Chong's a pair of slippers, a silk kimono, a quarter pint of whiskey and a cigar.

And the book makes its final commitment of feeling through sense, letting Doc read from *Black Marigolds*—"The whitest pouring of eternal light—"

> He wiped his eyes with the back of his hand. And the white rats scampered and scrambled in their cages. And behind the glass the rattlesnakes lay still and stared into space with their dusty frowning eyes.

This is the sentiment of *things,* which relaxes with them and leaves much to them and is carried away by them, in the sway of their

significance which is after all its own. The things of the novel are by
bulk much richer and fuller than the things of poetry. *Sky* can expand
to a whole chapter on weather, *tree* and *leaf* to forest and swamp,
street to a city, *hand* to vast anatomies; and these are not the scenic
backgrounds or the symbolic settings of earlier literature, but subject
matters on their own, necessary to the necessary burden of reported
fact. The author was there; he must say what he saw.

The author's main styles of saying are not far from the main styles
of verse in the decade. That is, we may distinguish clearly the piled-up
rhapsodic style of Steinbeck here, or of the followers of Thomas
Wolfe, like the style of Thomas, Sitwell, Shapiro, Spender. And we
may distinguish the more clipped and active style of some Hemingway, Hersey, Warren, and the briefer war novels, as closer to Auden,
Manifold, Millay, Cummings, Williams, charged with sentiment but
restricted in speech. And we may discern that minute scrutinizing of
motives and memorabilia in Porter, Welty, Wescott as in Stevens,
Eliot, Yeats.

In *The Best American Short Stories of 1947,* the editor, Martha
Foley, generalizes about the change of stories through the 1940's, emphasizing a growth away from the brief and active toward the full
and meditative kind. Though I am not sure that I see this change as
a whole, I do recognize its partial likeness to the tendencies of the
younger poets, Thomas, Shapiro, Wilbur, Horan, toward a richly
developed static interior fantasy. Miss Foley says, "This year the short
story writer has been primarily concerned with the 'internal man.'"
"First and foremost is a preoccupation with emotional frustration."
Freud and Proust are the men of influence.

From the standpoint of literary style, *per se,* the stripped, stark school of
understatement which prevailed for twenty years has almost vanished. The
tendency is to greater length and more elaboration. As with architecture,
writing seems to have its cycles of reverting to an extremely simple style,
then to add adornment until the rococo or Victorian is reached and a new
evolution begins. (P. ix)

Be these cycles as they may, the qualities of inwardness and elaboration which Miss Foley attributes to the short story now may be as well

attributed to poetry now. And the supports of outward fact and implicative statement are still strong in the work she selects for 1947.

He woke to the air-conditioned comfort of his apartment at the Attorneys' Club. In summer the enervating heat was shut out; in winter the temperature was held to an exact seventy degrees. Everything he wanted in life was here inside the sheltering walls of the club: food cooked to please his finicking appetite, obsequious servants who knew his little idiosyncrasies, physical fitness in the athletic department where he exercised daily for ten minutes and swam three times the length of the tank.

So begins Gerstley's "The Man in the Mirror," and ends by its title, after its hero's human failure,

A man across the room was looking at him. Such an unkempt man with thin, florid cheeks, dirt-streaked, and wildly working lips. But after a moment he recognized that he was alone and that there was no other man. It was only himself in the mirror.

The grimy details of the story come finally to this end of illusion. So from *Story;* and equally so from *Good Housekeeping;* with an additional irony of interpretive vocabulary like Pound's or Eliot's:

Shirley Docksteder and Thelma Bassler, both stenos, congenial yet with different interests, so there was always something to talk about, were loafing in the little back yard of their little apartment on this Sunday afternoon in May. It was an old-fashioned, brownstone house, and there was a tree in the yard and there were some terrace chairs, and if you looked carefully, at an angle, between the hotel and the brownstone house next door, you could catch a glimpse of Central Park. Shirley was drying her dark, pretty hair in the sun, rubbing it occasionally with a towel, which she would drop to the flagstones on top of the news section, which naturally you don't read but comes in handy to keep a towel from getting dirty.

In this story, Raphaelson's "The Greatest Idea in the World," the illusion is forced, and accepted at the end:

Rummaging among the cultural plenitudes of the newspaper, she found the classified section and turned to the help-wanted ads, to see the jobs she might be applying for if she weren't lucky enough to have such a good job—and to be engaged to Alvin Smiley.

If these fictive illusions are not to be left poised, at the ends of stories, upon objects, as so many of these stories, both 1941 and 1947, leave them—"for the rain fell between them like a curtain of splintered glass"—"The shadows leapt around them like frightened birds"—"Out of the bright circus, into the silence and darkness"—"The little group headed for the Automat at 47th and Eighth"—"Presently they began to play ball"—"He motioned toward the window and the falling rain outside,"—if these illusions are not to be suggested, but written out, then we get the fuller materials, the longer cadences, of the substantival poets, and then some of the elaboration to which Miss Foley refers. The objects become thicker, more loaded or more distorted. The prose lengthens to re-create the sense and substance, rather than the mere concept and accessory, of illusion.

The development is represented by the difference between the mere "falling rain outside" and the rain "like a curtain of splintered glass": in the first, the relationship set up to the people in the story is single in its predication; it is not what the rain is like but how the man misuses it that counts; in the second, the relationship is double and substantival, the representative quality of splintered glass, rather than the simple rain, being the important matter. Again, the writing of Jean Stafford, in her story "The Interior Castle," as in her novel *Boston Adventure,* represents the unfolding, substantiating qualities of contemporary style as it deals with mind's illusions, not working by touch and motion, but by detailed construction and accumulation. The single incident in her short story is an operation on a woman's nose, or, rather, it is the prolonged consciousness of the operation. This is but one small piece of the prose and the pain:

To be sure, it came usually of its own accord, running like a wild fire through all the convolutions to fill with flame the small sockets and ravines and then at last, to withdraw, leaving behind a throbbing and an echo. On these occasions, she was as helpless as a tree in the wind. But at the other times when, by closing her eyes and rolling up the eyeballs in such a way that she fancied she looked directly on the place where her brain was, the pain woke sluggishly and came toward her at a snail's pace. Then, bit by bit, it gained speed. Sometimes it faltered back, subsided altogether, and then it rushed like a tidal wave driven by a hurricane, lashing and roaring until she lifted her hands from the counterpane, crushed her broken teeth into her swollen lip, stared in panic at the soothing walls with her ruby eyes, stretched out her legs until she felt their bones must snap. Each cove, each narrow inlet, every living bay was flooded and the frail brain, a little hat-shaped boat, was washed from its mooring and set adrift. The skull was as vast as the world and the brain was as small as a seashell. (P. 422)

Then there is further interpretation:

Some minutes after she had opened her eyes and left off soothing her wrist, she lay rigid, experiencing the sequel to the pain, an ideal terror. For, as before on several occasions, she was overwhelmed with the knowledge that the pain had been consummated in the vessel of her mind and for the moment the vessel was unbeautiful: she thought, quailing, of those plastic folds as palpable as the fingers of locked hands containing in their very cells, their fissures, their repulsive hemispheres, the mind, the soul, the inscrutable intelligence.

The porter, then, like the pink hat and like her mother and the hounds' voices, loitered with her.

So the *mind,* the *head* of the 1940's. So *tree* and *sea,* devoted to their elucidation. So *time,* reaching from left to right, like space, in a moment.[1] These primary traits of the poetry are primary too for the prose. The varying styles, while they shade from brief immediacy to ironic analysis and to splendid encompassment, persist always in their emphasis on the pattern of things, made and natural, in the presence of mind; almost always their alteration, whether by hint, irony, or distortion, serves to tell something of the mind which has them in charge, so that, outward as they are, all do move inward by that concern.

The nonfictional work of the decade, including as it does much straight war reporting, and having less need to make anything of its discovered materials, nevertheless makes a good deal of them. It is surprising indeed to see how little take-it-or-leave-it presentation there is. The main force in White's *They Were Expendable* is the pride and wrath of Bulkeley. The power of Poncins's *Kabloona* is the adaptive power of human spirit. The allegories of C. S. Lewis painstakingly work out their detail, as detective stories do, for the sake of some degree of spiritual ratiocination. Ernie Pyle's *Here Is Your War* comes back in almost every paragraph from the facts of rations and

---

[1] See Joseph Frank, "Spatial Form in Modern Literature," *Sewanee Review,* LIII (1945), 221–240, 433–456, 643–653.

skirmishes, wounds and inventions, to the ideologizing of the home boy—Corporal Rogers, who lives in Twin Falls, Iowa, on Chestnut Street. The biographies and autobiographies, by Milne, Woolf, Heiser, Buchan, Freeman, Trilling, Bowen, Krutch, White, Schlesinger, Canby, Greenslet, Seagrave, Wright, and many others of equal variety, concern themselves most seriously with this boy: how he came to think what he thought, in the light of his home, his family, his town, the state of his nation, most primarily building up the *things* which will give clues by their accumulating pattern to mind and heart.

So, in leaving, I was taking a part of the South to transplant in alien soil, to see if it could grow differently, if it could drink of new and cool rains, bend in strange winds, respond to the warmth of other suns, and, perhaps, to bloom—. And if that miracle ever happened, then I would know that there was yet hope in that southern swamp of despair and violence, that light could emerge even out of the blackest southern night.

Different as this ending of Wright's *Black Boy* must be from the artifices of Sacheverell Sitwell's reminiscence, the two writers share the artifice of objects which tell their story, the prose of rich substantiality. For Sitwell ends,

This has been a vision of the golden age. Where every shepherd is a king and all men are giants, in the land of milk and honey, in long gowns, with the wand or sceptre in their ebon hands.

The golden age, the long gowns, the ebon hands, like the alien soil, cool rains, and blackest southern night, serve by their strong quality to convey at the conclusion the feelings and thoughts which have gathered to them, to be represented by them.

How both of these characteristic passages differ from an older discursive style not characteristic of the decade may be seen by a comparison with almost any passage from the memoirs of Santayana, who writes the prose of an era not identifiable with this. Note the constant analysis, the running abstraction, in chapter ii of *Persons and Places,* for example:

In approaching England I felt the excitement of a child at the play, before the curtain rises. I was about to open my eyes on a scene in one sense familiar from having heard and read so much about it. There was keen intellectual curiosity to discover the fact and compare it with my anticipations. There was my youthful hunger, still unappeased, for architectural effects, and picturesque scenes in general; and there was a more recent interest, destined to grow gradually stronger, in discovering and understanding human types, original or charming persons. And where were these more likely to be found than in England?

In such prose, *things* do almost no work at all. Always the material is presented in the metaphors and generalizations of interest. "Child at the play," "architectural effects," "human types," are the substantives, all brought far away from the levels of sense impression.

The modern reader reads again and again, by contrast, the purest sort of effortful reporting of sense. Heiser's popular *American Doctor's Odyssey* begins with ten minutes like ten hours of direct battering by the Johnstown flood, with the numbest minimum of stated reaction. The orphaned boy's learning is methodical, systematic, effective. The technique for recognizing trachoma in an immigrant child is a more live part of the text, as Heiser himself says, than the sorrow of the child's rejection. The symptoms of disease, the strategies of control, are side by side and without discussion the story of the life. In like fashion, even in so much more editorializing a book as William Allen White's, characters of parents, girls, friends, great acquaintances, the size and smell of offices, the look of open fields, the fish in the brook, the moonlight in trees, all make a sum of substance, a pattern by which one should read the man. The chair which his mother reupholstered before she met his fiancée is an example of the method; it takes more words and more attention than the meeting itself; through it the meeting is made plain, in the translation of tension.

Autobiography comes close to the heart of the matter for modern literature. There was little of it a century ago; now it is abundant, varied, close to fiction and to essaying, yet more representative than either in some ways, as it emphasizes time and truth. It subordinates both plot and discussion; its interest is in the single mind as it moves through things and the meanings of things, through trouble and through change, and is altered, and alters, as it moves. A hundred reminiscences of small towns are of this kind—Elliot Paul's *Linden on the Saugus Branch,* for example, or Woody Guthrie's story, or the English Schoolboy or the Country Doctor sort. A hundred stories of Jewish boyhoods recall from crowded city apartments every sight and smell. And in the devotion to heritage, parentage, first memories, streets, schooling, dust and dismay, the baffled older sense, fiction and nonfiction run together, because the laboring mind so earnest to record is not often willing or able to transform.

The most abstract prose in the same way runs fact into fantasy because of facts' newness and unbelievability. The many books of science, the reports on atomic structures and atmospheric pressures, run into science fiction, weird stories, and the comic books. The ratiocinations of pharmacists, psychiatrists, politicians, and intelligence staffs run into the highly technical mystery stories of the era. Historical fact becomes historical fancy in the long, popular, costume novels. Jury trials in court become jury trials on the stage. The technical studies of naturalists become the calendars of Donald Culross Peattie. Throughout prose the fact is the great value and marvel: the fact sensed, and changing, and therefore the fact in the sensing and changing mind.

Philosophy inscribes its recognitions of this emphasis. Bertrand Russell in *Twentieth-Century Philosophy* writes (p. 248):

Even chronometers and measuring-rods become subjective in modern physics; what they directly record is not a physical fact, but their relation to a physical fact. Thus physics and psychology have approached each other, and the old dualism of mind and matter has broken down.

The very juncture has made for a meticulous care in distinction, to draw every line as in fact and every seeming line as in mind, to tell the two apart the closer they come together. *Sign* becomes the word of juncture, more neutral, less mysteriously organic, than nineteenth-century *symbol*. And the relations between mind and object come to be of central interest: how fact and value are joined or separated, for example; how *is* yields *ought*. As Urban writes, in *Twentieth-Century Philosophy* (p. 71), "The metaphysical disjunction between value and existence is a wholly modern phenomenon."

In application to society, Stuart Chase in summary fashion sets up the problems again: the scientific method, the tradition of knowledge, the culture concept, common patterns of mankind, laws of social change. Max Lerner reasserts, in *Ideas Are Weapons* (p. 6), the need of context for ideas:

The meaning of an idea must be seen as the focus of four principal converging strains: the man and his biography; the intellectual tradition; the social context, or the age and its biography; the historical consequences of the idea, or the successive audiences that receive it.

Harvard's *General Education in a Free Society* again asks pattern (p. 49):

Modernism rightly affirms the importance of inquiry and of relevance to experience. But as scholasticism ran the danger of becoming a system without vitality, so modernism runs the danger of achieving vitality without pattern.

Pattern, context, field have become important descriptive and evaluative terms for the social scientist, with *tradition, law, custom, tendency, change, norm, variation* as the terms of the parts. The major vocabulary of poetry functions easily in this milieu, its *time* and *death, coming* and *going,* important for change; its *day, light, night, sun* for sensable context; its *eye, hand, head, heart, mind, world, thing, make, know* more anatomically human and intellectually constructive than before.

This constructive power the anthropologists stress in their culture concept. "Culture is the man-made part of the environment," Herskovits says in *Man and His Works* (p. 17). Even the total environment is made, as it is limited, by man:

the total environment of man, drawing on both the traditional heritage of his culture and the habitat in which he lives, is made up of no more than can be comprehended in the definitions of reality that he and his fellows draw out of their experience and the experience of those from whom they have descended. (P. 166)

Herskovits quotes the same from Cassirer in other terms:

Man lives in a symbolic universe.... No longer can man confront reality immediately; he cannot see it, as it were, face to face. Physical reality seems to recede in proportion as man's symbolic activity advances. (P. 27)

But even as men increasingly recognize their own limitations and controls, their interest in "reality," seen as separate from these, increases; and they try, even in human context, to isolate, by science the abstract, by art the concrete, realities they seem to discern, so as to bring the discernment to its fullest force.

With a means of probing deeply into all manner of differing cultural orientations, of reaching into the significance of the ways of living of different peoples, we can, however, turn again to our own culture with fresh perspective, and an objectivity that can be achieved in no other manner. (P. 78)

Along with man's construction of reality, then, goes this sense of objectivity toward it, and of self-objectivity, a sort of having cake and eating it too which is like the poets'—the artful creation which wishes to be pure report, the image made by and then scrutinized by mind.

II

The literary critics specifically are engaged in this sort of elucidation. They ask a "direct" reality, a "vivid" report, yet an "intense" and "significant" interpretation. They ask the facts and the meanings, and they must debate the relations between the two. A great many critics see clear specific social meanings, which they wish art to embody precisely and immediately; some feel that such embodiment is not by choice but is inevitable. Other critics take art as expressive gesture or transformation, and are concerned with the relation between source in mind and heart and resultant act or product. Most put a good deal of stress not only on the art as product, as complex or simple object and whole context, but on the object content of the work, the *things* in it. The abstracted or distorted forms of the painters, the "objective correlatives" of the poets, the connotative analyses of the critics, all emphasize key words and shapes and the items of observation, substitution, report, in their associations. All through, the stress is strongly substantival, upon the things related, more than upon the lines of relationship. Nevertheless, it is the problem of combination that is prime for the era.

A literary magazine makes a good representative of the running critical argument. Throughout the seasons, its return to certain main items of discussion, its playing of certain main themes, gives a clue to current interests. No single magazine can stand for all, of course, but the *Kenyon Review* should be fairly good to look at since it is one of the few to have had a continuous character through the 1940's, with a steadily literary concern under a single editor. To read through it is to recognize again and again a few main critical preoccupations, which are in part, of course, the preoccupations of the staff, but which reflect also, in their fashion, the thought of the time.

The leading articles in the quarterly are apt to consider a single literary figure: Wolfe, Auden, Housman, Joyce, Freud, Eliot, Hemingway, Mann, Kierkegaard, Yeats, Warren, Thomas, Stevens, Faulkner, James, Hopkins. A series of "Reconsiderations" goes back further to Johnson, Brontë, Coleridge, Flaubert, and others, and a series by Bentley deals with Wagner, Ibsen, Strindberg, Shaw, and other figures of drama. Further, there are articles on special problems, Nature and Society, Semantics and Basic English, Aesthetics, American Culture, the Modern Novel. Finally, there are scattered articles on music, painting, theater; there are prize stories and others, and poems by a half hundred poets—Auden, Brecht, Brinnin, De Jong, Engle, Eberhart, Blackmur, Ciardi, Garrigue, Horan, Humphries, Jarrell, Lowell, Millspaugh, Moss, MacNeice, Nerber, Nemerov, Moore, Prokosch, Schwartz, Spender, Stevens, Spencer, Williams, Viereck, Vazakas, Young, and so on. Clearly the aim is not popular, nor is it particularly ax-grinding; the combination is one of learning, theory, and experiment, with fair open-mindedness. It is much like the English *Scrutiny* in effect, with what seems to me far greater precision in the abstract statement of problems, and a fuller presentation of experimental materials.

The first number, for Winter, 1939, is opened by John Peale Bishop with an essay, "The Sorrows of Thomas Wolfe." Bishop chooses to consider just the problem which poetry too has raised, the relation of fact to the individual mind.

His aim was to set down America as far as it can belong to the experience of one man. Wolfe came early on what was for him the one available truth about this continent—that it was contained in himself.... (P. 7)

The most striking passages in Wolfe's novels always represent these moments of comprehension. For a moment, but a moment only, there is a sudden release of compassion, when some aspect of suffering and bewildered humanity is seized, when the other's emotion is in a timeless completion known. Then the moment passes, and compassion fails. (P. 14)

There is much of Wolfe, his home, his time and river, his leaf and stone, in the 1940's. His autobiography is retellable for others, in one shape or another. And the forms which Bishop points out, the continent in the mind, the timeless moment of compassion, are the great forms for poetry too.

Then Schwartz considers Auden and notes in him the same sort of symbols—mornings, islands, waters, frontiers, mountains, birds, stones. Schwartz calls these "romantic" and relates them to the Pre-Raphaelites as well as to younger poets like Barker, Thomas, Prokosch. At least they are romantic in a popular twentieth-century sense, which Winters also calls on in reviewing William Carlos Williams' concentration on concreteness, his "no ideas but in things." In turn, Williams on Lorca in the Spring issue writes of, as peculiarly modern, "Reality, immediacy, by the vividness of the image invoking the mind to start awake." Aldrich in Summer phrases:

The concept, then, of an expanding or expandable ego or self, incorporating parts of the environment into its own corpus—finally *being* such a body—and thereby extending the range of its immediate experience, will serve as our theory of visual and auditory perception. (P. 302)

Rahv states the danger in the modern "Redskin":

On the one hand he is a crass materialist, a greedy consumer of experience, and on the other a sentimentalist, a half-baked mystic listening to inward voices and watching for signs and portents. Think of Dreiser, Lewis, Anderson, Faulkner, Wolfe, Sandburg, Hemingway.... (P. 254)

And in Autumn, the survey of "The Present State of Poetry" fears for too much leftism, too much wit, too much violence and confusion, asking for, as in Yeats and Eliot, an attempt at an intellectual synthesis. Meanwhile, in the spring of the year, has begun the intermittent but continuing discussion of the relation of art to science. In writing for the "unified science" project, under Otto Neurath, Eliseo Vivas explains:

The history of modern philosophy may be envisaged from many points of view. One of these conceives of its development as an effort to mediate between the metaphysical conceptions of the universe which are part of our medieval heritage, and the naturalistic conceptions forced on the modern mind by the advance of positive science. (P. 159)

Positive science in considering meaning leads again to the problem of context. Signs have meaning in relation to other signs, in relation to the things they point out, in relation to the agent of interpretation. Charles W. Morris in the Autumn, 1939, issue distinguishes the language of science as statemental or predictive, the language of art as presenting values. Ransom in Winter, 1940, writing on "The Pragmatics of Art," says that the work of art "symbolizes the power of the material world to receive a rational structure and still maintain its particularity," and in Summer, 1940, praises Yeats' last poems for their great gift of images with absolutely local detail. The article by Wheelwright in the same issue again makes the distinction between science and art, in terms of prose and poetry and thus in terms of language, somewhat as Burke does: in monosignificance vs. plurisignificance: making an interesting connection with the preceding number on Freudian significances.

The series on American culture in Spring, 1941, continues, with Delmore Schwartz, to stress the specialization in the language of art:

The more the poet has cultivated his own sensibility, the more unique and special has his subject, and thus his method, become. The common language of daily life, its syntax, habitual sequences, and processes of association, are precisely the opposite of what he needs, if he is to make poetry from what absorbs him as a poet, his own sensibility. (P. 218)

Elucidations of scientific philosophies are played against Burke's "Master Tropes" and "Key Words" in the next three issues, to much the same point as that made earlier by Ransom (Spring, 1939), that science makes propositions, art makes tropes. The articles on Basic English, in Winter, 1943, bring vividly to view the dominance of Things over Qualities and of Qualities over Operations in the modern basic vocabulary; the bareness of essential predication, the richness of subject, in 600 of the total 850 terms. One must wonder about the reason for such emphasis: the nature of language, or of English, or of Basic, or of the sense of reality in our time?

When Ransom in the last two issues of 1947 devotes two long analyses to Poetry: The Formal Analysis and the Final Cause, he finds in his review of more than two decades of intensive literary criticism a central emphasis on language, on, specifically, "the total connotation of words." He rephrases his own favorite distinction: "Poetry is language in the pathetic mode, which is the mode not of logic but of feeling," and in his second section he reconnects feeling with things in his concept of "precious objects," human, natural, and institutional, objects *loved* as well as, or rather than, *used*. He builds up other parallel oppositions, ego vs. id, and thought-work vs. substance, and, throughout, his sensitive concern seems not with poetry in general but with the peculiar essences of poetry in his time. He draws even Aristotle to this service, as Barrett draws more recent philosophers in his review of Kierkegaard (Winter, 1943):

Within the small whirlpool of movements, counter-movements, dying ripples of the 19th Century's movements, that make up our century's philosophical background, we can disengage at least one large trend: in the direction of the existential, the immediate, "concreteness and adequacy." William James with his radical pluralism at the turn of the century, Bergson with his intuition, Whitehead with his feeling, the philosophies of *Existenz* of Heidegger and Jaspers, bear witness to this general movement. (Pp. 127-128)

Reviews of books of poems during the decade illustrate the application of such interest, in specific terms, and catch up here and there the qualities notable in contemporary verse. Berryman reviewing Dylan Thomas (Autumn, 1940) notes the fresh language of *things:*

The unmistakable signature of Dylan Thomas's poetry, so far as we have it in his three English volumes or in the forty poems here selected from them, is certainly its diction. Here are some of the key words: blood, sea, dry, ghost, grave, straw, worm, double, crooked, salt, cancer, tower, shape, fork, marrow, and the more usual death, light, time, sun, night, wind, love, grief.... One has the sense of words set at an angle, language seen freshly, a new language.

Some of the words Berryman lists are more "key" than others, and key in different ways, sometimes perhaps especially to Berryman, but his interest in listing them for their special value is itself interesting. They do represent Thomas, and more, they represent much of the decade.

Matthiessen directs attention in the work of Van Doren, on the other hand, to the meaning chiefly behind the objects (Autumn, 1939):

His chief subject in the lyrics of his last two books, which contain the major portion of his very best work, is symbolized in *The Tower,* "the hill of reason," the mind's "high play" over its own experience.

Yvor Winters in "T. S. Eliot: The Illusion of Reaction," Winter, 1941, and continued, weighs his own sense of the need for clear statement against Eliot's power of image, allusion, and revery; and Don Stanford in the same issue gives to Winters (along with Stevens, Crane, Tate, Williams) the credit for achieving that clarity and "hard dry classicism" not managed by the Imagists. Ransom in Autumn, 1941, comments on the younger poets, Ciardi, Garrigue, Herschberger, Nerber, Nemerov, Moss, Whittemore, and others, by reference to their handsome obscurity and their ignoring of metrics, and Mizener in Winter, 1944, points out again the rich baroque detail, the loose syntax, of Barker, Thomas, Shapiro. Matthiessen in "American Poetry Now" prefers to the persistent verb, the "I am," of Cummings, the *Noun,* the *Person, Place,* and *Thing,* of Shapiro; and Blackmur praises in Spring, 1945, such first lines of Garrigue's as "The moon has thinned; endurance wears it down," "That fish-shaped train, green headed," and "The dislocated person, feeling like a disease," saying, "No one could hope for better beginnings, more live in language, more brimming with their own achieved relationships of meaning."

These bits of selection from the critical articles of a decade make no more than a possible suggestion of direction, but they are helpful because they phrase in various ways the direction we have already seen poetry take. The critics in general seem to say: "These poets are writing rich materials in loose metric and syntactic form, and we are glad. We like a density of reference and connotation. We approve deep textures and sensibilities. The stuff signifies the reality we see." Of course not all critics are so sympathetic. The *Partisan Review* and the *Nation* would ask for more special sorts of reference, in social and psychological materials; *Harper's* and the *Atlantic* would need more form and less trouble; nevertheless, as characteristic a commentary as any runs through the sympathetic quarterlies because they see reasons for what is being tried. The opposing critics do not describe differently, but rather spend much less time in description, much more in opposition. The less "highbrow" poetry which they tend to favor is not a different kind, but rather simply an older kind, closer to the modes of the nineteenth century with which they have become securely familiar.

Critics as a kind in the 1940's are not homogeneous by any means; they write for widely varying audiences, and from widely varying preoccupations; but I think they share, even so, much of the concern emphasized in the *Kenyon Review*. Primarily they observe materials, list and weigh them, discuss their intrinsic interest and their suitability for a special time and audience. Secondarily they discuss theme, the work of mind and attitude in the materials. "Image" is their popular essential unit, and "intensity" their popular term of value.[2] They split most widely upon thoroughness of analysis. This decade and the last have been noted for their "closeness" of view; in the work of such men as I. A. Richards, William Empson, F. R. Leavis, R. P. Blackmur, Allen Tate, John Crowe Ransom, Cleanth Brooks, R. P. Warren, Yvor Winters; but at the same time there have been many sweeping social judgments, by Edmund Wilson, Van Wyck Brooks, Bernard De Voto, Archibald MacLeish, Horace Gregory, Christopher Caudwell, which, though they may have been close to the materials of literature, were far away from form. On materials and attitudes, then, the two schools best agree. Both are particularly troubled by the relationship between data and mind.

---

[2] Lillian Hornstein, "Analysis of Imagery," *PMLA*, 1942; Alice R. Benson, "Problems of Poetic Diction ...," *PMLA*, 1945.

MacLeish in *The Irresponsibles,* 1940, calls our failure "the division and therefore the destruction of intellectual responsibility" (p. 21). On the one hand, "The irresponsibility of the scholar is the irresponsibility of the scientist upon whose laboratory insulation he has patterned all his work" (p. 27). On the other hand, the writer is like the artist, in his devotion to the thing observed, in his desire to "write with such skill, such penetration of the physical presence of the world, that the action seen, the action described, will 'really happen' on his page" (p. 32). We have seen Steinbeck asking just this, most emotionally, and we have seen the strain of others' practice. But both writer and scholar, says MacLeish, are wrong to seek such objectivity. "They emerged free, pure and single into the antiseptic air of objectivity, and by the sublimation of the mind they prepared the mind's disaster" (p. 34). Tate in his selected essays *On the Limits of Poetry,* 1928–1948, states a like idea:

... I believe that all the essays are on one theme: a deep illness of the modern mind. I place it in the mind because that is the level at which I am interested in it. At any rate the mind is the dark center from which one may see coming the darkness gathering outside us. (P. 1)

And again:

The point of view here, then, is that historicism, scientism, psychologism, biologism, in general the confident use of the scientific vocabularies in the spiritual realm has created or at any rate is the expression of a spiritual disorder. (P. 4)

Tate believes with T. E. Hulme in a "radical discontinuity between physical and spiritual realms," and looks at poetry as "a focus of repose for the will-driven intellect" (p. 113), a "whole object," its meaning in its "tension," "the full organized body of all the extension and intension that we can find in it" (p. 83). Depth and complexity are therefore valuable to him, and objects are significant to focus upon.

If we look at critics like J. Donald Adams and Bernard De Voto, who regret the complexity of present critical interests and look back to standards of the past, we note that they draw their vocabulary from the past also. We get from them, in the 1940's, less of *mind* and *thing,* much more of nineteenth-century dignity, mystery, and *spirit*. For example, Adams says of his *The Shape of Books to Come,* in the Foreword, "This book derives from the profound conviction that literature, during the years immediately ahead, will seek above all else to restore the dignity of the human spirit." And De Voto in *The Literary Fallacy,* "One way is to think of literature as a fundamental expression of the human spirit, one of the activities of man which dignify his estate, illuminate his experience, work toward truth, pass judgment on life, and try to plumb the mysteries of fate" (p. 16). In turn, De Voto quotes Van Wyck Brooks (pp. 25–26), who uses even more of the old "organic" vocabulary in his statement that contemporary writers "had cut themselves off from mankind and formed a circle of their own that was wholly out of relation to the springs of life. They had broken their organic bonds with family life, the community, nature, and they wrote in a private language of personal friends;..." While the younger critics agree with these elders that the modern mind is "sick," they do not make so simple a diagnosis as isolation and idiosyncrasy, a diagnosis which is made of innovators in every era; rather they see themselves in the midst of the problem, in the difficulties of relation between the data of science and the sensibility of humanity.

The most technical literary focus of this interest is in the single word, and primarily in the word that names an object, the referential image or symbol word. Not the sound of literature—it is not intellectual enough; not the sentence structure—it is too intellectual; not even the figurative character of reference—it is too much involved in relation; not any of these complexities, but the complexity of simplest reference is the focus: what the word means. In 1920, Ogden and Richards set up the picture of the double connection of the word, to referrer and to referent; and that is, in small, the picture of reality with which the critics have since been struggling: the word as mediator between object and mind.

One discovered difficulty was the apparent power of words, through minds, to create objects. This was Korzybski's concern. Another was the power of minds to condense and displace: the interest of the psychoanalysts. Another was the power of objects to defy words: the difficulty of the poet in particular. Then the relations of words as signs to each other, to things, and to users were classified by the logical positivists; and poetry was apt always to be classified in one category or another on the basis of its words. Richards called its words emotive, Eastman and many others called them concrete, Empson, Wheelwright, and others called them ambiguous, plurisignificative, connotative; and poetry, with all its complexities, got caught in the toils of its simplest references. For the problem of reference is not simple now; it is one of the great difficulties of our day.

Meanwhile, through the nineteenth century, poetry was growing increasingly to fit this interest. The 1840's had moved as far as the atmospheres of objects. The critical theory of E. S. Dallas in the 1860's and of Pre-Raphaelite followers stressed objects particularly in their richness of relation and implication. An important part of the change in Yeats and in the poetry of his time was the gradual change from misty-edged to clear-edged objects, from atmospheric suggestion to a more wholly "objective" containment and signification.

No one is clearer than Yeats, and no one worked harder to become clear, on the nature of the change from nineteenth- to twentieth-century poetics, with its bearing on word, object, symbol. Not only did Yeats write poetry which is at the heart of poetry today; he wrote also explanations of the difficulties in achieving such poetry. The poets of the 1890's were still "romantic," still poets of mystery, blurred edge, and undertone, in the "soft modern manner," as Yeats called it, and as he scorned it; yet, on the other hand, hard abstraction seemed no more praiseworthy to him; he warned his Hermetic society against the dragon of the abstract. (Ellmann, pp. 40–42.) He said he had learned from Blake to hate the abstract (*Autobiographies,* p. 224), and he was to continue to learn to hate it from Pound (*Essays,* 1924, p. 128), so that still in *The King of the Great Clock Tower* in 1934 he published such commentary as, "We know the world through abstractions, statistics, time-tables, through images that refuse to compose themselves into a clear design. Such knowledge thins the blood."

Nevertheless, he was not content with the "soft modern manner" of his day. Though he wanted to seize upon the wealth of natural symbols, "the tumult of the sea, the rusted gold of thatch, the redness of the quickenberry," in his Introduction to *A Book of Irish Verse,* London, 1900, he was rebellious against the less grounded colors of Shelley, and he was dubious of his time's "slight sentimental sensuality," which pretended to many lingering connections between spirit and sense. (*Autobiographies,* p. 402.) So for almost twenty years he seemed torn between the style of his time, the symbolic allusiveness not only of the Rhymers but also of the school of Mallarmé, and, as an apparent opposite, the abstractness which he feared. Many students of Yeats, Ellmann with recent especial care, have traced this and other aspects of his quarrel with himself through its many philosophical, political, and personal manifestations.[3] For himself alone, and yet along with others like Pound and Eliot, in other countries, he was looking for clearer and more meaningful objects, a solider substance to deal with; he looked in Irish and in mystic lore because he did not want to compromise with any simple mechanical naturalism. He saw a "war of spiritual with natural order," in *The Secret Rose* of 1897.

Finally, after the turn of the century, he stated a sort of decision, a choice of his own, against the "modern" vagueness of his day. To Russell he wrote in 1900 against shadowy goddesses and terms like *haunted;* "... vague forms, pictures, scenes, etc. are rather a modern idea of the poetic & I would not want to call up a modern kind of picture.... All ancient vision was definite and precise." (Ellmann, p. 151.) In 1903 he wrote to Lady Gregory his new thoughts for verse. "My work has got far more masculine. It has more salt in it." (Ellmann, p. 153.) Later, in 1936, when he surveyed the turn of the century in his introduction to his *Oxford Book of English Verse,* he viewed the change in the same terms. "Then in 1900 everybody got down off his stilts." Hardy was "objective." Synge was "masculine." The earlier persistent image of "star" turned to a new persistent image of "bone."

---

[3] And see Thomas F. Parkinson, *Yeats as Critic of His Early Verse,* unpublished dissertation, University of California, 1949.

And Yeats understood the bone: "Does not intellectual analysis in one of its moods identify man with that which is most persistent in his body?" (p. xix).

Yeats was williing to come to terms with such intellectual analysis as well as with such hard symbol. He welcomed the quarrel between them, as they came closer together. Once he had feared the public tone, the intellectual argument of rhetoric, which he opposed to poetry (*Essays,* 1924, pp. 330–331, and "Per Amica"), but in the Oxford introduction of 1936 (p. xxi) he said he had erred in such antagonism, that not the rhetorical but the mechanical had been the fault of nineteenth-century naturalism. Indeed, even as early as 1913 he wrote to his father (Ellmann, p. 211, and Hone, p. 288) that he wanted to use a "speech so natural and dramatic that the hearer would feel the presence of a man thinking and feeling." Here is a striking agreement with the Senecan metaphysical rhetoricians of the seventeenth century, who wrote a plain, curt style, as opposed to the Ciceronian periodic style, in order to "portray not a thought, but a mind thinking."[4] The moving dramatic process of thought concerned Yeats, as it concerned the "curt," "masculine" poets and prose writers of the seventeenth century, more than did the substance of the thought.

Therefore, as we have seen in his poetry also, the matter of symbol was important, but not enough. He wanted "to include in my definition of water a little duckweed or a few fish. I have never met that poor naked creature H_2O." (Ellmann, p. 261.) But he did want his definition of water; he did want system. The whole *Vision* is his compromise. Like the poets of the 1940's, he sets his hard, clear objects in a pattern made by mind: his sun and moon, his bird and animal, his old man and young man, all themselves terms of contemporary force, he sets up in a great invented pattern of dynamic opposition and gyring motion, and proceeds to bring all history and psychology into the gyre. The abstract he hated was not the abstract of thought, but of thought without clear-cut objects. Rid of his mistiest pale terms, firm in his added verbs of construction, Yeats was able, with little other change

---

[4] Philip Smith, "Bishop Hall, 'Our English Seneca,' " *PMLA,* LXIII (1948), 1191–1204. See also Yeats, *Autobiographies,* p. 371.

of major materials, but with a clearer idea of how to control them, to assert and reassert in later life the power of interpreting mind.

"The moment had come for some poet to cry 'the flux is in my own mind'" (Introd. to *Oxford Book*, p. xxviii). "Even though we think temporal existence illusionary it cannot be capricious; it is what Plotinus called the characteristic act of the soul, and must reflect the soul's coherence" (*The Resurrection*). And, to Dorothy Wellesley on Mallarmé, "He escapes from history; you and I are in history, the history of the mind" (*Letters to Dorothy Wellesley*, p. 149). In such comments Yeats indicates the sort of reconciliation he learned to make between fact and interpretation. Dissatisfied with the nineteenth century's implicative blurred blend of them, he preferred to separate and clarify them and then face them direct, even if in antagonism. The questioning mind rather than the accepting spirit he had been looking for all along.

Pound and Eliot combined cannot construct so complete a view, so representative a self-consciousness. Perhaps because they were younger and had not worked with the Rhymers, perhaps because they were less tolerant of oppositions, they simply do not convey the feeling of transition so clearly. They set up their own standards and apply them.

Pound in his *Polite Essays*, 1937, takes us back to about 1912, in London. Then the "austere, bare, clear" standards of T. E. Hulme were coming into favor, though Pound discounts Hulme's force (p. 9), and rather gives to Hueffer the credit of stressing Rémy de Gourmont's "le mot juste." Hulme wrote in his *Speculations* (p. 132), "The great aim is accurate, precise, and definite description"; he favored the finite, the intensive; in the next years the manifestos of Imagism were to assert similar standards. In the 1920's George Moore went on to emphasize in his *Pure Poetry* "the poetry in things," and J. Middleton Murry in his *Problem of Style* to stress "crystallization" and "impersonality." These, and many others, supported the insistences of Pound.

Bad writing, or a great deal of it, drips down from an abstract received "idea" or "generality" held with fanaticism (twin beast with personal vanity) by men who NEVER take in concrete detail.

Men are good or bad in the year 1935 in proportion as they will LOOK AT the facts, new facts, any facts.

That is part of the new FORMA MENTIS. Forma to the great minds of at least one epoch meant something more than dead pattern or fixed opinion. "The light of the DOER, as it were a form cleaving to it" meant an ACTIVE pattern, a pattern that set things in motion. (P. 51)

Pound then allowed for mind, in this working form. Even more enthusiastically he takes it in the form of the Word.

The WORD built out of perception of the COMPONENT parts of its meaning reaches down and through and out into all ethics and politics. Clean the word, clearly define its borders and health pervades the whole human congeries, *in una parte più e meno altrove.* (P. 52)

It is a special sort of word, too, devoted to the object. Note the facets of the criterion: first, a separation from the earlier nineteenth century, "Wordsworth was so busied about the ordinary word that he never found time to think about *le mot juste*" (p. 60). Then a praise of William Carlos Williams' comment, "All I do is try to understand something in its natural colours and shapes" (p. 68). Then a humorous remark about the omission of Harold Munro from *Des Imagistes:* "Why he wasn't in it I cannot at this time remember, unless it was that I had called him a blithering idiot or because he had clung to an adjective" (p. 8). If *le mot juste* is to indicate something in its natural colors and shapes without being an adjective, it is apt to be a noun, with a specific reference to things with color and shape; and that is just the sort of word of major vocabulary which, as we have seen, Pound does employ extremely in his poetry, and which to a strong degree the 1940's share with him.

Eliot seldom brings his recommendations down to so fine a point. His analytical concern is not with the word, or even the poem, but, like his master Arnold's, with the conscience of the time, to which the quoted passage, the recognized convention, may be a guide. As in his poetry, *time* is the major term; it represents the power of tradition and continuity which individual poets variously adapt and intensify. Eliot sees Johnson as a die-hard in the midst of an altering sensibility, Massinger as representative of a sensibility too far shattered, Pound as an expert in the combining of freedom with form.[5] He agrees with Pound and others in the sense of his own time that poetry is for "actuality," prose for "ideas" (*After Strange Gods*, 1934); and once in a great while, in particular reviews, comes down to the "apparatus" of actuality in poetry. For example, in his introduction to Baudelaire's Journals, he writes that the "apparatus, by which I do not mean his command of words and rhythms, but his stock of imagery (and every poet's stock of imagery is circumscribed somewhere), is not wholly perdurable or adequate." Elsewhere, in his book on the *Metric and Poetry* of Ezra Pound, he gets down to words themselves (p. 14) as "perhaps the hardest of all material for art: for they must be used to express both visual beauty and beauty of sound, as well as communicating a grammatical statement."[6]

But as a whole the concept of cumulative continuity in poetry which he expressed in "Tradition and the Individual Talent" and which he has rephrased often, as in the "True originality is merely development" of his introduction to Pound's selected poems, is Eliot's most explicitly worked out, most meditated prose idea. Even his most recent essays, his work on Milton, for example, bend round this point, the value for a certain time, at a certain stage, of certain qualities partly defined but more fully felt. He has not the desire of the "close critics" for analysis; he says in "Hamlet," "*Qua* work of art, the work of art cannot be interpreted; there is nothing to interpret; we can only criticise it according to standards, in comparison to other works of art; and for 'interpretation' the chief task is the presentation of relevant historical facts which the reader is not assumed to know." He makes his temporal limitations very strict: "It must not be forgotten that a poet in a romantic age cannot be a 'classical' poet except in tendency. If he is sincere, he must express with individual differences the general state of mind—not as a *duty*, but simply because he cannot help participating in it." ("Baudelaire," *Selected Essays*.)

---

[5] Introduction to "The Vanity of Human Wishes"; essay on Massinger; essay on Pound.

[6] Such tripartite emphasis Pound makes the basis for his "kinds" of poetry: melopoeia (Greek, etc.); phanopoeia (Oriental, modern); logopoeia (Roman, satiric, in Heine, Laforgue, etc.). Pound's own poetry seems to me phanopoetic, with the other two forms used strongly as subordinate device: he stresses the precision of image, with sound and speech as supporting powers.

It is surprising, then, that Eliot's most famous statement about objective correlatives, exactly suited as it is to the major interest of his own age, should not be modified in its contexts by any temporal limitation, but should be applied to Shakespeare as well as to the twentieth century. "The only way of expressing emotion in the form of art is by finding an 'objective correlative'; in other words, a set of objects, a situation, a chain of events which shall be the formula of that *particular* emotion; such that when the external facts, which must terminate in sensory experience, are given, the emotion is immediately evoked" ("Hamlet"). Such a statement seems to me uncharacteristic of the steadiest thought of Eliot, his consistent concern for temporal sensibility and its expression in the intensities of form—for the very reason that it goes outside the bounds of time. Nevertheless, for our own time it has been a great blessing; it has deliberately phrased as a general psychological and artistic truth just that relation which has most interested poets in the twentieth century, the sensed object or event as correlate of emotion. This is not, it must be remembered, the seventeenth-century object of microcosmic instance; nor the eighteenth, of sympathetic correspondence, nor the nineteenth, of infinite implication; rather, it is especially the twentieth-century object of contextual significance.

Its basis is the psychological structure built up since the mid-nineteenth century in the work of Ribot and Galton and the psychoanalysts, in a world of "free-floating affects," "projections," "condensations," "displacements," in a philosophical world allied to German idealism as its interest is strongly in the world of phenomena as interpreted. So June Downey, in her book *Creative Imagination,* characteristically states the objectifying relation much as Eliot does, the emotions seeking attachments to objects, after having been cut off from the objects of their source. Miss Downey's own bias is a little pre-Eliot, but nonetheless sympathetic:

The point of crystallization for a poetic emotion is often in itself as insignificant as Wordsworth's daisy or Blake's little fly; but the wandering and homeless emotion more readily enters the empty chamber. (P. 130)

Accepting Pound's definition of image as "that which presents an intellectual and emotional complex in an instant of time" (p. 143), Miss Downey also emphasizes the present interest in the "word" alone, and the word which seems to be a noun.

We must emphasize the statement that one word used by itself is a much richer experience than the same word used in a sentence. The "Word" as detached consciousness has a tendency to blossom into all manner of images, feelings, impulses. It is a focus of associations, often of exceeding richness. It is haloed with meaning. (P. 60)

Being a poet committed to this doctrine, Edith Sitwell can say it again, more richly, even though negatively in a derogation of poets before 1900:

But not only did the texture of a line, the fabric of a poem mean nothing to them; the shape and weight or lightness of a word, itself as entity, these too were ignored. For these writers, words cast no shadows, had no radiance, were not of varying heights and depths. They did not know that a word can glitter like a star reflected in deep water, can be round and smooth-skinned as an apple. (*Aspects of Modern Poetry,* 1934)

Poet and critic and even advertiser agree on this focus on the richly connotative word. Not only does Aiken reviewing Rilke's poetry in the *New Republic* (October 19, 1942) make such a statement as "No other poetry of this century vibrates with so much of this *reference,*" but also the crowded statements of newspaper and magazine advertisements exploit such *reference.* And in the realm of art we get the same language, the "thick, tangled, radiant paste" (Frankenstein, San Francisco *Chronicle,* December 12, 1948) and the "destruction of illusionist effects and fictive depths" in the collage medium which is characteristic of modern art (Greenberg, *Nation,* November 27, 1948).

The briefest critical reviews of current poetry are now apt to point out, whether in praise or blame, the physical force and surface vividness, the transforming interrelations of reference.

There is the characteristic quasi-cryptic title; the traditional lyric form with individual metrical variations; the sensitive, brilliant originality of figure and image; the studied verbal assonance and dissonance; the theme developed not directly through a single, over-all image or specific emotion, but through the indirect succession of contrapuntally associated images within the framework. (Lechlitner on Moss, New York *Herald Tribune,* April 20, 1947)

Much the same, in negative:

Again and again I found the virtues of our new verse, its return to formal disciplines and metrics, spoiled by that persistent problem of lurid diction: "the hectic purple of a bruise." The infallible wrongness of contemporary diction lies in its reliance on the unimaginative clichés of revolt, the dully "daring" juxtapositions of incongruous adjectives for the purpose of startling or shocking. (Viereck on "Five Good Poets in a Bad Year," *Atlantic Monthly,* November, 1948)

The *Celebration for Edith Sitwell* published by New Directions in 1948 itself contains, among its many brief descriptions, both the new language of analysis and the older, in strong contrast.

This poem is an excellent example of the quality which I have called stone-like, made transparent with a passion as of light shining through it. The inner theme of Miss Sitwell's later poems is often transformation—the transformation of life into death, of warmth into coldness, of love into hatred. This sense of transformation is something which takes place within the images themselves. One must judge these images not as being derived from natural processes but from unnatural ones—chemical changes of one substance into another, identification of opposites one with the other.

This is said by Spender, at the end of his essay. Maurice Bowra in the next one makes what is close to the same point, the shining of interpretation through the sense of solid physical object in Miss Sitwell's verse, but his terms are from an older nineteenth-century critical frame:

With her acute and lively senses Miss Sitwell sees in the events of physical nature the manifestation of a spiritual power, and this is the inspiration of her faith and the object of her worship.

Most devoted in the *Celebration* seem those who echo and rearrange Miss Sitwell's golden terms of garden and myth to show how richly, fully, deeply they are laden with the costs of the decade and the troubles of reality.

As the significance of words and objects has come less and less *through* them, more and more *between,* the nature of nineteenth-century symbol has altered into twentieth-century context. Things, and their words of reference, do not now stand for ideas and mysteries of spirit so much as by interaction they create forms meaningful to mind. These forms then themselves become things, and even the perceiving acts of mind become scrutinizable as things. There are further and further progressions of objectivity, but always within the reach of interpretation. The very separation of mind and matter, the very stress on object words in poetic language, have the effect, are perhaps for the purpose, of bringing the one into the dominion of the other. Wallace Stevens' essay "The Noble Rider and the Sound of Words" exalts the process.

In its ultimate extension the truth about which we have been insane will lead us to look beyond the truth to something in which the imagination will be the dominant complement. It is not only that the imagination adheres to reality, but, also, that reality adheres to the imagination and that the interdependence is essential. We may emerge from our *bassesse* and, if we do, how would it happen if not by the intervention of some fortune of the mind? And what would that fortune of the mind happen to be? It might be only commonsense but even that, a commensense beyond the truth, would be a nobility of long descent. (*Language of Poetry,* p. 123)

Stevens ends with strong reasons for his "intervention" of mind:

It is not an artifice that the mind has added to human nature. The mind has added nothing to human nature. It is a violence from within that protects us from a violence without. It is the imagination pressing back against the pressure of reality. It seems, in the last analysis, to have something to do with our self-preservation; and that, no doubt, is why the expression of it, the sound of its words, helps us to "live our lives."

On the other hand, T. S. Eliot, who is still loyal to the interventions beyond the constructing power of mind, points out, in his recent essay, *From Poe to Valéry,* the dangers of their practice as it is allied to Stevens'. Eliot describes this *art poétique* (p. 26):

The subject matter exists for the poem, not the poem for the subject. A poem may employ several subjects, combining them in a particular way; and it may be meaningless to ask "What is the subject of the poem?" From the union of several subjects there appears, not another subject, but the poem.

Eliot quotes Valéry as saying, in *Variétés* V: "In my opinion the most authentic philosophy is not in the objects of reflection, so much as in the very act of thought and its manipulation," and remarks that the practice of such opinion has represented "the most interesting develop-ment of poetic consciousness anywhere in that same hundred years" (p. 31). But he concludes:

... it is a tenable hypothesis that this advance of self-consciousness, the ex-treme awareness of and concern for language which we find in Valéry, is something which must ultimately break down, owing to an increasing strain against which the human mind and nerves will rebel; ...

Opinion is divided, then, whether the strain of mind is a noble one. Should mind create, or should it discover? Should it learn through its own patterns, or by the revelations of symbol? Should it look *at,* or *through?* Certainly the alternatives are not exhaustive, but they exist in their present form because of the sources from which they derive as well as because of their indefinable goals. Having lost the physical and emotional associative agreements of the eighteenth cen-tury, on which the most mysterious implications of nineteenth-century symbol could rest with assurance of general meaning, the twentieth century has less sure grounds for common implication, and must in turn bring its inherited symbol back to some common ground. The ground it has chosen is not classical natural agreement, but modern fact, and it is still devoted to learning the nature of that fact. The learning is so difficult that Eliot, who in reaction doubts its value, fears for the strain it brings, and it is indeed often called an obsession, the "sickness" of our time, the separation of human nature from fact. So, for example, Diana Trilling speaks of Ira Wolfert's novel *An Act of Love* (*Nation,* January 8, 1949):

Yet here is the sickness of contemporary fiction—Mr. Wolfert's novel is but an example of it, the more striking because of his real gifts and proper am-bitions—that our writers would seem to be incapable of feeling that they are enough a part of the world so that if they explain or enlarge the world they are themselves enough explained and enlarged. Such is their sense of aliena-tion from their society that they must constantly assert their existence in it by virtue of the fact that they are in a position to have attitudes toward it: to be is to be perceived in the act of perceiving.

This dissociation which is on the one hand feared, on the other praised, is at any rate a characterizing force in modern thought, in poetry as in prose. Poetry brings the problem to its focus in the word: that word which had best be a noun and name a thing; that word which in itself like its object reveals nothing, but which in context gives and takes meaning; that word which is an employment of mind, not in active reasoning, but in naming and arranging. Poet, scientist, critic agree on the focus, the word as object, the object as sign, in the ordering mind. The terms of connection and relation, even of modification, are subordinated, so that things themselves may seem to be pure in their interactions. None builds so full and consciously contrived an order as Yeats. Most are able, like Pound, Eliot, Stevens, to make some special emphasis of the reality as they see it. Jung, Whitehead, Langer give us the "depth" of symbol; Freud, Baudouin, Burke give us the "condensation and displacement" of symbol; Dewey and Eastman give us its denoting force, its direct vividness apart from the organizing power of abstraction; Richards gives us its emotive "organizing, controlling, consolidating" force, apart from the reports of truth. Brooks gives us its paradox, Ransom its texture, Tate its tension, Leavis like Eliot its temporal suitability, Caudwell its social, and Blackmur and Winters its moral, representativeness. All the critics, for all their differences, share with the poets and scientists they would separate an absorption in the fact of object and the order of mind.[7]

---

[7] For essays making a basic distinction between poetry and prose in terms of language, see Balakian, Bateson, Baudouin, Brooks, Drew, Eastman, Hulme, Leavis, Moore, Pollock, Roberts, Rylands, Sampson, Tate, Winters, Matthiessen, Riding and Graves, and many others.

For psychological distinctions within language, see, as examples, Thurstone's verbal reasoning vs. verbal fluency; Russell's logic words vs. object words (*Inquiry into Meaning*, p. 33), Haugen's words talked-with vs. words talked-about; Lee's action vs. quality (p. 137); Pratt's human vs. natural color terms; the three functions of language as stated by C. W. Morris, by Russell (*Inquiry into Meaning and Truth*, p. 256), by Rynin in his introduction to Johnson's *Treatise on Language;* Vendryes' distinction between abstract and concrete, and his statement that "all languages are at one in distinguishing the substantive form from the verbal sentence" (p. 120); even those who decide what parts of speech are most "poetic." Hugh Ross Williamson in *The Poetry of T. S. Eliot*, p. 33, follows the Imagist line in saying: "Adjectival emphasis, the prerogative of the adolescent and the uneducated, is also a mark of senility and the failure of inspiration. Ivy is useful for concealing bad workmanship and may impart to undistinguished architecture a spurious romantic 'beauty'; but ivy would intolerably mar a building of classical perfection." With Hulme and Pound, Williamson would probably call most of the adjectival poetry of the eighteenth century "romantic"; he would then have to call Ovid and Virgil "ro-

Out of contextual analysis certain tendencies emerge, in certain philosophical shapes. The grouping of contexts is the problem, and one of the most common solutions is dichotomy. Those who argue against isolated meanings, who treat facts in orders, are apt at the same time to isolate Fact and Order as opposing poles. I suppose that lack of interest in the function of categories makes for such extremes, and that we are still, for all our experimental pluralisms, in the philosophical range of Kant and Hegel. At any rate, criticism seems to me to have made more difficulties for poetry than poetry has made for itself, by setting art against science and, in its special realm of interest, the language of poetry against the language of prose. So, while we have in the work of both Richards and Eliot good early

mantic" too. Gertrude Stein, on the other hand, thinks that nouns are the basis of poetry (*Lectures in America*, p. 234). "Words have to do everything in poetry and prose and some writers write more in articles and prepositions and some say you should write in nouns, and of course one has to think of everything" (p. 209). She thinks that verbs and prepositions are more exciting, but: "Poetry is I say essentially a vocabulary just as prose is essentially not. . . . Poetry is doing nothing but using losing refusing and pleasing and betraying and caressing nouns" (p. 131). Miss Stein thus neatly simplifies the modern attitude, both poetic and critical, which sees poetry as noun vocabulary rather than as verb sentence. See also Hatzfeld, "Language of Twentieth-Century Poetry."

Views of language, and of poetry and prose which employ it as medium for art, reflect views of reality. The *thingness* of reality and our interpretation of it are particularly strong in our time. The symbolists present things as connotative of feelings and ideas, and are not much interested in syntactic structures; for the metaphysical poet, on the other hand, syntax represents the working mind in its consideration of thingness and meta-thingness; for the neoclassical poet, the parallels between things and feelings are important. The *res-verba* debate is an ancient one (see A. C. Howell, " 'Res et Verba': Words and Things," *ELH*, 1946), and its seventeenth-century form took from classical oratory the notion of masculine sentence structure and feminine materials, according to which Donne, Jonson, Dryden were masculine because they firmly controlled material by structure. To the same notion Yeats came (Ellmann, p. 211); and Theodore Spencer in "Antaeus" makes an interesting comparison between Dryden and Yeats as poets who got back to the naturalness of speech structures. In all these senses, "verbal" is a complimentary term. On the other hand, for those to whom the "stuff" itself is important, "verbal" is derogatory, as in much eighteenth-century criticism and modern semantics. "What! are not our ideas formed by objects . . . ?" asked Voltaire's Master Simple. So Hulme "despised 'words,' regarding them as mere counters in a game, 'beads on a chain,' mere physical things carrying no reality. Against words he opposed the *image* as a unit and the *analogy* as an instrument of thought." (Read, quoted by O'Connor, p. 103.) This is part of the classicism Hulme professed. In like fashion, George Moore exclaimed, "So perhaps the time has come for somebody to ask if there is not more poetry in things than in ideas" (*Pure Poetry*, p. 19). Writing on Pound's *Pisan Cantos* in the *Hudson Review* (Winter, 1949), Hugh Kenner stresses Pound's emphasis on *res* over *verba*, but confounds tradition by calling this emphasis "masculine" in the line of Jonson, Landor, Browning. Perhaps, the sort of poetic strength has altered, but not enough thus to group Pound with these three.

twentieth-century examples of the emphasis on meaning in context, either artistic or moral, at the same time we have from both these leaders in criticism the split between object and feeling which has not helped, but hindered, the description of poetry as it is written. Poetry does not set the issue at this point. It has neither fused the operations of interpretation with objects, in Eliot's romantic sense, nor controlled report by suggestion in Richards' partly mechanical sense. Rather, as it has devoted its primary usage to mind, body, and objects both natural and created, poetry has emphasized the ordering and altering powers of human perception, with both feeling and abstraction more implicit than in any other century, and situation explicit.

Notice the discrepancies in the quarter-century debate. The American pragmatic idea that direct sensory experience is vivid, lively, aesthetic, qualitative, while thought generalizes and abstracts experience into science is, as expressed by Dewey in *Art as Experience,* or by Eastman in *The Literary Mind: Its Place in an Age of Science,* apparently in opposition to Richards' idea that sense is emotional, connotative, and organizing, while science directly reports, denotes. Both sides are interested in the distinction between fact and order; but the first makes fact an immediate experience within an abstract order, the second makes fact a reportable truth in an emotional order. So Eastman says (1932 ed., p. 301) that Richards has the matter upside down; that poetry, not science, points to things; that science, not poetry, "orders, controls, consolidates." What is the basis of such disagreement? I think it is the forcing of many factors into two groups; the groups contain different arrangements for different theorizers. Therefore, though object and order may seem stable enough poles, they are altered by combination with other factors; with emotion, for example. The present implicitness of our emotional statement makes the major discrepancy here; Richards allies emotion not to observation, not to truth, but to order, and so supports its implicativeness in shape and form and connotation. American pragmatic aestheticians ally it to immediacy, to fact in this sense of experienced fact, and so support its implicativeness in quality and image, in "surface" and "texture."

But the shifts of alliance suggest that the two poles have not made a stable basis for discussion; that the aspects of artistic and scientific and ethical practice are multiple and not to be dualized. When they are so dualized they raise more confusions than they allay, as they measure modern art by a standard alien to it. Even so general a book as Charles Stevenson's *Ethics and Language,* separating as it does statements of attitude from statements of belief, seems to me to impose upon art an alien polar position. It is as if some critics would identify the beautiful with the good because both are subjective and opposed to objective fact, and others would identify the beautiful with the true because both are objects of direct experience as opposed to rational thought; but none would allow, as the poets seem to try to do, the function of each in its own way. Possibly the poets of the 1940's are closer to a Dewey's scheme than a Richards', in their emphasis upon rich immediate sense as both true and beautiful; yet in their feeling of the goodness of order and pattern the emphasis changes, and the dichotomy comes to seem more and more arbitrary.

The difficulty is strong in a recent study, William Van O'Connor's *Sense and Sensibility in Modern Poetry.* Here the poles get new names but force the old grouping of Richards. The language of objects is logical, denotative, abstract; the language of emotions, evocative, symbolic, dramatic. But do we not get a joining, in the first group, of the very aspects which modern poetry has tended to separate, objects, abstractions, and categories; and do we not get in the second a more nineteenth-century than twentieth-century combination? O'Connor says that under the influence of symbolist and metaphysical poetry we have broken away from what he calls "verism" (p. 31): "Verism, which derives from the scientific point of view, implies that reality is only understandable in terms of abstract categories. The language which serves verism is necessarily logical, denotative, and abstract, which is not, certainly, the sole language of poetry." Later he says that denotative symbols make for pure statement, connotative and image symbols for dramatic statement (p. 40), and that logical categories not only killed metaphysical poetry but were foreign to symbolist poetry with its esoteric affinities of sensory appearances (p. 67). With Brooks, Tate, and others, O'Connor praises the drama of complexity (p. 145): "If the poet must work through a context of conflicting and heterogeneous elements, the resulting structure will of necessity be dramatic." Finally, he concludes that in consequence of their reaction against the objective, rational, and factual, modern poets, more aware of cultural pattern, will make a better synthesis.

His own acceptance of the metaphor of poles, of the simplified drama of reaction and synthesis, seems to me to make O'Connor more sympathetic than analytical. His opposition is a fiction of unity; verism, a compound of denotation and statement, from which connotation is forcefully separated, a combination of object and logic which leaves at the positive extreme a most tenuous symbol and myth, in a tension of conflict. Like Cleanth Brooks, O'Connor is sensitive to poetic multiplicities, and the concept of conflict, of paradox, of dialectic, seems imposed upon, rather than drawn from, these multiplicities, except in the sense that variety does yield contrariety.

The most articulate debaters against polar criticism are, as one would expect, the Neo-Aristotelians, like Olson, Maclean, Trowbridge, who argue for more than two categories, and for criteria suited to type. Yet because they have suggested few pertinent bases for categories, they must discuss each piece of art as individual, and thus subject its individuality to their own. We see, for example, in Maclean and Olson's analysis of poems (*University Review,* Vol. VIII), that the differences between them rise not from the differences between the poems merely, but also from their differing unexplicated premises. Like the polar critics, then, they represent extremes.

The most practicable and practiced modern suggestion for grouping or classifying and thus generalizing about works between extremes is the category of time, and it has not tended, like the category of type in prose and poetry, to get drawn to poles. Rather it still allows variety by standard "periods" in literature, and seems indeed the most orthodox sort of classification in our day. It is Eliot's primary sort, and that of the social critics, and that of relativists like Frederick Pottle, and that of departments of literature. It is the category which I have been examining through these studies of language, and it seems more descriptive than I had expected. It reflects, too, far more than poles or elements, a poetic preoccupation of our day.

But most thoroughly reflective is, I think, the simplest sort of contextual analysis which our critics have most thoroughly engaged in. Not Poetry capitalized, nor Poem, nor Period, is so characteristic of critical philosophy in the 1940's as the moderate scrutinizing lower-case studies of works as they work, of words in sentences, sentences in paragraphs, and paragraphs in the frame of construction and communication. Richards' *Practical Criticism,* Eliot's *Dante,* Blackmur's clearest descriptions, and more and more journal essays, have such a character. Like poetry itself, like narrative prose, they find difficulty in distinguishing what is from what seems in the work they consider, but like poetry too they find the distinction to be of interest and importance. The critics keep asking for myth in our time; some of them have already developed the myth of the poles from the lore of dialectic; all the while, they have, and are working in, the myth of their own poetry: the significance of a wealth of substance when it is given a human design.

III. COMPARISONS AND CONCLUSIONS

Now THAT we have come to the end of the 1940's, a backward look at the character of poetry in earlier centuries may tell us, by comparison, more about the character of what we have come to. There is inheritance in language and in poetic language, as well as innovation, and even the innovation may follow clear lines of development, as Eliot has emphasized.

To begin with the simple major vocabulary: the terms for the 1940's are, it will be remembered, the adjectives *little, old, white,* the nouns *day, death, eye, God, hand, head, heart, life, light, love, man, mind, night, sun, thing, time, world,* the verbs *come, fall, give, go, hear, know, lie, make, see, take.* If we look back to the 1540's, the decade of Wyatt and Surrey and their early century in general, we see an equal number of verbs and a majority of the same verbs; many fewer shared nouns, but a majority of those agreed on; and fewer and different adjectives.

Verbs are the most stable, the least changing. They persist through all centuries except the eighteenth, with about ten major terms, and of these *come, give, go, know, make, see, take* specifically, persist. Note the pairs of actions, *come* and *go, give* and *take, know* and *make.* The great change in the five centuries is the loss of *find, tell, think,* and the gain of *hear, fall, lie,* from the eighteenth and nineteenth centuries. The verbs have become more passive and receptive.

Of major nouns of the 1540's, eight, all but *king* and *lord,* are primary still for the 1940's. Indeed these are primary terms for almost the whole range of the poetry: basic *day, God, heart, life, love, man, time;* the eighth noun, *thing,* is less steady, but is taken up from across the centuries by the 1940's in its renewed awareness of human construction. From the 1640's we take persistent *eye,* but have dropped its *heaven* and *soul;* from the 1740's, *hand,* but not *air, friend, joy, nature, power, youth;* from the 1840's, *light, night, sun, world,* but not *spirit, thought,* and *word.* Finally, on our own, we have added *death, head, mind,* and possibly *sky.* So, of our many agreed-on nouns in the 1940's, about half are characteristic of English poetry through its history, and these are terms of human and spiritual love and sight in day and time; a fourth come from the nineteenth century as immediate predecessor, and these are terms of light, primarily; and a fourth are new, the terms of mind and death, with sky as parallel in nature, and thing as renewed construct. The main change in nouns, then, is a strong increase, which moves toward specification of thought and of external atmosphere, discarding in this progress the feelings of joy, soul, spirit, the realms of heaven, earth, and nature, thus specifying and intensifying by both abstraction and objectification.

The adjectives also represent this alteration. Of early *good* and *great,* one or another of which persisted through the nineteenth century as major, and of seventeenth-century *fair* and *sweet,* which were nearly as strong, none remains to the 1940's. *Little* and *white* are new, *old* comes from the preceding century; together they show the same increase of focus on detail of time and size and quality which we see in the rest of the vocabulary.

We see both a sustaining and a particularizing of poetic vocabulary. About half the words are steady throughout, and a fourth drops away as another fourth comes in. The thirty major terms of the 1940's when compared to the twenty-two of the 1540's are more detailed: *day* has added *light, night, sun; heart* has added *hand, head, mind; life* has added *death; earth* has changed to *world.* What are lost in the meantime are *people —king, lord, friend, youth—*and general forces and feelings. Fifteen of the present terms come from the 1540's, are, that is, lasting in the language of poetry from its beginnings in Tudor England; one present term, *eye,* comes specifically from the 1640's; two, *hand* and *hear,* from the 1740's; seven, *old, light, night, sun, world, fall, lie,* from the 1840's; five are its own, *little, white, death, head, mind,* with no verbs. We see, then, the continuity of the line of direction. The 1940's are closer to their preceding century than to any other. They reach back over it to an earlier time for only one word, the *thing* of the 1540's; otherwise they preserve no majority term which the 1840's have not also preserved. Between these two last decades there is agreement in twenty-four of the thirty terms; in addition, the particularizations of mind and quality have been carried further in the present, by innovation and by the giving up of agreements on such nineteenth-century words as *bright, spirit, thought, word, look, love,* and such inherited terms as *sweet, good, earth, heaven, soul, rise, think.* The abundance of nineteenth-century agreement on all these traditional general and thoughtful terms, as well as the new specializations, has been cut down by our own decade at the expense of tradition; in singling out our emphasis we have narrowed our agreement, though it is still greater than in any decade except the 1840's. From that most catholic yet individual of decades we draw and concentrate our resources.

The majority's emphasis in each decade, which has provided the basis of consideration, is supplemented by the types of terms emphasized by the minorities or by individual poets, types which do not alter, but rather extend, the generalizations to be made. Minority and individual terms in the 1540's and 1640's focused strongly, as one would expect, on social attitude and relation. Such adjectives as *bad, false, poor, rich, gentle, just, kind, noble, pious* were dominant; such nouns as named body or kind of man, *blood, body, ear, lips, sense, tear, tongue, voice,* and *daughter, son, poet, name, shepherd, swain, virgin, woman;* such verbs of communication as *call, prove, sing, speak, swear, shine, show, seem, kiss, weep.*

In the 1740's the emphasis divided, part inward to feeling, part outward to nature, with general terms of science and art to connect the two. Primary terms of feeling were *bold, conscious, free, gay, happy, lonely, lovely, mild, pensive, sad, solemn;* of nature, in a great access of scenery, *cloud, country, dust, flame, flood, flower, hill, land, mountain, shade, sheep, sky, snow, storm, winter.* At the same time, a great sense of general and ceremonious bond tempered the connections between these, in such adjectives as *divine, endless, eternal, generous, immortal, royal, sacred, various, virtuous,* and such nouns as *fate, fame, freedom, fancy, glory, honor, liberty, mercy, virtue, wit,* with *man* made various in *crowd, dame, name, foe, fool, king, monarch, maid, nymph, poet, priest, prince, shepherd, virgin,* and a handful of proper names like *Damon* and *Isis.* Furthermore, there were many terms of conscious artistic order, *art, beauty, charm, manner, muse, praise, ruins, strain, voice, way;* and the verbs were mainly attentive, *bear, behold, lead, leave, meet, move, please, pursue, view, yield.* The tone of pleasant general correspondence was constant. Modification was emotional; action, receptive.

In the 1840's, with greater variety of agreement, innovation, and renewal, came more shades of emphasis in the individual primary terms. Feeling greatly lessened, in favor of sense: *awful, beautiful, brave, glad, sad, hope, faith,* were subordinate to the new colors and objects, natural and man-made, *blue, brown, grey, loud, silent, bell, bough, bridge, door, dust, flower, home, house, river, rose, sea, shadow, sky, star, stag, stream, wall, wood.* The words of *man* maintained importance, and grew more inward in *breast, dream, prayer, humility, wisdom, smile,* more minute and particular in *babe, child, father, mother, bride, fool, giant, knight, maid, nymph, page, saviour, teacher, woman,* and in more than a dozen proper names, *Artemis, Christ, Margaret.* The verbs are personal and expressive: *feel, forbear, haunt, ride, seem, speak, sing, learn, laugh, pray, work.* In every kind we see that the central emphasis on sense carries the terms on the one hand outward to things, on the other inward to individual sensitivity and expression.

These ways the vocabulary moves even further in the 1940's, in substantiation of the terms of the majority. Adjectives are now almost wholly of sense, not of standard or of feeling. *Beautiful* is closest to feeling. The rest are of specified color and quality, *black, dark, green, blue, bright, cold, deep, dry, golden, grey, red, high, open, still,* with certain groupings further into space, *great, long, big, large, small, fine,* and into time, *ancient, new, last, young,* and in some uses *dead.* The nouns triple their emphasis on natural objects, on *bird, fire, flame, flower, land, sea, sky, river, snow, stone, wood, weather, wind,* and then specify these yet further, *bird* to *wing, land* to *hill, sky* to *moon* and *star, weather* to *spring* and *summer, tree* to *leaf, flower* to *rose, water* to *wave* and *rain*. Further, there are the made objects of *thing, nothing, everything, glass, ice, home, house, ship, tower, wall,* along with the continuing made *rhyme, song, verse, music* of art. The words of *man* take on a more precise anatomy in addition to inward being, *blood, body, bone, face, foot, ear, mouth, neck, tongue,* along with *brain, dream, being, soul, spirit, sleep, thought, word, name;* and man's kinds come closer home in *child, boy, father, friend, king, lord, poet, mother, soldier, stranger, woman,* as in the lessened proper names. For the major *mind* there are a handful of abstract terms, *real* and *true,* for example, and *faith, fate, innocence, luck, power, truth;* but these are from few poets. The verbs have increased again their individuality of motion, as in *ask, breathe, feel, cry, grow, move, sit, run, stop, turn, try, stare, walk,* and they have added actions which seem to deal with objects rather than people, like *get, keep, leave, lose, hold, break, drop, drive, ring,* with renewed emphasis on *make* as major.

While continuing and narrowing the particularizations of the nineteenth century, both inward to individual sensibility and outward to the natural world, the poetry of the 1940's has made, then, another specialization, that represented by the major terms of *mind* and *thing* and *death* and *old* and *little,* a more precise orienting in terms of time and space and in man's mental relation to physical structure. This change is innovative; it is characteristic of the 1940's; yet it also renews, as in the word *thing,* some emphasis from the Tudors. *Old,* too, was stronger for them than later, *death* and *mind* moderately so, *time* strongest until the present; *make* also. In this shading of temporal and objective concept we find an aspect of return or renewal in twentieth-century verse.

The primary words which, used by a majority or strong minority, most distinguish the 1940's from other periods have not just suddenly become poetic; they have grown gradually in power. Consider the new adjectives, *little, old, white. Old* is strongest and is also most conventional, primary for Chaucer and for the most traditional poets in the next centuries. *Little* early belongs to the affectionate tradition of

Spenser, Shenstone, Dyer, Wordsworth, and then is carried over by the Brownings into twentieth-century lyricism. *White* is a more fully modern term, from the Brownings, Clough, Longfellow, Tennyson, the active forces in their era; but even *white* gleams earlier, in the poetry of Herrick.[1]

Of the major modern nouns, *eye, man,* and *time,* the first two have declined from fullest usage, but *time* has risen. *Death* and *thing* return slowly after an eighteenth-century lapse, from the metaphysical poets, through Young, through the active nineteenth-century users of *white,* to Auden and the substantival poets. *Head* and *mind,* on the other hand, weak metaphysical terms, though strong in Wyatt and Surrey, are important for Pope and a number of his contemporaries and survive through Mrs. Hemans and Tupper into the main twentieth-century practice. The special *child, dream, sky, water, wind* of this practice are more abrupt in appearance, as still minor; *child* and *dream* from the Longfellow-Lowell-Keble group, *sky* from these and others and back to Akenside, Blacklock, Armstrong, Dyer, Thomson; *water* and *wind* most purely of the 1940's and of Pound, the water once in a while, as in pastoral Quarles, earlier, the wind only in Thomson. Even when we deal with such individual inheritances, we see a continuity of substantival emphasis, the nouns of nature through Thomson, of mind through Pope. So, in like fashion, the strongest verb, *go,* has a foundation in the predicative poetry of the preceding century; the less active, *seem,* in less active predecessors. When the force of great usage does not sustain the poetic term from one century to the next, the persistence of a style of practice, along with the force of individual treatment, may sustain. Through the rich general innovations of the eighteenth century, for example, we see three other lines surviving: mind and age in Pope, death and thing in Young, the special particularity of Thomson. These renewed together in the twentieth century help make its characteristic style.

These relationships in vocabulary are pertinent to the common consideration of the "romantic," the "classical," the "metaphysical" char-

---

[1] A. E. Pratt, *The Use of Color in the Verse of the English Romantic Poets,* p. 31, says that the *white* group has been most constant in English poetry.

acter of modern verse. Since Grierson's edition of Donne in 1912, the school of Donne, some of the best of poets and critics, including perhaps Eliot, Spencer, Brooks, and many others, has asserted the closeness of the modern to the metaphysical sensibility, the "sort of thought in sense." At the same time T. E. Hulme, and later Pound, Eliot, Winters, and others, were asserting the new classicism of clear objectivity in reaction against the blurred lines of Georgian romanticism. And all along, especially by Imagist admirers of Keats and by the reviewers of young poets now, the richness of neoromanticism is praised.

I think that the simplest view of primary vocabulary shows first of all that the poetry of an era does not in any whole sense return to the poetry of another. The line of development is largely one-directional. We probably do not have, then, major fluctuations in poetry which can be labeled by recurring names; time itself is too strong a forward-carrying force. If to apply the names of older styles is to note one or two major elements which carry over or reappear, it is possible easily to call an era's poetry by all the names at once; but their relation and proportion thereby become important.

The vocabulary of the 1940's is, first of all, the vocabulary of poetry, and perhaps of prose, through five centuries of the language. It is just "English." Secondly, it is "1940" or thereabout, itself and very different from any other. Thirdly, it is very "romantic" if we may identify that term at all with practice in the early nineteenth century; it is closest in terms as in time to its atmospheric predecessor. Fourth, it is somewhat neoclassical, as it retains the full sensuous line, the physical and *head-mind* terminology of the 1740's. Finally, it is somewhat metaphysical and humanistic as it calls up the temporal sense of the seventeenth century, the constructive sense of the sixteenth. Only the just relation of all these traits can begin to define it.

Contexts of terms may suggest part of the distinction. The terms which are steadfast through five centuries, *great, day, eye, God, heart, life, love, man, come, find, give, hear, know, make, see,* may alter in aspects of reference, as they alter in emphasis. The leading *good* and *heart* of the 1540's, the added *eye* and *see* of the 1640's, the outward *fair* and *day* of the 1740's, the *light* and *come* of the 1840's, have turned finally to *old* and *time* and *go,* and in the turning have altered association a little. For example, Ben Jonson's *eyes* were bright in simple sight, *minds* and *things* but toys, *world* to be forsworn, *day* apt to be the *last day,* feelings and perceptions strongest as abstract and in relation to God. The heart can be broken and torn, but God remains "still one God, in Unitie," and "Poets, though divine, are men," and one may love Truth as well as a person or a thing. The lines of thought steadily interally the human perceptions with metaphysical goods, in the metaphoric mode of "Unless my heart would as my thought be torne," and "mistaking earth for heaven."

The generalizing power of Gray's similitude or personification removes the physical eye and heart from such personal context, either by bringing more of cosmos in—"Some heart once pregnant with celestial fire," or by reëmbodiment—"To contemplation's sober eye / Such is the race of man." Both the spiritual and the emotional are naturalized in such a way that God and gods blur, and passions may be called vultures, the soul a genial current, life a little day. Sight sees fewer relations, more persons, objects, trains, and troops; hands and eyes, especially for Collins, take the qualities of sense in *balmy, dewy, haggard, throbbing, darting;* and even mind is *glowing.* Sense makes man in nature and nature in man.

For a poet like Arnold such interpretations must be more tentative, the bonds often illusory, and symbol more justly suggestive than conceptual figure. Joy "comes and goes," men are old, things are vague, death "dissevers all," seas and stars suggest the flux. "A light that, shining from the blest abodes, / Did shadow somewhat of the life of Gods" is characteristic in the hints of its phrasing, the glancing quality of its image. "Blest abodes," or "face to face with God," or "eagle eyes," like Tennyson's Pilot in "Crossing the Bar," are not figures or images which allow for further work of intellect or sense; they too function as symbols, suggestive and not to be examined. The particularity of sense grows in Arnold, as in his *white* shoulder, neck, hair, robe, dawn; but its relation to statement is oblique. In statement, at the other extreme, we get a growing force of flat abstraction, at once more impersonal and more personal than before: "My father lov'd injustice and liv'd long," or, "man can control / To pain, to death, the bent of his own days." The nineteenth-century mystery, while it divides sense from soul, makes each more self-reliant.

By the 1940's this reliance has got so strong that it seems ready to compromise again; not in Tudor humanism or in Jacobin microcosm or in Augustan cosmos, but in some sort of construction of its own, which the contexts indicate. Yeats' adjectives for *man, bitter, blind, powerful, violent,* as well as *old* and *young,* are at odds with an accepting man; his nouns for *old,* similarly, quarrel with the associations of the epithet, in *thorns* and *tricks, rascals* and *rooms, clothes* and *marvels,* as well as *friends, memories,* and *songs.* His *heart* is neither a mortal nor a physical nor a spiritual heart, but all these confused, in *ambitious, blown, brutal, burst, cold, driven, empty, outworn, resinous, sick, weary, wild, wrung.* It is at times a thing. The poem, not the epithet, reveals the character. The quality is not in the word but in the context.

The same for Stevens. "Look round at the head and zither / On the ground"; "the great space of your age"; "a foyer of the spirit"; "Angry men and furious machines"; "the whole experience of day"; "Eyes dripping blue"; "the green mind bulges." And for Spender: "These questions are white rifts"; "With human bodies as words in history"; "Their deeds and deaths are birds"; "Those brothers who we were lie wrapped in flannel." For Lowell: "this cymbal of a hand"; "The world, this ferris wheel." For Williams: "A tune nameless as Time." For Cummings: "five wishes are five / and one hand is a mind." For H. D.: "and every concrete object / has abstract value, is timeless / in the dream parallel." For Crane: "I saw the frontiers gleaming of his mind"; "Though other calendars now stack the sky"; "lend a myth to God." For Moore: "There never was a war that was not inward"; "the mind feeling its way as though blind"; "small things go / as they will." For Sitwell: "The dead disguised as a living man." For Thomas: "Where, punctual as death, we ring the stars"; "Time's jacket"; "The kissproof world"; "the god of beginning in the intricate seawhirl"; "I am the man your father was."

When the poetic statements do not so literally interrelate men and things, time and space, feelings and ideas, they keep them as coldly separate as possible, in order to present the "purest" quality. Facts are facts, like Williams' "A big young bareheaded woman / in an apron." Ideas are spoken as ideas, with their own limitation, like his "I suppose it's my mind—the fear of / infection." Much of Frost's meditation is treated as meditation *per se*—this is how meditation runs along; and much of Jeffers' action is treated with equal objectivity—violent as it is, this is the way it happens. "She heard a crash far away down the mountain / And saw a cream-colored car go through the bridge-head / Guard-rails ..." The actions, things, ideas, numb as they may seem, must, to be truthful, speak for themselves. Then, by their arrangement in the whole context, they may be interpreted.

Therefore, not only the immediate associations, not only the used denotations and connotations, of the words are important to the poetry. We see the connotations of relation important in the seventeenth century, the connotations of generality in the eighteenth, the connotations of allusion in the nineteenth, and all these now come together. But they are used most particularly now in relation to each other, and plain juxtaposition clashes and controls them. In other words, placement, both spatial and temporal, is the strong organizing principle of the modern poet; placement works with a sense of objectivity; it arranges words, statements, ideas, as if they were colors or things, as if they could be ordered into a physical pattern of sight and sound and thus treated both "in themselves" and in interaction. The pattern carries the meaning. In this sense, the poetry of the 1940's is more manipulative than that of the nineteenth century in its "wise passiveness," than that of the eighteenth century in its natural correspondences, than that of the seventeenth in its metaphysical thought. The *mind* of the 1940's is not so much a reasoning thought, a passion or a spirit, as it is an organizing state, an area of space and time which must see to significant arrangement.

The arrangement, in language, must consider more than reference, with the interacting of its denotations and associations; the sound and the syntax too provide a strong part of significance, and they too have associations. The mind, time, and color of the 1940's do not work in argumentative structures upon the heavenly and earthly planes of the seventeenth century. Nor do they invoke the cosmic reaches of eighteenth-century similitude. They are far too inert for either of these other functions. Yet they are not so inert, at least not so accepting, as the nineteenth century's lyrical spirit and narrative persistence; they move and make their way with difficulty, because each is conditioned by the other and none is free to soar; but they achieve a complex harmony of interaction.

The syntax of the 1940's puts emphasis on phrases, as reference does on things and qualities. Clauses, especially clauses of subordination, are of relatively less importance; *though,* and *because,* and *if* are not the prime thematic relations that they were in the seventeenth century. Subordination itself makes assumptions of value and relation which the mind is now not willing to allow, for fear of robbing any object of its objectivity; rather, the interest is in the results of a co-ordinating relation, as that may expose or alter. Modifications of place, time, and quality, in word, phrase, or clause, are pertinent, and indeed most commonly provide the setting of the characteristically simple statement.

Consider, for example, the structural simplicity and phrasal quality of Stevens' "Holiday in Reality," Part 2: the richness of reference, the constancy of short periods, the close confinement and depth of odd combination, the bodily presentation of man and nature to the sense, as if in declarative definition.

> The flowering Judas grows from the belly or not at all.
> The breast is covered with violets. It is a green leaf.
>
> Spring is umbilical or else it is not spring.
> Spring is the truth of spring or nothing, a waste, a fake.
>
> These trees and their argentines, their dark-spiced branches,
> Grow out of the spirit or they are fantastic dust.

> The bud of the apple is desire, the down-falling gold,
> The catbird's gobble in the morning half-awake—
>
> These are real only if I make them so. Whistle
> For me, grow green for me and, as you whistle and grow green,
>
> Intangible arrows quiver and stick in the skin
> And I taste at the root of the tongue the unreal of what is real.[2]

The poetic statement is characteristically thus declarative, in third and first person, in the 1940's. Frost is somewhat more complex in syntax, Pound more colloquially fragmentary, Williams and Moore more compact, Crane and Eliot and Sitwell more allusive and exclamatory; but these are shades of quality, the center of which has this solid pattern.

Notice the sound pattern also. Some in the decade are closer to the echo of speech; some have a longer liquid roll, or make more of external bounds of rhyme; but again, this arranged internal modification by sound is most moderately characteristic. Placing is important, as in sense. The initial sound in *breast* alliteratively confirms the startle of *belly* as flowering source, and the strong spondee of *green leaf* asserts as it presents. At the end of every unrhymed couplet, such a doublet of sound takes the place of rhyme in confirming the close— *waste, fake; fantastic dust;* and so on to the thematic *unreal, real.* As the tradition of couplet rhyme is adapted to phrasal stress, so blank verse, alliteration, and other repetitions are turned inward to accent sense. See, in comparison, the structure of an early thinking poet like Surrey ("Description of the Fickle Affections"):

> Such wayward ways hath Love, that most part in discord
> Our wills do stand, whereby our hearts but seldom do accord.
> Deceit is his delight, and to beguile and mock
> The simple hearts, which he doth strike with froward, diverse stroke.
> He causeth the one to rage with golden burning dart;
> And doth allay with leaden cold against the other's heart.

Or Jonson, "Against Jealousie":

> Wretched and foolish Jealousie,
> How cam'st thou thus to enter me?

---

[2] Reprinted from *Transport to Summer,* by permission of Alfred A. Knopf, Inc. Copyright by Wallace Stevens.

> I ne'er was of thy kind;
> Nor have I yet the narrow mind
>   To vent that poore desire,
> That others should not warme them at my fire,
>   I wish the Sun should shine
> On all men's Fruit, and flowers, as well as mine.

And Gray, "To Adversity":

> Daughter of Jove, relentless Power,
> Thou Tamer of the human breast,
> Whose iron scourge and tort'ring hour,
> The Bad affright, afflict the Best!
> Bound in thy adamantine chain
> The Proud are taught to taste of pain,
> And purple Tyrants vainly groan
> With pangs unfelt before, unpitied and alone.

And Arnold, "Religious Isolation":

> Children (as such forgive them) have I known,
> Ever in their own eager pastime bent
> To make the incurious bystander, intent
> On his own swarming thoughts, an interest own;
> Too fearful or too fond to play alone.
> Do thou, whom light in thine own inmost soul
> (Not less thy boast) illuminates, control
> Wishes unworthy of a man full-grown.
> What though the holy secret which moulds thee
> Moulds not the solid Earth? though never Winds
> Have whisper'd it to the complaining Sea,
> Nature's great law, and law of all men's minds?
>   To its own impulse every creature stirs:
>   Live by thy light, and Earth will live by hers.

These are all lines not extreme of their kind, but moderate as Stevens' are. They are alike as possible in their several ways, concerned with feeling as it conveys reality, using a measured, meditative beat, rhyming in couplets mainly, or quatrains, making serious statements of a general human theme. They are taken to represent not the strongest distinguishing characteristics of their respective eras, but the soberest continuity. Yet see, even so, how differently each speaks in sound and structure.

Surrey is working out a thought about love, and the measure of language is arduously bent to this thought. *Most part* is difficult to accent but is necessary to a reasonable sense; and *the one, the other,* while awkward to balance in sound, has an important balance in meaning. Apart from rhyme, the repetition of syllables works only in a little alliteration, of which "Deceit is his delight" is most successful in stressing love's duplicity. Hyperbole first in abstract state and then in concrete metaphor intensifies for us the nature of the emotion. The generalization is thoughtfully borne out through action and instance, through personification and imported sense, the logic developed with rhetorical consistency.

Jonson is easier; he takes the liberties of tradition and experience. First, he is more familiar, addresses his own personification of feeling, varies his line length and his tone, rhymes lightly, uses no set repetitions except in the last line, ends with a flourish; second, his question and abstract assertion he follows, like Surrey, with a metaphor, but a delicate transitional one, in "narrow" mind, which prepares without forcing the domain of fire and garden, the generous sharing of sun. The rhetorical development of reason is eased, but the process is still firm, the flexibility of both accent and personal argument working within the rational frame.

Gray has changed; he has submitted to tremendous emotion and scope, and his exclamatory mode is adapted not to the working out of thought but rather to the accumulating of qualities for passion. The address is invocative, the progress additive, with balance giving an effect of inclusiveness, and the heavy epithets, alliterations, and figures suiting substantially the substantial state of sensation. The participial constructions are characteristic, and the richly distributed syllables, the full vowels.

Arnold has accepted the literal, simple description of his era and turns it, as his era did, to symbolic account. His children, his man, his holy secret are considered at a pedestrian pace, the meter and rhyme deliberate, but varied into the light and shade of sonnet development, His deliberated instance is released, after the octave, into questions, freer syllables, natural objects, until the final couplet has, rather than the laboriousness of Surrey, the assurance of Jonson, in its assertion of individual light. The poem has not the lyrical smoothness and subtlety of Arnold's "Merman," but it is more consistent than many of his in its characteristic progression from narrated situation to lyrical spiritual release.

Out of all these modes, the mode of Stevens and his time has moved, toward harmony of vocal detail and visual detail, away from external orders of rhyme and meter in organization, and away from progression, toward presentation. There is continuity also: from the easy tone of Jonson, the open and reflective vowel patterns of Gray, the reportorial fidelity and sense of significance of Arnold. These qualities are altered as they come together. The easy speech, the sense of thought, are not now following a reasoning process. The richness is not so involved in ostensive emotion. The significance is not discovered, but made.

We see, then, how sound has informed sense. As argument and prayer in poetry have altered into exposition and invocation, and then to narrative and lyrical exclamation, and finally to declarative presentation, moving from second to first to third person, and from subjunctive imperative and exclamation to indicative declaration, sound has moved increasingly into the structure, from its boundaries. In its forms of measure, sound has lightened, giving up the regularities of the primary iambic foot for an increasing number of lighter dactyls and anapests in the nineteenth century, and many extra unaccented syllables in the twentieth. Measure is released from unaccent to accent alone, and even there is varied in amount and interval by the principle of placement which works for reference. In its forms of repetition, or rhyme, sound has lessened its marking of the ends of lines, lets one line move more imperceptibly or variously into another, but nevertheless preserves the line as unit by setting up a pattern of assonance and consonance within it. In its relation to structure, sound tends to comply, emphasizing phrasal interconnection. In its relation to sense, sound is neither so harmonized in onomatopoeia as in the eighteenth century, nor so melodized in expressiveness as in the nineteenth; it returns, as for some poetry in the nineteenth century, to the catching up of speech tones and accents, but, because of its phrasal sense, does so in more fragmentary fashion. Devoted to the quality of things, it yet creates some whole effect of the mind which perceives the things.

All the traits of language—sense, syntax, sound—have been modified by their concentrated association in poetry toward the ends of the poetry in its progress. Innovations of vocabulary, cadence, off-rhymes, assonantal patterns, have been delicate and gradual. Renovations, as of ballad measure, alliterative stress, roughened speech tones, have been turned directly to new uses, and so altered. Individual poets have at times adopted most thoroughly and consciously an old poetic mode, in which sound and meaning seem to be allied with a peculiarity suitable again in the new era to a personal need; but always the force of the contemporary mode to modify seems greater than that of the revived mode to persist.

The forces of language are apparently more interallied and more allied temporally than they are bound by school or by individual choice. The major terms and tones are definable rather by time than by type or person. The language which is the medium for the art is most readily describable as the language of general use; and even its most technical qualities of linear composition, setting it apart from prose, are closely conditioned by its qualities of syntax and reference.

Therefore, it is not only difficult to label the work of the present era by an old term like "romantic" or "metaphysical," when the old qualities have been turned to a new whole; it is even more difficult to think of groups or individuals in these special terms. Eliot calls himself classical; Winters calls him romantic. Younger poets like Thomas and Shapiro are called romantic or baroque. Even apart from the mixtures of meanings in the labels as they are applied, is there any good way to distinguish the endurance of schools or types in poetry into the 1940's?

Proportioning seems a useful basis, as it involves both structure and vocabulary. We have seen that the proportions in the 1940's vary from the 5A–8N–4V of Williams to the 15A–28N–16V of Jeffers, for both of which extremes some allowance must be made on the basis of line length. As a whole, there are three groups of poets in the period: those who, like Millay, Auden, Frost, Warren, and others, use a proportion of about 8–14–11, with more verbs than adjectives; those who, like Yeats, Stevens, Eliot, tend to balance adjectives and verbs at about 9–18–9; and those who, like Thomas and Sitwell, at about 10–23–8, use more adjectives than verbs, with a high number of nouns. For the first group the substantival dominance is 2 to 1; for the second, 3 to 1; for the third, 4 to 1.

The first group is similar in proportion to the Wyatt and Surrey group in the 1540's, to the Donne and Cowley group in the 1640's, to none in the 1740's, to the Emerson-Browning group in the 1840's. Knowing the general interests of all these poets, we may fairly call them all "metaphysical": they are active in thoughtful predication; they are least interested in substance and quality; they use the tones and the roughnesses of speech; their vocabulary deals with the double, the physical and metaphysical, values of man and God.

Then the second group, from Yeats to Spender, we may fairly call "romantic." These poets carry on the balanced mode which came into being after, not during and not before, the 1740's, and which found its first expression in the poetry of Wordsworth, Bryant, Long-fellow, Poe, Arnold, Clough. These poets maintain a lyrical poise between modification and predication; they are devoted to quality as few sixteenth- or seventeenth-century poets were, but they are also devoted to meditation upon that quality; they are literal, common-place, domestic in observation, but lofty and allusive in conclusion. They work in storied scene as well as in speech, and make it romantic as they make it fictive.

The third group, finally, has its fullest sources in the 1740's. Crane, Sitwell, Shapiro, Thomas, like their predecessors Hemans and Camp-bell, Keble and Lowell, and the later Wordsworth, draw from the full and general descriptive abundance of the eighteenth century, and before that from the stores of Dryden, Crashaw, Waller, Milton, back to Spenser. They are the smoothest of poets, most concerned with the flow of the verse, the harmony of onomatopoeia, the pleasure of open vowels and liquid consonants. They are, in addition, the most picturing of poets, the most brilliant with image. Theirs is the aesthetic of direct sense, rather than of form or relationship. The planes of reference are simplified, the gods treated as personification, unlikenesses brought to similitude, symbol enjoyed in its quality and substance. Whether such poetry is rightly to be called "classical," I cannot tell without further knowledge of classical practice itself, and of earlier eighteenth-century decades. A truer sort of classicism may be expressed in the full balance of Shakespeare and Dryden than in the qualitative emphasis of the line from Spenser through Waller and Milton, Pope and Collins, to Lowell. But much Virgilian and Ovidian practice is of this sort, and it seems not misleading to think of it as a version of neoclassicism at least, foreign as it may seem to the common definitions.

Granting, then, that the 1940's may have drawn one order of poetry from the dominantly metaphysical 1540's and 1640's, another from the dominantly neoclassical eighteenth century, and a third and strongest from the dominantly romantic nineteenth, in a sense we are no one of these, but must take some new label for the combination we have arrived at. Further, no one of these major proportions brings with it the whole of its poetic language. Some of the major terms, and the sound and sentence patterns, as we have seen, do not survive together. The neoclassical couplet, for example, and descriptive blank verse and soaring ode, are lost to Shapiro and Thomas, though both, in the tradition of this mode, do preserve more external measure and rhyme than is common in our time. Alteration in new context is everywhere visible. A few words representative of type, like the meta-physical *good,* the neoclassical *head,* the romantic *light,* persist to distinguish the groups, but no group maintains a solid block of in-herited vocabulary of its own. Nor does an individual poet. The least conforming to the practice of their period are Marianne Moore and H. D. and Pound. But these are all eccentric as they accentuate one or another of the period's emphases; that is, they go further into specialization, as Cleveland did in his day, rather than back into an earlier mode. Of no single poet can it be said that he is closer to another period than to his own, in his choice of language. His time defines him better than his type.

We learn of this time, the 1940's, that its interest in objective truth and subjective interpretation determines its language and distinguishes its poetry from that of other centuries. We learn that the sound, the structure, the vocabulary are interallied, and allied to the concept of truth in art which makes for specific objects and qualities in interacting juxtaposition, for tonal pattern, for phrasal presentation, for a moderation of both verbs and adjectives in favor of nouns, for a laden and ordered cadence in which mind observes things and considers them. We may speak, through poetic language, of a strong homogeneity in the poetry of the 1940's.

At the same time, we may define the diversities of the period as they bear upon the likenesses. The most individualistic contribution is one of specification, of carrying further into particular detail the interests of the whole. Or, in another sense, the individualism of Yeats, rather than of Pound for example, is one of integration, the inclusion and ordering of more than a usual number of the materials of the whole, in profounder relationship. The "wildness" of Yeats, the concreteness of Williams, the fragmentary irony of Pound, the anatomy of Thomas, lead us, further, to the modes in which they participate. They bring some of the vocabulary and some of the tone of other poetries into the 1940's: romantic symbolism, classical simile, metaphysical metaphor, into twentieth-century context. They show how poetic convention functions, first by enduring emphases (the five-accented meditation upon the love of man); second, by direct continuity (the nineteenth century's lyric atmosphere); third, by minor survivals and reconsiderations (the metaphysical argument, the eighteenth-century sense); fourth, by the reordering and thus the modifying of all these into a newly varied mode.

Language, the medium of the poem, is not the whole. Through the nature of its sound and meaning speaks the idea of the poet, and that idea is the greater whole. Only in the single poem in its fullest working of attitude through material does poetry come to be directly known. The abstraction which this study has made, the abstraction of the material from the intent, and of the most elementary traits of sound and structure from the whole complex character of language, can have therefore at best an indirect and provisional virtue for the reading of contemporary poetry. But its direction toward at least a partial self-knowledge should be perceivable. Some twenty leading poets of our day, idiosyncratic as they seem, eccentric in relation to each other and, as a group, to their present and their past, are, in the view of their major materials, not so separate after all. Jeffers and Millay share much significance; Frost and Auden span an ocean and a generation in their meditative concern. The linear experiments of Williams, H. D., Sitwell, the syntactical experiments of Cummings, the phrasal experiments of Pound, the reversions of Eliot and Warren, the elastic conventions of Shapiro, all are versions of a shared concern. And the concern is shared too with other writers of the time, with novelists, biographers, journalists, essayists; the concern speaks in the language of the time and of times past as they pertain.

The study of materials does not indicate to us that a poet has special interests to convey. Rather, it indicates that he speaks in the common interest, in terms of the commonest materials. These concepts, objects, qualities, actions he emphasizes and formalizes, trying, in all ways of measure, stress, tone, order that he knows, to make them memorable.

THE CONTINUITY OF ENGLISH POETIC
LANGUAGE

UPON THE assumption that the five decades of the 'forties may represent their respective five centuries, as the thousand lines of twenty poets in each of these decades represent the poets and their eras, one may base some brief and tentative generalizations about the nature and development of English poetic usage.

Most generally, one may assert the homogeneity of five centuries of practice and at the same time the details of singularity. None of the hundred poets seems to work outside the frame of the whole; he always has companions. But none is close to complete likeness to any other, even in major vocabulary, or even in proportioning, which is necessarily limited by the capacities of the poetic line and the common sentence structure.

Second, one may note that groupings of poets are based more solidly on time than on type. Each decade has its own homogeneity, though each has a different degree of heterogeneity. There is, moreover, a clear direction of development from one century to another, not a mere moving back and forth of tendencies. This directional force is what alters type and revises it to temporal ends. A type does prevail and progress, but as it progresses it seems to merge with other types into the specific mode of the new day, and therefore is only partly recognizable, in new shape.

Rearrangements within time and type are flexible because of the adjustability of the various characteristics of the medium used. The sound, reference, and sentence structure of language may not all change at once or in regular parallel, but may make numerous small changes in interrelation. Internal proportions may be stabilized, as external controls decline; sound in qualitative reflection may take over some of the function of qualification by epithet. The stresses and strains of material seem to alter and readjust themselves to new modes of thought and feeling.

The table of proportions (table A) shows even at one glance the

TABLE A

PROPORTIONS: ADJECTIVES–NOUNS–VERBS

1540's (7-15-11)	1640's (8-15-10)	1740's (12-19-9)	1840's (10-17-9)	1940's (9-18-9)
Skelton 4-10-7				Williams 5-8-4
Sternhold 4-11-8				
Breton 5-11-8				
Googe 5-12-9				
Ballads 6-13-11				
Turberville 5-13-10				
Langland 6-21-18				
Lindsay 6-13-9	Harvey 6-12-10			Cummings 6-11-7
	Suckling 6-13-12			H. D. 6-13-6
Lydgate 6-16-9	Wither 7-14-11			
	Jonson 6-14-12			
	Donne 7-13-12			Millay 8-13-11
Wyatt 7-12-11	Vaughan 7-13-9			
	Cowley 7-13-11			
	Shirley 7-14-11			
	Herrick 7-13-11		Landor 8-16-12	Auden 8-16-10
Chaucer 7-15-11	Denham 7-15-9		Emerson 7-15-8	
Surrey 7-18-13	Cleveland 7-17-10		Macaulay 7-15-7	R. Lowell 7-21-10
Baldwin 7-20-12				Frost 8-15-11
	Lovelace 8-13-10			Manifold 8-17-11
Douglas 8-18-9	Carew 8-15-11		R. Browning 8-16-12	Warren 8-18-11
Gascoigne 9-18-12	Sandys 8-17-9		E. Browning 8-16-10	Pound 7-20-6
Barclay 8-22-12				
			Clough 9-13-9	Yeats 9-16-9
			Arnold 9-15-9	Moore 9-17-6
			Poe 9-16-8	

Heywood	9-17-15			
Sackville	9-18-10			
Shakespeare	10-17-10			
Spenser	12-16-11			

Dryden	10-16-10
Quarles	10-17-13
Crashaw	10-18-11
Waller	11-19-10
Milton	12-16-8
More	12-18-10

Cooke	9-21-11
Gray	10-17-8
Akenside	10-17-8
Young	10-20-10
Johnson	9-21-10
Blair	11-17-9
Blacklock	11-18-9
Montagu	11-18-12
Walpole	11-19-9
Pope	11-22-10
Collins	12-17-9
Mason	12-18-10
Lyttelton	10-17-9
Shenstone	12-19-11
J. Warton	13-19-8
Dyer	13-17-8
Armstrong	15-18-9
Thomson	15-18-7
T. Warton	15-19-8
Somerville	17-19-8

Hawker	9-18-9
Bryant	9-17-9
Longfellow	9-19-10
Hood	10-14-6
Tennyson	10-14-6
Campbell	10-21-12
Keble	11-16-8
Wordsworth	11-19-9
Horne	12-13-9
Lowell	12-19-11
Hemans	13-20-9
Tupper	13-30-15

Spender	9-18-9
Stevens	9-19-10
Eliot	9-19-8
Crane	10-20-8
Shapiro	10-?
Thomas	10-23-8
Sitwell	10-23-9
Jeffers	16-28-16

separate characters of eras. The 1540's were, as Chaucer had been, and as the ballads had been, centered in a mode of 5–12–10 or 7–15–11, a roughly 1–2–2 proportion, scant in substantive forms and probably proportionately strong in connectives. Theirs was a verse of fairly laborious thinking process, a language of logic more than names. Gascoigne and Sackville notably moved toward greater richness, toward the era of Spenser which a later decade would define.

In the 1640's, poetry consolidated at two mid-points: at Donne, Jonson, and Cowley's following of Wyatt and Surrey, and at Dryden and Milton's use of the Shakespeare, Spenser tradition. The relative subordination of this mode turned in the 1740's to a total domination of about 12–19–9, with even further extensions to almost 2–2–1, by half a dozen poets. By the 1840's the adjectival mode was spread out, varied, and tempered, a transitional poet like Bryant striking the average, and new poets like Lowell on the one hand and Emerson or the Brownings on the other renewing the eighteenth century or carrying it back to the metaphysical poets of the seventeenth century. The young majority gathered at a new center, about 9–17–9, or 1–2–1; and the 1940's made even further consolidation at this middle point, moving a little away from eighteenth century toward seventeenth, as its predecessor had done.

We see, then, a fairly steady rise toward an extreme, marked by adjectival quantity, and then a slower decline, moving toward moderation and not far beyond it, not back to the starting point. Each decade has made a different sort of contribution: the 1540's, variety of predication; the 1640's, the consolidation of two separate types, predicative and qualitative; the 1740's, the consolidation and furtherance of the single mode, the qualitative; the 1840's, innovation of a new central mode, unlike almost any preceding, working between extremes; and the 1940's, consolidation of this innovation.

The basis of the table primarily in adjectival quantity establishes three groups: 7 adjectives or less, sixteenth and seventeenth; 11 or more, eighteenth; 8–10, nineteenth and twentieth. Further, the basis is in the main more than adjectival, because certain proportions tend to work together: first, seventeenth century, 1–2–2; then eighteenth, 2–2–1; then nineteenth and twentieth, 1–2–1. Through this simplification of proportion we see another aspect of the tendency toward balance. Adjectives and nouns first rose, while verbs declined; then, in the nineteenth century, adjectives and nouns decreased while verbs were constant. Now, in the twentieth century, a balance between adjectives and verbs is set up, but on a foundation of nouns again increased. Nouns, which have long been most stable in proportion, may now be due to change, toward such a pattern as Robert Lowell's 1–3–1.

Balance itself may be considered a kind of mode, and we may see traces of it through the centuries: in Sackville and Shakespeare; in Dryden, Crashaw, Waller; in Young, Johnson, Pope, and others; in Emerson, Macaulay, Clough, Arnold, Poe, Hawker, Bryant, Longfellow, Campbell, Lowell; in Williams, Cummings, H. D., Yeats, Stevens, Eliot, Shapiro, Sitwell, Jeffers: its force for modern verse is patent. Modern verse seeks not only a mid-point in historical practice, but also a literal point of balance which it seems to have derived from a somewhat richer and fuller classicism. Most out of balance, the ballads, Langland, Suckling, Jonson, Milton, Thomson, Warton, Somerville, Landor, Hood, Tennyson, Millay and Moore in lesser degree, represent either a special form much used and established for certain purposes, or a kind of innovation which will later be tempered, as the *Lyrical Ballads,* especially Wordsworth's, tempered to qualification the strong predication of the fifteenth-century stories.

In the process of changing and then stabilizing and then changing again, the table of proportions shows the poetry of the 1940's at a point of stability. It is a point taken straight from the nineteenth century and further emphasized; and it is a point which was itself innovative, distinguishing recent balance of forms from the two strong imbalances of earlier centuries. The present mode is different from, yet participating almost equally in, the two modes of the past.

Reading horizontally, we get no such clear view of type as of time. We can see, first, the Wyatt and Donne tradition in Cummings and

Millay; second, the less spare metaphysical tradition in Landor, Emerson, Auden; third, Sackville and Shakespeare as nineteenth- and twentieth-century predecessors; and fourth, the line of Spenser, now lessened. Each one of these not very persisting lines undergoes much alteration by its mere passage through time, for vocabulary alters, and sound modulates. Millay uses a vocabulary of nature and an easy lyrical suggestion foreign to Donne's argument. Collins moved the noble world of Spenser out into the fields of imagination. Eliot sharpens and heightens Longfellow. Nevertheless, the lines of inheritance have meaning as they suggest basic modes of thought. The Herrick, Landor, Auden line is such a one, with its sharp delivery of accepted thought; or the Baldwin, Lowell, with its world's estate; or the Carew, Browning, Manifold, with its vigor; or the Bryant, Longfellow, Stevens, Eliot; or the Crashaw, Young, Crane, Shapiro, and Thomas line of rich meditation; or Horne's representation of Keats' Miltonism; or the scrutinizing moral observations of Thomson, Tupper, and Jeffers, in their plenitude.

Sound pattern and sentence show us the transformations these modes have undergone. For Auden, Herrick's stanza has loosened and at the same time become sonorously complicated, more out in the world, speaking less its author's tones. The awkwardness of Robert Lowell seems more conscious and objective than the awkwardness of Baldwin. The intricacy of Crashaw and the scope of Young have been turned outward; the explicitness of Thomson's and Tupper's interpretations turned to the solidity of rock. As sentence patterns have grown external, away from first- and second-person exclamation and argument toward third-person declaration, sound has grown internal in the line, away from metrical foot and end rhyme toward cadence and inner repetition. So even the most external of formalizers, like Frost and Shapiro, use patterns more inward than would have suited their type in the past.

The summary table of the approximately 150 words most used in poetry through five centuries (table B) shows a similar yet varying pattern of development. While each century has a characteristic set of terms, two lines of progressive change are visible: one in the number of terms agreed upon by the poets, reaching its height in the 1840's; and the other in the content or reference of the terms, which grows more externally particular straight through the 1940's. To the tendencies of proportion toward centering the sixteenth- and eighteenth-century extremes, and to the tendencies of sound and structure steadily more inward, we must add the tendencies of reference steadily outward, the 1940's narrowing and consolidating the most various agreement of the 1840's.

We see, then, that change is not a simple line, because different constituents of the poetry move with different speeds and emphases, as they make adjustments to each other. As extremes of predication or qualification are moderated, other extremes of substantial reference and internal order are reached. The nineteenth century, as it subsided from the peak of eighteenth-century qualification, picked up other variations in sound and reference both old and new, providing the full reservoir from which a more concentrating twentieth century could select the special elements of internal sound and external sense.

Note the table itself. The first column under each date is the column of majority usage: words used 10 times or more in 1,000 lines by each of ten poets or more in the decade. The second column represents use by at least four poets. The 150 words on the page therefore are the words agreed on for primary use by at least four poets of one decade, and only a few of them are limited to one decade, since most persist. Adjectives and verbs are equal in number; nouns, twice as many; as in proportioning, a balance in variety has been reached through the centuries. Italicizing represents the first appearance of the word on a majority list, or on a minority list preceding majority. It will be noted that the 1540's provided some 10 adjectives, 24 nouns, 19 verbs for primary use, and that these were, as a whole, terms of human station and relation. Of this material, the 1640's preserved most except the negatives of *cruel, fortune,* and *woe,* strengthened many of the minority terms to majority, and added major oppositions like *earth* and *heaven,* with lesser ones in quality, anatomy, and expressive ap-

TABLE B

Primary Vocabulary in Five Centuries: Majority and Minority

1540's Maj.	1540's Min.	1640's Maj.	1640's Min.	1740's Maj.	1740's Min.	1840's Maj.	1840's Min.	1940's Maj.	1940's Min.
good	*cruel*	fair	*bright*	fair	*divine*	bright	*dark*	*little*	*black*
great	*dear*	good	*dark*	great	*gay*	good	*dear*	*old*	*dark*
	fair	great	*full*	*soft*	*happy*	old	*deep*	*white*	*dead*
	high	sweet	*happy*	sweet	*new*	sweet	*dim*		good
	old		*high*		*proud*	long	*fair*		great
	poor		*new*		*tender*		*golden*		green
	sweet		*old*		*vain*		*great*		long
	true		*poor*				*happy*		new
			rich				*high*		*young*
			true				*holy*		
							human		
							little		
							mighty		
							poor		
							proud		
							soft		
							strong		
							true		
							white		
							wild		
							wise		

1540's Maj.	1540's Min.	1640's Maj.	1640's Min.	1740's Maj.	1740's Min.	1840's Maj.	1840's Min.	1940's Maj.	1940's Min.
day	*beauty*	day	*blood*	*air*	*art*	day	*air*	day	air
God	*death*	earth	*death*	day	*beauty*	earth	*beauty*	*death*	*bird*
heart	*eye*	eye	*face*	eye	*breast*	eye	*breast*	eye	child
king	*fortune*	God	*fire*	*friend*	*fate*	God	*child*	God	dream
life	*gold*	heart	*grace*	God	*flower*	hand	*death*	hand	earth
lord	*hand*	heaven	*hand*	hand	*head*	heart	*dream*	*head*	face
love	*heaven*	love	*king*	heart	*hour*	heaven	*father*	heart	heaven
man	*lady*	man	*life*	heaven	*king*	life	*flower*	life	*leaf*
thing	*mind*	soul	*name*	*joy*	*land*	light	*friend*	light	moon
time	*night*	time	*nature*	life	*maid*	love	*hope*	love	*nothing*
	pain		*night*	love	*mind*	man	*hour*	man	sea

sky
stone
thought
tree
water
wind
word

die
find
grow
live
look
love
seem
speak
stand
think

---

mind
night
sun
thing
time
world

come
fall
give
go
hear
know
lie
make
see
take

---

joy
king
Lord
maid
mind
mother
nature
power
prayer
sea
sky
song
star
thing
youth

bring
feel
find
live
seem
sing
speak
stand
tell

---

night
soul
spirit
sun
thought
time
word
world

come
fall
give
go
hear
know
lie
look
love
make
rise
see
take
think

---

muse
name
night
scene
sky
song
thought
time
virtue
world

bear
behold
call
die
find
fly
love
make
stand
take
tell
think

---

man
nature
power
soul
youth

come
give
hear
know
rise
see

---

part
power
sin
son
sun
tear
thing
world
year

appear
call
die
fall
fly
grow
hear
keep
lie
live
look
love
shine
show
sing
seem
speak
stand
weep

bring
come
find
give
go
know
make
see
take
tell
think

---

woe
word
world

bring
die
hear
lie
look
love
seek
show
speak

come
find
give
go
know
make
see
take
tell
think

pearance. The eighteenth century minimized a great many adjectives and verbs by then traditional, and focused on its own qualities, its nouns of person and scene. The nineteenth century, not content with these specializations, renewed many seventeenth-century terms, so that the body of shared material was increased to twice that with which it began. Color and size and time were particularized, nouns of nature and family, and receptive verbs. All these the twentieth century reduced somewhat, removing generalities of feeling and atmosphere and human relation, and stressing more particular color and size, smaller objects, drawing back *thing* and *mind* from earlier centuries.

The continuity seems gradual and regular. Words used by a majority in one decade are usually drawn from the minority usage of the preceding century. In only 10 of 32 innovations by the majority is there no precedent minority appearance, and 6 of these are in the eighteenth century, a fact which suggests perhaps that more variation was going on between the 1640's and 1740's than later. The metaphysical poets created the force of *earth* and *soul;* the romantics, *light* and *spirit;* the rest are the eighteenth century's: *soft, air, friend, joy, youth, rise,* a characterizing list for which we see least evidence of preparation. Like the usual preparation, the discarding too is gradual, almost every majority term declining through the next century's minority before it disappears. Minority terms are less stable, at least 50 of them, or a third of the whole tabulation, appearing only once. Another third keeps to common minority usage. The rest reach major agreement. About 100 terms, then, half nouns, half adjectives and verbs, are so strong in their time and so persistent through time as to characterize the fullest referential vocabulary of English poetry.

What is the general nature of these words? They are monosyllabic, with the exceptions of *heaven, nature, power, spirit, little.* They range through all degrees of abstraction and concreteness. They provide a number of easy rhymes and echoes: *great, sweet, night; fair, dear, hear; lord, word; love, give, live, high, eye; find, mind; king, thing; look, seek, speak; woe, go, know; sweet, bright, night; face, grace; call, fall; eye, fly; hear, tear* in the early centuries; *fair, air, bear; eyes, rise; great, fate; flower, hour, power; hand, land, stand* in the eighteenth; and in recent years, *bright, light, white, night; old, gold; head, dead; mind, find; mother, father; sky, lie; sea, tree; sun, moon, stone; dream, seem.* No large change in type of sound seems apparent; the long *i* is consistently strong; initial sounds like final ones are various.

Since the words do not seem to be in themselves any special type, either of form, source, reference, or sound, we cannot consider them an especially "poetic" vocabulary. That is, there seems nothing in the formal demands of poetry which conditions their choice except their simplicity in form and familiarity in meaning, which are criteria for prose and speech also. Indeed, the present-day word-frequency lists, compiled by Thorndike, Dewey, Eaton, and others, show among the words of highest frequency now in common use all of the 100 major poetic terms and most of the 150. Primary English poetic vocabulary is therefore primary English prose vocabulary also, the simple, lasting terms of interest and value.

Thorndike's list of the 2,500 words of "most wide and frequent occurrence" (*The Teacher's Word Book*, 1921, pp. 127 ff.) shows even in its first 500 the force of the terms of poetry. Of these 500, about 100 are the connectives, pronouns, adverbs, articles, which are distinguished from terms of reference. Another 100 are the very common auxiliaries of the verb *to be, to have, to do,* the various verb forms, and the limiting modifiers like *all, some, no, many,* which we have counted for quantity but not listed for reference. Of the remaining 300, the clearest terms of reference, 100 are the terms of poetry. The other 200 words, less active in poetry, are, in example, *answer, apple, arm, bad, ball, bank, beautiful, bed, begin, believe, big, blow, blue, body, book, box, boy, bread, brother, build, burn, buy, carry, case, cause, certain, change, church, city, clear, close, cold, color, company, country, cover, cross, cut, door, draw, dress, drink, drive, drop, ear, east, eat, egg, end, family, fear, feet, field, fine, floor, follow, food, form, free, fresh, garden, general, girl, glad, ground, hair, hard, heavy, help, hill, hold, home, horse, hot, house, kill, kind, large, late, laugh, law, lead, learn, leave, length, letter, line, low, mark, matter, mean, measure, meet, might, mile, milk, miss, money, mouth, morning, mountain, move,* and so on. I do not see that this is a vocabulary differing deeply from that stressed in poetry. There seems much potential poetry here also. Perhaps the many words beginning with *b* and *m,* and later *p* and *r* and especially *s,* indicate some selection by sound of which I am unaware. Or perhaps, since this is a frequency list for the twentieth century, these terms ignored by poetry in its history are the more modern, the ones just growing into poetic power. Many are already primary for a number of poets in the 1940's. At any rate, I find no clear split in kind between the primary vocabulary of poetry and the primary vocabulary of modern language in which it is fully included.

Time does have some importance in determining those few words which have once been primary for poetry but which are not among the first 1,000 for present prose. These are the terms which appear in only one decade, as used by a minority: *cruel, fortune, woe,* and *seek* in the 1540's; *appear* in the 1640's; *youth, divine, gay, tender, vain, breast, fate, maid, muse, scene, virtue, behold* in the 1740's; *dim, holy, human, prayer* in the 1840's; *leaf* in the 1940's. Most of these represent the extremes in major usage of the decade's special character: the negative sense of fate in the 1540's, the emotional scene of the 1740's, the spiritual suggestiveness of the 1840's, our own particularity. From the point of view of usage today, the eighteenth century is clearly most special, the classical emotions and personages most out of date, carrying to our ears, therefore, a lingering sense of past poetry. But we have not frequency lists for the prose of the past by which to make a check on the currencies of the past.[1]

The reader may suggest that if the primary language of poetry is the primary language of prose as it is tabulated in the twentieth century, the material is inevitable, not a matter of choice, and so not useful in any way in defining the poetry. But, first, the very identity is useful in showing that poetry is not to be set apart from prose in its

---

[1] But see Diederich's *Frequency of Latin Words* for 300 most frequent in Latin prose and verse. About 60 of these are paralleled in table B.

major materials; and second, the relative smallness of the poetic selection, and its variation from century to century, from poet to poet, shows that choice is made, that emphasis is established, that certain reference is considered most worthy of design and most fit for it.

Further, this selectivity itself is related more closely to the use of language, the changing choices in language, than to the limitations of poetic practice. The word books, the word-frequency lists, which have been made in the past few years all tend to substantiate the point which Godfrey Dewey made explicitly in his *Relativ Frequency of English Speech Sounds,* 1923 (p. 133): "The outstanding feature of this study is the degree to which a comparatively small part of the commoner words, syllables, or sounds of English form by their frequent repetitions, a large part of our ordinary speech." Of 100,000 words of representative writing, he has found that the 10 or so most frequent make up 25 per cent of the total; 100, about 50 per cent; 1,000 (more than 10 times apiece), about 75 per cent. Einar Haugen in *Norwegian Word Studies* (1942) found in representative Scandinavian works that the leading 10 different words make 22 per cent of the total of different words, and 100, 60 per cent. Yule found much the same for Latin and English literary prose, in his *Statistical Study of Literary Vocabulary,* 1944. Edmund Andrews reports from Zipf's studies of telephone conversations a proportional use of 6A–10N–5V among leading terms, which is very like the balance in poetry, especially since Zipf included adverbs with adjectives, so accounting for a little heavier emphasis. At least, evidence points to a selective emphasis in speech and prose which is similar, quantitatively, qualitatively, and proportionally, to the selectivity of poetry. The one may well establish and include the other.

Two more specific word books provide specific exemplification, one in the poetry of another language, one in the language of another form, narrative prose. W. T. Bandy's *Word Index to Baudelaire's Poems,* 1939, besides quoting Baudelaire on the poetic import of a few frequent terms, presents those terms, *œil, cœur, beau, ciel, âme, plein, noir, amour, nuit, soleil, vieux, soir, connaître, esprit,* and so on, which, as we

have seen, are very close to the most characteristic English primary
poetic words of the same period, mid-nineteenth century, so that we
may speculate upon the possible extensions in space of such vocabulary. Miles L. Hanley's *Word Index to James Joyce's Ulysses,* 1939,
shows that the most frequent 100 words of this supposedly strange
prose are not only like Godfrey Dewey's first 100 of common language,
with the exception of some 20 proper names and such, but are also like
their contemporaries in poetry, with their special emphasis on *old, see,
man, time, eyes, hand, little, know, come.* From most counts available,
then, we gather both the dominance of time over type and the participation of poetic choice in the general choices of language.

Turning back to the table of primary terms of five centuries, we may
see that, slight as it looks, it is rich also. The words represent choice so
constant and repeated that it makes for a strong proportion of the
whole. If the leading 100 words in 100,000 make 50 per cent, or more,
of all, then in the 100,000 words which each decade here represents,
the primary words, from about 50 to 90, may make at least 30 per cent
of all.

These, it must be remembered, are words agreed upon by at least
four poets of a decade. In each decade are also 100 terms or more upon
which fewer than four poets agree, but which are primary, used 10
times or more by some one poet at least. In all, there are roughly 200
primary terms in each decade, without any great variation between
decades, and with, as we have seen, a good deal of continuity from one
to the next, so that the total number of primary terms for all five is
only about 500: 150 agreed on by majority or minority, 350 close to
individual.

Of these 350 words, 215 are literally individual, stressed by only one
poet of the 100 poets observed. We see, then, how much emphasis is
steadily personal, in each decade. Another 122 words are shared, in
one, two, or even three decades, and there are 8 terms, *false, gentle,
sad, ear, tongue, truth, way, sit,* which may be distinguished because,
though they are never stressed by a minority, they persist in some importance through at least four centuries.

The total 500 words of primary usage in 100,000 lines of verse through five centuries are, in other words, about half individual, half shared. And of the half shared, less than a half again, or about 100, are so strong in interest for poetic choice that they persist not only from one poet to another in one decade, but from one century to another. These are our inheritance of "poetic" language, and they are our inheritance of prosaic language as well. If analogies between prose and poetry proportions are warrantable, these main words by their repetition make up at least a third of all different nouns, adjectives, verbs used in the poetry. They provide a substantial portion of the stuff of which poetry is made.

Another substantial portion we have not looked at. This, made up of the most frequent pronouns, adverbs, connectives, the "logical" aspects of language, rather than the referential, probably varies its proportional relation to the referential from poet to poet and from time to time. Certainly it is the sort of language of least interest to critics today, and probably subordinate in our verse. Such terms as *or, and, if, because* are condensed to "the crisis of the object," in surrealist terms, the placing of opposites, the merging of unlikes, or the hazard of a juxtaposition where there is no room for prepositional interpretation. Though I have followed the present fashion, in observing referential rather than logical terms, I think that some view of the latter is provided by proportion itself. That is, it seems possible to surmise, granting a fair stability of line length, that the most substantival poetry has least room for predications and connections; that the substantival eighteenth century, for example, is not strongly logical. Its fame for "reason" rises not from the logical relations stated and argued in the verse, not from hypothesis and subordination, but from the power of generalization, as that is based on qualities, drawn out and balanced. So, in our own day, the process of thought is less important than the state of mind; and relation, at least for many poets and critics, subordinate to "transformation."

Limiting adjectives, those of number, amount, degree, like *some, all, one, many,* are closest of all the terms here observed to logical terms, and they have shown a decline through the five centuries. At the same time, participial adjectives, which reduce logical subordinations, have increased, while simple descriptive adjectives have maintained a regular proportion through the centuries. The relation of participial to limiting forms therefore is an additional clue to the relation of the referential terms we have observed to the connective terms we have assumed, and it bears out the idea that a style of substantial reference, like the eighteenth century's and ours, is especially weak in logical terminology. In the sixteenth and seventeenth centuries, the ratio of kinds of adjectives was about 20 per cent limiting, 20 per cent participial, 60 per cent descriptive. Just a few individual poets, like Marlowe, Fletcher, Cleveland, Sandys, Milton, moved toward the greater emphasis on participials which was to characterize the 1740's: the proportion of 10–30–60 per cent. This reduction of numerical limiting terms to a mere 10 per cent has persisted ever since, and indeed has been carried almost to a vanishing point by extremists from Thomson, Dyer, and the Wartons to Williams, Lowell, Crane, Shapiro, Thomas, as participial, especially present-participial, modification has increased for some of these to 40 per cent or more.

This is a minor point of language, but a significant one as it indicates a certain consistency in style in the whole of language, as well as in the parts we have undertaken most closely to observe. If the most adjectival and the most substantival poets tend to use not only fewest verbs but also fewest of those very adjectives which are closest to logical connection, then we may surmise that the whole language of connection and explicit interrelation will be a more important vocabulary for predicative poets than for the others; the strong use of adjectives of limitation is a simple clue to the distinguishing of type. We may be led further, too, from this distinction, into a consideration of the resources of English. The predicative style may be less classical than a substantial one, as it makes use of more native particles of connection. Certainly the best-known classical poets, Ovid, Virgil, Homer, Pindar, Horace, correspond more closely in proportional usage to the "classical" poets of the 1740's than to others. Dryden, when he asked specifically for fewer words and richer ones (Pref. to *Aeneid*), meant nouns and adjectives, not the English small particles which seemed to him unpoetic, as apparently from our usage they seem to us unpoetic today.

These speculations about language as a whole lead us past the bounds of our investigation, but they have the virtue of suggesting the close connections as well as the boundlessness of inquiry. We should need more word books, more studies of common usage, more interlanguage comparisons, more descriptive observations of art and language of every sort, before we could make any full attempt to characterize poetry's use of its medium, or people's use of poetry. In specific reference to my studies of primary vocabulary in structural context through five decades, we should need, the reader must be reminded, more proof of the justness of representation, more checking of the accuracies of count, more extension into other poets and decades, more deepening into quality of vocabulary and device, more examination of stresses other than quantitative. The study through all its course has been most tentative. It has undertaken by one narrow and concentrated line of observation to trace a relationship between the general nature of language and the specific nature of poetic language: poetry's sorts of formal selection from the social emphases of language, and the continuity of the relation. However tentative are the methods and the conclusions, the importance of the inquiry seems to me sure, if we wish to understand our thought and art.

In concluding this series of studies of poetic language in five centuries, I should like, as a sort of afterword, to assert again the provisional quality of the work and the care of those who have helped with it. From those friends and students who counted and checked the counts of words, to those committees, of the University of California and of the Guggenheim Foundation, who financed such chores, and to those participators in speculation and patient readers of a struggling prose who have helped argue the problems of method and pertinence, there is such a range of names and aids that I cannot list them. Beyond the Berkeley names, moreover, are those of the Bibliography, of scholars known mainly through their books, of critics debated mainly by implication.

My interest has been in the similarities, rather than the differences, of poetic practice, and so has run counter to much of the best work done in our time. I have asked, not what sets one poem or poet apart from another, not what distinguishes a style, not what separates poetry from prose, but rather, what in frequency and abundance most centers and joins. Such observation, among the close scrutinies of our day, is apt to seem superficial. At the same time, its quantitative aspect, its attention to frequency, appears to be mechanical and pettishly unliterary.

Most readers of one or another of the studies in proof have been troubled by what seems to them a great gap between the tables and the prose continuity of analysis. The few main words of the tables do not make the quoted poems what they are, nor do they give very new views of the periods they represent. Much is said that has been said before, and what is newly counted might well have been guessed. But this is just my interest, in a sense to record the obvious, to indicate how much general obviousness and commonness as well as how much subtlety there is in poetry. I do not quote poems to reveal new entities, but rather to repeat, over and over, the main lines of agreements in the various forms they take, the recurring *God* and *man* in declarative pentameters, as they are successively combined with *good* and *lord* in argument, with *nature* and *power* in exclamation, with *light* and *spirit* in symbolic suggestion, with *time* and *mind* in arranged association. Such a procedure assumes a certain amount of stability in language, a persistence in the meanings of *man* and *God* which allows their careers to be traced. Of course a twentieth-century *God* is not the same word as a sixteenth-century *God;* but there is enough likeness to make comparison possible; and indeed much of the very significant difference between them is to be seen in the comparison of contexts: the God of soul, the God of mind.

Moreover, the obvious, to-be-guessed continuities need still to be seen in the shades of their combination. They are so open, so basic to every poem that without some arbitrary isolation they are difficult to observe. Those qualities of artistic emphasis which are marked by accents of form like the frame, the focus, the climax, the rhyme, by singular and accented choice, most vividly meet the attention; the characteristics which continue and underlie, which by very mass and repetition may subordinate themselves, are the more apt in the long run to pervade attention. Quantity is not alien to art. In its form of repetition it is a primary organizing as well as substantiating force. Art uses quantity just as it uses quality, to make the effect it chooses. If the form of exclamation is used just once by a poet, and then in a position of great emphasis, that is one effect. If exclamation is used steadily and frequently throughout the verse, that is another effect. If the poet once exclaims *day!* there is one quality. If he uses *day* in sentence after sentence, there is another. If most frequent *day* appears in poems where *light* also is most frequent, there is one effect; if *day* appears rather with *night*, there is another. And the structure may easily reflect the difference, a difference, for example, between continuity of atmosphere and opposition of conception.

In many ways, observations of such extension of material must be partial. Attempting to answer the central question about extension, they must select decades in centuries, poets in decades, and poems in poets, which are only provisionally representative. They must select just one poetic quality, frequency, from among many. But at least the question of continuity may be answered. Poetry varies and persists as the art of a live language.

BIBLIOGRAPHY

(Works named below have been selected on the basis of direct use in this study. Poetry used is listed in table 1, p. 389. Many other works on poetry and language have had a general bearing; a good many of these are listed in earlier bibliographies. At no time has a single poet's work, or the work on him, been presented as a whole.)

Prose

Agar, Herbert. *A Time for Greatness* (Boston, Little, Brown, 1942).

Bellow, Saul. *The Victim* (New York, Vanguard, 1947).

Foley, Martha, ed. *The Best American Short Stories, 1947* (and *The Best [American] Short Stories of 1941,* ed. Edward J. O'Brien), (Boston, Houghton Mifflin, 1947 and 1941).

Gordon, Caroline. *The Women on the Porch* (New York, Scribner's, 1944).

Gunther, John. *Inside U. S. A.* (New York, Harper, 1947).

Heiser, Victor. *An American Doctor's Odyssey* (New York, Norton, 1936).

Hemingway, Ernest. *For Whom the Bell Tolls* (New York, Scribner's, 1940).

Hersey, John. *A Bell for Adano* (New York, Knopf, 1944).

—— *Hiroshima* (New York, Knopf, 1946).

Herskovits, Melville J. *Man and His Works: The Science of Cultural Anthropology* (New York, Knopf, 1948).

Lerner, Max. *Ideas Are Weapons* (New York, Viking, 1939).

Liebman, Joshua Loth. *Peace of Mind* (New York, Simon and Schuster, 1946).

Lewis, C. S. *Out of the Silent Planet* (New York, Macmillan, 1943).

Lewis, Sinclair. *Kingsblood Royal* (New York, Random House, 1947).

Meyer, Cord, Jr. *Peace or Anarchy* (Boston, Little, Brown, 1947).

Northrop, F. S. C. *The Meeting of East and West* (New York, Macmillan, 1946).

Porter, Katherine Anne. *The Leaning Tower, and Other Stories* (New York, Harcourt, Brace, 1944).

Pyle, Ernie. *Here Is Your War* (New York, Holt, 1943).

Santayana, George. *Persons and Places,* Vol. II: *The Middle Span* (New York, Scribner's, 1945).

Sitwell, Sacheverell. *The Hunters and the Hunted* (London, Macmillan, 1947).

Steinbeck, John. *Cannery Row* (New York, Viking, 1945).

Toynbee, Arnold. *A Study of History* (abridged ed.; Oxford Univ. Press, 1947).

Warren, Robert Penn. *All the King's Men* (New York, Harcourt, Brace, 1946).

Welles, Sumner. *The Time for Decision* (New York, Harper, 1944).
Welty, Eudora. *Delta Wedding* (New York, Harcourt, Brace, 1946).
Wescott, Glenway. *The Pilgrim Hawk* (New York, Harper, 1940).
White, William Allen. *The Autobiography of* ... (New York, Macmillan, 1946).
White, W. L. *They Were Expendable* (New York, Harcourt, Brace, 1942).
Willkie, Wendell. *One World* (New York, Simon and Schuster, 1943).
Woolf, Virginia. *Roger Fry* (New York, Harcourt, Brace, 1940).
Wright, Richard. *Black Boy* (New York, Harper, 1945).

Problems in Criticism

Adams, J. Donald. *The Shape of Books to Come* (New York, Viking, 1944).
Bensen, Alice R. "Problems of Poetic Diction in Twentieth-Century Criticism," *PMLA,* LX (1945), 271–286.
Blackmur, R. P. *The Double Agent: Essays in Craft and Elucidation* (New York, Arrow Editions, 1935).
Bowra, C. M. *The Heritage of Symbolism* (London, Macmillan, 1943).
Brooks, Cleanth. *Modern Poetry and the Tradition* (Univ. of North Carolina Press, 1939).
—— *The Well-Wrought Urn: Studies in the Structure of Poetry* (New York, Reynal and Hitchcock, 1947).
Burke, Kenneth. *The Philosophy of Literary Form: Studies in Symbolic Action* (Louisiana State Univ. Press, 1941).
Cassirer, Ernst. *An Essay on Man: An Introduction to a Philosophy of Human Culture* (Yale Univ. Press, 1944).
Crane, R. S. "Two Essays in Practical Criticism: Prefatory Note," University of Kansas City *University Review,* VIII (1942), 199–219.
Cunningham, J. V. "The Poetry of Wallace Stevens," *Poetry,* LXXV (1949), 149–165.
Daiches, David. *Poetry in the Modern World: A Study of Poetry in England between 1900 and 1939* (Univ. of Chicago Press, 1940).
De Voto, Bernard, *The Literary Fallacy* (Boston, Little, Brown, 1944).
Dickinson, Asa Don. *The Best Books of the Decade, 1936–1945: Another Clue to the Literary Labyrinth* (New York, Wilson, 1945).
Downey, June E. *Creative Imagination: Studies in the Psychology of Literature* (New York, Harcourt, Brace, 1929).
Drew, Elizabeth, in collaboration with John L. Sweeney. *Directions in Modern Poetry* (New York, Norton, 1940).
Eastman, Max. *The Literary Mind: Its Place in an Age of Science* (New York, Scribner's, 1931).
Eliot, T. S. *Selected Essays, 1917–1932* (New York, Harcourt, Brace, 1932).
—— *After Strange Gods* (New York, Harcourt, Brace, 1934).

Eliot, T. S. Introduction to "London" and "The Vanity of Human Wishes" (London, F. Etchells & H. Macdonald, 1930).

—— *From Poe to Valéry* (New York, Harcourt, Brace, 1948).

—— Introduction to *Baudelaire's Intimate Journals* (London, Blackamore Press; New York, Random House, 1930).

—— *Ezra Pound, His Metric and Poetry* (New York, Knopf, 1917).

—— "Milton," *Sewanee Review,* LVI (1948), 185–209.

Ellmann, Richard. *Yeats, the Man and the Masks* (New York, Macmillan, 1948).

Foster, Genevieve W. "Archetypal Imagery of T. S. Eliot," *PMLA,* LX (1945), 567–585.

Frankenberg, Lloyd. *Pleasure Dome: On Reading Modern Poetry* (Boston, Houghton Mifflin, 1949).

Hatzfeld, Helmut A. "The Language of the Poet," *Studies in Philology,* XLIII (1946), 93–120.

Heringman, Bernard. "Wallace Stevens: The Use of Poetry," *ELH,* XVI (1949), 325–336.

Hone, Joseph. *W. B. Yeats, 1865–1939* (New York, Macmillan, 1943).

Hornstein, Lillian H. "Analysis of Imagery: A Critique of Literary Method," *PMLA,* LVII (1942), 638–653.

Horton, Philip. *Hart Crane: The Life of an American Poet* (New York, Norton, 1937).

Howell, A. C. " 'Res et Verba': Words and Things," *ELH,* XIII (1946), 131–142.

Hughes, Glenn. *Imagism and the Imagists: A Study in Modern Poetry* (Stanford Univ. Press, 1931).

Hulme, T. E. *Speculations: Essays on Humanism and the Philosophy of Art,* ed. Herbert Read (London, Kegan Paul, Trench, Trübner, 1924).

Jarrell, Randall. "Changes of Attitude and Rhetoric in Auden's Poetry," *Southern Review,* VII (1941), 326–349.

Koch, Vivienne. *William Carlos Williams* (Norfolk, Conn., New Directions, 1950).

Langer, Suzanne K. *Philosophy in a New Key: A Study in the Symbolism of Reason, Rite, and Art* (Harvard Univ. Press, 1942).

Leavis, F. R. *New Bearings in English Poetry: A Study of the Contemporary Structure* (London, Chatto and Windus, 1932).

MacLeish, Archibald. *The Irresponsibles: A Declaration* (New York, Duell, Sloan and Pearce, 1940).

MacNeice, Louis. *The Poetry of W. B. Yeats* (Oxford Univ. Press, 1941).

Matthiessen, F. O. *The Achievement of T. S. Eliot: An Essay on the Nature of Poetry* (Oxford Univ. Press, 1935).

Mizener, Arthur. "Some Notes on the Nature of English Poetry," *Sewanee Review,* LI (1943), 27–51.

Monroe, Harriet. *A Poet's Life: Seventy Years in a Changing World* (New York, Macmillan, 1938).

Moore, George, ed. *An Anthology of Pure Poetry* (New York, Boni and Liveright, 1925).

O'Connor, William Van. *Sense and Sensibility in Modern Poetry* (Univ. of Chicago Press, 1948).

—— *The Shaping Spirit: A Study of Wallace Stevens* (New York, De Regnery, 1950).

Parkinson, Thomas. *Yeats as Critic of His Early Verse* (Univ. of California dissertation, 1949).

Pepper, Stephen C. *The Basis of Criticism in the Arts* (Harvard Univ. Press, 1945).

Poetry, the editors of. *The Case against the Saturday Review of Literature* (Chicago, 1949).

Pound, Ezra. *Polite Essays* (London, Faber and Faber, 1937).

Prall, David. *Aesthetic Analysis* (New York, Crowell, 1936).

Quarterly Review of Literature. Ezra Pound Issue (Vol. V, No. 2, 1949).

Rajan, B., ed. *T. S. Eliot: A Study of His Writings by Several Hands* (London, D. Dobson, 1947).

Ransom, John Crowe. *The New Criticism* (Norfolk, Conn., New Directions, 1941).

Richards, I. A. *Practical Criticism: A Study of Literary Judgment* (New York, Harcourt, Brace, 1929).

—— *The Philosophy of Rhetoric* (Oxford Univ. Press, 1936).

Ross Williamson, Hugh. *The Poetry of T. S. Eliot* (London, Hodder and Stoughton, 1932).

Runes, Dagobert, ed. *Twentieth-Century Philosophy: Living Schools of Thought* (New York, Philosophical Library, 1943).

Russell, Bertrand. *An Inquiry into Meaning and Truth* (New York, Norton, 1940).

Schwartz, Delmore. "The Literary Dictatorship of T. S. Eliot," *Partisan Review,* XVI (1949), 119–137.

Shapiro, Karl. *Essay on Rime* (New York, Reynal and Hitchcock, 1945).

—— "Prosody as the Meaning," *Poetry,* LXXIII (1949), 336–351.

—— "English Prosody and Modern Poetry," *ELH,* XIV (1947), 77–92.

Sitwell, Edith. *Aspects of Modern Poetry* (London, Duckworth, 1934).

—— *A Celebration for Edith Sitwell,* ed. by José García Villa (Norfolk, Conn., New Directions, 1948).

Spencer, Theodore. "Antaeus, or Poetic Language and the Actual World," *ELH,* X (1943), 173–192.

—— "The Poetry of Sir Philip Sidney," *ELH,* XII (1945), 251–278.

Spender, Stephen. "The Making of a Poem," *Partisan Review,* XIII (1946), 294–308.

Stein, Gertrude. *Lectures in America* (New York, Random House, 1935).

Stevens, Wallace. "The Noble Rider and the Sound of Words," pp. 91–125 in *The Language of Poetry,* ed. Allen Tate (Princeton Univ. Press, 1942).

—— "Effects of Analogy," *Yale Review,* XXXVIII (1948), 29–44.

Tate, Allen. *On the Limits of Poetry* (New York, Morrow, 1948).

Trilling, Lionel. *The Liberal Imagination* (New York, Viking Press, 1950).

Trowbridge, Hoyt. "Aristotle and the 'New Criticism,' " *Sewanee Review,* LII (1944), 537–556.

Vinograd, Sherna S. "The Accidental: A Clue to Structure in Eliot's Poetry," *Accent,* IX (1949), 231–238.

Watts, Harold H. "H. D. and the Age of Myth," *Sewanee Review,* LVI (1948), 287–303.

Wellek, René, and Austin Warren, eds. *Theory of Literature* (New York, Harcourt, Brace, 1949).

Williams, William Carlos. "An Approach to the Poem," *English Institute Essays, 1947* (Columbia Univ. Press, 1948), pp. 50–75.

Wilson, Edmund. *Axel's Castle: A Study in the Imaginative Literature of 1870–1930* (New York, Scribner's, 1931).

Wimsatt, W. K., Jr. "Comment on 'Two Essays in Practical Criticism,' " University of Kansas City *University Review,* IX (1942), 139–143.

Winters, Yvor. *The Anatomy of Nonsense* (Norfolk, Conn., New Directions, 1943).

Witt, Marion. "A Competition for Eternity: Yeats's Revision of His Later Poems," *PMLA,* LXIV (1949), 40–58.

Yeats, W. B. *Essays* (New York, Macmillan, 1924).

—— *Autobiographies* (New York, Macmillan, 1927).

—— *Oxford Book of Modern Verse* (Oxford, Clarendon Press, 1936).

—— *Letters on Poetry to Dorothy Wellesley* (Oxford Univ. Press, 1940).

PROBLEMS OF LANGUAGE AND VERSIFICATION

Bandy, W. T. *A Word Index to Baudelaire's Poems* (Madison, Wis., 1939).

Barkas, Pallister. *A Critique of Modern English Prosody (1880–1930)* (Halle, M. Niemeyer, 1934).

Baum, Paull Franklin. *The Principles of English Versification* (Harvard Univ. Press, 1922).

Dewey, Godfrey. *Relativ Frequency of English Speech Sounds* (Harvard Univ. Press, 1923).

Diederich, Paul Bernard. *The Frequency of Latin Words and Their Endings* (Univ. of Chicago Press, 1939).

Eaton, Helen S. *Semantic Frequency List for English* ... (Univ. of Chicago Press, 1940).

Hanley, Miles L. *Word Index to James Joyce's Ulysses* (Madison, Wis., 1937).

Haugen, Einar. *Norwegian Word Studies* (Univ. of Wisconsin Press, 1942).

Hoijer, Harry. "Linguistic and Cultural Change," *Language,* XXIV (1948).

Lee, Vernon [i.e., Violet Paget]. *The Handling of Words, and Other Studies in Literary Psychology* (London, Lane, 1923).

Morris, Charles. *Signs, Language and Behavior* (New York, Prentice-Hall, 1946).

Pratt, Alice Edwards. *The Use of Color in the Verse of the English Romantic Poets* (Univ. of Chicago Press, 1898).

Roberts, Murat H. "The Science of Idiom: A Method of Inquiry into the Cognitive Design of Language," *PMLA,* LIX (1944), 291–306.

Roberts, Paul. *The Influence of Sir Walter Scott on the Vocabulary of the Modern English Language* (unpublished dissertation, Univ. of California, 1948).

Rynin, David, ed. *A Treatise on Language by Alexander Bryan Johnson* (Univ. of California Press, 1947).

Sapir, Edward. *Language: An Introduction to the Study of Speech* (New York, Harcourt, Brace, 1921).

Schneider, Wilhelm. *Ausdruckswerte der deutschen Sprache* (Leipzig and Berlin, Tuebner, 1931).

Skard, Sigmund. "The Use of Color in Literature: A Survey of Research," *Proc. Am. Philos. Assoc.,* 90 (1946), 163–247.

Smith, Philip A. "Bishop Hall, 'Our English Seneca,'" *PMLA,* LXIII (1948), 1191–1204.

Spitzer, Leo. *Linguistics and Literary History: Essays in Stylistics* (Princeton Univ. Press, 1948).

——— "Why Does Language Change?" *Modern Language Quarterly,* IV (1943), 413–431.

Stewart, George R. *The Technique of English Verse* (New York, Holt, 1930).

Stevenson, Charles L. *Ethics and Language* (Yale Univ. Press, 1944).

Thorndike, Edw. L. *The Teacher's Word Book* (New York, Teachers College, Columbia Univ., 1921).

Wheat, Leonard B. *Free Associations to Common Words . . .* (New York, Teachers College, Columbia Univ., 1931).

Yule, G. Udny. *The Statistical Study of Literary Vocabulary* (Cambridge Univ. Press, 1944).

Zipf, George K. *Human Behavior and the Principle of Least Effort: An Introduction to Human Ecology* (Cambridge, Mass., Addison-Wesley Press, 1949).